Financial Management in a Managed Care Environment

Delmar's Health Information Management Series

Claudia R. Campbell, PhD
Homer H. Schmitz, PhD
Linda C. Waller, RRA

Shirley Anderson
Series Editor

Delmar Publishers

an International Thomson Publishing company I(T)P®

Albany • Bonn • Boston • Cincinnati • Detroit • London • Madrid
Melbourne • Mexico City • New York • Pacific Grove • Paris • San Francisco
Singapore • Tokyo • Toronto • Washington

NOTICE TO THE READER

Cover Design: Brucie Rosch

Publishing Team:
Publisher: Susan Simpfenderfer
Acquisitions Editor: Marlene McHugh Pratt
Developmental Editor: Jill Rembetski
Project Editor: William Trudell

Art and Design Coordinator: Rich Killar
Production Coordinator: Cathleen Berry
Marketing Manager: Darryl L. Caron
Editorial Assistant: Marla Perretta

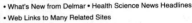
COPYRIGHT © 1998
By Delmar Publishers
a division of International Thomson Publishing Inc.

The ITP logo is a trademark under license

Printed in the United States of America

For more information, contact:

Delmar Publishers
3 Columbia Circle, Box 15015
Albany, New York 12212-5015

International Thomson Publishing Europe
Berkshire House 168-173
High Holborn
London, WC1V7AA
England

Thomas Nelson Australia
102 Dodds Street
South Melbourne, 3205
Victoria, Australia

Nelson Canada
1120 Birchmount Road
Scarborough, Ontario
Canada M1K 5G4

International Thomson Editores
Campos Eliseos 385, Piso 7
Col Polanco
11560 Mexico D F Mexico

International Thomson Publishing Gmbh
Königswinterer Strasse 418
53227 Bonn
Germany

International Thomson Publishing Asia
60 Albert Street
#15-01 Albert Complex
Singapore 189969

International Thomson Publishing - Japan
Hirakawacho Kyowa Building, 3F
2-2-1 Hirakawacho
Chiyoda-ku, 102 Tokyo
Japan

1 2 3 4 5 6 7 8 9 10 XXX 02 01 00 99 98

Library of Congress Cataloging-in-Publication Data

Campbell, Claudia R.
     Financial management in a managed care environment / Claudia R.
Campbell, Homer H. Schmitz, Linda C. Waller.
         p. cm. — (Delmar's health information management series)
     ISBN 0-8273-8133-6
     1. Managed care plan (Medical care)—United States—Finance.
     2. Managed care plans (Medical care)—United States—Cost control.
     3. Capitation fees (Medical care)   I. Schmitz, Homer H.
     II. Waller, Linda C.   III. Title.   IV. Series.
     RA971.3.C25   1998
     36Z.1'04258'0681—dc21

                                        98–3061
                                          CIP

Contents

Preface   ix

Chapter 1   **The Emergence of Managed Care**   **1**
Learning Objectives   *1*
Key Terms   *1*
Introduction   *2*
U.S. Health System Reform   *2*
Trends in National Health Care Spending   *9*
Fundamental Causes of Rising Health Care Prices   *13*
Other Reasons for Rising Health Care Spending   *17*
Policy Options to Control Health Care Costs   *19*
Financial Management Under Managed Care   *19*
Conclusion   *21*
Case 1-1: Performance of St. Louis Area Hospitals, 1983–1992   *21*
References   *24*

Chapter 2   **Risk and Insurance in Health Care: The Health Maintenance Organization**   **27**
Learning Objectives   *27*
Key Terms   *28*
Introduction   *28*
Risk and Insurance   *28*
Profitability and Costs of Health Insurance   *36*
Emergence of Managed Care Organizations   *40*

Managed Care Plan Characteristics   42
Criticisms of the HMO Model   47
Premium Rate Development   48
Capitation Using Community Rating   49
Conclusion   53
Case 2-1: Establishing a Capitation Rate for Hometown HMO   53
References   56

Chapter 3   Inpatient Delivery Under a Managed Care System   58
Learning Objectives   58
Key Terms   59
Introduction   59
The Evolving Managed Care Market   59
Pluralistic Payment Systems in the United States   68
The Evolution of Risk   74
Conclusion   78
Review Questions   79
References   79

Chapter 4   Ambulatory Care in a Managed Care Environment   81
Learning Objectives   81
Key Terms   82
Introduction   82
Growth of Ambulatory Care   82
Models of Ambulatory Care   86
Quality and the Managed Care Effort   91
Conclusion   100
Review Questions   100
References   101

Chapter 5   The Emergence of Integrated Delivery Systems   102
Learning Objectives   102
Key Terms   102
Introduction   103
The Basics of an IDS   103
Types of Integration   106
Information Needs of an IDS   108

The Role of Governance   114
A Look at the Future   116
Conclusion   118
Review Questions   119
References   119

Chapter 6   Third-Party Payment Systems   120
Learning Objectives   120
Key Terms   121
Introduction   121
Traditional Payment Systems   122
Alternatives to Fee-for-Service Reimbursement   124
Hospital Reimbursement   125
Physician Reimbursement   141
Conclusion   149
Case 6-1: Centerville Health Center   149
Case 6-2: To Participate or Not to Participate in Medicare   152
Case 6-3: Pricing a Medicare Risk Contract   153
References   154

Chapter 7   Understanding Financial Performance   156
Learning Objectives   156
Key Terms   157
Introduction   158
Financial Statements   158
The Balance Sheet   162
The Income Statement   169
Effects of the Income Statement on the Balance Sheet   172
Capital Structure Decisions   176
Statement of Cash Flows   177
Financial Statement Analysis   179
Operating Ratios and Financial Performance   190
Conclusion   195
Case 7-1: Accounting versus Economic Depreciation   195
Case 7-2: Columbia/HCA Healthcare   196
Case 7-3: St. Mary's Hospital   196
References   197

Chapter 8   Operating Budgets Under Capitation   198

 Learning Objectives   198
 Key Terms   198
 Introduction   199
 The Pluralistic Reimbursement Environment   199
 Budgeting Under Capitation   202
 Other Issues   215
 Conclusion   219
 Case 8-1: County Primary Care Practice   219
 Case 8-2: Global Managed Care Company   220
 Case 8-3: Claims Administration   221
 Review Questions   221
 Reference   221

Chapter 9   Investing and Financing Decisions   222

 Learning Objectives   222
 Key Terms   223
 Introduction   223
 Opportunity Costs and Capital Budgeting   224
 Cash Flows and Time Value of Money   225
 Evaluating a Series of Lump-Sum Payments   230
 Evaluating Annuities and Perpetuities   233
 Opportunity Costs Once More: The Required Return on Stocks and Bonds   234
 Finding the Opportunity Cost of Debt   237
 Stock Valuation and the Opportunity Cost of Equity   239
 Weighted Average Cost of Capital   244
 Capital Budgeting in the Health Care Organization   247
 Using Decision Tools to Assess Capital Projects   261
 Conclusion   265
 Case 9-1: Finding the Present Value of an Annuity— the Hard Way   266
 Case 9-2: Break-Even Enrollment in a Managed Care Plan   266
 Case 9-3: Using Capital Budgeting Tools to Assess Project Profitability   267
 Case 9-4: What Is the IRR and the MIRR of an Investment?   268
 Case 9-5: Finding the Weighted Average Cost of Capital   269
 References   270

Chapter 10 **Cash Budgeting and Working Capital Management** **271**

Learning Objectives   271
Key Terms   272
Introduction   272
Cash, Working Capital, and Net Working Capital   273
Cash Budgeting   274
The Cash Conversion Cycle   274
Financing Working Capital   290
Conclusion   297
Case 10-1: Developing a Cash Budget for a Physician Group Practice   297
References   299

Chapter 11 **Utilization Management Under Capitation** **300**

Learning Objectives   300
Key Terms   300
Introduction   301
Objectives of a Utilization Management System   301
The Utilization Process   308
Conclusion   312
Review Questions   313

Chapter 12 **Cost Accounting and Control Under Capitation** **314**

Learning Objectives   314
Key Terms   314
Introduction   315
Understanding Costs   315
Cost Definitions   323
Accounting for Costs   325
Managing Costs   328
Case 12-1: City Hospital Managed Care—Part I   336
Case 12-2: City Hospital Managed Care—Part II   337
Case 12-3: City Hospital Cardiac Catheterization Department—Part I   338
Case 12-4: City Hospital Cardiac Catheterization Department—Part II   338
Case 12-5: City Hospital Budget Variances for a Managed Care Group   339
Review Question   340

Chapter 13 **Quality and Outcomes Management** **341**

Learning Objectives 341
Key Terms 341
Introduction 342
Participants and Quality Concepts 342
Using Continuous Quality Improvement 344
Quality Indicators 348
Conclusion 358
Review Questions 359
References 359

Chapter 14 **Future Impact on Managers of Health Care Organizations** **360**

Learning Objectives 360
Key Terms 361
Introduction 361
The Perspective of History 362
The Global Health Care System 363
The Impact of Technology 366
Prevention Services 367
Changing Methods of Treatment and Delivery 368
The Policy Perspective on Health Care Availability 370
The Role of Government 372
The Patient's Perspective 375
The Financial Perspective 376
Conclusion 377
Review Questions 379
References 379

Appendix **381**

Glossary **387**

Index **407**

Preface

The health care industry is in the midst of a paradigm shift in the way health care is being delivered and financed, and this is affecting the role of all of the stakeholders. Within five years the health care industry is likely to look like something quite different from what we know it as today. There is no road map showing exactly where the industry is going or what strategies will be successful. Nonetheless, health care professionals need to recognize the significant changes underway in economic and clinical management of patient care and anticipate how these changes are likely to affect their work. Health services managers, no matter in what area of the industry, must know the contours of this changing environment in order to move forward and be successful.

As a result of this paradigm shift, health care no longer can be neatly segregated into separate and independent units, such as inpatient acute care providers, ambulatory care providers, physician providers, allied health professionals, third party payers, employers, and patients. Instead, providers are attempting to become third party payers; third party payers are attempting to become providers. Employers are trying to have a greater say in the health care decisions of their employees. Patients are becoming much more aware of their rights, and demanding them. Allied health professionals are seeking a larger role in health care decisions. Accrediting agencies are becoming more involved with day to day operations. The health care industry today is coalescing into large, integrated systems that provide a continuum of services from wellness and prevention programs to acute and extended care and into health plans that are responsible for creating a package of comprehensive services and accepting risk.

Target Audience

This transformation of the health care system points to a need for a new textbook. *Financial Management in a Managed Care Environment* focuses on managed care and the significant role it plays in the changes underway in the system. The text is written primarily for undergraduate and beginning graduate students who are pursuing health professions careers that involve managing some facet of the health care delivery system whether it be clinical or administrative, provider-based or payer-oriented. Students in allied health programs, health administration and MBA programs, medical schools, and nursing schools are targeted users. Current practitioners also may find the text beneficial for enlarging their knowledge of the fundamentals of managed care.

Content and Scope

Many allied health and other health professions programs currently rely on textbooks that deal with core financial management concepts covered in health and non health-related management texts. This book is different from these other texts in four respects:

- It deals exclusively with the health care sector.
- It emphasizes managed care and its impact on financial management, decision making, and the information requirements of the health care system.
- It provides a view of managed care from the perspective of both health plans and providers rather than exclusively from one side or the other.
- It places significant emphasis on the newly emerging ambulatory care component of managed health care.

To adequately cover managed care, the scope of the text is, of necessity, broad. Basic principles from economics, finance, accounting, organizational behavior, and payment methodology are addressed. The book is meant to serve as an introduction to these areas. Learners are encouraged to do additional work in these disciplines to deepen and expand their knowledge and understanding.

This text also retains relevant information on the traditional reimbursement systems used by Medicare and Medicaid, which are swiftly incorporating or adopting features of managed health care into their programs. The Balanced Budget Act of 1997 signed into law in August, for example, authorizes the creation of provider sponsored organizations—managed care plans run by health care providers, and will encourage Medicare beneficiaries to enroll in the managed care plans. To understand these changes, one needs to be familiar with how the system currently operates.

Chapter Organization

Each chapter in the text is arranged and structured to focus the efforts of the learner on the subject matter of the chapter and to reinforce the concepts introduced.

- The chapter overview provides a general understanding of the direction that the chapter will take and the subject matter that will be treated within the chapter.
- Learning objectives are provided at the beginning of each chapter so the learner can anticipate the direction of the instruction and have measurable goals against which to evaluate progress through the chapter.
- Key terms are listed at the beginning of each chapter to focus the learner's understanding on some of the terminology that is central to the subject, or new to the

learner. These terms have been bolded for emphasis. All boldface terms are defined in the glossary at the end of the text.

- Review questions are provided at the end of some chapters to allow the learner to test the extent of the knowledge gained. These range from questions that require recall of straightforward bodies of knowledge to questions that require the learner to integrate concepts that have been presented in the chapter. The health-related review questions at the end of some chapters focus the application of these financial and managed care concepts on the health care field.

- In some chapters, simple cases, questions, and exercises that require computer spreadsheets are used where the content lends itself to problem solving and analysis. The cases and problems enable the learner to integrate the knowledge gained in the chapter and apply it to a new situation. These cases and problems also are found on a 3.5 computer disk that accompanies the text.

- References are provided in each chapter and focus on external information that bears on the subject being presented.

- At the end of the text is a glossary containing terminology that is common to the field. Definitions are provided for easy reference and recall. These terms are bold-faced in the chapters where they first appear in the text.

Each chapter is self-contained and can be used independent of other chapters, permitting the instructor to select those chapters that best address the subjects contained in the course syllabus. The book is organized into three general content areas. These include a overview of the health care system in Chapters 1 and 2, the impact of managed care on the delivery system in Chapters 3 to 5, and general topics in financial management (Chapters 6 to 14).

Chapters 1 and 2 deal with many of the foundation issues related to managed care and its evolution. Chapter 1 places the emergence for managed care into its historical context and provides an overview of the current state of affairs in health care spending in the United States. The chapter gives an economic rationale for the rise of managed care in the wake of previous failed attempts to contain health care costs. Chapter 2 explores the nature of health insurance and the creation of the health maintenance organization as the prototype managed care organization that combines health insurance with a comprehensive and integrated system of health care delivery.

Chapters 3, 4 and 5 concern the impact of managed care on both the inpatient and ambulatory care delivery systems and the emergence of integrated delivery systems in response to the growth of managed care. The similarities and differences between the inpatient acute care environment and the ambulatory care sector are outlined and the structure and importance of the newly emerging integrated delivery systems are explained. Particular attention is given to the critical role of information and information management in these developments. Finally these chapters address the tension created between the cost reduction strategies of managed care and the maintenance of quality in health care.

The final section of the book contains nine chapters that apply financial management concepts and tools to diverse health-related organizations operating in a managed care environment. Once again, significant differences between the inpatient acute care environment and the ambulatory care environment are addressed. Financial management techniques required to successfully operate a health care organization are discussed in some detail, including managing reimbursement, capital investment and financing, operating budget development, working capital management, utilization management, cost accounting, quality assurance, and outcomes management. The final chapter speculates on the changes that will occur in health care delivery and visualizes the environment in which a health care manager might operate in the future.

Optional Chapter Uses

Selected chapters of this book can be used alone as they apply to specific content areas in the health care curriculum, or they can be used in total for a fully integrated managed care course. Chapters 1 and 2 are well suited to an introductory health care finance or economics course, as special readings related to the emergence of managed care. Chapters 1 to 5 provide a framework for understanding the organization structures, incentives, and health system changes brought about by managed care. These chapters can be used in general management courses related to health care organization, managing with professionals, or organizational theory and behavior. Chapters 3 to 5 together with chapters 13 to 15 focus primarily on major financial concerns under managed care from the perspective of the health care provider with a special emphasis on ambulatory care. These chapters would be an appropriate component of an ambulatory care management course. Chapters 6 through 12 cover the core topics found in standard financial management courses with applications to health care providers and health plans operating in a managed care environment. These chapters could be included in a more general course focused on health care financial management.

Special Features of the Text

A 3.5 diskette is included at the back of this text to aid the learner in working through the chapter cases. This disk contains 1) document files with instructions on how to use the disk, 2) document files containing relevant case material and review questions, and 3) computer spreadsheet files that can be used for analyzing the chapter cases and problems.

Using the Disk

A commercially available word processing software program, such as Word for Windows or Wordperfect for Windows, and a spreadsheet software program, such as Excel or Lotus 1-2-3, must be previously loaded on the user's computer before working with the disk. The disk contains the following files.

- A README.doc file that explains how to use the disk. Before beginning to work with the disk, the users should open this file in their word processing program and read it carefully.

- A narrative version of the cases and problems that appear in Chapters 1, 2, 6, 7, 8, 9, 10, and 12. These are found in document (.doc) files labeled by the chapter in which they are found. For example, the first case in Chapter 1 would be Cs1-1.doc. If a chapter contains more than one case, they are labeled first with the chapter number and then by the case number according to their appearance in the text. For example case 3 in chapter nine would be Cs9-3.doc.
- A spreadsheet for each problem or case. These have the same names as the narrative files but are labeled Ch1-1.xls (if you are using Excel) or Ch1-1.wk4 (if you are using Lotus) instead of .doc files. In order to work through the questions in the text, you will need to enter data and formulas into the cells found on the spreadsheet.

These cases and problems help enhance the learning process by reinforcing concepts through application. Learners are encouraged to develop their competence in using computer technology by accessing the Internet to obtain additional information on the cases and other topics in the book.

For example, you will find a tutorial file that illustrates the basic spreadsheet operations needed to solve the problems and questions posed in the cases. This file is particularly helpful to those just learning about spreadsheet programs. To access this tutorial and other resources, visit the web page for this book on the Delmar Publishers Allied Health website: www.delmaralliedhealth.com.

We hope that users of this text will gain as much as the authors did in researching and writing it. Health care is a challenging and interesting field, made more so by the emergence of managed care.

Acknowledgments

The authors would like to thank the following reviewers for their helpful assistance during the development of this text, although any errors that remain are ours alone.

Fevzi Akinci, MHA
Ph.D. Candidate
Saint Louis University
St. Louis, MO

Shirley Anderson
Formerly of Saint Louis
  University
St. Louis, MO

Paul Bell
Health Information
  Management
East Carolina University
Greenville, NC

Sue Ellen Bice
Health Services
Mohawk Valley Community College
Utica, NY

Marjorie McNeil
Division of Health Information
  Management
Florida A&M University
Tallahassee, FL

Joan Rines
Director, Health Information Management
Stephens College
Columbia, MO

Hanh Trinh
Health Information Administration Program
University of Wisconsin, Milwaukee
Milwaukee, WI

Nicholas M. Borho, CFO
Daughters of Charity National Health
    System—West Central Region
St. Louis, MO

Virginia S. Dill
Executive Vice President/ CFO
Franklin Equity Leasing Company
St. Louis, MO

Kathleen N. Gillespie, Ph.D.
Department of Health Administration
Saint Louis University
St. Louis, MO

Rik W. Hafer, Ph.D.
Department of Economics
Southern Illinois University at
    Edwardsville
Edwardsville, IL

John Kysar
Director of Employee Benefits
Saint Louis University
St. Louis, MO

Steven Weiss, CFO
SLUCare
St. Louis, MO

Dedication

To Steven, whose continued support and encouragement lifted my spirits and kept me going in the long months of writing.

Claudia R. Campbell

To my family. They were patient . . . Patient . . . PATIENT with the amount of time I stole from them in writing this book.

Homer H. Schmitz

Chapter 1

The Emergence of Managed Care

This chapter addresses the historical developments and economic forces that have shaped the U.S. health care system. Rising prices and costs are shown to be the primary catalyst for the development of the new forms of payment and health care delivery known as managed care. The chapter concludes with a brief overview of how managed care affects the roles and responsibilities of health care financial managers.

Learning Objectives

Upon successful completion of this chapter, the learner will:

- Identify the long-run trends in health care spending.
- Analyze the major sources of rising health care spending.
- Measure inflation in the economy and in health care.
- Explain why U.S. third-party payers are adopting managed care alternatives.
- Recognize the financial management skills that health services managers need in a managed care environment.

Key Terms

community rating	managed care
Consumer Price Index	managerial (cost) accounting
corporate finance	market failure
financial management	Medicaid
financial accounting	Medical Price Index
gross domestic product	Medicare
health maintenance organizations	moral hazard
inflation	national health expenditure
inflation rate	supplier-induced demand

Introduction

"Why does health care cost so much?"
"Why do some people lack health insurance?"
"Why must choice of physician be restricted?"
"Will the health insurance fund for the elderly go bankrupt?"

To understand why the new forms of health care organization and financing known as **managed care** have become so important in the U.S. health care system, these questions need to be addressed. Concerns about cost and access to health care did not arise overnight. They are the result of various forces that have contributed to a persistent rise in per capita spending for health care over time. Managed care is a market response to these forces.

U.S. Health System Reform

The United States is the only nation among the major industrialized countries in which lack of health insurance creates a barrier to basic health care services for a large minority of its citizens. In 1994, over 17.8 percent of Americans under the age of 65 were uninsured (National Center for Health Statistics, 1996). The United States is also noted for having the most expensive health system in the world as measured by per capita **national health expenditures.** As Table 1-1 shows, health spending per person in 1992 was $3,144 (National Center for Health Statistics, 1996). The next most expensive systems were Canada, at $1,912, and Germany, at $1,831. Given the high level of spending on health care, one would expect that the U.S. health care system would significantly outperform other countries with respect to basic health outcomes. In fact, the United States records higher infant mortality rates and lower male life expectancy rates at birth as compared with nine other industrialized countries. Where universal access is the same across the ten health care systems for citizens over sixty-five years of age, the United States, with its high level of spending, outperforms only two of these countries—Germany and England—in terms of male and female life expectancy at age sixty-five. When surveyed about the performance of the U.S. health care system, 89 percent of Americans believed that major changes were needed. In contrast, only 43 percent of Canadians and 48 percent of Germans voiced major dissatisfaction with their health systems (Blendon, Leitman, Morrison, and Donelan, 1992).

In an effort to respond to citizen dissatisfaction, the Clinton administration in 1994 proposed a major reform of the U.S. health care system. The Health Security Act of 1994, based in part on the German model, was a comprehensive piece of legislation that attempted to provide health insurance coverage for all citizens, including the 37 million Americans who were uninsured. The proposal contained the following elements:

1. Employers would provide full or partial insurance to all employees.
2. States would create insurance pools for the unemployed or uninsured.

Table 1-1   Comparative Performance of U.S. Health Care System

| Country | Health Care Spending per Capita[b] | Infant Mortality Rates[c] | Life Expectancy (Male) | | Life Expectancy (Female)[d] | | Health System Needs Major Changes |
			At Birth (years)	At 65 years (years)	At Birth (years)	At 65 years (years)	
United States	**$3,144**	**8.52**	**72.3**	**15.4**	**79.1**	**19.2**	**89%**
Australia	1,415	6.91	74.8	15.6	80.1	19.6	60
Canada	1,912	6.1	74.9	16.1	81.4	20.4	43
Japan	1,411	4.53	76.3	16.6	83	21.1	53
Netherlands	1,494	6.29	74.3	14.7	80.5	19.4	51
France	1,789	6.82	73.8	16.4	82.3	21.1	52
Germany[a]	1,831	6.17	72.7	14.5	79.3	18.3	48
Italy	1,553	8.19	73.7	15.2	80.5	19.2	86
Sweden	1,300	5.19	75.5	15.7	81.1	19.6	64
England and Wales	1,181	6.58	73.9	14.6	79.5	18.5	69

[a]Data are for unified Germany, which came into being in 1990.
[b]In 1992 measured in U.S. dollars. Data for England and Wales are for United Kingdom.
[c]Number of deaths of infants under 1 year per 1,000 live births in 1992. Data for Italy are for 1991.
[d]Data for Italy are for 1991. All other countries are for 1992.
Sources: National Center for Health Statistics (1996); Blendon et al. (1992).

3. Large health plans would sell insurance to firms.
4. Standard packages of benefits covered were stipulated.
5. Premiums would be based on **community rating** derived from the average cost of all enrollee groups covered by the insurer.
6. A national health board would monitor system spending and quality.

Besides providing all citizens with access to health services regardless of income or employment status, health reform promised to reduce inappropriate use of hospital emergency rooms by providing everyone access to a physician's care. In addition, all children would have access to health care services through their parents' health plans, workers between jobs and the unemployed would retain health insurance benefits, and persons under sixty-five with preexisting conditions would no longer be denied health insurance coverage.

Major barriers to passage of the Health Security Act arose as concerns grew about how the system would work. The actual cost of reform was unclear, and there were concerns that these costs might not be fairly distributed among workers, employers, and taxpayers. Providing health insurance for uninsured and underinsured families had the potential to be more costly than projected. Experience with previous expansions of health insurance to the elderly and poor suggested that families newly enfranchised by health reform might initially go to the doctor more frequently than those already covered by insurance. Potential losers from reform were small insurance companies, since large insurance plans were likely to dominate the reformed health insurance market. Small businesses, businesses using part-time employees, and young and unskilled workers were also likely to lose from health care reform. The costs of health insurance, some charged, would reduce profits and jobs in highly competitive companies. The wages of newly insured workers were likely to be cut to off-set the 80 percent contribution to workers' insurance premiums that the Health Security Act would require of employers.

Perhaps the greatest impediment to reform was the fear of loss of physician choice among insured workers, who were generally content with their own doctors and their current health insurance coverage. The proposed reform would encourage enrollment of workers into large, managed health care plans, where choice of physicians and hospitals was likely to be restricted to control costs. It is not surprising that the initiative failed as various interest groups worked successfully to defeat its passage.

Previous Health Reform Efforts

Notably, 1994 was not the first time that the federal government had initiated major health system changes. Several times during the post–World War II period, attempts to expand access and provide universal insurance coverage had been made, with only partial success. Immediately after the war, in 1946, the Hill-Burton Act provided access to low-cost government financing for the expansion of hospitals and hospital beds throughout the country. Hospitals were required to provide free care to the poor in exchange for access to financing. This resulted in the construction of hundreds of hospital beds from 1946 to 1966, especially in the South and in rural areas (Berman, Weeks, and Kukla, 1986).

Reform in the 1960s

By the mid-1960s, many workers and their families received tax-subsidized health insurance coverage for major medical expenses through their employers. But the poor and elderly often lacked insurance because of preexisting conditions or low incomes or because they were not employed. In 1965 Congress passed legislation that provided health insurance to the elderly through **Medicare,** a federally funded and administered program, and to the poor through **Medicaid,** a program jointly funded and administered by the states and the federal government. Retired workers over age sixty-five who were eligible for social security were automatically covered by Medicare, regardless of income. The small number of the elderly who did not qualify because of inadequate work history could purchase health insurance through Medicare. Hospital insurance under Medicare–Part A was financed by a payroll tax on workers. Physician services were insured under Medicare–Part B and funded by insurance premiums paid for by the elderly. These premiums were kept low, so they had to be subsidized by government general tax revenues. In 1997, 64 percent of the premium was funded by general tax revenues (Health Care Financing Administration, 1997). Medicare has been a major success in ensuring access. Based on the 1992 census, less than 1 percent of the uninsured were over age 65 (Health Care Financing Administration, 1995).

In contrast to Medicare, Medicaid is funded jointly by the states and the federal government. Poorer states receive a larger percentage of federal matching funds than wealthier states in order to encourage parity in state programs, and each state has different eligibility criteria for access to Medicaid. Prior to the Personal Responsibility and Work Opportunity Act of 1996, also known as the welfare reform act, Medicaid eligibility was determined by AFDC income thresholds set by the state, which varied widely. Under the AFDC eligibility criteria in California in 1991, families of three with annual incomes up to $13,932 were eligible for Medicaid. In Louisiana, similar-sized families who earned more than $4,872 a year were denied access to Medicaid coverage (U.S. House of Representatives, 1991). As a result, the working poor in many states continued to be uninsured after the implementation of Medicaid. The welfare reform act eliminated Aid to Families with Dependent Children (AFDC) and replaced it with Temporary Assistance for Needy Families (TANF). In general, families meeting the AFDC eligibility criteria before the welfare reform law was enacted are still eligible for Medicaid (Gundling, 1997). Although Medicare provides access to acute care services for the elderly and the disabled, long-term-care services for these groups remain a responsibility of the states under Medicaid. The elderly and the disabled make up only about 26.4 percent of Medicaid beneficiaries, yet they consume 69 percent of the costs of the program (Health Care Financing Administration, 1995).

Reforms in the 1970s

During the inflationary 1970s, health care expenditures and health insurance premiums rose significantly. Health reform efforts turned from expanding access to containing expenditures. The Nixon administration encouraged the formation of federally qualified health plans under the Health Maintenance Organizations Act of 1973. The **health maintenance organizations (HMOs)** created by this act are the prototype for the managed care organizations that are being formed today. HMOs integrate delivery of health services with health insurance. HMO built-in incentives are to provide health care at the lowest cost. Competition between HMOs would provide consumer alternatives and make health providers price conscious while maintaining quality. With funding subsidies from Congress, start-up HMOs meeting federal requirements could compete with commercial health insurance plans offered to workers by employers. Under the 1973 law, businesses with more than twenty-five employees were required to offer workers a choice of a federally qualified HMO or a traditional health plan in areas where such HMOs operated. The HMO experiment is still underway.

Reform in the 1980s

The Medicare program, which cost $4.2 billion in 1967, its first year of operation, grew to $33.6 billion by 1980, a 17.3 percent annual increase (Health Care Financing Administration, 1995). Three reasons account for this significant rate of growth: (1) increased enrollment, (2) increased utilization, and (3) increased costs. The number of people entitled to Medicare benefits grew about 2.9 percent per year from 1967 to 1980, but the number of persons actually receiving health services during this time grew by 7.4 percent annually. Average costs per person served rose even faster, at 9.2 percent (Health Care Financing Administration, 1995). It was predicted that if Medicare costs continued to rise at these rates, the insurance fund from which payments were made would be depleted by 1987.

To slow expenditure increases, Congress in 1983 implemented a new pricing system for Medicare hospital reimbursement. Under the prospective payment system (PPS), the federal government set hospital prices. Hospitals were paid a preestablished, single price per admission based on the classification of the patient into one of over 500 diagnosis-related groups (**DRGs**) (see Chapter 3). In 1989, Congress altered Medicare reimbursement further by introducing volume-adjusted, prospectively set, standard fees for physicians who cared for Medicare patients. In 1991, hospital capital reimbursement for building and equipment was added to the per case price.

PPS had a short-run effect on expenditures. Medicare spending growth moderated during the late 1980s, rising only 9 percent per year from 1985 to 1990. But growth accelerated again, at 10.4 percent per year, from 1990 to 1994 (Health Care Financing Administration, 1995). Although the government was able to set prices, it was unable to control the quantity and intensity of services delivered in hospitals. Moreover, health care providers shifted care to ambulatory and home settings, where prices were not fixed by prospective payment. Although Federal Insurance Contribution Assessments (FICA), or payroll taxes, for Medicare were increased several times from 1983 to 1993, the Congressional Budget Office in 1996 was again warning of depletion of the Medicare Trust Fund by 2001 (Gardner, 1996). Cutting the growth in Medicare spending became a central concern for the federal government in political debates in the mid-1990s. For this, Congress increasingly turned to managed care alternatives already being tried by business and state governments.

Managed Care Initiatives to Curb Health Spending

In the late 1980s business and state governments also attempted to curb rising health care costs. Health insurance benefits averaged about 6.4 percent of total private worker compensation (wages plus benefits) in the early 1990s (National Center for Health Statistics, 1995). In addition, employers and workers finance Medicare–Part A through payroll taxes. These taxes were increased in the early 1990s to maintain the viability of the Medicare Trust Fund. In 1983, payroll taxes for both Social Security and Medicare were indexed to general **inflation.** In 1991, the maximum income subject to the Medicare portion of the payroll tax was raised from $51,300 to $125,000. In 1992, the threshold was again raised, to $200,000, and, in 1993, it was eliminated. Thereafter, all wage income was subject to the 2.9 percent tax, which was split fifty-fifty between employer and employee. Income subject to the payroll tax for Social Security continued to rise with inflation but was capped at a maximum level. In 1998, income above $68,400 is not subject to the payroll tax. Payroll taxes, measured in constant dollars, increased 27 percent from 1977 to 1992. At the same time, real income taxes declined 7 percent, and corporate taxes fell 35 percent. If both the employer and employee contributions to payroll taxes in 1992 are counted, 70.5 percent of tax-paying families paid more in social insurance taxes, which entitled them to Social Security and Medicare benefits at age sixty-five, than in income taxes (U.S. House of Representatives, 1991, Table 33).

Business tried several approaches to control health benefits costs. Large companies elected to insure their own workers to avoid state-mandated health care benefits, which tended to raise premium costs. In addition, they controlled costs by paying premiums based on the actual cost incurred by their own workforce, called experience rating. In this way, firms with younger, healthier workers could lower their health insurance premiums. Another strategy, given the impetus by the dual-option mandate in the Health Maintenance Act of 1973, was to encourage greater employee enrollment in managed health care plans. This approach did not take off until the 1990s, however.

HMOs showed great promise in their ability to contain health care costs for those under age sixty-five. They made significant inroads primarily in the Pacific region (California and Washington) and in Minnesota. By 1988, 30.3 million people were enrolled in HMOs across the country (Wrightson, 1990). Under the Health Maintenance Organization Amendments of 1988, Congress relaxed many restrictions placed on federally qualified HMOs, enabling them to compete more aggressively with insurance programs that were themselves adopting managed care strategies. By 1993, HMO plans had spread to nearly 25 percent of the population (National Center for Health Statistics, 1996).

In the early 1990s, all types of managed care plans, including HMOs, were promising to deliver large provider discounts to businesses contracting with them, to lower hospital utilization, and to contain, or reduce, health insurance premium costs. The failure of federal health care reform in 1994 accelerated private business's contracting with managed care plans nationwide. From 1993 to January 1995, the percentage of workers in companies with 10 or more employees enrolled in some form of managed health care plan was estimated to have risen from 46 percent to 57 percent ("Managed care enrollment grows," 1996). Another survey found that 75 percent of all insured workers were enrolled in some type of managed care plan in 1995 (Jensen, Morrisey, Gaffney, & Liston, 1997).

States also attempted to rein in health care costs. Medicaid spending accelerated at the end of 1980s for two reasons: (1) the growth of federally mandated benefits for pregnant women and children and (2) increased unemployment created by the 1990–1991 economic recession. From 1980 to 1988, Medicaid expenditures across the nation had risen approximately 10 percent annually. Then they accelerated, from 13 percent in 1989 to 26 percent in 1991 (Long, 1993). As of 1990, twenty-eight states had managed care plans, which enrolled about 14 percent of all Medicaid recipients (Herrick, 1995). An increasing number of states sought waivers from the federal government to allow them to provide Medicaid coverage through alternative delivery systems, most of which employed some form of managed health care. From 1994 to 1995, Medicaid managed care enrollment grew by more than 50 percent. According to the Health Care Financing Administration (HCFA) data, forty-nine states were using managed care strategies in the delivery of health services by mid-1995 (Wolf and Gorman, 1996).

The expansion of Medicaid managed care coincided with significant reductions in spending growth. From 1993 to 1995, total Medicaid payment growth slowed to 8.7 percent per year from its double digit rates in the previous period; Medicaid spending growth per person served fell to 4.3 percent per year in the same period (Health Care Financing Administration, 1997).

In the mid-1980s the federal government also broadened the availability of managed care to Medicare beneficiaries as a part of the Tax Equity and Fiscal Responsibility Act of 1982. At the time of implementation in 1985, there were only about 300,000 Medicare enrollees in Medicare HMOs under Medicare risk contracts (Zarabozo and LeMasurier, 1995). Enrollment enabled the elderly to reduce their growing out-of-pocket medical costs. HMOs eliminated the need for supplemental insurance to cover the 20 percent co-payments and other expenses not covered by Medicare. In these plans, those over age sixty-five often received health care benefits for prescription drugs and routine physical examinations. As of 1992, 1.4 million elderly, or about 4 percent, were enrolled in Medicare risk plans (Brown and Hill, 1994). By 1996, 4 million, or one in ten Medicare beneficiaries, were receiving health services through an HMO (Wolf and Gorman, 1996).

The Dominance of Managed Care

With the failure of serious health reform at the federal level, managed health care has emerged as the dominant model for private and public sector initiatives to contain health care spending in the United States. To understand how managed care works to contain costs, it is helpful to look at the major components of spending increases for health-related goods and services. National health care expenditure growth (NHE) results from three factors: population growth (N), increased utilization of health services per capita (Q), and rising prices per unit of service provided (P):

$$\text{NHE} = N \times Q \times P.$$

Dividing NHE by population growth provides a measure of per capita spending growth (NHP) that depends solely on the behavior of prices and utilization over time:

$$\text{NHP} = Q \times P.$$

Many managed care organizations that accept a fixed amount of reimbursement per enrollee regardless of services used are at risk that they will lose money if costs are higher than expected. Thus, they have financial incentives to control both the price and the quantity of health care services used. They control P by negotiating price discounts with physicians and hospitals, employing their own doctors, and/or purchasing and operating their own clinics and hospitals. HMOs control Q by altering physician practice patterns and restricting consumer choice to doctors and hospitals that have agreed to price discounts and utilization review. When physicians and hospitals are fully capitated—that is they agree to be paid a given amount per month for each plan enrollee regardless of services provided—then $Q \times P$ is fixed, and there can be no unexpected spending growth per enrollee over the duration of the contract.

As managed care plans grow and compete with one another for consumer business, pressures to reduce premiums charged by all health insurance plans and providers are created (Zwanziger and Melnick, 1996). This requires successful cost cutting in service delivery and pricing. In 1990, private per capita spending for health care rose 10.5 percent. By 1994, this rate of growth had fallen to 3.6 percent. Government spending increases per capita for Medicare and Medicaid slowed less radically, from 11.6 percent in 1990 to 7.6 in 1994 (National Center for Health Statistics, 1995). There is growing evidence that the significant drop in national health care spending growth in the mid-1990s stems primarily from the rapid adoption by private payers nationwide of managed care ("Managed care does it again," 1996; Levit et al., 1995).

Trends in National Health Care Spending

National health care spending as a percentage of total spending, or nominal **gross domestic product (GDP),** was 5.7 percent in 1965. Nominal GDP measures total current domestic expenditures for goods and services by consumers, business, and government. Over thirty years, this percentage more than doubled. By 1995, 13.6 percent of nominal GDP was for health-related goods and services (National Center for Health Statistics, 1995). Growth in the share of national output produced by the health care industry indicates the change in the composition of the national market basket of goods and services that we as a nation produce and consume. Whether social welfare has been improved by this shift will depend on the extent to which these increases were made up of greater quantities of services offered or higher prices.

If the source of increased health care spending is primarily higher prices charged for the same services over time, then consumers are likely to be made worse off, and health professionals and insurers as a group are better off. If health care spending is rising primarily because more and better health services are being provided and used over time, consumers are better off and rising health care expenditures are not a major concern. However, higher consumption of health services does not necessarily represent an increase in consumer welfare. If increased utilization is found to be inappropriate or ineffective, then patients have given up scarce resources for a service from which they have gained little or no additional benefit. Resources have been wasted.

Price Changes in Health Care Spending

The **Consumer Price Index (CPI),** which reflects the average prices charged for goods and services normally purchased by consumers, is commonly used to measure inflation. The **inflation rate** is the rate at which prices increase from year to year. Representative items are selected to be included in what is known as the "market basket" of the average consumer. Consumer price increases for all consumer goods and services are based on this represented group in constructing the CPI. The percentage of income spent on each item in the market basket is held constant over time, only the prices of each component are allowed to change. Thus, changes in the CPI reflect overall increases (or decreases) in a weighted average of the prices of goods and services that consumers are observed to purchase in a specific base year. Periodically, the market basket and base year are adjusted to reflect changes in consumption patterns. For example, the CPI was rebased in 1982–84.

Table 1-2 shows that the average level of prices facing U.S. consumers has risen 5.6 percent annually since 1965, although the annual rate has slowed to 3.1 percent since 1990. One component of the CPI is the **Medical Price Index (MPI),** which is measured in the same way as the CPI, using price increases for a fixed market basket

Table 1-2   Measures of Inflation in Health Care

Year	CPI for Current Year, All Items	% Change for Current Year, All Items[a]	MPI for Current Year	% Change for Current Year, Medical Care[a]
1965	31.5	4.3[b]	25.5	5.6[b]
1970	38.8	6.8[b]	34.0	6.6[b]
1975	53.8	5.8[b]	47.5	12.0[b]
1980	82.4	10.3	74.9	11.0
1985	107.6	1.9	113.5	6.3
1990	130.7	5.4	162.8	9.1
1995	152.4	2.8	220.5	4.5
1996	156.9	2.9	228.2	3.5
Average				
1965–1990		5.6		7.8
1990–1996		3.1		5.8
National Health Expenditures		**Nominal**	**Real (CPI)[c]**	**Real (MPI)[d]**
1990		$2,686	$2,055	$1,649
1995		3,621	2,376	1,642

[a]Average annual percentage change in current year.

[b]Five year average annual percentage change.

[c]Nominal national health expenditures divided by CPI and multiplied by 100.

[d]Nominal national health expenditures divided by MPI and multiplied by 100.

Source of CPI and MPI for 1990, 1995, and 1996: Sensenig et al. (1997).

Source for 1996 NHE: Medicare and Medicaid Statistical Supplement: 1 (1997).

Source for NHE for 1990 and CPI and MPI for 1965–1990: National Center for Health Statistics (1996).

containing only health-related goods and services. This index is used in constructing the overall CPI. As measured by the MPI, prices charged for health care have risen more rapidly over the past thirty years—by over 2 percent per year—than the prices of the average of all other goods in the consumer's market basket. Since 1990, annual medical care price increases have moderated to 5.8 percent from 7.8 percent, in part due to a slowing of general inflation in the economy, as seen in the drop in CPI growth. Nevertheless, at 5.8 percent, this is nearly over 3 percentage points faster than price increases in all other consumer goods. Also the significant fall in health care prices in 1995 and 1996 may be temporary. Health plans are losing money in part due to price competition and higher administrative costs (Hamer and VanAntiwerp, 1997). Health plans are expected to raise premiums in 1997 and 1998 (Ginsburg and Pickreign, 1997). Thus, after the temporary lull, price increases in health care may continue to absorb a greater portion of each dollar spent when compared with other consumer goods purchased.

If national health expenditures per capita are adjusted for consumer price increases, an estimate of real spending on health-related goods and services can be obtained. Real spending estimates try to remove price changes from dollars spent to allow for a more accurate comparison of consumption over time. To create these real spending estimates, health expenditures are first divided by the CPI. Because the CPI is an index, the adjusted amount must then be multiplied by 100 to obtain a dollar amount, as reflected in the following formula:

$$\text{Real NHP} = \frac{\text{Current NHP} \times 100}{\text{Price index}}.$$

In 1995, national health expenditures per capita were $3,621, and the CPI was 152.4. Applying the formula, real spending in 1995 was $2,376 per person, somewhat less than suggested by the unadjusted numbers.

Because health care prices have risen much faster than those in the general economy, dividing NHP by the MPI reduces real health spending per capita even more than does deflation using the CPI. In 1995, real national health expenditures per capita were only $1,642 using this adjustment, slightly less than real spending in 1990. If the MPI accurately measures health care price increases, health care price inflation remains a major problem for consumers. Attempts by third-party payers to contain health care costs through price discounts from providers seem warranted.

Problems with the MPI

The MPI may exaggerate health care inflation. Prices actually paid by purchasers of services may not be accurately represented by this index. (Note that similar concerns exist for the CPI. Some economists believe that the CPI may overstate inflation by up to 1.5 percentage points. Moreover, if the medical care component overstates inflation, this will contribute to the bias in the CPI.) The MPI includes quoted hospital and physician prices, individual health insurance premiums, and retail prices paid directly by consumers. It does not reflect the "markdown" received by some third-party payers—that is special contractual arrangements negotiated by government and managed care companies that result in effective prices that are much lower than those shown on the bill. These discounts may result in price cuts as high as 50 or 60 percent for some payers. As hospitals and doctors try to raise prices charged to other patients to compensate for these lower payments from the government and managed care plans, quoted rates may rise. This depends on the lack of resistance to price increases by other payers. Therefore, health care price inflation as measured by the MPI is overstated for the majority of health care consumers whose third-party payers are able to negotiate aggressively with doctors and hospitals for reduced fees. As managed care has expanded, these payers represent a greater proportion of consumers of health services. Billed charges become increasingly irrelevant.

Effect of Quality on Measured Health Care Prices

A price index like the MPI or the CPI does not capture price changes alone. Improvements in the quality of goods or services purchased are also embedded in price increases. For example, the development of better drugs, improved medical procedures, and increased physician skill may be picked up as price inflation by the MPI. Periodic adjustment of the basic market basket attempts to control for these changes but cannot do so completely. Therefore, rising health care prices may be attributable in part to the rising quality of health care goods and services. The omission of quality may be true of other goods and services in the CPI, however, so other components of the consumer's market basket may be similarly overstated. Therefore, quality improvement and effectiveness must be relatively greater and more highly valued in health care than in other sectors of the economy to explain the persistent divergence between medical prices and all other consumer prices.

Distribution Effects of Health Care Inflation

One of the consequences of rising health care prices relative to other prices in the economy is that health services and health insurance become less affordable to those whose incomes are rising more slowly than average in the economy. As commercial premiums rise, workers elect not to purchase insurance coverage, and businesses with very low profit margins decline to offer it to their workers. For people whose medical expenses are not fully covered by insurance, out-of-pocket costs will increase. As shown in Table 1-3, the number of uninsured Americans has steadily risen since 1980, suggesting that financial access, and not quantity or quantity of services, may contribute to the less than adequate relative performance of the United States in several national health indicators.

Utilization per Capita

U.S. consumers with financial access to care appear to have used increasing quantities of health services over time. Although admissions to hospitals and average lengths of

Table 1-3   Insurance Coverage, as a Percent of Civilian Population

Year	Private insurance	Medicaid recipients	Uninsured persons
1960	68.8[a]	N/A	N/A
1965	72.4[a]	N/A	N/A
1970	78.7[a]	N/A	N/A
1975	82.1[a]	N/A	N/A
1980[b]	78.8	5.9	12.5
1984[b]	76.9	6.0	15.4
1989[b]	76.6	6.4	15.7
1994[b]	70.1	10.2	17.8

[a]Hospital insurance only, for all age groups. Source: U.S. Bureau of the Census, 1989.
[b]For persons under age 65 only. Source: National Center for Health Statistics, 1995 and 1996.

stay have declined, intensity of treatment during a hospitalization has increased. Previously unavailable diagnostic and treatment services, such as CT scans, new and more effective drugs, coronary artery bypass grafts, and cataract procedures, have contributed significantly to real growth in health care spending. Among men, diagnostic and other nonsurgical procedures rose from 31.3 per 1,000 population in 1980 to 60.6 per 1,000 in 1993. Among women, the rate was 27.5 per 1,000 and 71.9 per 1,000 over the same period. (National Center for Health Statistics, 1996). U.S. consumers have greater access to advanced techniques than the citizens of Canada, as measured by the use per person of open heart surgery, cardiac catheterization, organ transplantation, radiation therapy, and magnetic resonance imaging (Rublee, 1994).

Although the number and types of services delivered to consumers have grown, it is not clear that these additional services improve the fundamental health status of the population or of individual patients. Results of case-controlled experiments in which the cost-effectiveness of more treatment is compared with the cost-effectiveness of less treatment can be used to improve resource allocation decisions. As was indicated in Table 1-1, in terms of basic health status indicators, the U.S. population fares no better and sometimes is worse off than are citizens in other countries that spend less on health care. More information on the cost-effectiveness of treatment alternatives based on health outcomes is critically important if individual and community resources are to be used wisely.

Fundamental Causes of Rising Health Care Prices

Regardless of how they are measured, health care prices have risen faster than the general level of consumer prices since the mid-1960s. This persistence of higher inflation rates in health care over such a long period of time needs to be explained in order to understand the phenomenal growth of managed care in the 1990s.

A persistent rise over time in prices occurs because of either (1) a continuing reduction in supply or (2) a continuing increase in the demand of a good or service over time. Restriction of supply does not seem to be a problem in the U.S. acute health care system (see Table 1-4). Although the number of hospital beds per 1,000 population has steadily declined since the mid-1960s, the available capacity has remained more than adequate. Average occupancy rates were above 76 percent before 1980. In the 1980s and 1990s, available capacity grew as changes in reimbursement moved the site of care to outpatient departments, ambulatory care clinics, doctors' offices, and home services, leaving hospitals one-third empty. The supply of physicians has grown markedly since 1970 as well. Physicians per 1,000 population rose from 1.42 in 1960 to 2.63 in 1995, or 2.4 percent per year. Over the same period, the supply of registered nurses grew from 2.82 per 1,000 to 7.26 per 1,000, a 218 percent increase, or 8.8 percent annually. Thus, the rising relative prices of medical care cannot be attributed to a reduced supply of health professionals or available hospital beds relative to the population served.

Another possibility is that health care providers can raise their prices without deterring patient use. Normally this situation occurs when suppliers have a monopoly or cartel in a good for which there are few available substitutes. Physicians and hospitals, however, do not have monopoly power to set or raise prices. Nevertheless, the fee-for-service reimbursement system and third-party payers have failed to penalize providers who raise prices. Price increases of health care providers were simply passed on to third-party payers and then transferred to workers through lower wages, to consumers in higher prices, and to taxpayers in higher taxes.

If supply shortages and monopoly power do not explain rising prices, this leaves rising demand as the main source of health care inflation. Several factors have in-

Table 1-4   Supply of Health Professionals and Beds, 1960–1995

Year	Physicians per 1,000[a]	Registered Nurses per 1,000[b]	Hospital Beds per 1,000[c]	Occupancy Rate[d], in Percent
1960	1.42	2.93	9.3	84.6
1965	1.48	3.19	8.9	82.3
1970	1.61	3.68	8.0	80.3
1975	1.80	4.46	6.9	76.7
1980	2.02	5.60	6.0	77.7
1985	2.28	6.47	5.5	69.5
1990	2.44	6.90	4.9	69.7
1994	2.63	7.93	4.1[d]	67.7[d]

[a]All federal and non-federal physicians. Source: American Medical Association, 1996.

[b]Active registered nurses. Sources: Data for 1994 are from ACHE, 1996. All other years are from U.S. Bureau of the Census, 1980, and 1995.

[c]For all hospitals. Source: U.S. Bureau of the Census, 1980, and 1995.

[d]For 1995. Source: The Universal Healthcare Almanac, 1997.

creased demand for health services and made consumers less resistant to price increases over time: national income growth, expansion of insurance, and increases in the intensity of services initiated and ordered by physicians, called **supplier-induced demand.**

National Income Growth

In the absence of increased money income, persistent price increases are not likely to occur in any one sector of the economy. The reason is that consumers must give up the purchases of less important goods and services to buy more expensive and necessary goods if their incomes are fixed. At some point, they will stop increasing the amount of income they devote to a good whose price continues to rise faster than their incomes. Continued price increases in one good or service above that experienced in other goods and services will be self-limiting.

To get a continued rise in spending for goods and services whose prices continue to go up requires a growth in consumer incomes. This will be true whether the spending is initiated by individuals or by the government. Because the government must tax or borrow money from citizens to pay for expanded services, such as health care, the government's ability to spend is ultimately limited by the growth in the money income of its citizens.

As consumers have more income and wealth, they may choose to spend a greater proportion of their incomes individually and collectively on relatively scarce goods and services, like larger homes, leisure time, higher education, and advanced health care services, and less on basic and more abundant goods, like food and clothing. An increased willingness to pay for longevity and the maintenance of health appears greater among wealthier nations (Newhouse, 1977). Through private or government financing mechanisms, citizens have elected to increase the share of national spending going for health care. Because additional and more advanced health care services are costly to supply, the prices of these goods and services rise.

The United States is not unique in this respect. Other wealthy, industrialized countries are also experiencing an acceleration in health care spending growth (Schieber, Poullier, and Greenwald, 1994). In Canada, for example, NHE spending had grown to over 10 percent of GDP by 1993, up from 4 percent in 1973 (National Center for Health Statistics, 1996). Unlike the United States, where market-based, managed care systems are being tried, other nations are seeking government interventions to slow the growth of national health care spending (U.S. GAO, 1993).

Expansion of Insurance

Although a life-threatening medical emergency eliminates consumer willingness to search for a lower price, most of the time consumers' lack of resistance to higher prices in health care is due to the incentives created by health insurance. Over time, reimbursement for health care services in the United States increasingly has been the responsibility of third-party payers, both public and private. In 1950, 65.5 percent of personal health spending was funded out of pocket by individual patients. By 1994, individuals paid only 21 percent of the cost. Of the 79 percent of spending financed by third parties in 1994, 35.5 percent was from private health insurance and 43.5 percent from government (National Center for Health Statistics, 1996).

With the emergence of third-party payers, dollars spent for health care have become increasingly separated from the delivery of services. Insurance is now more comprehensive, covering many medical services outside the hospital. Doctor visits and treatments, ambulatory care services, prescriptions, and dental care have been added to many benefit packages. The consumer pays a fee, or copayment, usually at the time of service, but this is only a fraction of the full price. Although insurance coverage has eliminated the public's concern that doctors or other health care practitioners might prescribe fewer services for less affluent patients, it has also reduced pressures on health professionals to deliver care at the lowest cost.

Insurance introduces **moral hazard** (or insurance-induced demand): the risk that individuals will use more services simply because they pay little or nothing at the time of service. (In insurance, *moral* hazard normally refers only to fraudulent behavior on the part of the insured, while *morale* hazard applies to situations in which those who are insured tend to be less careful because they are insured. In health care, *moral* hazard refers to the latter type of behavior, as well as the tendency to use medically less important services simply because of their lower relative prices with insurance.) Although it is absurd to suggest that people are more likely to get sick if they have health insurance, once they do become ill, more services are likely to be consumed if the insurance is available. High Cesarean section rates in the U.S., many of which are considered unnecessary, may be influenced by patient demand and insurance coverage. One study found that "women who have opted for one C-section opt for another because they prefer a 'scheduled' delivery" (Rose, 1996). C-section rates in Missouri hospitals were found to be the lowest in a hospital that treated medically indigent patients, who normally have more high-risk births (Carlton, 1996). Doctors defend the use of C-sections to prevent being sued (Lutz, 1989). Moreover, since most consumers are risk averse, they may accept potentially ineffective treatment—antibiotics for viral infections, for example—rather than risk inadequate treatment, especially when they bear little or none of the additional cost.

Insurance also reduces consumer resistance to higher prices. Research indicates that consumers are more responsive to price increases in health care the more they pay out-of-pocket and for services that are less urgent, such as in primary and preventive care (Manning, Newhouse, Duan, Keeler, and Liebowitz, 1987). Further evidence of moral hazard is found by looking at the use of covered services across countries. In Germany, where there are no co-payments for doctor visits, the population goes to the doctor far more frequently than they do in the United States, where co-payments on doctor visits exist (U.S. GAO, 1993).

To maintain the viability of the insurance fund, moral hazard must be controlled. In most developed countries, this responsibility falls on government as the primary insurer. In European nations, for example, public coverage averages 77 percent of total insurance, as compared with only 41 percent in the United States. In these countries, government must institute mechanisms to control moral hazard. For example, the government of Ontario, Canada, initiated a public information campaign in 1993 to discourage unnecessary visits to the doctor by describing available home remedies to treat the common cold (Greenberg, 1994). Merely encouraging people to change their behavior often does not work, however. Another avenue that governments take to constrain moral hazard is to restrict the supply of hospital beds and physicians, which results in patients' queuing for services. Germany recently instituted health reform designed to limit the number of licenses granted to physicians.

Commercial insurance companies usually have financial incentives to contain moral hazard of their insured population, such as co-payments or deductibles or limits on coverage for certain services that are more price sensitive, such as outpatient mental health and substance abuse services (Buck and Umland, 1997). Managed care goes even further to hold back insurance-induced demand. In addition to co-payments and deductibles, these insurers reduce the choice of physician specialists and hospitals available to plan members and alter physician practice patterns. By changing physician practices, managed care plans influence another source of rising spending: supplier-induced demand.

Increases in the Intensity of Services Initiated and Ordered

Once a patient is covered by insurance, the financial costs of excessive or inappropriate care are borne by the insurer, or third-party payer, to which the physician is not directly responsible. Physicians with no fiduciary responsibility to the payer, but who initiate or provide 70 percent of all health care services consumed, may be more willing to offer additional treatment than risk a dissatisfied patient or, worse, a malpractice suit for inadequate care. Moreover, there is a difference in information available to the buyer and seller in this transaction. Experienced and trained physicians are in a better position to determine the number and type of services to be used for treatment. The patient, or the patient's payer, often has no way of verifying that prescribed services are appropriate and necessary without considerable additional time and expense. Under these circumstances, there is a potential for physicians to influence patient demand inappropriately.

Evidence of supplier-induced demand comes from studies of the response of physicians to fee restrictions. When physicians are unable to raise fees over time, they are observed to increase the number of services offered to each patient they see (Rice and LaBelle, 1989). The HCFA has attempted to control supplier-induced demand through fee schedules for physicians treating Medicare patients. Included in the physicians' fees are "volume performance standards," which adjust physician fees downward for expected volume increases in specialties where there is greater likelihood that physicians will prescribe additional treatment to offset the effect of fee controls.

Other Reasons for Rising Health Care Spending

Three additional reasons have been given for the significant rise in spending for health services: the aging of the population, the growth of technology, and **market failure.**

Aging of the Population

Older citizens need additional health services. Need does not equate with demand, however. Only if the elderly are able to pay for these services will expenditures associated with age increase. In poorer countries, the aging of the population does not alter the amount spent on health care. Once financial access is assured, however, we would expect to see greater use of services among the elderly. The aging postwar baby boom generation will begin to be eligible for Medicare starting in 2010, and its size will grow significantly over the next thirty years. For this reason, concern about the growth in health spending for the elderly has become of major concern for the federal government.

Growth of Technology

Many policymakers attribute rising prices in health care to the development and use of advanced medical technology. This, too, may be the result of rising incomes and wealth, augmented by insurance-induced demand. With fixed incomes and no insurance, consumers would tend to choose technology that is cost saving or leads to no increase in costs without a significant demonstrated benefit. Therefore, growth in money income may fuel the demand for new techniques in health care. If money incomes are low and not expected to grow, there would be a small market for advanced, cost-increasing techniques. Innovative firms will bear the financial risk of developing a new medical technique only if a sufficient return is expected. A higher return is more likely in wealthy nations and among consumers whose purchasing power has been augmented by insurance.

Market Failure

A final reason given for escalating health care costs is **market failure.** When a market fails to operate correctly, it does not achieve the lowest price or maximum output possible. Among the reasons for market failure in health care, in addition to the problems created by insurance, are informational disparities between physicians (the sellers) and patients (the buyers) and the inability of consumers to search for lower prices and higher quality in a medical emergency. As a result, it is argued, government regulation is necessary to monitor and control prices charged and the quality of available services.

Managed care is a market alternative to government regulation to eliminate market failure. It allows consumers to select physicians in advance and contractually obligates the physicians to provide all needed services at a prenegotiated price. Quality is maintained by competition where comparable information on the performance of competing health plans is available to consumers and third-party payers. Without standards of treatment and verifiable outcomes of treatment, however, managed care will only partially eliminate market failure. Moreover, if health insurance markets become oligopolistic—that is, if there are only two or three health plans in a market—market efficiency may not be attained.

Policy Options to Control Health Care Costs

Although managed care is now being adopted by third-party payers as a means to contain health care spending, there are other options, including a national health insurance plan, such as a single-payer system, and medical savings accounts. Both of these approaches increase consumer choice of physicians and maintain the physician-patient relationship.

In the case of a single-payer system, the government is largely responsible for setting prices, paying providers, and allocating capital (facilities and equipment) to the system. One of the arguments in favor of a single payer is the ability of government, or its agents, to negotiate and set prices unilaterally with all health care providers and to reduce the administrative costs of billing, collecting, and paying for services. In fact, it is argued that a major portion of the difference in health care spending across nations may be due to differences in administrative costs, *not* the quantity and quality of health services rendered.

At the other extreme are medical savings accounts (MSAs). With MSAs, the private competitive market dominates; individuals use before-tax income to purchase health insurance and medical services directly from providers and insurers. Here, the individual consumer, not the employer or the government, makes the decision about the type of insurance to purchase, providers to employ, and services to use. With an MSA, the consumer can accumulate savings that earn interest, tax free for use on health care in future years, or withdraw funds from the MSA to use for other purposes. Funds withdrawn for nonmedical goods and services are subject to normal taxation. MSAs create strong incentives for the consumer to reduce ineffective and unnecessary utilization, to search more aggressively for lower prices and higher quality, and to monitor billing errors. Critics of MSAs point out that they discourage the use of preventive health services and may benefit healthier and wealthier members of society.

Financial Management Under Managed Care

Financial management is the efficient and effective use of financial resources to achieve the mission of the health care organization. Financial resources are derived from profits or surpluses, bank loans, and the proceeds from the sale of bonds and stocks to outside investors. In the not-for-profit organizations found in health care, donations are also a source of financial capital. These financial assets must then be employed, or invested, in real assets—personnel, inventory, plant and equipment—so as to achieve the goals and objectives of the organization.

Knowledge in three core disciplines is typically used by financial managers: **financial accounting, managerial (cost) accounting,** and **corporate finance.** Financial accounting is concerned with keeping accurate records of the performance of the organization. These records or financial statements are used by external agents, such as creditors, government, the governing board, and community stakeholders, to assess the financial performance and viability of the organization. Financial accounting information is also important internally for keeping track of tax obligations and other financial liabilities, so that cash is available for timely payment. Financial accounting information is used for monitoring the behavior of assets like cash, securities, accounts receivable, inventories, plant, and equipment and for developing budget projections. Cost, or managerial, accounting focuses on developing measures of the internal performance of the organization. The information it generates is used for pricing, budgeting, and operations management. Both cost and financial accounting are *backward looking* and involve developing standardized and consistent measures of the real activity of the firm.

Corporate finance focuses on the investment and financing decisions of the firm. Although this aspect of financial management relies on accounting information for developing models and examining alternatives, it ultimately relies on market-based information on competitors, potential customers, reimbursement regimes, inflation, and interest rates for making strategic investment decisions. Corporate finance is *forward looking*; that is, decisions must be made for actions that will be carried out in an uncertain future. As such, analysis of cash flowing in and out of the organization and the assessment and management of risk receive a great deal of attention in corporate finance.

The financial management of health care organizations has undergone several transformations in response to the changing environments that health care providers face. During the period of expanded access in the 1960s and 1970s, financial managers focused on accounting functions to measure and capture expenses for the purposes of maximizing reimbursement. Health care provider competition was based on quality rather than price, and there were few concerns about correctly measured costs and strategic pricing. Providers faced little financial risk because expenses were fully reimbursed. Cost accounting and corporate finance functions were less important to financial managers during this period. Because the hospital was the locus of the most expensive care, financial management techniques were in greater demand in hospitals and hospital systems than in doctors' offices, group practices, and nursing homes.

The second period of financial management was during the shift from fee-for-service and cost reimbursement of the 1970s to the cost-containment strategies of the 1980s. Business and financial risk increased significantly as revenues became more uncertain and financing became more costly. The need for corporate finance skills came into prominence during this period. Also, health care organizations began to manage assets more carefully, so short-term cash management became more important. Investment decisions, which locked the organization into a long-term commitment of resources, became increasingly critical. Hospital strategic pricing and maximization of reimbursement made the mix of hospital third-party payers important for financial viability. During this period, many rural and inner-city hospitals closed or became financially weakened.

Cost accounting has now emerged as an important function of the financial manager, and corporate finance is critical to health care operations. Today, better financial management tools are needed in organizations other than hospitals as large physician group practices are formed. The management of risk under managed care contracts has grown in importance in financial management. Finally, more than ever before, health care finance requires the integration of clinical information with financial data to manage and control both the utilization and cost—the medical risk—associated with the delivery of patient care under a managed care contract. Under managed care, this risk is largely shifted from the third-party payer and insurer to the provider. As a provider and bearer of increased financial risk, health care professionals today need a broad and sophisticated understanding of the elements of health care financial management.

Conclusion

In a managed care environment, health care managers require expanded financial management skills. In this chapter, we have shown how growing health care expenditures have created higher prices, growth in the uninsured, and the adoption of managed health care as a strategy for containing health care costs. We reviewed the changes in financial management that accompanied changes in the health care environment. In the next chapter, we examine the prototype managed care organization—the health maintenance organization—and investigate the new dimension of health care financial management—the insurance function—that is undertaken when a provider accepts a capitated contract with a managed care organization.

Case 1-1: Performance of St. Louis Area Hospitals, 1983–1992

Information taken from the financial statements of St. Louis area hospitals for the period 1983 to 1992 is presented below and on your student diskette in a file called Case 1. Included are aggregated data for all hospitals on gross charges, contractual allowances, net revenues, expenses and gain (loss) from operations, average cost per discharge and cost per visit and how much prices have been marked up over cost during this period. The table provides information on inpatient statistics and inflation rates in the St. Louis area over this period as well. To answer the questions below, create formulas in the blank cells on the second page of the Student Worksheets using the table entries on page one as input values. To help you get started, several formulas are already set up for you.

Case 1-1 Questions

1. In the table, "allowances" refers to special payment arrangements and price discounts with third-party payers, as well as bad debt expenses and charity care. Gross charges (total revenues) are listed prices (P) times the number of services provided (Q). Net patient service revenue (R) is actual amounts paid to hospitals

Case 1 Totals for Missouri and Illinois (All Figures Are in Millions of Dollars)

	1983	1984	1985	1986	1987	1988	1989	1990	1991	1992
Income Statement										
Total Gross Charges	1,938	1,987	2,129	2,432	2,727	3,041	3,458	4,010	4,564	5,234
Less: Allowances	388	360	379	549	725	896	1,131	1,322	1,653	1,979
Net Patient Service Revenue	1,550	1,627	1,750	1,883	2,002	2,145	2,327	2,688	2,910	3,255
Other Operating Revenue	46	51	58	64	76	87	95	106	132	153
Total Operating Revenue	1,596	1,678	1,808	1,947	2,078	2,232	2,422	2,794	3,042	3,407
Total Operating Expenses	1,525	1,569	1,690	1,882	2,046	2,205	2,398	2,752	2,996	3,335
Gain (Loss) from Operations	71	109	118	65	33	26	24	42	46	72
Costs										
Cost per Day	$401.59	$452.64	$501.53	$544.83	$592.55	$645.39	$702.84	$792.57	$875.18	$986.74
Cost per Discharge	$3,193	$3,413	$3,699	$4,085	$4,452	$4,817	$5,122	$5,707	$6,005	$6,528
Mark-up Percent (Charges over cost)	27.1%	26.7%	26.0%	29.3%	33.3%	37.9%	44.2%	45.7%	52.3%	56.9%
Inflation Indexes										
Consumer Price Index	99.6	103.9	107.6	109.6	113.6	118.3	124.0	130.7	136.2	140.3
Medical Price Index	100.6	106.8	113.5	122.0	130.1	138.6	149.3	162.8	177.0	190.1
Inpatient Statistics										
Average Daily Beds Available	12,518	12,281	11,977	11,973	11,830	11,860	11,756	11,383	11,214	11,033
Discharges	423,547	401,056	387,775	382,368	372,044	361,654	362,205	360,512	364,050	362,917
Patient Days	3,367,169	3,024,070	2,859,660	2,866,949	2,795,298	2,699,489	2,639,507	2,595,949	2,497,917	2,400,780
Occupancy Percentage	73.7%	67.3%	65.4%	65.6%	64.7%	62.2%	61.5%	62.5%	61.0%	59.6%
Average Length of Stay	7.9	7.5	7.4	7.5	7.5	7.5	7.3	7.2	6.9	6.6

Carry out to 3 decimal places

for services. In a single year, the only difference in the two numbers is between prices charged (P) and reimbursement received (R), not in the utilization of services (Q).

a) What is the average annual change in gross charges from 1983 to 1992? (Hint: Find the percentage change in each year, sum them, and then divide the result by nine.) Below are formulas for the yearly percentage change, from the end of 1983 to the end of 1984, and for the ten-year average.

$$\text{Yearly percentage change (YPC)} = \frac{\text{(gross charges ('83) - gross charges ('84)}}{\text{gross charges ('83)}}$$

$$\text{Annual Average (1983–1992): } \text{YPC}_{1984} + \text{YPC}_{1985} + \text{.......} \text{YPC}_{1992}) / 9$$

b) Using the same approach as in (a), what are the yearly percentage change and the annual average change over the ten-year period in net patient service revenue?

c) What is the average contractual allowance as a percent of gross revenues each year? What is the average for the ten-year period? Has the size of this difference between gross charges and net patient service revenues grown over time? Why do you think this is has occurred?

diff = gross charges - net serv. rev.

MPI

d) By how much are average hospital prices overstated if gross charges, instead of actual reimbursement, are used to calculate price changes for the MPI?

2. Although hospitals in your area gained $72 million from operations in 1992, you are concerned as to whether area hospitals are making the same amount of money, in real terms, as they were in 1983, considering general price inflation in the economy. To find out, adjust your gain from operations using the Consumer Price Index provided in the table. What has happened to earnings over time? Would it be appropriate to use the Medical Price Index for this purpose? Why or why not?

3. Operating margin is the percentage of revenues remaining as profit (or surplus) after expenses have been met. The operating margin is calculated by the following formula:

$$\frac{\text{gain(loss) from operations}}{\text{patient revenues}}$$

What is the operating margin using net patient service revenue in the denominator of this formula? Using gross charges? Which better reflects financial performance? Why?

4. What is the average annual percent change in the CPI and the MPI over the ten-year period. (Hint: See formulas in Question 1a.) How much faster have medical prices relative to general prices risen over the ten-year period?

5. Cost per day has risen from $401.59 to $986.74 during this ten-year period while cost per discharge has grown from $3,193 to $6,528. Adjust these costs for aver-

Cost per day × 100
_____
CPI

age inflation using the CPI and for medical price inflation using the MPI. Are costs per unit higher in 1992 than in 1983 after these adjustments? Assuming that the MPI accurately reflects changes in medical care prices, how do you explain the changes in costs per day and per discharge?

6. Create a formula in your spreadsheet to calculate the ten-year average annual percentage change in beds, discharges, inpatient days, occupancy and average length of stay. (Hint: See formulas in Question 1a.)

    a) What has happened to inpatient utilization over this period?

    b) Based on the discussion in the chapter, why do you think this has occurred?

    c) Given this information, is utilization a source of the increases in gross charges and net patient revenues observed during this period?

References

American College of Healthcare Executives. (1996, Sep/Oct). Key industry facts. *Healthcare Executive*. Chicago, IL: American College of Healthcare Executives.

American Medical Association. (1996). *Physician characteristics and distribution in the U.S.* (1995–96 ed.). Chicago, IL: American Medical Association.

Berman, J. B., Weeks, L. E., & Kukla, S. F. (1986). *The financial management of hospitals* (6th ed.). Ann Arbor, MI: Health Administration Press.

Blendon, R. J., Leitman, R., Morrison, I., & Donelan, K. (1992). Satisfaction with health systems in ten nations. *Health Affairs, 9*(2), 185–192.

Brown, R. S., & Hill, J. W. (1994). *The effects of Medicare risk HMOs on Medicare HMOs and the elderly*. In H. A. Luft (Ed.), *HMOs and the elderly*. Ann Arbor, MI: Health Administration Press.

Buck, J. A., & Umland, B. (1997, Jul/Aug). Covering mental health and substance abuse services. *Health Affairs, 16*(4), 120–126.

Carlton, J. G. (1996, Oct. 14). No delivery: Regional closes obstetrics. *St. Louis Post Dispatch*.

Gardner, J. (1996, May 6). Trust fund report turns up pressure. *Modern Healthcare, 26*(19), 8.

Ginsburg, P. B., & Pickreign, J. D. (1997, Jul/Aug). Tracking health care costs: An update. *Health Affairs. 16*(4), 151–155.

Greenburg, J. (1994, Feb. 22). Take two tablespoons of mustard and call if you don't feel better. *Wall Street Journal*, B1.

Gundling, Rick. (1997, May). Welfare reform's effect on Medicaid eligibility. *Healthcare Financial Management, 51*(5), 88–89.

Hamer, R., & VanAntiwerp, S. (1997, Jun). Study results show decline on HMO operating margins. *Healthcare Financial Management, 51*(6), 78–84.

Health Care Financing Administration. (1995). *Health Care Financing review: Medicare and Medicaid statistical supplement*, 1995. (HCFA Pub. No. 03348). Baltimore, MD: Health Care Financing Administration.

Health Care Financing Administration. (1997). *Health Care Financing review: Medicare and Medicaid statistical supplement*, 1997. (HCFA Pub. No. 03399). Baltimore, MD: Health Care Financing Administration.

Herrick, R. R. (1995). Medicaid and managed care. In P. R. Kongstvedt (Ed.), *Essentials of managed care*. Gaithersburg, MD: Aspen.

Jensen, G. A., Morrisey, M. A., Gaffney, S., & Liston, D. K. (1997, Jan/Feb). The new dominance of managed care: Insurance trends in the 1990s. *Health Affairs, 16*(1), 125–136.

Levit, K. R., Lazenby, H. C., Braden, B. R., Cowan, C. A., McDonnell, P. A. et al. (1996, Fall). National health expenditures, 1995. *Health Care Financing Review, 18*(1), 175–214.

Long, S. H. (1993). Causes of soaring Medicaid spending, 1988–1991. In D. Rowland, J. Feder, & A. Salganicoff (Eds.), *Medicaid financing crisis: Balancing responsibilities, priorities, and dollars*. Washington, DC: American Association for the Advancement of Science Press.

Lutz, S. (1989, Feb. 3). Providers forced to defend C-section rates. *Modern Healthcare, 19*(5), 66–67.

Managed care does it again. (1996). *Business and Health, 14*(3), 10.

Managed care enrollment grows: Plans become profitable with small premium hikes. (1996). *Employee Benefit Plan Review, 50*(8), 24–26.

Manning, W. G., Newhouse, J. P., Duan, N., Keeler, E. B., & Liebowitz, A. M. (1987). Health insurance and the demand for medical care. *American Economic Review, 77*(3), 251–277

National Center for Health Statistics. (1995). *Health, United States, 1994*. Hyattsville, MD: Public Health Service.

National Center for Health Statistics. (1996). *Health, United States, 1995*. Hyattsville, MD: Public Health Service.

Newhouse, J. P. (1977). Medical care expenditures—A cross-national survey. *Journal of Human Resources, 12*(1), 115–125.

Overview of the Medicare and Medicaid Programs. (1997). *Health Care Financing Review: Medicare and Medicaid Statistical Supplement: 1*.

Rice, T., & LaBelle, R. (1989, Fall). Do physicians induce demand for medical services? *Journal of Politics, Policy and Law, 14*, 587–600.

Rose, J. R. (1996, Mar. 25). Too many C-sections? Hospitals blame patients. *Medical Economics, 73*(6), 23.

Rublee, D. A. (1994). Medical technology in Canada, Germany and the United States. *Health Affairs, 13*(4), 113–117.

Schieber, G. J., Poullier, J. P., & Greenwald, L. G. (1994, Fall). Health system performance in OECD countries, 1980–1992. *Health Affairs, 13*(4), 100–112.

Sensenig, A., Heffler, S. K., & Donham, C. S., (1997, Summer). Hospital, employment and price indicators for the health care industry: Fourth quarter 1966 and annual data for 1988–96. *Health Care Financing Review, 18* (4).

Trends in age and uninsured status in the United States. (1995). *Health Care Financing Review* (Medicare and Medicaid Statistical Supplement), 128–129.

The Universal Healthcare Almanac. (1997). Phoenix, AZ: Silver & Cherner.

U.S. Bureau of the Census. (1980). *Statistical Abstract of the United States: 1980* (101st ed.). Washington, DC.

U.S. Bureau of the Census. (1989). *Statistical Abstract of the United States: 1989* (109th ed.). Washington, DC.

U.S. Bureau of the Census. (1995). *Statistical Abstract of the United States: 1995* (115th ed.). Washington, DC.

U.S. General Accounting Office (GAO). (1993, July). *1993 German health reforms: New cost control initiatives* (GAO/HRD-93-103). Washington, DC: Government Printing Office.

U.S. House of Representatives, Committee on Ways and Means. (1991). *Overview of entitlement programs: 1991 green book*. Washington, DC: Government Printing Office.

Welch, W. P. (1994). HMO market share and its effects on local medicare costs. In H. A. Luft (Ed.), *HMOs and the Elderly*. Ann Arbor, MI: Health Administration Press.

Wolf, L. F., & Gorman, J. K. (1996). New directions and development in managed care financing. *Health Care Financing Review, 17*(3), 1–5.

Wrightson, C. W. (1990). *HMO rate setting and financial strategy*. Ann Arbor, MI: Health Administration Press Perspectives.

Zarabozo, C., & LeMasurier, J. D. (1995). Medicare and managed care. In P. R. Kongstvedt (Ed.), *Essentials of managed health care*. Gaithersburg, MD: Aspen.

Zwanziger, J., Melnick, G. A., & Barnezai, A. (1994). Costs and price competition in California hospitals, 1980–1990. *Health Affairs, 13*(4), 118–126.

Zwanziger, J., & Melnick, G. A. (1996, Summer). Can managed care plans control health care costs? *Health Affairs, 15*(2), 185–199.

Chapter 2

Risk and Insurance in Health Care: The Health Maintenance Organization

The purpose of this chapter is to develop an understanding of insurance and how insurance companies price their services. As providers take the role of health care insurers by accepting risk contracts, they must understand how to evaluate these risks from the perspective of insurers. In this chapter, risk is defined, and the function of insurance in increasing consumer welfare is explored.

Learning Objectives

Upon successful completion of this chapter, the learner will:

- Describe why people buy and insurers sell health insurance.
- Distinguish among types of risk faced by a managed care organization.
- Calculate the expected value and standard deviation of the outcomes of an uncertain event.
- Evaluate the objective risk of an insured group.
- Outline the characteristics of different types of health maintenance organizations.
- Relate the financial incentives of health maintenance organizations to their organizational structure.
- Construct a capitation rate for a hypothetical group of enrollees in a managed health care plan.

Key Terms

adverse selection	medical care risk
business risk	medical loss ratio
capitation rate	objective risk
community rating system	premium rate setting
expected value	pure risk
experience rating system	risk aversion
financial risk	speculative risk
health status risk	underwriting risk
loading	

Introduction

Effective financial management under the incentives produced by managed care has become increasingly important with the growth of managed care organizations. In this environment, the health care professional needs to understand not only the financial management concerns associated with the delivery of health care services but also the financial management issues of providing insurance services. In this chapter, the nature of insurance and risk is explored, and the health maintenance organization (**HMO**), as a prototype of managed care, is described. In an HMO, the valuation, pricing, and management of medical expense risk are added to the traditional responsibilities of the health care financial manager. The informational requirements of managed health care are illustrated by developing a capitation rate for a health insurance plan.

Risk and Insurance

The primary concern of health professionals is providing high-quality health care services to patients. Under fee-for-service medicine, the patient is charged whatever the market will bear to provide the best care possible. Physicians, acting on behalf of their patients, determine which services are appropriate and necessary. With about 85 percent of consumers insured by a third-party payer, a majority of today's health care professionals bear low risk that they will not be paid for treating patients. One of the consequences of the growth of health insurance coverage since World War II is that the financial uncertainty associated with adverse health events has been transferred from patients, doctors, and hospitals to private and public third-party payers. While other nations have chosen to transfer virtually all of this risk to government, exposure to medical expense risk in the United States continues to be more widely, and unevenly, distributed among different segments of the population.

What Is Risk?

Life has many uncertainties that result in financial loss and unhappiness—for example, loss of a job, of one's possessions, of health, and of life. Voluntarily purchased insurance increases individual welfare because it creates less uncertainty and concern about financial losses that may accompany these types of adverse, and unpredictable, future events. Insurance buys financial security and peace of mind before such events occur. It also reduces the financial burden associated with an adverse event if it does come about, although it cannot, of course, restore to the individual exactly what has been lost.

Risk is defined as uncertainty about the outcome of a future event. Uncertainty is present in a speculative or a pure risk. **Speculative risk** is uncertainty surrounding a chance event that can result in a gain or a loss. For example, the owners of stock are exposed to speculative risk; stockholders can lose part or all of their investment or receive more than the original amount invested. With **pure risks,** uncertainty involves the outcome of a chance event that results only in a loss. The question is how big or small the loss will be. The uncertainty of future medical expenses associated with an unpredictable poor health state or loss of family income from premature death of a wage earner reflects pure risk because no possible gain arises from these chance occurrences.

A simple example of a pure risk helps to illustrate the problem facing consumers. Suppose a consumer is offered a certain loss of $500 today, or he can take his chances on an uncertain future loss. The uncertain loss is represented by a 95 percent chance of losing nothing and a 5 percent chance of losing $10,000 during the coming year. Let us say that the $10,000 loss will occur if the consumer finds himself in a poor health state and has to pay doctor and hospital bills. There is a 5 percent chance that this adverse event will occur. The **expected value** of a risky alternative can be measured by the average of the possible financial outcomes weighted by their probability of occurring. With n alternative outcomes, the expected value is

$$\text{Expected value} = \sum_{i=1}^{n} (\text{Probability of a loss}_i) \times (\$ \text{ Amount of a loss}_i)$$

In our example, the expected value of the risky alternative is $500:

$$\text{Expected value} = .95(0) + .05(10,000) = \$500.$$

Note that the expected value of this gamble is the same as the certain loss of $500. Most people dislike uncertainty; they prefer to know their losses in advance rather than to worry about what they might be. If the consumer accepts the risky alternative, he may lose up to $10,000 if he is unlucky. The greater the size of a possible loss and the greater the uncertainty surrounding that loss, the more likely it is that the consumer would choose to pay a certain amount today to avoid financial worry.

Statistical Properties of Risk

There are two types of uncertainty. The first is simply not knowing anything about the odds of a chance event. This usually occurs in situations where there is no experience. For example, what is the likelihood that aliens will come to earth in your lifetime? Is it 0 percent, 5 percent, 50 percent, or 100 percent? There is no history of verified exposures, or occurrences, on which to base an estimate of this probability. Suppose you believe the odds are 50 percent. How certain are you about this prediction? While you might believe in your forecast, it is difficult to convince others without supporting data or facts. Your opinion or belief is as good as anyone else's. It is impossible to predict the odds of this type of event, much less objectively quantify the amount of uncertainty that the prediction entails.

A second type of uncertainty exists when the odds can be predicted from prior experience but some uncertainty exists about the accuracy of the prediction. For example, from numerous observations and a fairly complete model about why the sun comes up each morning, it is easy to predict with a very high level of confidence—virtually no uncertainty, in fact—that the sun will come up tomorrow, a year from now, or even a hundred years from now. It is more difficult to predict with certainty whether it will rain tomorrow morning. Uncertainty about the accuracy of a future prediction can be quantified. A greater number of prior observations with the same outcome reduces the second type of uncertainty and increases confidence in predictions.

With past observations on a chance event, it may be possible to identify a **probability distribution** to represent the outcomes of the event and use the properties of the distribution to predict future occurrences. A probability distribution shows a pattern of different possible outcomes along with the relative frequency, or probability, that each outcome will occur. What are the possible outcomes of tossing a coin? Given enough trials, 50 percent of the time, a fair coin will turn up heads, and 50 percent of the time, it will turn up tails. Coin tossing can be represented by a **binomial distribution.** Another familiar distribution of outcomes is the **normal distribution,** better known as the bell-shaped curve. If the outcomes of an event follow a normal distribution, most of the observations are expected to group in the middle of the distribution, with a gradually diminishing number of observations occurring in its upper and lower tails. When instructors "grade on the curve," they assign a C to a large majority of the students and F's and A's to a very small percentage of the class.

If a chance event is assumed to follow a known probability distribution, the outcomes of the event can be characterized by its **mean,** μ, or expected value, and its **standard deviation,** σ, which measures the average dispersion of outcomes around the mean. The standard deviation is obtained from the square root of the **variance** (σ^2) of the distribution. The variance is the sum of the squared distance of each observation from the mean divided by the number of observations of the event. The formulas for the mean, the variance, and standard deviation of these outcomes are:

$$\mu = \text{Mean or expected value} \quad = \sum_{t=1}^{n} \frac{(\text{Outcome}_t)}{v}$$

$$\sigma^2 = \text{Variance} \quad = \sum_{t=1}^{n} \frac{(\text{Outcome}_t - \text{Mean})^2}{v}$$

$$\sigma = \text{Standard deviation} \quad = \sqrt{\sum_{t=1}^{v} \frac{(\text{Outcome}_t - \text{Mean})}{n}}$$

These formulas use the arithmetic mean for a population. If a sample from a population of outcomes is used, then the variance and standard deviation are divided by $n-1$ rather than n to obtain a better estimate.

For example, assume three outcomes are observed: 10, 50, and 90. Assuming each outcome is equally likely, then the mean is

$$\mu = \frac{10 + 50 + 90}{3} = 50.$$

The variance and standard deviation are derived as follows:

$$\sigma^2 = \frac{(10-50)^2 + (50-50)^2 + (90-50)^2}{2} = \frac{3,200}{2} = 1,600.$$

$$\sigma = \text{square root of } 1,600 = 40.$$

The standard deviation provides a way to measure the quantifiable risk surrounding drawing the number 50, the mean or expected value, from this population in the future.

In health care, uncertainty arises from a combination of two chance events, each of which can be described by a known probability distribution. The first event is the chance of becoming ill in some future period, and the second is the expected treatment costs if one is ill. In insurance, the combination of these two distributions is called the **total loss distribution**. The mean, variance, and standard deviation of the total loss distribution are, respectively (Rejda, 1986):

Mean: hm (2.2)

Variance: $s_{hm}^{2} = s_{h}^{2}m^{2} + s_{m}^{2}h$ (2.3)

Standard deviation: $s_{hm} = \sqrt{(s_{h}^{2}m^{2} + s_{m}^{2}h)}$ (2.4)

where

s_{h}^{2} = variance in the expected frequency of a loss (health status risk)

s_{m}^{2} = variance in the size of a loss (medical care risk)

h = mean probability, or expected frequency, that a loss will occur

m^2 = mean, or expected value, of treatment costs squared

The standard deviation of the first event, s_h, reflects **health status risk**—uncertainty about the likelihood of becoming ill. The standard deviation of the second event, s_m, is **medical care risk**—the uncertainty surrounding actual treatments and related costs, conditional on becoming ill. An increase in the odds of a poor health state, h, and in the average cost of illness, m, amplifies the amount of uncertainty about the financial consequences of an adverse health state.

A Case in Point. The probability of becoming ill , h, can be represented by a binomial distribution, which reflects the probable outcome from events with two distinct results (e.g., heads or tails, fire or no fire, sickness or health, married or single). Using the example of the risky alternative, the mean likelihood, h, of becoming ill, is 5 percent. Five in 100 people will become ill, and 95 will not. The variance in the expected frequency of a loss is

$$s_h^2 = h\,(1 - h) = (5/100)(95/100) = 475/10{,}000 = .048.$$

To calculate m and s_m^2, assume for simplicity that in 25 percent of cases, medical expenses are expected to average $5,000, in 50 percent of cases $10,000, and the remaining 25 percent of cases $15,000. The expected value of medical expenses, m, is therefore $10,000:

$$m = .25\,(\$5{,}000) + .5(\$10{,}000) + .25(\$15{,}000) = \$10{,}000$$
$$m^2 = 100{,}000{,}000.$$

The variance in medical care expenses is:

$$s_m^2 = .25(5{,}000 - 10{,}000)^2 + .5(10{,}000 - 10{,}000)^2 + .25(15{,}500 - 10{,}000)^2$$
$$= 12{,}500{,}000.$$

Using the formula for the standard deviation of two distributions,

$$s_{hm} = \sqrt{s_h^2\, m^2 + s_m^2\, h}.$$

first find the variance of the total loss distribution:

$$s_{hm}^2 = (.048)\,100{,}000{,}000 + 12{,}500{,}000\,(.05) = \$5{,}425{,}000.$$

The standard deviation for the combined distributions using the formula in Equation (2.3) is $2,329. The mean is simply hm, or $.05(10{,}000) = \$500$.

The standard deviation of the combined distributions measures **objective risk:** the average difference between expected and actual losses arising from an adverse, but not perfectly predictable, future event. Objective risk of a loss is different from the chance of a loss. The chance of a loss is the expected, or predicted, loss from an event whose outcome is not certain. Objective risk is uncertainty about the prediction itself.

As can be seen from Equations 2.3 and 2.4, when an insurance company accepts a group insurance premium from an employer, it accepts the uncertainty about how many group enrollees will in fact become ill, s_h^2, and about the actual costs of their treatment, s_m^2. This is important for understanding the risks faced by a health insurer, a self-insured employer, or a health care organization that contracts to provide services for an enrolled population for a fixed amount per member per month—under managed care. Providers who accept capitation are exposed to objective risk. Understanding and managing of objective risk is therefore crucial to health care providers who are negotiating with managed care plans.

Reducing Objective Risk Through Group Insurance

Individual uncertainty about a future loss can be reduced by the formation of a mutual insurance association. Suppose long-run historical data indicate that women over age sixty are likely to be hospitalized once in their remaining lifetime at an average cost of about $10,000 per admission, assuming no inflation. If the average life expectancy is eighty years and the odds of hospitalization do not increase with age, then the expected annual frequency that hospitalization will occur before death is 1 in 20, or 5 percent. Therefore, the expected cost of this hospitalization is $500 per year. In theory, women in this risk class could save $500 each year and have amassed just enough to cover the expected future loss. (This assumes no inflation in health care costs or accumulation of interest earnings on each year's annual savings.)

Although each woman in this risk class knows her average chance of hospitalization, she is nonetheless uncertain about what her actual odds, timing, and cost of hospitalization will turn out to be. Before the fact, she does not know (1) how many hospitalizations she will actually have during her remaining lifetime and (2) by how much actual medical expenses will differ from the average expected today. Even if costs are known to range from $5,000 to $15,000, she does not know which outcome she will draw. Uncertainty about future inflation in medical care costs only adds to the financial insecurity she faces. Furthermore, she does not know in which of the twenty years she might be hospitalized. If it is early in the period, she will not have saved enough money, so she will have to pay borrowing costs or reduce her consumption of other items, or both.

If a group of women aged sixty agrees to share the risk of hospitalization, uncertainty for each member can be reduced. Some members will have more than one hospitalization during this period, offset by others with none. Among those hospitalized, some will experience higher costs than average, subsidized by some with lower costs. For a sufficiently large group, the actual outcome will be close to the predicted average of $500 per woman per year. Now each woman can pay this amount annually into a pool and be certain that whatever the actual outcome, uncertainty about financial losses from hospitalization will be eliminated.

Risk Reduction and the Law of Large Numbers

Pooling of risks reduces the uncertainty about an expected future loss, or the objective risk, facing each individual member of the group. Why does this work? Risk pooling reduces objective risk because of the **law of large numbers** (Rejda, 1986). This law states that in a given sample of individuals in a similar risk class, the standard error (**SE**) of the estimated loss will decline as the sample size increases:

$$SE = \frac{s^2}{n} = \frac{s}{\sqrt{n}}. \qquad (2.5)$$

The SE is the standard deviation of the population risk divided by the square root of the number of individuals in the sample. Being in a similar risk class guarantees that each individual in the group faces the same likelihood of illness and variability in outcomes. For only one individual, the amount of objective risk is the standard deviation of the risk found in the population of people in the same risk class.

> *A Case in Point.* Let the objective risk of the population be $2,329, the standard deviation estimated from the previous example. For one woman, the SE will be $2,329 ($2,329/1), the same as the population risk. For 100 women, the SE will be $233 ($2,329/10), ten times less than the population risk. At 10,000 members, the objective risk drops to $23 ($2,329/100) per member.
>
> As the group covered becomes sufficiently large, uncertainty about the expected outcome for the group and its members approaches zero. For a pool with 1 million members, the average difference between the actual and expected loss is $2.33 per member per year. The advantage of pooling risks is that actual losses can be more accurately predicted. Notice, however, that reduced risk has no effect on the expected medical expenses, which remain at $500 per member per year. Also, even though risk per member declines as members increase, the total amount of loss to the pool rises by n times the standard error. In the case of 10,000 members, total risk to the pool is $232,900. At 1 million members, it is $2,329,000.

Role of Insurance Providers

In theory, voluntary risk pools consisting of a large number of members can be formed without a health insurer acting as an intermediary between consumers and health care providers. In practice, though, there are transactions costs associated with forming and managing risk pools. Members of the risk pool must employ administrators to identify new and current members, report the financial status of the pool to members, collect and invest premiums, pay providers, verify that member claims are legitimate and accurate, prevent moral hazard and fraud, and set new premiums when necessary. Without administrators, plan members would have to carry out these tasks themselves.

Furthermore, plan members now bear the objective risk of the group, which although considerably reduced by pooling, is still present. In some years, the pool will have a surplus and in others a deficit. Plan members can add an extra amount to the $500 fee (or premium) to cover the risk of higher-than-expected medical expenses. Alternatively they may pay for these losses as they arise.

Members of the risk pool may prefer to transfer this uncertainty to a third party, who accepts it in exchange for a fee. This additional fee is provided to the third party as compensation for accepting and managing the objective risk of the plan. When insurers accept the objective risk of a specific group, they underwrite the risk. **Underwriting risk** is measured by the standard error in Equation 2.5 for a specific group to be covered. The insuring agent must invest capital to guarantee fulfillment of its contract to accept risk. Invested capital is used as reserves to pay for unexpected medical claims of subscribers. Insurer's capital is subject to **financial risk,** which depends on accurate predictions of the expected medical expenses for the group and efficient management of the plan. The lower (higher) the administrative costs of the plan and the more (less) accurate the prediction of medical expenses, the greater (less) the profits and returns to investors are likely to be.

The underwriting risk of a health plan can be reduced by increasing the number of plan enrollees. Insurance plans with too few enrollees to diversify risk will have to charge a higher premium in order to cover the objective risk of the plan. Market forces will tend to drive out plans that are too small to spread risk effectively (Ambrose and Drennan, 1994; Stone and Hefferman, 1989). On the other hand, there are fixed administrative costs associated with each new group enrolled. As the number of different groups covered increases, plan administrative expense rises. There is a trade-off between these benefits and costs. Large employers in particular have taken advantage of the gains from risk pooling. They bear lower administrative expenses per enrollee and are large enough to reduce the underwriting risk of a self-insurance plan by covering their own workers. Furthermore, self-insured companies can gain financially from the savings if the plan operates efficiently to reduce health care costs. Usually a third-party administrator is employed by the firm to administer its plan.

Government insurers, like private insurers, accept financial risk and manage it on behalf of citizens. Because of the law of large numbers, government, or social, insurance achieves maximum benefits from pooling by spreading risks across large population groups. With national health insurance, maximum possible risk reduction is obtained so that objective risk per citizen is virtually zero. Given the benefits of risk pooling, why has the United States failed to adopt a national health insurance system? Equations 2.2 and 2.3 provide part of the answer. Pooling alone does not ensure that the sources of population risk will remain the same over time. Although social insurance may reduce objective risk to an insignificant amount per capita, pooling by itself does nothing to control changes in the chance of illness, h, or growth in expected medical care expenses, m, which arise from moral hazard. Furthermore, each citizen bears the direct and indirect costs of government's attempt to contain the growth in the total cost of the system (Danzon, 1992). Potentially higher total costs of social insurance are transferred to society as a whole. Medicare payroll taxes, for example, have been increased to cover the rising expected costs of the Medicare program over time. Thus, reduced risk from social insurance may come at a higher price.

Profitability and Costs of Health Insurance

The demand for insurance depends on the individual's preference for financial security. People for whom financial uncertainty is particularly unpleasant are characterized by **risk aversion.** They are willing to pay more than the expected value of a possible future medical expense ($500 in the example above) to transfer risk to a third party. People who would pay no more than the expected medical expense loss of $500 for financial security are called **risk neutral.** They are indifferent to purchasing insurance with a premium of $500 or accepting the risky alternative. People who would be willing to pay less than the expected medical loss are **risk lovers.** Because of their higher tolerance for risk, risk lovers would not *voluntarily* purchase insurance unless it were priced below cost. Instead, they put themselves at risk for higher actual losses in the unlikely event that they require medical treatment. It is generally assumed that most people are risk averse and willing to pay more than the expected cost of medical expenses for financial security. If everyone were risk lovers or risk neutral, there would be no insurance market.

With the transfer of risk to a third party, administrative expenses, taxes, and profits for bearing risk must be added to the expected medical expenses of group members. The medical expenses of an insurance plan make up the **pure premium** charged to subscribers. Any amount added to the pure premium is called the **loading.** Suppose administrative costs, taxes, and a normal return for bearing risk are $100, and expected medical expenses are $500. Under competitive market conditions, the premium rate would be $600. What if risk-averse consumers are willing to pay as much as $200 per year more than the expected cost of medical expenses to avoid financial worry? In the absence of competition, the health insurer could charge a $700 premium and earn an excess profit of $100 per enrollee. With competitive pressures from other plans, however, the price will be bid down to $600, driving profits to a level just sufficient to compensate owners of capital for the financial risk and administrative costs of the plan (Wickizer and Feldstein, 1995; Szpiro, 1985). Consumers would gain $100 more in financial security benefits than they cost, making them better off.

The loading reflects the price of insurance. One way to measure this price is to examine the **medical loss ratio (MLR):** the ratio of realized medical expenses—the pure premium—to total premiums received by the health insurance plan. In managed care plans, this ratio averages about 86 percent (Touby, 1993). Some individual plans have reported MLRs as low as 70 percent (among them are Oxford, WellPoint Health Networks, and U.S. Healthcare) while others report an MLR as high as 96.5 percent (reported by Kaiser Foundation Health Plan of California) (Spragins, 1996; Touby, 1993). A 70 percent MLR means that the insurance company keeps 30 percent of the total premium for administration, taxes, and profits and uses only 70 percent for medical expenses. This translates into a price of $0.43 for a dollar of medical benefits (.30/.70).

At 96.5 percent, the plan is charging only about $0.5 for each dollar of medical claims expense incurred.

A low MLR does not indicate whether the plan has higher profits (or surplus) or higher administrative expenses. High profits would indicate lack of sufficient competition in the market; high administrative costs would suggest inefficiency in plan administration, although more aggressive cost management may result in higher administrative cost and a lower MLR (Touby, 1993). Similarly, the MLR does not reveal the total premium charged by the plan. A plan may have a higher MLR and commensurably higher premiums because plan expenses are not well managed or because the risk pool has higher medical expense risks than the norm. For the same reasons, a plan may have a lower MLR and lower premiums. Without information on relative premiums and plan risks, it is difficult to assess plan efficiency fully (Robinson, 1997). Furthermore, a low or high MLR in any given year may be the result of unanticipated low or high medical care expenses in the plan, resulting from objective risk. The average MLR over a longer period of time is a better indicator of plan performance and pricing. In general, employers and other payers should negotiate aggressively for lower premiums in plans with high premiums and low MLRs.

Several other factors have been found to be associated with greater consumer willingness to buy health insurance (Holmer and Weinberg, 1987):

- Tax deductibility of insurance premiums, which reduces the effective price of health insurance relative to other goods and services.
- Higher incomes and wealth.
- Size of the expected loss.
- Higher odds of a loss.

Together with a lower plan loading (the price of insurance) and higher risk aversion, these factors will increase individual demand for health insurance.

Health Status Risk, Medical Care Risk, and Total Risk

The chance of an individual entering an adverse health state that requires treatment can result from genetic, environmental, and behavioral risk factors. Health scientists such as epidemiologists, psychologists, and biologists learn about the risk factors that increase the odds of illness and disease among a given population. Although many risk factors that lead to greater health services use are outside the control of the individual, such as biological and genetic characteristics, the chance of illness may be altered by individual behavior—for example, smoking cessation, exercise, use of seat belts, and better nutrition. Use of effective preventive health services also reduces the odds of an adverse and more costly future health event. Among these are immunizations, prenatal care, use of high blood pressure medication, and estrogen replacement therapy. Although less controllable than behavioral factors, environmental factors also play a role in sickness and can sometimes be avoided. Living in a hazardous environment or working in a hazardous industry or a highly stressful job may increase one's chance of illness.

Uncertainty about the odds of experiencing an adverse health event, or health status risk, is related to what is known about the relationships between these risk factors and illness. Uncertainty about these relationships reduces the predictability of future medical expenses arising from exposure. Health plans may institute measures to change the odds of an illness when sufficient empirical and scientific evidence of their cost-effectiveness has been accumulated. In the past, commercial insurers merely provided the benefits of pooling to reduce risk and make a profit; they placed little or no emphasis on changing the odds of illness by altering lifestyle behavior. With rising average treatment costs and better understanding of their relationship to behavioral and environmental health risks, however, more health plans are using prevention and health promotion to reduce or avoid these costs (Hyland, 1992). Managed care plans provide wellness programs and health education to alter behaviors that lead to poor health outcomes. Financial incentives, like lower premiums for nonsmokers, have also been employed by employer-created self-insurance plans. Greater market penetration of health plans offering prevention and wellness benefits is likely to encourage this trend throughout the industry as plans capture the benefits of offering prevention services and improving lifestyle choices that were previously lost when subscribers switched plans.

In addition to health status risk, insurers face medical care risk. Medical care risk arises because actual utilization and treatment costs among those who become ill deviate from what is expected for the group being covered. Medical care risk has two sources of uncertainty: (1) variability in expected prices per unit of service and (2) variability in expected quantity of services used by each member of a covered group. Lack of homogeneity among group members increases the uncertainty about the cost of treatment. The insurance company bases its estimate of underwriting risk and the resulting premium rate on expected medical expenses of the group (or groups) covered, depending on the risk rating system used. If more treatments are prescribed than expected or if costs per treatment are higher than anticipated, the insurance company is forced to pay more than it charged members for medical expenses, and the plan will lose money. If medical expenses are lower than expected and administrative costs are held in check, the plan will make money.

Managing Health Plan Risks

Physicians play a central role in the determination of medical care provided and thus contribute to medical care risk. They act as agents of patients in directing care. They decide whether and which diagnostic procedures are warranted and referrals to specialists are needed, determine whether patients need to be hospitalized, and recommend treatment. There is considerable evidence that physician treatment practices vary widely for the same symptoms and conditions in difference geographical locations (Billings and Eddy, 1987; Wennberg, 1988). Outcome studies that reflect the effectiveness of various practice styles and treatment approaches are needed to reduce the uncertainty about which treatments are cost-effective. Management and control of medical care risk depend fundamentally on influencing and improving the treatment decisions of physicians.

Besides lowering health status and medical care risk, other factors can alter the total risk of a plan over time. For a contract to be financially viable, expected use and cost must remain the same over time. New enrollees must replace disenrolling members in the same risk class (no adverse or favorable selection), and member use of health services must not change once one is covered by insurance (no moral hazard).

When the likelihood of illness varies significantly across individuals within the same risk pool, it creates the potential for **adverse selection** (Browne, 1992; van de Ven and van Vliet, 1995). Adverse selection arises when those most at risk for a particular adverse health event join the risk pool and those with the least risk withdraw from it. If not anticipated in advance and built into the premium charged, adverse selection will increase actual medical expenses above those expected, creating a loss for the plan. Insurers attempt to reduce adverse selection by screening new members for preexisting conditions and marketing to healthier employer groups. The practice of an insurance company's offering insurance exclusively to companies with healthier workers is called **cream skimming.** Recent congressional legislation, the Kennedy-Kassebaum Health Insurance Portability and Accountability Act of 1996, effectively eliminated the ability of insurers to refuse insurance to previously insured workers because of preexisting conditions.

Another mechanism to prevent adverse selection is a regulation that all health insurers must use the same rating system to price insurance. If the same rate is charged to all enrollees, there is no other plan available at a lower premium to induce low-risk enrollees to switch. Using a single medical expense rate to set the premium for all groups is a **community rating system.** At the other extreme, separate risk pools can be formed that reflect different probabilities and expected costs of utilization for each group enrolled. This is an **experience rating system.** Experience rating reduces opportunities for adverse selection because enrollees are charged a premium that is more closely related to their expected medical expenses. No other plan can offer coverage at a lower rate.

Two other sources of rising medical expenses and risk to the insurer are moral hazard and fraud, traditional problems facing insurance companies. Moral hazard, or insurance-induced demand, occurs because health insurance coverage reduces the relative cost of health services with respect to other goods and services. If not anticipated or prevented, moral hazard raises actual use above the predicted level. Insurance companies attempt to reduce moral hazard by imposing copayments and deductibles on plan members. More recently, insurers, especially those using managed care techniques, have attempted to reduce moral hazard through direct intervention in consumer and physician decisions. Fraud typically involves unscrupulous providers who bill for services that did not occur or otherwise misrepresent claims for services rendered. Periodic claims audits and utilization reviews are used to control fraud.

Government insurers, like any other insurer, incur added administrative costs to monitor and control the potential for moral hazard and fraud in the system. Failure to do so puts its insurance reserves, such as the Medicare Trust Fund, at risk of being underfunded. Recently the federal government instituted major audits of health care providers, designed to find evidence of fraudulent billing and other improper practices. Moreover, the federal and state governments are seeking ways to reduce the cost of Medicare and Medicaid. Ironically, they are turning increasingly to some form of privately managed health care to assist them in this task. Danzon (1992) argues that private insurers have strong incentives to control moral hazard and fraud, as they compete for business. Increasingly, growing federal entitlement obligations of Medicare, Medicaid, and Social Security and dramatically rising state Medicaid obligations have placed similar pressures on government.

What can a health insurer do when actual medical expenses are higher than predicted, and they are not the result of fraud or mismanagement? First, it can raise its premium in the following year to make up for losses in the current year, using **prospective experience rating.** This was the primary response of commercial insurers throughout the 1970s and early 1980s, until payers began to resist and sought cheaper health benefit plans. Second, it can stop offering coverage to high-cost groups. Third, it can go out of business and refuse to provide health insurance. Small health insurers are more likely to exit the market in response to variability in medical expenses (Stone and Heffernan, 1989). Fourth, the insurer can change its contract with the employer (payer) to share more risk. At the end of the year, if the insurance company loses more than a certain amount on the contract, it receives an extra payment from the payer; if it makes more than a certain amount, it returns some of the premium. This is called a **retrospective experience rating** system. Finally, the insurer can negotiate price discounts from providers and/or monitor or influence treatment patterns in order to predict medical expenses better; in other words, insurers can manage care.

Emergence of Managed Care Organizations

Prior to the 1980s, commercial insurance companies, Blue Cross plans, and the government were not concerned with controlling medical expense risk and costs of their health insurance plans. Today managed care has been embraced by insurers and payers eager to stem the rise in health care costs and reduce the business and financial risks they face. The most aggressive model for managing health services use is the HMO, given formal definition in the Federal HMO Act of 1973. Managed care applies to a wider group of plans than those that received federal qualification under this legislation. For example, preferred provider organizations (**PPOs**) are considered to be managed care organizations even though they do not accept and manage risk. This section reviews the history of managed health care and discusses different approaches to managing health care expenses that are used by three types of health insurance plans. Finally, alternative HMO structures are related to the financial risk produced by the integration of insurance with the efficient provision of medical services.

Early Forms of Managed Care

The earliest form of managed care, prepaid physicians practice plans (**PPP**), accepted financial risk for the medical care services used by plan enrollees. Begun as early as 1910 in the state of Washington, prepaid group and individual practice plans accepted payment in advance in exchange for providing a defined set of health care services to a group of subscribers for a given period of time. Like health insurers, these plans assumed the financial risk associated with covering the cost of medical expenses of enrollees in exchange for a prepaid premium. Unlike health insurers, they also provided the services that were being covered.

Endorsement of these types of plans as cost-effective alternatives to fee-for-service medicine came from two blue-ribbon panels in the 1930s and 1960s: the Committee on the Costs of Medical Care (1932) and the National Advisory Commission on Health Manpower (1967). These endorsements led to the creation of well-known group practice plans, including Group Health Association in 1937; Kaiser-Permanente, Group Health Cooperative of Puget Sound, and Health Insurance Plan of Greater New York in 1947; Group Health Plan of St. Paul in 1957; and Harvard Community Health Plan in 1969 (Wright, 1990).

In contrast to PPPs, the not-for-profit Blue Cross plans that were formed in the 1930s were created to generate cash for financially strapped hospitals. Small, monthly member prepayments ensured access to a hospital bed if illness struck. As opposed to the risk of a doctor's visit and related treatment, hospitalization was a very unlikely, but highly costly, event for most people. Coverage for treatment of an unpredictable and expensive episode of illness—catastrophic coverage—was the fundamental purpose of hospital insurance plans that arose after World War II. The expense per member per month was minimal because costs were shared among many subscribers and the likelihood of hospitalization was low. Except for unionized workers, who negotiated comprehensive health insurance coverage as part of their labor contracts, most consumers continued to pay for doctor visits and outpatient treatment out of pocket, purchasing first-dollar coverage for hospital services only.

Meanwhile, the early prepaid practice plans evolved into what is now called the HMO. This name was coined by Paul Ellwood, the physician who proposed the HMO concept to President Nixon in 1976. The name emphasizes the organization's responsibility not only for effective treatment of acute illness but also for ongoing maintenance of the health status of enrollees. These plans were comprehensive, covering both physician and hospital services. Inherent in the HMO concept was the acceptance and management of medical expense risk, an aspect of health insurance coverage largely ignored by commercial insurers and Blue Cross–Blue Shield plans. Traditional insurers focused primarily on managing the insurance function: reaching optimal plan size, effective rate setting and underwriting of risk, containment of moral hazard, and minimizing administrative expenses. Being at financial risk, HMOs had structural and financial incentives to constrain and manage costs arising from the medical care and health status risks of an enrolled population.

Typology of Health Insurers

In recent years, commercial health insurers, Blue Cross–Blue Shield, and the government have adopted many of the attributes of managed care organizations. By definition, any intrusion by the insurer into the practice of medicine may be considered managed care. Insurers have always been involved minimally in their very legitimate role of monitoring fraud and moral hazard. Commercial health insurers, however, have shown the least involvement in influencing treatment decisions and choices of enrollees. Just like casualty and property insurers, commercial health insurers are **indemnity insurance plans** (Wrightston, 1990). They reimburse members directly for losses (medical expenses) that have been incurred. In these plans, the consumer's choice of provider and the physician's choice of treatment are unrestricted. The only controls are in the types of treatments covered by the plan, the maximum benefits available for designated services, and the imposition of deductibles and co-payments to discourage unnecessary utilization (moral hazard). Precertification of a hospital admission, for example, reflects recent attempts by commercial insurers to manage care.

A second type of insurer, called a **service benefit plan,** pays providers directly for services rendered to members. Consumers are required to make payments to providers only for services or amounts not covered by the insurer. Monthly premiums are viewed as advance payments, which entitle beneficiaries to services from participating providers in the event of illness. Again, consumer choice and physician autonomy are maintained because few barriers to being designated a participating provider exist in these plans. Service benefit plans negotiate prices and acceptable reimbursement formulas with providers in advance. Through these contractual relationships with providers, service benefit plans attempt to control costs.

Blue Cross and Medicare are prime examples of service benefit plans. Originally plan providers were reimbursed on the basis of full cost plus a profit margin and then on a cost basis. More aggressive constraints on reimbursement and rules about the appropriate sites of care are now employed by these plans to control excess utilization and costs. Medicare's prospective payment system, for example (see Chapter 3), certifies participating providers and sets prices prospectively to control costs. A new type of service benefit plan is the PPO, which provides a panel of physicians and hospital services to payers and insurers at a discount.

The third type of intermediary is the **direct service delivery plan.** In these organizations, the insurer not only reimburses providers directly for services and establishes prices and reimbursement in advance, but it also restricts eligible service providers and in some models oversees the delivery of health services to members. Some of these plans have also adopted the co-payments imposed by indemnity insurance plans to curb excess utilization of ambulatory care. PPPs and HMOs are typical of such plans. By being both an insurer and a provider, these plans impose greater control over risks and costs. But these controls come at the expense of a reduced choice of providers and of physician autonomy (Morrison and Luft, 1990).

Managed Care Plan Characteristics

Managed care can most accurately be defined as the practice of medicine that seeks to provide health care at a quality acceptable in the community, in the most efficient and effective way possible. This does not always mean the least expensive on a unit basis, nor does it mean that services are inappropriately rationed. At the same time, it does put pressure on physicians and other health professionals to practice in ways that are different from traditional ways. The aim of managed care is to encourage care of the patient in a fairly consistent way, given the diagnosis, and to encourage, if not force, physicians who practice outside the community norms to change their practice.

Managed care organizations (**MCOs**) are not identical in structure or approach. The PPO, for example, attempts to control medical expenses primarily by reducing the rates charged by its member providers in exchange for increases in their market share. At the other extreme is the staff model HMO, which controls utilization and prices through direct provision of health services. In comparison to indemnity plans, MCOs have been successful at controlling health care costs (Johnson, 1994).

Preferred Provider Organizations

PPOs create a delivery network of physicians and institutions, which is then brokered to other risk takers, such as insurance companies, union trusts, and self-insured employers. The primary service a PPO provides to the health delivery system is the construction of these networks and the establishment of a fee structure and prices of services delivered by the network. Early on, PPOs were less successful in controlling costs because of less stringent utilization management and provider selection criteria. Without these controls in place, PPO physicians and hospitals had an incentive to increase the number of services provided to offset fee reductions (Alkire and Stolz, 1993; Ellis and McGuire, 1996).

The profitability of a PPO arises not from receiving premiums and managing risk but by charging access fees for use of the network and collecting other fees for services provided to the payer, such as utilization review and quality assurance of participating providers. A PPO differs from an HMO in a number of respects. Most important, PPOs do not accept risk, nor are they directly involved in the delivery of care. Moreover, health care professionals who contract with payers as part of a PPO generally are not at risk for the provision of health care, although they will sometimes be put at limited financial risk by the withholding of a portion of the fee or a similar reimbursement mechanism to discourage unnecessary use.

Capitation is a rarely encountered reimbursement vehicle for members of a PPO. Reimbursement to institutional and individual health care providers in a PPO is usually on the basis of a contract, which uses either a fee schedule or a usual and customary standard. Although a discount from billed charges is still used sometimes, it is a declining method of reimbursement because it effectively allows the health care provider to increase the billed charge to offset a fee discount.

Typically, enrollment in a PPO plan allows the enrollee to use either network or nonnetwork physicians and hospitals. Enrollees are offered the financial incentive of a lower deductible and co-insurance amount to use network providers. Thus, the enrollee has the freedom to choose a provider outside the network, although there will be some financial costs associated with making that choice. Physician autonomy is not generally affected, but when utilization review is in place, physician's reimbursement claims may be questioned for services deemed inappropriate. Thus, the greatest impact of PPOs on the medical care expenses comes from reduced fees rather than changes in physician behavior.

Health Maintenance Organizations

An HMO contracts with providers for health care services to a defined population on a prepaid basis. The ideal HMO would operate in a competitive market environment, where information about differences in quality and price would be freely available to employers and enrollees and plans would be required to accept all enrollees at stated premiums.

Typically a beneficiary or employer pays the HMO a specific monthly premium in return for guarantees to provide a previously agreed-on range of health care services. HMOs offer comprehensive benefits and encourage the use of prevention services and a continuum of care. Like the commercial insurer, the HMO bases the premium charged to payers on the expected utilization and cost of the enrolled population. Thus, HMOs of insufficient size bear additional insurance risk. In addition, the HMO identifies and contracts with a panel of health care professionals from whom care may be sought by enrollees. Finally, the HMO is at risk for the efficient and effective provision of services delivered by these providers. If the HMO provides services for less than the aggregate premium amount, the HMO is profitable; if services cost more than the aggregate premium, the HMO loses money.

An HMO may attempt to shift some of its risk to providers by paying them a fixed fee per member per month—a capitation rate—in return for a provider guarantee to provide a predefined range of health services. Thus, if actual services used by enrollees cost more than the total capitation amount, there is a loss to the physician or hospital, or both. If the physician or hospital can provide the services for less than the total received under capitation, there is a profit.

A further consideration in the relationship between providers and the HMO involves volume risk (Hillman, Pauly, and Kerstein, 1989). If a minimum volume of enrollees is guaranteed to the provider, the downside variability in total revenues is reduced. Without volume guarantees, the contracting provider accepts the uncertainty about the number of HMO members who will select it under capitation. With insufficient and unpredictable enrollment, the provider is subject to much greater risk than otherwise. Insufficient enrollment may reduce the provider's ability to cover fixed costs. Moreover, by accepting the objective risk of enrollees, the provider must require a capitation rate that includes both expected medical expenses and a premium to compensate for the objective risk of the contract.

Recall that objective risk is the variation of actual medical expenses from expected medical expenses. The accuracy of the projected expenses will be greater the higher is the number of HMO enrollees who select the provider. Thus, a lower number of enrollees than expected reduces total revenues to the provider while raising the objective risk, or uncertainty, about actual expenses of the plan. In this situation, **business risk** will be higher than under a discounted fee-for-service contract. Business risk results from greater variability in total revenues and net income. This risk to the provider can be attenuated by accepting a greater number of capitated contracts from different managed care plans or by joining with other physicians to create a group practice that accepts capitation. This will diversify the risk of low group enrollment rates from individual plans. Also, providers can cap their loses through reinsurance or other risk reduction strategies (Bond and Marshall, 1994).

An HMO that transfers all risk to providers has an opportunity to earn a risk-free return per enrollee—the difference between the premium it receives from employers and the capitation it pays to providers—regardless of the utilization patterns of enrollees. Moreover, capital will be attracted to proprietary HMOs that have transferred risk to providers, since investors can earn a higher-risk free rate of return on their investment. So long as providers undervalue the risk they accept and fail to account for it in their capitation rates, the HMO investors and stakeholders will benefit at their expense.

It is not surprising that HMOs seek out physicians who offer quality service and practice cost-effective medicine and that they attempt to shift their financial risk to the health care providers. Furthermore, the HMO, or the health care provider who accepts risk, has an incentive to see that the care is managed across the entire insured population in such way that quality is acceptable and costs are controlled. HMOs that fail to do so may lose enrollees and market share.

HMOs are not homogeneous organizations. The incentives to produce cost-effective care differ across plans based on their structure. HMOs can be structured in a variety of ways, and usually the structure is defined by the relationship with physicians and the amount of risk transferred to them by the plan. We will examine the most common structures.

Staff Model

In this model, the physicians work for the HMO usually as full-time, salaried employees and do not individually experience risk in providing health care services. Some plans may include bonuses to physicians when a profit is returned to the plan. Most staff model HMOs own their own clinics. Some also own hospitals, thereby gaining greater leverage over hospital utilization by restricting the number of beds available to the plan. The staff model HMO is at financial risk for the medical expenses of the plan members. Enrollees face highly restricted choices of providers. Physicians, as employees, have much less discretion in their practice patterns. Treatment protocols and standards of care are often dictated by the HMO medical staff management. Because physicians are salaried, they have less incentive to provide additional treatment or work long hours. The staff model HMO must maintain the medical quality standards of the community to retain enrollees if membership is voluntary and other health insurance options are available.

Group Model

An HMO is a group model when the organization contracts for the services of one or more large multispecialty physician groups to deliver and direct care of plan enrollees. The physicians' group may dedicate its services solely to the HMO, or it may provide a percentage of its services to patients not enrolled in the HMO. Also, the HMO may provide the clinical facility for the group practice and furnish support personnel. Typically reimbursement from the HMO to the group practice is capitated, with risks and profits being shared among the HMO and participating physician groups. Like the staff model HMO, the incentives of the group model are to reduce costs while maintaining quality.

Network Model

In this model, the HMO contracts with a number of smaller physician groups rather than a few large multispecialty groups, as in the group model. Also, the physician groups provide their own facilities and support personnel. The HMO usually reimburses on the basis of a capitation rate to each practice, but payment may be on a discounted fee-for-service basis as well.

Independent Practice Association

The independent practice association (**IPA**) model is one in which the HMO contracts with a large number of small group and solo practitioners to provide services. This model is fragmented and offers the least ability to control resource use in the practice. There is little interaction between the physicians on an organized basis, so patient care plans often approximate the level of coordination experienced in fee-for-service practice. Sometimes this results in costs that are higher than other medical staff models for HMOs.

The degree of control in resource use is often determined by the reimbursement mechanism of the IPA. Reimbursement is typically on a discounted fee-for-service basis with a **withhold**. This means that a prospectively determined amount of the reimbursement the provider receives is "withheld" by the payer as a contingency against overuse of resources. In the event that it is retrospectively determined that there was not an overuse of resources, the withhold is given to the provider. In this way, the HMO transfers some of the utilization risk to IPA physicians to encourage greater efficiency. The rationale for the IPA model is to offer plan enrollees greater choice of physicians and practice location.

Point of Service Plans

Point-of-service (**POS**) plans, also called triple option plans, attempt to maximize consumer choice of provider but adjust co-payment and deductibles to reflect the differences in plan costs of each provider. Enrollees may elect to use HMO providers, PPO providers, or fee-for-service providers but will pay higher co-payments commensurate with negotiated rates charged to the plan by the provider.

Exclusive Provider Organizations

The exclusive provider organization (**EPO**) is managed care's response to accusations by the provider community that PPOs have not been effective in directing patients to network providers. In contrast to POS plans, EPOs attempt to restrict enrollee choice to PPO providers and thereby improve their market share. In this model, enrollees are required to use the network providers, or no payment will be made by the payer, effectively making the enrollee responsible for 100 percent of the health care bill. Thus, EPOs have some characteristics of an HMO and some of a PPO. The EPO is distinguished from the HMO in that it does not accept or manage medical care risk.

Criticisms of the HMO Model

Major concerns have arisen about the possibility that HMOs reduce their risk exposure by transferring it to other payers, that they compromise quality to reduce costs, and that poor market information invalidates a major assumption needed for markets to be competitive.

Favorable and Adverse Selection

Many critics of managed care argue that the historical success achieved by HMOs in reducing costs stems from their ability to encourage favorable selection. Through marketing and strategic pricing of their premiums and benefits, it is suggested, people with lower health status risks voluntarily enroll in the HMOs and people with high health status risks choose to disenroll, or decline to join HMOs at all. There is evidence that HMOs and PPOs initially attract lower-risk enrollees when they compete with other plans (Billi et al., 1993). Evidence of selection bias in mature plans and in mature managed care markets is less clear. Favorable selection of healthier enrollees into Medicare managed care plans may increase overall Medicare costs, as the less healthy elderly remain in the FFS system, and as plans discourage enrollment of the very old and chronically ill (Newcomer et al., 1996).

Compromising Quality for Cost

Given the financial incentives of the HMO, some ethical questions have been raised as to whether the economic incentives of the reimbursement system promote inappropriate rationing of services. Although there have been isolated instances of poor care, these practices are not believed to be widespread or inherent in the HMO model. Being at risk enhances incentives to provide medical care in the most cost-effective manner (Hillman, Pauly, and Kerstein, 1989). The compromise of quality and access subjects HMO physicians to litigation by patients and payers. With sufficient bad press about poor-quality performance of HMOs, market share will be lost to higher-quality providers and more responsible insurers. While a great deal of research has been done, there is little evidence of a reduction in quality of care in HMOs (Retchin et al., 1992; Tussing and Wojtowycz, 1994; Appleby, 1995).

Poor Market Information

Market pressures to maintain quality while reducing costs depend significantly on the free flow of information about prices, quality, and outcomes. Without such information, the possibility exists that HMOs and other managed care plans will be able to compromise care in order to maximize profits. Under fee-for-service medicine, the only variable reported and monitored by the public was quality of care. Indeed, competition among providers was on the basis of high quality of care, not price. For HMOs and other managed care plans to operate efficiently and effectively, however, information about quality and price differences among HMOs must be available to consumers and third-party payers.

The HMO market is still in its infancy in producing information adequate for people to make informed choices about their medical care providers. Major payers are now demanding that HMOs produce report cards on quality and price performance to enable selection of high-quality, low-cost plans. Until this occurs, the potential for lowered quality exists. It is therefore incumbent on health care workers, as well as managed care employees, to ensure that the potential to reduce quality in search of lower costs does not materialize.

Premium Rate Development

The difference in types of managed care plans is primarily in the degree of the organization's involvement in managing the delivery of care and motivating changes in physician behavior. This can affect overall plan costs and, ultimately, premium rates. A successful managed care organization has the potential to reduce actual medical expenses and objective risk, and thereby charge a lower premium to all subscribers (Zwanziger et al., 1994; Schmid, 1995).

The process of constructing a premium to charge an individual or group subscribers for insurance is called **premium rate setting.** Premiums charged to subscribers are based on a capitation rate, which reflects the amount of revenue that the insurer needs to receive from each member each month to cover expected medical costs, plan administration, and profits. The capitation rate may pertain to the expected costs of an individual, of a group, or of all groups in an insurance plan, depending on the type of rating system used. Different premiums may be constructed from the same capitation rate to reflect the tiered structure of coverage: single, family, or multiple. For example, a composite premium is based on a single tier structure, whereby the same rate is charged for all subscribers regardless of the number of family members covered under that subscriber. A two-tiered premium rate structure charges one rate for single subscribers and another for family subscribers. A three-tiered structure has a single rate, a rate for the subscriber and one dependent, and a family rate.

Suppose the capitation rate is $98 per member per month. This is based on the revenues required to cover the costs of all plan enrollees—subscribers as well as their families. In a two-tiered group plan, single subscribers might pay $88, and subscribers with family coverage might pay $250; in a three-tiered system, an $82 rate might be charged for singles, $145 for the subscriber and one dependent, and $265 for family coverage. No matter what premium rate structure is used, however, the premium will depend on the same underlying capitation rate used for the plan, or group covered.

The type of pricing, or rating, system used by the insurer dictates the way that required revenues needed to cover costs are spread over plan enrollees to construct a capitation rate. Moreover, different rating systems have different information requirements. **Medical underwriting** refers to basing the premium rate on the individual's own risk of needing health services. Most rating systems are on the basis of group risks, however, including the following categories:

- *Community rating,* which refers to developing a capitation rate based on the average risk and costs of all the plan's enrollees, regardless of the employer group to which they belong. Community rating maximizes the risk sharing across all plan enrollees and groups so that low-risk groups subsidize high-risk groups. Community rating systems were traditionally used by HMOs and not-for-profit Blue Cross plans.

- *Community rating by class,* which allows for each group's capitation rate to be adjusted for differences in expected expenses associated with identifiable group characteristics like age and sex. For example, using community rating by class to determine the capitation rate would mean that a group enrolling more older men would have a higher rate than a group with a higher percentage of young men.

- *Adjusted community rating (ACR),* which adjusts the community rate for the actual experience of large groups. Premiums for ACR-insured groups are based on the group's past utilization and cost. ACR, which had already been used in Medicare managed care contracts, was first allowed for federally qualified HMOs after 1988.

- *Experience rating,* like ACR, bases premiums on previous group-wide experience. The major difference between the two approaches is that an ACR is set in advance—prospectively—while experience rated plans may allow for adjustments at the end of the contract year, or retrospectively. Retrospective experience rating is typically used by commercial insurers.

Community rating encourages adverse selection, if markets make lower-priced insurance options available to lower risk enrollees. Experience rating eliminates the sharing of costs among different risk groups that enroll in the plan and prevents adverse selection. Community-rated systems require less information about specific group utilization behavior and costs. Experience-rated systems need much more information about differences in medical expenses expected for groups covered by the plan.

Capitation Using Community Rating

Two approaches are used to calculate the capitation rate in a community rating system: the expense-budget approach and the actuarial approach. The expense-budget approach, typically used by staff and group model HMOs, bases the capitation rate on planwide medical and administrative expenses. The actuarial approach calculates and sums the dollar cost per member per month for each benefit covered by the plan.

The Expense-Budget Approach

Under this approach, total revenues and total expenses for plan operation are projected for the coming year (see Table 2-1). Since a staff model HMO provides health services directly, medical services costs are part of the operating expenses of the plan, typical of the operating budget of any other health care provider. The major difference is that most revenues will be derived from fixed monthly insurance premiums, which depend solely on the number of plan enrollees, not actual utilization. Projected expenses for each item in the budget are based on prior planwide expenses adjusted for expected cost and utilization changes over the next year.

Projected expenses will depend on expected enrollment changes for the plan. In highly competitive markets, particularly in small plans, variability in actual plan enrollment may be greater. Based on projected membership and costs, the total amount of revenue needed to cover costs is calculated. Typically a premium rate increase to cover projected expenses is calculated for the coming year and then implemented though partial rate adjustments on a quarterly basis.

Actuarial Approach

The actuarial approach uses estimated costs for each service on a per member per month basis to derive medical expenses of the plan (see Table 2-2). This approach to rate setting is more likely to be found in plans using some type of adjusted community rating. Moreover, it is suitable for rate setting in managed care organizations that provide few direct medical services, such as in group, network and IPA models.

The components for rate setting using this approach are similar to the expense-budget approach (see Table 2-1). First, costs are projected for medical expenses, as shown on Table 2-2. Next, plan expenses are estimated and added to medical expenses, as shown on Table 2-3. The major difference between the expense budget approach and the actuarial approach is that projected medical expenses are broken out by type of service, which requires much more information on use and costs for each benefit covered. Medical expenses will normally include (1) hospital services, (2) physician services, (3) and other services (e.g., rehabilitation services, home health care, specialty referrals, ambulance services). Hospital services expenses can be broken down by service site, such as emergency room services, outpatient surgery, out-of-state services, or subacute care. Physician services can be decomposed into service types like office and hospital visits, surgical services, emergency room encounters, and laboratory services.

For each type of service, the following information is needed:

- Expected use per enrollee (based on planwide or specific group data).
- Expected charge per unit of service (based on contractual rates).

From these data, a basic capitation rate for each service is calculated, summed, and adjusted for co-payments, outside referrals, discounts, and other revenues. Co-payments

Table 2-1   Expense-Budget Approach (in millions)

	Current	*Projected*
Expenses		
Medical services		
Salaries	$19,000	$20,900
Supplies/equipment	1,500	1,635
Rent	2,800	3,300
Contracted services		
(Inpatient, specialty care)	35,000	39,200
Subtotal:	$57,000	$65,035
Administration		
Salaries	$ 3,500	$ 3,850
Supplies/equipment/rent	1,200	1,308
Marketing	500	575
Information processing	2,900	3,350
Subtotal	$ 7,100	$ 9,083
Total	**$64,100**	**$74,118**
Revenues		
Premium revenues	$62,500	$72,375
Third party payments	800	1,000
Fee-for-service	850	1,100
Co-payments	620	720
Reinsurance	300	320
Total	**$65,070**	**$75,515**
Excess revenues over expenses	**$ 970**	**$ 1,397**

Table 2-2   Capitation Rate for Medical Services Expenses

	Annual Rate/1,000	*Expected Charge/Unit*	*Cost per Member per month*[a]
Hospital days	350	$600	$17.50
Nursing days	40	100	.33
Physician ambulatory visits	3,000	25	6.25
Physician hospital visits	400	50	1.67
Surgery	200	350	5.83
Specialty referrals	60	80	.40
Copayments adjustment			(.50)
Fee discounts			(1.20)
Total medical expenses			**$30.28**

[a]Cost per member per month = [(annual rate per 1000 × expected charge per unit)/1000]/12

Table 2-3   Capitation Rate—Medical and Plan Expenses

	Cost per Member per Month
Medical expenses	$30.28
Loadings	
Plan administration	5.75
Premiums and recoveries	.60
State reserve requirements	.75
Profits	4.00
Total capitation rate	**$41.38**

reduce the capitation rate since providers collect this part of their reimbursement directly from patients. Referrals to providers outside the plan increase the plan's medical expenses and the required capitation rate needed to cover them. Discounts from providers reduce the capitation rate. Other revenues might come from reinsurance recoveries and coordination of benefits, which refers to billing another insurance company for claims against a plan enrollee when an enrollee is dually covered by health insurance coverage from a second health plan. These recoveries reduce the required revenues needed to cover costs.

To the medical cost capitation rate must be added administrative costs and required returns (profits) for investor-owned firms (see Table 2-3). These are the components of the premium that make up the loading. The loading is also calculated per member per month. It includes (1) plan administration, marketing, claims processing, debt service, and overhead costs; (2) reserves required by the state to meet unanticipated medical expenses; (3) reinsurance premium payments and recoveries; and (4) taxes and profits where applicable. It is also permissible to adjust the loading for differences in administrative costs of a group covered. Smaller groups may entail higher administrative costs per member per month. Finally, using the capitation rate for the group, premium rates are developed based on a tiered structure. Although subscribers in the plan might pay different premiums for single or family coverage, the underlying revenue required per member per month—the capitation rate—will be the same for each enrollee covered.

Community rating by class permits the calculation and use of a percentage adjustment to the capitation rate for specific classes of enrollees. Suppose females aged forty-five to sixty-four are found to incur twice the hospital services costs of the average enrollee served by the health plan. The capitation rate for hospital services for the average group in the plan has been found to be $18.00 per member per month (**PMPM**). Using an adjustment factor of 2.0, the capitation rate for hospital services for women aged forty-five to sixty-four would be $36.00 per member per month. Assume an employer has 25 percent of its workforce in this age/sex category and 75 percent in the average group. The capitation rate for this employer's enrollees would be a weighted average of these two classes of employees as follows:

Group hospital days capitation rate: .25(36.00) + .75(18.00) = $22.50.

Whereas a plan with the average enrollee demographics would pay $18.00 PMPM for hospital services, this employer group with more older females would pay $22.50 PMPM for hospital services.

The construction of capitation rates based on adjusted community rating (**ACR**) involves a similar approach. Under this method, the actual cost experience of each group's enrollees would be used to determine the adjustment factors. Utilization and cost data would have to be collected for each service category for each employer group to receive an ACR. The capitation rate for each group is then calculated by adjusting the community rate for the cost differences of each group.

Conclusion

The concepts of risk and insurance have been explored in this chapter. In a managed care environment, health care providers are likely to take on the responsibilities of insurers. The financial risk this creates requires that health care executives find ways to manage the costs and medical care utilization of patients they serve. To reduce total costs and manage total medical expense risk of an enrolled population, managed care encourages the coordination and integration of care. As a result, health providers are creating integrated health care delivery systems. Like the staff and group model HMOs, integrated delivery systems replicate HMO delivery systems by combining and coordinating all care components under a single organization. Moreover, capitation encourages physicians to form larger groups and to join with hospitals and other providers to negotiate a single price for a comprehensive package of health services. The next three chapters describe the impact of managed care on the organizational structure of the health care delivery system.

Case 2-1: Establishing a Capitation Rate for Hometown HMO

Hometown, a not-for-profit HMO, has experienced major growth in the past 7 years. With the adoption of managed care by local business, it has grown from 10,000 enrollees in 1990 to 80,000 in 1997. In the past year, Hometown has experienced increasing competition from new entrants into the market, which threaten to take away some of Hometown's enrollees by offering lower premiums to healthier employer groups.

Hometown has been using a community rating system to set its premiums. Under community rating low-risk groups subsidize high-risk groups in Hometown's portfolio of business. Hometown's managers are considering the use of experience rating for some of the larger groups it covers.

Case 2 Table   Hometown HMO (Enrollment and Utilization Statistics)

Plan Members

All groups	80,000
Group 1	6,000
Group 2	12,000
Group 3	8,000

Medical Expenses

	Hospital Services			Medical Group Services			
	Hospital days	Skilled nursing days	Outpatient surgeries	Office visits	Inpatient visits	Surgical procedures	Referrals
Utilization Statistics (per 1,000 enrollees)							
All	300	10	30	2500	250	80	200
Gp 1	325	14	40	2700	300	90	200
Gp 2	250	7	35	2200	200	75	175
Gp 3	310	8	30	2500	220	85	190
Treatment costs per unit							
All	$1,000	$500	$1,200	$60	$90	$1,200	$150
Gp 1	1,200	490	1,100	60	95	1,150	175
Gp 2	900	410	1,000	60	80	1,200	130
Gp 3	950	500	1,250	60	90	1,100	150

You have been asked by the CEO of Hometown to calculate the community rate for the plan as a whole and then to determine the experience rate for three large groups that you cover.

As a group model HMO, you contract with hospitals and doctors for services. Therefore, you use the actuarial approach to setting the capitation rate for your plan. From analysis of past health services use and cost for Hometown's enrollees, you have gleaned the information presented in the case table.

Using the spreadsheet model provided on diskette (studcs2), enter the values and create the formulas to answer the following questions. Be prepared to present your results and recommendations to Hometown's executive management team.

Case 2-1 Questions

1. What is the current medical expense capitation rate for all groups enrolled in Hometown. This rate is its community rate.

2. Hometown uses its medical expense capitation rate (found in question 1) to set premiums it charges to subscribers. How much premium revenue is currently received under the community rating system to cover medical losses of plan members?

3a. Calculate the per member per month (PMPM) rate of each medical expense component for Employer Groups 1, 2, and 3 based on their historical utilization and average cost experience.

3b. What differences are there in the medical expenses in the capitation rates across the three large employer groups?

3c. Which of these three groups are likely to be bid away by competing HMOs that use an experience rating system? *largest # + lowest cst-*

4. Calculate the total revenues that would be received from Employer Groups 1, 2, and 3 if the experience rates (found in 3a) are used instead of the community rate to set their premiums.

5a. How much total revenue must be collected from the remaining community rated plan members to cover total medical expenses of the plan after excluding the revenues received from Employer Groups 1, 2, and 3 under experience rating?
Total Expense – Exper-Rate group Reve = net Rev. needed-

5b. What is the community rate for the remaining plan members if these three groups are excluded from the community rated risk pool? (*Hint:* Subtract revenues expected from Groups 1, 2, and 3 under experience rates from total revenues received currently. Then divide this net revenue by the number of members whose premiums will be based on a community rate.) *80,000 – 26.00 u*

5c. Based on your analysis, should Hometown use experience rating? Explain.

6. Suppose that medical cost inflation is expected to be 7 percent next year and utilization is expected to remain the same for each group. What is the 1998 capitation rate needed from each group and from the community rated groups to cover plan expenses? *ie- 658.50 X 1.07 (7%)*

7. Assume that administrative costs are 8 percent and the required surplus needed to manage objective risk of the plan is 1 percent of medical expenses. What are the premium rates (medical expenses plus load) charged to each group of subscribers after adding the loading and adjusting for inflation? *9% + cst for each group-*

8. What is the impact on your premium rates if you attempt to lower utilization rates through more aggressive utilization management?

References

Alkire, A. A., & Stotz, S. W. (1993). The employers' view of managed health care: From a passive to an aggressive role. In Peter R. Krongstvedt (Ed.), *The managed health care handbook* (2nd ed.) (pp. 255–264). Gaithersburg, MD: Aspen.

Ambrose, J. M., & Drennan, R. B. (1994). Plan, market and regulatory considerations in HMO insolvency prediction. *Journal of Insurance Regulation, 12*(3), 416–433.

Appleby, C. (1995). Report cards: Giving consumers the scoop on quality and cost. *Hospitals and Health Networks, 69*(24), 84.

Billi, J. E., Wise, C. G., Sher, S. I. , Duran-Arenas, L., & Shapiro, L. (1993). Selection in a preferred provider organization enrollment. *Health Services Research, 28*(5), 563–575.

Billings, J., & Eddy, D. (1987). Physician decision making limited by medical evidence (part 1). *Business and Health, 5*(1), 23–28.

Bond, M. T. , & Marshall, B. S. (1994). Offsetting unexpected healthcare costs with futures contracts. *Healthcare Financial Management, 48*(12), 54–58.

Browne, M. J. (1992). Evidence of adverse selection in the individual health insurance market. *Journal of Risk and Insurance, 59*(1), 13–33.

Chernick, H. A., Holmer, M. R., & Weinberg, D. H. (1987). Tax policy toward health insurance and the demand for medical services. *Journal of Health Economics, 6*(1), 1–25.

Danzon, P. M. (1992). Hidden overhead costs: Is Canada's system really less expensive? *Health Affairs, 11*(1), 21–43.

Ellis, R. P., & McGuire, T. G. (1996). Hospital response to prospective payment: Moral hazard, selection, and practice-style effects. *Journal of Health Economics, 15*(3), 257–277.

Hellinger, F. J. (1995). Selection bias in HMOs and PPOs: A review of the evidence. *Inquiry, 32*(2), 135–142.

Hillman, A. L., Pauly, M. V., & Kerstein, J. T. (1989). How do financial incentives affect physicians' clinical decisions and the financial performance of health maintenance organizations? *New England Journal of Medicine, 321*(2), 86–92.

Hyland, S. L. (1992). Health care benefits show cost-containment strategies. *Monthly Labor Review, 115*(2), 42–43.

Johnson, D. E. (1994). Lewin shows how MCO, IHS competition will cut costs. *Health Care Strategic Management, 12*(6), 2–3.

Morrison, E. M., & Luft, H. S. (1990). Health maintenance organization environments in the 1980s and beyond. *Health Care Financing Review, 12*(1), 81–90.

Newcomer, R., Preston, S., & Harrington, C. (1996). Health plan satisfaction and risk of disenrollment among social/HMO and fee-for-service recipients. *Inquiry, 33*(2), 144–154.

Rejda, G. E. (1986). *Principles of insurance* (2nd ed.). Glenview, IL: Scott Foresman.

Retchin, S. M., Clement, D. G., Rossiter, L. F., Brown, B., Brown, R., & Nelson, L. (1992). How the elderly fare in HMOs: Outcomes from the Medicare competition demonstration. *Health Services Research, 27*(5), 651–669.

Robinson, J. C. (1997, July/August). Use and abuse of the medical loss ratio to measure health plan performance. *Health Affairs, 16*(4), 176–187.

Schmid, S. G. (1995). Geographic variation in medical costs: Evidence from HMOs. *Health Affairs, 14*(1), 271–275.

Spragins, E. (1996). Examining HMOs. http://www.bloomberg.com/personal/oct95/hmo.html.

Stone, D. L., & Heffernan, D. (1989). 1988 Survey on regulation of HMOs and HMO solvency: Findings and recommendations. *GHAA Journal, 10*(1), 28–39.

Szpiro, G. G. (1985). Optimal insurance coverage. *Journal of Risk and Insurance, 52*(4), 704–710.

Touby, L. (1993, May 31). Who's afraid of health reform? *Business Week*, 96–97.

Tussing, A. D., & Wojtowycz, M. A. (1994). Health maintenance organizations, independent practice associations, and cesarean section rates. *Health Services Research, 29*(1), 75–93.

van de Ven, W. P. M. M., & van Vliet, R. C. J. A. (1995). Consumer information surplus and adverse selection in competitive health insurance markets: An empirical study. *Journal of Health Economics, 14*(2), 149–169.

Wennberg, J. E. (1988). Improving the medical decision-making process. *Health Affairs, 7*(1), 99–106.

Wickizer, T. M., & Feldstein, P. J. (1995). The impact of HMO competition on private health insurance premiums, 1985–1992. *Inquiry, 32*(3), 241–251.

Wrightson, C. W. (1990). *HMO rate setting and financial strategy.* Ann Arbor, MI: Health Administration Press.

Zwanziger, J., Melnick, G. A., & Bamezai, A. (1994). Costs and price competition in California hospitals, 1980–1990. *Health Affairs, 13*(4), 118–126.

Chapter 3

Inpatient Delivery Under a Managed Care System

This chapter examines the impact that the implementation of managed care has had on the delivery of inpatient care in the U.S. health care system. This impact has not been just economic. It has also included fundamental changes in the way that medicine is being practiced. This includes the movement of medical procedures from an inpatient basis to an ambulatory setting. It has also included significant reductions in the length of stay for inpatient procedures and the creation of critical paths in establishing best practices for treatment of patients.

Learning Objectives

Upon successful completion of this chapter, the learner will:

- Understand that the stakeholders in the competitive managed care environment are in competition.
- Understand who the players are and the role that each plays in the pluralistic payment system of the U.S. health care system.
- Understand the nature of participation in a pluralistic payment system and the reasons that some kinds of reimbursement schemes are more beneficial than others.
- Understand the types of economic risk involved and the nature of the transition that has occurred.
- Understand how to determine the level of payment from each of the types of inpatient reimbursement.

Key Terms

at risk

carve-outs

co-payment, co-insurance

deductible

for profit

individual providers

institutional providers

integrated delivery networks

not-for-profit

payer fiat

pluralistic payment system

point of service

precertification

provider panel

relative value unit (RVU)

risk-based Medicare programs

staff model

stakeholders

unbundling

usual and customary (U&C)

Introduction

Managed care means different things to different people because the stages of development vary across the United States. In many instances in this chapter, generalizations are made for the purpose of illustration; they usually reflect either the status of managed care in some of the more mature markets or characteristics that managed care is likely to manifest in the future. However, this approach is subject to some skepticism because even in mature markets, the nature of the health care delivery system has evolved in different ways in various parts of the country due to the unique characteristics of a local area. These unique characteristics can include any or all of such factors as the number or strength of **institutional providers,** the cohesiveness of the **individual providers,** the will and organizational structure of the business community, and the attitude of the general population toward health care. Thus, readers should recognize that a general characterization of managed care is being given here. Not every market will evolve in exactly the same way and not all markets will exhibit the same characteristics as they evolve. Indeed, it has been argued that because each market has unique characteristics, the development of the networks should take this uniqueness into account (Sevell, 1995).

The Evolving Managed Care Market

There are basically four **stakeholders** in the health care delivery system of the United States: (1) the institutional providers (hospitals and ambulatory care centers), (2) caregivers (physicians and other allied health professionals), (3) employers, and (4) risk takers (insurance companies, managed care companies, and self-insured companies). These stakeholders are often in competition with one another to control the health care marketplace (Enthoven and Singer, 1995). The managed care companies have become a rapidly growing force in this competition, and it is important that they be understood.

Managed care companies come in many varieties. Some are **for-profit** entities, while others have **not-for-profit** status. Some are part of nationwide organizations, while others are local in their coverage, ownership, and organization. Some are owned and controlled by health care providers, while others are responsible to individuals or corporations that have no ties to the actual delivery of health care but are stockholders interested in a profit. Some managed care companies are strict **staff models,** allowing little provider choice to the enrollees, while others are **point-of-service** entities, which allow much more freedom of choice to the users of the services. The variety in the nature of managed care world is not exhausted by this brief listing, but it does provide a perspective into the amount of diversity that exists among them.

Given this high level of diversity, it is useful to have a perspective into the way managed care is being defined for this book. The health maintenance organization (HMO) is often viewed as a prototype managed care organization, although it is by no means the only type that exists. Going beyond the introductory insights given there, it is useful to understand the environment in which managed care organizations are currently operating in communities across the nation.

The health care delivery marketplace is exhibiting enormous competition: between institutional providers and other institutional providers, between institutional providers and physicians (and other caregivers), between institutional providers and caregivers, and payers; and in some instances there is competition between providers, payers and employers. The most important party, the patient (customer), is often left out of the equation of considerations, and the issues of convenience, satisfaction, and clinical outcome are frequently not even items of discussion for the interested parties.

It is little wonder that the delivery of health care generally, as contrasted to specifically the managed care segment, is fragmented, inefficient, and in some cases ineffective, as in the case of large numbers of Americans with no access to the health care system. This is not to say that the managed care segment does not have any responsibility in this matter or that it is performing well. Rather, it means only that the entire delivery system, of which the managed care segment is one part, has been ineffective in this set of responsibilities to the population.

Unlike some other sectors of the economy, the incentives for the various stakeholders in the delivery of health care are not aligned. In addition, the patient, who is central to the entire issue, is often not involved in the decision-making process except to respond to patient satisfaction questionnaires from the provider, the payer, and sometimes the employer. Ultimately, at some point in this process, the patient must be given more meaningful representation. Until this alignment of incentives for providers, payers, employers, and patients takes place, there is little reason to expect any significant improvement. This alignment of incentives could take place in several ways, but it is not at all clear how the situation will ultimately resolve itself. The resolution could come as the result of economic market forces that create a solution among all of the stakeholders, legislative action at state or national levels, consumer revolt, or all the parties forming cooperative alliances and rationally reaching mutually advantageous decisions.

So far, the primary changes in the managed care environment have resulted from economic pressures, although there have been some limited successes in the area of collaboration of interested parties. In general, the changes caused by the economic pressures have addressed the limited self-interest of one or more of the parties rather than embracing the needs of all of the stakeholders. For example, the driving down of costs has largely benefited managed care companies and in some cases employers. It has not resulted in coverage for people who have no access to health care. To the extent that reductions in reimbursement to health care providers have been accomplished, it has correspondingly reduced the ability of the health care providers to provide care for the poor. The beneficiaries of this reduction in reimbursement, the managed care companies and to some extent the premium payers, have not generally translated these financial windfalls into help for the health care system as a whole.

Reform of the health care system has not generally been viewed as a team effort by the stakeholders. It should be noted that the threat of reform from the federal legislative level has had an undefined, but nevertheless real, effect on the shape of the marketplace but has not actually been the locus of the change. Rather, the threat of federal intervention has caused local interests to review their methods of operation and to make cost reduction a focal point of operations. However, as noted, the cost reductions have not always been coordinated for the benefit of the total system, including the indigent patient population.

Economic pressures tend to be exerted by the dominant player in a market; in health care, this could be provider or payer, depending on the market and how it evolved. Thus far, neither employers (who pay for much of the health care services consumed) nor patients (who consume health care services) have achieved the status of dominant players and are not involved with the decision-making process in a meaningful way. At some point the economic pressures are almost always accompanied by concerns about antitrust issues or restraint of trade issues.

The relationship of the four stakeholders in the health care delivery system—the institutional providers, caregivers, employers, and risk takers—is shown in Figure 3-1. In this model, the employer becomes the proxy for the patient's interests. The employer can play a dual role of purchaser of the services and risk taker. Historically, the risk taker has held the dominant position and has contracted with the other entities for needed services.

Here, the risk taker contracts with (1) the institutional provider for facilities and services to provide health care and (2) the caregivers to provide the framework for access to health services. Finally, when the employer is not also the risk taker, the risk taker contracts with the employer to provide health care services to the employees in return for a premium paid to the risk taker for providing this service.

This model is changing, and it is no longer clear who is at the center of the model coordinating the health care delivery process. The characteristics of the relationships between the entities are changing. Institutional providers and caregivers are moving closer together, risk takers are getting into the business of becoming health care pro-

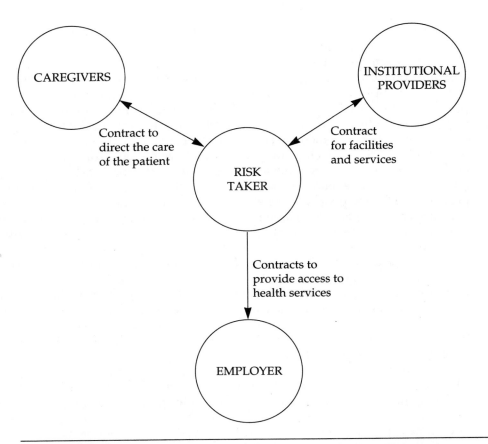

Figure 3-1   Relationship of Stakeholders in the Health Care Delivery System

viders, and health care providers are getting into the business of becoming risk takers and insurers of health care services. Thus, there is extraordinary ambiguity concerning the relationships of the stakeholders in the health care delivery system.

Perhaps the best way to portray the current status of inpatient delivery under a managed care system is to outline the relationships between the various players and describe the environment within which these relationships exist. In general, these relationships are often less than cordial, and in many instances they represent distrust and direct competition.

Competition of Institutional Providers with Institutional Providers

The health care market in the United States has changed substantially over the past decade. Many procedures have moved from an inpatient setting to an ambulatory setting. There has been an emphasis on reducing the length of stay for patients treated on an inpatient basis. Medical technology, while expensive, has affected the delivery of health care by providing noninvasive means of diagnostic and therapeutic treatment. Changes like these have focused on reducing the costs of health care, which have been escalating for three decades (Vincenzine, 1995). The financial sector of the U.S. economy has taken a significant interest in the health care market and has begun introducing innovative financing vehicles, which have similarities to agricultural futures markets (Ray, 1995). In the face of these pressures, health care providers have sought ways to become more competitive. The formation of **integrated delivery networks (IDN),** groups of institutional and individual providers who have organized themselves into a single vertically integrated health care delivery network, has been a response of many institutional health care providers (Bushick, 1995).

The development of IDNs resulted from the perception of many providers that they could gain a competitive advantage by combining a number of previously unrelated existing entities into a single institutional provider. Most believed that the competitive advantage to be gained would arise from either economies of scale from more efficient operations or the larger size of the resulting organization, with the ability to leverage negotiations, or both. The economies of scale have been slow in demonstrating themselves, although there is some evidence that they are beginning to emerge in mature markets. Certainly the financial sector of the United States economy sees this development as attractive and has been following it closely in the for-profit sector (Cerne, 1995).

Even when IDNs have not been the dominant form of competition in a particular market, where there are two or more health care providers, there has generally been more competition as the health care market has consolidated. Thus, the nature of the current health care environment is one of competition among the institutional providers, and in many instances competition has also emerged between institutional providers and the caregivers.

There are a number of issues surrounding the choices related to whether an IDN should be developed and, if so, what strategies should be used. In many instances, these choices will be governed by the environmental circumstances of the local health market. Issues that will bear on the ultimate success of the organization include the development strategies that will be used. For example, will the network concentrate on the acquisition of facilities as contrasted to building alliances (Coile, 1995). Another important issue is the type of governance that is adopted, which will have significant implications for the relationships between the institutional provider and the individual provider (Pointer, Alesancer, and Zuckerman, 1995). Finances are an important determinant in the success or failure of a network, so the methods used to finance the undertaking are enormously important (Pallarite, 1995).

Thus, the formation of an IDN is not only a strategic decision for an organization, which must include consideration of whether this is the correct approach for the community, but there are also a number of important tactical decisions that must be made. The leadership of the organization must be sure that all of the important issues bearing on the issue have been considered.

Competition of Institutional Providers with Individual Providers

The competition between institutional providers and individual providers (physicians and other individual caregivers) is of relatively recent origin. In the past, there was ample opportunity for each to provide his or her services without impinging on the other's turf. However, as competition has changed the utilization of health services, as well as reduced the reimbursement for those services, considerable competition to provide those services has emerged. It is not unusual now for physicians to build and operate their own ambulatory surgery centers, thereby engaging in direct competition with institutional providers. And institutional providers are moving into the practice of medicine by acquiring and building primary and specialty physician practices. Thus, the traditional lines of demarcation are vanishing, and direct competition between the institutional provider and the individual provider is increasingly common.

As an emerging model, competition between the institutional provider and the individual provider is more difficult to describe than is the case with some of the other competition in the health care market. It also varies widely around the country and is a function of the environment at the local level as well. It has become an issue of importance because managed care companies in the more mature markets have often preferred to deal with a single contracting entity. In less mature markets, managed care companies have preferred a fragmentation strategy, which seeks to contract separately with physicians and institutions and sometimes will not contract with large physician organizations. This fragmentation strategy tends to be used in the less mature markets in order to promote the market power of the managed care companies and minimize the negotiating power of institutions and physicians. As markets move to maturity, managed care companies eventually make a conscious decision to work with the networks in a partnership or are forced to do so by the evolving market conditions. Part of the evolution sometimes sees the accusation and counteraccusation of antitrust activity by government and other interested parties.

As health care systems form themselves, there is the inevitable issue between the institutional provider and the individual provider of who will control the process (Unland, 1995). Typically the institutional providers have had the economic resources that are necessary to capitalize the effort. In many instances, physicians have been either unwilling or unable to provide the capital necessary for such an effort, although capital sources from the capital markets in the form of venture capitalists have been used in some instances and physicians have taken control of the process (Vavala, 1995). When the physicians have not been involved with capitalizing the venture, they are sometimes given positions of influence within the governance of the organization in return for the important role they play in bringing patients to the institution and in managing cases efficiently.

In some markets, physicians are the focal point of the consolidation process (Coile, 1995). These arrangements can take a variety of forms in terms of ownership, relationships, and organizational structure (Ellerson and Nelson-Morrill, 1995). They can be owned and capitalized by the physicians themselves, or the physicians can share the ownership with an outside venture capitalist. The relationships to the provider organization can range from the physician's being an employee to being part of an association of independent physician practices. The organizational structure can be a multispecialty venture or a specialty group. Whatever form the venture takes, the intent is to position the entity to be an indispensable part of the health care delivery system of the community and thereby provide it with leverage in negotiating contracts with the risk takers. If an entity wishes to become part of a managed care panel, leverage is important not only to negotiate inclusion in the panel but also to negotiate prices. When the physician-based organization is the focal point of the health care delivery network, clearly the physicians are in a position of power; the institutional providers then become vehicles of the delivery system with which the physicians contract as part of their responsibility to provide for the health needs of the community.

The issue of who controls the process often has its roots in the economic relationships that are being defined and ultimately in how the reimbursement will be accomplished. The matter is not a trivial one from either side's point of view.

As a community advances along a managed care continuum, it is almost inevitable that there will be struggles between the individual providers and the institutional providers for control of the process.

Competition of Providers with Payers

As a community evolves through the managed care process, payers (the risk takers) become involved in a variety of skirmishes with the provider community. These skirmishes ultimately have their locus in control of the process of delivering health care to the community. There are many ways in which this struggle will manifest itself, but in the final analysis most contentions between these parties resolve into issues of cost and management of costs.

Most managed care companies, for example, insist on a **precertification** program for inpatient hospitalizations and sometimes for outpatient procedures. While this activity is done in the name of quality, it is ultimately focused on resource consumption and control of costs. This is a process in which the physician is required to receive approval from a managed care company before an elective admission or procedure will be reimbursed. This kind of control is not inherently bad; overuse can have adverse financial impacts and even an adverse quality impact on the care of patients. Nevertheless, control of the process is an issue that the health care delivery system constantly grapples with and is one of the principal focal points of contention between the risk takers and the provider community.

Rate negotiation is the second issue that is often contentious between risk takers and the provider community. The issue is the fine balance between the provider community's being able to provide the services in a way that is acceptable to all of its constituents and the risk-taking community's being able to sell the product to the consumers of health care.

A third area where control of the system is at stake is formation of the **provider panel,** which are those caregivers who are contracted and authorized to provide services to beneficiaries of a managed care company. The risk taker usually forms its own

provider panel and selects certain institutional and individual providers while reject-
ing others. The rationale for acceptance or rejection is usually on the basis of geographic coverage and having the appropriate number of providers. In this context, the
provider community must be on as many payer panels as is possible, given that the
reimbursement is acceptable. Thus, being rejected becomes an issue of significant
contention because it restricts or reduces access to a block of patients. From the risk
taker's perspective, it is important to have the appropriate geographic distribution of
providers, as well as to have providers who are efficient in their use of resources while
maintaining an acceptable level of quality. Again, the issue of control of the health care
delivery process comes into focus.

There are other issues too on which risk takers and providers are in contention.
The point is not to list them exhaustively but to note that control of the process is central to the interactions of all of the stakeholders, and the core of the issue is usually
economic.

Competition of Providers with Employers

In some parts of the country, there has been movement toward direct contracting
between providers and employers (Cave, Home, and Mahoney, 1995). In these settings, the provider has sometimes taken on the payer responsibilities. This means that
the provider provides the administrative services, such as paying the claims and
maintaining information systems that do statistical analysis for both the health care
provider and the employer, and takes on the responsibility for risk and all of the issues
attendant with that function. Taking on the risk function usually means meeting the
insurance standards for the state or states in which the activity is taking place.

It is sometimes argued that this kind of relationship is a natural conflict of interest
for the health care provider because one of the traditional roles of the payer has been
to negotiate competitive fees, control resource use, and ensure that acceptable quality
is being maintained. In this new model, the health care provider plays all of the roles,
including provider of health care services and guardian of the interests of the employer
or consumer of the services. By contrast, the health care provider seeking to assume
these multiple roles will argue that consumers of the services can contract independent
third parties to ensure competitive prices and adequate quality if they do not wish to
carry out these roles themselves. This newly emerging relationship is a complex one
and not yet well defined. Time will determine whether it is acceptable to the marketplace of health care consumers.

In these situations, it is not uncommon for there to develop a tension between the
provider and the third-party payers who formerly played the respective roles of
insurer and provider of administrative services. Thus, the decision by a provider to
take on this new function is a calculated risk, which includes not only the question of
whether additional business can be obtained by this mechanism but also a consideration of whether business will be lost from the payers who formerly had the business
but used this provider in their network. The calculated risk that the health care
provider takes is that the entire book of business that would be obtained by direct con-

tracting with a particular employer (i.e., other providers or provider networks would not participate in the business) will outweigh any business that might be lost if the third-party payer, who was formerly responsible for the business, decides to terminate the provider contract. Obviously there are additional considerations associated with this decision, including the issue of the relative strength of the provider or provider network and the degree of indispensability associated with the particular market.

An additional dimension of this competition has been the development of close partnerships between employers and managed care companies (Reiff and Sperling, 1995). These are often developed with the aim of containing health care costs by managing the health care of the employees more closely but without sacrificing quality of care.

The Disenfranchised Patient

In all of this discussion thus far, little has been said about the patient and the role of the patient in the process. Unfortunately this is the case; it is not an oversight. The truth of the matter is that individual patients have relatively little leverage in the process. The providers have leverage because they provide the necessary service. Although different providers have different degrees of leverage, depending on their position in the marketplace, the providers are indispensable. The employer has leverage because a large part of the bill is being paid as a benefit of employment, although increasingly workers themselves are being asked to pay a larger part. The third-party payers have leverage because of their historical position in the equation, including the longstanding relationships with the employers. The third-party payer's relationship tends to be stronger when the employer has a multilocation health care requirement, particularly when the requirement is widely dispersed in multiple states. With few exceptions, the patient has little leverage, although there are some indications that this might be changing with the help of certain advocacy groups, such as the American Association of Retired People. The question of whether the patient will have a larger voice in the future evolution of health care delivery will be a function of whether groups will be able to consolidate and speak as a unit on issues of importance.

In a few areas of the country, patients have been sufficiently dissatisfied to create lobbying efforts that produced legislation or the threat of legislation such that the managed care companies changed their position on restricting services. One of the best examples of this relates to the length of inpatient stay for a normal vaginal delivery.

Nevertheless, with very few exceptions, the nature of the health care delivery system has been shaped and defined by some combination of risk takers—insurers, employers, and providers—probably because these are the entities that have been organized well enough to speak as a single entity. Their communications have been directed effectively to a combination of lobbyists, politicians, regulators at both the state and national levels, and the public at large. Through this ability to communicate a message that engendered confidence in the system, the insurers, employers, and providers have historically been able to shape and control the health care delivery system. The inability of patients to communicate their message effectively has resulted in that group's having relatively little influence on the process. There are some indications that this might be changing.

Pluralistic Payment Systems in the United States

For purposes of illustration, the discussion that follows is limited to an examination of risk in the inpatient setting. The principles that are illustrated are nevertheless equally applicable to the outpatient setting, although the models are much more complicated and have occurred in a more delayed time frame. In addition, the changes in the inpatient, acute care managed care market have evolved in different time frames in various parts of the country. Therefore, the generalizations we make should be understood to approximate the market as it has evolved in various parts of the United States.

The current **pluralistic payment system** in the United States creates significant costs in the health care delivery system. It does so because of the requirement that every health care provider be aware of, and comply with, the multiplicity of rules and regulations that are indigenous to each plan, and the obvious corollary that it takes people and systems to comply with those disparate regulations. In addition, costs are introduced because of the duplication of efforts and administrative services that exist within the many payment systems. A General Accounting Office report stated, "If the universal coverage and single-payor features of the Canadian system were applied in the United States, the savings in administrative costs alone would be more than enough to finance insurance coverage for the millions of Americans who are currently uninsured. There would be enough left over to permit a reduction, or possibly even the elimination of the **co-payments** and **deductibles,** if that were deemed appropriate" (U.S. General Accounting Office, 1991). If this is true, it is a compelling reason for decision makers to consider seriously how the system can be improved both from a delivery and a financing point of view.

The payment system in the United States has evolved as a pluralistic model, with multiple payers in both the private and public sectors. In the public sector, Medicare, Medicaid, and CHAMPUS (Civilian Health and Medical Program of the Uniformed Services) are the most prominent. In the private sector, there are many different models, ranging from indemnity insurance to various managed care prototypes.

Government Reimbursement Systems

Price setting in the government payment sector is largely by **payer fiat.** The most obvious examples are the Medicare and Medicaid programs, where the health care provider has no negotiating power in setting the reimbursement rates. Because of the high volume of patients in these programs, most health care providers elect to accept the payment rates. They are not in a position to ignore a payer (the federal government) that represents over 40 percent of the market. In conjunction with the fiat prices, there is the issue of the multiplicity of rules that must be observed in both the actual delivery of health care and the reimbursement arena. The press is full of stories about the ramifications of not following the rules. Enforcement is strict, and in most cases there is little latitude for negotiation.

Medicare

Medicare, the largest payer group in the United States, has traditionally focused on the inpatient hospital sector but is now beginning to give significant attention to the ambulatory care sector as well—both the institutional-based ambulatory care facilities and the physician sector. In order to control costs, the focus is moving in the direction of the resource-based **relative value unit** (RBRVU) which defines the amount of resources that are believed to be appropriate for a given procedure. This RVU allows for reimbursement of the appropriate resources involved with the procedure, but also precludes **unbundling** the charges and at the same time establishes an expected unit price for the procedure.

The reimbursement strategy of the Medicare system is to reduce the overall reimbursement to health care providers and thereby stabilize the budget. Part of the reason is to squeeze fraud and abuse out of the system, but part is also clearly focused on reducing the costs of traditional health services.

Because of the enormous leverage the Medicare program has in terms of its buying power for the population it controls, most health care providers determine that they have little choice but to accept the fiat prices that are offered and the payment mechanisms that are unilaterally invoked.

A relatively new trend in Medicare reimbursement is the evolution of **risk-based Medicare programs,** administered by private sector payers under a managed care protocol. As these programs evolve, it will be interesting to note whether the elderly will elect to obtain their care in a private managed care environment or to remain in the relatively familiar, if not secure, environment of the government-administered program. The managed care approach by the federal government is similar to the evolution of managed care in the private sector. It is fundamentally a matter of shifting the risk from one part of the system to another; in this case, the risk is shifted from the federal government to the private sector. Ultimately all or part of the risk gets shifted to the health care providers. As a result, the Health Care Financing Administration (**HCFA**) has a fixed, capitated cost for each Medicare recipient, and the private sector takes the risk of managing the health care benefits guaranteed under the capitation. In some instances, the payer retains the entire risk; in other Medicare-managed care models, some or all of the risk is shifted to the medical providers.

It will be interesting to follow the evolution of this program and see whether the anticipated savings materialize and, if they do, how they are administered. One way would be to reinvest them back in the program, by either lowering the premium to the users or expanding the benefits by lowering or eliminating current deductibles and co-payments. Another use of the savings could be to take them back in the general budget of the federal government and disburse them in the usual political ways. Time will demonstrate the level of success in redesigning this very complex program.

Medicaid

Medicaid is often thought of as a program of the individual states, but it is actually a federal program that is administered by states, often in very different ways and with widely varying benefit and reimbursement programs. Certain entitlements, such as aid to dependent children, are required of all Medicaid programs, but there are also substantial differences in the way that the programs are administered, financed, and reimbursed. Perhaps the most common thread that runs through the way various states administer the program is that it is inadequately funded. Because of the low reimbursement and unwieldy bureaucracy associated with reimbursement in many of the state-administered programs, many physicians elect not to participate in the Medicaid program of the state in which they reside.

Like the Medicare program, many states are electing to migrate toward a managed care environment, and for the same reasons. In these instances, state Medicaid programs have subcontracted with private sector organizations to administer the Medicaid program on a risk basis. As in the case of Medicare, there are anticipated savings associated with shifting the financing risk to the private sector. If these savings materialize, it will be interesting to see whether they accrue to the medical delivery system for indigent patients, which almost everyone agrees is underfunded, or whether it will accrue to the general fund of the state budgets, to be disbursed in the usual political way.

CHAMPUS

This program is designed to care for retired military personnel and their dependents. Most prices are established on a **usual and customary (U&C)** basis—that is, the methodology for arriving at the reimbursement is to keep track of the charges that are made for each health care service by the community of providers and to calculate the mean price and quartile breaks for pricing each procedure in the community. The distribution of the charges is therefore known. The reimbursement is usually established at the seventy-fifth or ninetieth percentile of the distribution for each service.

Veterans Administration

The Veterans Administration system is designed to provide health care to veterans of the armed services (this is different from CHAMPUS, which covers retired military personnel and their families). Private sector physicians sometimes participate in this system on a contract basis, but the inpatient acute care services and ambulatory services are performed in government-owned facilities under the management of the Veterans Administration. The basis for reimbursement to private physicians can be either salary or fee for service.

Military

Each service of the armed forces of the United States has its own medical service. The institutional facilities, both inpatient acute care and ambulatory, are almost always owned and operated by the military service branches. Like the Veterans Administration system, private sector physicians sometimes provide services, and on a contract basis. The methodology of reimbursement can be salary, fee for service, or, in some cases, capitation.

The Private Sector

Indemnity Insurance Reimbursement Systems

This reimbursement mechanism is rapidly disappearing, but it is found, though in limited scope, in some parts of the country. For the most part, this sector of the reimbursement system is moving to various managed care models.

In its original form, this reimbursement method pays the health care provider on the basis of billed charges, or sometimes on discounted billed charges, after the deductible and co-payments are met—from a provider's point of view, one of the most desirable payment mechanisms. It is rapidly disappearing because there are few cost control mechanisms built into it other than the inclinations of individual physicians as they practice medicine. For all practical purposes, the price is set by the provider, and there are few controls set on resource consumption. In some instances, indemnity companies are limiting their reimbursements up to the U&C limits, which usually means that they will pay up to a stated percentile, often the seventy-fifth or ninetieth, of the norms of the community.

Managed Care Reimbursement Systems

Managed care comes in many forms and addresses both the ambulatory and inpatient acute treatment of patients. It had its beginnings in the inpatient, acute side of the industry, but is now rapidly expanding to the ambulatory area. The most common organizational structures are health maintenance organizations (**HMO**) and preferred provider organizations (**PPO**).

Managed care could most accurately be defined as that practice of medicine that seeks to provide health care at a quality acceptable in the community, in the most efficient and effective way possible. This does not always mean the least expensive on a unit basis, nor does it necessarily mean that services are inappropriately rationed. At the same time, it does not mean that pressures are not brought on physicians and other health professionals to practice in ways that are different from traditional practice. The aim of managed care is to encourage care of the patient in a fairly consistent way, given the diagnosis, and to encourage, if not force, physicians who practice outside the community norms to change their practice.

Health Maintenance Organizations

An HMO contracts to provide health care services to a defined population on a prepaid basis. The premium is paid on the basis of the enrolled population of the HMO, and the HMO is **at risk,** although it often shifts that risk to the provider by the reimbursement mechanism. Typically a beneficiary or employer, or both, pays the HMO a specific monthly premium in return for guarantees to provide a previously agreed upon range of health care services. If services can be provided for less than the aggregate premium amount, the HMO is profitable; if it costs more than the aggregate premium amount to provide the services, the HMO loses money. In those cases where the HMO shifts the risk to the providers, the formula is the same except that the HMO pays the provider a fixed fee per member per month (a *capitation*) in return for a guarantee from the provider to provide a predefined range of health services. If the physician or hospital can provide the services for less than the capitation, there is a profit; if the services cost more than the capitation, there is a financial loss to the physician and/or hospital.

Thus, it is not surprising that HMOs seek out physicians who offer quality service and practice cost-effective medicine or that they attempt to shift the financial risk to the health care providers. Furthermore, the HMO or the health care provider who has taken risk obviously have an incentive to see that the care is managed across the entire insured population, in a way that ensures that the quality is acceptable and the costs are controlled. Hence, there has been an evolution to the concept of managed care.

Given this model, some questions of ethics have been raised along the lines of whether the economic incentives of the reimbursement system promote inappropriate rationing of services. Although there have been isolated instances where this has been demonstrated, it is not believed to be a widespread practice; nevertheless, it is incumbent on health care workers, as well as managed care employees, to ensure that this potential does not escalate into a problem.

An HMO can be organized in a variety of ways. Usually the organizational structure refers to the way that the physicians relate to the organization. The most common structures are:

- *Staff model.* The physicians work for the HMO as full-time, usually salaried employees and do not individually experience risk in providing health care services, although the HMO would be at financial risk and subject to the potential ethical problems already cited.

- *Group model.* The organization contracts for the services of one or more large physician groups. The HMO provides the facility for the practice and furnishes the support personnel. The reimbursement can be on a capitated basis or fee for service.

- *Network model.* The HMO contracts with a number of smaller physician groups (rather than a few large multispecialty groups), and the physician groups provide their own facilities and support personnel. The HMO usually reimburses on the basis of a capitation fee to the practice, but it can be on a fee-for-service basis as well.

- *Independent practice association (IPA).* This model is fragmented and offers the least ability to control the resource use in the practice. There is little interaction between the physicians on an organized basis, so patient care plans often approximate the level of coordination experienced in private sector practice. The results can be costs that are higher than other medical staff models for HMOs. The degree of control in resource use is often determined by the reimbursement mechanism. The model is one where the HMO contracts with a large number of group and solo practitioners to provide services. The rationale of this approach is to give the enrollees more choice in their use of physicians and the location of the practices.

Preferred Provider Organizations

A PPO differs from an HMO in a number of respects. For example, PPOs generally are not at economic risk for providing health care, although they will sometimes put providers at limited financial risk by the vehicle of a withhold or other reimbursement mechanism. This means that a prospectively determined amount of the reimbursement the provider receives is "withheld" by the payer as a contingency against excessive use of resources, which would result in higher-than-expected reimbursement for health care services. In the event that it is retrospectively determined that there was not an overuse of resources, the withhold is given to the provider. The withhold is usually deducted from the agreed-on reimbursement schedule. Thus, if a provider had a contract that called for a 25 percent discount from billed charges and a 10 percent withhold, the provider would be paid at the rate of 65 percent of billed charges with 10 percent going into a withhold pool whose disposition would be decided later on the basis of the provider's use of resources. Capitation is a rarely encountered reimbursement vehicle for PPOs.

The service a PPO provides to the health delivery system is to construct a delivery network of physicians and institutions. This network is then brokered to other risk takers, such as insurance companies, union trusts, and self-insured employers. Thus, the profitability of a PPO often arises not from receiving premiums and managing the care to produce a profit on operations, but rather by charging access fees for use of the network and collecting other fees for services provided, such as utilization review and quality assurance. Reimbursement to institutional and individual health care providers is usually on the basis of a contract that uses either a fee schedule or a U&C standard. A discount from billed charges is still used in some cases, but it is a declining method of reimbursement because it effectively allows the health care provider to set the fee.

Typically a PPO managed care plan allows the enrollee to use network or nonnetwork providers. A financial incentive to use a network provider usually takes the form of a lower deductible and **co-insurance** amount to be paid by the enrollee using a network provider. Thus, the enrollee has the freedom to choose a provider outside the network, although there will be some financial costs associated with making that choice.

Exclusive Provider Organizations

Exclusive provider organizations, **(EPO)** are organizations that have some characteristics of an HMO and some likeness to a PPO. It is a managed care response to accusations by the provider community that PPOs have not been effective in directing patients to network providers. In this model, the enrollees are required to use the network providers, or no payment will be made by the payer, effectively making the enrollee responsible for 100 percent of the health care bill. The EPO is distinguished from the HMO in that it does not take risk as the HMO does.

Self-Payment Systems

In this reimbursement mechanism, the patient has direct responsibility for the health care services bill. There is a significantly higher probability of nonpayment of the bill than is the case with insured patients. It thus has come to mean risky reimbursement to health care providers, but sometimes self-pay is a lucrative and reliable source of reimbursement. One of the best examples of this is cosmetic surgery. Most risk takers do not cover cosmetic surgery as a benefit, so people who wish to have cosmetic procedures performed must assume the financial burden associated with it. Many cosmetic surgeons require that all or part of the fee be paid in advance, so the reimbursement becomes reliable. Nevertheless, this condition is a relatively small proportion of the self-pay population, and reimbursement for this category of health care is relatively uncertain.

When a patient is determined to be responsible for the bill but is unable to pay, the unpaid amount is categorized as bad debt, not charity. Thus, it is critical that the financial personnel of an organization be able to determine the patient's ability to pay early in the episode because the ability to classify the care as charity is determined by whether there was an expectation of receiving the payment (Schmitz, Weiss, and Melichar, 1992). When a patient is unable to pay, it is far more desirable for the care to be classified as charity rather than bad debt because of Internal Revenue Service requirements that not-for-profit entities provide certain levels of charity work to the community. Guidelines for this responsibility are determined by current approaches that have not yet been defined by specific algorithms. Patients who fall into the self-pay category of the reimbursement system make up a relatively small proportion of the total system, although the total dollars involved are significant.

The Evolution of Risk

In the late 1960s the dominant payment system was a combination of indemnity insurance in the commercial sector and cost-based reimbursement in the government sector. In this setting, health care providers experienced very little risk. In the commercial sector, institutions were paid for services that were rendered, at whatever price the provider charged. In the government sector, institutions were paid on the basis of costs, so effectively there was no way to lose money on these patients. Actually Medicaid patients are in the governmental sector, and the reimbursement was generally low, but since these patients composed a relatively minor portion of the total patient population, it had little effect on total reimbursement received, and the deficits experienced because of these patients were compensated by cost shifting to the commercial sector. For physicians, Medicare payments were generally a discount from billed charges, although a fee schedule came into practice later. In the commercial sector, reimbursement was on the basis of whatever the physician charged.

In the intervening years, the payers have systematically shifted the economic risk for providing health care from themselves to institutional and individual providers. (For purposes of illustration, inpatient acute care will be discussed, but the philosophy is the same for ambulatory care although it is happening at a different pace.) This risk comprises two parts: price risk and the risk associated with the volume of services used. In turn, the volume risk is made up of two parts: the actuarial risk of illness in the population that is being covered and the risk of overusing resources. Thus, the costs to a risk taker to insure a defined population will be a combination of the price that is charged for those services and the volume of services used. To the extent that either or both of these two variables can be rationally controlled, the risk taker stands a better chance of being successful and making a profit.

Providers and payers have attempted to manage these variables to minimize their exposure to the economic risk associated with them. Indeed, the evolution of managed care can be seen in the light of how this battle has been played out.

The Billed Charges Era

As late as the late 1960s, a major portion of the reimbursement mechanism for both institutional and individual providers was on the basis of billed charges. At the zenith of the billed charges era, the providers set the price, and the payer paid the bill. In this setting, the economic risk associated with the price level as well as the volume of services used was with the payer. For example, when a beneficiary was hospitalized, both the price and the volume of services were under the control of the providers, and the payer had the entire economic risk associated with the provision of services. Thus, the reimbursement was by this very simple equation:

$$\text{Reimbursement} = \text{Price charged by the provider.}$$

The Discount from Billed Charges Era

By the mid-1970s, some managed care was emerging across the country. Of course, there was managed care much earlier than this, but it was in isolated pockets of the country. Managed care companies, in the form of HMOs and PPOs, promised to direct patients to those providers who would become part of their networks. In return, the providers were expected to provide lower prices so the managed care companies could be competitive and gain market share with this new health care delivery vehicle. In the early stages of the evolution, these more competitive prices often took the form of discounts from billed charges. The discounts were usually calculated as a percentage of the billed charges, but sometimes fixed amounts were discounted from procedure prices.

A large proportion of the early managed care ventures were PPOs. Although there were also new HMO ventures, they were far less frequent, and their early growth rates were substantially lower than those of the PPOs. In retrospect, this pattern is not unexpected. The PPO model required less of a departure from the traditional health care delivery model than did the HMO because the PPO allowed the beneficiary to retain a choice in selecting providers. Thus, the modest growth curve of the HMOs in their early days can be seen as the typical human resistance to change.

In this era, the payer continued to have risk for both price and volume of services. Although the payer experienced some one-time cost reductions from the discounts, the provider effectively maintained control of the pricing mechanism by virtue of the fact that the prices could be changed. There were no controls on volume of services by utilization review vehicles or financial incentives. Thus the reimbursement algorithm was:

$$\text{Reimbursement} = \text{Price} - \text{discount}.$$

The Per Day Reimbursement Era

In this model, inpatient services were paid on the basis of a prospectively agreed upon price that would cover all costs for an inpatient day of service. This represented the first attempt to allocate some of the financial risk to the provider. This pricing was often stratified in that different reimbursements would be negotiated for critical care units, medical and surgical services, obstetrical services, and psychiatric services. For the first time, the provider had to consider how often a patient might have a surgical procedure and therefore to manage the risks associated with these variable costs in terms of both how many surgical patients there would be as well as the consumption of resources for those patients. Here the reimbursement algorithm was:

$$\text{Reimbursement} = \text{Negotiated rate per day} \times \text{number of days}.$$

The Per Stay Reimbursement Era

This era is also known as case rate reimbursement and further shifts the risk to the providers. In this model, reimbursement is made on the basis of the entire hospital stay for a patient. In the Medicare realm, this reimbursement mechanism is known as diagnosis-related groups (**DRGs**) and is stratified by various levels of medical complexity associated with the medical treatment of those groups of patients. In some instances, there is a provision for additional payments to be made as a result of outlier conditions for a patient. For example, if a patient exceeds the expected length of stay for a particular illness by a specified number of days, additional payments are allowed. According to this reimbursement mechanism, the payer shifts an additional volume risk to the provider by making the provider primarily responsible for the length of stay of the patient. Thus, the provider now has become responsible for the risk associated with the price, the consumption of resources, and, for all practical purposes, the length of stay. Only the risk for frequency of illness in the population remains with the payer for inpatient hospitalizations. The reimbursement algorithm is:

$$\text{Reimbursement} = \text{Established rate for inpatient stay}.$$

The Capitation Reimbursement Era

This change in reimbursement methodology takes the final step in shifting the economic risk for health care to the provider. There are multiple forms of capitation, ranging from global capitation to capitation for limited services, such as primary care or **carve-out** niches such as laboratory or radiology services. In global capitation, the provider receiving the capitation takes the agreed-on medical risks for the entire covered population. This represents a substantial shift in the level of risk for the health care provider, now responsible for the actuarial frequency of illness in the population. In addition, the contracting entity becomes responsible for the utilization of resources across the entire spectrum of care for a patient. For example, if the contracting entity for global capitation is an institutional provider, it also takes the risks for the physician component, which might be handled in turn by a variety of reimbursement methods ranging from subcapitation to discounted fee for service. If physicians take the global capitation, they take the risk for institutional costs and must be able to guarantee hospital and ambulatory services, either by owning them or by contracting for them. In those instances where the payer wishes only to capitate for primary care or other carve-out segments, risk is shifted for only those parts of the delivery system that are capitated or are in some other kind of risk-sharing agreement.

Where global capitation is in effect, the payer has effectively shifted all of the financial risk to the provider. The risk for the price, for resource use, and for frequency of illness in the population becomes that of the provider. The only risk remaining for the payer is the normal business risk associated with administratively managing the operations of the managed care company.

Thus, there are ranges of risk accruing to the provider, depending on the reimbursement mechanism that is invoked within the framework of capitation. However, generally the payers are moving to capitation, the final step in shifting the financial risk for providing health care to the provider. The reimbursement algorithm for capitation is:

$$\text{Reimbursement} = \text{Capitation rate} - \text{cost.}$$

A Recap

During the past thirty years, there has been a substantial shift of risk from the payer to the provider. Table 3-1 provides a compact view of this transition.

It is important to understand the rationale and strategies associated with this transition, as well as the timing accompanying it. Generally, shifting risk from the payer to the provider has occurred when it is advantageous to the payer. From the payer's perspective, it is not universally true that it is always desirable to shift the risk to the provider. Sometimes it is not financially desirable to make this shift.

In some parts of the country, there is still excess use of resources, particularly in the inpatient acute care sector. For example, in the Midwest, it is not uncommon to see inpatient hospital utilization rates for the employed population at over 300 inpa-

Table 3-1   Responsibility of the Provider to Bear Risk

Era of Reimbursement	Responsibility to Bear Risk		
	Price	*Volume*	*Population*
Billed charges	None	None	None
Discount from billed charges	Partial	None	None
Per day reimbursement	All	Partial	None
Per stay reimbursement	All	All	None
Global capitation	All	All	All

tient days per 1,000 population. In other parts of the country, where managed care is at a much more mature stage, the utilization rate for this same population is fewer than 200 days per 1,000 population.

If the utilization rate for the employed population in the Midwest eventually is driven down to the level where it is in the areas where managed care is mature, substantial savings in costs will occur as the excess inpatient acute care utilization is forced out of the system. The only question is who will experience the fruits of those savings. The answer is that the risk takers, whoever they are, will experience those savings and the financial windfalls associated with them. One could argue from a policy point of view that the savings should accrue to the system in the form of broader access, perhaps even universal access, for patients. The barrier has always been the argument that the economy cannot afford this kind of access. Perhaps if the funds are available but are simply being reallocated, there is a chance to engage in some comprehensive health care reform. The state of Washington has undertaken an attempt to provide comprehensive health care (Jacobson, 1995). This would suggest that the idea that all citizens of the United states should have access to the health care system still survives.

There is a financial incentive for the managed care companies to squeeze the excesses out of the system before they move to a capitated reimbursement environment. In that way, they experience the savings. The health care providers are not oblivious to this fact either, and in many communities where there is excess utilization, there are major contentions between the payers and the providers on the subject of capitation. In these instances, the providers wish to take the capitation because the savings that accrue as a result of driving out overutilization will accrue to the provider. Both the provider and the managed care companies want to experience the savings so the providers will seek capitation and the payers will resist it until they perceive that most or all of the excesses have been forced out of the system.

Conclusion

A discussion of the evolution of managed care is fundamentally one of how risk is being taken and who controls the process. At the heart of the issue is the question of financial incentive. The payer, the employer, and the provider all have a financial stake in how the system evolves. Patients have a stake, too, but they are rarely in a position to influence the outcome. Thus, the three major players are vying for control and the best possible financial outcome for their part of the equation. The process has moved from one where the payer was the coordinator for the employers, physicians, and health care institutions to one where all of the players, to a greater or lesser extent, are maneuvering to take over the other's role. Health care institutions want to become payers. Payers want to become providers. In some instances employers have attempted to become payers or providers, or both.

Whether the payers, the providers, or the employers end up in control of the system is yet to be determined. The future is far from certain, but it is likely that the next step in the evolution of the health care delivery system in the United States will take its form as a result of playing out this conflict on the grounds of financial advantage and control of the system.

Review Questions

1. In today's competitive health care environment, which stakeholder do you believe dominates the market? Why?

2. Do you think that managed care companies have an obligation to help resolve the problem of health care access where 30 percent of Americans do not have access to health care? Provide reasons for your answers.

3. What factors do you believe were instrumental in promoting managed care as a dominant reimbursement mechanism?

4. List and discuss some of the issues that make the pluralistic payment system economically inefficient.

5. As financial risk shifted from the payer to the provider, what factors stimulated this evolution?

References

Bushick, J. (1995). Creating an integrated health care system as a basis for managed care excellence: A health plan's perspective. *Managed Care Quarterly, 3*(1), 1–10.

Cave, D. G., Home, D., & Mahoney, J. J. (1995). Pitney Bowes: Using comprehensive cost information to build provider networks. *Benefits Quarterly, 11*(2), 19–25.

Cerne, F. (1995). Wall Street: Where health care is suddenly hot. *Hospitals and Health Networks, 69*(6), 38–40, 42.

Coile, R. C. (1994). Independent physician organizations: Medical networks put physicians in control of managed care. *Hospital Strategy Report, 6*(7), 1–3, 6–7.

Coile, R. C. (1995). Assessing health care market trends and capital needs: 1996–2000. *Healthcare Financial Management, 94*(8), 60–62, 64–65.

Ellerson, A., and Nelson-Morrill, C. (1995). Columbia/HCA's physician equity strategy. *Health System Leader, 2*(2), 12–13.

Enthoven, A., & Singer, S. (1995). Who will dominate HMO master contracting? *Journal of Health Care Finance, 21*(3), 1–5.

Jacobson, P. D. (1995). Washington State Health Service Act: Implementing comprehensive health care reform. *Health Care Financing Review, 16*(3), 177–196.

Pallarite, K. (1995). CFOs take new tack. *Modern Healthcare, 25*(10), 85–86, 88–90, 92–94.

Pointer, D. D., Alexander, J. A., & Zuckerman, H. S. (1995). Loosening the Gordian Knot of governance in integrating health care delivery systems. *Frontiers of Health Services Management, 11*(3), 3–37.

Ray, R. (1995). Controlling America's health care costs via health care futures. *Health Care Management Review, 20*(2), 85–91.

Reiff, M. G., & Sperling, K. L. (1995). Measuring the savings from managed care: Experience at Citibank. *Benefits Quarterly, 11*(2), 9–15.

Schmitz, H. H., Weiss, S. J., & Melichar, C. (1992). A systematic method of accountability. *Health Progress, 73*(9), 46–51, 57.

Sevell, R. (1995). An integrated delivery systems review: Common problems to be addressed. *Health Care Law Newsletter, 10*(1), 3–8.

U.S. General Accounting Office. (1991). *Canadian health insurance: Lessons for the United States.* Washington, DC: U.S. Government Printing Office.

Unland, J. (1995). Hospitals versus physicians, POs versus PHOs: The providers' struggle for control of managed care contracting. *Journal of Health Care Finance, 21*(3), 17–36.

Vavala, D. (1995). Fighting fire with fire: Physicians blazing new paths to autonomy. *Physician Executive, 21*(4), 3–6.

Vincenzine, J. (1995). Health care costs: Market forces and reform. *Statistical Bulletin—Metropolitan Insurance Companies, 76*(1), 29–35.

Chapter 4

Ambulatory Care in a Managed Care Environment

This chapter discusses the dynamics of managed care in the ambulatory setting. Many of the issues are quite different from managed care in the acute care inpatient setting. One of the primary differences between the inpatient and ambulatory delivery settings relates to how quality concepts are applied and how risk is evaluated.

Learning Objectives

Upon successful completion of this chapter, the learner will:

- Be able to identify and discuss the differences between the inpatient and ambulatory delivery systems.
- Be able to recognize and discuss the elements that have been instrumental in driving the growth of the ambulatory sector.
- Be able to discuss the newly emerging ambulatory care delivery models.
- Understand the complex relationships that exist between measuring risk and measuring quality.
- Understand the role of quality improvement in delivering health care in the ambulatory care setting under a managed care model.
- Understand how quality is being applied to the ambulatory care setting by some managed care companies.

Key Terms

best practices

continuous quality improvement

critical path

EAP programs

Introduction

Managed care has evolved much more slowly in the ambulatory care setting than has been the case with the inpatient acute care setting. This is partly because there were many fewer dollars being expended in the ambulatory sector and partly because managing care in the ambulatory care setting is much more complex than is the case with the inpatient acute care setting. Given this combination of circumstances, managed care in the ambulatory care setting is only now beginning to get the same intensity of scrutiny from the managed care companies as was given to the inpatient acute care setting a few years ago. Of course, as in the case of inpatient acute care managed care efforts, in some parts of the country managed care in the ambulatory sector has been practiced for some time. However, in general, including Medicaid and Medicare's role in the process, the ambulatory sector is just being organized as a site of delivery under the managed care mantle.

The evolution of managed care in the ambulatory environment has occurred in different ways and at differing paces. Thus, the discussion that follows does not represent an expectation of what will happen or has happened in every market or that particular markets will exhibit the same characteristics as others as they evolve. In general, the local market will determine the nature of the managed care market, and that is a function of all of the organizational dynamics discussed in Chapter 3.

Growth of Ambulatory Care

Three primary forces have been driving the shift from the inpatient acute care institution's being the site of delivery to a number of alternative forms of ambulatory care organizations' being the site of delivery: (1) the incentives by Medicare to shift the delivery site, (2) incentives by the managed care companies to do the same, and (3) the logistical issues with making managed care work in the ambulatory care setting.

Incentives Under Medicare to Shift Delivery Site

The initial thrust by Medicare a few years ago was to move certain procedures out of the more expensive acute care setting into the relatively less expensive ambulatory care setting. Having done this, there was a realization that just as there was the potential for overutilization in the inpatient acute care setting, there is also the same potential in the ambulatory setting. This problem was exacerbated by the fact that many of the procedures were paid on a discount from billed charges basis, which means there was little control over the price paid. As more and more medical services were passing into the ambulatory realm, with corresponding increases in cost, it became obvious that a need was developing for managing utilization and prices in the ambulatory setting.

Thus, some of the same types of managed care controls are being sought in the ambulatory setting as had been the case in acute care. Although the form is sometimes different, the intent of Medicare is the same: to control the price of the medical services being offered and the volume used. The vehicles used to exercise both of these controls are currently evolving.

In the area of pricing, the resource-based relative value unit (**RBRVU**) is being developed and refined. This concept, which originated in Medicare, increasingly is being viewed by managed care companies in the private sector as a tool to control price. It is a pricing vehicle that attributes value to the resources that are consumed in delivering ambulatory health care. It gives higher value to the cognitive activities of physicians—those activities achieved through analysis—than had been the case in the past, while reducing some of the reimbursement to surgeons and other physicians performing invasive procedures requiring significant physical dexterity and proficiency. In addition, Medicare has begun defining what items are included in the prices and does not permit unbundling the prices, which means the provider makes a separate charge for each supply or service provided.

In addition, Medicare policies are being put in place to control the volume of services. For example, reimbursement for defined numbers of office visits is permitted for specific spells of illness, but utilization beyond that point is not normally reimbursed. Further, as in the case of inpatient admissions, a second example of controlling the volume of services is the requirement for precertification of specified ambulatory procedures. When this precertification is not obtained, reimbursement is in question.

Like Medicaid, Medicare is experimenting with the concept of contracting with private sector managed care companies to provide medical services for Medicare beneficiaries. A number of these contracts are in place and are being evaluated for their effectiveness. Under these arrangements, Medicare capitates the private sector managed care companies to provide a defined level of benefits to Medicare beneficiaries. The advantage to Medicare is that it fixes the costs and transfers the risk to the managed care companies. Just as the private sector managed care companies capitate health care providers in order to limit their risk, Medicare is capitating private sector companies to cover Medicare beneficiaries in order to limit governmental risk to cover this population. In order to gain enrollees, the managed care companies sometimes add benefits to the package, and it is not uncommon for the benefits to exceed those of the beneficiaries under the traditional Medicare program. These increases in benefits can include vision benefits, smaller deductibles and co-payments, and more generous pharmacy benefits. The private sector is testing the market and at the same time is being tested by the market in terms of its ability to respond to the health care needs of the Medicare population within the economic framework (capitation), being imposed.

Incentives by Managed Care Companies to Shift the Delivery Site

Most of the Medicare incentives discussed in the previous section are applicable in the case of the private sector managed care companies. The actual techniques are not always the same, but the functional activities of controlling price and utilization are nevertheless present.

The intent of private sector managed care companies, as is also the case with Medicare and Medicaid, is to move the delivery of health care to the most appropriate level. When this is achieved, advocates believe, the costs associated with the delivery of health care should be reduced while the quality of care is maintained or increased.

Whether quality can be maintained at the same time costs are being reduced is a hotly debated issue. Some argue that the costs of doing an ambulatory procedure in an inpatient setting are no more or less than doing them in a strict ambulatory setting. They suggest that the issue of cost is simply a matter of how institutional activities are allocated to the medical procedure, and the real issue is therefore no more than a question of how the procedure is priced. This line of reasoning concludes by asserting that costs are really not a primary issue when debating the merits of providing care in an inpatient or ambulatory setting. Rather, the issue is one of quality of care and safety for the patient in receiving the medical procedure.

A second argument is that quality is not being maintained as some medical procedures are moved from the inpatient to ambulatory settings and that there are excesses in terms of moving health care procedures too far down the level-of-care chain. The matter of patient safety is sometimes cited as an issue in this debate. There is some validity to most of these points on both sides of the debate. Examples can certainly be found of inappropriate outcomes with regard to both quality and pricing.

On the other side of the debate, the rising trend in health care costs has been curbed, and some would attribute much of the success to shifting the site of health care delivery.

This debate will continue, and the market will ultimately decide what is appropriate. Interestingly this decision, which will be rendered by the market, will probably be made on the basis of the same two factors—price and quality of outcome—and a balance will ultimately be found that reflects what satisfies the customer.

Logistical Issues in the Growth of Managed Care in the Ambulatory Setting

The growth of managed care in the ambulatory setting has been occurring at an increasing rate. This raises the question of why this was not a growth in parallel with the inpatient acute care setting instead of lagging by a number of years. Several reasons can be postulated for this phased growth of managed care.

First, at the time that managed care began its growth phase in the acute care setting, few major medical procedures were being performed in the outpatient setting, and there were relatively few dollars being expended or costs incurred in the ambulatory sector. The bulk of costs in the ambulatory sector were associated with primary care and specialist physician office visits. Most of the medical procedures were being performed in the inpatient acute care setting and thus formed the initial focus of Medicare and the managed care companies in moving those procedures to the ambulatory setting. Once that happened, and there were significantly increased expenditures being made in the ambulatory sector, the next logical step, from the managed care perspective, was to establish policies and procedures that would place controls on any excess utilization. Thus, one of the primary reasons that managed care was not initially active in the ambulatory setting is that there was very little care to manage, other than the individual physician office visits and some ancillary services utilization. When the site of delivery for many of the medical procedures was shifted to the ambulatory setting, it became necessary to manage them too.

This highlights the second reason that ambulatory care was not immediately active in the ambulatory sector: the providers in that sector were much more scattered and independent, and there were many more of them. Thus, there would be many more provider entities to manage than was the case with the inpatient sector, and the dollar volume on a unit-of-service basis was much lower. Of course, physicians were paid for their inpatient services, as well as their ambulatory services, by Medicare and the managed care companies in the private sector, but the focus of managing the care as well as the reimbursement penalties targeted the institutional providers.

At that time, the operational systems of Medicare and the managed care companies in the ambulatory setting were evolving and did not have the level of sophistication to manage such a complex array of providers and services as existed in that setting. In addition, the technology of the information systems was much more primitive than it is today, and often the systems were incapable of embracing the volume and complexity of ambulatory health care. The system concepts related to quality and risk management are quite different for the inpatient acute care setting than in the ambulatory setting, yet another set of factors that became barriers to implementing managed care in this setting. The concept of quality assurance and risk management in the ambulatory setting will be discussed in greater detail later in this chapter.

A final issue is the concept of accountability. The issues related to accountability are much different in the inpatient acute care setting than in the ambulatory setting. Making the inpatient acute care institutions responsible for the economic outcome of the patient care experience effectively made them responsible for physician actions, even though most institutions had no effective mechanisms in place to influence physicians in their treatment of patients. At that time, most of the penalties for overutilization focused on the reimbursement mechanism for the institutional providers. Medicare and the managed care companies were therefore able to control the costs of the inpatient acute care episodes by concentrating their efforts on institutions.

It was much easier to try to deal with 6,000 hospitals and health care institutions than 250,000 individual physicians and ambulatory care delivery sites. It was economically more sensible to deal with $1,000 medical procedures than $30 office visits. If the choice had to be made about where to begin the effort of managing the delivery of health care, it was much more logical to work on the inpatient acute care side first. The task would be simpler because the number of providers was a definable group of manageable size, and the economic paybacks would be greater.

Models of Ambulatory Care

To this point the two polar extremes of health care have been used. The institutional model has been used to describe inpatient acute care, even though individual physicians and contracting entities are engaged in that system of health care delivery. And the individual physician has been cited as the example of ambulatory care delivery even though many institutional entities deliver health care in the ambulatory setting. This section explores a variety of models used in delivering ambulatory health care.

In many ways, these models correspond to the way managed care companies have created reimbursement mechanisms to address specific carve-out sectors. That is, these ambulatory health care sectors are often taken out of the general contracts with physicians or health care institutions, (hence "carved out" of the contract), because the payers feel it is easier to control the volume of services used and the price paid for each unit of service, when this methodology is adopted. Thus, the carve-out evolves as one of several methodologies aimed at controlling resource use.

Each of the models discussed here can take multiple forms. They can exist within a hospital setting, or they can be freestanding. They can be owned by health care institutions or individual investors. They can be not-for-profit entities or for-profit organizations. Thus, the number of combinations and permutations of ambulatory health care delivery vehicles is large.

Physician Services

Perhaps the most common ambulatory health model is physician services. It has existed for the longest period of time and is familiar to most health care consumers.

The form of this model has changed considerably over the past two decades, from one of individual and small group practitioners to the current trend of large groups of physicians practicing in either multispecialty or specialty models. The nature of these groups is also changing from being independent physicians, usually owning their own practice, to practices that are owned by institutions or investors. A distinguishing factor is the changing relationship that physicians are having with hospitals and other institutional health care organizations. In the 1970s and 1980s, most physicians were financially and organizationally independent of hospitals. Today they are much closer in order to cope more effectively with the control issues discussed in Chapter 3.

Table 4-1 compares some physician practices of the 1970s and 1980s with the current situation. (Note that these are generalizations aimed at describing the predominant form of physician practices in each era and that all of the forms existed to some

Table 4-1   Comparison of Physician Practices

	1970s and 1980s	*Current*
Form	Individuals and small groups	Large groups
Ownership	Independently owned	Investor or institution owned
Nature	Freestanding	Freestanding and institutional based
Type	Partnerships or individual ownership	For-profit, not-for-profit corporations
Compensation	Self-pay	Salary and self-pay
Relation to institutions	Independent	Owned, independent practice association, physician–hospital organization

degree in both eras.) These shifts in the nature of physician practice have enormous implications from an economic and a clinical practice point of view.

Economic Impact

The economic impact of these changing relationships occurs at several levels. It affects the economic status of the individual physician practitioner and has an impact on the general population.

Population impacts arise in part from the consolidation of the health care industry, including physician practices. Some view consolidation as a method by which health care costs can be reduced, thus benefiting society. The expected cost reduction outcomes are expected to result from efficiencies arising from economies of scale in the administration of the practice, as well as savings resulting from more efficient methods in treating certain illnesses. One approach directed at reducing the costs for treating specific illnesses is a methodology called a **critical path** or **best practices,** which are the generally accepted treatment norms for a given diagnosis. (These two terms are synonymous and can be used interchangeably, along with several other similar terms.)

When one speaks of the economic impact on individual physicians, it should be noted that the economic status of the physician is often changed by virtue of the way in which he or she is compensated. As consolidation occurs, physicians often become salaried employees of an institutional entity and as such protect downside risk to their incomes, but at the same time limit their upside potential for earnings. In addition to the direct economic effect on the individual physician when this compensation method is in place, there is sometimes also an impact on productivity and motivation, which has an economic impact on the owning entity. As a result, more enlightened organizations usually include some form of incentive pay in physicians' compensation packages.

Thus, a complex array of economic relationships has resulted from the evolution of the structure of physician practices during the past two decades. They have an impact on both the individual physician and society. It is not unusual for these forces (individual practitioner and society) to be at odds with each other, so they must reach resolution by finding the equilibrium between the two countervailing forces. The environment wants lower cost health care; health care providers, including physicians, prefer more income. A balance must be found that both parties find acceptable. The market usually decides this equilibrium.

Clinical Practice Impact

Given the changes in physician practices over the past two decades, it must also be noted that there are significant changes in the environment in which the practices operate; some of them are the stimuli that caused the changes in the way physician practices operate. For example, the fact that physician practice entities have become much larger and more formal has had some fallout in terms of day-to-day clinical practice in that approaches to caring for patients have been standardized for purposes of cross-coverage. In addition, standardization of clinical practice is also becoming a significant issue from a quality and economic point of view. Environmental dissatisfaction from employers, patients, and payers increasingly has put pressure on health care providers to reduce costs. Yet at the same time that reduced costs are being demanded, no reduction in quality is being expected. Thus, best-practices protocols are being adopted because there is a recognition that every approach to clinical management does not yield the same outcome. These best practices have emerged primarily in the acute care inpatient setting but will undoubtedly become common in the ambulatory setting as well.

Usually the best practices are established as a consensus of the physician practitioners who are treating the disease entity, based on the most current literature. Consequently, establishing specific protocols to treat certain illnesses is being promoted as an approach to improving clinical outcomes. At the same time, treatment according to these disease-specific protocols is often adopted as a strategy for reducing costs.

Thus, the economic impact is intertwined with the clinical impact and cannot be separated from it. To the extent that the use of best practices can be demonstrated to produce better clinical results at lower cost, society is obviously better off, and the stakeholders who are demanding lower costs at the same or better level of quality should be satisfied. It is a clear demonstration of the market in action.

Other Models of Ambulatory Health Care

There are numerous other models for delivering ambulatory care besides physician practices. The dynamics of the ambulatory delivery setting, and the effect of managed care on health care delivery in these additional models, is similar to the issues discussed in the section on physician practices. For example, they can be either hospital based or stand-alone, for profit or not for profit, individually owned or corporate owned. The sections that follow identify some the more important ambulatory models for health care delivery.

Outpatient Surgery

Outpatient surgery facilities, for surgical procedures that do not require that the patient stay overnight, exist in both the hospital setting and a stand-alone setting. There has been a steady trend of more complex procedures being moved from the acute care inpatient setting to this one. There has been considerable discussion about how far this trend should go and at what point the patient's safety comes into play.

Imaging

Imaging facilities provide a wide range of diagnostic radiologic services, from simple radiographic images to more complex computed tomography and magnetic resonance imaging scans. In addition, some centers engage in therapeutic services, such as radiation therapy for oncology patients. When managed care companies carve these services out, it means that the patient cannot have imaging done at the physician's office but must go to the imaging center(s) holding the contract. This has the potential for considerable inconvenience to the patient in terms of additional time and travel. This inconvenience is balanced against the anticipated reduction in costs by using this carve-out approach.

Laboratory Services

Laboratory services entities provide clinical and anatomical pathology services and are characterized by low-cost, high-volume operations with numerous convenient locations for patients where the specimen can be obtained. When managed care companies carve these services out, it is not as serious a problem as in the case of imaging because the physician can often obtain the specimen in his or her office and send it to the appropriate laboratory. However, in the case of **integrated delivery networks (IDNs),** which will be discussed in Chapter 5, this does present certain organizational and logistical problems that work against the efficiencies and intended strategies of an IDN.

Psychiatric Services

Psychiatric and behavioral services (for sleeping or eating disorders, substance abuse, and other behavioral disorders) are usually characterized by a variety of behavioral medicine services ranging from psychiatrists, to clinical psychologists, to clinical social workers. The aim is to treat the patient in the least expensive setting consistent with clinical needs. Ambulatory psychiatric services may be either hospital based or independent.

Vision Services

These are services defined as dealing with routine vision treatment in the population. They include vision testing and prescription of corrective vision devices. The services can involve a range of clinicians, from ophthalmologists to optometrists. Diseases of the eye are in a different category and are normally addressed by ophthalmologists in a physician practice setting.

Occupational Health

This is an ambulatory health delivery model designed specifically to address issues of occupational and environmental health in the workplace—for example, treatment for job-related injuries, substance abuse testing, ergonomic analysis, health screening, prevention programs, and **employee assistance programs (EAP).** These activities are not normally part of the general health delivery system and vary from state to state because they are governed by specific legislation and regulation at the state level. Worker's compensation laws in each state govern the way the services are delivered. In most states the worker's compensation programs are governed separately from general health insurance, but there is a trend among many managed care companies to include occupational health as one of their products.

Home Health

Home health services have evolved as a methodology for giving certain kinds of care in the home that require skills that the patient or the patient's caregiver do not have— for example, administration of medications, intravenous therapy, changing dressings on surgical wounds, and obtaining specimens for diagnostic testing. They are provided when the patient does not require care in an institutional setting, such as an acute care hospital or a skilled nursing facility, but still requires services that are typically given in the institutional setting. Home health services have also expanded into the area of domestic services.

Disease Prevention and Health Promotion Services

These are activities aimed at reducing the incidence of disease in the population, which in the case of a managed care company relates primarily to its insured clients. Historically this activity has been a public health endeavor, but more recently it has also become the focus of some managed care companies. This change of focus is not surprising when the managed care company is in an environment where increases in the premium are difficult because of competitive forces and is made responsible for the total care of the patient under certain reimbursement programs that extend all of the risk to the managed care company. When the managed care company is made responsible for all of the health care needs of its insured base and finds it difficult to increase the premium because of competitive forces in the market, reducing the incidence of disease makes very good sense. Examples of wellness and disease prevention activity are screening programs for disease (e.g., mammograms and PAP smears), smoking cessation programs, and benchmarking disease rates for selected diseases and comparing them to the population.

Quality and the Managed Care Effort

Quality issues are ever-present in the subject of managed care, partly because there is an inherent issue of distrust: that is, the belief that if the focus of an activity is to reduce costs, the quality of those services will likely be reduced. Nevertheless, we know from other sectors of the economy that costs and quality can be inversely related and need not necessarily be locked in a relationship where decreases in cost result in decreases in quality. Indeed, the **continuous quality improvement (CQI)** concept holds that increases in quality arise from taking waste out of the system, and elimination of re-work in the system results in both reduced costs and increases in quality. Thus, quality measurement is central to a discussion of managed care because it allows for a determination of whether quality is increasing or decreasing and thus is able to address people's confidence and trust in the system.

Accreditation and What It Means

In order to address the issue of quality in managed care organizations realistically and independently, an accrediting body is needed that is independent of the bodies it is evaluating. The most prominent of these is the National Committee for Quality Assurance (**NCQA**), which conducts rigorous on-site and off-site reviews of managed care organizations. It evaluates how well the managed care company manages its delivery system. Its evaluation is made on the basis of over 50 standards that fall into six groups:

1. Quality improvement—How well the managed care company evaluates the quality of care it provides its members. It evaluates the coordination of the delivery system and the efficiency with which it operates, including the ease of access that the members experience in receiving health care services.

2. Physician credentials—The extent to which the managed care organization evaluates physician performance and whether that information is used in the periodic evaluation of the physician. In addition, it looks at how the organization investigates the training and experience of physicians in the network and the extent to which there might be patterns of malpractice or fraud.

3. Members' rights and responsibilities—How well the plan informs its members about such issues as how to register a complaint, how to access the plan, and how to choose a physician. In addition, the level of satisfaction of the plan members is evaluated.

4. Preventive health services—The extent of the plan's participation in various preventive health services. It assesses whether physicians deliver these services and whether they encourage plan members to avail themselves of the services.

5. Utilization management—The process used to determine the appropriateness of services for the plan members. It assesses whether the approach is reasonable and consistent in its application and evaluates the methodology for appeals on denial of payment for services.

6. Medical records—The extent to which the plan's physicians comply with documentation standards.

As a result of the accreditation process, NCQA issues a determination of the plan's accreditation status at one of the following levels:

- *Full accreditation*, granted for a three-year period to plans that demonstrate excellent quality improvement programs and meet the NCQA standards.
- *One-year accreditation*, given to plans that meet most of the NCQA standards and have an established quality improvement program.
- *Provisional accreditation*, given for one year to plans that meet some NCQA standards and have adequate quality improvement plans. Progress must be observed before either the one-year or the full accreditation is granted.
- *Denial*, the status of plans that do not qualify for any of the other categories.

The nature of this program and the impact that it has on the delivery of health care are discussed in more depth in Chapter 13.

It is obvious that the quality theme plays prominently in the accreditation of managed care plans. It provides a vehicle that consumers and purchasers can use to assess the plan. The process certainly does not guarantee quality, but it does demonstrate the extent to which a plan provides the quality and consumer protection that are embraced in the NCQA standards. The accreditation of the plans applies to both inpatient acute care and ambulatory care.

Quality Measures in the Ambulatory Care Setting

There is a complex relationship among the concepts of quality management, case mix adjustment, risk management, and clinical outcomes. The specific nature of all of these relationships has not been definitively identified in the literature, but that there is a link between the concepts is clear. The literature demonstrates links between isolated sets of these elements, but an integrated model that links all of them has not yet evolved.

In the inpatient acute care setting we have observed that diagnosis-related groups, as a measure of case mix severity, are a link between outcomes and costs (Kolb and Clay, 1994). It has been postulated that the best way to develop the tools for physician profiling, and hence reduce risk and improve outcomes, is through a quality improvement process (Goldfield, 1994). Macnee and Penchansky (1994) suggest that a method is needed in the ambulatory setting that provides a classification model allowing for identification of highly productive areas for quality review and risk management. These views imply a link between a case mix adjustment model for classification and risk management as well as quality management.

The extension of these insights is that a better understanding of these phenomena, and the relationships between them, in the ambulatory setting are necessary if patient care is to be managed cost-effectively at appropriate levels of quality. The ability to manage health care in the ambulatory setting is limited by the fact that mechanisms to measure quality, resource consumption, risk, and outcomes are much more primitive than is the case in the acute care inpatient setting, which in itself is not stellar in its ability to measure these variables. Only recently has definitive research emerged that seeks to establish a link between case mix severity, outcomes, and costs (Kolb and Clay, 1994). Establishing a link between health status and variations in resource consumption in the ambulatory setting is in the early stages of research (Goldfield, 1994). Research linking quality measures with cost data in the ambulatory setting is beginning to emerge (Harris, 1994).

This work suggests that there are relationships between these elements and that it will be necessary to describe and measure them with some level of reliable precision if care is going to be managed effectively in the ambulatory setting. In order to appreciate the nature of the issues facing managed care in the ambulatory setting, a discussion of these concepts is helpful.

Adjusting for Risk

Kolb and Clay (1994) assert that there is a need for managed care companies to be much more sophisticated in the way they adjust for risk as they set capitation rates for providers. They point out that managed care companies usually try to explain risk with the dual variables of age and sex, but note that these two factors actually explain only about 6 percent of the difference in ambulatory utilization of resources (Starfield, Mumford, and Steonwachs, 1991). Thus, when managed care companies are able to explain only a fraction of the risk with the variables they are applying to the model, but attempt to establish reimbursement rates on the basis of those models, there is inherently something wrong with the system. This is a particularly troublesome issue when the reimbursement methodology is capitation, because it passes the risk from the managed care company, which has historically been in the business of taking risk, to the health care provider, who is relatively inexperienced in these matters and has relatively less to say about the reimbursement. Health care providers must become much more knowledgeable about measuring risk and understanding the variables that go into the models that explain risk.

The authors (Kolb and Clay, 1994) describe a new model being developed and tested at Johns Hopkins that uses a list of criteria to assign diagnostic codes into ambulatory diagnostic groups (**ADGs**). The following concepts are part of this model:

- Expected persistence or recurrence of the condition
- Likelihood of return visit(s) for the condition
- Likelihood of a specialty consultation or referral
- Expected need and cost of diagnostic and therapeutic procedures associated with the condition
- Likelihood of an associated hospitalization
- Likelihood of an associated disability
- Likelihood of associated decreased life expectancy

The model is then described, and the authors conclude by indicating that the initial research shows that at this early stage of development, ADGs can explain more than 50 percent of the variance in consumption of ambulatory resources when used retrospectively. Although these results are far from ideal, they nevertheless suggest a promising direction for describing and managing risk in the ambulatory setting and certainly demonstrate better results than the current widely used methodology being applied by managed care companies, which applies only age and sex factors to adjust for risk.

The Role of Quality Improvement

The success of managed care programs in the ambulatory setting depends on the ability to perform accurate, risk-adjusted profiles of physician activities. These profiles must include both resource consumption and quality. These profiles can be used for several purposes, including more accurate adjustment of capitation rates and physician feedback. Certain kinds of profiling, such as resource utilization and limited quality measures, are currently available for physician feedback. However, the missing link that would allow use of the information for accurate adjustment of capitation rates is an ability to account for risk and the attendant issues related to differences in acuity in the patient mix. Goldfield (1994) argues that given this state of the marketplace, a quality improvement process (plan, do, check, act) is the most appropriate approach to developing the tools to perform physician profiling. Goldfield goes on to say that physician profiling based on quality improvement shares the following characteristics:

- Individualized feedback
- Peer comparison
- Face-to-face communication
- A continuous program
- An understanding of the costs of overused services

Systems that allow for analysis of resource use in the ambulatory care setting are in a primitive state. As they are being developed, it is appropriate that they be developed in a way that allows them to be most productive to the entire health care delivery system. Historically, data of this type have been used in a recriminatory way as contrasted to being used constructively. Thus, Goldfield's proposal that case mix systems be used in a continuous quality improvement (**CQI**) model seems most appropriate. CQI seeks to improve processes over time, thereby improving quality. When change is needed, process improvement is achieved by a collegial approach of all interested parties. Significant investments of time and resources are required to make this methodology work. Using other sectors of the economy as a guide is likely to yield better results.

Unfortunately the managed care sector of the health care market has not been unanimous in embracing the quality improvement process because of the amount of time and other resources that it takes to produce results. It seems much more interested in how the stock market will assess performance in terms of growth of market share and profitability on a quarterly reporting basis, and thus a recriminatory approach to weeding out the bad apples seems preferred over CQI.

Goldfield points out that a key issue in determining the adequacy of a case mix system is the use to which it will be put and suggests the following uses:

- Quality improvement, including outcomes management
- Utilization management (physician resource utilization)
- Capitation adjustment
- Technology assessment
- Network determination and updating

Quality improvement is often not the central focus of managed care in the ambulatory care setting, although the long-term potential seems significant. The entire health care industry, including payers and providers, must come to grips with the question of whether it wishes to operate on the basis of short-term gains or long-term infrastructure.

The Quality of Care Issue

Tools for measuring the quality of care in the ambulatory care setting are just being developed (Harris, 1994; Macnee and Penchansky, 1994). In this context, it is argued that the best way to evaluate quality of care is to measure the ability to deliver quality care, as contrasted to evaluating individual providers (Harris, 1994). On the other hand, the pressures of the health care system promote fragmentation. For example, managed care companies, particularly in immature markets, often pursue a strategy of provider fragmentation. Antitrust laws favor a fragmented system when the providers are in economic competition. Even provider systems, in their formative stages promote fragmentation as it relates to institutional versus caregiver competition. Thus, evaluating quality on the basis of a health care system's ability to deliver care is sometimes difficult because the systems are not in place to measure the health status of the population it serves.

The consolidation of the provider community into large health care systems is beginning to provide a meaningful laboratory where the hypothesis of whether integrated health care systems can improve quality can be tested. One such system is California Care, an integrated network of providers to serve California's Medicaid population, which has developed a quantitative score card for measuring the quality of care of 130 managed care organizations, with 19,000 physicians and 270 hospitals (Harris, 1994). This study describes a methodology that defines quality measures having the following characteristics:

- *Face validity.* The variable must be acceptable to the providers as a legitimate subject of measurement.
- *Statistical validity.* In order to differentiate, the measure must occur often enough that important differences are unlikely to be happening by chance.
- *Reliability.* The measure must be standardized in a way that permits people to achieve the same results when reviewing the same data.
- *Generalizability.* Quality measures must reflect an organization's quality of care and be applicable to other organizations.

This tool is being used as a large-scale CQI process to improve the quality of care in California Care. Some of the preliminary results are encouraging in that they show that a negative correlation exists when quality data are compared with cost data in which as costs are reduced, quality is increased. This suggests that the CQI model existing in the industrial setting is appropriate for the health care delivery system. That is, the CQI model postulates that higher quality and lower costs are parallel outcomes of a good management process.

There is still a lot of work to be done in this area before we have reliable measures and conclusive outcomes of managed care in the ambulatory care setting. Other preliminary findings of the study suggest that the inter-rater reliability is a significant problem, but that providers accept this process if it is done in an open and nonpunitive way.

The Quality Improvement Process

In a recent article, Goldfield (1994) suggests that the success of managed care programs depends on a physician profiling mechanism that includes consideration of the quality and utilization of physician practice on a risk-adjusted basis. While the techniques are imperfect, physician profiling attempts to measure the amount of resources a physician uses in treating a patient, compared to the clinical outcomes of that physician. Physician profiling has become a topic of significant importance to many managed care companies, but there is little agreement on what should be evaluated by the profiles or how the results should be used. The profiles that are being used by a cross-section of managed care companies evaluate a wide variety of variables, and the results are used for a range of reasons. For example, some plans adjust for risk when looking at the physician profile, but most do not. Furthermore, the results of the profile can be used for a variety of reasons, including adjusting the reimbursement of physician providers, being used as a basis for forming or adjusting networks, or as a basis to providing feedback to physicians. When looking at uses to which the results can be put, it becomes apparent that they can be at cross-purposes, ranging from punitive to collegial and educational.

When the profiles are used as the basis for forming or adjusting networks, the motivation of the managed care company appears to be punitive in nature and geared to short-term gain. The motivation for short-term gain arises from the fact that some managed care companies appear to be more interested in immediate results arising from using physicians who consume the fewest resources in their treatment of patients than in making structural changes in the system with longer-term results—both better efficiency and higher quality. Of course, this latter approach can be recognized as the CQI approach, which is widely and effectively used in other sectors of the economy. Furthermore, the potential punitive nature of the activity can be seen in the fact that the past history of the physician is used to make decisions about the present and future, often without any adjustment for adverse circumstances or risk anomalies and without the physician's having had the opportunity to explain the circumstances, learn from the experience, or modify behavior. This is fundamentally a management decision-making process that neither attempts to explain the behavior nor to give an opportunity to modify behavior. Moreover, given this superficial treatment of the very complicated subject of establishing profiles of physician practice, there is a very high potential for the managed care company to exclude highly qualified physicians from their panel when unadjusted data are used. An example is the case of highly qualified and distinguished university faculty physicians who sometimes receive the referrals that community specialists do not wish to treat. In these cases, it is sometimes possible that the risk profile of the cases would explain the additional use of resources when it is present, as contrasted to ignoring these factors and concluding that the physician is simply inefficient in the use of resources.

Goldfield (1994) reports that profiling tools are often used in harmful ways by organizations that have set them up and notes these complaints:

- Physicians have never seen the data.
- Physicians have not been provided with the ability to respond to the data.
- Physicians have not been given the opportunity to correct the patterns for which they are criticized.

On the other hand, when the profiles are used as feedback to physicians, there is a much higher potential for there to be a longer-range positive impact on quality for the population because the physician has the opportunity to change behavior and adjust to the best practices of the community. Furthermore, this approach is consistent with CQI principles, which, if other sectors of the economy are an indication, have a much higher potential to improve the quality of the long-range clinical outcomes while reducing the costs associated with treating patients.

Ultimately, success in implementing a meaningful quality process in the ambulatory setting depends on an ability to identify productive areas for quality review and then act on the results. Currently there are no standards by which this identification process can occur, although some promising developmental work is taking place. Unlike the acute care inpatient setting, where there is general agreement that structured case review can yield meaningful quality assessment results, this approach in the ambulatory setting is infeasible for a number of reasons, including:

- There are too many individual encounters to manage in this way.
- The encounters are spread over many locations.
- The nature of the illness is often not as well identified as in the inpatient setting.
- The illness might be treated by multiple unrelated entities.
- The information systems supporting the ambulatory care process are much less sophisticated than in the acute care setting.
- The information systems in the ambulatory care setting are generally not integrated across organizations, much less within organizations.

As a result, the methods that have evolved in the acute care setting are not necessarily transferable to the ambulatory care setting, resulting in a pressing need for the development of a generally accepted ambulatory care model of quality assessment.

Measuring these quality variables and having a better understanding of the models that tie them together is a significant challenge to all health care professionals, but it is particularly important that health information managers become intimately involved with this process and, in fact, take a leadership role.

Applying the Quality Concept in Ambulatory Managed Care

While comments in this chapter might be interpreted as being fairly critical of the ambulatory quality process of managed care companies, it should also be noted that they are part of an evolutionary process and are not solely responsible for the shortcomings of the ambulatory health care delivery system. Many of them are actively engaged in trying to develop improved methodologies.

An example of the interest in quality issues can be found on the home page of the Group Health Cooperative Web site (www.ghc.org). It points to a section on quality that has far-ranging and extensive content on the subject of quality. The content of the pages is focused at their enrollees and is clearly trying to convey the message that the managed care company is interested in quality from its own perspective and that of the enrollee as well. This information addresses both the inpatient acute care activities as well as the ambulatory care activities.

This organization clearly has a commitment to quality and its role in the organization's operations. It states Group Health's philosophy as follows (www.ghc.org/quality):

Quality of care and service activities are ongoing processes that must involve all staff in partnership with patients.

Long-term cost savings can't be sustained unless they are linked to quality assurance and improvements.

Traditional quality assurance activities, such as granting of medical privileges or case reviews, should be viewed as starting points.

The organization goes on to state that accreditation by NCQA is an important matter and points out, apparently as a marketing issue, that it is the only health care organization in its area to receive full NCQA accreditation; on a nationwide basis, only 33 percent of the plans reviewed have been given full accreditation. Group Health then cites many of the critical elements needed to make a quality program meaningful, including special emphasis on the information technology required. Although the points mentioned are fairly standard from an information management point of view, they are worth noting here because they form the foundation of the quality program and underscore the scope of Group Health's commitment.

The discourse on quality concludes with a discussion on quality measures being used. Group Health uses the Health Plan Employer Data and Information (HEDIS) data set to report on quality of care, member satisfaction, and utilization. Finally, the United States Public Health Service's national goals for the year 2000 are compared with Group Health measures. These measures include the following categories, with the United States Public Health Goals in parentheses:

- Breast cancer screening, women (ages 50+: >60 percent)
- Cesarean section rate (<15 percent)
- Cervical cancer screen rate, ages 21–64, at least one PAP in past three years (>85 percent)
- Childhood immunizations, 2-year-olds with completed vaccinations (>90 percent)
- Cholesterol screening, at least one screening in past five years, ages 18+ (>75 percent)
- Flu immunization rate, age 65+ (>80 percent)
- Low-birth weight babies (<5 percent)
- Tobacco cessation, age 20+ (<15 percent)

Many managed care companies across the country have a focus on quality and are willing to commit the economic resources and time to bring the concept to reality. On the other hand, there are also managed care companies with limited and self-serving interests in quality that have not committed the resources required to make quality measurement a reality in their delivery of health care. Group Health Cooperative is an example of what many managed care organizations are doing relative to quality.

Conclusion

The delivery of health care in the ambulatory setting is much different from the inpatient setting. The dynamics of managed care are different as well and have evolved in a different time frame and with different parameters. The issue of quality is a critical one to all of the stakeholders in ambulatory health care, but specific measuring tools are not well developed.

As managed care evolves in the ambulatory care field, significant emphasis will be placed on the quality issue with regard to both clinical outcomes for specific patients and the health status for the population. These are two different concepts of quality, and the issues are identified, measured, and acted on in different ways. For example, in the case of measuring quality relating to clinical outcomes for specific patients, variances from the norm must be specifically identified. This has proved to be a difficult task in the ambulatory setting. By contrast, quality relating to the health status for the population measures compliance with certain measures, such as immunizations, and is fundamentally a data collection and analysis task. Both views of quality are important, but they require widely varying approaches.

The issue of risk assessment will be a critical element in this evolutionary process of measuring quality because it affects rate setting as well as network development. Both rate setting and network development affect managed care companies, the health care providers, and the patients.

Review Questions

1. What are the differences between the inpatient and outpatient managed care models? What environmental factors do you believe account for these differences?

2. If you are the decision maker in a managed care company, would you seek NCQA accreditation? Why or why not?

3. What reasons do you believe best account for the growth of managed care in the ambulatory care sector?

4. To what extent can "best practices" be viewed as a quality improvement process?

5. What factors influenced the slower evolution of managed care in the ambulatory care setting?

6. Select a World Wide Web health site, and analyze it with regard to its focus on such factors as:

   a. Patient satisfaction
   b. Quality

      c. Confidentiality
      d. Patient knowledge

Note: One Web site is that of Group Health Cooperative, at http://www.ghc.org. Others can be located by using any of the Internet search vehicles with a query of "managed care."

References

Goldfield, N. (1994). Profiling of health care professionals, quality improvement, and ambulatory case mix systems: A commentary on the article by Douglas Cave. *Journal of Ambulatory Care, 17*(3), 82.

Group Health Cooperative. http://www.ghc.org.

Harris, J. M. (1994). Managing the quality of managed care delivery systems. *Journal of Ambulatory Care Management, 17*(4), 59–66.

Kolb, D., & Clay, S. (1994). Ambulatory care grouping: When, how and the impact on managed care. *Journal of Ambulatory Care Management, 17*(1), 29.

Macnee, C., & Penchansky, R. (1994). Targeting ambulatory care cases for risk management and quality management. *Inquiry, 31*(1), 66–75.

Starfield, B., Mumford, L., & Steonwachs, D. (1991). Ambulatory care groups: A categorization of diagnoses for research and management. *Health Services Research, 26*(1), 150–173.

Chapter 5

The Emergence of Integrated Delivery Systems

This chapter discusses the dynamics of integrated delivery systems. These dynamics are different in many respects from the traditional view and understanding of health care systems. These systems have significant implications for the delivery of health care, the infrastructure required to operate such a delivery system, and the governance required to make it work.

Learning Objectives

Upon successful completion of this chapter, the learner will:

- Understand the differences between an integrated delivery system (IDS) and a traditional health delivery system.
- Understand why an IDS might be formed.
- Understand the organizational structures used to form an IDS.
- Understand the information requirements for an IDS.
- Understand the way information is used in an IDS.
- Understand the governance issues in forming an IDS.

Key Terms

active repository	data warehouse
capitation	diversification strategy
clinical integration	economies of scale
continuum of care	functional integration

health system

horizontal integration

independent practice associations (IPA)

managed care integration

organized delivery system (ODS)

passive repository

physician integration

primary care

repository

vertical integration

Introduction

Integrated delivery systems (IDSs) have been viewed by some as the solution to lead to a higher level of efficiency and effectiveness and an approach to health care delivery that addresses the question of being economically competitive in the market.

Most of what has happened in the formation of IDSs has had its origin at the local or regional level rather than resulting from federal or state regulation. Of course, the threat of federally mandated reform in 1992 and 1993 certainly did have an effect in that it hastened the activities of health care organizations that might have been contemplating these moves previously. An additional factor is that at the same time that there was a federal threat of reform for the health care system, there was significant expansion of the managed care phenomenon with all of the attendant effects that were discussed in Chapters 3 and 4. This became an increasingly important economic factor in stressing the importance of more efficient operations. A final related pressure was the significant merger activity in the for-profit sector, which included such companies as Columbia HCA, Tenet, Health South, PhyCor, and MedPartners.

All of these forces are creating a new paradigm for health care delivery. In the United States health care system, one of the more prominent new organizational structures that is evolving is the IDS also known as an **integrated delivery network (IDN)** or an **organized delivery system (ODS)**. Regardless of the acronym assigned to the evolving organization, it is important to note its properties and consider the operational issues associated with this developing entity.

The Basics of an IDS

The emphasis in an IDS is on the integration of entities. One description defines an IDS as "a network of organizations that provides or arranges to provide a coordinated continuum of services to a defined population and is willing to be held clinically and fiscally accountable for the outcomes and health status of the population served" (Shortell, Gillies, Anderson, Mitchell, and Morgan, 1993).

Those constructing these networks usually seek to make them as inclusive of the **continuum of care** as possible in that they attempt to have them cover as wide a spectrum of services as is possible. This includes the obvious services, like inpatient acute care and traditional ambulatory care, as well as some lesser profile delivery systems, such as nursing homes, home health organizations, and durable medical equipment vendors.

People sometimes confuse a **health system** and an IDS, and certainly there are many similarities, including the fact that sometimes they are part of the same organizational entity or there is sometimes common ownership. Often the health system and the IDS have quite different operational strategies, however. Indeed, these fundamental strategic differences highlight one of the important reasons for creating an IDS.

Most health systems are primarily focused on a single delivery strategy. This means that they are interested in integration of similar entities, which in many instances is acute care hospitals. They seek to assemble similar entities that are geographically distributed in a way that gives them a market advantage. This strategy is known as **horizontal integration.** By contrast, the organizational strategy of an IDS is usually to align many different types of operational units in a way that provides a continuum of care across a wide spectrum of services for a defined geographic area. Indeed, the aim is often to be able to provide all health care services that would ever be needed within the framework of the IDS. Location is important in the use of this strategy, but the most important factor in developing this different kind of organization is the range of the spectrum of services that allows for "one-stop shopping" for health care within the IDS. This strategy is known as **vertical integration.**

Students of organizational behavior and organizational structure are often critical of this latter strategy of diversification employed by the IDS because there is a danger that an organization that does one thing well (for example, run hospitals) might not be as successful at operating a dissimilar line of business (like running physician practices or insurance companies). Many business entities outside the health care sector are moving away from diversification and are tending to consolidate their organization in the operation of their core business. For example, at considerable cost to itself, AT&T in 1996 divested itself of what was formerly the NCR Corporation, after acquiring and holding the company for only two years. The reason given for this business decision was that the computer development and manufacturing business was not consistent with the core business of AT&T, which is communications. These changes in strategic direction are happening throughout the business world and should not be ignored by the health care sector.

One can see some of this same type of behavior in the for-profit sector of health care. Columbia HCA, for example, is primarily interested in its core business of hospitals and has not seriously engaged in physician practice management; PhyCor and other similar physician management companies are primarily interested in the operation of physician practices and have generally not entered into the hospital business. As the health care industry evolves, it will be interesting to see whether the **diversification strategy** will be successful. Many health care executives believe that the IDS strategy will work and that they will be able to manage the diversity of health care products. Others are not as sure. The business principle of specialization versus diversification will be tested in the health delivery field.

It is too early to predict the outcome, but it is an enormously important issue. Ultimately the market will decide whether it values "one-stop shopping" over a more specialized (and fragmented) delivery system that has very efficient operational units providing high-quality services. We should not necessarily assume that these two concepts—that IDSs are more convenient, while organizations tending to core unit operations are more efficient and effective—are mutually exclusive, but the non–health care business sector seems to be in general agreement that this is the case with their operations. Indeed, this dichotomy flies in the face of one of the motivating forces for establishing an IDS, which is that integration will provide for **economies of scale.**

An organization might form an IDS for a variety of reasons. They are most predominant as local organizations, but in some instances they are beginning to evolve as regional organizations. The most probable reason that most are still local in scope is that they often grow out of local circumstances. Only when the founding entity is regional in scope, such as might be the case with a regional health care system, does the IDS tend to exhibit regional tendencies.

IDSs are formed for a variety of reasons—for example:

- To be more competitive in the market and to gain managed care contracts
- To provide appropriate geographical coverage for health care services
- To improve the quality of health care
- To provide a continuum of health care
- To lower the costs of health care

When they are formed, these are some of the basic beliefs held by the founding entities (McQueen and Marwick, 1995):

- Services should be provided along a continuum of care in convenient delivery sites.
- Emphasis is placed on primary (managed) care rather than acute (hospital) patient care.
- The system should own or be affiliated with an HMO.
- Care delivery sites should be in close geographic proximity.
- Care should be provided at clinically appropriate, lower-cost sites of care.
- **Clinical integration** focuses on patient care systems used to manage care in a capitated payment environment.
- **Physician integration** focuses on developing physician leadership, formation of **primary care** group practices, and negotiating risk-based capitated contracts.
- **Functional integration** is the extent to which professional and support services are integrated into the care process within and across all units of the system.
- A continuous quality improvement (CQI) process enables dynamic ongoing improvements in all aspects of the IDS.

Types of Integration

Integration of health care delivery systems has occurred in a number of ways, and there are various perspectives from which the types of integration can be addressed. Some are addressed in the literature, while some are intuitive. The perspectives range from a typology that views the integration from the position of the way services are delivered to a typology that enunciates how it is organized.

Clinical Integration

This is an approach to integration that focuses on systematizing the services to the patient in a way that produces the best possible outcome at the lowest possible price. In the inpatient acute care setting, critical pathways and other vehicles designed to standardize the methodology for delivering the services to patients are often part of this method of integration. As this model evolves, the methodology must also embrace ambulatory services. In the ambulatory care setting critical pathways and ambulatory care groupings have been slow to develop because of the methodological difficulties related to adjusting for case mix (Kolb and Clay, 1994) However, eventually clinical integration of health care delivery must embrace both the inpatient acute care events and the ambulatory episodes if clinical integration is to be accomplished. Physicians must be part of the integrated entity because they control the way the services are used and delivered.

From an organizational perspective, integration of physicians into the clinical process can be accomplished by contract or practice ownership. This integration sometimes also includes other entities that interact clinically with the patient across the entire continuum of care rendered to the patient. However, at this time, the primary focus is on inpatient acute care events and ambulatory episodes. In addition to the physician component, clinical integration could include such services as durable medical equipment, skilled nursing facilities, pharmacy services, rehabilitation services, and home health care.

Clinical integration often includes a goal relating to patient convenience. This is in contrast to some managed care models that carve out services like laboratory medicine and radiology services, thereby sometimes requiring the patient to schedule separate trips to other locations to complete the diagnostic or therapeutic process.

The clinical integration approach requires that there be appropriate quality measures to ensure that quality is maintained in the face of the countervailing pressure to reduce costs. The issue of quality and its role in delivering health care will be discussed in more detail in Chapter 13.

Physician-System Integration

"Primary care physicians are the likeliest candidates to control master **capitation** contracts" (Johns, 1995). Many people see the physician as the most likely candidate to control managed care contracting under a capitation model because the physician is in the best position to control the use of resources. Within the physician constellation, the primary care physician usually sees the patient first and is in the best position to prevent unnecessary specialty services. Of course, this creates the potential for competition between primary care physicians and the specialists. Many specialty groups and specialty **independent practice associations (IPAs)** have been formed for the expressed purpose of getting managed care contracts within their specialty areas.

Ultimately the market will have to decide whether it is better to have a single point of responsibility for the entire system or whether the system can be controlled at multiple points, which is to say that individual specialty groups and IPAs will receive managed care contracts for those particular specialties. It is readily apparent that specialty contracting is inconsistent with the clinical integration model, which seeks to integrate the delivery of health care across episodes of illness and, in some cases, across the entire continuum of care. In order to accomplish this in an efficient and effective way, sophisticated communication protocols are required. At the same time, specialty contracting can be consistent with the functional integration model, which seeks to integrate services by functional area.

Physician system integration, whatever form it takes, differs from clinical integration in that the physician entity becomes the focus of the health care delivery activities from both a clinical delivery point of view and a managed care contracting perspective. That is, with this model the physician entity controls the operation of the provider delivery system. In the clinical integration model, the physician, the institution (hospital), or some other entity can control the clinical integration.

In the physician system integration model, a physician entity organizes the network. This embodies not only the physician network itself, but also all other elements required to satisfy the continuum of care, including the availability of hospital beds, ambulatory services, and other required services.

Functional Integration

In this model, the focus is on integration by service line or function. That is, the physician entity is integrated, the acute care delivery is integrated, the ambulatory care is integrated, and the management services function are integrated, as are all other functional areas within the health care delivery system. In this approach, integration is viewed as making the individual functions of the total organization as efficient as possible while attempting to gain efficiency by specialization within the functions.

In order for this model to be successful, a management process ensuring that the individual specialized functions are working toward the same organizational objectives must be in place. In some ways, this approach could be viewed as the classical matrix management model where individual functions of the organization (such as marketing, manufacturing, research, and finance) are brought together to achieve specific organizational objectives. In the case of health care, the organizational objective might be to provide the most cost-effective quality health care to a target population. The individual functional areas then organize their activities to achieve that objective.

Continuum of Care

In this model, the objective is to put together a network that is capable of providing all of the health care required by the community. The motivating factor in creating the integrated network is to achieve the vertical integration needed to provide this continuum of care. It must embrace not only hospitals and physician groups, but also ambulatory care and subacute facilities of various kinds. It can be achieved by either ownership or contractual relationships.

Managed Care Integration

Finally, the fact that in some parts of the country insurers are actively engaged in forming health care delivery networks cannot be overlooked. They are competing with hospitals and health care systems to form alliances with physician groups, and in some cases they own and operate physician groups. In this model of integration, the managed care companies establish relationships with physicians that range from straightforward provider contracts to outright ownership and operation of physician practices. The objective is to forge a relationship that will allow the two entities—the insurer and the physician groups—to control the provision of health care in a particular market while eliminating hospitals and health care systems from active involvement as stakeholders in delivering health care in that community. These models are relatively rare and have not enjoyed significant success.

Information Needs of an IDS

The issues relating to the information needs of an IDS have many similarities to those relevant to the governance process. These similarities include the fact that dissimilar organizations and cultures must be brought together into a single entity just as dissimilar information systems must be brought together. In addition, control is often a pivotal issue, and information systems are frequently the fulcrum around which control revolves. Thus, the integration of information systems within the framework of an IDS demands considerable attention.

Standardization of Data Elements

At its most basic level, the integration must standardize the data elements across the entire network so that the information systems can communicate with each other and report the same data. That is, a common database must be defined so that the reporting systems are able to access the same data elements regardless of the system from which they are drawn. This process of integration goes further than simply using the same data elements. It includes standardizing the definition of the data elements. For example, the data element "visit" can mean different things to different people. If one entity of the organization defines a "visit" as a registration event—a person arrives at a clinic to receive services—and another defines it to mean a service rendered—a person might receive a laboratory test and a radiology examination as a result of seeing his or her physician—it is quite clear that they are not reporting the same thing when they report a "visit." Thus, when an IDS begins to integrate its information systems, it must standardize the data elements within the database as well as standardize the definition of those elements.

Coordination of Clinical Services Across the Entities

When an IDS integrates its information resources, it does so with the intent of being able to coordinate its clinical services across all of its entities. Unless the information resource can provide reliable data in a standardized format at all of the entity locations, the organization will have difficulty being efficient and effective in its delivery of clinical services to its public. If an IDS is unable to accomplish this integration, for all practical purposes it is unable to integrate the organization and it is no different than if the entities are operating independently. Several examples will illustrate this point.

Patient Scheduling Across Entities

One of the major reasons for forming an IDS is to gain efficiency across a number of entities that provide health services. This includes the condition where there is rationalization of services across the network and every entity within the network does not necessarily provide all of the services. As a result, if a patient requires a specialized ambulatory service, he or she may have to be scheduled to receive that service at another location within the network.

Suppose that a patient sees a primary care physician in a normal office visit, and the physician determines that the patient should have an MRI exam, which is located at another site within the network. This scheduling process would be significantly easier if the network had an enterprise-wide scheduling capability. If it did, the person doing the scheduling at the location where the patient saw the primary care physician could check the system for openings and make an appointment for the patient immediately. The alternative would be to accomplish this task by telephone, which can be much more time-consuming and also creates the possibility for error because of additional steps introduced into the process. The scheduling becomes even more complex if the patient is asked to make the appointment.

Enterprise-Wide Registration

Most people have experienced the annoyance of having to provide the same information repeatedly to an organization with each incremental visit. This repeated information-gathering process is not efficient from the organization's perspective because it requires significant duplication of effort, with the corresponding increases in cost and losses in efficiency. An organization with an integrated information resource requires that the information be gathered only once, and that certain key pieces of information can be verified with each service encounter.

Availability of Financial Information Across Entities

The ability to have financial information available across all of the entities of the network is important. It eliminates the problems in the registration process and also makes certain that key information is available across the entire network for personnel who are trying to manage the financial function. For example, it would be important to be aware at all network locations if there were special financial circumstances associated with a particular patient, such as installment payment agreements or nonpayment of previous bills. In addition, it would be important to know the status of co-payments and deductibles that might have been incurred at other locations within the network.

If this kind of information is unavailable on an enterprise-wide basis, the individual entities within the network are, for all practical purposes, working independently of each other. The result will be less efficient operations. The entity will therefore be less competitive and fail in one of the primary objectives for becoming an integrated delivery network. Furthermore, its measurement of quality will decline when patients become dissatisfied.

Resource Allocation

Ultimately the role of the information resource of the organization is to provide whatever information is needed to make rational decisions and manage the resources of the organization. One of the major reasons for organizing an IDS is that of resource rationalization and making allocations of resources that will lead to efficient, effective operations. A primary difficulty in forming the governance of these organizations is to find a method by which these allocation decisions can be made across formerly unrelated entities, while maintaining a level of comfort among the players that the resource allocation process is being conducted in a fair and impartial way.

In this context, information is a resource of the organization (the same as its economic resources, its human resources, and its facilities), and must be managed as such (Johns, 1995). The effectiveness of the information resources of an organization is often evaluated on a cost versus benefits basis, which is similar in concept to a profit and loss financial statement. That is, the evaluation takes the form of trying to determine whether the benefits of the system exceed the costs. If such is the case, the system is judged to be effective.

In actuality, the information resource is an asset and should be viewed in a balance sheet sense like its economic resources and the facilities. If it is viewed in this way, the information resource can be deployed so that it helps to optimize the use of the organization's other resources.

Most organizational behavior theory suggests that there are three basic functions of management: planning, operating, and controlling. For the organization to be managed effectively, it needs information to support decisions in these three management areas. The planning function, at either the strategic or the tactical level, is largely carried out at the executive level of the organization, although most organizations provide for input from all parts of the organization. Planning activities relate to allocating the always scarce resources in a way that will optimize operations. Obviously timely and accurate information is required to perform this management function.

The operational function relates to the day-to-day activities of the organization and focuses on coordinating individual activities into group accomplishments. For example, it requires a number of different people working together in order to provide an inpatient nuclear medicine procedure: the dietary department must be aware of the procedure so that the patient's test is not contaminated by having a meal; the transportation department must know so the patient can be transported to the appropriate place at the appropriate time; and the nuclear medicine department must know so that the equipment, personnel, and supplies are available. The quality of the outcome and the efficiency of the operation are all dependent on having timely and accurate information about the procedure.

The control function of the organization relates to determining whether the organization is performing its day-to-day activities (its operational function) according to its strategic and operational plans (its planning function). For example, the organization requires timely and accurate information to know whether it is reaching its volume budget or using supplies consistent with its budget.

If the IDS has not integrated its information systems, the process of providing information to support decision making for the planning, operational, and control functions of management is much more fragmented and certainly less efficient.

Management Decision Support Across the Network

In order to do effective strategic planning and carry out tactical decision making and implementation of plans, the organization needs timely, accurate, and cost-effective information. The information resource of an organization must provide the information required by decision makers at all levels of the organization for making planning, operational, and control decisions (Schmitz, 1987). Information takes on a different meaning in this context. It is a strategic weapon of the organization and the raw material from which rational decisions are made (Schmitz, 1991). Without reliable information, the decision-making process at any level of the organization becomes suspect. Although good information will not guarantee good decisions, it will most certainly increase the probability that good decisions will be made.

The organization's information resource must be able to produce the data required for decision making at the time it is needed and at any location within the network. If information is not available when it is needed, it might as well not exist. An integrated information system promotes the probability that the information will be available when it is needed because it will have already identified the location and availability of the information, thus reducing the time needed to make prolonged and costly searches across the organization. In addition to being available, the information must be accurate. Inaccurate information is worse than useless; it is dangerous. Under normal circumstances, when a decision maker is presented with information, he or she relies on it to be accurate. If no information is available, the decision maker is at least aware that there are risks associated with making a decision that lacks specific information on which to base an analysis. An integrated information system will promote the probability that the data contained in it will be accurate because there is a single source from which the data come rather than multiple sources, as is the case when there are multiple information systems that are not integrated.

Integration of Financial Information with Clinical and Outcomes Data

An additional level of organizational efficiency accrues when the network is able to integrate financial information with clinical information and outcomes data. It is one thing to be able to account for costs across the organization and quite another to link those costs to specific clinical activities and outcomes. The ability to integrate this information within the organization represents a significant step forward from where most health care organizations are, but the ability to do it across the entire IDS represents a paradigm shift. Most organizations are not yet able to link data in this way, but that they will be able to do so in the future is quite clear. Since patients are likely to be served anywhere within the network, the ability to reference the data across the entire network is clearly necessary. Similarly, the ability to determine costs and link them to clinical practices and outcomes across the entire network will be necessary. Without this ability, the IDS will not be able to make informed decisions about the costs of doing business or rational decisions about pricing its services. In addition, being able to link outcomes data to the previously cited information will allow the organization to make definitive statements about the quality of its clinical services.

Availability of Medical Record Information Across the Network

Integration of information in and about the medical record is very important. The most desirable condition is for most or all of the medical record to be in electronic form. Short of that optimum condition, an electronic tracking system is essential in ensuring that the medical record information be available across the entire network. Because the patient might be treated at any location within the network, the organization must have the ability to make the medical record information available at all patient contact points.

If the medical record information is in an electronic database, its availability is significantly simplified, but only if the network's electronic information system is integrated. If the medical record is in manual form, a centralized, preferably electronic, information system must be in place that can pinpoint the location of the record and make it available to the person treating the patient. For scheduled patient encounters, the record must be transported to the location of patient service. If the availability of the medical record is accomplished by use of an integrated electronic information system, the efficiency of the organization is greatly enhanced, as is the quality of the care rendered to the patient.

Moreover, most accreditation bodies require that medical records be centralized. This does not necessarily mean that all of the records must reside in one place but it does require a master patient index, with access to it by all potential users of the record. This accreditation standard can be satisfied much more easily if the network has integrated its information resource.

Architectural Constructs of Information Integration

Most IDSs come into being from diverse backgrounds, and only rarely do all of the entities have the same information systems. Integrating the information resource can be accomplished by several methods. The first is to choose the best system available and install it throughout the network. This could be a very expensive choice depending on the chosen system and the original mix of vendors. A second approach is for the organization to develop its own information system. This has been successfully accomplished by a few organizations, but it too is expensive and requires a number of highly qualified information system professionals. Nevertheless, when it is done successfully, the organization has an integrated information system tailored to its needs. A third approach is to choose a system architecture whose sole purpose is to devise interfaces for diverse existing systems. This choice could be a good one if all of the currently installed information systems meet the functional requirements of the network. The desirability of this approach is enhanced when the organization wishes to integrate other sources of electronic information, internal or external to the network. An example of another kind of internal information might be clinical monitoring data; an example of external electronic data might include census information or other kinds of demographic data.

This architectural design is often referred to as a **repository** or as a **data warehouse.** In general, it can (1) receive data from any system, (2) standardize and put the data in their proper location in the repository database, and (3) report the standardized and reformatted data in a user-friendly way.

This design allows an information user to retrieve data quickly and easily that were originally created in multiple diverse systems and format the information into a single customized report, it allows the organization to create a centralized database even though its production systems are diverse, and it is user friendly, a characteristic that many production systems do not possess.

There are two approaches to the repository architecture: **passive** and **active.** The **passive repository** is fundamentally a warehouse for data that gathers and stores the information in preparation for reporting requests. Its sole function is to provide an integrated reporting capability from diverse systems within an organization.

An **active repository** is a much more aggressive system design. In addition to the capabilities of the passive repository, this approach includes data manipulation capabilities. It can switch data from one system to another and in some cases becomes the primary system for some information users. In some instances the active repository is designed with the intent of having it replace the existing production system(s). This system design strategy can thus become a system replacement strategy as well as an integration strategy. This architectural design has the potential to serve as the vehicle for integrating diverse systems while positioning the organization to replace the originally diverse systems with a single integrated system to manage the information resource.

The Role of Governance

When previously unrelated organizational entities come together, the governance must be structured so that all of the parties are comfortable with it. A balance must be identified that gives the new entity adequate authority to discharge its responsibility while vesting enough decision making in the original entities. If the parties were distrustful in their previous relationships, the governance can be problematic. A core issue in this dilemma is control.

One of the first control issues to be resolved is whether the authority should be centralized or decentralized. Ultimately this decision has a direct impact on many of the other decisions related to organizational structure.

Decentralized Control

When control is decentralized, it creates multiple layers of organizational structure and in some instances seriously encumbers the decision-making process. That is, when there are multiple boards, it means that major decisions must be acted on at each board level, thus potentially introducing delays into the decision-making process. A second potential problem with decentralized control is that the local board might not share the same values as the system board, thereby potentially making decisions that are at cross-purposes with each other. This is a particular danger when bringing diverse entities together into a single organization. Thus there is a need at the outset to define the governance activities by each level of the boards and to coordinate the activities of all organizational entities within the IDS.

One of the advantages of this organizational structure is that it is often accepted because it allows previous stakeholders in the original organization to maintain a role in the decision-making process. Furthermore, it allows the central board to delegate certain decision-making authority, thereby relieving the central board of many routine decisions. In addition, the local board is likely to have a better understanding of and higher sensitivity to local issues.

Centralized Control

If the decision is to centralize control, other structures must be designed and implemented that will provide input from the individual organizational entities. One of the central points in this discussion is the issue of fiduciary responsibility of the governing board of the organization. These fiduciary responsibilities are defined by the organization's charter and bylaws, as well as by the laws of the land. This responsibility cannot be abrogated and cannot be delegated to other parts and levels of the organization. Usually this means that the role of boards in other parts and levels of the organization is advisory in nature; it provides advice to the governing board of the organization but does not act on its behalf on issues that are the responsibility of the governing board.

The advantage of centralized control is generally the converse of the disadvantages stated for a decentralized model. A centralized model is usually more effective in coordinating integrated actions on the part of the total organization because all major decisions flow through a single source. Furthermore, this model promotes the probability that timely decisions will be made because fewer decisions must be made in order to chart a course of action. The disadvantages too tend to be the converse of the advantages of a decentralized model. Here there is the potential that decisions will be made by a board that is more distant from an operational understanding of the individual entity. In addition, this structure is less likely to give comfort that the values of the original organization will be preserved in the decision-making process.

The Role of Physicians

One of the key issues in forming an IDS is that of the role of physicians in the governance of the organization. This is a particularly difficult process when the originator of the organizational process is a health care institution. Often there have been longstanding issues of distrust and competition between the physicians and the administration of the organization. Thus, the formation of the organization is faced with dealing with these animosities within the framework of developing a new organization.

The role of the physician is critical in reforming the health care organization to become more cost-effective and efficient. Indeed, physicians probably have a greater influence on the outcome than any other group of individuals in the organization. Therefore, it is almost axiomatic that physicians must be represented in the governance of the organization. The question is how this is accomplished. When institutions initiate the formation of an IDS, they are often reluctant to transfer part of the control to physicians. This reluctance can stem from the traditional adversarial relationship that often exists between institutional health care managers and physicians and possibly the fact that physicians often do not want to invest capital in such a venture. In addition to the superficial issue of equality of investment, this latter point is important from a fraud and abuse point of view as well. If physicians are given ownership in the network and a resulting role in its governance without having invested at a comparable level as the institution, it would not be viewed as an arm's length transaction. As such, it would be interpreted by governmental agencies as an enticement to bring patients to the entity and thus become the potential subject of a fraud and abuse investigation. (The issues of fraud and abuse are complicated. This explanation is intended only to familiarize readers with the concept. For specifics related to this issue, research the current literature or consult an attorney.)

Making a capital investment in the network is not the only reason that physicians might play a role in the governance of the organization. Other reasons that physicians might be on the board of an IDS formed by a group of hospitals could include the fact that they represent a particular interest group and that they have the greatest ability to influence the required changes in the efficiency of the organization or possess a particular expertise in governance.

Whatever the reason for the physician's role in the governance of the network, it is critical that they be a part of the decision-making, policymaking body of the organization because they exercise the most significant influence for making the needed changes.

A Look at the Future

People and organizations often are inclined to continue doing things the same way as they have always been done. Furthermore, they sometimes do not realize that the assumptions underlying their decision making are grounded in the past. For example, the medical delivery system has believed that the management structure revolves around institutions, and in particular around hospitals. In today's environment, the assumption persists that efficiency will come through control, and control comes through ownership and merged institutional assets. Yet the things that have worked in the past might not be approaches that will continue to work in the future.

In many ways it is difficult to talk about the future without simultaneously talking about the present and the past. The predominant organizational structure of today's health care delivery system is the IDS, based on the assumption that operational efficiency will come through control and control comes through ownership and merged assets. Essentially an IDS is an obligated group for debt. In some ways, this structure has so far done little to promote perhaps the most fundamental strategy of health care delivery, which is to make people healthier for less cost. Indeed, in some ways, this structure adds to the cost by building larger and more modern facilities for the new entity. The emerging IDS still has not shed itself of some of the older conventional wisdom:

- Bigger is better.
- Control is needed to get greater efficiency.
- Control is obtained by economic power (ownership).
- You must have better facilities than competitors.

These kinds of assumptions lead to thinking that the way to change the system and the way that it operates is to change the organization rather than change the strategy. It is not that health care systems do not understand that a fundamental change in the way that health care does business is required. The line of demarcation is how this change is to be accomplished.

One of the big barriers in the current system is that both health care providers and patients see it as an entitlement. They see the broad-based tenets of the health care system as continuing more or less unchanged. The excess money and capacity in the system are the biggest barriers to restructuring its operation. Although there is general agreement that some things within the system must change, the system itself is considered inviolate. The cynic would say that it is other parts of the system that must change. For example, almost everyone agrees that there is far too much capacity within the health care system. Yet no governmental or private entity has devised a comprehensive strategy that would allow for systematic and orderly reduction of capacity.

The way health care is organized and delivered is changing rapidly. Because of the excess capacity of the health care system, it will become increasingly competitive, and many of today's organizations will not survive. Although the trend today suggests that health care organizations are betting that successful integrated health systems of the future will be a single corporate structure, where the assets of diverse entities are merged together with common management and governance, there are some contrary views.

A health care environmental assessment made by Allina Health Systems, Deloitte & Touche, and the Voluntary Hospitals of America (VHA) suggests that the successful health care organization of the future will be "a combination of wholly owned operations, alliances, joint ventures, spinouts and acquired subsidiaries. Rather than being directed by a single board, these 'organizational networks' will be held together by shared values, people, technology, financial resources and operating styles" (Integrated system survivors, 1995). This study goes on to predict that:

- More than half of the newly formed IHSs (IDSs) will fail.
- The new markets for many health plans will be individuals, previously uninsured populations, and Medicare and Medicaid.
- Some health plans that cannot compete on a cost-effective basis will be regulated out of business.

There are two fundamental facts that must be better understood about the health care delivery system:

- There is no magic in the current approach that IDSs are taking, where ownership and economic control are seen as the method by which greater efficiency can be brought to the system. This approach has some vulnerabilities.
- Virtual integration is a possibility that is beginning to emerge and has enjoyed some success. This approach postulates that it does not matter who owns the facilities; the issue is to get the incentives of all of the stakeholders aligned. Virtual integration is accomplished by the membership ascribing to the goals of the organization as contrasted to imposing participation by ownership.

In both of these approaches, the ultimate goal is the same. The system must squeeze out inappropriate and unneeded health care and redeploy these resources to provide access to the many people who currently lack health care.

One view of the future envisions a virtual IDS that is already in existence. This view suggests that a number of the for-profit physician management companies currently operate as virtual networks by virtue of the fact that they link their organizations together with information systems and management services (Pallarito, 1995). This approach has not resolved all of the problems, but it provides some hope that new and innovative ideas might be worth trying.

Visualizing some extensions to this virtual network concept might include ideas that are emerging out of the research of public health entities in both educational and applied settings:

- Patients who are physically and mentally able to do so must be permitted to manage their own health care.
- A variety of ways must be found to give people information about their own health interests.
- Since a substantial portion of the population has accepted television and computers as reliable sources of information, innovative approaches to providing health information to the public can include these media.
- We must bring the technology of communication together with people's health care needs.

Research in these areas should be one of the most important tools in pointing the way to the future. The successful approaches to delivering health care in the future will apply the research of the past to patients' interests. Ultimately the focus of this approach should be to help patients help each other.

There is no unanimous view of what the structure of the health care delivery system will be in the future. Whatever systems evolve, it will be a costly process. It has been estimated that the cost of building a group or staff model IDS is between $50 million and $75 million (Pallarito, 1995, p. 85). A risk-bearing IPA model IDS is estimated to cost between $10 million and $20 million to create. If the vision for formation of these integrated organizations is to fulfill their promise, significant savings will have to be achieved simply to overcome the organizational costs. Perhaps this change in the nature of an IDS can be achieved. Perhaps different approaches will be employed. Perhaps ideas that have not been thought of will be discovered by the work of educational and applied researchers. It is certain that continuation of the current mode of operation is not an option.

Conclusion

Health care in the United States is in a state of rapid change, and it is difficult for anyone to predict how it will be organized in the future. The IDN may be the delivery model of the future, but it is equally possible that some other delivery model, more efficient and effective, will emerge. All that can be said with any degree of certainty is that the way health care is delivered five years from now will be significantly different than it is today.

Review Questions

1. Is there any difference between an integrated delivery system and a traditional health delivery system? Discuss your answer in detail.

2. Discuss the strengths and weaknesses of the horizontal integration and vertical integration strategies of health care integration.

3. Discuss the information systems issues you consider to be most critical in the formation of an IDS. Explain why you think these issues would be important.

4. If you are responsible for the health information management function in an IDS, what information system issues would you want to address first?

5. How do physicians typically relate to an IDS? What roles should physicians play in this process?

6. Do you believe the integrated delivery system will be the predominant health care delivery vehicle of the future? Explain your answer.

References

Integrated system survivors adopt revolutionary structures. (1995, February). *Health Care Strategic Management*, p. 7.

Johns, E. L. (1995). Who will dominate HMO master contracting? *Journal of Health Care Finance*, *21*(3), 1–5.

Kolb, D. S., & Clay, S. B. (1994). Ambulatory care groupings: When, how and the impact on managed care. *Journal of Ambulatory Care Management*, *17*(1), 29–38.

McQueen, J., & Marwick, P. (1995). Introduction: Evolution of patient-focused care within the contextual framework of an integrated delivery system. *Journal of the Society for Health Systems*, *51*(6), 5–9.

Pallarito, K. (1995). It's an integrated healthcare delivery system . . . virtually. *Modern Healthcare*, *25*(10), 85–88.

Schmitz, H. H. (1987). *Managing health care information systems*. Rockville, MD: Aspen.

Schmitz, H. H. (1991). Decision support: A strategic weapon. In M. J. Ball, J. V. Douglas, R. I. O'Desky, & J. W. Albright (Eds.), *Healthcare information management systems*, (pp. 42ff). New York: Springer-Verlag.

Shortell, S. M., Gillies, R. R., Anderson, D. A., Mitchell, J. B., & Morgan, K. L. (1993). Creating organized delivery systems: The barriers and facilitators. *Hospital and Health Services Administration*, *38*(4), 447–466.

Chapter 6

Third-Party Payment Systems

In highly competitive industries, prices are set in the marketplace containing many individual buyers and sellers; no one market participant can dictate prices. In health care, prices are often determined by large payers representing groups of workers, retirees, or the poor. Each large payer has its own system of payment, so providers face a complex structure of billing systems, accounting and regulatory requirements, quality standards, and conflicting behavioral incentives. Effective financial management in health care requires an understanding of this structure. This chapter describes the key components of the current reimbursement system, introduced in Chapter 3, and how it is being transformed by the movement toward alternative payment arrangements under managed health care.

Learning Objectives

Upon successful completion of this chapter, the learner will:

- Describe how third-party payers reimburse hospitals, doctors, and other providers of health services.
- Recognize the incentives of the fee-for-service, cost-based reimbursement, and prospective payment systems in use today.
- Become familiar with differences in provider payer mix.
- Estimate reimbursement from payers based on payment systems.
- Describe the information requirements of differing reimbursement systems.
- Explain the extent to which traditional reimbursement systems have been adopted by managed care plans to pay providers.
- Assess the shift toward managed care by traditional payers.

Key Terms

adjusted annual per capita cost

adjusted community rate

allowable costs

ambulatory patient groups

annual update factor

average payment rate

balance billing

blended rate

break-even analysis

case mix index

common procedural terminology (CPT) codes

contribution margin

conversion factor

cost finding

cost shifting

cost-based reimbursement

customary, prevailing, and reasonable charges

diagnosis-related groups (DRGs)

discounted fee-for-service (FFS) system

fee-for-service (FFS) system

fixed costs

geographic adjustment factor (GAF)

HCPCS codes

Medicare cost reports

Medicare risk contracts

nonparticipating physicians

opportunity cost

pass-through payments

payer mix

prospective payment system

prospective payment system (PPS) rate

resource-based relative value system

up-coding

variable costs

volume performance standards

Introduction

It is no coincidence that Canada, Germany, France, and England have moved to a universal and standardized system of paying health care providers in the postwar years, while the United States continues to maintain a mixed system of public and private financing of health services. Historical tensions between the rights of the individual and the rights of the community, the appropriate role of federal versus state and local government, and the distrust of powerful government and business interests have shaped the evolution of health care financing in the United States (Starr, 1982). These tensions have created resistance to the adoption of a single-payer, or even a single, uniform payment, system in this country. As is shown in Table 6-1, government payers, primarily Medicare and Medicaid, financed only 43.5 percent of personal health expenditures in 1994, while another 32.1 percent of health-related spending was funded by employer-sponsored health insurance (see Table 6-1). Individual households pay for 21 percent of personal health care spending out of their own pockets (National Center for Health Statistics, 1996).

The thrust of the traditional United States health care third-party payment system has been to expand comprehensive insurance coverage for acute care and hospital-

Table 6-1 Source of Personal Health Expenditures, 1950–1994[a] (as percent of total expenditures)

	Out of Pocket	Private Health Insurance	Other Private Funds	Federal	State and Local	Percent Government Funded
1950	65.5	9.1	2.9	10.4	12.0	22.4
1960	55.3	21.2	1.8	9.0	12.6	21.7
1970	39.0	23.2	2.6	23.0	12.2	35.3
1980	27.8	28.6	3.6	29.2	10.9	40.1
1990	24.1	32.8	3.5	29.0	10.6	39.5
1994	21.0	32.1	3.4	33.7	9.8	43.5

[a]Source: National Center for Health Statistics, 1996.

based services. Public and private insurance coverage for primary care, chronic conditions, and nursing home stays has remained incomplete, and partially dependent on tax-based state financing through Medicaid and public and community health agencies. As of 1994, consumers paid directly for only 2.9 percent of all spending for hospital-based acute and nursing care (National Center for Health Statistics, 1996). Third-party payers financed the rest of these expenditures. In contrast, 18.9 percent of physician services, 37.2 percent of freestanding nursing home stays, and 44.2 percent of all other health care spending, including dental care, home health care, prescription drugs, vision care, durable medical equipment, and personal health care, was paid for by patients. Preventive services are not necessarily covered by third-party payers. Interestingly, only about 3 percent of national health spending is for public health services, which include health education and health promotion, childhood immunizations and vaccinations, and prevention of the spread of communicable disease.

Traditional Payment Systems

Like payment for other services in the economy, reimbursement of doctors, hospitals, and other health care providers has largely been based on a **fee-for-service (FFS) system:** the seller charges a specific price for each identifiable and distinct unit of service or good sold.

Total provider revenues (TR) in an FFS system consist of the sum of each unit of health services provided, Q_i, multiplied by the price, or fee charged, per unit of service, P_i.

$$TR = \sum Q_i \times P_i.$$

Prices in the FFS system have usually been based on the following units of service:

- Per procedure, or service provided, when reimbursing health professionals like doctors and dentists
- Per day rates, for institutional care in hospitals or nursing homes

Reductions in fees charged per unit of service reduce total revenues to the health provider while increased services increase them. In the FFS system, each provider that participates in treatment submits a separate bill to the patient for services rendered. For example, a patient receives bills from the referring physician; other physicians involved in treatment, such as the surgeon, the radiologist, and the anesthesiologist; and other professionals, like rehabilitation therapists or home health nurses; as well as the facility or site in which treatment is provided, like an emergency room, an ambulatory care clinic, a freestanding surgery center, or a hospital.

In the days before government and private health insurance was widespread, family doctors and hospitals gave individual discounts on their fees to the less affluent and provided charity care to poor patients. Not-for-profit hospitals depended heavily on donations to cover their costs. Doctors hoped to earn a sufficient amount of revenues from fees on services to their wealthier patients to maintain sufficient revenues and income to cover the costs of treating poor patients. In essence, doctors were the first to shift costs to higher-paying patients to fund indigent care.

One way to increase total revenues and incomes in a fee-based system is to do more for each paying patient and to charge separately for each service provided. The process of charging separately for each service provided is called **unbundling.** Unbundling allows treatment and charges to vary for each patient depending on the services used. Imagine that your professor charged for each class lecture you attended, each paper or exam graded, each office visit for advising, each hour of instruction provided outside of class, and for any letters of recommendation written for you. Similarly the university would bill you for your seat in each class attended, your use of computer time, each book checked out of the library, and the time spent with the reference librarian. Currently these services are bundled into a single tuition payment, and every student pays the same rate per credit hour regardless of the amount of services used. In an FFS health payment system, each patient, or his or her payer, pays for the quantity and type of services consumed.

With the expansion of insurance coverage, the FFS reimbursement system rewarded doctors and hospitals for unbundling each individual encounter, service, procedure, or day of care provided. Incentives to do more, especially when the provider is confident of payment because of health insurance coverage, are inherent in an fully insured FFS system. Uncertainty about outcomes of treatment adds to the pressure to do more, not less, since the health care provider is subject to penalties for inappropriate or inadequate treatment. Finally, if fees are subsidized by insurance, consumers demand more services than they otherwise would want, or could afford, if they had to pay for them out of their own funds.

Alternatives to Fee-for-Service Reimbursement

Alternatives to FFS reimbursement were developed by third-party payers with market power, like Blue Cross, the federal government, and large, self-insured employers. Such payers could use their leverage to dictate reimbursement rates and define reimbursable units of service. Reimbursable units became broader, going from per day to per case rates, to minimize unbundling, and pricing shifted first to discounted prices and then to payer-set rates for an episode of care. Among these new forms of payment are the following:

- **Discounted FFS system**—Pays providers on the basis of a percentage discount from prices (i.e., their billed charges).
- **Cost-based reimbursement**—Pays the provider for the full costs of care associated with the payer's beneficiaries.
- **Prospective payment system**—Pays a fixed fee set in advance for a defined episode of treatment based on a patient's diagnosis.
- **Resource-based relative value system**—Pays physicians and other caregivers on the basis of fees derived from relative resource utilization and costs.

The proportion of total revenues expected from different payers is its **payer mix.** Payer mix has significant implications for pricing and the internal management of financial and clinical resources. The greater the proportion of payers paying full charges, the greater is the incentive to increase service volume, the ability to increase fees on services in greatest demand, and the likelihood that charity care can be financed by higher payers. Moreover, if fee-based systems coexist along side new capitated contracts, conflicting pressures to increase services on some and reduce them on others will be placed on the organization. Thus, physicians and hospitals that provide services to patient groups under different reimbursement systems face conflicting behavioral incentives and management issues.

Alternative payment systems have not been implemented uniformly across all provider groups. Hospitals receive 42 percent of the dollars spent annually on health care and were the first to be affected by the shift away from fee-based reimbursement. Twenty-one percent of all health care dollars now flow into physician practices and freestanding clinics. As a rapidly growing component of health care spending, physician reimbursement has more recently been subject to alternative third-party payment arrangements. Changes are now underway in the reimbursement of other health-related goods and services, including prescription drugs, nursing home care, durable medical equipment, and home health care.

Understanding alternative payment systems may seem less relevant in a system increasingly dominated by managed health care. Knowledge of these systems is important, however, because many health care organizations and caregivers have yet to accept capitation, so that a large percentage of reimbursement is derived from one or more of these alternative payment systems. While managed care's greatest expansion has been among employer groups and state Medicaid and other plans, some major payers, like Medicare, continue to use alternative systems of reimbursement. In addition, many managed care plans and provider groups that contract with managed care plans use these payment systems to reimburse providers and caregivers within their own networks. Thus, a physician-hospital organization that accepts capitation from a health plan may divide up the capitation payment internally, using, for example, the Medicare reimbursement system.

Perhaps the most important reason for understanding alternative forms of payment is the fact that these systems have largely failed to control total health care costs. The inherent flaws in these systems are revealed by understanding how they are constructed and used in the financing of health services.

Hospital Reimbursement

Since hospital care was the first to be financed predominantly through third-party payers, it was the first to experience payer efforts to contain costs that seemed to rise uncontrollably under an insurance-subsidized, FFS reimbursement system. From its inception in 1966, in fact, Medicare reimbursement of hospital care for the elderly and disabled was based on reasonable costs of its beneficiaries rather than on billed charges. Private payers, including Blue Cross/Blue Shield as well as commercial insurance companies, make up about one-third of hospital revenue sources. Most state not-for-profit Blue Cross plans adopted Medicare reimbursement methods, however, making these payers more like Medicare in terms of the behavioral incentives they created. Only a small portion of hospital revenues come from individual, uninsured patients who pay full charges, called "self-pay" patients.

Cost-Based Reimbursement

Prior to the Blue Cross plans that emerged during the Great Depression to maintain the financial viability of hospitals, hospital revenues were derived predominantly from per day rates charged to more affluent patients. Charity care was delivered with donated funds. With the growth of Blue Cross plans, hospitals continued to receive a flat rate per day, supplemented by additional fees for special services (Berman, Weekes, and Kukla, 1990). As the volume of these special services grew in proportion to the per day charge, third-party payers began to base hospital payment on "reasonable costs," that is, the accounting costs that the payer permitted the hospital to list on its bill to the payer. The health provider would be reimbursed only for the costs incurred, not the billed charges, unless the billed charges were lower than costs. These **allowable costs** included direct patient care costs of beneficiaries, plus some portion of hospital overhead expenses like human resources, general administration, research and teaching expenses, and plant maintenance costs. Generally payers disallowed recovery of bad debts, charity care expenses, and nursing education costs.

During the 1960s and 1970s, Blue Cross paid reasonable costs plus 2 percent or the billed charges of its subscribers, whichever was lower. Medicare and Medicaid, which came into being in 1966, usually paid the lower of reasonable costs, or charges, with state Medicaid payers often demanding a discount from this rate. Cost-based reimbursement required that hospital financial managers find and allocate overhead costs to patient care so that reasonable costs of each payer were at least equal to billed patient charges. The importance of **cost finding** to obtain the greatest amount of reimbursement was a key to maintaining financial viability and competitive position of hospitals that were paid on the basis of costs.

Under cost-based reimbursement, hospitals were paid retrospectively, that is, after all costs had been incurred. In order to be reimbursed, hospitals had to file annual **Medicare cost reports** documenting direct and allocated overhead costs on which payment would be made. Medicare hired intermediaries, typically Blue Cross plans, to administer claims and assess allowable costs. The intermediary laid out strict rules for counting and including costs. Adhering to these rules was similar to filing tax returns with the Internal Revenue Service. But rather than minimizing tax liabilities, hospital financial managers tried to maximize revenues through effective cost-finding strategies. Thus, a thorough knowledge of cost allocation rules and allowable costs is important for financial managers whose organizations operate under retrospective cost-based reimbursement systems.

Incentives Under Cost-Based Reimbursement

Cost-based reimbursement reduces managerial incentives to provide care at the lowest cost. Normally if managers make mistakes, they must bear the full effect of the loss; however, under cost-based reimbursement, poor forecasting of service use may not result in a financial loss to the hospital (Cleverley, 1992). For example, a hospital may choose to invest in equipment that, under a FFS system, would have to be used a minimum number of times to cover its full costs. **Break-even analysis,** a financial management technique, illustrates the effects of cost-based reimbursement on the performance of the hospital. Break-even analysis answers the question: How many units of service must be provided to cover all costs incurred in offering a service to patients? This technique can also be used to find out what price must be charged to cover all costs incurred if the volume of services that will be delivered is known.

To break even, total revenues must be just enough to cover total costs. In an FFS system, a profit will be made beyond the break-even point, Q^*. If there is not enough demand for the service to reach the break-even volume, the hospital will experience a loss. Total costs include **fixed costs** and **variable costs.** Fixed costs are costs that do not change with the number of units of service provided—for example, interest and depreciation expenses, the salaries of senior managers, and a minimum staffing level required to offer a specific service. Variable costs are costs incurred each time the service is provided—for example, nursing hours and supplies.

Break-even occurs when total revenues (TR) equal total costs (TC).

$$TR = TC \tag{1}$$

Total revenue expected by the healthcare organization consists of P, the price charged for each unit of service, times Q, the quantity of services provided

$$TR = P(Q) \qquad (2)$$

and total costs incurred by the organization include fixed and variable costs.

$$TC = FC + VC(Q) \qquad (3)$$

where FC are fixed costs which are independent of the units of service, VC are the costs associated with each unit of service, and Q is the number of services provided. Total variable costs, the second term in equation (3), are VC times Q. By substituting (2) and (3) into (1), we obtain

$$P(Q) = FC + VC(Q) \qquad (4)$$

To break even, total revenues represented on the left side of equation (4) must be high enough to cover total costs on the right side of the equation.

We can solve equation (4) for Q to find the volume of services needed to break even. First subtract $VC(Q)$ from both sides of the equation (4).

$$P(Q) - VC(Q) = FC + VC(Q) - VC(Q)$$
$$P(Q) - VC(Q) = FC$$

and since Q is found in both terms on the left side of the equation, we rewrite it as

$$Q(P - VC) = FC$$

Finally, dividing both sides of the equation by $P - VC$, the break-even volume is

$$Q = FC/(P - VC)$$

The break-even equation indicates that prices must be higher than variable costs. The positive difference between prices and variable costs is called the **contribution margin.** It tells how much each unit produced and sold contributes to recovery of fixed costs. Next, the number of units sold must be increased until the accumulated contribution margin is sufficient to offset fixed costs.

Under cost-based reimbursement, a portion of the hospital's total allowable costs can be charged to the payer based on the percentage of total hospital charges billed to the payer, or the share of admissions, or patient-days, attributable to the payer's clients or subscribers. As an extreme example, suppose a hospital had two patients: one of them is covered by a cost-based payer and one a charge-based payer. Under cost-based reimbursement, it is possible that 50 percent of the hospital's allowable costs, like management salaries and the costs of building and equipment, would be reimbursed by the cost-based payer.

A Case in Point. Applying some numbers to break-even analysis illustrates the effect of cost-based reimbursement. For a given medical test, let $FC = \$60,000$, $VC = \$1$, and $P = \$4$.

$$Q = \frac{60,000}{(4-1)} = \frac{60,000}{3} = 20,000 \ .$$

In this case, the contribution margin is $3. For each test administered, $3 is earned net of variable costs. Solving the equation yields 20,000 tests as the break-even volume. At 20,000 tests, total revenues would be $80,000 ($4 \times 20,000$). At this volume, $60,000 would be earned to cover fixed costs after paying the variable costs of $20,000 ($1 \times 20,000$). This level of utilization is just enough to recover total costs of providing care.

What happens to total revenues if the hospital has overestimated demand and performs only 10,000 tests, half the volume needed to break even?

$$TR = \$4 \ (10,000) = \$40,000$$
$$TC = FC + VC(Q) = 60,000 + 1(10,000)$$
$$\text{Profit(loss)} = TR - TC = 40,000 - 50,000 = (10,000)$$

In a fee-for-service system, the hospital would make only $40,000 in revenue and cover only half of its fixed costs of $60,000. The hospital would lose $10,000.

A Case in Point. Let us return to the hospital that has overestimated use of the new equipment and actual volume is 10,000 tests, resulting in a $10,000 loss. Suppose cost-based payers make up 50 percent of patient volumes in this hospital and pay the hospital based on the percentage of patients using the service. Then half of the fixed costs—$30,000—plus half of the variable costs ($1 \times 5,000$), or $35,000, would be reimbursed by the cost-based payer.

Cost-based payer: $50\% \ (FC) + 50\% \ (VC)$
$$5(60,000) + .5(1)(10,000) = \$35,000.$$

FFS patients would pay $20,000 ($4 \times 5,000$). Total revenues from all payers is $55,000. As a result, the cost-based payer has enabled the hospital to recover $5,000 of the $10,000 loss, and partially insulated management from its poor planning.

A strategic response to poor planning would be for the hospital to raise billed prices on each test to $5 each. Assuming other third-party payers are unresponsive to price increases, which was typical of commercial insurers during this period, the hospital could break even at this lower volume. In this case, commercial insurers would pay $25,000 ($5 × 5,000) of total revenues. When this revenue is added to the $35,000 from cost-based payers, the hospital would completely recover its costs. Managers would bear little or no financial risk for overly optimistic projections. There is a catch to cost-based reimbursement, however. To be reimbursed on the basis of costs, it is typically the case that costs must be less than billed charges. This creates an even greater incentive for the hospital to raise its prices—to $7 per test in this case. At $7 per test, costs of $35,000 to cost-based payers would equal charges.

A 100 percent cost-based provider would not be financially motivated to achieve an efficient use of resources. For example, suppose the hospital has three cost-based payers, each representing one-third of the hospital's patients. Each cost-based payer would pay its share of the $60,000 in fixed costs plus $1 per unit in variable costs incurred by their enrollees. Under 100 percent cost-based reimbursement, the full $70,000 in costs would be recovered at a volume of 10,000 tests. The provider is not penalized for its inefficiency since all costs are recovered, even at inefficient volumes.

Another behavioral effect of cost-based reimbursement is that a highly efficient hospital is penalized. If the hospital performed 30,000 tests, well above break-even, it would earn $120,000 and make a profit of $40,000 if all of its payers paid on the basis of billed charges. However, if 50 percent of patients pay costs, the hospital would receive only $45,000 from cost-based payers and $60,000 from FFS payers, for a total of $105,000—$15,000 less that it would earn in a FFS system.

Cost-based payers

$$\text{TR:} \quad .5(60,000) + .5(1)(30,000) = 30,000 + 15,000 = 45,000$$

Charge-based payers

$$\text{TR:} \quad \$4 \, (15,000) = 60,000$$

$$\text{Total Revenue} = \$105,000$$

This "tax" on efficient management also discourages optimal use of resources.

The effects of cost-based reimbursement on profits and losses are shown in Figure 6-1. If the hospital receives the lesser of costs or charges, hospital reimbursement is represented by the area *ABC*. Below Q^*, the hospital's revenues are less than its full costs. Above Q^*, the cost-based payer would pay only the amount along line *BC*, representing the hospital's costs. Thus, the hospital would just break even for any services provided above the break-even amount. The only way to increase total revenues is to raise expenses and shift the total cost line upward to the dotted line, *FG*. Thus the inherent incentive of cost-based reimbursement is to increase the organization's fixed costs.

In response to the perverse incentives of cost reimbursement, third-party payers adopted cost-containment strategies in the 1980s. Strategies included restricting the rate of growth in allowable costs and capping the amount of cost reimbursement that the hospital could receive. Payment shifted from retrospective reimbursement (establish-

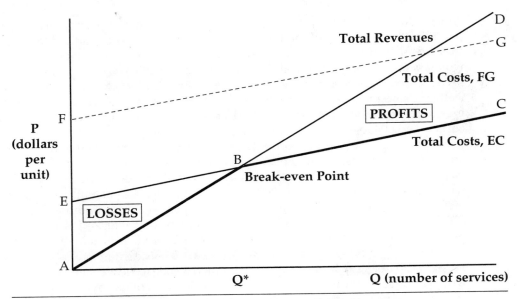

Figure 6-1   Effect of Cost-Based Reimbursement on Profits and Losses

ing payments after services have been delivered) to prospective reimbursement (setting payment rates before services are delivered). Also hospital cost-based payers moved to a rate-setting system of payment. Administered prices were based on average costs per discharge, with certain adjustments, experienced by all patients. Specific costs above the administered price would no longer be reimbursed. Finally, the unit of service to be priced was broadened to include all treatments associated with a specific illness. Specific services and treatments provided to individual patients could not be priced separately.

The Problem of Cost Shifting

A major problem with cost-based reimbursement is that it does not recognize the **opportunity cost** of funds invested by shareholders, sponsoring organizations, or the community. The opportunity cost of a dollar used for one purpose is the amount that could be earned in its next best use. If $20 bill is placed in a drawer for a year and could have been invested in a bank certificate of deposit over the same period at 5 percent interest, the opportunity to earn $1 over the period has been lost. Without a normal return on the funds invested, health care organizations cannot provide charity care, improve or maintain services, or survive the inherent risk and uncertainty of delivering health care. Thus, any surplus funds for these purposes must be obtained from higher charges to FFS payers.

A Case in Point. Cost shifting can be illustrated using break-even analysis. In this instance, we solve equation (4) for the break-even price by dividing both sides by Q.

$$
\begin{aligned}
TR &= TC \\
P(Q) &= FC + VC(Q) \\
P &= FC/Q + VC
\end{aligned}
$$

Price must equal fixed costs per unit of service plus variable costs. Suppose a hospital projects 1,000 admissions and 5,000 patient days of care based on an average length of stay of 5 days and $5 million in fixed and variable costs required to deliver this care. If all payers paid the same price, billed charges would be $5,000 (=5,000,000/1,000) per admission or $1,000 (=5,000,000/5,000) per day.

The hospital has different payers, however. Fifty-eight percent of patients are covered by commercial insurers who pay billed charges, 40 percent pay a percent of costs, and 2 percent are charity cases. Total revenues will be the sum of revenues from each payer.

$$TR = TR(\text{FFS payers}) + TR(\text{cost-based payers}) + TR(\text{charity care})$$

To use break-even analysis to set prices, revenues from the payers who do not pay charges must be subtracted from both sides of the break-even equation:

$$
\begin{aligned}
TR &= TC \\
TR(\text{FFS payers}) + TR(\text{cost-based payers}) + TR(\text{charity care}) &= FC + VC \times Q \\
TR(\text{FFS payers}) &= FC + VC(Q) - TR(\text{cost-based payers}) - TR(\text{charity care})
\end{aligned}
$$

Forty percent of total costs, or $2 million (.4 × 5,000,000), is expected from cost-based payers. Charity patients will pay nothing. To recover all costs, commercial payers must make up the $3 million difference.

$$TR(\text{FFS payers}) = 5,000,000 - 2,000,000 - 0 = 3,000,000$$

Since *TR* from FFS payers equals *P(Q)*, the charge to cover total remaining costs is

$$
\begin{aligned}
TR\ (\text{charge-based payers}) = P(Q) &= 3,000,000 \\
P &= 3,000,000/Q
\end{aligned}
$$

The payer mix of 58 percent indicates that 580 projected admissions (or 2,900 days) will be from commercially insured patients. The price for commercial payers must be

$$
\begin{aligned}
P \text{ per admission} &= 3,000,000/580 \\
&= 5,172.41 \\
P \text{ per day} &= 3,000,000/2900 \\
&= \$1,034.48
\end{aligned}
$$

Commercial payers pay $172.41 per admission, or $34.48 per day, more than cost-based payers. The cost of charity care has been shifted to charge-based payers. FFS payers can avoid the additional charge by encouraging their subscribers to seek lower cost providers or by negotiating their own discounted rates with the hospital.

Opportunity costs of funds supplied by equity investors are not found in the accounting costs of health providers used to construct their reimbursable costs. Recognition of the opportunity costs of capital in hospitals, however, was reflected in arrangements with some cost-based payers. Blue Cross used a system of reasonable cost plus 2 percent of charges. This reflected a willingness to provide a reasonable return on equity invested. And in the early 1980s, Medicare made an adjustment in its reimbursement of for-profit hospitals to compensate for the opportunity costs of funds obtained from market investors. It no longer does so.

Prices charged to FFS payers must be high enough to cover additional costs, including opportunity costs and the costs of bad debt and charity care that are not reimbursed by cost-based payers. Such a pricing strategy is called **cost shifting.** Cost shifting works only if payers to whom costs are shifted do not resist price increases.

Services Covered by Cost Reimbursement

Although third-party payers largely abandoned cost-based reimbursement for alternative reimbursement mechanisms in the 1980s, some services continue to be reimbursed on the basis of allowable costs. For example, until 1991, Medicare reimbursed hospitals for capital costs, including interest, depreciation, and lease payments, based on the percentage of Medicare hospital-days in total patient-days. Cost reimbursement of capital expenses allowed the purchase of expensive, state-of-the-art equipment that was often underemployed and encouraged the addition or renovation of space that qualified for cost-based reimbursement.

Medicare Part A, which covers hospital care, continues to pay on the basis of allowable costs for care delivered in the following settings:

- Rehabilitation hospitals (and distinct part-hospital units)
- Psychiatric hospitals (and distinct part-hospital units)
- Children's hospitals
- Long-term care hospitals (with average lengths of stay greater than 25 days)
- Veterans Administration hospitals
- Cancer hospitals (where 50 percent or more discharges must be diagnosed with cancer)

In addition, specialty hospitals and units, outpatient care, and home health care are typically reimbursed on the basis of costs. Thus, the inefficiencies of cost-based reimbursement continue to be present in payment systems of many payers. With the recent passage of the Balanced Budget Act of 1997, however, Congress asked HCFA to implement case-based and per diem reimbursement for some cost reimbursed Medicare providers. Skilled nursing facilities will be effected in 1998, long-term care hospitals starting in 1999, and rehabilitiation hospitals and units beginning in 2000. Home health services will lost cost reimbursement beginning in 1999.

In summary, reimbursing hospitals for their reasonable costs encouraged the following:

- Price increases (cost shifting to FFS payers) to cover disallowed costs and ensure the reimbursement of allocated costs under the lower of costs or charges reimbursement

- The maximum possible allocation of overhead expenses to patient services covered by cost-based reimbursement

- A reduction in incentives to use resources efficiently

- Competition among hospitals to provide more and better services and convenience to its doctors and patients, regardless of cost, since these expenses would be fully reimbursable

The Prospective Payment System

Until 1983, Medicare based rates on a share of the actual costs reported by each participating hospital. Because costs in the system were mounting, the HCFA, which administers Medicare, proposed another approach to hospital reimbursement, this one based on reimbursement per case. If a single national rate could be set in advance for each Medicare hospital discharge, HCFA could dictate how much the rate would be allowed to increase each year. Hospitals would bear the financial risk of providing services at a cost above the prospective, national rate. Hospitals that provided care at a lower cost than the national average would be rewarded with a surplus, or profit. Those that were relatively less efficient would experience poor financial performance. This method of hospital reimbursement, called the **prospective payment system (PPS)** was implemented by HCFA in October 1983. Since then, it has been adopted by other payers, including Blue Cross plans and many state governments.

HCFA developed a national rate per discharge using the average operating costs reported by all hospitals in their 1981 Medicare cost reports. At this time, capital costs were excluded from the new system of reimbursement, with the stipulation by Congress that eventually they would be incorporated. Once set, the **PPS rate** (or federal rate) would be adjusted annually for average inflation and improvements in cost efficiency in all hospitals through the **annual update factor.** Inflation would increase the update factor of the PPS rate; system-wide efficiency gains would reduce it. For example, if the inflation adjustment is 4 percent and improvements in efficiency are 2 percent, the net increase in the PPS rate projected for the coming fiscal year would be 2 percent. With a PPS rate this year of $2,000 per case, the annual update factor would raise it to $2,040 ($2,000 × 1.02) next year. All participating hospitals could expect to receive an increase of $40 per discharge for each Medicare patient treated.

The primary problem with a national case-based system is that patients require different treatments and services depending on their health status, age, and diagnosis. If payment rates were the same for each patient, treatment of very ill patients would be inadequately compensated. Some hospitals might choose to avoid treating complex, costly cases. What was needed was a simple way to classify patients to predict their resource utilization and costs during a hospital stay.

Diagnosis-Related Groups

A model was developed at Yale University to assign resource costs to patients based on clinically relevant criteria (Fetter, 1980; Mills et al., 1976). Researchers constructed 23 major diagnostic categories from the International Classification of Diseases, 9th Revision, Clinical Modification codes. From these diagnostic categories, 467 **diagnosis-related groups (DRGs)** were formed. DRGs took into account not only the principal diagnosis of the patient but also the patient's age, whether the admission was medical or surgical, and any patient comorbidities and complications. Relative resource cost weights were then assigned to each DRG. (Appendix I illustrates the cost weights effective 10/1/97 for 220 of the 503 DRGs now classified by the system.) An average hospital discharge would have a cost weight of 1. Inpatients who were assigned DRG codes requiring more resources than the average would have a cost weight greater than 1; patients in less costly DRGs would receive a cost weight less than 1. By averaging these cost weights, a **case mix index** of all patients treated in a specific hospital could be constructed. Revisions in cost weights and annual update factors are published each September in the *Federal Register*. This information helps hospitals establish budgets based on anticipated reimbursement.

The calculation of a simple case mix index and expected revenues for all Medicare discharges to a hospital during a fiscal year is illustrated in Table 6-2. To simplify the calculations, assume that Medicare discharges occur in only 5 DRGs. Typically, during the year, patients will be represented in most of the 503 DRGs, especially in large, urban hospitals. With an average PPS rate of $3,040, this hospital's reimbursement per case, adjusted for case mix, would be $3,736.13. The higher rate of reimbursement is justified because this hospital treats more costly cases, as reflected by its higher-than-average case mix index. Total Medicare reimbursement for the year is projected at

Table 6-2   Projection of Medicare Case Mix Index and Revenues

			Medicare Discharges	
DRG	*Cost Weight*	*Description*	*Number*	*Percentage*
82	1.3329	Respiratory neoplasms	400	20%
106	5.5843	Coronary bypass with coronary catheterization	100	5
127	1.0199	Heart failure and shock	800	40
140	.5993	Angina pectoris	500	25
211	1.2541	Hip and femur procedure without coronary catheterization	200	10
Total			2,000	

Case mix index = .20 (1.3329) + .05 (5.5843) + .40 (1.0199) + .25 (.5993) + .10 (1.2541) = 1.23

Adjusted federal rate per discharge: $3,040 (1.23) = $3736.13

Total projected Medicare revenues: 2,000 ($3736.13) = $7,472,259

$7,472,259. However, Medicare patients also pay the hospital directly for a portion of the bill. Deductibles and co-payments billed directly to the patient are subtracted from the amount expected from the government.

Hospital costs differ for reasons other than the case mix of patients treated. These cost differences are incorporated into Medicare's PPS rate or added as **pass-through payments.** As of September 1997, specific adjustments were made for

- Large urban hospitals
- Local area wage differences
- Recovery of unpaid balances (bad debts) of Medicare patients
- Excessively high costs of care (cost outliers)
- Transfers to other participating PPS hospitals
- Capital costs
- Medical education and teaching costs
- Hospitals serving a disproportionate share of the poor

Implementation

To avoid undue financial stress to hospitals, HCFA phased in its new payment system gradually. During the transition, adjustments were made for regional cost differences, excessively long lengths of stay, and rural hospitals. These adjustments are no longer in force. Rural hospital rates are now included in the other urban category, and regional adjustments and payments for unusually long stays (day outliers) are no longer made. In addition, from 1983 to 1987, hospitals were paid a weighted average of their own operating costs and the federal rate, called a **blended rate.** By so doing, hospital revenues from Medicare were much less volatile during the conversion process.

Table 6-3 calculates the Medicare payment for two hospitals. To adjust for urban location and local area wages, two PPS rates are calculated, representing average

Table 6-3 Medicare Reimbursement for Regional and Memorial Hospitals

	Regional (large urban)		Memorial (other urban)	
	Labor	**Nonlabor**	**Labor**	**Nonlabor**
PPS rate	$2,709.42	$1,085.29	$2,666.52	$1,068.10
Area wage index	× 1.03		× .94	
Wage-adjusted rate	$2,790.70	$1,085.29	$2,506.53	$1,068.10
	$2,790.70		$2,506.53	
+ Nonlabor	$1,085.29		$1,068.10	
Total PPS rate	**$3,875.99**		**$3,574.63**	
Case mix index	× .92		× 1.14	
Adjusted PPS rate	**$3,565.91**		**$4,075.08**	

costs of hospitals located in large urban areas and average costs of hospitals located in other urban areas. Each of these rates is partitioned further into a labor and a non-labor component. Only the labor component is adjusted for differences in local area wages. Regional Medical Center located in a large urban area, has a lower case mix than average. Memorial Hospital is located outside a large urban area and has a higher average case mix.

Adjustments for cost outliers, patient transfers, capital costs, medical education costs, and disproportionate share payments are more complex. The latter two payments are a pass-through of hospital costs, related to certain hospital characteristics, which cannot be apportioned directly to costs of treating specific patients, or patient groups.

Cost Outliers

Cost outlier payments attempt to compensate hospitals for unusual cases. With PPS reimbursement, hospitals are paid the national average costs, adjusted for case mix, of treating a Medicare patient. By paying the average, or mean, cost of treating a patient, it is expected that losses from high-cost cases in each DRG will be offset by profits from low-cost cases, so that a hospital performing at an average level of effi-ciency will just break even. In order for this averaging process to work, however, costs must be normally distributed; that is, the proportion of costs of cases below the mean must be equal to the proportion costs of the cases above the mean. In a small per-centage of patients, however, costs are very high—so high that they cannot be offset by the costs of very low-cost patients, violating the assumption of normally distrib-uted costs. HCFA pays an additional amount for these unusual cases, typically 80 per-cent of the hospital's costs above a threshold amount.

Transfers

Medicare pays more than the PPS amount for the treatment of patients who are trans-ferred from one participating PPS hospital to another. The federal payment rate is made only to the hospital where treatment was completed. The transferring hospital is paid on a per day rate, calculated as follows: the transferring hospital's federal rate is divided by the average length of stay for typical patients assigned to that DRG. Let us say that a transferring patient is coded in DRG 209, Major Joint and Limb Reat-tachment Procedure, which has a mean length of stay of 5.3 days (see geometric mean length of stay in Appendix 1). The per diem rate can be calculated from the transfer-ring hospital's expected DRG payment. Assume it is $11,653. The per diem rate would be $2,199 ($11,653/5.3). The transferring hospital receives twice the per diem rate for the first day and the per diem rate for any remaining days before the transfer. The hos-pital receiving the transfer gets the DRG rate. The transferring hospital would be paid this amount for each day of care prior to transfer.

Capital Costs

Prior to 1991, capital costs were passed through to hospitals on a reasonable-cost basis. Capital costs include interest, depreciation, leases, taxes on plant and equipment, improvements, and insurance. Capital cost reimbursement is still in transition from a cost-based system to a PPS system. Full incorporation of capital costs into the PPS rate, intended from the inception of PPS, was delayed a number of times during the 1980s while HCFA designed an equitable system of reimbursement. HCFA did not want to penalize hospitals that had just added or renovated facilities and equipment and therefore had high capital costs, nor did it want to discourage older hospitals from making needed improvements because of expected inadequate capital reimbursement rates.

As of the October 1991 cost reporting periods, hospitals began to be paid on a per discharge basis similar to the one already in place for operating costs per case. During the transition to a fully prospective rate, hospitals with lower than average capital costs per discharge are to receive a weighted average rate consisting of their own capital costs and the federal rate. These low-cost hospitals would experience slightly higher reimbursement under PPS. Each year during the ten-year transition to the 100 percent PPS rate, the portion of hospital-specific costs per discharge reimbursed would decline by 10 percent, while the share of the federal rate paid to the hospital would rise by 10 percent.

Hospitals with higher-than-average capital costs would be under a "hold harmless" rate. In this case, the hospital could elect one of the following, whichever was higher: 100 percent of the hospital's federal rate for capital expenses or 85 percent of the cost of "old" capital plus a percentage of the federal rate where the percentage is determined by the proportion of "new" capital costs in total capital costs. Under certain conditions, capital put in place and used in the treatment of patients by October 1994 could qualify as old capital. Special hospitals, like rural referral centers, cancer hospitals, and sole community providers, received special adjustments and exclusions under PPS.

The federal rate per discharge for capital costs is based on the average capital costs of all PPS hospitals. In the first year of implementation, 1991, the federal rate for capital was $415.59 per discharge. Like the PPS rate for operating costs, the federal capital rate is updated annually for efficiency and inflation and then adjusted for case mix, patient transfers, cost outliers, large urban area location, a geographic adjustment factor similar to the area wage index, disproportionate share, and medical education costs of the hospital. For fiscal year 1997, the federal payment rate on capital was $438.92 per discharge (*Federal Register*, August 30, 1996).

Medical Education

Until 1989, HCFA reimbursed teaching hospitals on a reasonable cost basis for the direct costs of training nurses, paramedics, and physicians. After 1989, the direct costs of training interns and residents were calculated as a fixed rate per intern or resident, updated annually for inflation. The percentage of this amount that could be charged to Medicare was based on the ratio of Medicare-days in total patient-days. Medicare's share of direct costs of residency training was then divided up among the hospital that submits Medicare Part A claims and physicians who submit Part B claims for care provided in the teaching facility.

In addition to payments for the salaries and overhead costs of interns and residents, the federal DRG rate was adjusted for indirect medical education costs that arise in a teaching hospital but cannot be apportioned to specific patients. The indirect medical education adjustment factor to the federal rate is derived from a formula based on number of full-time-equivalent interns and residents per patient-day.

Disproportionate Share

The federal rate is increased if the hospital serves a high number of indigent patients. The PPS rate for urban hospitals with more than 100 beds or rural hospitals with more than 500 beds is adjusted if treatment of Medicare patients on disability and Medicaid patients combined makes up 15 percent or more of the hospital's patient-days. The adjustment factor rises as the percentage of indigent patient–days increases. For urban hospitals smaller than 100 beds and more than 40 percent disproportionate share days, the PPS rate is increased by 5 percent. Rural hospitals with fewer than 500 beds and 30 percent or more indigent care–days also receive an adjustment, which varies by type of rural hospital and its bed size.

Table 6-4 illustrates the PPS rates for operating costs and capital costs of mix at St. Elizabeth's Hospital in 1997. The hospital is a 300-bed teaching hospital located in a large metropolitan area. Fifteen percent of its patient-days are delivered to the disabled and persons eligible for Medicaid. As a teaching hospital, it has a higher-than-average case mix. Area wages are also higher than average. The adjusted federal rate for operating costs is $4,666.59. The hospital has lower-than-average capital costs. Therefore it is reimbursed at a blended rate of its own costs and the national rate. Because 1997 is the sixth year of transition into a fully prospective capital rate,

Table 6-4 Calculation of PPS Rate for St. Elizabeth's Hospital

	St. Elizabeth's Hospital PPS Rates, 1997		
	Operating Costs		Capital Costs
	Labor	Nonlabor	
Federal rate (large urban)	$2,709.42	$1,085.29	$ 388.14
Area wage/geographic adjustment	× 1.01		× 1.02
Wage-adjusted rate	$2,736.51	$1,085.29	$ 385.90
Total PPS rate	$3,821.80		$ 385.90
Case mix adjustment	× 1.102		× 1.102
Indirect teaching adjustment	× 1.081		× 1.081
Disproportionate share adjustment	× 1.025		× 1.025
Adjusted federal rate	$4,666.59		$ 471.20
Hospital-specific capital costs			$ 402.26
Weighted average capital costs			$ 429.84
Total PPS rate	($ 4,666.59 + $429.84)		**$5,096.43 per discharge**

Misprint (handwritten annotation)

the hospital receives 40 percent of its own hospital-specific costs per discharge and 60 percent of the adjusted federal rate per discharge, resulting in a final capital rate of $429.84. Total expected reimbursement per discharge for St. Elizabeth's is $5,096.43.

Concerned that PPS might result in a lower quality of care—perhaps discharging patients sooner than is medically warranted—HCFA required that all participating hospitals submit to review and evaluation by a peer review organization (**PRO**). PROs screened hospital records for unnecessary and inappropriate admissions and treatments, incorrect DRG assignments, and evidence of poor quality of care. PROs could deny payment for cases deemed inappropriate. Hospitals could appeal PRO denials.

The Effects of PPS

The implementation of PPS for the reimbursement of hospitals by Medicare resulted in important changes in health care delivery. A significant result was the reduction in the average length of stay (LOS) of elderly inpatients and a movement of some hospital services into nonhospital treatment settings. In 1980, the LOS of discharges aged 65 and older was 10.7 days. As of 1994, it was 7.8 days. Discharges from short-stay hospitals among the same age group followed a similar pattern, dropping from 383.7 to 342.6 per thousand in the same period (National Center for Health Statistics, 1996). Shortened stays brought greater treatment intensity as needed services were delivered in a reduced time period.

Medicare billing under PPS also involved the coding of patients into appropriate DRG categories to ensure reimbursement. Patients were assigned to only one DRG category, regardless of the number of diagnoses or the actual procedures used. Hospital medical records coders quickly learned how to maximize reimbursement by assigning patients to the highest-paying DRG code. **Up-coding** created obsolescence in some DRGs.

Weak hospitals failed or were merged into more viable organizations. Rural hospitals that were not exempt or excluded from PPS were particularly vulnerable. Inadequate patient volumes in small rural hospitals made the averaging of high-cost discharges with low-cost discharges less predictable and attainable. Many hospitals found that they had excess capacity—unfilled beds—given the reduced number of patient-days needed to treat patients. Occupancy rates dropped from an average for nonfederal hospitals of 75.4 percent in 1980 to 64.4 percent in 1993.

Concerns that the quality of care would erode with PPS did not materialize. Neither did the anticipated decline in total Medicare expenditures. Although inpatient hospital spending declined from 65 percent to 52 percent of total Medicare spending, expansion in other spending categories outstripped this moderation in inpatient spending growth. As shown in Table 6-5, care was shifted out of the hospital into doctors' offices, outpatient clinics, ambulatory surgery centers, skilled nursing facilities, and home health (PPRC, 1996). Reflecting this trend, outpatient surgeries for all patients rose from 16.4 percent of total surgeries in 1980 to 54.9 percent in 1993 (National Center for Health Statistics, 1996).

Meanwhile, many nonhospital services continued to be reimbursed on the basis of costs. In 1989 Congress allowed Medicare coverage of 150 days of nursing care fol-

Table 6-5   Shares of Medicare Spending, by Type, 1983–1993

	Physicians	*Hospital Inpatient*	*Hospital Outpatient*	*Home Health*	*Skilled Nursing Facilities*
1983	23%	65%	6%	3%	1%
1984	24	64	6	3	1
1985	23	65	6	3	1
1986	25	63	7	3	1
1987	27	59	7	2	1
1988	28	57	8	2	1
1989	28	56	8	2	2
1990	27	55	8	3	3
1991	27	53	8	4	2
1992	25	54	8	5	3
1993	24	52	8	7	4

PPRC, 1996.

lowing a hospital discharge. Skilled nursing facilities (**SNFs**) are paid on the basis of costs , adjusted upward each year for inflation. To capture this additional reimbursement on their DRG patients, many hospitals built SNFs as distinct units within the hospital and allocated existing hospital overhead expenses to them. DRG reimbursement for a given Medicare discharge could be augmented by payment for skilled nursing care after discharge, without moving the patient out of the hospital. Although these subacute units have not proved to be highly profitable, they have sustained revenues otherwise lost under PPS (Anders, 1996).

The failure of DRGs to control total Medicare costs is reflected by the continued concern about the bankruptcy of the Medicare Trust Fund. Because nonhospital service volumes and prices remain uncontrolled, the DRG system's ability to restrict spending is weakened. It is interesting to note that a number of eastern states were allowed a waiver from HCFA to establish their own statewide hospital rate setting systems. They retained their waivers only so long as costs could be kept lower than they would have been under PPS. None of the seven state rate setting systems was successful in containing total hospital spending, and the states have abandoned them.

To plug in the holes that allow for expenditure leakages under PPS, HCFA is trying to bring other Medicare providers into DRG-type reimbursement systems. A **resource-based relative value system (RBRVS)** to set fees prospectively for physicians was implemented in 1992. Hospital-based ambulatory surgery is being converted from a cost-based to a PPS system. Finally, **ambulatory patient groups (APGs)** are being developed to pay for all outpatient services, whether in a hospital-based clinic or a freestanding facility (KPMG Peat Marwick LLP, 1995). Like DRGs, APGs classify patient encounters with a health care professional in an outpatient setting into clinically meaningful groups. Relative resource cost weights are developed and used to calculate reimbursement.

As HCFA has ratcheted down the rate of hospital reimbursement, some hospitals have tried to shift costs to other payers (ProPAC, 1993). In response, the DRG system of reimbursement has been wholly or partially adopted by a large majority of Blue Cross plans, nearly half of state Medicaid programs, and most government-run hospitals such as the Veterans Administration hospitals (Carter, Jacobson, Kominski, and Perry, 1994). Commercial insurance companies that indemnify their subscribers for their hospitals bills have been subject to the greatest price increases with cost shifting. In response, employers have been unwilling to absorb the higher premiums charged by their commercial health plans. Thus, growth of managed care may have been given added momentum by the efforts of other third-party payers to rein in costs.

Physician Reimbursement

The payer mix of physicians indicates that they are less dependent on government payers than hospitals are. In 1993, physicians received nearly 48 percent of their revenues from private payers and about 37 percent from government payers. They are therefore more reliant on private health insurance, including Blue Shield plans, and out-of-pocket payment from patients than hospitals are. Patients contributed directly to 15.6 percent of physician revenues (PPRC, 1995). Moreover, these payer groups have been less resistant to physician fee increases.

The DRG system encouraged greater use of nonhospital care, including services provided in physician offices. This shift augmented the rapid growth in nonhospital expenditures from 1975 to 1982, when Medicare Part B spending, which covers physician services and ambulatory care, rose 17 percent annually (PPRC, 1990). In addition to incentives created by PPS, the development of technologies that enabled the delivery of care in an outpatient setting, such as cataract and endoscopic surgery, helped to increase demand for and costs of physician services in the 1980s. Medicare expenditures reveal these impacts. As Table 6-5 shows, the physician share of total Medicare spending rose from 23 percent in 1983 to 28 percent in 1989, in spite of a Medicare freeze on physicians' fees between 1984 and 1986. Research suggested that physicians were able to maintain their revenues from Medicare in spite of the fee freeze by increasing the volume of services provided (Mitchell, Wedig, and Cromwell, 1989).

Rising patient demand for certain services allowed physicians to raise fees without a loss of patients. Some physicians could bill their patients for the balance not covered by third-party payers. With rising prices and use of services, out-of-pocket expenses associated with co-payments and balanced billing increased. In 1991, for instance, Medicare patients paid 17 percent out of pocket, up from 10.6 percent in 1972 (McCormack and Burge, 1994). Growing costs and out-of-pocket spending spurred the adoption of a prospective fee schedule for physicians treating Medicare patients. This new fee schedule, based on weighting units called relative value units, reflected resources used by physicians in treating patients. The RBRVS has attributes similar to the DRG system for reimbursing hospitals.

Medicare's Resource-Based Relative Value System

At the inception of the Medicare DRG system, physician payment remained on a fee basis for virtually all payers. Private payers reimbursed physicians their usual, customary, and reasonable charge and Medicare paid physicians in a similar fashion of **customary, prevailing and reasonable charges (CPR).** Under the CPR system, physicians received the lowest of three alternative fees: billed charges, the seventy-fifth percentile of customary charges of all local physicians, or the physician's median charge over a prior 12-month period. Failure to keep pace with price increases of one's peers could result in foregone income from third-party payers. **Nonparticipating physicians** in the Medicare system, who did not accept Medicare fees as payment in full, could attempt to recover some of these losses by **balance billing** patients for the difference between billed charges and CPR payments from third-party payers. Medicare constrained balance billing to some maximum amount of increase per year.

In response to rising physician costs, HCFA in 1992 implemented a five-year transition to a fee schedule for physicians treating Medicare patients Resource-based relative value system (RBRVS). This system of physician reimbursement had several goals:

- To slow the growth in Part B physician expenditures
- To discourage the use of procedures and encourage the use of physician time
- To reduce specialist fees for services deemed to be overvalued
- To limit balance billing by nonparticipating physicians

HCFA wanted to base physician reimbursement on resource costs, not market prices. Also the agency believed that higher reimbursement of time-intensive services, involving the cognitive skills of the physician rather than the use of diagnostic procedures, would lead to lower costs and better care. The new schedule therefore paid primary care physicians at a somewhat higher rate than they had received under CPR. Also some specialist services were considered overvalued and the fees too high. Therefore, overpaid physician services would be paid less than the CPR rate under RBRVS. Finally, balance billing would be limited to 115 percent of the fee expected under the new fee schedule.

Cost Adjustment Using Relative Value Units

RBRVS is based on a weighted average of the costs of three inputs employed by physicians in providing a unit of care:

1. The physician's time and skill required
2. The physician's overhead and practice support services
3. The physician's malpractice insurance

Each input factor is measured in relative value units (**RVUs**) originally developed by researchers (Hsaio et al., 1988, 1992) and refined by HCFA.

Standard resource units for physician time and skill inputs are assigned to physician codes in **HCFA's common procedure coding system** (HCPCS—"Hicpics"). **HCPCS codes** are based on the **common procedural terminology (CPT) codes** developed by the American Medical Association to classify physician services. HCPCS includes additional codes for nonphysician services.

To construct physician RVUs, an intermediate office visit is assigned an RVU of 1. All other HCPCS physician service codes are assigned RVUs that reflect differences in the amount of time and skill needed for the HCPCS coded service relative to the time and skill required in an intermediate office visit. Currently, practice expense RVUs are based on historical charges for physician overhead. HCFA calculated the malpractice RVUs. The latter two RVU groups are not based on true resource costs, although efforts are underway to create appropriate practice expense RVUs (PPRC, 1996).

To determine the amount of reimbursement, the RVUs for the physician's work, practice expense, and malpractice costs are summed and multiplied by geographic practice cost indexes (GPCIs) that reflect cost differences faced by physicians in different regions of the country. For example, if area wages are higher in certain locations, then practice expense costs are likely to be higher in that area than the national average. Finally, a standard national conversion factor, like the federal rate, or PPS rate, in the DRG system, is used to transform the GPCI-adjusted RVU inputs into dollars.

Table 6-6 illustrates the calculation of the Medicare physician fee using the RBRVS system. Additional adjustments to the conversion factor are made to offset the ability of physicians to make up any losses by increasing volumes in certain specialties. These are called **volume performance standards.** Different conversion factors are used to compensate primary care physicians, surgeons, and other physicians. Surgi-

Table 6-6   Physician Fees under RBRVs for Knee Arthroscopy/Surgery

(HCPCS (CPT) Code – 29875)			
	RVU	*GPCI*	*Adjusted RVUs*
Work	6.16	.994	6.12304
Practice	7.88	.944	7.43872
Malpractice	1.61	1.209	1.94649
Total adjusted RVUs			15.50825
Conversion factor (surgical)			$40.9603
RBRVS fee:			15.50825 × $40.9603
RBRVS fee:			**$635.22**

Note: The HCPCS (CPT) code identifies the type of procedure. The GPCIs are for the St. Louis area. While work and practice expense are below the national average, malpractice expense at 1.209 is higher than average. The conversion factor is the national payment rate set prospectively for a physician service during 1997.

cal procedures received a conversion rate of $40.9603 in 1997. Primary care services had a lower rate of $35.7671 in the same year (*Federal Register*, September 1996). As Table 6-6 indicates, the final RVU fee of $635.22 for knee surgery is the product of the three RVUs, the GPCIs, and the conversion factor.

Impact of RBRVS

HCFA has been partially successful in achieving the goals of RBRVS. According to Table 6-5, physician cost increases and the share of Medicare spending have declined since the implementation of RBRVS. Growth in spending for physician services slowed from over 10.6 percent in the 1986–1991 period to 3.8 percent from 1991 to 1993 (PPRC, 1995). Physicians' share of Medicare expenditures fell from 27 to 24 percent of the total. As planned, evaluation and management services (physician's time inputs) have received a greater share of Medicare payments, and certain specialties and subspecialties have experienced reductions in spending growth. RBRVS has also been successful in reducing balance billing through the limitation on nonparticipating providers to 115 percent of Medicare's allowable fee. In comparison with private payer reimbursement, Medicare RBRVS fees are about 68 percent of charge-based fees (PPRC, 1995).

Although physician spending has slowed, it has not slowed as much as was anticipated, for several reasons. First, conversion to national payment rates was not competed until 1996. During the transition, physicians received a blended rate, which was a weighted average of their own historical charge and the RBRVS fee. Now that the system is fully implemented, however, HCFA is in a position to tighten physician spending by lowering the conversion factor. As with PPS, there is evidence of inappropriate use of RBRVS codes and the possibility of up-coding of HCPCS codes for purposes of obtaining better reimbursement (PPRC, 1995). Finally, the automatic adjustments for lower volume than projected resulted in higher conversion factors for certain physician groups. This has helped to maintain Medicare spending levels and physicians' fees.

The shift to evaluation and management services requiring more physician time has also not been as great as expected, largely due to the use of separate conversion factors for surgeons, primary care physicians, and all other physicians. Being in separate pools allowed services of different physician groups to increase without forcing a substitution of one service group for the other. Volume adjustments in the surgical pool have been perverse, resulting in a larger conversion rate increase for surgeons than for primary care physicians. Policymakers have urged the adoption of a single conversion rate for all physicians (PPRC, 1995, 1996). Medicare implemented a single conversion rate effective January 1998.

Finally, because the practice and malpractice RVUs are based on historical charges, there is concern that they do not reflect resource costs and are too high. The Physician Payment Review Commission, which reports to Congress on recommended policy and payment changes, has proposed that RVUs based on costs be developed for these two components of RBRVS reimbursement (PPRC, 1996). These proposals have been adopted by HCFA.

Non-Medicare Use of PPS and RBRVS

The RBRVS fee structure has been adopted by other payers (McCormack and Burge, 1994), albeit not as widely as the DRG system for hospital reimbursement. Blue Cross/Blue Shield plans appear to be major users of RBRVS, with 79 percent of respondents to the McCormack and Burge study using this system of reimbursement. Commercial insurance companies continue to reimburse physicians their usual, customary, and reasonable charges. However, a number of managed care plans appear to be using Medicare fee schedules for managing utilization and costs and for paying network providers. According to the McCormack and Burge study, 50 percent of the IPA-model HMOs and 39 percent of the PPO plans responding to their survey had adopted an RBRVS-based payment system. Moreover, insurance companies that use RBRVS rates tended to apply them in their managed care insurance products. Thus, RBRVS is likely to continue to be an important component of physician reimbursement strategy under emerging managed care plans, as well as government insurers.

Medicaid Reimbursement

Up to this point the discussion has focused primarily on Medicare and not-for-profit Blue Cross/Blue Shield plans because of their rapid adoption of Medicare's reimbursement systems. Another important government payer is Medicaid, the jointly funded federal-state program, administered by each state that provides health care services to the poor and disabled. The federal government provides matching funds to participating states based on the relative income of each state. High-income states are paid 50 cents of each dollar they spend on Medicaid services. Matching rates go up to 82 cents on the dollar for states with lower relative statewide incomes.

In addition to hospital and physician services, Medicaid is the only major source of financing for long-term care services. Although two-thirds of Medicaid enrollees are younger women and children, two-thirds of Medicaid spending is allocated to long-term care services for the elderly and disabled. Accelerating costs in Medicaid since the late 1980s have prompted state-based initiatives for the reform of Medicaid programs. The federal government has considered conversion of Medicaid funds to a block grant to states to allow them greater flexibility in providing services to the poor. To date, such legislation has not been passed. The Balanced Budget Act of 1997, however, includes a provision, the Child Health Assistance Program, to expand health care coverage under Medicaid to all children in households without insurance with incomes up to 300 percent of poverty.

Although the federal government sets general rules for eligibility and coverage, these are implemented differently by each state. The actual package of benefits set by the state could be comprehensive or restrictive. Moreover, income criteria differ across states. Before 1989, for example, Medicaid eligibility for poor women and children was determined primarily by eligibility for Aid to Families with Dependent Children (**AFDC**). States with low AFDC income thresholds effectively limited the number of women and children who could apply for Medicaid. In the late 1980s, Congress enacted legislation that mandated coverage for pregnant women and newborns in households with incomes up to 133 percent of the federal poverty rate, thereby separating Medicaid eligibility from AFDC-set criteria. Finally, each state determines its own reimbursement system. Some have used cost-based reimbursement; others employ contractual fee-based systems, including Medicare DRGs and RBRVS. As of 1995, 22 states had adopted or planned to adopt RBRVS reimbursement systems for physicians (PPRC, 1995).

Use of Capitation by Government Payers

Capitation protects the payer from increases in volumes and more intensive treatment that may occur in an insurance-funded FFS system. Moreover, unlike cost-based reimbursement that encourages a health care organization to increase reimbursable costs, capitation rewards less costly and more efficient approaches to treatment. Since the mid-1980s, HCFA has allowed Medicare beneficiaries to enroll voluntarily in managed care "risk contracts" based on a single capitation rate per beneficiary.

Medicare Risk Contracts

Medicare risk contracts pay a managed care plan a monthly capitation rate that equals 95 percent of the projected costs that would be incurred by treating similar types of Medicare patients in the FFS system. The base capitation rate is estimated from average costs experienced by Medicare patients in the FFS system nationally and then adjusted for relative average cost differences in the county of residence and the risk characteristics of the Medicare population in the county. This adjusted rate is called the **adjusted annual per capita cost (AAPCC).** Ninety-five percent of the projected AAPCC is reported in the *Federal Register* and becomes the base rate of payment that a health plan can expect before adjusting for risk characteristics of plan enrollees. Each Medicare beneficiary is assigned to one of 122 risk categories to reflect the member's age group, sex, enrollment in Medicare Part A and Part B, Medicaid eligibility, institutional status (e.g., in a nursing home), and whether the enrollee has end-stage renal disease. After applying the risk adjustment factors to the AAPCC, there are 122 possible capitation amounts that a plan could receive for each Medicare beneficiary enrolled. In addition, the health plan receives a premium payment from Medicare enrollees equal to the deductible and co-insurance payments they would have made in the FFS system.

Federally qualified health maintenance organizations (**FQHMOs**) and competitive health plans (**CHPs**) are eligible to enter into risk contracts with HCFA. CHPs are similar to HMOs except that CHPs are not required to offer the breadth of services that FQHMOs must offer (Zarabozo and LeMasurier, 1995). Moreover, CHPs can charge co-payments and deductibles. An eligible health plan wishing to accept Medicare enrollees under a risk contract must first estimate the percentage of Medicare enrollees who will fall into each of the 122 risk classes. The cost factors for each class that will be served by the HMO are applied to the base rate. Then a weighted average of these rates is calculated to obtain the **average payment rate (APR)** expected from Medicare beneficiaries who enroll in the plan.

Next the plan compares the APR with the community rate that it would charge a commercial payer for the same group coverage after adjusting for expected utilization differences of Medicare enrollees. This rate is called the **adjusted community rate (ACR)** for the HMO or CHP. If the ACR is less than the estimated APR, then the plan must lower the APR capitation rate to the adjusted community rate, reduce Medicare enrollee premiums charged by the plan to make up the difference between the APR and ACR, or expand benefits to use up the difference. Once contracts are negotiated, they are in force for a year. Adjustments to the capitation rate as a result of over- or underestimation of the APR and ACR are made only in the next year. HMOs and CHPs can also contract to receive reasonable costs of Medicare enrollees. Health plans contracting with HCFA also have the option of accepting cost-based reimbursement for services provided.

Problems in Medicare Risk Contracts

Cost problems have emerged in Medicare risk contracts as a result of the incentives to participate. If a health plan can deliver services to Medicare beneficiaries in its service area at a cost that is less than 95 percent of the FFS cost, then it will choose to contract. But if the costs to the plan are found to be higher than 95 percent of the FFS costs, plans would not contract. As a result, sicker Medicare beneficiaries would remain in the FFS system, and participating HMOs and CHPs would be observed to experience favorable selection of healthier Medicare beneficiaries into their plans. Medicare ends up paying more overall than it would have under the totally FFS system (Brown et al., 1993).

Another problem with the current system of Medicare risk contracting is the variability in rates from year to year, especially in counties with few Medicare beneficiaries. An HMO or CHP will have difficulty contracting over time when rates are unstable and unpredictable.

Under the Balanced Budget Act of 1997, Congress initiated changes in Medicare risk contracting (Pauly, 1996). As of June 1998, all risk- and cost-based contracts will be phased out and replaced by Medicare+Choice plans. Three types of plans will be created: coordinated care plans, fee-for-service plans, and medical savings accounts. Each type of plan will be paid a per capita rate by Medicare. The coordinated care plans will be made up of HMOs, PPOs, and point-of-service plans—all managed care plans. The fee-for-service plans would pay providers on an FFS basis negotiated by the plan, the provider would not be placed at financial risk, and no withholds from providers would be allowed. Medical savings accounts are high deductible (up to $6,000) plans. The difference between the capitation from Medicare and the premium charged for the high-deductible plan goes into the enrollee's medical savings account, to be spent for health services. Medical savings accounts are limited to 390,000 Medicare beneficiaries.

Other features of the budget act are attempts to improve risk factor adjustments that result in higher payments by Medicare, a carve-out of direct and indirect medical education costs from the AAPCC, and a blended capitation rate based on national and area-specific rates to reduce yearly fluctuations in rates.

Medicaid Managed Care Initiatives

Many states, hampered in their efforts to expand health services to the poor and uninsured and facing rising costs, are requesting and obtaining waivers from HCFA to pay providers through managed care plans and providers. Twenty-five state Medicaid programs have sought waivers from the federal government to implement managed care plans for some or all of their enrollees. As of 1996, 13.3 million people, or 40 percent of the Medicaid population, were enrolled in managed care, up from 2.7 million in 1991, which amounted to 9.5 percent of the Medicaid population (www.hcfa). Enrollments vary across states. States like Tennessee with 100 percent enrolled stand in great contrast to Vermont and Alaska, where no Medicaid recipients are enrolled in managed care plans.

Medicaid managed care contracts tend to vary across states. Some states use a variation of the Medicare AAPCC rating approach to determine plan capitation. Others permit managed care plans to bid for contracts but compare those bids with the going rates paid in the FFS system. If managed care rates are greater than what would be paid the existing system, plans are often asked to resubmit their bids at a lower capitation rate. Medicaid recipients include women and children and the disabled. Providing services at a lower cost to the chronically ill and disabled has proved difficult. In general, states achieve savings on their managed care plans for pregnant women and children, who make up only 25 percent of expenditures but are 75 percent of enrollees.

Mandatory Medicaid managed care appears to be successful in reducing the costs to the states, especially for emergency room use and hospitalization. Recent data estimate Medicaid managed care savings at $350 per beneficiary (PPRC, 1997). It is likely to continue to grow as a system of payment and delivery of services to poor women and children. With state Medicaid expansions and federal expansions proposed under the Balanced Budget Act of 1997, Medicaid managed care plans are likely to be extended to the working poor and their families. Issues surrounding the quality and outcomes of Medicaid managed care plans have yet to be adequately addressed.

In states that have used cost-based reimbursement, allowable hospital costs are often lower than granted to Medicare patients. Moreover, Medicaid physician fees have often been set considerably below the fees of other payers. On average, Medicaid in 1993 paid 47 percent of private insurance fees and 73 percent of Medicare's fees under RBRVS (PPRC, 1994; Norton, 1995). As a result, some doctors and hospitals have been unwilling to provide services to Medicaid enrollees. Hospitals and nursing homes obtained congressional relief from low fees through the Boren Amendment, passed by Congress in 1981, which requires that states reimburse providers at least reasonable costs of caring for Medicaid patients. The Balanced Budget Act of

1997, however, nullified the Boren Amendment by allowing states the discretion to set rates.

Conclusion

While cost-based reimbursement encourages more abundant and costly care, rate-setting systems, like PPS and RBRVS, promote more efficient care without necessarily reducing total costs to the payer. This is because even though prices are fixed, the provider can increase total revenues by increasing the volume of services provided. When volume increases are constrained under an administered price system, care-givers may shift care to less restrictive sites and substitute services that are more adequately reimbursed. PPS, RBRVS, or any other rate-based regime fails to control both price and quantity of services provided to patients. Thus, these systems will succeed only partially and temporarily in controlling costs. Capitation provides yet another tactic in the payer's cost-cutting strategy. For a one-year period, total spending by payers will be fixed, and the responsibility for managing all health care costs and absorbing the uncertainty of those costs will be transferred to the managed care plan and its providers. Capitation may not solve the cost problems of a single payer like Medicare, however, when enrollment of all beneficiaries is voluntary and medical expense risk adjustment is inadequate. Because of favorable selection, total expenditures might rise as healthier beneficiaries join managed care plans, leaving the sick in the FFS system.

Case 6-1: Centerville Health Center

You are the new controller for Centerville Health Center, CMH, a 300-bed hospital located in a city of 200,000 in a South Central state. CMH was purchased by a national health care system, United Medical Mission, 5 years ago. UMM owns health care facilities throughout the South and Midwest. The town of Centerville has been steadily growing over the past fifteen years. With its proximity to rivers and lakes and its mild winter weather, Centerville attracted developers in the early 1980s who opened a large retirement community just outside of town. In addition, 7 years ago a new Japanese auto plant relocated to Centerville bringing in young workers and their families.

You have been asked to project CHC inpatient revenues for next year based on 1998 volume projections and contractual arrangements in place with third-party payers. Based on department-level projections, the hospital expects to treat 16,000 patients next year, down from 16,500 last year, reflecting a persistent, long-run downward trend in hospital utilization as more services are delivered on an outpatient basis. Currently CHC hospital beds are more than 73% occupied. Projected expenses for 1998 based on estimated volume are $4,800 per discharge. There are no other hospitals in town, but several small hospitals are located within a 30-mile radius of CHC, and a large academic medical center is 80 miles away by interstate.

Sources of Revenue

Fifty percent of CHC discharges are patients covered by federal or state payers. Of these, 40 percent are Medicare beneficiaries and Medicaid covers 10 persent. Your commercial payers include one large HMO whose members make up 20 percent of your discharges, a PPO with 10 percent of your discharges, and an indemnity insurer that reimburses 10 percent of your discharges. You expect another 10 percent of your discharges to be uninsured and to pay out of pocket. Two percent of them will be classified as charity patients.

Contractual Arrangements

Medicare

In 1997, the total PPS rate for a hospital like CHC was $3,400 per discharge. You have gone to the September 30th *Federal Register* and found that HCFA has announced an increase in the 1997 base rate of 2 percent to account for inflation and changes in technology. Case mix for Medicare patients in CHC is currently 1.2 but is expected to rise to 1.25 next year. Because the hosptial will be in the seventh year of transition of capital reimbursement to a fully prospective system, capital payment in 1998 will be determined by a 70 percent federal to 30 percent hospital-specific blended rate. The federal rate is calculated to be $446 per discharge and the hospital-specific rate will be $395 per discharge in 1998. All adjustments for case mix and geographic location have been taken into account in your capital rates. You are not entitled to extra payments for residency training or treating the poor. Medicare patients stay on average 6.25 days.

Medicaid

Medicaid pays the hospital its share of operating costs on a per day basis. To calculate its per diem rate for cost reimbursement, the hospital divides total budgeted expenses for 1998 by total expected inpatient days. Medicaid days are calculated by mulitplying Medicaid discharges by the average length of stay of Medicaid beneficiaries. Last year, the typical Medicaid patient spent four days in the hospital.

Managed Care Plans and Commercial Payers

Your HMO and PPO negotiations have resulted in an average discount of 25 percent off the charge per day. Billed charges for these patients in 1997 were $1,400 per day. Managed care patients have an average length of stay of four days. Other commercial payers pay billed charges and their patients average four days in the hospital.

Self-pay

Self-pay patients include the uninsured, some of whom will be able to pay out-of-pocket. Most of your bad debt expense has come from these "self-pay" patients. After several attempts at collection, you have only been able to collect on average 60 percent from self-paying patients. You expect to write off this amount next year. Self pay and charity care patients typically stay 5 days on average.

Budgeted expenses are expected to be $4,800 per discharge, CHC needs to earn at least an additional 15 percent, or $720, per discharge to cover principal payments on old debt, to provide cash for daily operations, to maintain buildings and equipment, and to invest in new technology. Thus net revenues need to average at least $5,200 per discharge to cover all costs.

Answer the questions below. To do so, you must complete the spreadsheet provided on diskette. It will allow you to calculate 1998 revenues using the information above. Initially, assume that billed charges and per diem rates remain the same next year. To do "what if" analysis, attempt to use formulas when ever possible in constructing the spreadsheet.

Case 6-1 Questions

1. What is the average length of stay of all CHC patients?
2. What are billed charged per day? 1400 only commercial + self pay 1997-
3. What is the expected total revenue and revenue per discharge from Medicare?
4. What is the expected revenue from Medicaid? Suppose Medicaid decides to pay you on a cost per discharge basis. How does this affect the amount you will collect from Medicaid?
5. What are expected revenues from self-pay patients?
6. Will you make positive net income next year if you keep billed charges per day unchanged? If not, what should your billed charge per day be to earn a surplus (profit)? (Hint: Vary the charge per day in the spreadsheet until you break even. Break even is the charge that causes total revenues to equal total costs including the 15 percent additional return.)
7. How does the hospital shift uncompensated care costs to other payers. (Hint: what happens to net revenue from each payer as you change your price per day?) Which payers are most affected?
8. What if you can reduce your average length of stay by one day for your Medicare patients? How would this affect your net income under the new price obtained in question 6?
9. What would happen to net income if you could reduce your length of stay on HMO patients from 4 days to 3 days?
10. Assume that the state is implementing a capitated plan for its Medicaid-eligible population. Among Centerville's population, 9,000 are enrolled in Medicaid and receive health care from CHC. What would you need to receive per member per month for each of these enrollees to be paid the same amount that you are currently receiving in revenues on Medicaid patients? What PMPM rate would you bid to cover all Medicaid costs?

Case 6-2: To Participate or Not to Participate in Medicare

Dr. Jones, an orthopedic surgeon with her own practice in Omaha, Nebraska, plans to do a total hip replacement on a Medicare-eligible patient. She currently charges $2,175 for this procedure.

As a participating physician in Medicare, Dr. Jones must calculate what she can expect to be paid by Medicare under RVRVS. She has obtained the most recent data on cost weights, geographic adjusters, and conversion factors from the *Federal Register*, which are shown for this procedure in the table below. In 1998, there will be only one conversion factor for all procedures. In 1997, however, she will be paid under the surgical conversion factor.

CPT Code for Total Hip Replacement: 27130

RVUs:	Work	18.68
	Practice	23.91
	Malpractice	4.58
GPCs:	Work	.951
	Practice	.872
	Malpractice	.444
Conversion factor (surgical)		$40.9603

Participating physicians agree to accept the Medicare RBRVS rate as payment in full. This entitles her to direct payment for 80 percent of the allowed charge from Medicare and for 20 percent from the patient. As a participating provider, she cannot bill her patients for the balance not covered by Medicare.

Dr. Jones has the option of being a nonparticipating provider. In this case, she could bill her patients for up to 115 percent of the Medicare allowed charge. There are costs to doing this, however. First, she risks nonpayment of more than just the 20 percent copayment of her patients. Second, she incurs additional billing costs. Finally, if her patients take longer to pay her, she needs additional cash to cover her practice expenses. Additional cash could be acquired through a bank loan or from her personal funds. Banks would charge interest. Use of her own funds entails an opportunity cost since she loses the option of investing that amount in an interest-earning asset.

Case 6-2 Questions

1. What can Dr. Jones expect to be paid under RBRVS?
2. What would she be paid under RBRVS if this procedure were done in St. Louis where the geographic conversion factors for work, practice, and malpractice expense are .994, .944, and 1.207, respectively?
3. What will she be paid if the conversion factor is lowered to $39.122?
4. Should she remain a participating provider?

Case 6-3: Pricing a Medicare Risk Contract

Hometown Health Plan is a federally qualified HMO located in Dade County, Florida. HHP wishes to contract with Medicare to accept risk. Based on county demographics and the age and sex of the elderly who are expected to enroll, HHP estimates that its Medicare enrollees will be 45 percent male and 55 percent female. You have been asked to calculate the PMPM payment you can expect from Medicare and report back to the finance committee with your recommendations.

To simplify the analysis, we have assumed only two risk classes in the contract: one for males over age 65 and one for females over age 65. The base rates (AAPCC) and cost adjustment factors needed to calculate the average payment rate (APR) are shown below.

chances of using the services

Base Rate	Rate Class	Risk Factors
$390	Males > 65	1.82
$390	Females > 65	1.40

Medicare will pay you the lower of the APR, or the adjusted community rate (ACR). The ACR is based on commercial rates in the plan adjusted for the expected utilization differences of Medicare enrollees. Commercial rates at HHP and Medicare utilization factors are shown below.

ACR

	Initial Rate ($)	Utilization Factor	
Inpatient hospital	51.50	5.62	289.47
Skilled nursing	.50	47.22	23.61
Home health services	.75	27.10	20.3
Physician services	65.25	3.12	203.58
Ancillary services	14.00	2.67	37.38
Other services	3.00	4.75	14.25
Subtotal, medical expenses, PMPM	135.00		

confidential rate— 90.18 588.55

Administrative costs for the commercial plans average $25.00 PMPM and you expect them to be $92.50 PMPM for Medicare risk contracts. Also other reimbursement, such as copayments and coordination of benefits from other insurance coverage, reduces the capitation rate by $22.50 PMPM for commercial plans. In Medicare risk contracts, $52.00 PMPM will be recovered.

Case 6-3 Questions

1. What is the APR for this contract assuming the age/sex distribution of your Medicare enrollees is correct? (Hint: First you must adjust the base rate for cost

differences resulting from the two classes of beneficiaries. Then you must calculate a weighted average of these adjusted rates. The weights are the percent male and percent female enrollees.)

2. What is your commercial rate and annual premium revenue from commercial payers? [37.50×12 1650]

3. What is the ACR for this contract? (To find the ACR for the Medicare risk contract, first adjust the commercial rates for utilization differences of Medicare enrollees using the utilization factors. Then sum these adjusted PMPM rates to obtain the medical expense component of the ACR for your Medicare enrollees. Finally add the administrative expense and recoveries to get the final ACR rate.) What annual premium payments can you expect from Medicare if you are paid the ACR?

4. Will you receive the APR or the ACR if you enter this contract? Why?

5. Do you want to contract with Medicare for this contract? Explain.

References

Anders, G. (1996, October 3). A plan to cut back on Medicare expenses goes awry: Costs soar. *Wall Street Journal*.

Berman, J. B., Weekes, L. E., and Kukla, S. F. (1990). *The financial management of hospitals* (7th ed.). Ann Arbor, MI: Health Administration Press.

Brown, R. S., Clement, D. G., Hill, J. W., Retchin, S. M., & Bergeron, J. W. (1993). Do health maintenance organizations work for Medicare? *Health Care Financing Review, 15*(1), 7–23.

Carter, G. M., Jacobson, P. D., Kominski, G. F., & Perry, M. J. (1994). Use of diagnosis-related groups by non-Medicare payers. *Health Care Financing Review, 6*(2), 127–158.

Cleverley, W. O. (1992). *The essentials of health care finance* (3rd ed.). Gaithersburg, MD: Aspen.

Federal Register. (1996, August 30).

Federal Register. (1996, November 22).

Fetter, R. B., Shin, Y., Freeman, J. L., Averill, R. F., Thompson, J. D. (1980, February). Case mix definition by diagnosis-related groups. *Medical Care, 18* (supplement).

Health Care Financing Administration. www.hcfa.gove/medicaid/ome1996.htm. Medicaid Managed Care Page.

Hsaio, W. C., et al. (1988, September). *A national study of resource-based relative value scales for physicians services: Final report*. Cambridge, MA: Harvard School of Public Health.

Hsaio, W. C., et al. (1992). An overview of the development and refinement of the resource based relative value scale. *Medical Care, 30*(11) (supplement), NS1–NS12.

KPMG Peat Marwick LLP. (1995, February). *The prospective payment system and outpatient payment reform: A current analysis of key Medicare rules and regulations*.

McCormack, L. A., & Burge, R. T. (1994). Diffusion of Medicare RBRVS and related physician payment policies. *Health Care Financing Review, 6*(2), 159–174.

Mills, R., Fetter, R. B., Riedel, D. C., Averill, R. F. (1976). AUTOGRP: An interactive computer system for the analysis of health care data. *Medical Care, 14*.

Mitchell, J. B., Wedig, G., & Cromwell, J. (1989). The Medicare physician fee freeze. *Health Affairs, 8*(1), 21–33.

National Center for Health Statistics. (1996). *Health, United States, 1995.* Hyattsville, MD: Public Health Service.

Norton, S. A. (1995). Medicaid fees and Medicare fee schedule: An update. *Health Care Financing Review, 17*(1), 167–183.

Pauly, Mark V. Will Medicare reforms increase managed care enrollment? *Health Affairs, 15*(3), 182–191.

PPRC (Physician Payment Review Commission). (1990). *Annual report to Congress 1990.* Washington, DC: PPRC.

PPRC (Physician Payment Review Commission). (1994). *Annual report to Congress 1994.* Washington, DC: PPRC.

PPRC (Physician Payment Review Commission). (1995). *Annual report to Congress 1995.* Washington, DC: PPRC.

PPRC (Physician Payment Review Commission). (1996). *Annual report to Congress 1996.* Washington, DC: PPRC.

ProPAC (Prospective Payment Assessment Commission). (1993). *Report and recommendations to Congress.* Washington, DC: ProPAC.

Starr, P. (1982). *The social transformation of American medicine.* New York: Basic Books.

Zarabozo, C., & LeMasurier, J. D. (1995). Medicare and managed care. In P. R. Kongstvedt (Ed.), *Essentials of managed health care* (pp. 209–233). Gaithersburg, MD: Aspen.

Chapter 7

Understanding Financial Performance

Data contained in the financial statements of health care providers reveal a great deal about their performance. This chapter explains the information contained in the financial statements of typical health care organizations. It identifies significant differences in financial statements among health care providers, insurers, and managed care plans; explains financial ratios derived from the financial statements; presents pertinent data available on operating performance; and describes the relationship between operating and financial performance.

Learning Objectives

Upon successful completion of this chapter, the learner will:

- Identify primary users and uses of financial information.
- State the key differences between cash and accrual accounting.
- Interpret the informational content of the balance sheet, the income statement, and the statement of cash flows of health providers.
- Construct composition ratios and key financial ratios from financial statements.
- Assess the financial performance of different types of health care organizations using horizontal and vertical analysis.
- Describe important relationships between operating and financial performance indicators.
- Link financial and clinical information to improve health care delivery and outcomes management.
- Recognize and account for limitations in financial statement data.

Key Terms

accelerated depreciation

accounts payable

accrual accounting

accrued expenses

accumulated depreciation

activity ratios

amortization

average age of plant

average collection period (ACP)

average payment period (APP)

balance sheet

bond covenants

book value

capital budgeting

capital structure

capitalization, or capital structure ratios

cash accounting

cash flow to total debt

common stocks

comparative analysis

composition ratio analysis

consolidated balance sheet

contingency reserve

contractual allowances

coordination of benefits

cost of goods sold

current assets

current liabilities

current portion of long-term debt

current ratio

days' cash on hand

debt service coverage ratio

deferred tax liability

depreciation expense

dividends

downgrade

DuPont analysis

efficiency

equity financing ratio

equity multiplier

excess revenue over expenses

financial leverage

fund accounting

general fund

goodwill

gross revenues

horizontal analysis

income statement

initial public offering

intangible assets

just in time

liquidity

liquidity ratios

long-term assets

long-term debt-to-equity ratio

modified cash basis of accounting

net assets

net income

net income margin

net operating income

net patient revenues

net working capital

net worth

nonoperating gains and losses

operating margin

paid-in capital

preferred stocks

prepaid expense

provision for bad debt	risk management
quick ratio	statement of cash flows
reinsurance recoveries	tangible assets
restricted funds	trend analysis
retained earnings	turnover ratios
return on equity (ROE)	vertical analysis

Introduction

Managed care requires an understanding of the relationships between financial results and clinical performance. Clinicians interpret the signs and symptoms of patient health status from data such as weight, height, age, blood pressure, temperature, blood chemistry, and results from computerized tomography scans. These are compared with clinical norms and the patient's health status on the last visit. If health problems are detected, the physician implements a plan to treat the patient. Like doctors, health care managers can examine their organizations for signs and symptoms of poor or favorable financial condition and take action to improve performance. Data from the financial statements provide owners and the community with the information they need to evaluate how well managers are doing in maintaining the financial health of the organizations with which they are entrusted.

Financial Statements

Among the users of the financial statements of health care organizations are:

- Stockholders, donors, and sponsoring communities
- Creditors and bond rating agencies
- Government taxing authorities
- Third-party payers
- Accrediting organizations
- Network contractors and subcontractors, and suppliers
- Managers and competitors

Financial statements are representations, in monetary terms, of the activity, obligations, and cash flows of an organization. Like the instrument panel in an airplane, financial statements reveal the position of an organization and can be used to guide and operate it to achieve overall mission and goals.

There are as many uses as there are users of these data. Managers of health care organizations must report information about financial performance to corporate or sponsoring boards to assure owners that managers are doing their jobs well. Federal, state, and local governments require an accounting of the organization's financial performance for purposes of tax assessment and maintenance of tax-exempt status if applicable. Through reported financial statements, health care organizations demonstrate compliance with contractual financial obligations to creditors such as banks, bondholders, and bond trustees, as well as their ability to meet payment commitments. Bond rating agencies base their assessment of the financial viability of an organization in part on the financial performance and condition found in the financial statements. Third-party payers require financial information to verify provider claims for reimbursement. Partners in joint ventures, members of provider networks, and managed care plans use financial statements to ascertain their partners' financial capacity to deliver promised services. Regulators, licensing agents, and accrediting organizations need financial information to assess compliance with financial regulations.

Generally accepted accounting principles (**GAAP**) have been established by the Financial Accounting Standards Board (**FASB**), so that data reported in financial statements are consistent, representative, and material (that is, important). In order to assure users that these statements conform with GAAP, organizations submit their financial statements to outside accounting firms for auditing.

Types of Financial Statements

Three financial statements are maintained and reported by health care organizations:

1. The **balance sheet,** which presents the dollar value of assets the organization has acquired and where it obtained the money to pay for them. If assets are worth less than liabilities, the organization may fail.

2. The **income statement,** which indicates what the organization earned and how much was spent in giving care over an interval of time, usually one year. The organization performs well if the money it received or expects to receive for services is greater than what they cost to provide.

3. The **statement of cash flows,** which reveals how much cash the organization has at the beginning and at the end of a reporting period and how it achieved those balances. To continue to operate, the organization needs to produce a positive amount of cash.

Financial Statements of Not-for-Profit Organizations

The primary difference between the financial statements of for-profit and not-for-profit organizations is that for-profit organizations pay income taxes and not-for-profit organizations are exempt from income taxes. Also, not-for-profit organizations account for the use of donated funds. Otherwise, the concepts and components of the financial statements are basically the same for both types of organization. Moreover, with the growth of managed care, the proportion of not-for-profit entities in health care is diminishing. Table 7-1 shows the percentage in each health industry group that is operating as a for-profit, not-for-profit, or government-run institution ("government" encompasses federal,

Table 7-1   Health Care Organizations by Ownership Status

	For Profit	*Not for Profit*	*Government*
Hospitals[a]	13.7%	56.3%	30.0%
Home health agencies[b]	43.8	36.8	19.5
Nursing homes[c]	71.4	23.7	4.9
Pure HMOs[d]	72.8	27.2	N.A.
Open-ended HMOs[d]	76.6	23.4	N.A.
Specialty PPOs[e]	85.2	14.8	N.A.
Specialty HMOs[e]	87.0	13.0	N.A.
Physician practices[f]	100.0		

[a]*Universal Healthcare Almanac* (1997). For 5,493 hospitals in 1996.

[b]*Statistical Abstract of the United States 1996*. For 9,800 agencies in 1994.

[c]*Statistical Abstract of the United States 1996*. For 14,744 nursing and related care facilities in 1991.

[d]*1997 Health Care Almanac and Yearbook*. For 628 pure HMOs and 291 open-ended HMOs in 1996.

[e]*Interstudy* (1996). For 149 specialty PPOs and 106 specialty HMOs in 1995.

[f]Applies primarily to solo practices. Approximately 7.32 percent of group practices are not-for-profits based on Medical Group Management Association member characteristics (MGMA Cost Survey, 1995).

state, and county institutions). In this chapter, the financial statements will be viewed initially from the perspective of the for-profit, or proprietary, firm. Effects of not-for-profit status on the presentation of the data will be discussed as needed.

Accrual Versus Cash Accounting

One of the most important conventions used in preparing financial statements for publicly accountable organizations is **accrual accounting,** which documents the activity of the organization, measured in dollars, at the time that services are performed. On the income statement, patient revenues are matched to related patient expenses. If 40 patients are seen by a physician in a day, the revenues expected from those patients and the expenses associated with their care are reported on that day, regardless of when the patient actually pays the bill or when physician reimburses the staff and suppliers.

In contrast, **cash accounting** reports activity only when cash is received (called *receipts*) and paid (called *disbursements*), regardless of when the related services were actually performed. For example, third-party payers might pay 30 to 60 days after care is provided, while workers and suppliers must be paid within 15 to 45 days of the date when services or supplies are delivered. Profits under a cash basis would fluctuate with differences in the receipt and payment of cash and could be very volatile if receipts and disbursements could not be synchronized. On the other hand, if patients paid at the time of treatment and physicians, nurses, technicians, and suppliers were paid on a daily basis, then accrual and cash accounting would report similar levels of activity and profitability over a given interval of time.

A Case in Point: Cash versus Accrual Basis of Accounting. Dr. Lopez is a family practitioner who has recently opened his practice. In July he saw 15 patients a day and charges $50 per patient visit. Total billed revenues for July were $15,000. Currently all his patients are insured by Medicare or commercial insurers. Third-party payers typically pay two months after care is delivered, so his actual receipts in July are zero. Dr. Lopez pays his nursing staff $1,500 twice a month. The rest of his expenses—rent, utilities, supplies, insurance, bookkeeping—are paid monthly. His total disbursements for July were $6,000, so on a cash basis, Dr. Lopez lost money in July.

Income Statement, Cash Basis, for the Month Ending July 31

Receipts	Disbursements
$ 0	$3,000 (staff salary and benefits)
	6,000 (other practice expenses)
$ 0	$9,000
Net income for July:	**–$9,000**

Contrast these results with those under an accrual basis of accounting. The charges billed for services provided in July—$15,000—are shown as revenues even though Dr. Lopez has yet to be paid. Now he has a $6,000 profit.

Income Statement, Accrual Basis, for the Month Ending July 31

Revenues	Expenses
$ 15,000	$3,000 (staff salary and benefits)
	6,000 (other practice expenses)
$ 15,000	$9,000
Net income for July	**$6,000**

Now assume that all of Dr. Lopez's patients paid at the time of service. Revenues in July would be the same as receipts. The income statement for July when everyone pays in cash is identical on a cash or an accrual basis.

Delay in payment is not the only problem that occurs when using a cash basis of accounting. Suppose a physician pays six months of rent in advance. On a cash basis, the entire amount would be shown as an expense in the first month, depressing actual profits earned in that month. On the other hand, the physician would find his practice to be more profitable than it actually was during the next five months of "free" rent. These profit fluctuations are merely an illusion resulting from cash accounting. On an accrual basis of accounting, only 1/6th of the amount would be an expense in the current month. The rest would remain on the balance sheet as a **prepaid expense.** Like a coupon book for ten free soft drinks, prepaid expenses under accrual accounting are reduced by the amount consumed (expensed) each month until they are totally used up.

A Case in Point. Prepaid expenses also affect Dr. Lopez's practice. He made insurance payments of $4,200 in advance to cover him for the next six months. In July he made such a payment. This depresses earnings in July. Suppose his patients still pay cash at the time of service.

Income Statement, Cash Basis, for the Month Ending July 31

Receipts	Disbursements
$ 15,000	$ 3,000 (staff salary and benefits)
	4,200 (insurance)
	6,000 (other practice expenses)
$ 15,000	$13,200

Net income for July: $ 1,800

Moreover, for the next five months, he would show lower practice expenses because insurance payments would not produce a cash disbursement. On an accrual basis, only $700 would be expensed in July and in the next five months. This stabilizes earnings and better reflects the actual activity in his practice.

Income Statement, Accrual Basis, for the Month Ending July 31

Revenues	Expenses
$ 15,000	$3,000 (staff salary and benefits)
	700 (insurance)
	6,000 (other practice expenses)
$ 15,000	$9,700

Net income for July: $5,300

Some health care firms, especially physician practices, use a **modified cash basis of accounting** (Doelling, 1996). Under this system, a cash basis is used, but certain non-cash expenses, like deferred taxes and depreciation, are also reported. Noncash expenses will be discussed in more detail later in this chapter.

The Balance Sheet

The balance sheet—or the statement of financial condition—is a financial snapshot of the organization taken at a moment in time. It shows what the health care organization owns—its *assets*—and its obligations to creditors and owners—its *liabilities* and equity—as of a certain date. Table 7-2 is a condensed balance sheet for a typical health care organization. Table 7-3 illustrates a condensed balance sheet for a health plan. A condensed balance sheet summarizes the typical items reported on the balance sheet.

Table 7-2   Hometown Health Provider
Condensed Balance Sheet (in thousands) as of June 30, 199X

Assets		Liabilities and Equity	
Current assets		**Current liabilities**	
Cash and marketable securities	$ 2,497	Accounts payable	$ 1,920
Accounts receivable (net)	9,748	Accrued expenses	4,522
Inventories	515	Notes payable	133
Prepaid expenses and other current assets	2,023	Current portion of long term debt	719
Total current assets	14,546	Total current liabilities	7,294
Other assets		**Long-term liabilities**	
Other assets	$ 2,436	Long term debt and leases	$16,605
Equipment, buildings and land (net)	23,080	Deferred income taxes	1,310
Long term investments	14,518	Common stocks outstanding	1,191
Intangible assets (net)	2,800	Paid in capital	4,900
	42,834	Retained earnings	26,080
Total assets	$57,380	Total stockholder's equity	32,171
		Total liabilities and stockholder's equity	$57,380

Table 7-3   Hometown Health Plan
Condensed Balance Sheet (in thousands) as of June 30, 199X

Assets		Liabilities and Equity	
Current assets		**Current liabilities**	
Cash and marketable securities	$ 93,001	Accounts payable	$112,340
Short term investments	85,381	Accrued claims (IBNR)	45,222
Premiums receivable	55,030	Other current liabilities	33,536
Total current assets	233,412	Total current liabilities	191,098
Other assets		**Long-term liabilities**	
Equipment, buildings and land (net)	$16,720	Long term debt and leases	$3,870
Long term investments	118,905	Total stockholder's equity	254,569
Intangible assets (net)	80,500	Total liabilities and stockholder's equity	$449,537
Total assets	$449,537		

Assets

Assets, shown on the left side of the balance sheet, represent the dollar value of resources available to the organization as of a certain date to provide services and generate a return. One of the financial manager's major tasks is to invest in assets that return more cash to the organization than is used in delivering patient care. This investment decision is called **capital budgeting** (see Chapter 9).

Asset Characteristics

Assets are **tangible** or **intangible,** and tangible assets may be real (e.g., office supplies, sterile gauze pads, examining tables, CT scanners, computers, hospital rooms, and physician's office buildings) or financial (e.g., cash, marketable securities, checking accounts, bank certificates of deposit, money market funds, accounts receivable, shares of stock, and government Treasury securities).

Intangible assets include name recognition, expected patient referrals, unexpired patents, or the quality of well-trained and experienced employees who add value to the organization but are not easy to quantify or document. For example, if Hometown Hospital is purchased by National Hospitals, a major health care system, for more than the

A Case in Point. Suppose Hometown Hospital has assets of $400 million and owes $300 million to the bank. As a result, net assets, or owner's equity, is $100 million. Suppose Hometown is purchased by National Hospital, a system with $600 million in assets, $100 million in liabilities, and $500 million in owner's equity. National pays $400 million for Hometown by obtaining additional funds from investors. The appraised value of Hometown's assets is $300 million.

After the purchase, the merged hospital system has $1,100 million in assets. Since National has paid $100 million more than Hometown's appraised value, the difference is shown as goodwill, an intangible asset, on the balance sheet. Owner's equity is increased by $100 million. (The numbers that follow are in millions of dollars.)

	Hometown Hospital	*National Hospital Before Purchase*	*National Hospital After Purchase*
Assets	$400	$600	$1,000
Goodwill	–––	–––	$ 100
Total assets	$400	$600	$1,100
Liabilities	$300	$100	$ 400
Equity (net assets)	100	500	$ 700
Net assets	$400	$600	$1,100

appraised value of its assets, then an intangible asset called **goodwill** is created. An equal amount of new equity is added to equity on the right side of the balance sheet.

Assets shown in Table 7-2 are representative of most nonmanufacturing organizations. Differences occur because of organizational mission and goals. A grocery store, for example, invests cash in inventories of canned goods and frozen foods and long-lived assets such as freezers and cash registers. If credit is given to customers, the grocer also invests in accounts receivable, which are nothing more than short-term, interest-free loans. A hospital or physician practice stocks inventories of syringes and medicines, catheters and bandages. Health providers invest in accounts receivable when payment is not collected at the time of service. Hospital long-lived assets are operating tables, nursing stations, and emergency rooms. In nursing homes, they are wheelchairs and patient beds. Physicians typically don't own their own buildings or offices unless they are in a large group practice. They nonetheless may invest in long-lived diagnostic and treatment equipment, examining tables, and other furniture and fixtures.

The financial statements of managed care plans and insurance companies differ somewhat from those of other organizations (see Table 7-3). The service that health insurers sell is financial security. To provide this security, health plans invest in assets that generate cash just in time and in sufficient amounts to pay providers for the health care claims of their members. Thus, managed care plan assets consist of real and financial investments like cash and money market funds, accounts (premiums) receivable, payments due from other insurance companies, stocks and bonds, and real estate. Principal and income from these investments generate cash to indemnify subscribers. As a financial services institution, an insurance company typically has no inventories.

A **consolidated balance sheet** reflects the aggregation of the balance sheets of all entities in an organization. In an integrated delivery system (**IDS**), for example, assets owned by all system members are shown on the left side, and their liabilities to owners and external creditors presented on the right. Interorganizational liabilities and assets are canceled out. A staff model HMO is a hybrid organization; it is both an insurance company and a provider of health services. The consolidated balance sheet would contain the assets (and liabilities) of its hospitals, ambulatory clinics, and other health care facilities, as well as financial investments made to support its insurance function.

Asset Liquidity

Assets can be characterized by their **liquidity**—how easily and quickly they can be turned into cash. If all assets of the organization had to be put up for sale today, the least liquid would be the most difficult to sell and the most likely to suffer a loss in value. Organizations using highly liquid assets are much less vulnerable to losses and financial distress when consumer demand is variable and uncertain. Hospitals and nursing homes have highly illiquid assets; physician practices and home health agencies use assets that are more easily disposed of or sold.

The loss in dollar value of the assets that would be realized if they had to be sold immediately reflects the asset's illiquidity. There is a direct relationship between the cost of an immediate conversion of an asset to cash and the liquidity of an asset. Cash and short-term securities, like government Treasury bills, are the most liquid of assets.

A Case in Point. If a hospital makes a loan from available cash to its home health agency to buy office equipment, the loan is an asset to the hospital, and the equipment is an asset to the home health agency. Here is the balance sheet entry from the consolidation of two entities within a single organization.

Home Health (HH) Agency		Hospital	
Assets	Liabilities and equity	Assets	Liabilities and equity
Equipment	Loan from hospital	Loan to HH	Equity
$5,000	$5,000	$5,000	$5,000

Consolidated Entry	
Assets	Liabilities and equity
Equipment	Hospital equity
$5,000	$5,000

In the consolidated balance sheet, including both the loan and the equipment as assets amounts to counting the same asset twice. Therefore, the internal loan would be eliminated. Only the equipment would be shown on the consolidated balance sheet, with corresponding external funding sources shown as the balancing liability.

Cash has no liquidity risk. Short-term government securities have little risk of a loss in value if they have to be sold quickly. Accounts receivable are less liquid. They can be sold quickly for cash to a collection agency, but at a discount. Although inventories can sometimes be returned to a supplier for cash or sold to other providers, these sales or returns are done at a discount as well. Patient beds, hospitals, and nursing homes are even more difficult to sell quickly without suffering a considerable reduction in cash value, and thus they are highly illiquid.

Assets are organized from top to bottom on the balance sheet from the most liquid to least liquid. **Current assets,** also called working capital, are shown at the top of the balance sheet. Under normal conditions, current assets are expected to be fully converted to cash in a year or less. These short-term assets—cash and marketable securities, accounts receivable, and inventories—are used to pay workers, stock supplies, and provide credit to maintain daily operations. **Long-term assets** take more than a year to be "used up" and returned as cash to owners. These long-lived, or capital, assets are shown below current assets on the balance sheet. Capital assets—primarily made up of facilities, equipment, real estate, and long-term financial investments—are used in conjunction with working capital to provide health-related services.

Insurance companies and HMOs are regulated by the state departments of insurance. Organizations accepting insurance risk are often required by state law to create and fund an asset called a *statutory reserve* that is dedicated to covering unexpected future subscriber claims.

Liabilities and Owner's Equity

Part of the financial success of the health care organization depends on how its asset investments are financed. The financial manager must find the least cost-method of acquiring funds to purchase assets that the organization needs. Liabilities and owner's equity—the right side of the balance sheet—reveal the sources of funds to purchase the assets shown on the left side. The mix of debt and equity used in financing assets is called the **capital structure** of the organization.

Liabilities

Like assets, outstanding liabilities are presented on the balance sheet according to how soon they must be paid for in cash. **Current liabilities** refer to all obligations that must be met within a year or less. **Accounts payable** are typically bills that the provider owes to medical care and office supply companies. Delaying payment to suppliers frees up cash, but at a cost. Suppliers often provide a discount if payment is made within a certain number of days. Failure to pay promptly results in the loss of the discount. Notes payable are payments due to banks and other creditors on short-term loans. Also included in current liabilities are **accrued expenses,** such as wages owed to workers who are paid on other than a daily basis. Between paychecks, workers provide services "for free," which allows the organization to use the cash released during this period for other purposes. These outstanding obligations to workers must be fulfilled for the health provider to remain in operation. The **current portion of long-term debt** is the amount of principal owed during the year on outstanding long-term loans and bonds.

In a managed care plan, short-term liabilities consist largely of claims to providers of care. Claims encompass those that have already been billed and reported to the plan and those that have been incurred by enrollees but not yet reported (**IBNR claims**) by the plan. Thus, IBNR claims are accruals, like payroll.

Recall that short-term assets are called working capital. The dollar difference between current assets and current liabilities is called **net working capital.** This difference reveals the dollar amount of short-term assets that is not financed by short-term liabilities. By definition, net working capital must be financed with long-term debt or equity.

Long-term liabilities are expected to remain outstanding for more than one year. They include long-term bonds, mortgages, and long-term lease contracts. Long-term contractual obligations are more difficult and costly to nullify or cancel. Also, they place restrictions on manager autonomy in the use of funds. Moreover, lenders may place limitations on the manager's ability to obtain additional debt financing. Both short-term and long-term debt obligations must be fulfilled before the claims of equity owners or community stakeholders can be met.

Owner's Equity

The difference between available assets and outstanding liabilities represents the net worth or owner's equity, defined as how much of what is owned belongs to the sponsoring organization, the community, or the shareholders after all outstanding debts have been paid. Because the balance sheet must always balance, owner's equity makes up the difference between total assets and total liabilities:

$$\text{Total assets } (TA) = \text{Total liabilities } (TL) + \text{Equity } (E).$$

If the dollar value of what an organization owns is more than it owes to creditors, then TA is more than TL, and owner's equity (E) will be positive. If the assets owned are worth less than debts owed, then TA is less than TL and E is negative. Unless the organization is subsidized by an outside entity or its debt obligations guaranteed or assumed by another entity, negative net worth means that the firm is bankrupt.

In for-profit organizations, components of owner's equity include additional paid-in capital, outstanding shares of stock, and retained earnings. **Paid-in capital** is the cash used to start up the company. As an organization's opportunities expand and internally generated funds become inadequate to support growth, additional capital will be sought. The firm may "go public." It does so by issuing new shares of stock to outside investors in an **initial public offering (IPO).** After the sale, stocks are traded among investors in secondary markets, resale markets where owners of securities can sell or exchange them. These resale markets are called *stock exchanges*, the best known of which is the New York Stock Exchange. As additional equity is needed, companies return to the markets to sell additional shares to investors.

Stocks are classified as either common or preferred. **Common stocks** have no stated dividends; **preferred stocks** pay regular, fixed dividends to stockholders. Preferred stockholders are paid dividends before common stockholders. In this respect, preferred stocks are more akin to debt than equity. With debt, the organization is obligated to pay fixed interest payments to lenders. Owner's equity is considered a long-term obligation to shareholders of the organization. Shares of a company's stock may be traded indefinitely in secondary markets.

In not-for-profit organizations, owner's equity consists of donations made by sponsoring communities, subsequent restricted and nonrestricted gifts, government and private grants, and retained earnings. Because not-for-profit organizations must account to donors and granting agencies, they use a reporting system called **fund accounting,** developed for government entities to account for the use of public funds. Under this system, gifts given for a specific purpose are placed in **restricted funds** and their use accounted for separately. Restricted funds are like individual balance sheets for each major donor. Unrestricted gifts are placed in the **general fund**. Thus, the general fund is like the balance sheet of the for-profit organization. Because financial performance and condition are more difficult to interpret from financial statements constructed using fund accounting, not-for-profit providers now report a consolidated balance sheet with all funds, restricted and unrestricted, shown on one statement.

Retained earnings, restricted gifts, and unrestricted gifts make up owner's equity, or **net assets,** of the not-for-profit organization. (Note that the term *net assets* is a change from the previous designation for equity in not-for-profit organizations. Before 1996, net assets were referred to as *fund balances*.)

The Income Statement

In contrast to the balance sheet, which shows the composition of assets and liabilities at a point in time, the income statement shows how owner's equity changes over time. Imagine a city's water tank. The balance sheet reports the level of water in the tank on a certain date. The water in the tank represents the city's equity at a point in time. The income statement indicates how much water has been used by the community (shown as an expense) and how much has been replaced (shown as revenue) since the last reported date.

Table 7-4 illustrates two income statements: one for the typical health care provider and one for a managed care organization, an HMO.

Total Revenues

Over time an organization's revenues replenish assets or reduce debt on the balance sheet. Prior to 1990, hospitals and other institutional providers reported **gross revenues,** which are billed charges, along with **net patient revenues,** which are what the provider expected to be paid. Hospitals and other health care providers rarely receive what they bill the patient. Reimbursement from third-party payers is likely to be based on a contractual amount, such as discounted charges, costs, or diagnosis-related groups. These price discounts, or **contractual allowances,** today make up a growing percentage of billed charges, so gross revenues are an increasingly inaccurate measure of revenues expected. In addition, many hospitals, clinics, and physicians provide uncompensated or charity care, and have uncollected bills, or bad debts. Before 1990, contractual allowances and deductions for bad debts and charity care were deducted from gross revenues to obtain net patient revenues. Since 1990, only net patient revenues are reported on the income statements of institutional health care providers. Contractual allowances with Medicare, Medicaid, and other payers and the value of charity care are now reported in footnotes to the financial statements. As in the financial statements of other organizations, bad debt is included as an operating expense rather than a deduction from revenue.

Operating revenues of other health-related organizations vary by the type of good or service provided. For example, the revenues of a physician or physician group practice are shown as professional fees collected from various third-party payers and patients. A pharmaceutical company reports revenues from sales of medicines to health providers and consumers.

Other operating revenues arise from nonpatient care activities like the gift shop, parking, cafeteria, and income on investments related to operation, such as malpractice trust funds, pension plans, and interest on funds held to repay outstanding bonds. Other revenues can come from research grants, educational programs, and donations.

As Table 7-4 shows, the operating revenue streams of a managed care organization or insurance company are very different from health care providers. They include subscriber premiums, coordination of benefits, and reinsurance recoveries (not shown).

Table 7-4   Statement of Revenues and Expenses (in millions of dollars)

Hometown Health Provider (for the year ending June 30, 199X)		Hometown HMO (for the year ending June 30, 199X)	
Operating revenues		**Operating revenues**	
Net patient revenue	47,500	Subscriber premiums	5,960
Other operating revenues	1,725	Coordination of benefits	39
Total revenues	49,225	Total revenues	5,999
Operating expenses		**Operating expenses**	
Wages and salaries	28,240	Capitation and professional fees	3,290
Fringe benefits	5,700	Hospital and out-of-area expense	853
Professional fees	350	(including IBNR expense)	
Supplies	749	Reinsurance premiums	78
Rent and lease payments	877	Plan administration costs	1,230
Interest expense	1,590	(wages, benefits, supplies, rent,	
Provision for bad debt	1,334	leases and interest)	
Depreciation and amortization	3,257	Depreciation and amortization	94
Total operating expense	42,097	Total operating expense	5,545
Operating income (rev. less exp.)	**7,128**	**Operating income**	**454**
Nonoperating gains (losses)	450	Nonoperating gains (losses)	NA
Net income (excess rev. over exp.)	**7,578**	**Net income**	**454**
Provision for income taxes	2,198	Income taxes	172
Net income after taxes	**5,380**	**Net income after taxes**	**282**

Coordination of benefits pertains to obtaining legitimate payment from other insurers, such as for worker's compensation, no-fault insurance, and spousal coverage, for the health care claims of plan enrollees. **Reinsurance recoveries** are payments to the health plan from its own insurer, which has accepted the medical expense risk of unpredictable high-cost enrollees in the plan. Finally, an HMO might also collect copayments as another source of revenue for the plan.

Nonoperating gains (losses) are revenues (losses) net of expenses resulting from activities or investments considered not directly related to the principal activity of the organization. For health care providers and insurers, these typically include income from investments in securities, real estate, and joint ventures with other organizations. The classification of some sources of revenue as a nonoperating activity is somewhat at the discretion of the health care organization. In one organization, for example, parking lot earnings might be classified as a nonoperating gain rather than other operating revenue, while another might include these earnings as part of operating revenues. Together, total operating revenues and nonoperating gains make up the total revenues of the organization.

Expenses

Operating expenses are costs incurred in providing health-related services. Expenses drain assets from or create liabilities on the balance sheet. Operating expenses include employee wages, salaries, and benefits; professional fees and other forms of payment to physicians and other providers who are not employed by the organization; supply costs; and rent and lease payments. Interest expense is paid on outstanding loans and other debts of the organization.

Some operating expenses involve no cash payments. These noncash expenses include depreciation, amortization, and provision for doubtful accounts, also called *bad debt expense*. **Depreciation expense** is the charge for average wear and tear on long-lived, owned real assets. **Amortization** expense is a reduction over time in the value of a financial or intangible asset on the balance sheet. For example, the total value of goodwill is amortized, or divided up, over a number of future periods. Remember that goodwill is the increase in the value of the organization's assets when one organization acquires another for more than its book value. Each period, a portion of goodwill is reduced on the balance sheet and shown as amortization expense on the income statement. In general, depreciation, amortization, and other noncash expenses are tax deductible in for-profit entities. Amortization of goodwill is not (Seitz, 1990).

The **provision for bad debt** is the estimated loss of revenue from uncollectable accounts. Bad debts arise when patients who are fully expected to pay and are billed for services fail to do so. Experience with patients in different payer groups can be used to estimate what percentage of the bills are likely to be uncollectable. This estimate is shown as bad debt expense.

Except for staff model HMOs, managed care organizations provide no direct patient services. Therefore, their expenses differ from a provider's income statement. In addition to plan administration costs, their expenses include capitation payments, reimbursement of professional fees of providers contracting with the health plan, reimbursement of out-of-plan services, and reinsurance premiums. Like the provision for bad debts, a portion of plan expenses must be estimated. The estimated IBNR claims that have been incurred in the current accounting period are included as a noncash portion of physician, hospital, and out-of-area medical care expenses. These estimated expenses are added to outstanding liabilities on the balance sheet.

Net Operating Income and Net Income

Net operating income, the excess of operating revenues over operating expenses, is important for stakeholders and other users of financial information because it shows how well the organization is performing in its principal activities. If income from operations is weak or negative, major concerns arise about its long-run organizational viability and ability to return cash to owners and sponsoring organizations. **Net income** is the "bottom line" of the organization; it shows how much income results after adding nonoperating gains to operating income. In not-for-profit organizations, net income is called **excess revenues over expenses.** Health care organizations that persistently rely on nonoperating gains to break even or to make a profit must find ways to improve operating performance.

Effects of the Income Statement on the Balance Sheet

The balance sheet and income statement are directly linked to one another. Entries on the income statement during a reporting period alter entries on the balance sheet at the end of the current reporting period. Three relationships—distribution of net income, depreciation of assets, and estimation of uncertain liabilities—are important.

Distribution of Net Income

Net income after taxes is added to retained earnings where it may be paid to investors or used as a source of funds for future investments that support the mission of the organization.

Dividends

Dollars of net income returned to investors in for-profit, or proprietary, organizations are called **dividends.** In for-profit corporations, net income paid out as dividends is taxed twice: first as corporate income and then as part of individual investor income. In physician practices, net income can be distributed to participating physicians under a compensation formula so that no net income remains for reinvestment after distribution. If the practice is a partnership or a special type of corporation (an S corporation), it avoids corporate income taxes altogether. Physicians pay taxes on net income only after it has been distributed as personal income to the partners.

Not-for-profits are exempt from taxes by federal, state and local governments. (Although not-for-profit organizations are exempt from federal income taxes, they may be subject to state or local taxes. In some states, provider taxes are levied on the gross revenues of health care organizations (Solomon, 1992). Not-for-profit health care organizations are granted an exemption from income taxes because they operate as charitible or educational institutions. Hospital systems often establish foundations to funnel net income into philanthropic activities or return profits to the sponsoring organization for the purpose of providing charitable benefits elsewhere when opportunities do not exist in their local communities.

The dollars used in providing charity care and community benefits are implicit dividends paid by a not-for-profit entity. They are implicit because charity care and community benefits are shown as part of ongoing operating expenses, not as a deduction from net income that otherwise would have been earned. Health care organizations typically report the value of charity and uncompensated care in footnotes to the financial statements. A word of caution is needed here: uncompensated care should not be reported on the basis of billed charges. Billed charges overstate the amount of income distributed for charity care. Average costs of uncompensated care more closely approximate the dollar value of these implicit dividends to the community.

Retained Earnings

Income that is not paid out as charity care and community benefits, taxes, or shareholder dividends is retained by the organization. Net income that is kept in the organization is called **retained earnings.** Retained earnings become part of the equity base of the organization and help finance the replacement and expansion of the assets. Lenders and donors are more likely to provide funding when the health care organization has sufficient equity to ensure that it can fulfill its commitments. Retained earnings are an especially important source of funds to not-for-profit organizations that have no access to equity financing.

The decision to pay dividends—the organization's dividend policy—and not retain earnings may affect investor valuation of the organization. On one hand, dividend payments may be a signal from managers to market investors that the organization ha good prospects for future earnings growth, which will enhance stock prices. Also, dividends provide a more rapid return of cash which investors may desire. On the other hand, a payment of dividends may indicate the lack of profitable investment opportunities. Also dividends are subject to personal income taxes which investors may wish to avoid, especially if they are in higher income tax brackets. In this case, the payment of dividends will not be valued by market investors.

Depreciation and the Value of Assets

The amount of assets shown on the books is directly affected by the amount of non-cash expenses reported on the income statement each period. By accounting convention, the dollar value of long-lived assets like buildings and equipment is the price paid when assets were purchased, adjusted for their use. This adjusted, or net, price is called the **book value** of an asset and the accounting adjustment to the purchase price is called depreciation. **Accumulated depreciation** (depreciation added up over the years of ownership and use) is subtracted from the original price and the net amount reported on the balance sheet as the asset's book value.

Accounting depreciation is not necessarily the same as economic depreciation. The book value of an asset may not equal its market value. *Market value* is what the assets could be sold for today. *Book value* would equal the asset's market value if the original price of a long-lived asset were adjusted each year for its actual use and for changes in expected ability of the asset to generate future benefits for its owners. Future benefits of owning an automobile include, for example, the transportation services it provides and the "intangible value" or desirability of the car. Economic depreciation takes both of these factors into account.

Since depreciation is considered an expense, which is tax deductible to a tax-paying organization, government places restrictions on how much of an asset's purchase price can be depreciated and counted as an expense each year. The proportion of the cost of other investments, such as research and development costs, that can be expensed each period is also restricted. Thus, methods of depreciation and amortization are largely dictated by tax law, not economic depletion of the asset's value. Third-

A Case in Point. You plan to purchase a used automobile to get you through the last two years of school. You have found an eight-year-old car that, when new, cost $20,000. The owner tells you that, according to the manufacturer, the car has an expected life of 10 years of normal driving, assumed to be about 15,000 miles per year. Also, the car will have to be junked at the end of its life, so it has no salvage value.

You can use the straight line method of depreciation, which assumes that an asset is used up at a constant rate each year, to get an estimate of the amount the car has depreciated. To determine this, first figure out how much the car depreciates each year, or its *annual depreciation rate*. Divide the purchase price by expected life less expected salvage value. Since salvage value is zero, annual depreciation is 20,000/10 = $2,000 per year. Next, multiply by the age of the vehicle to get accumulated depreciation of $16,000 (8 × $2000 = $16,000). Finally, subtract accumulated depreciation from the purchase price to get its current book value of $4,000. Summarizing,

Car's book value (new)	$20,000
Accumulated depreciation ($2,000 per year)	16,000
Current book value (after eight years)	$ 4,000

party payers that reimburse health care providers on the basis of costs also restrict allowable depreciation methods.

In addition to straight line depreciation, which assumes that an asset will be used at a constant rate over its life, several other methods are allowed for tax purposes. These methods employ some form of **accelerated depreciation** that gives the investing organization a higher tax deduction by increasing the percentage of an asset's cost that can be expensed early in its life. The Tax Reform Act of 1986 required that firms use the modified accelerated cost recovery system (**MACRS**) to depreciate assets acquired after 1986. Under MACRS, the useful life of an asset must first be determined. Based on its useful life class, a specific depreciation schedule is applied.

Under MACRS, the asset is assumed to be acquired in the middle of the first year and used through the middle of the year following the last year of its useful life. Thus an asset with a three-year life will show depreciation expense for four years; one with a 7-year life will show it for eight years. As shown in Table 7-5 more than half the cost of an asset with a useful life of 3 years can be charged as depreciation for tax purposes in the first year (Gapenski, 1996). Depreciable amounts for an asset with a twenty-year life are much closer to straight line depreciation. For a twenty-year asset, straight line deprecation, assuming no salvage value, would be 5 percent per year.

To avoid reporting lower profits when using accelerated depreciation, financial statements reported to shareholders often are different from what is reported for tax purposes. A **deferred tax liability** representing future tax liability from lower future depreciation expense is reported on the balance sheet, and depreciation expenses based on straight line method are reported as expenses on the income statement.

The value of inventories on the balance sheet and supply expenses on the income statement (called the **cost of goods sold** in manufacturing firms) are also affected by accounting methods. Organizations may use first-in first-out (**FIFO**) or last-in first-out (**LIFO**) methods to account for their inventories. As inventories are used in providing health services, FIFO reduces their value on the balance sheet by the amount paid for the oldest supplies in stock. This amount is shown as an expense on the income statement. LIFO reduces inventory value using the costs of the most recent supplies purchased and charges this as an expense. If the prices of inventories rise over time, FIFO will show higher dollar values of inventories remaining on the balance sheet and report lower supply expense on the income statement, while LIFO will show a lower amount of inventory on the books and charge a higher supply expense. Organizations must stick with one method of accounting for inventories—either LIFO or FIFO. Otherwise they could reduce their tax liability by alternating accounting systems with changes in prices of supplies.

As suppliers have developed more efficient systems, such as **just-in-time (JIT)** delivery of supplies, major users of medical supplies need to hold and account for fewer inventories as assets on their books. Under a JIT system, the medical supply companies deliver supplies as they are needed so that the hospital does not have to stock and pay for them in advance. JIT systems require a high level of coordination between the medical care provider and the supplier. Among noninstitutional providers like physician practices, home health agencies, insurance companies, and managed care organizations, however, inventories are not a major component of current assets.

The dollar value of accounts receivable (**AR**) is also adjusted to reflect the actual amount that is expected to be collected from patients or payers. If the health care organization expects a certain percentage of its bills to be uncollectable, it shows a deduction for bad debt or doubtful accounts as an expense. AR are commensurably reduced on the balance sheet.

Estimation of Uncertain Liabilities and Risk Management

Many of the organization's liabilities, like leases, mortgages, and long-term bonds, are fixed by explicit dollar contract and thus impose no uncertainty as to the future obligation they impose on the organization. The amount due on these outstanding liabilities is shown on the balance sheet. They reflect the actual cash obligation to the organization at the time they become due and payable.

Outstanding liabilities on the balance sheet pose a problem if their future value is uncertain. The size of such obligations must be estimated. Uncertain liabilities are typically those that relate to the insurance function. Managing these uncertain liabilities is called **risk management.** Job-related injuries, consumer lawsuits, and theft are but a few of the risks the organization must manage. The importance of properly estimating and reporting outstanding liabilities is nowhere less apparent than in accounting for possible future malpractice expenses, which can be large and highly variable.

Table 7-5   MACRS in the First Four Years of a Short- and Long-Lived Asset

	Asset with a 3-Year Life	*Asset with a 20-Year Life*
Year 1	58.3%	6.6 %
Year 2	27.8	7.0
Year 3	12.4	6.45
Year 4	1.5	6.0

Note: Percentages are approximate.
Source: Gapenski (1996).

Managed care introduces additional risk management functions to the firm. Managed care plans must accurately estimate IBNR provider expenses and include them in their accounts payable and as monthly expenses of the plan. Managed care plans must have information systems capable of tracking all expenses in a timely manner to avoid underfunding of IBNR claims. Incorrect estimates of outstanding liabilities can result in major blows to the balance sheet when unpredicted and inadequately funded obligations must be met.

Capital Structure Decisions

The mix of debt and equity used to purchase assets is the capital structure of the organization. Capital structure decisions can affect the cost of financing an asset. Investors who provide cash to the organization expect to be adequately compensated for the use of their funds through stock price appreciation or dividend payments. An organization's outstanding bonds and stocks are obligations to owners and creditors on its balance sheet, but are assets in the portfolios of outside investors.

When the net income, or earnings, of a health care organization is uncertain, owners of hospital equity bear more financial risk than lenders do. This is because creditors get paid before owners and the amount they are to be paid is fixed in advance. Since owners bear greater financial risk of losses from swings in earnings, they expect to receive a greater return to induce them to supply funds to the organization. Under normal circumstances, debt financing will be less costly than equity financing.

If debt increases the owner's financial risk, then why do health care managers, especially in not-for-profit organizations, borrow money to finance their activities? There are several reasons:

- *Tax deductibility of interest expense.* For-profit health care providers may deduct interest expense, but not dividend payments, from their taxes. Even if there were no uncertainty about future earnings, this deduction alone would lower the relative cost of using debt over equity (Modigliani and Miller, 1963).

- *Cost reimbursement of interest expense.* Like taxes, cost-based reimbursement returns a portion of interest expense, but not dividend payments, to the provider. This additional financial incentive magnifies the tax benefit to the use of debt in for-profit health care organizations (Wheeler and Smith, 1988). Furthermore, cost-based reimbursement of interest expense explains why not-for-profit health care organizations, which do not get a tax benefit from debt, would find debt less expensive than equity.

- *Tax-exempt status of not-for-profit organizations.* Tax-exempt status gives not-for-profits two incentives to use more debt than they otherwise would. First, the interest payments on their bonds are tax exempt to investors. If an organization's debt is tax exempt, lenders do not have to pay taxes on the interest they earn on these bonds. Therefore to get the same after-tax rate of return, they require a lower interest rate than they do on taxable bonds. Interest expense to a not-for-profit organization is generally about 2 percentage points lower than a for-profit enterprise with similar risk. Therefore, tax-exempt status lowers the cost of debt relative to equity. Second, not-for-profits are unable to obtain additional cash by issuing stock. Thus they must rely on debt, along with grants and donations, as primary sources of external financing when opportunities to expand and fulfill their missions arise.

If debt is cheaper than equity, then why don't tax-exempt health care organizations finance entirely with debt? First, debt becomes more expensive, the greater the amount of debt financing used by the organization. As the organization reduces the amount of equity in its capital structure, creditors have reduced protection against loss from variability in the organization's net income and possible bankruptcy-related costs. With greater risk exposure, creditors must bear increasing costs of monitoring the behavior of managers. If a health care provider used 100 percent debt, creditors would bear all of the financial risk and costs of liquidating the organization. For this risk exposure, creditors would require the same return as an equity owner and probably want considerable voice in management as well.

The health care financial manager typically uses an intermediate amount of debt to finance investments. The maximum percentage of debt allowed is often set by the board of directors of the health care organization (Cleverley, 1992). Through **bond covenants,** however, creditors place restrictions on the total amount of debt the organization can have at any one time. Bond rating agencies assign a lower rating to, or **downgrade,** organizations that take on an excessive amount of debt. Investors require higher interest rates from organizations with lower bond ratings.

Statement of Cash Flows

The balance sheet and income statements provide an incomplete picture to investors, who are the beneficiaries of the net income of the firm. Under accrual accounting, the balance sheet and income statements measure the revenues and costs associated with the delivery of services during a period of time by a health-related organization. By measuring activity and not cash flows, these statements fail to show investors how cash was generated and spent over time. Cash is spent only when a capital asset is acquired, not when it is shown as depreciation expense on the income statement. Cash is received only when a bill is paid. Until accounts receivable are collected, the organization does not have cash earnings.

Investors and stakeholders want to know how cash from operations and from external financing sources is being used by managers. Was it invested in new assets, used to pay investors, or employed to reduce debt? Moreover, owners are interested in whether financing and investing activities produced or consumed cash. Assets may be bought or sold by managers for a loss or a gain of cash; the capital structure might be changed by repayment of debt and issuance of an equal amount of new equity resulting with no change in cash availability. All of this information is documented in the statement of cash flows, which shows the sources and uses of cash in an organization over the same period on the income statement.

Table 7-6 illustrates the key components of a cash flow statement. At the top are the cash flows resulting from operating activities. Nonoperating gains (or losses) are excluded from net income when they relate to investing and financing activities. Next, noncash expenses like depreciation are added back to net income for a reporting period. These expenses do not represent a current use of cash. Finally, adjustments for changes in operating assets and liabilities are made to net operating income. When inventories or accounts receivable increase (or decrease), for example, this is a use (or source) of cash. This amount would be subtracted from (or added to) net income. When accounts payable, or accrued expenses, are increased (or decreased), this is a source (or use) of cash. These changes would be added back to (or subtracted from) net income from operations to obtain cash provided (or used) by operations.

The next component of the statement of cash flows summarizes the cash flows that result from investing activities. Investments result from capital budgeting decisions of the organization. (Capital budgeting is discussed in Chapter 9.) Investing activities include purchases or sales of real and financial assets that earn income for the organization. In stable or growing organizations, investing activity is a net user of available cash, as assets are replaced or new investments are made. Downsizing by selling assets frees up cash. Hospital systems can generate cash by selling hospitals and removing excess beds from service.

The final source or use of cash is from financing activities. Financing activities provide cash to an ongoing organization. They are partially affected by capital structure decisions and by the organizational needs for funds to support investments. Thus, cash can be generated by issuing new debt or equity and by obtaining donations. Cash is used when debt is repaid (retired) or outstanding stocks are repurchased.

Net cash provided (or used) by the organization over the reporting period is added to (or subtracted from) cash available at the beginning of the period to obtain ending cash balances. In this way, investors can assess managerial decisions in the obtaining and using of cash and the consequences of these decisions on the amount of cash available at the end of the reporting period. Low cash balances may put the organization at risk of not meeting payment commitments, if funds are not available in short-term marketable securities.

Table 7-6   Condensed Statement of Cash Flows (for the year ending June 30, 199X)

Cash flows from operating activities	
Net operating income	7,578
plus non-cash expenses	3,257
plus adjustments for changes in operating assets and liabilities	(1,433)
Cash provided (used) by operations	9,402
Cash flows from investing activities	
Decrease (increase) in buildings, equipment and land	(2,590)
Sale (purchase) of securities and other financial assets	(3,640)
Disposal (acquisition) of other assets	340
Cash provided (used) by investing activities	(5,890)
Cash flows from financing activities	
Issuance (repayment) of long term debt	4,678
Issuance (repurchase) of common or preferred stocks	(2,211)
Cash provided (used) by financing activities	2,467
Increase (reduction) in cash from operations, investments and financing	**5,979**
plus cash at the beginning of the period	93,001
Cash at the end of the period	**98,980**

Financial Statement Analysis

Information contained in the financial statements is historical in nature; it reveals past events and activities. To the extent that the future can be predicted from the past and current problems are revealed in past information, analysis of financial statements can help users assess organizational problems and performance. A number of ratios can be constructed from the financial data and operating statistics of health care organizations. This section discusses composition, financial, and operating ratios. The behavior of these ratios can be viewed over time using **vertical,** or **trend, analysis** and compared to industry standards using **horizontal,** or **comparative, analysis.**

To do comparative analysis of peer groups requires access to industry standards. Aggregated data on financial and operating ratios are available from various sources. First is the Center for Healthcare Industry Performance Studies (**CHIPS**), which provides national medians on hospital and other health provider financial and operating ratios. Health Care Investment Analysts (**HCIA**) publishes the annual *Sourcebook,* which supplies aggregate data constructed from hospital Medicare cost reports filed with the Health Care Financing Administration. The American Hospital Association's *Hospitals* reports information from its member hospitals on revenues, operating costs, and utilization by hospital and for the industry.

HMO and PPO financial ratios are available from the American Association of Health Plans (formerly Group Health Association of America), which administers an annual survey of the industry that is reported in its *HMO and PPO Industry Profile*. Physician group practice statistics are produced by the Medical Group Management Association in the annual *Cost Survey*. Also *The Almanac of Business and Industrial Financial Ratios* reports data derived from taxable enterprises. Representative stan-

---

A Case in Point. Below are common size ratios derived from the condensed balance sheet of Hometown Health Plan (in thousands of dollars).

Assets

Current Assets		% of Assets
Cash and marketable securities	$ 758	24%
Premiums receivable	1,612	52
Total current assets	2,370	76
Office equipment and furniture	420	14
(less accumulated depreciation)	(218)	7
Net office equipment and furniture	$ 202	7
Long-term investments	530	17
Total assets	$ 3,102	100

Liabilities

Current liabilities		% of Liabilities
Medical claims payable	$ 1,634	53
IBNR liabilities	916	30
Total current liabilities	$ 2,550	82
Outstanding shares	$ 362	12
Retained earnings	190	6
Total shareholder equity	$ 552	18
Total liabilities and owner's equity	$ 3,102	100

Common size ratios are found by dividing each entry by total assets. Rather than comparing the dollar value of entries on the balance sheet, only the percentage of total assets is examined. Thus, relative and not absolute differences are to be examined. In Hometown Health Plan, IBNR claims are 30 percent of assets. Suppose this ratio has been increasing over time. Hometown's higher IBNR liabilities could mean that it is not managing utilization as well as it once did. On the other hand, it might indicate slow billing by providers or that the plan is growing rapidly. Further investigation would be warranted.

dards for physician practices can be found there. Finally, *Industry Norms and Key Business Ratios* is available through Dun and Bradstreet Information Services.

As with any other diagnostic process, financial statement analysis provides a broad array of information that must be used wisely and judiciously. Confirmation of a diagnosis usually requires in-depth investigation to understand the underlying causes of the symptoms and signs presented in the financial data. Financial statement analysis provides a starting point in identifying and addressing organization performance issues and concerns.

Composition Ratios

The standardized composition of a financial statement is revealed in **common-size ratios,** created by dividing each entry on the financial statement by some common denominator. For example, for hospital data, total revenues can be used as the denominator for entries from the income statement, total assets as the denominator for the balance sheet, and net changes in cash as the divisor for the statement of cash flows. Common size ratios permit vertical analysis of changes in the composition of assets, liabilities, revenues, expenses, and cash flows of the organization over time. If entries are not normalized by a common denominator, changes in dollar values might be solely the result of growth or downsizing of the organization.

Financial Ratio Analysis

More common than composition ratio analysis is financial ratio analysis. Stockbrokers and investors, bond rating agencies, creditors and suppliers, governing boards, and health services managers use financial ratios to assess performance, compliance with bond covenants, and financial condition.

Financial ratio analysis looks at four fundamental concerns of investors and stakeholders:

1. Liquidity
2. Efficiency
3. Financial leverage
4. Profitability

How these concerns are measured by financial ratios and the relationship between these ratios and financial performance is described below.

Table 7-7 summarizes industry standards on selected financial ratios for hospitals, physician practices and health maintenance organizations. The industry medians are shown for hospitals in 1996 (from CHIPS data) and for HMOs in 1996 (from AAHP data). Medians reveal that 50 percent of all organizations had ratios below the reported ratio and 50 percent had ratios above it. Physician practice ratios were obtained from the 1997 *Almanac of Business and Industrial Financial Ratios*. These are the mean rather than the median ratios for 39,760 proprietary physician practices in 1993–1994. The industry median equals the mean only when the ratios are normally distributed (see Chapter 2).

Table 7-7   Financial Ratios: Industry Standards by Type of Firm

	Hospitals[a]	Physician Practices[b]	HMOs[c]
Selected liquidity ratios			
Current ratio			
Current assets	1.96	1.3	1.17
Current liabilities			
Quick ratio			
Cash, marketable	1.8	1.1	N.A.
securities, and receivables			
Current liabilities			
Days' cash on hand			
Cash and marketable securities	26.8 days	N.A.	N.A.
(Total operating expenses less			
noncash expense)/365			
Cash and marketable securities	N.A.	N.A.	28.81 days
(Total medical expenses)/365			
Selected activity ratios			
Total asset turnover			
Total revenues	1.01	4.6	3.18
Total assets			
Current asset turnover			
Total revenues	3.57	N.A.	5.8
Current assets			
Fixed asset turnover			
Total revenues	2.2	N.A.	N.A.
Long-term assets (net)			
Average age of plant			
Accumulated depreciation	8.5 years	N.A.	N.A.
Depreciation expense			
Efficiency/liquidity ratios			
Average collection period			
Accounts receivable	56.7 days	29 days	9.47 days
Total revenues/365			

Table 7-7   *(cont.)*

	Hospitals[a]	Physician Practices[b]	HMOs[c]
Average payment period			
Accounts payable	57 days	N.A.	52.73 days
Total expenses/365			
Leverage ratios			
Equity financing			
Equity (net assets)	52	.304	.192
Total assets			
Long-term debt to equity			
Long-term debt	55	.746	2.12
Equity (net assets)			
Cash flow to total debt			
Cash flows	.21	N.A.	.264[d]
Total liabilities			
Debt service coverage			
Cash flow + interest	$3.3	$3.8	N.A.
Principal + interest			
IBNR expense			
IBNR expenses	N.A.	N.A.	.641
Current liabilities			
Profitability Ratios			
Operating margin			
Net operating income	2.7%	3.0%	3.8%
Total revenues			
Net income margin			
Net income	3.8%	2.0%	N.A.
Total revenues			
Return on equity			
Net income	7.4%	35%[e]	N.A.
Equity (net assets)			

[a]Industry medians for 1996. (CHIPS, 1996)
[b]Industry means for 1995. (Troy, 1997)
[c]Industry medians for 1993. (AAHP, 1996)
[d]Represents total debt to equity ratio for HMOs.
[e]Before distribution to officers and payment of taxes.

Sources: Center for Healthcare Industry Performance Studies (1996); Troy (1997); American Association of Health Plans (1996).

Liquidity Ratios

Liquidity is the ability of the organization to meet short-term payment commitments to workers, suppliers, and creditors. Even a profitable organization can experience financial distress and higher financing costs if insufficient cash is available. Most **liquidity ratios** are constructed by comparing some component, or group of components, of current assets with current liabilities. Three common ratios to measure liquidity are the current ratio, the quick ratio, and days' cash on hand.

Current Ratio

Are the organization's short-term assets sufficient to cover current liabilities in the coming year? The answer will be dictated largely by how quickly revenues are converted to cash. This will differ by type of health care organization. Hospitals must bill major third-party payers, which may not pay for 30 to 60 days or more, so they typically require $2 of current assets to cover $1 of current liabilities for a **current ratio** of about 2. The current ratio indicates dollars that will be converted to cash within the year as a percentage of bills coming due within the year. HMOs have current ratios closer to 1 because premium payments that support current expenses are received within 30 days of billing. Although not directly comparable because they are means rather than medians, the current ratios of physician practices lie somewhere in between hospitals and HMOs. Like hospitals, their retrospective billing systems result in delayed collections. On the other hand, physician practices have lower dollar amounts outstanding on each account receivable and a greater percentage of collections occur at the time of service.

Quick Ratio

The **quick ratio** relates ability to meet short-term liabilities with more liquid components of current assets. In the quick ratio, inventories are subtracted from current assets, leaving cash, marketable securities, and accounts receivable as future payment sources. This ratio indicates ability to meet payroll and pay suppliers and creditors without having to liquidate inventories. Since most managed care organizations carry few inventories, there will be little difference between their quick and current ratios.

Days' Cash on Hand

A third ratio to evaluate liquidity is **days' cash on hand.** This ratio calculates the ability of the organization to pay its ongoing expenses with cash and short-term marketable securities, the most liquid of their assets. Marketable securities are those that can be readily sold in secondary markets. The denominator of this ratio is calculated by dividing total operating expenses by the number of days in the year to get average daily expenses. Total cash and marketable securities are then divided by average daily expenses. Enough cash to pay about one month's bills is the industry norm in hospitals and HMOs. This ratio for HMO as constructed by AAHP excludes plan administrative expenses. Thus, HMO daily operating expenses consist of medical expenses only—payments to hospitals, doctors, and other providers.

Movement away from industry norms, either higher or lower, over time may signal liquidity problems. Declining levels of current assets relative to current liabilities may indicate increasingly poor performance and inability to make payments to suppliers and employees. On the other hand, a rising current or quick ratio may be the result of increased volume of activity, revenues, and profits. If an increase in current assets relative to liabilities is the result of poor collections—growth in accounts receivable—rather than better performance, then a larger current or quick ratio relative to industry norms suggests inefficient asset management. Such trends need to be assessed and managed.

Changes in individual sources of liquidity over time also warrant attention. While large and growing amounts of cash on hand relative to other current assets provide greater liquidity and less risk, they also reduce profitability. Cash and marketable securities pay a lower return than other investments. While creditors to the organization appreciate a large cash holding to protect them from losses, accumulating cash may not be a wise use of owner's invested capital.

Efficiency Ratios

Efficiency looks at how well the organization's assets and liabilities are being managed. Efficiency can be viewed from two perspectives. The first is how well individual assets are employed to produce revenues. These ratios, called **activity** or **turnover** ratios, measure how many dollars of revenue on the income statement are associated with a dollar of assets, or some component of assets, on the balance sheet. Turnover ratios can also be constructed to relate dollars of expense to some component of liabilities. A second view of efficiency looks at how much time, measured in days, it takes to convert an asset (or a liability) to cash. These ratios, which are created from turnover ratios, measure how long it takes the organization to collect and pay its bills, and so they provide a measure of liquidity as well.

Numerous turnover ratios can be constructed from individual items on the balance sheet. Only three will be examined here: total asset turnover, current asset turnover, and fixed asset turnover. Two other turnover ratios, accounts receivable turnover and accounts payable turnover, will be described from the second perspective: How many days it takes to convert these balance sheet entries to cash. Table 7-7 shows these ratios for the three representative providers.

The **total asset turnover, current asset turnover,** and **fixed asset turnover ratios** measure dollars of revenue generated by total, current, and fixed assets, respectively. The first ratio is much higher in physician practices and HMOs than in hospitals. The average hospital generates $1.01 in revenues for every dollar of assets. Physicians get about $4.60 in revenues, while HMOs receive $3.18 in premiums per $1.00 of assets. Current asset turnover, which was not available for physician practices, is $3.60 in hospitals and $4.51 in HMOs. The fixed asset ratio, reported only for hospitals, reflects the efficiency in using the building and equipment in generating revenues. Only $2.20 of revenues are produced by $1.00 of fixed assets.

The higher average turnover ratios in physician practices and HMOs arise because the asset base in HMOs and physician offices is much lower relative to hospitals; hospitals own more of the assets used in producing services. If office space and equipment are leased or rented, they will not appear as an asset of the practice or HMO. Accounting practices across types of organizations also create differences as well. For example, nearly 80 percent of physician group practices used a cash or modified cash basis of accounting in 1994 for internal management, and 86.5 percent used these methods for tax reporting purposes (Doelling, 1996; Schafer, 1991). This underscores the need to compare financial ratios of similar types of health care organizations and to pay attention to the way the ratios are calculated and reported.

In general, rising (falling) turnover ratios over time are favorable (unfavorable) to the organization, reflecting improved (worsening) use of assets. One problem with this conclusion is the distortion created by accounting conventions surrounding building, equipment, and fixtures. Recall that the value of fixed assets on the books is based on cost at the time of purchase, adjusted for accumulated depreciation. Older real assets have more accumulated depreciation and lower book value. Because the denominator in the fixed asset and total asset turnover ratios will be larger in a new facility, a relatively new hospital or nursing home may appear less efficient than an older facility, everything else being equal.

One way to compensate for the distortion in measuring long-term assets is to look at the **average age of plant**, found by dividing accumulated depreciation on the balance sheet by depreciation expense on the income statement. If the health care facility's fixed assets are older than the mean age of its peers, then its efficiency ratios should be higher, everything else being the same. Because physician practices and HMOs own fewer fixed assets, this distortion is not as great a problem in using turnover ratios to compare efficiency. Only in staff model HMOs and large group model HMOs that own their clinics will the age of plant be relevant in making peer comparisons about asset efficiency.

Accounts receivable turnover (total revenues/accounts receivable) and accounts payable turnover (total expenses/accounts payable) can be converted to days in accounts receivable, also called **average collection period (ACP),** and days in accounts payable, or **average payment period (APP).** To calculate the ACP, divide total revenues by 365 days to get average daily revenues:

$$\text{Average daily revenues} = \frac{\text{Total revenues}}{365}.$$

Next, divide accounts receivable by average daily revenues:

$$\text{Average collection period (ACP)} = \frac{\text{Accounts receivable}}{\text{Average daily revenues}}.$$

The same calculation is used for the APP except that accounts payable and average daily expenses are used. In HMOs, ACP measures how many days it takes to collect premiums, and APP indicates how many days it takes to pay providers participating in the plan.

$$\text{Average daily expenses} = \frac{\text{Total expenses}}{365}.$$

$$\text{Average payment period (APP)} = \frac{\text{Accounts payable}}{\text{Average daily expenses}}.$$

As indicated on Table 7-7, the APP is similar for HMOs and hospitals; it is not available for physician practices. The major difference occurs in the ACP. Hospital bills typically take nearly two months to collect, physicians about 1 month, and HMOs a little more than nine days. Moreover, according to industry norms, the average hospital is just matching the timing of payments to suppliers with the arrival of reimbursement from payers, at about fifty-seven days. A matching strategy minimizes the need to borrow in order temporarily to fund working capital: cash on hand, accounts receivable and inventories. HMOs pay for medical and hospital services about forty-three days after the receipt of premiums. HMOs can earn interest on premium revenues while claims are in process or incurred but not yet reported. Claims payable are a major source of temporary financing of working capital in HMOs.

Rising trends in the ACP and APP relative to industry norms are usually bad signs for health care organizations. Poor collections reduce liquidity; they indicate poor management of accounts receivable. Delay of payment to suppliers may be one way that managers deal with a cash shortage. There are costs, however. By delaying payment, the health care organization gives up a favorable discount offered by most suppliers for prompt payment. Moreover, suppliers may become wary if payment delays are repeated and excessive. It may be a wiser and less costly strategy to borrow from the bank than delay supplier payments. HMOs that delay the reimbursement of claims may find that future contract negotiations with providers include cash advances on expected claims.

Sometimes rising ACP trends reflect industry-wide factors. If a significant third-party payer, like Medicare, slows payments, the ACP of all providers with a high proportion of Medicare receivables will be adversely affected. Other environment factors may result from poor economic conditions. During economic recessions, patients may pay their bills more slowly or be unable to pay at all, resulting in higher bad debt percentages than expected. Uncontrollable external factors cannot be attributed to poor asset management. Comparison of an organization's trends with industry trends helps to uncover the extent to which lengthening payments and collection periods are occurring throughout the industry.

Financial Leverage Ratios

Financial leverage is the amount of debt financing used to acquire an organization's assets. Leverage ratios are also called **capitalization,** or **capital structure,** ratios. Because shareholders and stakeholders receive the residual cash flows after all other bills have been paid, greater financial leverage increases the risk of the return of cash to owners, sponsors, and the community. Up to a certain point, however, greater financial leverage also increases the average return to investors. Recall that tax deductibility of interest expense reduces its cost relative to equity. Since debt enables owners to acquire more income-earning assets with their invested dollars—to "leverage" their investment, so to speak—the residual earnings, or net income, available to investors will be split among a smaller number of individuals, so that each earns more per dollar invested. If too much debt is assumed by owners, however, creditors worry about the safety of their investment and raise the required interest rate, thereby nullifying the favorable tax treatment of debt on the returns to equity investors.

Among the ratios used to assess leverage are the equity financing ratio, long-term debt-to-equity ratio, cash flow to total debt, and the debt service coverage ratio.

Equity Financing Ratio

The **equity financing ratio** measures the percentage of the organization's assets that is funded by equity. Table 7-7 shows that hospitals use less total debt than do physician practices and managed care plans to support their asset base. Fifty-two percent of the average hospital's total assets is purchased with equity, while only 20 percent of an HMO's current and long-term assets is acquired with owner's funds. The rest is borrowed either short or long term. The physician equity financing ratio lies in between, at 30 percent.

Long-Term Debt-to-Equity Ratio

The **long-term debt-to-equity ratio,** or simply the debt-to-equity ratio, reveals the relative use of debt and equity to finance assets. Long-term debt consists of long-term bonds, mortgages, and loans that do not have to be repaid (do not mature) for at least one year or more. Hospitals use 55 cents of long-term debt for every $1.00 of equity invested. Thus, about 36 percent (.55/1.00 + .55) of long-term financing comes from long-term debt. Physicians use the most leverage to finance long term: $0.746 of debt for each $1.00 of equity, or 43 percent (.746/1.746) long-term debt financing. HMOs carry very little long-term debt. The total debt-to-equity ratio reported here is 2.12 to 1 in HMOs, or 68 percent (2.12/1.00 + 2.12). For-profit HMOs can issue new shares of stock to raise equity funds and avoid the use of debt, a funding source that is not available to the predominantly not-for-profit hospital industry. Individual practices tend not to retain earnings in the practice and also have less access to equity capital as a source of funding.

Staff and group model HMOs are more likely to own their own assets. Also staff and group model HMOs are more likely to be not-for-profit organizations with no access to equity capital. According to Palsbo and Gold (1991), the average long-term debt-to-equity ratios is .76 to 1 in the staff model HMO and .73 to 1 in the group model HMO, considerably higher than in the hospital industry currently. In contrast, network and IPA model HMOs have long-term debt-to-equity ratios of .10 to 1 and .22 to 1, respectively, much lower than the industry median for HMOs and hospitals. Finally, for-profit HMOs are found to have lower debt-to-equity ratios—.168 to 1—than not-for-profits—.6 to 1 (Palsbo and Gold, 1991).

Cash-Flow-to-Total-Debt and Debt-Service-Coverage Ratios

Cash-flow-to-total-debt and **debt-service-coverage** ratios indicate the ability of the organization to meet payment commitments to creditors. Cash flow to total debt measures cash balances relative to short-term and long-term financial obligations. Hospital net cash provided, which can be found on the cash flow statement, is 21 cents for every $1.00 of liabilities outstanding. HMOs have 26 cents in cash for each $1.00 of liabilities. This ratio was not reported for physician practices.

Debt service is total amount of principal and interest that must be paid to creditors during the year. The debt-service-coverage ratio measures the ability of the organization to make these payments. The similarity of this ratio in hospitals and physician practices, about $3.3 and $3.8 to every $1 of debt service, respectively, may reflect margins of safety imposed by creditors, banks and debt rating agencies on these more highly leveraged organizations.

IBNR-Expense-to-Current-Liabilities Ratio

The **IBNR-expense-to-current-liabilities** ratio shows the estimated amount of incurred but not yet reported claims expense as a proportion of current liabilities. IBNR is a non-cash expense. Higher ratios indicate inefficiency of hospitals and doctors in billing the health plan for services. Managed care plans can invest premium dollars until the claims are received and paid. Thus HMOs can "borrow" temporarily from IBNR claims outstanding at zero interest cost to fund working capital. The use of IBNR payables accounts for higher total debt financing observed in HMOs. Managed care plans that use capitation to pay providers will have a lower amount of IBNR expense, less ability to leverage their IBNR payables, and less uncertainty about their outstanding claims liability.

Like liquidity ratios, leverage ratios should be neither too high nor too low. Divergence from industry norms over time can result in poor performance and greater bankruptcy risk. Taking advantage of low-cost debt financing improves performance. Too much debt and its counterpart, too little equity, can expose the provider organization to the risk of being unable to meet fixed payment commitments, like debt service, rent and lease payments, and payroll when revenues decline unexpectedly.

When HMOs accept premiums from subscribers, they assume liability for the medical expenses of enrollees. Since their revenues are fixed, they are at risk for unexpected expenses—the objective risk of the plan. Too little equity to cushion the HMOs against higher-than-predicted claims expense threatens their solvency. If HMOs lock in their medical expense liabilities with capitated contracts, they forgo the opportunity to leverage premiums for higher earnings, but at the same time they lower their risk. State insurance regulators require that HMOs set aside a certain percentage of their assets as reserves to cover unexpected claims. In essence, statutory reserves set the minimum level of equity that must be maintained in the capital structure of the managed care plan to ensure its solvency. Good financial managers must balance the higher return with the higher risk of debt (or claims payable) financing. This trade-off exists for both health care providers and managed care plans.

Profitability Ratios

The bottom line of the organization is profitability. Profitability reveals how well managers are generating returns to owners and the community. Without positive net income, no organization can survive over the long run. An organization whose revenues just equal expenses is unable to deal with uncertainties and respond to opportunities in the environment. Key profitability ratios include operating margin, net income margin, and return on equity.

Operating and Net Income Margins

Operating margin measures the income from operations, and **net income margin** shows income from operations plus nonoperating gains as a percentage of total revenues. Total revenues include both operating revenues and nonoperating gains. In physician practices, operating and net income margins shown in Table 7-7 are after the earnings of the practice have been distributed to physicians.

Return on Equity

The **return on equity (ROE)** is the amount of net income earned on owner's equity investment in for-profit organizations and on the net assets supplied by donors and the community in not-for-profits. No ROEs were available for HMOs. ROEs are much higher in physician practices than hospitals, reflecting significantly higher net income margins before distribution to partners and officers of the firm.

The following equations show that ROE is composed of three ratios:

$$\text{ROE} = \text{Net income margin} \times \text{total asset turnover} \times \frac{1}{\text{equity financing ratio}}.$$

$$\frac{\text{Net income}}{\text{Equity}} = \frac{\text{Net income}}{\text{Total revenues}} \times \frac{\text{total revenues}}{\text{total assets}} \times \frac{1}{\text{equity/total assets}}.$$

$$\frac{\text{Net income}}{\text{Equity}} = \frac{\text{Net income}}{\text{Total revenues}} \times \frac{\text{total revenues}}{\text{total assets}} \times \frac{\text{total assets}}{\text{equity}}.$$

Differences in ROE in similar organizations can be analyzed using **DuPont analysis,** which these three underlying components of performance: profitability, efficiency, and financial leverage. Net income margin is used to measure profitability, total asset turnover is used to measure efficiency, and the inverse of the equity financing ratio, called the **equity multiplier,** is used to measure leverage. The ROE is the product of these three ratios.

Operating Ratios and Financial Performance

Operating statistics provide key information on sources of revenue, utilization, and costs. These data help to fill out the picture of the organization revealed in financial ratio analysis. While industry standards for operating ratios are generally available for hospitals so that comparisons can be made, fewer data are available for other providers.

Operating Ratios for Hospitals

Financial performance among hospitals depends heavily on the adequacy of reimbursement. A key operating statistic that illuminates this is net price per unit of service. Net prices are payments expected per case, per patient-day, per visit, or per member per month. Although these data are not always available publicly, they can be used internally to improve revenues and manage costs.

Payer mix is the proportion of revenues from Medicare, Medicaid, managed care, and other third-party payers. A payer mix with a high percentage of low- or slow-paying payers can adversely affect the provider. Each payer creates specific and unique behavioral incentives—more volume but short stays under DRGs, more volume but longer stays under per diem rates, and more volume of specific services for discounted fees. If a proportion of revenues is capitated, the incentives are reversed, resulting in less volume, less intense treatment, and shorter stays.

Payer mix not only provides insight into the adequacy and behavioral incentives of reimbursement but also indicates the types of patients treated. Medicare patients are predominantly elderly; Medicaid patients are typically young mothers, their children, and the disabled. Currently, managed care and commercial payer enrollees are workers and their families, but this may change as more states and the federal government move beneficiaries into managed care.

Another factor important for hospital financial performance is the management of expenses. Information on costs per unit is valuable for understanding where operating efficiencies might be gained. When comparing costs to industry norms, they should be adjusted for differences in patient types and severity of illness. This can be done using the case mix index, derived from DRG weights (see Chapter 6). Costs are likely to be higher than average the higher the case mix index.

A third factor that influences hospital financial performance is efficiency in the use of inputs. Key statistics to measure hospital and nursing care efficiency include full-time-equivalent (**FTE**) employees used per bed, average length of stay, and occupancy rates. Lower quantities of inputs employed—labor, time, and beds—reduce costs. High occupancy rates suggest efficient use of fixed resources. Today most hospital service areas are overbedded, as reflected in low occupancy rates that have resulted from managed care and PPS.

Operating Ratios in HMOs and Other Managed Care Plans

Because managed care organizations are primarily financial intermediaries, operating performance is driven by effective management of financial risk. Two key ratios are indicative of operating performance: the health care expense ratio and the administrative expense ratio. The health care expense ratio is the same as the medical loss ratio

A Case in Point. Representative hospital operating statistics for a group of St. Louis area hospitals located in Illinois are presented below.

Trends in Illinois Hospital Operating Statistics , 1988–1995

	1988	1989	1990	1991	1992	1993	1994	1995
Payer mix								
Discharges Medicare (%)	33.9	35.0	37.7	38.5	40.2	41.7	41.9	44.6
Discharges Medicaid (%)	21.0	22.6	22.5	22.8	24.6	23.8	23.6	21.6
All other payers (%)	45.1	42.4	39.7	38.8	35.2	34.5	34.4	33.8
Gross charges($)/discharge	4,865	5,413	6,257	6,968	7,771	8,278	9,212	9,867
Allowances (%)	31.5	35.6	35.1	36.6	38.5	40.7	43.4	46.1
Cost ($)/discharge	3,425	3,680	4,165	4,481	4,903	5,030	5,304	5,475
Available beds	2,485	2,479	2,158	2,120	2,094	2,037	1,944	1,861
FTE employees/bed	2.87	3.02	3.39	3.45	3.59	3.71	3.85	3.91
Occupancy rate	54.8	53.2	56.9	54.2	51.9	52.0	51.3	48.8
Average length of stay (days)	6.5	6.7	6.8	6.5	6.2	6.1	5.8	5.5

Source: St. Louis Area Business Health Coalition.

An analysis of trends in hospital operating statistics in this region indicates that Medicare beneficiaries make up an increasing proportion of hospital discharges. Similar trends in payer mix (not shown) appear in patient-days. Gross charges per discharge have been steadily increasing, at 10.6 percent per year in the face of growing contractual allowances. Costs per discharge have gone up nearly 7 percent per year over this period. FTEs per bed have risen even as discharges, occupancy rates, and beds have declined. Discharges (not shown) declined from nearly 73,000 in 1988 to 61,200 in 1995. Without information on case mix, it is difficult to know whether increased use of labor is the result of rising patient acuity or managerial inefficiency. While 624 available beds in the region have been eliminated since 1988, it was not enough to maintain occupancy rates at their 1988 levels. Operating efficiencies are observed by the falling average length of stay of all patients treated in area hospitals. It is interesting to note that net income margin and return on equity (not shown) have risen from 3.4 percent to 7.65 percent and 4.56 percent to 10.95 percent, respectively, in these hospitals. Obviously they were doing much better financially in 1995 than they did in 1988.

discussed in Chapter 2, except that total revenues include co-payments, coordination of benefits, and fee income in addition to premiums. The administrative expense ratio is dollars of revenue spent on plan administration.

HMO Operating Ratios, 1993 medians

a medical loss
Health care expense ratio: $\dfrac{\text{Medical and hospital expenses}}{\text{Total revenues}}$ = 83.5%.

Administrative expense ratio: $\dfrac{\text{Total administrative expense}}{\text{Total revenues}}$ = 10.7%.

Without an adjustment for the health risk of enrollees, comparisons of these ratios between HMOs may be problematic. Plans with older enrollees or enrollees with poor health status are likely to have higher health care expense ratios. More aggressive utilization management will lower health care expense ratios but raise administrative expense ratios. Plan size and age also affect these ratios. Larger and more experienced plans are likely to have lower ratios overall.

Other performance indicators for HMOs can be found in the Health Plan and Employer Data Indicator Statistics (**HEDIS**) data set, which is used by employers to measure outcomes and quality of care. These indicators are discussed in more detail in Chapter 13.

Operating Ratios in Physician Practices

Gross revenues used to be the key performance indicator of physician productivity. Because of this, physicians were rewarded on the basis of gross charges in the net income distribution formulas of the practice. With higher discounts from charges, gross revenues are no longer necessarily a good measure of physician ability to generate revenues for the practice. Like hospitals, physicians must take into account payer mix and net (medical) revenues resulting from the provision of services.

Physician practice expenses must be managed. These include staffing costs, space, and other midlevel provider costs. Units of service are ambulatory encounters, ambulatory and inpatient surgeries, inpatient visits, and laboratory procedures. Practice costs per unit will be affected by patient characteristics, case mix, geographical location, and other factors.

Efficiency in physician practices requires minimizing input costs and maximizing physician and other provider services per patient. Conflicting incentives arise when part of the practice is capitated. Capitation requires that patient encounters and procedures be optimized; they should be neither excessive nor inadequate. Thus, inpatient and outpatient visits and procedures per patient should reflect utilization norms among peers. Rising practice and malpractice expense when compared to similar practices is indicative of poor management and control of costs.

Medical Group Management Association (**MGMA**) provides detailed operating data on single and multispecialty group practices in their annual *Cost Survey*. These data have been collected since 1955. Table 7-8 provides a small sample of operating statistics available for assessing financial and operating performance in group practices. As the table indicates, about 17 percent of group practice revenue in 1994 was capitated, 38 percent was discounted fee for service, and 42 percent was commercial. Group practices collected $318 per patient on billed charges of $406, or about 78 percent. Expenses from operating the practice were 55 percent of total expense, and total expense per patient was $182. The data on efficiency provide insight into typical utilization patterns. The typical multispecialty group practice provided 2.68 ambulatory encounters per patient with each physician providing 4,238 encounters each year. The typical practice employed 3.3 FTE support staff. Clinics allotted 1,253 square feet of space per patient.

Limitations in the Use of Financial Ratio Analysis

The major problems associated with the use of comparative data obtained from the financial statements of health care organizations are the reliability, accuracy, and comparability of the data. Reliability depends on the number of organizations used to derive industry norms. Too small a sample relative to the population will provide unreliable and variable normative information. Accuracy depends on whether financial statements from which data are derived have been audited and follow GAAP. Even if proper methods are used and the data are accurate, some ratios will be

Table 7-8   Physician Multispecialty Group Practices, Selected
Operating Statistics, 1994

	Mean
Payer mix, % of gross revenues	
Medicare, capitated	9.79%
Medicare, fee-for-service	26.10%
Medicaid, capitated	7.56%
Medicaid fee-for-service	8.93%
Managed care, at risk-discounted fee for service	21.51%
Managed care, discounted fee for service	16.87%
Commercial	41.56%
Gross charges per patient	$406.06
Net medical revenue per patient	$317.97
Costs	
Total operating expense/total expense	.55
Total provider expense/total expense	.45
Total operating expense per patient	$182.69
Efficiency	
Ambulatory encounters per patient	2.68
Ambulatory encounters per physician	4,238
Inpatient visits per physician	904
FTE support staff per 1,000 patients	3.312
Square feet per patient	1,253

Source: MGMA *Cost Survey*, 1995 report based on 1994 data.

affected by remaining accounting differences across firms, such as the use of FIFO or LIFO in valuing inventories or the use of a cash or accrual basis of accounting.

For comparability, industry norms must come from similar organizations using similar accounting practices. To improve comparability, it is sometimes possible to acquire aggregate data that reflect the performance of one's peers. For example, median financial ratios for all not-for-profit hospitals in the South-Central region with 200 to 300 beds could be used to analyze a 250-bed not-for-profit hospital in Tennessee. Similarly, financial ratios on large, for-profit, network model HMOs might be used to assess the financial performance of Humana.

Trends in financial ratios over time are affected by inflation because of the way that inventories and long-term assets are valued on the balance sheet. With inflation, market values and replacement costs rise relative to the book value of an asset. Under-valuing the cost of assets used to provide services overstates profits. As a result, insufficient funds may be retained for replacement. Comparisons to peers at a point in time are distorted by differences in the age of assets used by the organization. Careful use of financial ratios requires that these factors be taken into consideration.

Conclusion

In this chapter, three financial statements used by health care organizations were described: the balance sheet, the income statement, and the statement of cash flows. Financial ratios were constructed from these data to measure liquidity, efficiency, leverage, and profitability, and the financial performance in different types of health-related organizations was analyzed. Financial ratios sometimes present only signs and symptoms of underlying problems, so operating statistics must be used to provide further illumination. Ultimately an accurate diagnosis of financial difficulty requires further investigation of underlying causes. Only then can appropriate corrective action be taken.

Case 7-1: Accounting versus Economic Depreciation

Recall the example of straight-line depreciation of a car you were considering in this chapter. You found the book value of the car was $4,000. Set up a simple spreadsheet that will allow you to answer the following questions:

1. Would you be wiling to pay $4,000 for the car if you learn that the car has 145,000 miles on it? What about 80,000 miles?

2. What if it were a Honda Accord or Ford Taurus station wagon? How would these facts affect your estimate of its market and salvage value?

3. How might you estimate its economic value—transportation plus tangible benefits?

4. Based on these questions, how well does straight-line depreciation account for changes in the market value of the car?

Case 7-2: Columbia/HCA Healthcare

Columbia/HCA Healthcare is a for-profit, healthcare services company that owns and operates 344 acute and specialty care hospitals in 36 states and in Europe. According to the May 1996 financial statements, Columbia/HCA had a net income of $961 million for the year ending December 1995.

The balance sheet and income statement for Columbia/HCA are provided on the spreadsheet that accompanies your text. Using this information, construct the ratios you need to complete a DuPont analysis of Columbia/HCA for 1993–95. Then compare Columbia's financial performance to that of all hospitals, shown on Table 7-7. Note that the equity financing ratio in the industry was .52. This ratio first must be inverted to obtain the equity multiplier, which is 1.00/.52 or 1.92, that is needed to analyze this component of the ROE.

Case 7-3: St. Mary's Hospital

St. Mary's Hospital is a not-for-profit, inner-city community hospital located in a poor neighborhood of a major metropolitan area in the Midwest. Sponsored by a religious order and part of a small hospital system, Saint Mary's has served its community since 1890. During the late 1980s, St. Mary's experienced declining profitability as a result of a number of environmental factors. These included the change in Medicare reimbursement from cost-based to prospective payment, slow and inadequate payment for the delivery of care to Medicaid recipients, increasing amounts of bad debt, rising numbers of uninsured patients, and a poor economy. Threatened with closure, St. Mary's board decided to bring in new management to turn the hospital around.

In late 1989 the board hired Mr. Charles Windsor, a nationally known and well-respected hospital administrator, to be the chief executive officer (CEO). Mr. Windsor and the board agreed that part of his job would be to groom his successor. Mr. Richard Mark, who had demonstrated excellent managerial and community development skills while working for state and local government, but who had little healthcare experience, was asked to join Mr. Windsor as the new chief operating officer for St. Mary's in early 1990.

It is now December of 1993. You have just joined the board of St. Mary's Hospital and have been presented with the summary financial statements and operating statistics for the hospital and for a peer group of hospitals in the region. You are to assess the performance of St. Mary's under its new management team and provide a report to the board. Since Mr. Windsor plans to retire soon, you must make a recommendation whether or not Mr. Mark should be retained and promoted to CEO.

On the spreadsheet for the case provided on disk, construct the financial and operating ratios for St. Mary's Hospital. Then prepare an executive summary for the board with your evaluation of Mr. Mark's performance and your recommendations for or against retention and promotion based on what is revealed in the data.

References

American Association of Health Plans (AAHP). (1996, June). *HMO and PPO industry profile*, (1995–96 ed.). Washington, DC.

Center for Healthcare Industry Performance Studies (CHIPS). (1996). *Hospital performance data*. Columbus, OH.

Cleverley, W. O. (1992). *Essentials of health care finance* (3rd ed.). Gaithersburg, MD: Aspen.

Doelling, P. M. (1996, September–October). Using financial ratios to assess physician practices. *Medical Group Management Journal*, pp. 42–55.

Gapenski, L. C. (1996). *Understanding health care financial management*. Ann Arbor, MI: AUPHA Press/Health Administration Press.

Medical Group Management Association (MGMA). (1995). *MGMA cost survey: 1995 report based on 1994 data*. Englewood, CO.

Modigliani, F., & Miller, M. H. (1958, June). The cost of capital, corporation finance and the theory of investment. *American Economic Review*, pp. 261–297.

Modigliani, F., & Miller, M. H. (1963, June). Taxes and the cost of capital: A correction. *American Economic Review*, pp. 433–443.

Palsbo, S. J., & Gold, M. (1991). *HMO industry profile: Vol. 3. Financial performance 1989*. Washington, DC: Group Health Association of America.

Schafer, E. L. (1991). Financial management of medical and dental practices. In A. Ross, S. J. Williams, & E. L. Schafer (Eds.), *Ambulatory care management*. Albany, NY: Delmar.

Seitz, N. (1990). *Capital budgeting and long-term financing decisions*. Toronto: Dryden Press.

Solomon, C. M. (1992, May/June). Alternatives to Medicaid provider taxes. *Health Systems Review*, 25(3), 45–46.

Troy, L. (1997). *Almanac of business and industrial financial ratios*, (28th ed.). Englewood Cliffs, NJ: Prentice Hall.

Wheeler, J., Smith, R. C., & Dean, G. (1988). The discount rate for capital expenditure analysis in health care. *Health Care Management Review*, 13(2), 43–51.

Chapter 8

Operating Budgets Under Capitation

This chapter discusses the economic dimensions of managing a capitated contract under managed care. Given that the health care manager must deal with a pluralistic payment system, the essentials of managing a budget under capitation will be examined. Underlying issues and assumptions about the nature and impact of capitation in physician practices and hospitals will be explored.

Learning Objectives

Upon successful completion of this chapter, the learner will:

- Understand the scope of the pluralistic payment system.
- Understand the nature of risk in health care reimbursement.
- Understand the economic environment of managed care companies.
- Understand the economic environment of health care providers.
- Understand how revenue streams are determined for physicians under capitation.
- Understand how revenue streams are determined for hospitals under capitation.

Key Terms

case rate pricing	primary care physician (PCP)
covered services	risk pool
downside risk	specialty care physician (SCP)
gatekeeper	stop loss insurance
per diem pricing	upside risk
per member per month (PMPM)	withhold

Introduction

Financial statements are the evidence by which management determines whether its activities are producing the desired economic results. In the current health care environment, most provider organizations must deal with a pluralistic payment system (Schmitz, 1992, pp. 30–59). Because the incentives under the various payment systems vary, it is difficult to chart a homogeneous course for an operating budget. If the reimbursement was strictly capitation, a single strategy could be undertaken, or if the reimbursement was solely fee for service, the budget strategies could be homogeneous. But this is not the case, so it is necessary that health care organizations adopt a hybrid approach that makes the best of the pluralistic payment environment.

Although there are numerous kinds of health care provider organizations that operate under this mixed reimbursement system, the discussion in this chapter focuses primarily on physician organizations and hospital-based systems along with the health delivery systems that they support. Nevertheless, the ideas presented in this chapter can be generalized to other kinds of providers, such as independent ambulatory care facilities, home health services, and other service organizations within the framework of the health care delivery system.

The Pluralistic Reimbursement Environment

Although many of the concerns about coping with future reimbursement mechanisms focus on capitation, it is nevertheless necessary to understand the complexity of the total health care reimbursement environment and the wide variety of payment systems that currently exist in the health care environment.

The Health Care Environment

In addition to governmental payers, there are many independent payers that make up the pluralistic payment market. In almost every case, the reimbursement protocols differ from payer to payer. The institutional provider and individual provider behaviors must take into consideration individual payer rules with regard to the following (Schmitz, 1992, p. 32):

- Pre-admission certification
- Surgical second opinions
- Various utilization review mechanisms
- Documentation of need for treatment
- Pre-procedure certification (outpatients)
- Levels of benefit coverage
- Data requirements for billing
- Time frame for billing

Institutional and individual health care providers must contend with various payment systems (see Schmitz, 1992, for a complete explanation of these mechanisms):

1. Government payment systems:
   Medicare: Traditional and managed care
   Medicaid: Traditional and managed care
   CHAMPUS
   Veterans Administration
   Military

2. Indemnity insurance payment systems

3. Managed care payment systems:
   HMOs, PPOs, and EPOs

4. Self-payment

And within each of these payment mechanisms, there are multiple permutations. For example, the once-standard Medicare program is now as variable as the number of managed care companies offering a Medicare managed care program. If there are three managed care companies offering Medicare benefits to potential enrollees of a particular metropolitan market, the providers of that area must be familiar with four different Medicare products: the traditional Medicare product and the three different Medicare managed care products. The same is true with each of the other categories of payers, except that in the indemnity and managed care categories, there are literally hundreds of different benefit and payment options that health care providers must be familiar with.

The Payment Methodologies

The incentives associated with payment systems must be viewed from the perspective of the economic risks being taken by the providers. In general, the more economic risk the provider has for the population served, the more conservative will be the services rendered. This does not mean that the provider will withhold needed health services, but it could mean that the frequency of services could be modified. Furthermore, when pharmaceuticals or medical supplies are the issue, substitutable generic drugs or lower-cost supplies might be considered. Finally, when the risk for the health status of the population being served is undertaken by a health care provider, the incentives relative to wellness initiatives change.

In Chapter 3 the equations for various forms of inpatient reimbursement were given, along with Table 3-1 that delineates the extent to which the provider bears economic risk for each of the reimbursement systems. As the reimbursement system for health care evolves from the billed charges reimbursement methodology to the global capitation era, the provider takes on more and more economic risk, until, finally, all of the economic risk is taken under global capitation. The economic risk is broken into three categories: risk for price, risk for volume of services given, and the risk for the health status of the population.

Risk for Price

The risk for price addresses the extent to which the provider sets the price prospectively and the extent to which the provider is therefore able to change the price unilaterally. Health care providers lost the ability to change price fairly early in the evolution of payment systems and thus took on the risk for price. As a result of this pricing inflexibility, incentives evolved that encouraged certain cost-cutting behavior on the part of providers. The incentives to change behavior in matters related to pricing take into consideration the ability to substitute generic pharmaceuticals or substitute less costly goods and supplies. When the price that will be paid for a good or service is fixed, there is greater incentive to use less costly drugs and supplies. These changes became pronounced with the change to **per diem pricing** and the change to **case rate pricing** when Medicare implemented the diagnosis related groups (**DRG**) reimbursement methodology.

Risk for Volume of Services Given

The risk for volume looks at the issues related to the amount of services rendered to a patient under each episode of illness. In this scenario, the payer pays the same amount regardless of the amount of services rendered. There are sometimes adjustments for the intensity of the illness, as is the case with DRGs, but this is not always true, as is the case with capitation. As the reimbursement methodology transfers the risk for volume of services rendered, there is an incentive for the health care provider to render only services that are required to maintain the level of quality designated by community standards of care. While DRGs certainly place the risk for price on the provider, the primary change in moving to DRG payments was that for the first time (except for limited geographic areas where capitation existed), it shifted the risk for volume to providers on a large-scale basis.

Risk for Health Status of the Population

The risk for the health status of the population being served relates to the frequency that subscribers will use the health care system. Economic risk for the health status of the population generally accrues to the provider only under capitation. For example, under a case rate reimbursement mechanism like DRGs, the number of times that a patient accesses the system is generally unimportant because the provider is paid each time the patient accesses the system. Readmission for the same diagnosis within a specified period of time is usually reimbursed under the original admission with no additional payments made. However, except for this condition, it is generally true that under DRGs, the provider is paid regardless of the number of times that the patient accesses the system.

Under capitation, the provider is paid a single amount **per member per month (PMPM)**, regardless of how often the patient uses the system. Here, the provider has taken on the economic risk for the health status of the population being served, and it is in the best interest of the provider for the population to be as healthy as is possible. In this environment, health status programs such as smoking cessation, weight reduction, exercising, and other lifestyle changes take on much more importance to the provider because it is in the health provider's best interest that the population of patients being served be healthy.

An additional dimension of this issue is that in the pluralistic payment system that currently exists, the incentive for providers to maintain a healthy population exists primarily in the capitated setting, and not under other reimbursement schemes. Thus, when people in the population have the ability to move from one plan (with one kind of payment system) to another plan (with another payment methodology), there is the potential for one plan to expend significant resources in raising the health status within the covered lives in their plan, only to have those persons move to another plan, which will benefit from the healthiness at no cost to itself. Thus, there is a significant disincentive to promote health in the population when the positive results might be reaped by a health plan other than the plan initially providing the services. Unless there is a single payment methodology within a population, this "leakage" will remain a problem.

Budgeting Under Capitation

Budgeting under capitation is entirely different from budgeting under a fee-for-service reimbursement system. Saying this is equivalent to saying that budgeting when the payer is an indemnity insurance payer or a preferred provider payer is much different from budgeting when the payer is an HMO. This is not to say that HMOs always pay on a capitated basis, because they do not, but various other ploys are sometimes exercised by HMOs to shift the risk from the payer to the provider, and this can have some of the same effects as shifting the risk by capitation. The degree to which the risk is shifted to the health provider is most often a function of the level of maturity of the local market. Managed care organizations typically do not wish to shift the risk and move to a capitated model until the market is mature. The reason is that until the market is mature, there are inefficiencies to be squeezed out of it, and to the extent that the managed care companies are able to control the process, they wish to be the beneficiaries of gaining the efficiencies.

There are many varieties of capitation, and the form that it takes is a function of variables that include the level of maturity of the market, the willingness of various providers to take risk, the position of control that the payer(s) or provider(s) maintain over the health care market, and the relative position of power exercised within the provider community between institutions and physicians. Reimbursement can take the form of capitating only primary care services, or it can take a more evolved form of capitating all physician services (both primary and specialist care). Finally it can take the form of capitating all health services, which would include **primary care physicians (PCPs)**, specialist physicians, hospitals, and other health services, such as home health services and durable medical equipment. This latter form is sometimes called global capitation because the economic risks for all health services are assumed by the provider. In any of these reimbursement forms except for when the PCP is the only provider capitated, there remains the question of who takes the risk, which is equivalent to who signed the contract. For example, when all physician services are covered by capitation, theoretically either the primary physician or the specialist could be the contractor having subcontracts with the other to provide the remaining services. Alternatively, with a multispecialty group with primary care capabilities, the entire entity takes the risk. And when all health care services are covered by capitation, there is the question of whether the hospital is the contractor or whether some part of the physician component is the contractor with the managed care company. Only when there is an integrated delivery system with a fully integrated physician component can there be a single contract for global services. This is one of the conditions that makes an integrated delivery system an appealing option for organizing health care delivery.

The Economic Scenario for a Managed Care Company

In simplified form, the flow of funds through an HMO is that funds are received from two sources and expended in two areas.

The Revenue Stream

The largest part of the revenue stream is from premiums paid by subscribers who expect to be able to access health care through the relationships established by the managed care company. (For a complete discussion of the relationships between the managed care company and the provider community, see Chapters 3 and 4.) The other revenue stream for the managed care companies arises from interest income on the premiums before they are paid out and earnings on other idle funds. There are two ways in which the managed care company can optimize this source of income: (1) collect the premium as far in advance as is practical or (2) delay payment for services by health care providers as long as possible. This latter condition has become a significant problem in some local instances and forms the basis for yet another reason that managed care organizations and health care providers are at odds with each other. It is in the best interest of the health care provider to get paid as quickly as possible, while it is in the best interest of the managed care company to delay payment as long as possible.

The Expenses

The expenses of an HMO fall into two primary categories: (1) payment made to health care providers for medical services and (2) administrative expenses required to run the organization. The medical loss ratio, which is the percentage of the premium dollar paid out in medical claims, is the most difficult to predict. It is therefore not surprising that as the local market matures and the efficiencies have been squeezed out of it, the managed care companies will seek to shift the economic risk for the health of the population being covered to the health care providers. In this way, they are able to be more assured that they will meet their financial operating objectives because the least predictable element (payment for medical services) is no longer their responsibility. It is interesting to note that managed care companies are tending to spend a higher percentage of the premium dollar on administrative services as contrasted to spending it on health care services for their subscribers. Over the past 10 years, the percentage of premium dollar spent on administrative services has ranged from 14 to 18 percent in the earlier years to 17 to 20 percent or more recently. So far the literature has not reported any studies that establish a cause-and-effect relationship with these spending patterns. One could hypothesize various scenarios. One could link the change to an actual need for more administrative services, particularly that of marketing as the local environments become more competitive. One could hypothesize that as the managed care companies have shifted the risk from themselves to the providers, they are no longer worried about that sector and have simply focused on increasing their profitability by retaining more of the premium. Along similar lines, one might theorize that the costs have actually been squeezed out of the system and there is simply less money being spent on providing health care and that the premiums have been reduced while the administrative expenses have remained constant. Any of these theories must consider not only the way that the expenses are occurring but also whether the amount of the premium is changing. It remains for some research studies to establish a cause-and-effect relationship between the elements that contribute to the percentage of premium allocated to administrative services.

The Economic Scenario for the Health Care Provider

As the economic risk is shifted to the health care provider, it becomes more and more difficult for the provider to predict accurately either the revenue streams or the expenses of the organization. The problem is compounded by a lack of precision in cost finding for health care providers. This lack of precision can arise not only from poorly conceived cost-finding systems but also from the fact that estimation must often be involved in allocating commonly used services and facilities across the inpatient acute care and ambulatory care entities of the organization. Something as simple as a chest radiograph can vary in cost depending on whether it is an inpatient or ambulatory exam, even if it is done on the same equipment with the same technicians.

For purposes of this discussion, capitation is assumed to be the predominant reimbursement model. Under capitation, the revenue streams are difficult to predict not because the unit reimbursement is unknown but rather because the organization is often not in a position to predict accurately the number of patients it will serve. For both the hospital and the physician, the unit price is known and is usually given as a **per member per month (PMPM)** figure. That is, for the particular services contracted to be delivered, the provider is paid a specified amount PMPM.

In the case of a hospital, it is sometimes difficult to know exactly which patients represent the lives being covered unless the contract is written as a global capitation contract, usually for an integrated delivery system (**IDS**). For example, in the case of an IDS holding a global capitation risk contract, the network is paid a specific amount PMPM to provide for all of the health care needs of the population of covered lives. It therefore makes little difference to the organization whether the patient goes to Hospital A or Hospital B if they are in the same IDS. However, when the hospital is independent, it is virtually impossible to predict which patients will go to a particular hospital, so paying the individual hospital on a PMPM basis is not a realistic option. In those cases, the managed care organization or IDS usually contracts on either a per diem basis or a case rate basis. A per diem reimbursement means the managed care organization agrees to pay the hospital a particular amount of money for each day a patient of the health plan spends in the hospital. A case rate means that the hospital is paid a specified amount for each hospital stay; the amount is based on the intensity of service and is usually defined by the diagnosis or DRG.

Setting the Price

From the perspective of both the managed care company and the provider, this activity is probably the most critical issue in the entire contracting process. Recall that in general, indemnity plans provide the broadest range of choices to the insured with regard to the use of providers and HMOs provide the narrowest range of choices. Conversely, indemnity plans provide the narrowest range of medical benefits to the insured while HMOs provide the widest range of choices. Thus, there are trade-offs to all of the parties involved: the payer, the provider, and the patient. The following paragraphs outline the pricing issues that face the physician provider and the institutional provider under a capitation contract when they act independently and are not part of the same organization.

Pricing Physician Services

Pricing physician services under capitation is a complex issue. In general, PCPs are paid by one methodology and **specialty care physicians (SCP)** by another reimbursement system. There are many combinations and permutations of the various methodologies for physician reimbursement under capitation, but we examine only the most common one here. One of the things that makes the reimbursement system complex is that under the pluralistic payment system, the fee-for-service method imposes a different set of economic incentives than the capitation system does.

Figure 8-1 demonstrates that income under a fee-for-service reimbursement system is optimized by doing as much for the patient as is possible and ethically correct.

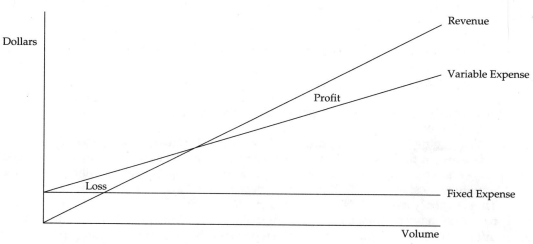

Figure 8-1   Profitability Under Fee-for-Service

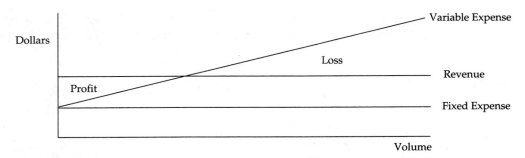

Figure 8-2   Profitability Under Capitation

In this paradigm, break-even is achieved when a volume of business is reached that is sufficient to cover all fixed and variable costs. All additional volume makes a contribution to a higher level of profit. In this reimbursement methodology, revenue varies with the volume of services provided, as do the costs.

Figure 8-2 shows that income under a capitated reimbursement environment is optimized by doing as little for the patient as is possible, given that quality of care will be maintained. In this scenario, break-even is achieved when no more services are provided than are covered by the fixed reimbursement. Income is therefore optimized by providing as few services as is possible, given that the quality of care is maintained. In this reimbursement methodology, the revenue is fixed, and the costs vary with the volume of services provided.

Primary Care Physicians

In a capitation environment, PCPs are usually the ones who are capitated, while SCPs are most often paid on the basis of a fee schedule.

There are several key pieces of information that are needed in order to determine the appropriate price under a capitated payment system:

- The expected number of encounters per member per year
- The cost per encounter
- The profit margin required

Each of these requires significant thought and planning prior to negotiating the price for capitation.

Obtaining the information about the expected number of encounters per patient per year is by far the most difficult information to obtain. In some cases, the managed care company is the only source for this information, and in some instances they are unwilling to share it with the practice because they are in negotiations with them. Thus, the only other real source of this information is other experience that the practice might have or national norms. Either of these has the potential to produce biased information because they might not be representative of the population of patients for which the contract is being negotiated. A further difficulty is determining whether the expected utilization is being projected on the basis of all encounters that the practice might have or whether it is stratified on the basis of types of encounters.

The questions related to the cost per encounter are technical; they address the level of sophistication of the cost finding system being used by the practice. For example, should the practice determine the average cost per encounter, or should it calculate the cost of each individual health care service that the practice provides? Finding the average cost for all services rendered is the least resource intensive, but it is also the least sophisticated in terms of being able to isolate individual causes for cost overruns. The practice must make this decision based on their view of the cost of providing the information versus the value of that information in decision making.

The profit margin required for the contract must take into consideration whether the costs include such nonexpense items as charity care. Generally charity care is not an expense item in the profit and loss statement and as such might not be included in the cost finding methodology that determines the costs of doing business for each health care procedure performed by the practice. Rather, charity care is a reduction of revenue. In that physicians often find themselves in the position of having to provide charity care or give health care below cost to indigent patients, there is a need to determine the extent to which the overall profitability of the practice will allow for these kinds of activities. This is actually a seriously debated health care policy issue. On the one hand, the managed care company generally contends it is not responsible for the well-being of society but rather is responsible only to the lives it insures and to its stockholders if it is a for-profit entity. Managed care companies have systematically reduced the reimbursement to health care providers, thereby reducing the ability of the provider to give health care to the medically indigent. To the extent that providing care to the medically indigent is a responsibility of health care providers, some financing mechanism must be provided, and building it into the profit margin is one of these mechanisms.

Thus, the data elements required to determine the appropriate level of reimbursement in a capitation contract are difficult to obtain. By far the most difficult information to obtain, in terms of reliability, is the expected number of encounters for the lives being covered.

If a PCP negotiating a capitated contract had the following information, the actual calculation would be straightforward:

- Type of service is office visits
- Average number of encounters per member per year
- Average cost per office visit

The PMPM cost is found by the following formula:

$$\text{PMPM cost} = \frac{(\text{Average encounters per member per year})(\text{average cost per visit})}{12}.$$

Here is the calculation if the average number of encounters per year is 4.5 and the average cost of an office visit is $60:

$$\text{PMPM cost} = \frac{(4.5)(\$60)}{12} = \$22.50.$$

Thus the PCP would have to receive $22.50 PMPM in order to break even economically, given that the assumptions about the cost per visit and the average number of visits per patient per year are accurate. Other issues must be part of the negotiation too:

- Are hospital visits included in the 4.5 average encounters per year?
- Are catastrophic diseases like AIDS covered in the capitation, or are they carved out?
- Are routine inoculations included in the capitation? This is a particularly important question when the covered lives include a large number of children.
- What other items are carved out and thus not part of the capitation? Potential candidates are pharmacy, laboratory, and radiology services. If they are not carved out, this represents a significant additional economic exposure to the practice, and the average cost per visit must be modified.

In order to understand the sensitivity of this equation, let us make the assumption that it is one year later and the following data represent the actual experience of the PCP:

- Average visits per member per year is 4.3.
- Number of patients enrolled with the PCP is 600.
- PMPM capitation is $22.50.

$$\begin{aligned}
\text{Total reimbursement} &= \text{Enrolled patients} \times \text{PMPM capitation} \times 12 \\
&= 600 \times \$22.50 \times 12 \\
&= \$162,000
\end{aligned}$$

$$\begin{aligned}
\text{Total cost} &= \text{Enrolled patients} \times \text{average visits per year} \times \text{cost per visit} \\
&= 600 \times 4.3 \times \$60 \\
&= \$154,800
\end{aligned}$$

$$\begin{aligned}
\text{Annual profit} &= \text{Total reimbursement} - \text{total cost} \\
&= \$162,000 - \$154,800 \\
&= \$7,200
\end{aligned}$$

By contrast, if the utilization was higher than the rate used when calculating the capitation rate, the practice would experience a loss. Let us assume the following data describe the actual experience of the practice in treating this group of patients:

- Average visits per member per year is 4.9.
- Number of patients enrolled with the PCP is 600.
- PMPM capitation is $22.50.

Applying the same formulas, the results are as follows:

$$\text{Total reimbursement} = \text{Enrolled patients} \times \text{PMPM capitation} \times 12$$
$$= 600 \times \$22.50 \times 12$$
$$= \$162,000$$

$$\text{Total cost} = \text{Enrolled patients} \times \text{average visits per year} \times \text{cost per visit}$$
$$= 600 \times 4.9 \times \$60$$
$$= \$176,400$$

$$\text{Annual profit} = \text{Total reimbursement} - \text{total cost}$$
$$= \$162,000 - \$176,400$$
$$= (\$14,400)$$

With this shift in utilization from an average of 4.3 visits per member per year to 4.9 visits, the profitability of the practice in treating this group shifts from a profit of $7,200 to a loss of $14,400. It becomes readily apparent why health care providers are becoming increasingly sensitive to the volume of services rendered when they operate under capitation.

This exercise also makes apparent the importance of accurate cost finding for the practice. For example, if the actual average cost per visit was $62 when the practice thought it was $60 per visit, the capitation rate would still have been set at $22.50 PMPM. However, the actual costs for serving the population would be represented as follows if we make the assumption that the average number of visits was as predicted at 4.5 per year:

$$\text{Total Cost} = \text{Enrolled patients} \times \text{average visits per year} \times \text{cost per visit}$$
$$= 600 \times \$62 \times 4.5$$
$$= \$167,400$$

$$\text{Annual profit} = \text{Total reimbursement} - \text{total cost}$$
$$= \$162,000 - \$167,400$$
$$= (\$5,400)$$

In this scenario, the costs were not accurately determined, and the practice lost money on this covered group even though the actual utilization was exactly what had been predicted.

Specialty Care Physicians

The reimbursement methodology most frequently used with SCPs is some form of fee schedule. The type of schedule can range from the use of relative value units (**RVU**), to a fee schedule that is part of the contract, to a schedule that represents a discount from billed charges. This last mechanism is becoming rare because a discount from billed charges gives the physician the ability to increase compensation by changing prices. The other two mechanisms, and permutations of them, fix the reimbursement prospectively for a defined set of services.

Generally a **gatekeeper** is used to prevent overutilization of specialty services. This means that a patient is not able to see a specialty physician, nor is a specialty physician reimbursed, unless a PCP from the plan refers the patient to the specialist. In addition, the PCP is often made economically responsible for overutilization of specialists by participation in the specialist **risk pool,** a mechanism used by the managed care organization to have the health care providers participate in the economic risk of insuring the population of patients covered by the plan. When the managed care company has no economic risk, as in the case of global capitation, there is no risk pool unless the contracting provider sets one up. However, where economic risk remains for the managed care organization, as in the case with hospitals being paid on a per diem basis or specialists being paid by a fee schedule, the use of a risk pool is common.

Assume that there is a managed care plan with 100,000 members and that a budget to cover specialty services is $18 PMPM has been actuarially established. This means that the total budget to cover specialty care is:

$$\text{Annual SCP budget} = \text{Number of members} \times \text{PMPM reimbursement} \times 12$$
$$= 100,000 \times \$18 \times 12$$
$$= \$21,600,000$$

A formula often used is that 10 percent of the budget is set up as a risk pool. In this case, $2,160,000 is set aside as the risk pool, and $19,440,000 is actually available to pay for specialty services before the risk pool is invaded:

$$\text{Funds available to pay SPC services} = \text{Annual SCP budget} - \text{withhold}$$
$$= \$21,600,000 - \$2,160,000$$
$$= \$19,440,000$$

Normally, three parties participate in the risk pool: the PCP, the SCP, and the managed care organization. The PCP participates because he or she controls utilization by the number of referrals made as the gatekeeper. The SPC controls utilization by providing only those specialty services that are needed.

To demonstrate how this mechanism works, assume that the amount paid out for specialty care was $18,500,000. This means that the budget was underspent by $940,000 ($19,440,000 − $18,500,000). This also means that the risk pool is distributed to the three parties participating. The PCPs, SCPs, and HMO will each receive $720,000 ($2,160,000/3). Generally the amount of the budget that was underspent (in this case, $940,000) accrues only to the HMO, although this could be a matter of negotiation in setting up the contract. Since the physicians usually do not participate in **downside risk,** which is the risk associated with experiencing losses in providing health services, the HMO generally is unwilling to allow them to participate in upside risk, which is the risk associated with gains in providing health services.

Assume that instead of paying out $18,500,000 for specialty services, $22,000,000 was paid out. In this case, the budget has been exceeded by $2,560,000 ($19,440,000 − $22,000,000), and the risk pool is used to make up the deficit but still exceeds the annual SPC Budget of $21,600,000 by $400,000. In this case, none of the risk pool is returned to the participants. Whether the PCPs and SCPs participate in the $400,000 loss is a matter of negotiation in setting up the original contract.

Assume a middle ground experience: $19,800,000 is paid out for specialty services. In this case, the budget of $19,440,000 is exceeded, but the risk pool is only partially invaded to cover the loss. In most cases, the remainder of the risk pool is distributed to the participants, but this is also a matter established by the negotiated contract. If the remainder of the risk pool is distributed, each of the three participants would receive $600,000:

$$\text{Risk pool distribution} = \frac{\text{Risk pool} - \text{budget deficit}}{\text{Number of participants}}$$
$$= \frac{\$2,160,000 - \$360,000}{3}$$
$$= \$600,000$$

Issues that must be determined and made part of the contract include the following:

- How the risk pool proceeds will be distributed among individual physicians
- Whether the physicians participate in downside risk
- Whether the physicians participate in upside risk
- Whether the physicians participate in partial risk pools

Pricing Hospital Services

As with the case of physician services, pricing hospital services under capitation varies with the degree of capitation. For example, if a global capitation contract is involved, the issue of establishing a risk pool or a withhold is moot because the risk resides with one party and there is no risk to share. Except for organ transplantation procedures, a global capitation is rarely used in large metropolitan areas because patients want choice not only with their physician but with hospitals as well. In areas where IDSs have matured, managed care organizations sometimes establish insurance products that use a particular IDS exclusively. In those cases, global capitation could be the reimbursement model if both parties agree.

In most cases, the market is still fragmented enough that the managed care organization must provide the flexibility for the insured lives to select different hospitals. This means that it is virtually impossible to predict in advance which patients would select a particular hospital, and thus pure capitation becomes a very difficult reimbursement model. The usual approach is to pay the hospital on a per diem or a case rate basis, which means that the hospital is paid a negotiated rate either for each day the patient is in the hospital or for the entire patient stay, as is the case with DRGs. For purposes of illustration, assume that the PCP is capitated, the SCP is paid on a fee schedule basis, and the hospital is paid on a prospectively negotiated per diem rate.

As in the case of physician rates, the key issue for hospitals is knowing what costs are experienced in providing health care. In this example, where the contract will reimburse on a per diem basis, it must be determined whether the costs will be stratified by types of services rendered. Critical care units will experience substantially higher costs than routine medical or surgical admissions, and both will be higher than psychiatric and obstetrical services. The question arises whether the contract should be stratified with per diems for each category of service. If this is the case, the hospital must be able to know the specific costs associated with each service, thus requiring a sophisticated cost finding system within the institution.

In this example, the hospital is part of an IDS that holds the contract to provide services exclusively to this health plan. (For purposes of simplicity, a single average per diem for all services will be assumed, but the methodology can be readily adapted to a stratified reimbursement system.) The plan has the following characteristics:

- Plan size: 100,000 members
- Plan utilization: 350 days per 1,000 population
- Hospital use: 10 percent of the plan's members
- Average cost per day: $1,000
- Risk pool: Yes
- Withhold: 10 percent
- Parties in risk pool: Hospital only

The expected total number of hospitalized days for the plan would be 35,000, (350 days/1,000 population × 100). The hospital expects to serve 10 percent of these patients, so the expected number of patient-days is 3,500. Since average cost per day for the hospital is $1,000, the total cost for serving these patients is $3,500,000 (3,500 patient days × $1,000 cost per day). Therefore, the hospital would be interested in negotiating a contract that would at least cover the total costs of $1,000 per day. Alternatives would be to view this business as marginal revenue if it represents new business or to anticipate that during the life of the contract, the organization would be able to reduce the average cost per day.

Marginal revenue is a complex concept that cannot be treated in detail here, but in general it holds that if the business being contracted is new business that the organization would otherwise not have and if the organization has excess capacity, then a lower price can be accepted because the only incremental costs that will be experienced in serving these patients will be the variable costs associated with the service, such as supplies and food. The fixed costs are already being covered by other patients. The danger of this approach is that if relatively large numbers of patients are contracted on a marginal cost basis, at some point in time, the organization will not have enough patients who are budgeted to cover the fixed costs of the organization.

In this example, the hospital would receive only $900 per day because the contract calls for a 10 percent withhold that becomes part of the risk pool. In the event that the hospital meets its volume objectives, the withhold is returned and made part of the reimbursement. If not, the withhold is forfeited.

Assume that the hospital actually experienced 3,400 patient-days and that projected average costs of $1,000 per day were accurate. How would this affect the total reimbursement of the hospital?

$$\text{Hospital target budget} = \text{Projected patient-days} \times (\text{rate} - \text{withhold})$$
$$= 3,500 \times (\$1,000 - \$100)$$
$$= \$3,150,000$$

$$\text{Routine hospital payments} = \text{Patient-days} \times (\text{rate} - \text{withhold})$$
$$= 3,400 \times (\$1,000 - \$100)$$
$$= \$3,060,000$$

Since the hospital was under its target by $90,000 (hospital target budget – routine hospital payments), it is eligible to participate in the withhold. However, depending on the structure of the contract, the withhold might be distributed only if all of the other hospitals (the other 90 percent of the patient-days) also meet their objectives. Alternatively, as in the case of some physician contracts, the participants might receive a prorated discount if the target deficit is less than the total withhold.

If we assume that the entire network met its patient-days target, the following pay-out would occur for the withhold. The risk pool (withhold) amounted to $350,000 (10 percent of the target budget of $3,500,000). The withhold distribution would be as follows:

$$\text{Withhold distribution} = \text{Risk pool} - \text{budget deficit}$$
$$= \$350,000 - \$0$$
$$= \$350,000$$

Assume that instead of the target of 3,500 patient-days, the hospital experienced 3,600 patient-days. This means that instead of the targeted costs of $3,150,000 for patient-days, $3,240,000 was expended, for a deficit of $90,000. Assuming that the other hospitals in the IDS met their target and that the contract allows for a prorated distribution of the withhold, the pay-out would be as follows:

$$\text{Withhold distribution} = \text{Risk pool} - \text{budget deficit}$$
$$= \$350,000 - \$90,000$$
$$= \$260,000$$

Note that to the extent that the hospital does not receive its entire withhold, it is not covering its anticipated costs. That is, the projected costs per day were $1,000. The withhold constituted 10 percent of that cost, or $100 per patient day. In the case just cited, the hospital received only $240,000 instead of the entire $350,000, so its costs were underpaid by $90,000.

Other scenarios could occur that would further complicate the reimbursement and would include conditions where the hospital exceeds its withhold or where other hospitals in the IDS miss their target.

Depending on how the contract is written between this hospital and the IDS, it is possible that other hospitals in the IDS would make up the deficit for the particular health plan under contract. Alternatively, this hospital would simply have to make up the deficit from their other operations.

If other hospitals in the IDS miss their target, a variety of outcomes could occur with regard to targeted volume outcomes. This hospital could (1) make its target, (2) miss its target but not exceed the withhold, or (3) exceed the withhold. And any other hospital in the IDS could (1) make its target, (2) miss its target but not exceed the withhold, or (3) exceed the withhold. If there are ten hospitals in the network, the number of combinations and permutations of outcomes is enormous. Nevertheless, it is important to be aware of this level of complexity because setting up the operating budget of an organization must make estimates of the most likely outcomes and act accordingly.

Building the Budget

In its simplest form, a budget consists of planning for and anticipating the revenue that is expected by the organization and the expenses it will experience in providing services to its clients. The profitability of the organization depends on two management actions: (1) optimizing the revenue of the organization and (2) minimizing the expenses. In a capitation environment, these two activities are interrelated. For example, in the case of hospitals in the typical capitation model, revenue is optimized by minimizing expense. This is the precise role of the withhold. By virtue of minimizing expenses, the withhold may be obtained, thereby increasing the revenue of the organization. The same is true with the typical SCP reimbursement model, where efficient operation (minimizing expenses) can result in the risk pool's being distributed, thereby increasing the revenue of the organization. Finally, in the case of global capitation, efficient operations do not increase revenue directly because revenue is fixed, but it does directly affect the net profit of the organization.

Given this environment, it is little wonder that health care professionals are acutely aware of expense management. Their operating budgets must consider this activity as a major strategy in maintaining the profitability of the organization.

Creating an operating budget in the capitated environment is a challenging and difficult task. Many of the factors determining the budget are unknown or at best subject to probabilities of occurrence. Unless the population being served under capitation is large enough to be subject to statistical and actuarial rules, the outcomes are likely to be unreliable. But when the population is large enough to be subject to statistical and actuarial rules, the potential for substantially increasing the profitability of the organization by effective management is good.

Observations About Operating Budgets Under Capitation

Only the most straightforward examples have been given in this chapter. Hints have been given about the extraordinary levels of complexity that can occur in a typical health care environment. Standardization in capitation reimbursement has not yet occurred, nor is it likely to occur in the near future, so the issue of trying to create an operating plan (budget) is complex and uncertain, built on many assumptions about what might happen in the environment. The level of uncertainty increases with the amount of economic risk that is transferred to health care providers out as one moves along the reimbursement continuum from withholds and risk pools to global capitation.

Reliable information is the most effective weapon against this uncertainty. Health care organizations must have cost-finding systems that produce accurate information about the organization's operations. They must have environmental information about the health status of the population, as well as the health choices that the population is likely to make. This information is difficult to obtain, but that does not mean it should not be pursued. The successful organizations of the future are likely to be the ones having these types of information on a timely, accurate, and cost-effective basis.

Other Issues

This chapter has discussed only the conceptual framework of operating budgets under capitation. There are many additional issues that have tangential effects on the process that we will mention briefly to provide insight into the complexity of the overall process.

Other Financial Factors

Withholds

Withholds—funds withheld from the reimbursement of the physician or hospital and designed to provide a pool of funds that can be used if the medical service costs exceed the managed care organization's budget—might or might not be part of a risk contract. When a withhold is part of the contract, the actual agreed-on total reimbursement is reduced by a specified amount, resulting in a lower reimbursement unless economic targets are met and the withhold is returned at the end of the accounting period. For example, assume that a hospital has a 10 percent withhold on an agreed per diem payment of $1,000. This means that the hospital is actually paid $900, and $100 is withheld by the managed care organization. At the end of the year, if the hospital has met its economic and utilization objectives, the withheld amount is returned. If the criteria have not been met, the funds are retained by the managed care organization. When constructing an operating budget, health care managers must consider the budgetary impact of a withhold, which includes the cash flow effects, as well as consideration of whether it seems likely that the funds will be returned to the entity.

Risk Pools

A risk pool is a mechanism to administer withholds. (Risk pools can be funded by methods other than withholds, although this is rare.) In general, a risk pool is set up as an incentive to encourage lower utilization and to provide some financial protection to the managed care organization. A simplified risk pool arrangement was discussed earlier in this chapter. The conditions under which the pay-out occurs can be complex, particularly if physicians and/or hospitals are independent of each other. Triggering the risk pool has three possible outcomes by the providers. Each individual provider can (1) achieve the budgeted economic objectives in total, (2) not achieve the budgeted economic objectives but also not exceed the risk pool, or (3) not achieve the budgeted economic objectives and also exceed the amount in the risk pool. Each outcome will have a different economic impact on the provider as defined by the contract. Depending on how the contract is written, the issue can be complicated by the fact that what other providers do affects the outcome of all of the participants.

In the context of this chapter, the issues associated with how a risk pool is administered must be considered by health care managers in constructing a budget. Particularly important is an assessment of whether management believes that the risk pool funds will be received and thus be transformed into real revenue. Secondary considerations relate to cash flow implications.

Deductibles

A deductible is the amount that must be paid by the patient before any benefits are paid by the health plan and usually is part of a fee-for-service environment for physicians or part of a per diem or case rate environment for hospitals. Capitated contracts usually do not have deductibles. A $250 deductible would mean that the patient must pay $250 before the health plan begins paying benefits. The deductible usually resets itself annually and applies to each member of a family. While this amount is considered normal reimbursement under the health plan, the provider is responsible for collecting it from the patient, and the health plan has no responsibility for the amount. This means that there is the potential for some or all of a deductible amount to become a bad debt to a provider. When constructing a budget, the health care manager must have some insight into the amount of deductibles that will be collected, in contrast to the amount that becomes bad debts. The accuracy of this estimate will have a direct impact on both the revenue (and ultimately the profitability) of the organization, as well as its cash flow.

Co-Insurance

Co-insurance is the amount of money that a patient pays with each service event. For example, a health plan might have a $5 co-payment with each office visit. This means that the patient must pay $5 each time he or she sees the physician. Alternatively, the co-insurance could be a percentage of the agreed-on reimbursement for the service event. For example, if the health plan agrees to pay a hospital $3,000 for an appendectomy and has a 20 percent co-insurance, the patient would be responsible for $600 of the $3,000 obligation, assuming all deductibles had been met. As is the case with a deductible, co-insurance is considered to be part of the reimbursement. It is the responsibility of the provider to collect this amount; the health plan has no responsibility for it. A co-insurance can be part of a fee-for-service plan as well as a capitated plan. As in the case of a deductible, the dimensions of collecting the co-insurance must be considered by the health care administrator when constructing a budget.

Defining Covered Services

When a physician practice or hospital enters into a capitated contract, it is essential that both parties clearly understand what is covered by the capitation amount and what is not. Services included in the reimbursement are referred to as **covered services.** Examples of items that are sometimes not part of the capitated amount are services out of the area, immunizations, pharmaceuticals, laboratory services, vision services, and radiology services. Each of these services carries with it a price, and it must be clear whether it is the responsibility of the health plan or the provider to cover these services. When a health care manager budgets under capitation, it is essential that he or she knows exactly what services are expected under the capitation. Slight variations in utilization can change a profit to a loss.

Use of Stop Loss Insurance

When a physician practice or a hospital takes on a risk contract, it is sometimes unwilling to accept all of the economic risk associated with the plan. Concerns about risk are particularly pronounced relative to catastrophic acute care cases and when the risk contract involves relatively small groups. In these cases, one solution is to purchase **stop loss insurance** in the commercial sector to cover potential losses. The more exposure that the external insurer takes, the more costly is the premium. Therefore, in most cases, the practice or hospital will purchase stop loss insurance to cover only those amounts that the entity itself could not sustain.

Environmental Factors

There are environmental factors at work that affect how capitation works but are not directly related to it. The following paragraphs draw attention to the fact that these factors exist and should be considered by any health care manager working with capitation.

Integrated Delivery Systems

When discussing capitation, IDSs play a very important role. They facilitate the capitation process because it is possible to get the geographic coverage that is necessary to create an exclusive relationship with a managed care organization for a health plan product while providing a range of physician and institutional health care services that meet the needs of the population being covered. That is, a managed care organization requires wide geographic coverage for any health care product that it markets to a metropolitan area, and dealing with a number of independent health care entities is not an attractive option if an IDS is available. Contracting with a number of independent entities requires additional administrative resources at the managed care organization, whereas working with an IDS is focused and requires relatively fewer administrative resources.

In addition, an IDS facilitates the capitation process because it can be the focal point for administering withholds and risk pools. When all of the physician practices and hospitals are aligned with a single IDS, the risk can be taken by the IDS and then distributed among its members in any way that seems appropriate and desirable. Thus, the administrative process involved with overseeing the risk pool is considerably simplified but at the same time transfers some of the control and autonomy out of the local provider to the IDS.

Capitating the Specialist

Earlier discussions described the typical capitated relationship with physicians as one where the PCP is capitated and the specialist is paid by some form of fee for service. The conventional wisdom is that this structure will control utilization because the PCP acts as a gatekeeper and refers to specialists only when necessary. This reasoning is extended to suggest that the PCPs will minimize usage because they have an economic incentive to reduce utilization. All of this is true, but there is another side to this issue that takes a longer view of the process.

If the objective of managed care is to offer care to its covered lives at the lowest possible cost, consistent with community standards for quality, it follows that it is in the best interest of the organization taking the economic risk to maintain the highest level of health that is possible among its population. One way to achieve this is to have the people covered by the plan receive as much preventive care as is possible, and most of this is likely to come from the PCP. However, since the PCP is capitated, he or she will minimize the number of visits. Obviously this is backward from the way it ought to be if the plan is interested in health promotion. The PCP should be paid on a fee-for-service basis. This will encourage the PCP to see the patients as often as is necessary, even when the illness is relatively minor, and it will also encourage the PCP to provide health promotion programs that will enhance healthiness in the population. By contrast, in this scenario it would make more sense to capitate the specialist in order to discourage unnecessary specialty work.

This model is not the generally accepted one for capitation of physicians, but it shows the alternatives to managing the health of a population and that the conventional wisdom is not always the only way to do things.

Productivity

Increasing the efficiency of an organization is one way to improve its profitability. As managed care organizations continue the trend to lower reimbursement, an organization must consider ways to become more productive. As the maturity of a health care market moves along a continuum from having the providers assume little risk to a position where they assume higher levels of economic risk, there are fewer options for an entity to increase the revenue stream of the organization. If one assumes a finite number of patients in a market, there are a number of options for increasing the revenue in a fee-for-service reimbursement environment, including doing a higher volume of services and in some cases providing a higher level of testing. However, as one moves to capitation, revenue cannot be increased by doing a higher volume of services or more intensive diagnostic and therapeutic procedures. The revenue is fixed for the finite population. The only other way to improve the profitability of the organization is to increase its productivity (lower costs).

The Shift to Ambulatory Sites

An additional environmental factor that plays a part in budgeting under capitation is the fact that more and more procedures are being shifted from an inpatient acute care site to ambulatory sites. If the capitation is global under a single provider (i.e., an IDS), the site of delivery makes little difference. However, if the provider is not integrated, it can make a great deal of difference in budgeting because ownership of the sites might be different and thus the revenue stream would change.

Adverse Selection and "Leakage"

Adverse selection must be considered in evaluating economic risk for a health plan. Adverse selection holds that less healthy individuals select a particular health plan at a higher than normal rate for some particular reason(s)—perhaps the price, location of services, or reputation. Whatever the reason, sometimes a health plan will end up with a less healthy group than would be actuarially expected from the population, a situation referred to as adverse selection. This obviously has serious consequences for budgeting because utilization rates will be higher if the health status of the group is lower.

A second event that must be considered is when a health plan engages in various kinds of health promotions (smoking cessation, weight reduction, breast screenings, etc.) in order to promote the overall health status of the group being covered but then finds those same patients changing to another health plan after a year or two. The initial idea of improving the health status of the group is sound, but it will pay dividends to the health plan only over the long term. If individuals switch out of the plan that offered the health promotions, some other health plan (often a competitor) will be the beneficiary of the work that was done. This phenomenon is referred to as *leakage*. This also has consequences in constructing operational budgets as well as organizational philosophy and mission. The strict economic issue is whether the health plan believes it can retain its members long enough to experience the long-term health benefits of the health promotions. The organizational mission issue relates to the beliefs the health plan has about whether health promotion is the correct organizational approach to improving the overall health status of the population.

Conclusion

Constructing an operating budget under capitation is a complex task. It must correctly predict the levels of utilization, identify and allocate the costs of serving the capitated health plan, and allocate the revenues back to the appropriate cost centers to determine whether service to the health plan is profitable. Having done this, there are a variety of internal, external and financial factors, as well as other kinds of environmental factors, that must be considered by the health care manager. These items are usually not directly associated with constructing an operating budget under capitation, but they nevertheless have a tangential effect on the profitability of the organization.

Case 8-1: County Primary Care Practice

You are the practice manager of a five-physician primary care practice in a metropolitan area that is just beginning to experience capitated reimbursement from managed care companies. A managed care company has approached the County Primary

Care Practice to determine whether it would be willing to provide primary care services on a capitated basis.

The managed care company indicates that it is rounding out its network and in all likelihood will close their panel within the next thirty to sixty days. County Primary Care Practice currently serves approximately 500 patients from this managed care company. The managed care company indicates that it is willing to pay a capitation rate of $15.00 PMPM for each covered life selecting County Primary Care Practice.

You take this information to the governing board of the practice along with the current operating statistics for the practice. These are as follows:

- Cost per procedure = $37.50
- Historical average patient visits per member per year = 4.5
- Members served = 500

The governing board has an interest in entering into a relationship with the managed care company on a capitated basis, but feels that it requires additional information before making a final decision. They request that you provide the following information at its next meeting:

1. What are the advantages and disadvantages of entering into a capitated relationship with the managed care company? 500 × 15 × 12 (Rev)
   37.50 × 4.5 × 500 (cost)
2. What is the expected annual profit or loss for the practice on the business for this managed care company? 90,000 − 84,375 = 5,625 (profit)
3. Suppose the actual cost per procedure for the year was $40.50. What is the actual profit or loss? 40.50 × 4.5 × 500
   90,000 − 91,125 = −1,125 (loss)
4. Suppose the actual cost per procedure was $41.00 and average visits per year were 4.1. What is the actual profit or loss? 41 × 4.1 × 500
   90,000 − 84,050 = 5,950 (profit)
5. Under the initial set of assumptions, what is the average cost to provide health services PMPM? 37.50 × 4.5 / 12 = $14.06

Case 8-2: Global Managed Care Company

You are working for a managed care company as a reimbursement specialist. In order to reduce the inappropriate utilization of services by physicians, the managed care company is contemplating introducing a withhold for primary care and specialty care physicians.

The CFO of the managed care company has asked you to prepare a report that will show what the financial outcome would be if a withhold is implemented. You know that the specialty care budget is $15.00 PMPM to cover 125,000 lives and that the company is thinking of setting aside 10 percent of the specialty care budget as a withhold to be shared equally by the primary care physicians, specialty care physicians, and the managed care organization.

Rev = 125,000 × 15 × 12 = 22,500,000   20,700
10% withhold = 2,250,000 (22,500 − 2,250)   20,250
withhold = 2,250 − 450 = 1,800 / 3 = 600,000   450

deductible – amount paid out of pocket before the insurance pays per year.
coinsurance – % of covered payment paid by the subscriber.

The CFO has asked you to assume that $20,700,000 is actually paid out in medical claims for specialty care. Your report to the CFO should indicate how much will be paid to the PCPs, SCPs, and the MCO if the physicians do not share in either up-side or down-side risk.

copay – fixed $ amount.

Case 8-3: Claims Administration

You just changed jobs and your insurance coverage has changed. You are not sure what your financial responsibilities will be so you call the managed care company providing the health care coverage at your new job. As a result of the conversation you are now aware that the new conditions of your coverage stipulate that your health care policy provides 100 percent coverage provided that you receive services within the managed care company network. The exception to this coverage is that you must personally pay a $250 deductible each year and are also responsible for paying a 10 percent co-insurance coverage on all health services.

Three months ago you experienced $150 of health care benefits and have just incurred $500 of additional charges. You want to determine how much of the newly incurred bill you are responsible for paying. You need to determine the following:

1. How much must you pay for this encounter for which there were $500 of charges?
2. How much will the managed care company pay?
3. Does it make any difference to the health care provider who pays?

Review Questions

1. How is the amount of risk taken by a provider likely to affect the behavior of the provider?
2. Discuss the effect of price risk, volume risk and population risk on the DRG method of reimbursement.
3. Discuss some possible explanations for the fact that administrative costs are becoming a higher percentage of the premium dollar.
4. As a health care manager, would you want a single average cost per encounter or costs for specific types of encounters as you attempt to determine the price? Provide reasons for your answers.

Reference

Schmitz, H. H. (1992). The financial dynamics of the health care market. In J. C. Edwards & R. M. Donati (Eds.), *Current medical practice: A handbook for residents and medical students* (pp. 30–59). St. Louis: Group Health Foundation.

Chapter 9

Investing and Financing Decisions

Capital budgeting is used to make decisions about spending for facilities: hospitals, nursing homes, outpatient clinics, physician office buildings, computer and information systems, major diagnostic and treatment equipment, and the development of new systems and products. Managed care organizations, operating solely as financial intermediaries, typically make major investments in information systems. Staff model HMOs build or buy clinics and sometimes hospitals. Capital budgeting techniques also can be used to assess major human capital investments in training and continuous quality improvement processes. This chapter describes the essential steps in capital budgeting. In so doing, it revisits the concepts of cash flows, valuation, and capital structure decisions introduced in previous chapters.

Learning Objectives

Upon successful completion of this chapter, the learner will:

- Understand the time value of money and discounting of cash flows.
- Be able to identify the cash flows relevant to an investment decision.
- Know which costs to exclude from the investment decision and why.
- Learn about the operation of financial markets that provide financing.
- Understand the creation of a portfolio to reduce systematic risk.
- Calculate the cost of capital appropriate to a specific project.
- Use appropriate decision criteria to select the best projects.

Key Terms

annuities	market portfolio
arrearages	market risk
call option	maturity
call premium	modified internal rate of return (MIRR)
capital asset pricing model (CAPM)	mutual fund
compounding	net present value (NPV)
corporate risk	par value
coupon rate	payback period (PP)
coupons	perpetuity
discount bonds	present value
discounted cash flow analysis	pro forma income statement, cash flow statement, and balance sheet
discounted payback period	profitability index (PI)
economic profit	put option
effective annual rate (EAR)	reinvestment risk
face or par value	secondary markets
flotation costs	spillover effects
incremental costs	sunk costs
interest rate risk	time line
internal rate of return (IRR)	time value of money
investment bankers	weighted average cost of capital (WACC)
issuance costs	yield to maturity
marginal cost of capital	

Introduction

Most financial management texts dedicate a number of pages to capital investment and financing decisions because it is such an important topic. One way to think about this is to look at how much thought is put into the purchase of a new car, a home, or a college education versus a decision about the purchase of clothing or food. Capital investments by definition are long-term investments. Moreover, they typically involve a major expenditure of funds. Long-term investments commit the organization's resources to certain activities over an extended period of time, thus reducing organizational flexibility and the ability to adjust and adapt to environmental changes. Large resource commitments require adequate up-front analysis to reduce the possibility of a mistake that can put the health care provider in financial jeopardy.

Opportunity Costs and Capital Budgeting

A major issue in capital budgeting is determining how much profit must be earned, or charitable benefits delivered, to attract potential investors, or donors. In a free market economy, owners of financial capital must be given an incentive to put these resources to work in productive or socially beneficial activities. With inadequate opportunity for gain or benefit, investors will simply hoard cash or spend it. Thus, investors and donors seek out the best available opportunities to earn a return, or to do good. The additional return the investor requires is the opportunity cost on those funds—that is, the profits or social benefits that the investor's capital could have earned in its next best use.

Many investments, especially in not-for-profit health care organizations, may be financed out of retained earnings. In this case, no new investors are needed. When the organization uses its own funds, it may seem that opportunity costs are irrelevant to the decision, but this reasoning is invalid. Capital investment decisions must be made *as if* outside investors were sought for each project. Otherwise the equity of current investors, or stakeholders, in the organization may be eroded by poor financial decisions. Opportunity costs reflect what could have been earned had the funds been placed in another investment. Thus, capital budgeting can be thought of as an exercise that improves financial decisions because managers must look at projects from the perspective of investors, sponsors, and donors who make funds available to the organization.

A Case in Point. Assume that Healing Healthcare, a major hospital system, plans to use retained earnings to invest in a new magnetic resonance imager (MRI) for one of its hospitals. Mr. Fisk, the financial manager of Healing Healthcare, does some market research and finds that equity investors currently are earning a 10 percent return on similar projects. As a result he argues that the project needs to earn at least 10 percent more than invested. By his calculations, the project only manages to break even. Some members of the management team suggest that since these funds have already been earned, the hospital does not have to pay anything to investors to finance the project. Moreover, since the hospital is not for profit, it should not make money on this project. It only needs to break even. What do you think? How much does Healing Healthcare need to earn on its MRI project to assure efficient use of funds? If you said 10 percent, you are right. Even if retained earnings are used, the project must cover opportunity costs. No organization can survive in the long run without doing so. This applies equally to for profits and not for profits.

The focus of capital budgeting on a sufficient return of cash to cover opportunity costs does not preclude investment of funds in "unprofitable" projects. Indeed, some health care services are not financially profitable but are socially valued. The capital budgeting process forces managers to consider the size of losses if the decision is made to invest in a socially beneficial project that does not earn a positive return. Responsible budgeting requires that management decide how these losses will be covered by earnings from profitable projects or by charitable donations.

Cash Flows and Time Value of Money

When assessing the merits of an investment project, health care financial managers try to estimate how much cash the project will generate in the future and compare this amount to cash required initially to pay for the investment. If the expected return of cash is greater than cash used, the project is deemed profitable. The problem is that dollars earned in different years are not of equal value to investors. Thus, the worth of a stream of future dollars depends on not only *how much* but *when* cash arrives. The difference in the value of money arriving at different times is called the **time value of money.** To understand the time value of money requires an introduction to the mathematics of compounding and discounting. With these tools, **discounted cash flow analysis** can be used to assess the financial implications of alternative investment opportunities available to health care providers.

Simple Compounding and Discounting

Suppose a dollar is placed in a bank savings account in 1998 that pays 3 percent interest each year. How much is earned by 2008 if the interest earned is withdrawn each year? Because interest is withdrawn, the initial investment stays the same. The cash flows from the bank saving account can be represented by a **time line,** which shows the dollar amount of cash paid or received during each year of an investment. A cash outflow is shown below and a cash inflow is shown above the time line. The interest rate, i, prevailing over the period when the funds are being used is shown above the time line in year zero. For the savings account, the time line is:

Year	0	1	2	3	4	5	6	7	8	9	10
Cash Inflow	3%	+.03	+.03	+.03	+.03	+.03	+.03	+.03	+.03	+.03	+$1.03
Cash Outflow	−$1.00										

The cash inflows in years 1 through 10 total $1.30. Subtracting the original amount of $1.00, a bank savings account returns a total of $0.30 over the ten-year period. If annual interest payments are left in the account so that the amount invested grows, the account would pay $1.331 at the end of ten years, for a return of a little over $0.33. The time line for this investment would be:

Year	0	1	2	3	4	5	6	7	8	9	10
Cash Inflow	3%										+$1.331
Cash Outflow	−$1.00										

Since no money is taken out by the saver in years 1 through 9, the time line shows nothing above the line in these years.

Where do the additional $0.03 come from in the second case? From the interest earned on reinvested interest, or the **compounding** of interest. The mathematics of compounding is represented by the following formula for calculating the future value of any cash investment today.

$$\$FV = \$PV\,(1 + i)^n. \tag{1}$$

A Case in Point. This example illustrates the effect of interest compounding on an original investment of $1.00. Each year, the initial investment of $1.00 and the $0.03 interest earned is left in the investment. At the end of the first year, $1.03 is in the account. At the end of the second year, $1.061 has been accumulated. This includes the (1) original $1.00, plus (2) $0.03 earned on that dollar in years 1 and 2, plus (3) 3 percent earned on the $0.03 in interest earned in the first year. At the end of the third year, each term is compounded once again.

Beginning of Year		**End of Year**
1998: $1	$1(1 + .03) = **$1(1 + .03)^1**	
FV(yr1) =	1 + .03	= $1.03
1999: $1.03	$1(1 + .03)(1 + .03) = **$1(1 + .03)^2**	
FV(yr2)=	1 + .03 + .03 + (.03)(.03)	= $1.061
2000: $1.0611	$1(1 + .03)(1 + .03)(1 + .03) = **$1(1 + .03)^3**	
	1 + .03 + .03 + .03 +	
	(.03)(.03) + (.03)(.03) + (.03)(.03)	
FV(yr3) =	+ (.03)(.03)(.03)	= $1.093

These calculations are repeated seven more times to obtain $1.331 in 2008. The numbers in bold type highlight the application of the formula for calculating the future value of a lump-sum investment: $\$FV = \$PV\,(1 + i)^n$.

The formula for calculating the future value of an investment has two parts: $\$PV$, the present value term, or initial cash provided, and $(1 + i)^n$, the compounding factor. This factor includes n, the number of years the money remains invested, and i, the stated market rate of return, or interest rate, on the investment. Substitute the amount of the investment today for $\$PV$—in this case, $1.00—the interest rate for i, or 3 percent, and the number of years the funds will be invested, n, or 10, to obtain the future value of $1.331.

The formula for the future value of an investment can be used to find the **present value** of a future cash amount. To do this, divide both sides of formula 1 by $(1 + i)^n$:

$$\frac{\$FV}{(1+i)^n} = \frac{\$PV(1+i)^n}{(1+i)^n} \tag{2}$$

$$(\$FV)\frac{1}{(1+i)^n} = \$PV.$$

Thus, the present value of a future cash flow is its future value divided, or discounted, by the compounding factor. Another way to do this is to multiply the discount factor, $1/(1+i)^n$, by the future value of the investment to obtain its present value. This equation reveals how much must be paid today to receive a specified future dollar amount in year n, assuming invested funds are earning at least as much as the going market interest rate, i. Formulas 1 and 2 can be solved for any one of the four variables—PV, FV, i, and n—if the other three values are known. An investor who knows the initial amount, the number of years that funds will be needed, and expected payment at the end of the project can calculate the annual rate of return on an investment and compare it with other available market opportunities.

A Case in Point. Suppose Dr. Rao will require $10,000 in cash in 2008 to purchase new office furniture for her practice. Health providers sometimes create a funded depreciation account for this purpose. How much must be invested in 1998 if the interest rate is 3 percent for it to grow to $10,000 in ten years? To get this answer, she can use formula 2:

$$\$PV = \frac{\$10,000}{(1+.03)^{10}} = \$10,000 \times \frac{1}{(1+.03)^{10}}$$

$$= \frac{\$10,000}{(1+.03)^{10}} = \$10,000 \times (.7441) = \$7,441.$$

Now suppose Dr. Rao has the opportunity to invest in a virtually risk-free project that costs $10,000 today and will pay $11,000 at the end of five years. What is the annual rate of return if the funds stay invested for five years? Solving the PV formula for i, the project will return 1.925 percent per year to Dr. Rao over the five-year period:

$$PV:\ -\$10,000 = \frac{\$11,000}{(1+i)^5}$$

$$i = 1.925\%.$$

Would this project be a wise investment if the going market interest rate on a five year investment were 2 percent per year? No. She would be better off putting the $10,000 in the financial markets and earning the higher return.

Periodic Compounding and Discounting

The compounding and discounting factors in formulas 1 and 2 assume that interest is earned and reinvested at the end of each year. Financial markets, however, offer investments that are compounded more frequently—semiannually, quarterly, monthly, daily, and even continuously. Periodic compounding of earnings during the year changes the effective annual rate of interest earned by the investor, and the amount paid by the users of these funds.

The more frequent compounding of interest can be incorporated into the PV and FV formulas. If an investment pays interest semiannually, then there are two periods in the year, so n becomes $2n$. At an annual interest rate of 3 percent, 1.5 percent in interest is earned at six months on a dollar invested. Then 1.5 percent is earned again at one year and every six months thereafter. In the compounding formula, the interest rate becomes $i/2$. Thus, the compounding factor becomes $(1 + i/2)^{2n}$. For monthly compounding, the formula is $(1 + i/12)^{12n}$. For any number of periods within the year, the compounding factor can be generalized to,

$$(1 + i/m)^{mn} \tag{3}$$

where m is the number of periods in the year and n is the number of years. Notice that in a 1-year investment compounded annually, m is 1 and n is 1, giving the same formula as in formula 1. If interest is compounded continuously, the formula changes slightly. For compounding a present investment to a future value, the compounding factor becomes $(1 + e^{rt})$, and for discounting a future amount to a present amount, it becomes $1/(1 + e^{rt})$.

A Case in Point. Aunt Matilda gives you $1,000 as a gift. You plan to invest it in a five-year bond that pays 5 percent interest semiannually and interest earned is reinvested. What will you earn if you hold the bond for five years?

Since interest is paid every 6 months, the number of periods within a year, m, is 2 and the interest rate paid is i/m, or 2.5 percent. The number of years, n, is 5. Substituting $i/m = 2.5$ percent, $mn = 10$, and $1,000 for PV into formula 3, $1,280.09 in cash will be received from this bond at the end of year 5, reflecting the initial investment of $1,000 plus accumulated interest of $280.09:

$$FV = PV (1 + i/m)^{mn} = 1,000 (1 + .025)^{10} = \$1,280.09.$$

In a similar fashion, the discount factor, which incorporates more frequent compounding of interest, becomes:

$$\frac{1}{(1 + i/m)^{mn}} \tag{4}$$

A Case in Point. Suppose $100,000 will be needed ten years from now to pay for a child's college education. How much must be invested today in a security paying 8 percent interest, compounded daily?

Using formula 4, first find i/m and mn. Since m is 365, i/m will be .022 percent and mn will be 3,650. Substituting these into formula 2,

$$\$44,802.26 = \frac{\$100,000}{(1 + .022)^{3650}}$$

$44,802.26 must be invested today to grow to $100,000 in cash in ten years. How much more must be invested if interest is compounded annually?

$$\$46,319.35 = \frac{\$100,000}{(1 + .08)^{10}}.$$

Again solving using $n = 10$, and $i = 8$, an additional $1,517.09 (46,319.35 − 44,802.26) will have to be invested today. This difference illustrates the amount gained on an investment that has the same quoted annual interest rate but is compounded daily rather than once a year.

This factor can be used to evaluate the present value of an investment that pays returns to investors more frequently than at the end of the year.

Tables at the back of many managerial accounting and finance textbooks contain the periodic compounding and discounting factors that can be used in evaluating future cash flows. Calculators are much easier to use, though. They have keys for PV, FV, n, and i that often can be set for periodic compounding. Also, you can simply calculate $i = i/m$ and $n = nm$ and then enter these values for i and n into the calculator. When you use a calculator, enter the dollar amount for the PV as a negative number, reflecting a cash outflow when the investment is made. After you have entered three of the four values, press the fourth key. The solution will appear in the window. Computer spreadsheets like Excel and Lotus 1-2-3 have built-in programs to do these calculations as well.

Periodic Compounding and Effective Annual Rates

An investment paying the same annual interest on a semiannual basis earns slightly more than one paying interest annually because interest is earned on interest more frequently. According the formula 4, a dollar invested at an annual interest rate of 10 percent paid at the end of the year earns 10 percent, the stated interest rate. Using formula 4, if interest is paid semiannually, the dollar earns 10.25 percent. This result shows that the **effective annual rate (EAR)**—in this case, 10.25 percent—is higher than the stated annual rate when interest is compounded more than once during the year. Another way to calculate the EAR when you know the quoted annual interest rate or the nominal interest rate is as follows:

$$EAR = (1 + i/m)^m - 1. \tag{5}$$

A Case in Point. Suppose three different investment opportunities are available. All three pay 3 percent interest annually, but the second investment compounds interest semiannually and the third compounds interest daily. Which of the three is the best investment?

If the stated annual rate of interest is 3 percent and interest is compounded annually, then $m = 1$. In this case, the interest rate and the *EAR* are the same—3 percent:

$$EAR = (1 + .03)^1 - 1 = .03000, \text{ or } 3 \text{ percent.}$$

If 3 percent interest is compounded semiannually, then $m = 2$, and the *EAR* is 3.023 percent:

$$EAR = (1 + .015)^2 - 1 = 1.030224 - 1 = .03023, \text{ or } 3.023 \text{ percent.}$$

At a daily rate of compounding, *EAR* is 3.045 percent, the highest *EAR* of the three:

$$EAR = (1 + .000842)^{365} - 1 = 1.030453 - 1 = .030453, \text{ or } 3.045 \text{ percent.}$$

Although all three quote the same annual interest rate, periodic compounding increases the EAR. Daily compounding provides the best investment.

Suppose a local bank offers a certificate of deposit paying 3.046 percent annually? Now the bank CD is the best investment. It pays a higher EAR than the other three investments.

Because of differences in periodic compounding, EARs can differ on alternative investment opportunities. Rational investors should compare EARs rather than nominal rates and choose the highest one. Similarly, when borrowing money, it is the EAR, not the nominal or quoted rate, that reveals how much the borrower actually pays annually on the loan.

Evaluating a Series of Lump-Sum Payments

The preceding sections illustrated how to calculate the present and future values of investments of single, lump-sum amounts with different maturities (*n*) and different periodicity (*m*). The **maturity** of an investment is the length of time that cash is left invested. At maturity, the investor receives the initial amount plus interest earned. Cash flows produced by the typical investment project are often made up of a series of lump-sum payments of varying amounts that are paid out over time. Because of the time value of money, each payment to the investor must be discounted separately to obtain its present value and then summed to find the present value of all the cash flows of the project.

A Case in Point. Suppose a project is expected to pay the investor $100 at the end of the first year, $500 at the end of the second year, and $1,000 at the end of the third year. If the project must earn at least 5 percent to cover the opportunity cost of funds, what is the present value of these cash flows adjusted for their opportunity costs?

The time line of this investment is:

Year	0	1	2	3
Cash Inflow	5%	+100	+500	+1,000
Cash Outflow	–PV			

The problem can easily be solved by treating the project cash flows in year 1, year 2, and year 3 as if they were separate investments. After discounting each of these lump sum cash flows to present values using formula 2, the resulting present values can be summed to get the present value of the investment project.

Year 1 cash flows ($n = 1$, $i = 5$, and $FV = \$100$):

$$\$PV = \frac{\$100}{(1.05)^1} = \$95.24.$$

Year 2 cash flows ($n = 2$, $i = 5$, and $FV = \$500$):

$$\$PV = \frac{\$500}{(1.05)^2} = \$453.52.$$

Year 3 cash flows ($n = 3$, $i = 5$, and $FV = \$1,000$):

$$\$PV = \frac{\$1,000}{(1.05)^3} = \$863.84.$$

Sum *PV*	**$1,412.60**

Discounted cash flow analysis suggests that informed investors will pay (invest) no more than $1,412 to receive the series of cash flows expected from this investment when the interest forgone—or the opportunity cost—on other investments with similar risk is 5 percent.

Cash flows invested in a project at different times can be converted into a common future value by compounding each amount invested to the last year of the project. Using the numbers from the example, the investor invests $100 at the end of year 1 and 500 at the end of year 2 and adds $1,000 at the end of year 3. To find out the future value of these accumulated dollars, calculate the *FV* of $100 invested for two years ($110.25) and $500 invested for one year ($525.00), and add $1,000 since this amount is at its future value when invested.

Cash Invested Year 1	$FV = \$100\ (1.05)^2\quad = \$110.25$
Cash Invested Year 2	$FV = \$500\ (1.05)^1\quad = \$525.00$
Cash Invested Year 3	$\underline{FV = \$1,000\ (1.05)^0 = \$1,000.00}$
	Sum *FV* $\$1,635.25$

The future value of these three cash flows at the end of year 3 is $1,635.35.

Although many problems encountered in analyzing cash flows can be solved by breaking them down into single, lump-sum payments, evaluation of long-term projects in this way can prove to be very time-consuming. Financial calculators can be programmed to solve problems with variable lump-sum cash flows in each year. Spreadsheets are the easiest approach, especially if you wish to derive a discount rate from a given set of variable lump-sum payments expected over time.

A Case in Point. Suppose you purchase a security in year 1 for $1,000. At the end of the first year, you will receive $100, at the end of year 2 you will be paid $500, and at the end of year 3 you will get $1,000. What is your rate of return on this investment?

The rate that solves this problem is referred to as the **internal rate of return (IRR)**, defined as the discount rate that will make a series of future cash flows exactly equal to an initial dollar amount invested. Below is the time line for these cash flows. IRR is the interest rate that must be found.

Year	0	1	2	3
Cash Inflow	IRR%	+100	+500	+1000
Cash Outflow	−$1,000			

The same problem represented algebraically is:

$$\$1,000 = \frac{\$100}{(1+\mathrm{IRR})^1} + \frac{\$500}{(1+\mathrm{IRR})^2} + \frac{\$1,000}{(1+\mathrm{IRR})^3}.$$

$$0 = -\$1,000 + \frac{\$100}{(1+\mathrm{IRR})^1} + \frac{\$500}{(1+\mathrm{IRR})^2} + \frac{\$1,000}{(1+\mathrm{IRR})^3}.$$

continued

After entering these cash flow values in the cells of a spreadsheet, select IRR from the financial functions in the menu. Financial functions can be found by locating the button at the top of the computer spreadsheet labeled *fx*. Clicking this button will show you the available formulas. Simply click on the correct function listed there, in this case, the IRR function, and enter the appropriate values and solve. The IRR is found to be 20 percent. This means that you must discount these cash flows by 20 percent to make the initial investment just equal to the present value of future cash flows received.

What if market opportunities are paying 18 percent? Is this a good investment? Under certain conditions, discussed later in this chapter, if the calculated IRR on an investment is higher than the opportunity cost of funds, then the project is profitable.

Evaluating Annuities and Perpetuities

Annuities are another type of investment available in financial markets. **Annuities** pay a fixed lump-sum payment (*PMT*) each period for a given number of periods, in exchange for the original amount invested (*PV*). Here is the time line for a ten-year annuity with a PMT of $30 annually:

Year	0	1	2	3	4	5	6	7	8	9	10
Cash Inflow		+$30	+$30	+$30	+$30	+$30	+$30	+$30	+$30	+$30	+$30
Cash Outflow	−$PV										

An annuity is a truncated **perpetuity**. A perpetuity is an annuity that never ends; it provides a fixed cash payment to the owner forever. Through the mathematics of a geometric infinite series, one can prove that the present discounted value of an perpetuity is:

$$PV = \frac{\$PMT}{i}. \qquad (6)$$

Intuitively, a perpetuity is simply a fixed interest payment, *i*, on an initial amount invested today—its present value—that remains invested forever:

$$PV \times i = \$PMT.$$

Therefore the difference between a perpetuity and, say, a bond or a bank certificate of deposit is that the initial investment (*PV*) is never paid back. Dividing by *i* produces formula 6, for the present value of a perpetuity.

Applying the formula for a perpetuity, what amount would have to be invested forever in order to receive $100,000 in interest each year (forever) if the interest rate is 5 percent? Answer: $2 million. The ability to assign a finite value to an infinite process results from the time value of money. Future cash flows from a perpetuity become increasingly less valuable to the holder the further into the future they are received. To see this, determine what cash flows of $100,000 are worth today, i.e. their present value, if they are received in 10 years, 50 years, and 100 years at a discount rate of 3 percent:

$$PV \ (n = 10, i = 3, FV = 100,000) = \$74,835.90.$$
$$PV \ (n = 50, i = 3, FV = 100,000) = \$24,097.20.$$
$$PV \ (n = 100, i = 3, FV = 100,000) = \$ 6,783.23.$$

It is easy to calculate the present value of a perpetuity; it is more difficult to determine the present value of an annuity in which fixed payments are received for a defined period. You can always resort to discounting each identical annuity payment by the same method used to discount single lump-sum cash flows.

Fortunately, in addition to published financial tables on the present and future values of annuities at differing interest rates and payment periods, financial calculators are equipped to solve these problems. A key for *PMT* allows you to enter the annual cash flow on an annuity. Next, enter *n* for the number of years (periods) the payment will be made (or received) and *i* for the opportunity cost of funds. Pressing *PV* returns the present value of an annuity. Again any three of the four values—*PV*, *PMT*, *i*, or *n*—can be entered and the fourth value obtained. Suppose an annuity paying $400 per year for five years is being sold for $1,600. What is the underlying interest rate (the rate of return) on this investment? Entering $400 for *PMT*, 5 for *n*, and –$1,600 for *PV*, the answer is 7.93 percent. This rate can be compared to other investments of similar risk to learn whether this annuity is priced too high given the rate of return on similar investments currently available in the market.

Opportunity Costs Once More: The Required Return on Stocks and Bonds

A project's cash flows must at least cover the opportunity costs of funds it uses. A project found to make more than its opportunity costs earns **economic profit** and is viewed as a highly valuable investment. If the project returns less than the opportunity costs of funds used, then either it should not be undertaken or, if it provides social benefits, cash to make up the expected loss should be identified.

Health care organizations fund their long-term projects with proceeds from the sale of stocks (for-profit only), issuance of tax-exempt (not-for-profit only) and taxable bonds, retained earnings, government grants, and donations (not-for-profit only). Cash raised from the sale of securities depends on how much an investor is willing to pay for the future cash flows expected from a stock or a bond issued by a health care organization. The time value of money indicates that this amount will be equal to the present value of the expected cash flows, discounted by the market-determined opportunity cost of funds. The opportunity cost may be observed in prices that investors currently pay for similar investments in the financial markets. For this reason, financial markets provide valuable information about discount rates to use in capital budgeting decisions.

Stocks and bonds do not have the same opportunity costs. Bondholders are paid before stockholders. As residual claimants to the organization's cash flows, the stockholders bear the risk of uncertain returns to the organization. For bearing this risk, they expect to be compensated. Otherwise, they would invest their funds in bonds or risk-free assets. In the next two sections, discounted cash flow analysis is used to derive the opportunity cost of debt and equity.

Bond Valuation

Bonds are securities that pay a fixed cash amount—its **face** or **par value**—at a specified maturity date, or, simply, at maturity. Most bonds provide cash payments, called **coupons,** over the life of the bond. The interest rate that establishes the amount of the coupon is its **coupon rate,** which is set at the going market rate at the time the bond is issued. If the coupon rate is set too high or too low, the bond will not sell at its par value. Bonds that do not pay coupons and return only the face value at maturity are **discount bonds.**

The purchase price of a bond is equal to the present value of the bond's future cash flows discounted by the opportunity cost of funds. Cash flows from discount bonds are single, lump-sum payments. Therefore formula 2 can be used to determine their selling price and the anticipated cash proceeds to the issuer for each bond sold. For example, a one-year government Treasury bill (a discount bond) paying $10,000 to investors at maturity would sell for $9,174.31 at the beginning of the year if the opportunity cost of funds were 9 percent:

$$\text{Current price} = PV \text{ of discount bond} = \frac{\$10,000}{(1+.09)^1} = \$9,174.31.$$

If market rates fall to 8 percent, the PV, or price, of this bond rises to $9,259.26. At the higher discount rate of 10 percent, the price of the bond would decline to $9,090.91. This discount from face value reflects the return, or yield, required by bond investors. The selling price of discount bonds will always be less than the face value on the bond.

The example reveals an important fact: market rates of return and the price of bonds are inversely related. Reports of a rising (falling) bond market may signal falling (rising) market opportunity costs. If major corporations, or the government, for example, need to borrow money and therefore issue (sell) new bonds, the price of existing bonds must fall. This is because coupon rates on the new bonds are raised slightly to entice market investors to buy more bonds. When interest rates on new bonds go up, the future cash flows on outstanding bonds, discounted by these higher market opportunity rates, are now less valuable. This depresses outstanding bond prices. On the other hand, suppose the Federal Reserve buys existing bonds in the secondary market. To get bondholders to sell, the Fed pays a slightly higher price for them. As bondholders reinvest the proceeds from the sale of bonds in other assets including existing bonds that pay a return—since cash pays no interest—market rates are driven down.

Cash flows from bonds that pay coupons can be modeled by a combination of two types of investments: a lump-sum plus an annuity. Thus present value of a coupon bond is the sum of the discounted present value of its face value at maturity plus the present value of the level coupon payments over the life of the bond.

A Case in Point. Suppose a bond is trading in the market with five years left until maturity and a par value of $1,000. Bonds pay interest semiannually. If the stated coupon rate is 10 percent, then the coupon is $100 per year, or $50 every six months. There will be ten coupons ($mn = 2 \times 5$) of $50, each paid over the remaining life of the bond. The time line for these cash flows is:

Year	0		1		2		3		4		5
Cash Inflow	+$50	+$50	+$50	+$50	+$50	+$50	+$50	+$50	+$50		+$50
8%											+$1,000
Cash Outflow	−$PV										

Assume financial markets are paying 8 percent annually on similar investments, so the opportunity cost of funds is 8 percent. How much should an investor pay for this bond? To obtain this answer, find the PV of the bond.

First, break the problem down into its two parts. The coupon payments are like an ordinary annuity paying $50 every six months for five years. Since coupons are received semiannually, the opportunity cost in the market is 4 percent (8 percent/2) for a six-month period. Entering $50 for *PMT*, 10 for *n*, and 4 for *i*, the present value of the ten level coupon payments (*PV* of an annuity) is $405.54:

Price = *PV* of annuity (*PMT* = $50, *n* = 10, *i* = 4%) = $405.54

Next, determine the present value of the bond at maturity. This is simply a discount bond with a par value of $1,000 at the end of five years. To add the *PV* of the lump sum to the *PV* of the annuity requires that the same effective annual rates be used here. Thus, to take into account the effect of semiannual interest compounding, use 4 percent (8 percent/2) for *i* and 10 (2 × 5) for *n*. The present value of this cash flow is $675.56:

$$\text{Price} = PV \text{ of the face value of bond} = \frac{\$1,000}{(1 + .04)^{10}} = \$675.56.$$

The price paid for this bond today is the sum of the present value of its par value at maturity and the present value of the ten coupons, or $1081.11:

Price = *PV* of coupon bond = $675.56 + $405.54 = $1,081.11.

Again financial calculators and spreadsheets are programmed to make these calculations in one step. To find the present value of this bond, enter $50 for *PMT*, $1,000 for *FV*, 10 for *n*, and 4 percent for *i*. Then push *PV*. The calculator will return −$1,081.11, the same answer as above.

Call and Put Options

Some bond contracts include call or put options. A **call option** gives the issuing health care organization the right to buy back the bonds before maturity, usually for a stated fee, or **call premium.** And some bonds permit investors to put, or sell, the bonds back to the health care organization before maturity. This is called a **put option.** If market interest rates go below the coupon rate on the bond, a call option is likely to be exercised by the issuer. If interest rates rise above the coupon rate, investors will enforce their put options and sell the bonds back to the health care organization.

Callable bonds are valuable because they permit the health care organization to escape the **interest rate risk** of being locked into high coupon payments on long-term debt when market interest rates fall. Interest rate risk is greater the longer the maturity of the bond. On the other hand, investors who own callable bonds risk the loss of their relatively high fixed rates if market rates fall. Therefore they face **reinvestment risk,** the loss of higher returns when funds received from one investment must be reinvested in the market at a lower rate of return. Because callable bonds reduce an organization's interest rate risk at the expense of the investor, they are sold at a higher discount, or require a higher coupon rate, at the time they are issued.

In contrast, putable bonds are valuable to investors who can liquidate bonds issued when market interest rates were low to take advantage of subsequently higher market rates. The issuing organization now must refinance at the higher interest rate prevailing in the market. Investors avoid interest rate risk when they purchase putable bonds and the organization faces higher reinvestment risk. Thus investors are willing to pay more for a putable bond when it is issued and thus receive a lower rate of return.

Finding the Opportunity Cost of Debt

In budgeting for a capital investment, managers need to know the opportunity cost of funds that will be borrowed to finance the project. The opportunity cost is the rate that must be paid to attract investors. How might one determine the cost of debt? There are four options:

1. Look at the coupon rate on the organization's outstanding bonds. If the coupon rate was established when opportunities and going market rates were different, however, this will provide an inaccurate estimate of current cost of debt.

2. Estimate the current rate of return on the organization's own publicly traded bonds. The current rate of return on a bond is its **yield to maturity,** the discount rate that equates the current market price of a bond with the present value of its future cash flows. Investors reveal the opportunity costs they face when they buy or sell bonds in the **secondary markets,** markets in which securities that were previously issued are bought and sold by market investors. The price for which outstanding bonds are traded is their present value. Using discount cash flow analysis, the opportunity costs facing investors can be found. If the organization's debt is not publicly traded, however, this will not be an option.

A Case in Point. Suppose Hometown Health System (HHS) has twenty-year coupon bonds outstanding that were issued ten years ago and pay 10 percent coupons semiannually. If its $1,000 bonds are currently selling for $1,297.55 in the secondary market, what is required rate of return on HHS debt, k_d, representing the opportunity cost to investors who have just purchased bonds at that price? Using the financial calculator, input the following values:

$$PV \text{ (price)} = -\$1,297.55 \text{ (the price paid in the bond market today)}$$

$$FV = \$1,000 \text{ (face value of bond at maturity)}$$

$$n = 20 \text{ periods } (2 \times 10 \text{ years until the bonds mature)}$$

$$PMT = \$50 \text{ every six months } \frac{\text{(annual coupon rate} \times \text{face value)}}{2}$$

Solve for i.

The calculator will return an answer of 3 percent. This is not the opportunity cost of funds for a year, however, but the rate paid every 6 months. To convert the answer to an annual rate, i must be multiplied by 2. Thus, the current cost of debt to HHS is 6 percent ($k_d = 2 \times 3$ percent), reflecting the annual rate of return required by buyers willing to purchase the future cash flows produced by HHS bonds.

Now assume Hometown's debt is not publicly traded, so that option 2 is not possible. Hometown will use option 3 to assess the price of debt. National Health System (NHS) is a tax-exempt integrated delivery system similar to Hometown. It has not purchased bond insurance and has risks similar to Hometown. Currently, NHS has thirty-year bonds outstanding that mature in fifteen years. Market investors are paying $1,459.80 to receive the cash flows from these bonds. The bonds have a face value of $1,000 at maturity and pay semiannual coupons based on a coupon rate of 12 percent. What is the underlying rate of return investors require on NHS bonds? Put these values in the calculator:

$$PV \text{ (price of bond)} = -\$1,459.80$$

$$FV = \$1,000$$

$$n = 30 \text{ periods } (2 \times 15 \text{ years until the bonds mature)}$$

$$PMT = \$60 \text{ paid every 6 months } (.12 \times 1,000/2)$$

solve for $i = k_d/2$.

As reflected in the price investors are willing to pay for NHS outstanding bonds, the required return is $3\frac{1}{2}$ percent semiannually, or 7 percent annually. This reflects investor assessment of the opportunity cost of their cash and the risk of NHS's debt. Since NHS cash flows have risk similar to Hometown's, then 7 percent can be used to represent its opportunity cost of debt, k_d.

3. Examine rates of return required on similar health care organization bonds that are publicly traded. Public information on current bond prices and their yields is available from financial publications. One problem in using rates on similar organizations that are publicly traded is whether the organization's bonds are insured. Bond insurance allows an issuing organization to buy insurance to pay off bondholders in the event that the issuing organization experiences financial distress (Demby, 1995; Pallarito, 1997). Yields on insured bonds are lower than on uninsured bonds and will distort the true opportunity cost of funds. Call and put options will affect the estimated yield as well.

4. Seek the advice of **investment bankers,** who help organizations find buyers and place (sell) their bonds. To do so, they must estimate the opportunity cost of funds. This option can be used in conjunction with the other three.

Stock Valuation and the Opportunity Cost of Equity

Determining the opportunity cost of debt is a far simpler task than calculating the cost of equity. There are several categories of equity: retained earnings, preferred stock, common stock, and donations. The major difference between retained earnings and other types of equity is that there are no **issuance costs** on retained earnings. Issuance costs include marketing and selling the stock, fulfillment of legal requirements and Securities and Exchange Commission regulations, and underwriting the issue. Investment bankers underwrite the issue when they accept the risk of the price at which stocks will be sold. Donations costs include all the costs of soliciting gifts from donors. Issuing bonds involves **flotation** costs. These tend to be considerably lower than the cost of issuing stocks.

Stocks are either common or preferred. Common stocks pay no fixed dividend to shareholders, while preferred stocks guarantee a fixed dividend payment based on the par value of the stock when dividends are paid. The board of directors that represents shareholders typically votes to pay a dividend to common stockholders typically when earnings are good. In a profitable organization, common stockholders expect regular dividends to be paid. A growing organization, however, may retain earnings to support expansion and therefore not pay, or increase, dividends when profits are earned.

In contrast to common stocks, preferred stocks are similar to debt because they obligate the organization to pay fixed dividends over time. If the organization is unable to meet a required dividend payment, then these overdue obligations, called **arrearages,** are accumulated and must be cleared before common stockholders can receive dividends. Thus, preferred stock is less risky than common stock but riskier than debt. Moreover, preferred stockholders usually cannot vote on the officers who will sit on the governing board of the corporation and exercise control over the decisions of management.

Applying Discount Cash Flow Analysis to Stock Valuation

How can the cash flows of stocks be modeled in order to find their discounted present value? Preferred stocks that are issued for a specified time period have cash flows much like those on a coupon bond. Preferred stocks are issued at a par or face value, usually $100, a lump-sum payment. Dividends are paid quarterly on each share outstanding based on a fixed percentage, or dollar amount, set at the time the stock is issued. Therefore, these payments can be modeled as an annuity:

With market information on the price (*PV*) of preferred stock, dividend payments, and par value, this model can be used to derive the opportunity cost of preferred stocks.

$PV (preferred stock) = $PV (fixed dividend payments) + $PV (par value).

This is the same model used to find the opportunity cost on coupon bonds. The fixed dividend payments are like the coupon payments (an annuity), and is like the par value of a share of stock the face value of the bond (a lump-sum payment).

In contrast to preferred stocks, a share of common stock produces a stream of future but uncertain dividends for its owner—in perpetuity. Most companies expect to operate forever, or at least for a very long time, so their common stocks remain outstanding forever. Of course, the organization can buy back some of its shares to change its capital structure (reduce the debt-to-equity ratio). It can also repurchase all of its shares and go private, thereby forgoing the opportunity to raise funds in public markets, but this would not eliminate the stream of future dividends to private owners.

Given the expected future dividends on shares of stocks, the cash flows from a share of common stock would be a perpetuity equal to:

$$PV \text{ of a share common stock} = \frac{E(Div)_i}{k_s},$$

where k_s is the opportunity cost of equity in company i and $E(Div)_i$ are the expected future dividends arising from future earnings of company i. Individuals do not expect to hold stocks in perpetuity; rather, they plan to sell their shares at some time in the future. Indeed, the ability to sell their shares adds value to investors, who otherwise would bear enormous interest rate risk on their investment.

What are the expected cash flows to these investors? Suppose the investor plans to buy and hold stocks for one year and then sell them to another investor. The second investor has similar intentions: to hold for one year and then sell to a third investor; and so on. The expected cash flows to the first investor would be the dividends received during the first year, $E(Div_1)$ plus the selling price of the stock at the end of the year. If k_s is the opportunity cost of equity, the present value of these cash flows at the end of year 0 would be:

$$PV = \text{purchase price (year 0)} = \frac{E(Div_1)}{(1 + k_s)^1} + \frac{\text{sale price (year 1)}}{(1 + k_s)^1}.$$

The next investor in year $t + 1$ would face the same cash flows, but they would be received one year later, in year 2. To convert year 2 cash flows to their present values, they would have to be discounted by $1/(1 + k_s)^2$:

$$PV \text{ (in year 0) of purchase price (in year 1)} = \frac{E(Div_2)}{(1 + k_s)^2} + \frac{\text{sale price (year 2)}}{(1 + k_s)^2}.$$

As this process continues, the price for which a stock will sell in each year must be equal to the dividends the next buyer expects, plus the sale price at the end of the year. Therefore, the present value turns out to be equal to the stream of future dividends expected by all future investors. This can be easily illustrated. Substituting the purchase price at the beginning of each year for its sale price at the end of the previous year and discounting these future cash flows, the purchase price in year 0, or the present value of future dividends of a share of stock, turns out to be:

$$PV = \frac{E(Div_1)}{(1+k_s)^1} + \frac{E(Div_2)}{(1+k_s)^2} + \frac{E(Div_3)}{(1+k_s)^3} + \frac{E(Div_4)}{(1+k_s)^4} + \frac{E(Div_5)}{(1+k_s)^5}, \ldots, + \frac{E(Div_n)}{(1+k_s)^n}.$$

This equation approaches the *PV* of a perpetuity as *n*, the number of years, approaches infinity. Therefore, a share of common stock or a perpetual preferred stock must sell at:

$$\text{Price} = PV \text{ share common stock} = \frac{E(Div_i)}{k_s}, \tag{7}$$

where $E(Div_i)$ is the average expected future dividend in organization *i* and k_s is the opportunity cost. With an estimate of expected future dividends and the current price at which the stock is trading—its *PV*—the opportunity cost is:

$$k_s = \frac{E(Div_i)}{PV}. \tag{8}$$

Notice that this model assumes that there are always future buyers of the stocks. But stocks in a company are bought and sold only as long as the company is viable and investors expect to receive the stream of future dividends paid out of future earnings. Financial distress and the risk of bankruptcy lower the price, or present value, of a stock. Much like the game of hot potato, as a company approaches bankruptcy, its price approaches zero and if the company cannot be restructured and returned to financial health, the last buyer ends up holding a worthless piece of paper—forever.

Incorporating Cash Flows of a Growing Company

How does this model handle the cash flows of a company whose future dividends are expected to grow? Recall that the profits, or earnings, of an organization can either be paid out as dividends or retained. If earnings are retained, they are reinvested in new projects. If the organization is well managed and opportunity for growth exists, retained earnings will increase its expected future dividends. In this case, another formula can be used to calculate the present value of the stock or the required rate of return and equity. If *g* is the rate of growth in future dividends, then:

$$\text{Price} = PV \text{ (growth company)} = \frac{E(Div_i)}{k_s - g}, \tag{9}$$

reveals that the required return on a growing company is equal to dividends expected in the next period. This equation can be solved for k_s:

$$k_s = \frac{E(Div_i)}{PV} + g.$$ (10)

If dividends are not expected to grow, g equals 0, and the formulas are the same as in formulas 7 and 8.

The Capital Asset Pricing Model

A second method for estimating the opportunity cost of equity is derived from a theory of investor behavior called the **capital asset pricing model (CAPM),** which explains how investors value securities as part of a portfolio of assets they hold. A portfolio of stocks or bonds is called a **mutual fund.** Because of the law of large numbers, discussed in Chapter 2, owning shares in a portfolio of stocks of different companies has less risk than owning shares of stock in a single company. Like the health plan that reduces its objective risk by increasing the number of enrollees, the investor reduces market risk by increasing the number of different securities in his or her portfolio. This is an important point. With reduced risk through portfolio diversification, investors require a lower rate of return on their investments. This, in turn, lowers the opportunity cost of capital prevailing in the market.

The CAPM theory is represented in the following model:

$$k_{si} = k_{rf} + (k_M - k_{rf})\,\beta_i$$ (11)

where:

k_{si} = the rate of return required by investors to induce them to own shares of stock in firm i.

k_{rf} = the rate of return on a risk-free investment.

k_M = the return required by investors who hold shares in a portfolio of all securities available in the economy, called the **market portfolio.**

$k_M - k_{rf}$ = the market risk premium, which is the additional return above the risk-free rate required by market investors who hold shares in the market portfolio.

β_i = the exposure of firm i to market risk. (β is pronounced "beta.")

This equation basically says that the required rate of return on funds invested in company i is equal to the rate of return on a risk-free asset plus a market risk premium $(k_M - k_{rf})$ multiplied by the degree to which the individual organization's earnings are exposed to market risk. **Market risk** is measured by the variability in the returns on the market portfolio that cannot be eliminated by diversification. The exposure of a single company to market risk is measured by its beta.

To use this model to estimate the opportunity cost of equity capital requires that managers obtain an estimate of the risk-free rate, usually the current interest rate on government long-term bonds, and the market rate of return, which can be measured by returns on an index like the Standard & Poor's composite index of 500 stocks or the Wilshire index of the returns on stocks of 5,000 companies. Finally, an estimate of beta must be obtained from the historical relationship between the company's stock returns and the returns on the market portfolio. Company betas on publicly traded firms are available from securities brokers or through the Internet. New companies, however, have no historical data on returns with which to estimate their betas. Similarly, not-for-profit organizations, like hospitals, and privately owned companies, like many nursing homes, have no historical data on market prices of their equity and therefore have no estimate of beta. In these cases, it may be possible to use the estimated beta on a similar, publicly traded company so long as that company's capital structure—that is, its use of debt financing—and income tax rates are the same. Methods are available to adjust the estimated beta for differences in capital structure and tax rates, but they are beyond the scope of this book (Hamada, 1969; Rubinstein, 1973).

A Case in Point. Hometown Doctors Clinic, a not-for-profit 70-physician multispecialty group practice, needs an estimate of its cost of equity financing to use in capital budgeting for new capital projects in the clinic. Hometown's practice manager, Ms. Chen, has obtained the estimated beta for a proprietary ambulatory care clinic chain, Patient Care Associates (PCA), whose shares trade on the NASDAQ stock exchange. Since PCA uses more debt than does Hometown Doctors Clinic, she has adjusted PCA's beta for differences in financial leverage. The resulting adjusted beta is 1.8. The *Wall Street Journal* reports the current required rate of return on a risk-free asset, measured by the yield on long-term government bonds, which is 6.75 percent, and the rate of return on the S&P 500, a portfolio of shares of 500 major corporations, which is 8.8 percent. With this information she plans to estimate what investors would require as an expected return on Hometown's investments. Using the CAPM, $k_{si} = k_{rf} + (k_M - k_{rf}) \beta_i$, she finds that the required return is 10.75 percent:

$$k_{si} = 6.25 + (8.75 - 6.25)\,1.8 = 6.25 + 4.50 = 10.75.$$

She plans to use this rate as the cost of equity for Hometowns Doctors Clinic financing.

Discounted Cash Flow Analysis versus the Capital Asset Pricing Model

Different estimates of the opportunity cost of equity may result from using the two methods of analysis: (1) discounted cash flow analysis and (2) CAPM. In this event, the financial manager may use an average cost of equity, or his or her best judgment, about which measure of k_s to use. This reveals the fact that capital budgeting is both an art and a science. Ultimately these decisions involve uncertain future outcomes, which cannot be known in advance. Experience and good judgment play as much role as market information and thorough financial analysis in capital investment decisions. Managers must come up with their best estimates, adjusted for the uncertainty surrounding those estimates, and proceed on that basis.

The capital markets impose discipline on the financial decisions of health care managers. If the estimate of the cost of equity is too low, publicly traded organizations will be unable to sell their shares for the amount expected and the cash they receive will be less than they require. Moreover, if they use retained earnings on projects that do not return their opportunity costs, then the price of their stock will fall as shareholders reassess future dividends. Market discipline is not directly imposed on organizations that are not publicly traded or are not-for-profit.

Weighted Average Cost of Capital

Once estimates of the opportunity cost of debt and equity have been obtained, the financial manager must come up with a single measure of the opportunity cost of funds used to finance the organization's investments. To do this requires an assumption about the organization's targeted capital structure, that is, how much investment should be financed by debt and how much by equity. These targeted percentages can then be used to weight the cost of debt and the cost of equity, creating a **weighted average cost of capital (WACC)** (Wheeler and Smith, 1988).

Assumed weights in the WACC should be those deemed appropriate by the governing board of the organization. Why must the health care organization target its capital structure? The amount of debt it uses affects the risk to shareholders and equity owners. This alters the required rate of return relative to less risky opportunities available in the market. Therefore the estimate of k_s will be too low or too high, and the organization will underestimate or overestimate the cost of equity and the cost of capital in its capital investment decisions. To avoid this and to minimize the cost of capital, the board should establish a targeted capital structure that is maintained over time. Capital structure weights are not totally discretionary, however. Lenders often dictate the level of debt permitted the organization by bond agreements, or covenants, and mortgage contracts. Also, the risk aversion of the governing board of the health care provider and its management will affect the amount of debt the organization may be willing to carry.

In addition to setting capital structure weights, adjustments must be made in capital costs to reflect the impact of taxes on the expected returns to shareholders in a tax-paying organization. Since interest expense can be deducted from income while dividend payments cannot, the cost of debt must be adjusted for the differential tax

A Case in Point. Suppose the proportion of debt used in financing new projects is targeted to be 40 percent and the proportion of new equity is set at 60 percent. The cost of capital will be:

$$\text{Cost of capital} = \frac{\text{Debt}}{\text{Debt + equity}} \times k_d + \frac{\text{equity}}{\text{debt + equity}} \times k_s$$

$$= 40\% \times k_d + 60\% \times k_s.$$

protection it affords to the owner's earnings. The after-tax cost of debt is $(1 - t)k_d$. In a tax-exempt entity, t is 0. Although this would suggest that debt costs are lower for a tax-paying organization than a not-for-profit, this is not the case. Because investors who buy tax-exempt securities pay no taxes on earnings from these investments, the rate of return they require is lower than on a taxable investment. Therefore the before-tax cost of debt to a tax-exempt health care organization is lower than the before-tax cost of debt to a taxable organization. To the extent that these two effects cancel out, the cost of debt may be similar in a for-profit and a not-for-profit organization. Note that cash recoveries of interest expense from cost-based reimbursement also can be accounted for in the discount rate. Taking taxes and cost reimbursement into account, the WACC becomes

$$WACC = \frac{Debt}{Debt + equity} \times (1 - t)(1 - p)k_d + \frac{equity}{debt + equity} \times k_s$$

The term $(1 - p)$, where p is the percentage of interest expense reimbursed by thirty-party payers, represents the percentage of interest expense that is not recovered by cost-based reimbursement. If the effect of cost-based reimbursement is included in the WACC, then cash inflows from cost-based reimbursement of interest should be omitted from project cash flows.

A Case in Point. Hometown Health System is a tax-exempt health care system whose cost of debt is 6 percent. National Hospital Corporation has a cost of debt of 8 percent and a tax rate of 25 percent. It has the same after-tax cost of debt as the Hometown Health System:

Hometown Health System

$$k_d = 6 \text{ percent.}$$

National Hospital System

$$(1 - t)k_d = (1 - .25)\, 8 \text{ percent} = 6 \text{ percent.}$$

With information on the cost of debt, the cost of equity, the tax rate, and the targeted capital structure, the WACC can be constructed. This single value incorporates the capital structure weights and the relative cost of debt and equity to the organization:

$$WACC = \frac{Debt}{Debt + equity} \times (1 - t)k_d + \frac{equity}{debt + equity} \times k_s.$$

The WACC may be expanded to incorporate the opportunity costs on each source of funds the health care organization uses to finance its projects: debt, retained earnings, stocks, and donations. Let the organization obtain long-term financing for three sources: debt, equity, and donations. Thus total = debt + equity + donations. The cost of raising charitable donations is k_c. With three sources of financing WACC becomes:

$$\text{WACC} = \frac{\text{debt}}{\text{total}} \times (1 - t)k_d + \frac{\text{equity}}{\text{total}} \times k_s + \frac{\text{donations}}{\text{total}} \times k_c.$$

At a *minimum*, project cash flows need to be large enough to return the opportunity cost of capital to investors, captured by the WACC. If net cash flows of an investment discounted by the WACC are positive, then this project returns economic profit to the organization and its owners. Positive net cash flows are earnings over and above what would have been earned had funds been invested in other projects available to market investors.

A Case in Point. Assume that the board of National Hospital Corporation (NHC) has targeted its capital structure at 50 percent debt and 50 percent equity; based on previous analysis of financial markets, it found the opportunity cost of debt to be approximately 8 percent and the risk-adjusted cost of equity to be about 12 percent. The tax rate is .25 percent. The WACC for NHC is:

$$\text{WACC} = .50 \, (8\%)(1 - .25) + .50 \, (12\%)$$
$$= 3\% + 6\%$$
$$= 9\%.$$

Suppose a project that it is evaluating has the expected future cash flows of $250,000 per year for five years and requires an initial investment of $1 million. Does the project earn economic profits? To answer this, calculate the present value of an annuity. On a financial calculator, enter $PMT = 250,000$, $i = 9$, $n = 5$, and solve for PV. The PV is –$972,412.82. Since this is less than the initial investment of $1 million, the project will not return enough cash to cover the opportunity costs of the investment.

What if the targeted capital structure were 70 percent debt and 30 percent equity? Substituting these capital weights into the WACC formula for NHC produces a WACC of 7.8 percent (4.2 + 3.6). Discounting the project cash flows by 7.8 percent produces a PV of –$1,003,461. Since this is greater than $1,000,000, the positive difference of $3,461 is pure profit to the organization over and above what could have been earned on other investments available in the market. Assuming the increase in debt has not increased risk to owners—and thus the required return on equity—the ability to use more financial leverage makes this project profitable for NHC.

Capital Budgeting in the Health Care Organization

Thus far, this chapter has focused on identifying the future cash flows of market investments, such as stocks and bonds, in order to derive the underlying opportunity costs on these sources of funds as revealed by investor behavior in the capital markets. The WACC was calculated to provide a measure of the cost of financing of capital projects for an individual organization.

In this section, discounted cash flow analysis is applied to specific projects being considered by the health care organization. The tools that investors use to value stocks and bonds and make efficient use of their financial resources are the same as those that health care managers need to make efficient capital investment decisions for their organizations.

Process Overview

When a project is undertaken within an organization, it can be viewed in much the same way that market investors assess the addition of a single stock to their portfolio of securities. In essence, the existing health care organization is a portfolio of ongoing projects and services—surgeries and procedures, physician exams and visits, lab tests and treatments—that generate cash flows. This portfolio of projects is under one management and organizational structure. When a new health service or product is added, it is as if a new stock (service) is being added to a portfolio of stocks (services).

Maximization of shareholder wealth is one of the stated goals of for-profit enterprises. This goal provides direction to the decisions of proprietary managers. Health care organizations need to ask how the new project supports their stated mission, goals, and objectives. In addition, managers who wish to receive funds for new capital investments need to submit a business plan and cash flow projections for the project. Creation of new services and expansion of existing services also require documented support of future demand, as well as expected revenues and expenses of the project.

Renovation and replacement of existing assets usually require less justification because typically they have little or no impact on revenues; rather, they tend to lower costs or maintain existing services. In fact, failure to replace worn-out equipment and buildings may result in a loss of revenues. Thus, the downside risk of revenue loss can be reduced by appropriate replacement decisions.

In proposing a new project, the manager must find out how much it will cost to purchase and install needed plant and equipment and to purchase inventory. Also, cash to support operations until reimbursement is received must be estimated. These costs are included in the project's initial cash flows.

A **pro forma income statement, the cash flow statement,** and **balance sheet** for the project must be developed. Pro forma financial statements are hypothetical financial statements that show a project's expected performance over a future time period. These projections require assumptions about revenues and expenses. These include:

- Volume of services demanded
- Reimbursement per unit of service
- Payer mix to assesses timeliness and types of payment
- Fixed and variable costs per unit of service (labor, supplies, equipment, space, utilities, insurance, support and administrative services related to the project)

Depending on the project, similar assumptions about individual capital investment projects undertaken by managed care plans would include the following:

- Estimated number of enrollees
- Premium or capitation payment received per enrollee
- Payer mix to assess the timeliness of expected claims from providers or subcontractors
- Fixed and variable costs per enrollee: medical expenses in the form of capitation or discounted fee-for-service payments to providers and plan administration costs (e.g., labor, supplies, equipment, space, utilities, insurance, support and administrative services related to the specific project)

These projections provide the basis for deriving the operating cash flows of the project.

While a project might, in fact, be operated indefinitely, capital budgeting delineates a "project life" over which the cash flows will be estimated and profitability determined. As future cash flows become more distant, estimates become less certain and therefore riskier to investors. Specifying a termination date for a project's cash flow projections, within a reasonable time horizon, can reduce this uncertainty. Care must be taken in setting the time horizon. If a project's proposed life is made too short, one may underestimate total profitability, especially if most profits come in later years. On the other hand, a project's life may be dictated by the physical life of its capital assets. These assets will have to be replaced for the project to continue. Also, if a project is performing poorly, the decision may be made to abandon it prior to the time period in the original business plan. Financial decision tools have been developed to deal with longer time horizons, the economic life of an asset, capital replacement decisions, and abandonment of a ongoing project. These techniques are beyond the scope of this book (see, for example, Gapenski, 1996).

Finally, to provide a complete picture of the cash flows expected from a project, the estimated sale or salvage value of project assets at the end of the specified period of analysis should be included in the final year of cash flow projections.

Capital budgeting entails four essential steps:

1. Estimating the projected future cash flows of a project
2. Determining the opportunity costs of capital to be used to discount the project's future cash flows
3. Assessing and adjusting the discount rate for project risk
4. Employing appropriate decision rules to evaluate the value of the project to the organization

A Case in Point. Hometown Health Center, located in a downtown area, is planning to acquire a new ambulatory care facility in the city's growing northern suburbs. The strategic objectives of opening Metro Clinic are to attract new patients, enhance system referrals to the hospital, and expand the ability to contract with managed care organizations by being closer to where families reside. Hometown's chief financial officer has developed a pro forma income statement for the new venture based on information obtained from a marketing survey, as well as costs that other outpatient clinics in the area experience. The pro forma income statement shows that Metro Clinic breaks even in year 2 and becomes profitable in year 3.

Metro Clinic's Pro Forma Income Statement for Three-Year Project

	Year 0 ($)	Year 1 ($)	Year 2 ($)	Year 3 ($)
Net patient revenues		5,000	5,800	6,800
Total operating expenses		5,000	5,300	5,500
Depreciation		**500**	**500**	**500**
Earnings before interest and taxes (EBIT)		–500	0	800
Interest		0	0	0
Taxes		0	0	0
Net income		–500	0	800

From the pro forma income statement, the operating cash flows can be found. Hometown has no debt, so it incurs no interest expense, and it is tax exempt. Therefore, earnings before interest and taxes (**EBIT**) are the same as net income. Because depreciation expense is a noncash expense, it must be added back to EBIT to get cash flows from operations:

	Year 0 ($)	Year 1 ($)	Year 2 ($)	Year 3 ($)
EBIT		–500	0	800
Add back depreciation		500	500	500
Operating cash flows		**0**	**500**	**1,300**

The initial cash outlay as well as the estimated salvage value of the clinic at the end of year 3 must be included to get projected cash flows from the clinic:

	Year 0 ($)	Year 1 ($)	Year 2 ($)	Year 3 ($)
Operating cash flows		0	500	1,300
Initial outlay	–2,000			
Salvage value				800
Projected cash flows	**–2,000**	**0**	**500**	**2,100**

Estimating Future Cash Flows of the Project

The first step in capital budgeting for new projects, or the expansion of existing services, requires cash flow projections for:

- initial cash flows (ICF)—expenses incurred to start up the project
- operating cash flows (OCF)—cash generated from operations once the project is up and running
- salvage value (SV)—the cash obtained from sale of the assets at the project's end

Initial Cash Flows

Most capital investment projects require a major up-front cash outflow. These initial costs are obvious: the acquisition of land, the purchase and installation of equipment and facilities, the expenses of a major marketing campaign, or the purchase and reorganization of an existing company. Several pitfalls can be encountered, however, when identifying the initial cash flows of a project. Among these pitfalls are the following:

- The inclusion of sunk costs
- The omission of opportunity costs
- The exclusion of changes in net working capital

Inclusion of Sunk Costs

A temptation exists to add **sunk costs**—cash expenses that have already been incurred—to the initial cash outflows. After all, a new project may be a way to make up for previous losses. This reasoning is faulty. If sunk costs were added to the costs of future projects, then many projects that are profitable on their own merits would be rejected if they were saddled with sunk costs. An opportunity to increase shareholders' wealth would be lost. To determine whether a cost is a sunk cost ask, Will the decision to invest or not to invest in this project change these costs? If not, then they should be excluded from the project's cash flows.

For example, prior spending for research and development of a product is a sunk cost; it is unchanged by the decision to move forward to production and sales. Sunk costs impose no additional use of cash with the implementation of the project. It is the use of new funds that is relevant to the capital budgeting decision. Nor can these dollars be recovered, whether or not the project is implemented. Cash flows relevant to the project should include costs that will be affected by the decision to invest. Costs that arise as a result of the investment are **incremental costs.** Only incremental costs and lost revenues should be included in cash outflows.

Omission of Opportunity Costs

A second pitfall is the omission of opportunity costs. By moving forward with a project, other options are ruled out. For example, suppose Hometown Health Center owns a parcel of land that it will use as the site of the new ambulatory clinic. The project's cash costs will be understated if cost of the land is omitted from initial cash out-flows. But how is this possible since no cash payments are being made? By building on this site, the opportunity to sell the land at market value and use the cash generated in an alternative project is no longer available. This loss of an opportunity to receive cash for the land results in an outflow of cash, even though the organization has no intention of selling it. The efficient use of resources implies that the new clinic should generate cash flows sufficient to cover the opportunity cost of the land—*as if* the land had been purchased specifically for this investment.

Changes in Net Working Capital

A third pitfall is the failure to include cash needed to support changes in net working capital. The funds to launch a new operation include not only the cost of long-term physical assets but also the acquisition of short-term assets (e.g., additional inventories, cash to pay employees, and the ability to extend credit to payers who do not pay at the time of service). Recall that net working capital is the dollar difference between current assets and current liabilities. To the extent that increases in current assets are not supported by "spontaneous liabilities," such as accrued payroll, IBNR expenses, or accounts payable, and by additional short-term credit from banks and other lenders, net working capital (**NWC**) will increase. (Spontaneous liabilities are discussed in Chapter 10.) Increases in NWC result in a use of cash—a cash outflow. Decreases in NWC produce a cash inflow. Failure to account for changes in net working capital means that a project could be underfinanced and out of business long before enough cash is collected to make it viable.

Cash to support increases in NWC at the beginning of and during the project will be automatically offset by a recovery of cash in the last year of the project as invento-

---

A Case in Point. Hometown Health estimates that changes in NWC associated with Metro Clinic will equal approximately 10 percent of the annual change in revenues over the life of the project. As shown in Metro Clinic's pro forma income statement, the projected change in revenues from year 0 to year 1 is $5,000 (0 to 5,000). Therefore the cash needed to support increased NWC in the first year is 10 percent of $5,000 or $500. Working capital expenses are shown in the period before they are incurred. Thus in year 0 there is a cash outflow of $1,000. From year 1 to year 2, this cost is 10 percent of $800 or $80 (where the change in revenues is 5000 to 5800 = 800) and from year 2 to year 3, the same calculation is $100 (.10 × 1000 = 5800 to 6800). At the end of year three when the project terminates, revenues go from $6800 to $0 for a change of $6800. Working capital requirements decline by (.10) × $6800, or $680. This is a cash inflow in year 3 of the project.

(continued)

Cash Flow Projections for Metro Clinic: Changes in New Working Capital

	Year 0	Year 1	Year 2	Year 3
Changes in WC	–$500	–$80	–$100	+$680

Notice that the present value of cash outflows associated with changes in NWC during the first three years of the project is less than the present value of the cash inflows from the reduction in NWC in the last year of the project. This difference reflects the impact of the time value of money on a project's NWC requirements.

	Year 0	Year 1	Year 2	Year 3
Changes in WC	–$500.00	–$80	–$100.00	$680.00
PV of cash flows	–$500.00	–$72.73	–$82.65	$511.28
Sum of increases in NWC	(–$500.00) + (–$72.73) + (–$82.65)		= –$655.38	
Reduction in NWC			= $511.28	
Difference in PV of NWC outflows and inflows			= –$144.10	

ries are depleted, accounts receivable are collected, and payroll expenses cease along with the termination of services. If it were not for the time value of money, changes in NWC could be omitted from capital budgeting analysis. Dollars spent in earlier years would equal dollars recovered in later years. The present value of cash returned later, however, is lower than the present value of cash spent earlier. This is why changes in NWC must be included in the cash flows of the project.

Operating Cash Flows

The second set of cash flows to be included in budgeting for capital needs are those that arise from operating the project. Operating cash flows are basically the net cash provided by operations shown on the statement of cash flows. One cannot simply take net income from a project as a measure of cash provided from operations, however. A number of important adjustments must first be made.

Add Back Noncash Expenses

Expenses like depreciation and amortization are noncash expenses and must be added back to earnings to calculate cash flows from operations accurately. Depreciation expense is an accounting convention for tax and reimbursement purposes that

A Case in Point. Suppose Metro Clinic is a taxable organization subject to a 30 percent tax rate. Assume the salvage value is the same as book value.

Metro Clinic's Pro Forma Income Statement for Three-Year Project (with taxes and depreciation)

	Year 0	Year 1	Year 2	Year 3
Net patient revenues		$5,000	$5,800	$6,800
Total operating expenses		5,000	5,300	5,500
Depreciation		**500**	**500**	**500**
Earnings before interest and taxes (EBIT)		–$ 500	$ 0	$ 800
Interest		0	0	0
Taxes		0	0	240
Net income		**–$ 500**	**$ 0**	**$ 560**
EBIT		–$ 500	$ 0	$ 560
Add back depreciation		500	500	500
Operating cash flows		**$ 0**	**$ 500**	**$1,060**

Metro Clinic's Pro Forma Income Statement for Three-Year Project (with taxes and no depreciation)

	Year 0	Year 1	Year 2	Year 3
Net patient revenues		$5,000	$5,800	$6,800
Total operating expenses		5,000	5,300	5,500
Earnings before interest and taxes (EBIT)		$0	$500	$1,300
Interest		0	0	0
Taxes		0	150	390
Net income		**$0**	**$ 350**	**$ 910**

Although net income is higher without depreciation expense, operating cash flows are lower:

	Year 1	Year 2	Year 3
Operating cash flows without depreciable assets	$0	$350	$ 910
Operating cash flows with depreciable assets	0	500	1,060
Tax shield (provided by depreciation)	N.A.	150	150

does not represent a use of cash. Cash is used when the asset is purchased. In capital budgeting, the cash outlay for the capital asset occurs in the year before the project is implemented and is part of initial cash flows. To include depreciation expense in operating cash flows would be to double-count cash used for the investment.

Calculating the Tax Shield from Noncash Expenses

Noncash expenses affect cash flows indirectly, by reducing the amount of income tax that must be paid on profits made by a taxable organization. Income tax payments are reduced by the organization's tax rate, t, times the depreciation expense. Since depreciation is included as an expense, taxable income is also reduced, shielding a part of net income from taxation. These additional dollars can be used to pay creditors and shareholders instead. Similarly, noncash expenses generate cash revenues under cost-based reimbursement. The portion of depreciation and other noncash expenses that are reimbursed at cost should be included in cash inflows of the project.

Remove Interest Payments from Project Cash Outflows

Interest expense is definitely a cash expenditure, but it is a use of cash that is already taken into account in the discount rate used to convert cash flows to their present values. One component of the WACC is the after-tax cost of debt—the interest paid to bondholders after subtracting the interest savings from its tax deductibility. Therefore, to include interest payments in operating cash outflows would be to count interest payments twice.

Incorporating Expected Inflation

In an inflationary economy, the rates of return that investors require include an inflation risk premium. Suppose investors need a 3 percent rate of return to compensate them for the opportunity costs associated with giving up the use of their cash for one year. Assuming no inflation, they will require $1.03 at the end of the year on a $1.00 investment:

$$FV = \$1.00\ (1.03) = \$1.03.$$

Now assume that 2 percent inflation is expected over the next year—that is, goods and services purchased one year from now on average will be 2 percent more expensive. To achieve the same purchasing power with their funds at the end of the year as they have today, investors will need to receive cash returns from an investment that are 2 percent higher to compensate for inflation. Thus, the rates of return they require will include an inflation premium of 2 percent:

$$FV = \$1.00(1.03)(1.02) = \$1.0506.$$

The WACC, which reflects the required returns of investors, is used to discount the cash flows of a project to their present values. Required rates of return reflect both opportunity costs and expected inflation risk. Failure to estimate the impact of infla-

A Case in Point. Assume Hometown Health Center has a project that requires initial cash outlays of $1,000. To simplify the example, it plans to finance the project solely with debt. The bank will lend the needed $1,000 and expects a return of principal plus 10 percent interest at the end of the project. Since k_d is 10 percent, the WACC for the project is:

$$WACC = 100\% \times k_d + 0\% \times k_s = 100\% \times 10\% = 10\%.$$

Cash flow projections show that the project will earn $1,100 in cash by the end of the year. Thus, the project should make just enough to break even—returning the principal of $1,000 plus interest of $100 to the lenders. Using discounted cash flow analysis,

$$PV \text{ of earnings before interest is paid} = \$1,100/(1.1) = \$1,000$$
$$\text{Net cash flows} = -1,000 + 1,000 = \$0$$

According to the *PV* calculations, if interest expense is not deducted from operating cash flows, the project breaks even, just as expected.

What if interest is subtracted from operating cash flows, so that projected earnings are $1,000 instead of $1,100? Here is the discounted cash flow analysis:

$$PV \text{ of earnings after interest is paid} = \$1,000/(1.1) = \$909.09$$
$$\text{Net cash flows} = -1,000 + 909.09 = -\$90.09$$

By deducting interest expense, the analysis indicates that there is not enough to pay the bank at the end of the year. In fact, the project would have a loss of $90.91. The problem with this analysis is that interest expense is counted twice: (1) when interest is subtracted from operating cash flows and (2) when remaining cash flows are discounted by $1/(1.1)$. The discount rate, 10 percent, takes into account the 10 percent interest expense that will be paid to the bank at the end of the year. By discounting future dollars using a 10 percent discount rate, the present value is reduced by exactly $100. Thus, if interest is not subtracted from operating cash flows, the correct result is obtained.

tionary pressures on future prices and costs, and thus revenues and expenses in the pro forma income statement, can result in excessive discounting of future cash flows. If cash flows are not adjusted upward to incorporate these inflationary effects, profitability will be underestimated and viable projects rejected.

Include Only Incremental Revenues and Expenses

Organizational overhead expenses in the project pro forma income statement that do not arise as a result of the new activity should be excluded from the project's operating cash flow projections. Like sunk costs, existing overhead expenses that are unchanged by undertaking the project are irrelevant in determining whether the project is profitable on its own merits. There is one exception, however: existing overhead costs that are allocated to a new project may be recovered if these cost allocations are allowed by third-party payers who pay on the basis of costs. Indeed, impetus for shifting sites of care to locations that receive cost-based reimbursement was to recover some of capital cost reimbursement lost under PPS (Boles, 1986). (See Chapter 6.) These cost recoveries are cash inflows to the project and should be included in project cash inflows. Reductions in cost reimbursement will remove these incentives.

A Case in Point. Suppose Hometown is tax exempt but qualifies for 30 percent capital cost reimbursement. Capital costs include depreciation and interest expenses. In this project, depreciation expenses are $500 per year, and debt is assumed to cost 7 percent per year. For simplicity, assume that interest expense is $35 per year. Hometown is eligible for capital reimbursement equal to 25 percent of capital expenses. Thus, 25 percent of depreciation expense and 25 percent of interest expense will be reimbursed each year.

Pro Forma Income Statement for Three-Year Project (with taxes and depreciation)

	Year 0	Year 1	Year 2	Year 3
Net patient revenues		$5,000	$5,800	$6,800
Total operating expenses		5,000	5,300	5,500
Depreciation		**500**	**500**	**500**
Earnings before interest and taxes (EBIT)		−500	0	800
Interest		35	35	35
Taxes		0	0	0
Net income		**−$535**	**−$35**	**$765**
Add back depreciation		500	500	500
Add back depreciation expense recovery		125	125	125
Add back interest expense recovery		8.75	8.75	8.75
Projected cash flows		**$98.75**	**$668.75**	**$1,398.75**

Hometown will recover some of its capital expenses from third-party payers Operating cash flows are projected to be higher for Metro Clinic if some payers pay on the basis of costs.

Include Spillover Effects

While a pro forma income statement represents the expenses and revenues directly re-lated to a project, there may be secondary project effects, called downstream or **spillover effects.** Spillover effects are consequences that the project has on the revenues and costs of other ongoing activities in the organization. For example, a project may involve the use of a new technology that makes an existing technology operated by the health care provider obsolete. The net loss in revenues from abandoning the old technology for the new should be included in the cash outflows. Similarly, if the new venture is expected to generate referrals to other services, these additional net revenues can be added to net cash inflows of the project. Failure to account for spillover effects can understate or over-state the net value of the project to the profitability of the entire organization. Spillover effects were not considered in the case of Metro Clinic, although one of the goals of open-ing the clinic was to increase hospital referrals, a positive spillover effect.

Salvage Value

Any cash inflows from anticipated sale or recovery of assets should be included in cash flows in the last year of the project.

Determining salvage value is not necessarily a simple task. Although historical market information is available, there will be some uncertainty about the future value of land, buildings, and equipment. At least three factors can affect salvage value esti-mates: (1) the general desirability of the location, (2) the reliability and longevity of the assets, and (3) the risk of technological obsolescence. In a good location with a growing population, land values are likely to appreciate, raising cash returned to the

A Case in Point. Assume that Metro Clinic is a for-profit entity rather than a not-for-profit. At the end of the project, the salvage value of the ambulatory care clinic was estimated to be $800,000. As a not-for-profit, Metro will pay no cap-ital gains taxes on the sale. As a for-profit, Metro Clinic is assumed to be subject to a 30 percent tax rate on capital gains.

Book value of building (purchase price less accumulated depreciation)	$2,000,000 1,500,000 $ 500,000
Sale price of the building	800,000
Capital gain ($800,000 – 500,000)	300,000
Capital gains tax (30% × $300,000)	90,000
Salvage value (sale price – capital gains tax)	$ 710,000

As a for-profit facility, Metro Clinic would show cash flows of $710,000 rather than $800,000 for the salvage value of the clinic.

project. A health care facility (or an ambulatory clinic or physician offices) situated in a good location will have more salvage value, especially if the facility is highly adaptable to other uses.

Next, if the asset turns out to be a "lemon"—say, construction was poor—it will not produce as much upon resale. Finally, equipment and space in health care are particularly subject to obsolescence if new techniques or modes of delivery are developed, reducing the salvage value of specialized health care assets at the termination of the project. In the case of Metro Clinic, the salvage value was estimated to be $800. It was added back to project cash flows at the end of year 3.

In for-profit enterprises, taxes must be paid on capital gains from the sale of assets. Capital gains are the appreciation in the value of assets over their book value. Note that the value of land on the books remains at its purchase price; land is not depreciated. Similarly, if there is a capital loss—if assets sell for less than their book value—this loss can be deducted from taxes. Capital gains taxes reduce net cash inflows from selling assets, while capital losses are offset by tax deductions.

Determining the Opportunity Costs of Capital

In addition to estimates on initial costs and future cash flows for a project, the appropriate discount rate must be found to convert future cash flows to common present dollar amounts. Should the WACC for the organization as a whole be used to discount cash flows of individual projects? The answer is yes, if an individual project has the same business risk as the organization as a whole. Business risk is the variability of net income of an organization with no debt. Net income variability can arise from uncertainty of revenues, amplified by the degree to which the expenses of the organization are fixed. The organization can use its estimated WACC as the discount rate, or "hurdle rate," for all projects that have similar business risks as the organization as a whole.

Adjusting the Discount Rate for Project Risk

Any organization is a basically a portfolio of projects. The health care organization's overall cost of capital is the average of required returns on each of its existing projects based on investor assessment of risk and opportunity costs. The relevant cost of capital to be used in capital budgeting is the **marginal cost of capital**—the opportunity cost of the next dollar raised to finance a project. The marginal cost of an investment with higher risk than the organization's portfolio of assets will be higher than the cost of funds on the organization's current investments. Similarly, if an individual project is less risky than the organization's portfolio of projects, the marginal cost of funds will be lower than average. Moreover, differences in business risk of individual investment projects alter their capacity for debt financing. Highly risky projects must use less debt or incur a higher financing cost. Thus, project risk alters the cost of capital and the appropriate WACC to be used in project evaluation.

Obtaining estimates of project risk is sometimes more difficult than finding those for the organization. If individual companies that specialize in the same service as the project under consideration exist in the market, then information on these companies

A Case in Point. Assume that the cost of debt for Hometown Health Center is 7 percent, the cost of equity is 12 percent, and the proportion of debt used is 25 percent. Hometown is tax exempt, so *t* is 0.

$$WACC = \frac{\text{Debt}}{(\text{Debt} + \text{equity})} \times (1 - t)k_d + \frac{\text{equity}}{(\text{debt} + \text{equity})} \times k_s$$

$$= .07(.25) + .12(.75) = .105, \text{ or } 10.50\%.$$

If Metro Clinic is expected to experience the same degree of business risk as Hometown Health Center, then the discount rate to use to find the present value of Metro Clinic's expected cash flows is 10.5 percent:

Metro Clinic

	Year 0	Year 1	Year 2	Year 3
Projected cash flows	−$2,000	$ 0	$ 500	$2100
Present value	$\dfrac{-2{,}000}{(1.105)^0}$	$\dfrac{0}{(1.105)^1}$	$\dfrac{500}{(1.105)^2}$	$\dfrac{2100}{(1.105)^3}$
Present value	−2,000	0	409	1,556
Sum of PVs	−$2000 + $ 0 + $409 + $1,556 = −$35			

Using discounted cash flow analysis, the expected cash flows from Metro Clinic using the Hometown's WACC are negative. The project does not return sufficient cash flows over the three-year period to cover opportunity costs of funds. Based on this analysis, Hometown Health Center should not invest funds in Metro Clinic.

may provide a model to approximate the marginal cost of capital for the project. Suppose Hometown Health Center is planning to open a home health agency. Rather than use the WACC for Hometown Health Center to discount the cash flows of the project, Hometown's financial managers could use the CAPM and obtain the market beta on publicly-traded home health agencies to estimate the risk-adjusted cost of equity for a home health agency. Using the cost of debt to Hometown and its targeted capital structure, a risk-adjusted WACC for the home health agency could be approximated.

Often market prices and market risk information on a comparable stand-alone organization are not available to derive an appropriate WACC for a project. Another approach is to use the CAPM model to measure the **corporate risk** exposure of the new project—the degree to which the project's rate of return is correlated with the rates of return on the cash flows of the portfolio of projects that make up the entire organization, the corporate portfolio. Corporate risk exposure is measured by the project's corporate beta, the correlation of project returns with returns on the firm.

In the corporate version of the CAPM, k_c is the required return on equity for the organization as a whole, and k_{rf} is the risk-free rate of return. The risk premium imposed on the cost of equity is measured by $k_c - k_{rf}$, the difference between the cost of the organization's equity and the risk-free rate of return in the market:

$$k_s = k_{rf} + (k_c - k_{rf})\ \beta.$$

If project returns, k_s, have no more risk than those of the organization, then its corporate beta will be equal to 1, and its cost of equity, k_s, will be the same as for the organization, as measured by k_c. The WACC can be used. If the corporate risk exposure, beta, is greater (less) than 1, then the cost of equity in the WACC should be adjusted by the estimated k_s. Use of the corporate CAPM requires historical data on organization and project cash flows in order to derive a corporate beta and estimate the project's cost of equity. With a new project, however, it is typically the case that historical data are not available to calculate the corporate beta and the risk-adjusted WACC for the project.

Finally, project risk can be assessed by projecting net income and investor returns expected under differing future conditions. One method is to project the future scenarios for the project cash flows and assign a probability to the likelihood that each scenario will occur. The estimated standard deviation of cash flows from their mean reflected by these subjective projections can provide a measure of project risk. If the risk is deemed higher than average, the organization's WACC can be adjusted upward. If the risk is lower, the WACC can be reduced.

A Case in Point. Suppose Hometown Health Center has estimated its WACC to be 10.5 percent. It plans to add a service using a very profitable new technology but one that has a great deal of uncertainty about demand, especially if managed care organizations do not pay for these services. Hometown has projected three different scenarios for the future cash flows of the project: the most likely scenario, the worst case, and the best case. Each scenario is weighted by the odds that it will materialize. Because of this uncertainty, the risk of this project is considered to be much higher than that of Hometown as a whole. It has projected a distribution of profitability outcomes to reflect this uncertainty. If the standard deviation of these outcomes is sufficiently high relative to expected returns, then management can recommend that the WACC be increased, say, by 4 percent to account for this risk. The adjusted WACC for this project would be 14.5 percent.

In contrast, suppose Hometown plans to improve the physical surroundings, parking, and access to the facility. Patients and physicians have complained about the lack of these amenities in the past. This project is considered much less risky than the Hometown's overall risk. In fact, its future revenue uncertainty is actually reduced by this investment. Therefore, the WACC to be used for this project would be lower than 10.5 percent—say, 6.5 percent. In each case, the opportunity cost of capital, as measured by the WACC, must reflect the risk of the project, not the risk of the organization as a whole.

As this discussion indicates, finding the appropriate discount rate to use in valuing the cash flows of a project requires consideration of a number of factors: the costs of each source of funding at the margin, the capital structure weights, and risk. Some of these factors are estimates rather than true values. Each contains a chance of error and the chance of over- or underestimating the true cost of capital for a project. If the project's profitability is highly sensitive to the discount rate, then care should be taken in obtaining the best estimate for the particular project. Financial managers should recognize the limitations of this methodology when using this capital budgeting tool (Luehrman, 1997).

Using Decision Tools to Assess Capital Projects

With information on projected net income, cash flows, and risk-adjusted WACC for a proposed project, expected performance and profitability can be assessed using a number of decision tools:

- Break-even analysis
- Payback period and discounted payback period
- Net present value
- Internal rate of return and modified internal rate of return
- Profitability index

Break-Even Analysis

The pro forma income statement is built around the information used in break-even (**BE**) analysis. Recall from the discussion in Chapter 6 that break-even volume of services is the amount of patient utilization required for total revenues to equal total costs. BE enrollments in managed care plans can also be analyzed using a similar model (Boles and Fleming, 1996) (see Chapter 8). These uses of BE analysis to estimate volume, or enrollment, sufficient to return revenues to cover costs enable health care managers to decide whether a project under consideration seems feasible and merits further analysis. If BE quantity seems unrealistic, then further financial assessment of the project may not be warranted.

Payback Period and Discounted Payback Period

When BE analysis is used to find BE volumes, no assessment as to how much time it will take before the project becomes profitable is involved. Once revenue and expense projections of the project are completed, however, it becomes possible to evaluate the BE point with respect to time. First, one can examine when the project is expected to break even in an accounting sense by looking at the pro forma income statement. When net income is zero, the project breaks even.

Another indicator to assess to BE with respect to time is **payback period (PP)**, which measures the number of years until the project's cash outflows just equal the project's cash inflows. The more rapid the return of cash, the less risky the project. The PP provides an estimate of this risk.

A Case in Point. From the pro forma income statement for Metro Clinic, the net income for the project can obtained and operating cash flows derived. Break-even is examined in terms of net income projections. Payback period for Metro Clinic is calculated using its projected cash flows. The original cash projections for Metro Clinic are used.

Metro Clinic's Pro Forma Income Statement for Three-Year Project

	Year 0	Year 1	Year 2	Year 3
Net Patient Revenues		$5,000	$5,800	$6,800
Total operating expenses (including depreciation)		5,500	5,800	6,000
Earnings before interest and taxes (EBIT)		−500	0	800
Interest		0	0	0
Taxes		0	0	0
Net income		**−$ 500**	**$ 0**	**$ 800**

The income statement indicates that the project breaks even in an accounting sense in year 2 of the project. To find PP, cash flows received (spent) each year are added to the cash flows received (spent) in the previous year to obtain cumulative cash flows in each year. The year when cumulative cash flows become zero is the project's payback period.

Metro Clinic's Projected Cash Flows for Three-Year Project

	Year 0	Year 1	Year 2	Year 3
Projected cash flows	−$2,000	$ 0	$ 500	$2,100
Cash flows to date	$2,000	−2,000	−2,000	−2,000
		0	0	0
			500	500
				2,100
Cumulative cash flows:	**−$2,000**	**−$2,000**	**−$1,500**	**$ 600**

Although the project is profitable in year 2, it does not break even on a cash basis until year 3. Specifically, this occurs in mid-August of the year, assuming cash flows of $2,100 arrive in constant amounts each month. This is calculated by dividing cumulative cash shortfall in year two, which is $1,500, by total cash flows of $2,100 arriving in year 3. The resulting percentage—71.43 percent—is the proportion of year 3 revenues needed to pay back remaining cash used in the project. Therefore, the PP for Metro Clinic is 3.71 years. To covert this to months, multiply .7143 times 12 to obtain 8.57, the eighth month of the year, which is August.

The PP provides an estimate of the amount of time it takes a project to break even with respect to cash. It does not account for the time value of money—that is, differences in the present values of cash spent and received at different times in the future. For this, the **discounted payback period (DPP)** can be used. The discounted payback discounts future cash flows of the project by the project's WACC. Then cumulative cash flows for these discounted values are obtained. The year in which the present value of cumulative cash flows is zero is the discounted payback period.

Net Present Value

The most important decision tool for capital investment decisions is **net present value (NPV)**, the discounted present value of a project's future cash flows after subtracting the initial cash outflows of the project. A positive NPV signals that a project will earn a return after recovering initial capital outlays and paying investors a rate of return equal to their opportunity costs. Whenever NPV is greater than zero, the project is viable from a financial standpoint (Boles and Glenn, 1986). It earns an economic profit for the organization.

Internal Rate of Return and Modified Internal Rate of Return

The **internal rate of return (IRR)** is the rate of return that will be earned from a project's projected cash flows if the investor leaves the cash invested until the project terminates. Mathematically, the IRR is the discount rate that makes the NPV of the

A Case in Point. Using the present values of cash flows for Metro Clinic using a discount rate of 10.5 percent, the NPV of the cash flows of Metro Clinic is found to be negative.

Metro Clinic's Projected Cash Flows for Three-Year Project

	Year 0	Year 1	Year 2	Year 3
Projected cash flows	−$2,000	$ 0	$ 500	$2,100
Present value	−2,000	0	409	1,556
NPV of cash flows	−$2,000 + $1,965 = −$35			

A positive NPV would indicate that the clinic is profitable and should be undertaken. It is possible that the analysis should be carried out for one more year because cash flow projections are increasingly positive in years 2 and 3. For example, suppose cash flows for year 4 including $400 in salvage value are projected to be $4,000 if the project were continued for another year. In this case, cash flows in year 4, discounted at a 10.5 percent rate, are $2,683. After removing salvage value from year 3 cash flows, the NPV of Metro Clinic is positive:

NPV of cash flows   −$2,000 + $1,965 − $593 + $2,683 = $2,055.

A Case in Point. Finding the IRR for Metro Clinic. Using the future cash flows and initial cash outlays for Metro Clinic, the IRR for this project can be found. The calculation of the IRR solves the following equation:

Initial outlays   Future cash flows

$$-\$2,000 = \frac{\$0}{(1 + IRR)^1} + \frac{\$500}{(1 + IRR)^2} + \frac{\$2,100}{(1 + IRR)^3}$$

$$IRR = 9.82\%$$

With a financial calculator or a spreadsheet formula, the IRR for this project is found to be 9.82 percent. The IRR is lower than the opportunity cost of capital—the WACC of 10.5 percent for Metro Clinic. Because the IRR is less than the WACC, Metro Clinic is not a profitable project, confirming the NPV results.

project equal to zero. This requires finding the discount rate, the IRR, such that future cash flows just equal initial cash outlays. Once an IRR has been found, it must be compared to the opportunity costs of funds on the project, as reflected in the project's WACC. If the IRR is greater than the WACC, the project should be undertaken.

The IRR has several problems that may lead to false conclusions. First, the estimate of the IRR assumes that the organization will earn the IRR on cash earnings received over the life of the project as they are reinvested in other projects. This is incorrect because the likelihood of finding other projects with rates of return that are equal to those on the project is low. Highly profitable projects are, by definition, rare because they pay a return that is higher than the average rate of return available in the market. Therefore, funds that are reinvested are likely to earn returns close to or equal to the returns available in the market. Because of reinvestment risk, the IRR will overstate (or understate) the rate of return actually earned by investors over the life of the project.

A second problem with the IRR involves projects that are expected to have negative cash flows in future years. Mathematically, the solution for the IRR equation will produce multiple IRRs when one or more future cash flows are negative. Because the NPV is neither affected by negative future cash flows nor reinvestment risk, it always produces the correct assessment.

The **modified internal rate of return (MIRR)** is an alternative decision rule for capital budgeting that removes the overstatement or understatement of expected returns in the IRR. The MIRR calculation assumes that all future cash inflows will be reinvested at the WACC, the market opportunity cost of funds (Anderson and Barber, 1994). Thus, the MIRR adjusts the IRR from a profitable project for the lower returns from cash that must be reinvested during the project's life. On the other hand, the MIRR will be higher than the IRR in a project that is found to be unprofitable. As cash inflows are reinvested at the higher market rate, the effective return over the project's life will be higher than it would have been if cash inflows were reinvested at the lower IRR rate.

Profitability Index

The last tool that can be used to decide whether a project merits funding is the **profitability index (PI)**, used when the organization has limited access to funds and must ration available cash among several competing projects, all of them profitable. The PI is calculated by dividing the NPV of a project by its initial cash outflows. The initial cash outflow is the amount of funding that will be absorbed by the project. All projects under consideration can be ranked by their PI. The PI measures how many dollars of economic profits are returned for each dollar invested. Starting with projects with the highest PI, each project is funded according to its PI ranking, until all available cash has been used.

Conclusion

In for-profit enterprises, management's objective is encapsulated in the often-heard phrase, "maximization of shareholder wealth." This means that investors are concerned with earnings over time, not just one-time gains. Also investors are risk averse; they prefer higher returns and lower risk. The same is true for investments by charitable or religious organizations; stakeholder "wealth" maximization requires that the organization achieve and sustain its charitable mission or community purpose over time or that it spin off sufficient cash to allow the attainment of community goals by reinvestment in other

A Case in Point. Metro Clinic is not profitable when viewed for three years. Therefore an analysis of its PI is not necessary since it would not be funded on this basis. If an additional year of operations is considered, however, then the NPV is positive and the PI for Metro Clinic is:

$$PI = \frac{NPV}{\text{Initial investment}} = \frac{\$2,055}{\$2,000} = 1.03.$$

Suppose this project is competing with three others for funding. The organization has $5,000 available for investment. Each project's PI and initial costs are:

> Project 1: $PI = 1.40$; cash outlay, $3,000
> Project 2: $PI = .61$; cash outlay, $2,000
> Project 3: $PI = .90$; cash outlay, $2,000

Given the capital constraints, Metro Clinic, which has a PI of 1.03, will be funded along with project 1, thereby consuming all the capital available to Hometown Health Center.

worthwhile projects. Risky investments must be adequately addressed by both for-profit or not-for profit organizations in their capital budgeting decisions.

This chapter has introduced the process and tools of capital budgeting in health care organizations. The health care industry poses some unique problems in capital budgeting related to reimbursement, tax-exempt status, and the charitable purpose of its participants. Nonetheless, the same incentives and decision rules that govern the behavior of other industries are found to apply in health care. Health care providers who understand the principle of opportunity costs and can apply it to their financial decisions will have greater access to the capital markets and perform better over time. Effective capital budgeting can improve the organization's performance and future viability, whether it is for-profit or tax exempt, accepts donations or sells stock, or is capitated or cost reimbursed.

Case 9-1: Finding the Present Value of an Annuity— the Hard Way

You have just won the lottery for $1,000,000. The state has agreed to either pay you $100,000 per year for the next ten years or give you $614,000 today. You don't have a financial calculator. Illustrate on the spreadsheet how to evaluate these options without using the formula for calculating the present value of an annuity. Hint: What is the present value of the sum of the ten $100,000 payments? Then check your answer using the PV formula. Which will you take: the annuity or the $614,000? Explain your reasoning.

Case 9-2: Break-Even Enrollment in a Managed Care Plan

Break-even analysis can be used by health plans to assess enrollment targets. Assume that you are employed by a health plan to analyze its contracts. The plan has decided to participate in a state managed care plan to provide health services to children and pregnant women eligible for Medicaid. There are thirteen other plans bidding for the contract and the state indicates that there will be a total of about 140,000 prospective Medicaid enrollees. The state has told all bidders that it will pay no more than it pays under the existing fee for service system, which you estimate to be about $98 pmpm, or $1,176 annually per recipient.

You have obtained historical utilization and cost data on the Medicaid population of children and pregnant women from the state. These data are based on utilization under a discounted fee-for-service system in which the rates paid by the state were very low. You have decided that you will have to pay commercial rates to attract physicians to your health plan. Also, emergency room and hospital use may be too high in these statistics. Medicaid recipients, lacking access to a primary care physician frequently use the emergency room for primary care services. Finally, many Medicaid women received inadequate prenatal care under the traditional Medicaid system. You expect they will use more services under managed care.

You have information on utilization and costs among women enrolled in your commercial group plans. You have decided that these rates may be a better estimate of the medical expense expected per member per month for this group but since you have never served this population before you are uncertain about this assumption.

The utilization rates and costs per unit for the commercial and Medicaid population are provided on your diskette. You plan to create three scenarios for your pmpm calculations for this state contract:

Scenario 1: Medicaid enrollees will have the same utilization rates as commercial enrollees.

Scenario 2: Medicaid enrollees will have the same utilization rates as they did under traditional Medicaid.

Scenario 3: Utilization rates will be the average of these too rates.

Further you assume that the cost per unit on medical and hospital services will be the same as in your commercial contracts.

Aside from the uncertainty surrounding utilization rates, there are fixed costs associated with participating in the Medicaid managed care plan.

- You must hire new staff to administer the plan at an annual cost of $225,000.
- You must invest in an information system to meet the state's data requirements. It is expected to be a one-time cost of $862,000.
- You must provide access to a twenty-four hour nurse telphone hot line at an annual cost of $55,000.

Set up the three scenarios and estimate the costs for each. Then answer the following questions about the contract.

1. How many Medicaid recipients must you enroll in your health plan for the contract to be profitable under low, average, and high utilization scenarios?
2. What might you do if you accept the contract but fail to enroll enough members to break even?
3. If you break even in the first year, how much will you make on the contract in the second year, assuming your information system is a one-time cost?
4. Would you bid for this contract? Why or why not?

Case 9-3: Using Capital Budgeting Tools to Assess Project Profitability

Seven Oaks is a not-for-profit nursing home sponsored by a religious congregation. It plans to add an assisted living unit that will cost about $1.1 million to build and equip. Seven Oaks already owns the land valued at $250,000. The project will need working capital equal to 8 percent of the increase in annual revenues. The CFO has come up with a pro forma income statement for the project. For purposes of capital budgeting the project is given a five-year time horizon.

Seven Oaks Nursing Home Assisted Living Unit Pro forma Income Statement (in thousands)

Year	1	2	3	4	5
Net revenues	$350	$650	$650	$650	$650
Operating expenses	320	345	345	345	345
(including depreciation)	55	55	55	55	55
Total expenses	375	400	400	400	400
Excess of revenue over expenses	**–$25**	**$250**	**$250**	**$250**	**$250**

At the end of five years, the salvage value of the building and equipment is expected to be $900,000. The project will be funded with cash so there will be no interest expense. The CFO estimates that the cost of capital to Seven Oaks is 7.6 percent.

Using the spreadsheet for the case, find the payback period, discounted payback period, net present value, internal rate of return, and modified internal rate of return on this project.

Case 9-3 Questions

1. What does each decision tool reveal about the profitability of this investment?
2. Should Seven Oaks move forward with this project as a not-for-profit?
3. What is the effect on investment profitability if Seven Oaks is for-profit and subject to a 25 percent income tax?
4. Suppose Seven Oaks can borrow and lower its cost of capital to 6 percent but incurs an interest expense of $12,500 per year.
   a. How does the use of debt affect its profitability as a not-for profit?
   b. How does the use of debt affect its profitability as a for-profit?
   c. How does depreciation affect your cash flow and profitability projections under different ownership status?
5. How might higher inflation alter your projections of revenues and expenses?

Case 9-4: What Is the IRR and the MIRR of an Investment?

Mr. Scott, the CFO of Hometown Healthcare, has calculated the MIRR for Metro Clinic. He has been told that it is a better estimate of the rate of return on the project because it takes into account the rate earned on future cash flows as they are reinvested at the going market rate. He does the calculation as follows:

Metro Clinic Future Value of Reinvested Cash Flows

	Year 1	Year 2	Year 3	FV in Year 3
FV:	$0(1.105)^2$			= $0
FV:		$+ 500(1.105)^1$		= 552.50
FV:			$+ 2100(1.105)^0$	= 2100.00
Terminal value of reinvested cash flows				= 2652.50

The MIRR is the interest rate that makes the terminal value (the sum of future reinvested cash) flows just equal to the initial investment.

$$-2000 = \frac{+2652.50}{(1 + MIRR)^3}$$

$$MIRR = 9.87\%.$$

1. Verify Mr. Scott's results on your spreadsheet.
2. The MIRR is higher than the IRR of 9.82% found for Metro Clinic. Explain why this is the case?

Hometown Healthcare has just recalculated the cost of capital for Metro Clinic. After adjusting for risk, Metro Clinic is estimated to have a WACC of 11.25 percent. It plans to use a four-year planning horizon so that projected cash flows are as follows:

Year	0	1	2	3	4
Cash flows	−$2,000	$ 0	$500	$1300	$4000

1. What is the IRR of Metro Clinic using the new risk-adjusted cost of capital and the additional project year?
2. What is the terminal value of the project, assuming future cash inflows are reinvested at the WACC?
3. What is the MIRR of the project?
4. The MIRR was higher than the IRR when the cost of capital was 10.5 percent. Why is the MIRR lower than the IRR in this situation?

Case 9-5: Finding the Weighted Average Cost of Capital

You are the CFO of Planetary Pharmaceutical, a for-profit drug company. You have been asked to estimate the weighted average cost of capital from information provided by your staff. You have bonds outstanding with twenty years left to maturity that pay 5 percent coupons semi-annually on a face value of $1,000. They are currently being exchanged in the secondary markets at $833.44 each. The bonds are not callable and they are not insured, so you believe that the semi-annual rate of return, or yield, implied by this market price is a good estimate of the interest rate market lenders would require if you issued new bonds today.

You plan to use the capital asset pricing model to estimate the required rate of return on equity. An examination of the correlation of your stocks with the return on a market portfolio of stocks reveals a historical market beta of 1.2. This tells you that when the stock market goes up by 1 percent, your stock returns have gone up by 1.2 percent. When market returns fall by 1 percent, your stocks decline even more, by 1.2 percent. Long-term US Treasury bonds, considered a risk-free investment, are now paying 6.5 percent and a portfolio of stocks made up of the S & P 500, which will be used to represent the required return on a market portfolio of stocks, is currently yielding 12.2 percent.

You plan to keep your debt financing at no more than 50 percent of total assets. Also your income tax rate is 40 percent. What is your weighted average cost of capital?

References

Anderson, G. A., & Barber, J. R. (1994). Project holding-period rate of return and the MIRR. *Journal of Business Finance and Accounting, 21*(4), 613–618.

Boles, K. E. (1986). Implications of the method of capital cost payment on the weighted average cost of capital. *Health Services Research, 21*, 189–212.

Boles, K. E., & Fleming, S. T. (1996). Breakeven under capitation: Pure and simple? *Health Care Management Review, 21*(1), 38–47.

Boles, K. E., & Glenn, J. K. (1986). What accounting leaves out of hospital financial management. *Hospital and Health Services Administration, 31*(2), 8–27.

Demby, H. J. (1995). Overcoming financing challenges with bond insurance. *Healthcare Financial Management, 49*(3), 48–49.

Gapenski, L. C. (1996). *Understanding health care financial management: Text, cases and models* (2nd ed.). Chicago, IL: AUPHA Press-Health Administration Press.

Hamada, R. S. (1969, March). Portfolio analysis, market equilibrium and corporation finance. *Journal of Finance,* 13–31.

Luehrman, T. A. (1997). Using APV: A better tool for valuing operations. *Harvard Business Review, 75*(3), 145–152.

Pallarito, K. (1997). MBIA offers guidelines on bond insurance for faculty practice plans. *Modern Healthcare, 27*(9), 26.

Rubinstein, M. E. (1973, March). A mean-variance synthesis of corporate financial policy. *Journal of Finance,* 167–181.

Wheeler, J. R C., & Smith, D. G. (1988). The discount rate for capital expenditure analysis in health care. *Health Care Management Review, 13*(2), 43–51.

Chapter 10

Cash Budgeting and Working Capital Management

Financial management concerns managing the cash flows of the organization. Capital budgeting and financing, discussed in the preceding chapter, involve major, periodic financing decisions to purchase long-lived assets. Cash budgeting, on the other hand, focuses on managing daily and monthly expenditures and receipts of cash associated with the delivery of services. While poor capital investment decisions may lead to financial insolvency, inadequate cash budgeting and management may result in the lack of liquidity, with equally devastating results. A profitable organization may experience financial distress or fail because of a shortage of cash. This chapter discusses the elements of short-term financial management in health care provider organizations and in managed care plans.

Learning Objectives

Upon successful completion of this chapter, the learner will:

- Recognize the components of working capital.
- Identify the cash conversion cycle of the organization and the operating cash requirements of the health care organization.
- Be able to develop a cash budget.
- Understand the matching principle in financing assets.
- Be able to manage operating cash flows in a managed care plan.
- Be able to manage provider cash flows under capitation.

Key Terms

aging schedules	lockbox services
cash conversion schedule	maturity matching
cash equivalents	money market mutual fund
certificates of deposit	periodic interim payments
commercial paper	precautionary demand for money
compensating balances	schedule of revenues outstanding
completion factors	securitization
concentration banking	specific inventory method
depository transfer checks	speculative demand for money
duration	spontaneous liabilities
factoring of receivables	sweep accounts
lag report	transaction demand for money
line of credit	

Introduction

Why do health care organizations hold cash? Like individuals who carry money in their wallets or have checking accounts with the bank, all organizations hold cash for daily transactions—paying bills. This is called the **transactions demand for money.** Physicians, hospitals, nursing homes, and managed care plans keep cash on hand (in a bank account) to meet payroll, pay suppliers, and cover other ongoing operating expenses. Cash in checking accounts pays no interest as compared with other assets, so there is an opportunity cost to holding too much cash relative to other assets. Cash management attempts to minimize the time and proportion of total assets invested in cash without compromising the ability to meet payment commitments in a timely fashion. Since there is also a cost to liquidating other, longer-term assets prematurely in order to pay bills, holding too little cash is expensive for the organization as well.

Uncertainty about future cash flows makes the determination of a minimum inventory of cash much more problematic. Uncertainty encourages the holding of a greater quantity of unproductive cash balances as safety stocks. Holding cash as a buffer against uncertain timing and the size of unpaid bills is called the **precautionary demand for money.** Managed care plans experience uncertainty as to the arrival of outstanding bills from providers. Physicians and hospitals experience uncertainty about the timing of reimbursement and the amount of bad debt expense they will incur.

Some organizations hold additional cash to take advantage of investment opportunities when they arise. Holding cash for future investment is the **speculative demand for money.** Suppose a hospital system has initiated a strategic plan to acquire physician practices to expand its referral network. To work quickly and without undue constraints from the capital markets, the health system might maintain excess cash balances in short-term securities that are readily available for promising future acquisition opportunities as they arise.

Cash, Working Capital, and Net Working Capital

To understand the issues in cash management, a brief review of the concept of working capital is in order. For this, we will return to the balance sheet. Table 10-1 illustrates the upper portion of the balance sheet, which shows the current assets and current liabilities of the typical health care organization. Working capital, or *gross* working capital, includes cash on hand, short-term securities, accounts receivable, inventories, and prepaid expenses. Short-term securities that are readily converted to cash without a loss in return are called **cash equivalents.** Cash equivalents are made up of short-term financial assets that mature in three months or less. Excess cash may be stored for short periods (even overnight) in these types of investments.

Working capital management requires balancing the costs of holding too much of a current asset with the costs of holding too little. Investing in too much inventory, for example, imposes purchase and storage costs, as well as the opportunity costs of the interest that could be earned on funds tied up in inventory. On the other hand, inadequate inventory prevents timely delivery of service and forces the provider to buy off the shelf and give up volume discounts. Similarly, maintaining high levels of accounts receivable creates holding costs—billing patients and payers and keeping track of collections—and opportunity costs amounting to the lost interest that could have been earned had bills been collected sooner. As we have said, cash holdings incur similar costs. Too little cash forces the organization to liquidate other assets at a loss or borrow at high interest rates. Too much cash imposes opportunity costs of forgone interest income.

Besides investing wisely in current assets, managers must implement efficient working capital financing strategies as well. This will depend on the relative costs of alternate sources of funds. Reflecting the way that current assets are financed, the expression "working capital" sometimes is used to refer to current liabilities: accounts payable, accrued salaries, benefits and other expenses, and short-term loans. The use of less expensive financing sources reduces the costs of maintaining adequate working capital balances. Note that the current portion of long-term debt, while part of cur-

Table 10-1   Balance Sheet for a Health Care Provider (thousands of dollars)

Current Assets		*Current Liabilities*	
Cash	568	Accounts payable	3,843
Short-term securities	882	Accrued expenses	1,988
Accounts receivable	10,545	Notes payable	3,200
Inventories/supplies	1,525	Current portion of	
Prepaid expenses	1,250	long-term debt	1,896
Total	14,770	Total	10,927
Net working capital	3,843		

rent liabilities used to support current assets, arises from long-term rather than short-term financing decisions.

Long-term financing requirements to support the organization's working capital are measured by its net working capital, defined as the *difference* between current assets and current liabilities. This is shown at the bottom of Table 10-1. By definition, this difference indicates the amount of working capital that the organization has *chosen* to finance with long-term debt or equity. For this reason, changes in net working capital associated with an investment project are included as part of the incremental cash flow analysis in a capital investment decision. (See Chapter 9.)

Cash Budgeting

Cash budgeting seeks to estimate the minimum amount of cash that must be held to maintain operations efficiently (Hauser, Edwards, and Edwards, 1991). To do so requires calculating on a monthly or daily basis the amount of cash that remains after all anticipated expenses have been covered and all expected revenues have been collected. If there is high uncertainty about these predictions, then safety stocks would be added to the minimum amount of cash required. Projections of monthly and daily cash balances that result from expected cash inflows and outflows allow the organization to plan for temporary shortages and surpluses of cash that result from seasonal and cyclical factors.

Temporary surpluses of cash can be invested in cash equivalents and used to fund temporary shortages. When the stock of short-term financial assets is inadequate to cover cash shortfalls, then additional cash must be obtained temporarily from commercial banks, suppliers, or long-term funding sources. If the shortfall is temporary, short-term financing can be used. If the shortfall is found to be permanent, then long-term sources of funds are more appropriate. Similarly, if the organization finds it is permanently accumulating cash, then it should be invested in higher-paying assets. Financial ratios that identify a shortage or surplus of cash were discussed in Chapter 7. They include the days' cash on hand, the quick ratio, and the acid test.

The Cash Conversion Cycle

To predict cash flows for cash budgeting, the health care organization must understand its **cash conversion cycle**, which traces out the pattern of cash outflows and inflows over time. The cycle is highly dependent on the internal and external operating environment. Assuming no significant changes in receipts and disbursements in the recent past, patterns of the cash conversion cycle can be derived from historical data. The cash conversion cycle differs for providers and payers.

The Provider Prospective

The provider's cash conversion cycle depends critically on the type and efficiency of the health care organization in providing services, preparing bills, and collecting payment. The amount of external cash needed to maintain a targeted cash balance in the cash budget will be affected not only by the *length* of the cash conversion cycle but also

A Case in Point. St. Clair Surgery Center has monthly and daily cash budgets. The monthly cash budget, shown below, allows it to plan for cash needs over the year as surgery services fluctuate each month.

At St. Clair, most patients do not pay at the time of service. Based on experience, St. Clair receives payment for 30 percent of its bills during the month of service. Another 60 percent of accounts are paid within sixty days of service. Ten percent are paid in ninety days. These percentages are used along with the service forecast to estimate monthly collections from payers.

St. Clair's revenue forecast for surgery services, February through June, are as follows: February, $10,000; March, $14,000; April, $16,000; May, $12,000; and June, $10,000. Because of shortfalls in cash inflows in the preceding months, St. Clair has accumulated $2,876 in outstanding loans by the beginning of April. The cash budget shows a beginning cash balance without supplemental bank loans.

Cash Budget for St. Clair Surgery Center, April–June

	April	May	June
Beginning cash balance	$3,300	$4,770	$ 5,970
Cash inflows			
Collections			
In 30 days of service	4,800	3,600	3,000
In 60 days of service	8,400	9,600	7,200
In 90 days of service	1,000	1,400	1,600
Total	14,200	14,600	11,800
Cash outflows			
Supplies	4,480	3,360	2,800
Wages	6,200	5,240	4,800
Rent	800	800	800
Equipment		4,000	
Taxes	1,250		
Total	12,730	13,400	8,400
Net cash gain (loss)	1,470	1,200	3,400
Ending cash balance	4,770	5,970	9,370
Targeted cash balance	5,000	5,000	5,000
Surplus (shortage)	(230)	970	4,370
Cumulative investments (loans)	(3,106)	(2,136)	2,234

St. Clair's financial manager predicts a shortfall in desired cash balances of $230 in April. She will need an additional $230 in loans in April, for a total of $3,106 owed to the bank. In May and June, cash surpluses will develop. St. Clair will be able pay off its short-term bank loans in May and June. At the end of June, in fact, St. Clair will have a $2,234 cash surplus to invest in cash equivalents. These funds will be used to finance future cash shortages until they are depleted and bank financing is accessed once again.

by the *amount* of dollars tied up in each stage of the cycle. The cash conversion cycle consists of four ongoing stages:

1. The start-up stage (cash outflow)
2. The service delivery stage (cash outflow)
3. The billing stage (cash outflow)
4. The collections stage (cash inflow)

The cycle traces dollar outflows through these four stages until the stock of cash is restored in the final collections stage. Once returned to the organization, excess cash balances may be reinvested in short-term financial assets until they are needed again for the production of services.

The Start-up Stage

Prior to providing services, the health care organization must hire staff and obtain supplies and stock inventories in addition to acquiring space and equipment. On the balance sheet, available cash acquired for the project is reduced and converted to in-

A Case in Point. Suppose a start-up medical supply firm receives $500,000 from investors. The balance sheet after this transaction shows:

Mission Medical Supplies (in thousands of dollars)

Assets		Liabilities and Equity	
Cash	$500	Equity	$500

With these funds, supplies are purchased, employees are hired, and insurance and three months' rent are paid in advance. The rest is conserved as cash. Now the balance sheet shows:

Assets		Liabilities and Equity	
Cash	$200	Accrued payroll	$120
Inventory/supplies	180	Accounts Payable	180
Prepaid Expenses	220	Current liabilities	$200
Current assets	$500		
		Equity	$300
Total assets	$500	Liabilities and equity	$500

The composition of assets and liabilities has been changed to prepare Mission Medical for business by spending some of the cash initially invested. No revenues or expenses have been incurred.

ventory, supplies, and prepaid expenses, like insurance and rent. These investments in working capital are made *before* the first patient or client comes in for services. On an accrual basis, start-up involves no operating expense or revenue because no services have been delivered. Nonetheless, there is a net cash outflow that must be financed by funds secured from sources external to the project.

A new project has higher start-up costs than does the expansion of an ongoing activity. Not only do new projects involve marketing and development expenses, but minimum staffing and supply levels may be necessary to fulfill regulatory and licensing requirements. The uncertainty of success of the new service is greater, perhaps requiring larger precautionary cash balances. Building excess capacity at start-up by employing too much permanent staff and stocking surplus inventory can threaten the success of a new project.

Once a project is up and running, however, expansion merely requires building current assets sufficient to support the higher level of operations. Just-in-time inventory systems and the ability to employ nurses and doctors on a temporary basis may help a health care provider to reduce the up-front costs of new projects and the expansion of existing services.

The Service Delivery Stage

The service delivery stage begins when patients enter the system for health services. During this period, labor, supply, and overhead expenses are being incurred. Although matching revenues related to these services are shown on the income statement, bills may be incomplete or in process. Cash balances continue to be drawn down as funds are used to support health care operations until bills are submitted to payers or patients.

Everything else remaining the same, the cash conversion cycle will be longer and the amount of cash outstanding greater among hospitals than other providers. Tertiary and quaternary care hospitals, which include academic medical centers, have longer and more expensive stays than other hospitals because of the types of patients they treat. Hospitals as a group have longer and more expensive treatment episodes than primary care facilities, ambulatory care clinics, and outpatient surgery centers where no nursing care is required. Efficient providers that use fewer resources and time to provide patient care have a shorter cash conversion cycle and a reduced need for cash balances when compared with other organizations.

The Billing Stage

As service delivery is completed, bills are submitted to payers for reimbursement. Again cash is used temporarily to support the salaries and related expenses of the business office or billing department. More complex billing systems increase this cost because additional staff and/or staff time and better information systems are required. When providers must submit claims to many different payers and follow diverse rules to receive payment, the process takes longer and there is a greater chance for error. Delays in preparing and submitting the bill and errors that result in a rejected claim that must be resubmitted are costly and time-consuming. The existing system of multiple payers and nonstandard billing systems and benefits packages increases the cash conversion cycle, the need for cash, and the working capital requirements of the health care organization.

If services are covered under capitated contracts, the billing and subsequent collections stages of providers are significantly reduced. Funds to pay for services are received on a monthly basis based on enrollment data. Payers and health plans that pay the provider on a capitation basis may require data on encounters with patients as part of the contractual agreement. Patient encounters include office visits, specific treatments, lab work, and other documentable services. Such information requirements preclude the provider's ability to avoid the cost of preparing bills and documenting utilization.

A number of operational strategies can be used to shorten the billing stage of the cash conversion cycle. Providers can obtain insurance information prior to treatment. With accurate and real-time billing systems, charge data can be captured as services are delivered, with a final bill ready when treatment ends. Incentives for physicians to complete medical charts promptly and attest to the patient's diagnosis need to be in place. Moreover, the patient accounts manager should be well informed about different payer requirements. Computer information and coding systems should be created to ensure proper data are obtained, entered, and submitted to each payer. Well-trained medical records coders and other health information management specialists are very important in this stage, not only in hospitals but also in physician group practices and ambulatory care clinics with large volumes of patients. Finally, electronic claims submission reduces the time it takes to submit a bill for payment by eliminating paper claims generation, processing, and mailing time, and the possibility of coding error that this entails.

The Collections/Accounts Receivable Stage

Once the bill is complete, it must be submitted to the patient or payer for payment. Most health care providers allow patients and third-party payers to pay at a later time rather than at the time of service. In other words, providers provide credit—interest free—to patients. Unpaid bills become accounts receivable on the balance sheet. For most organizations, providing short-term credit is part of the necessary cost of doing business. People are more willing and able to buy an expensive good or service when they do not have to pay the full amount immediately.

In health care, credit is especially necessary when an acute illness or an accident requires immediate attention. Emergency services by definition are provided on a credit basis; normally there is no time to establish the patient's ability to pay or creditworthiness. Moreover, disability associated with recovery from a major and costly illness may prevent the patient from going back to work, thus hampering the ability to pay hospital and doctor bills promptly. The high dollar amount of most hospital bills and the predominance of third-party payers in the industry make credit a normal and necessary cost of providing medical care services.

For more predictable, less urgent services, like a physician prenatal office visit or nonemergency surgery, payment arrangements can be made in advance. The patient may be asked to prepay, pay at the time of service, or demonstrate third-party insurance coverage. Also, patients may choose to use credit cards instead of cash as a means of financing health services that must be paid for in cash.

Payment delays vary by payer type, size of the bill, credit policy, and quality of information management. Uninsured patients may take longer to pay than the insured. Larger bills increase this risk. Being insured is no guarantee of timely payment either. Receiving and processing of claims by third-party payers is slowed by inadequate information systems and payment technologies. Disputed claims can result in major delays in payment from third-party payers. State government payers that are temporarily short of cash also may delay payment to providers. Finally, weak credit policies will also extend the collections period. These include poor follow-up of uncollected accounts, lack of incentives for prompt payment, and failure to identify bad debt and charity care patients.

The collections stage may be shortened by a number of approaches that reduce the dollar amount and average collection period of accounts receivable:

- Implementing a more restrictive credit policy
- Monitoring outstanding balances
- Purchasing cash management services from banks
- Selling accounts receivable to a collection agency
- Offering a discount to payers for earlier payment

Implement a More Restrictive Credit Policy

One approach to shorten the collections process is to implement a more restrictive credit policy. Requiring payment in cash or by use of a credit card reduces accounts receivable and the costs of collecting outstanding balances. Penalties for late payment may also be imposed. For some payers, like Medicare, there is little that can be done to force speedier payments, however. A large third-party payer has a stronger negotiating position and the ability to set its payment terms.

The use of credit cards speeds up collections considerably, but cash is not immediately available to the provider. The provider must first collect from the credit card company. Credit card companies may take up to ten days to reimburse providers. Then the credit card company collects payment from patients just as they collect for other credit card purchases. The provider pays a fee to the credit card company for the billing and processing of charges. Fees also offset the cost of bad debt, or losses from uncollectable accounts, that the credit card company now accepts. For most providers, the fee imposed by credit card companies is minimal and the collection period relatively short when compared with the costs of collection and the average collection period. Health care entities are unable to achieve the economies of scale attainable by credit card companies in billing and collections. Economies of scale are operational efficiencies gained by producing a higher volume of goods and services.

Monitor Delinquent Accounts

More aggressive monitoring and follow-up of uncollected accounts may uncover problems that can be quickly remedied and free up a bottleneck in payment. Several reports are helpful for understanding payment patterns and identifying delinquent accounts: aging schedules, schedules of revenues outstanding, and the average collection period.

The average collection period (**ACP**) measures the average number of days that revenues are outstanding (in accounts receivable). This is a highly aggregated measure of credit and collections policy that can be obtained from the financial statements (see Chapter 7). An increase in the ACP may indicate that problems are developing in collections. A higher ACP than one's peers may indicate a need for stricter credit policies and improved billing and collections processes.

Aging schedules show how many months current unpaid bills have been on the books at a given point in time. Aging schedules can be prepared for individual accounts as well as the organization as a whole. Monitoring the aging of accounts of individual payers allows the health care organization to identify slow payers and detect delinquent accounts. With this information, corrective action can be taken. Very old bills may need to be written off.

A Case in Point. St. Ambrose Mental Health Center observed the following aging schedule for its outstanding accounts in the first quarter:

Aging Schedule

	January	*February*	*March*	*First Quarter*
Charges (accounts receivable, **AR**)	$100,000	$100,000	$100,000	$300,000
Outstanding at end of quarter	0	$ 15,000	$ 40,000	$ 55,000
Age of receivables outstanding	0%	5%	13.3%	18.3%

According to St. Ambrose's aging schedule, 18.3 percent of its quarterly charges are unpaid at the end of the quarter. Of these, 5 percent of unpaid accounts are two months old and 13.3 percent of its quarterly accounts are one month old.

Aging schedules are affected by changes in the volume of services. The percentage of total balances outstanding for the quarter by the month they were billed will vary if monthly charges change. Thus, accounts receivable may appear to be aging simply because the amount outstanding has increased over the quarter, not because payers are paying more slowly. If the health care organization knows the payment patterns of its payers, this problem can be avoided. One way to measure payment patterns is to calculate the charges outstanding as a percentage of the amount originally billed. A **schedule of revenues outstanding** provides this information.

A Case in Point. Suppose St. Ambrose's March receivables are $200,000, and $80,000 is unpaid at the end of the quarter. Using an aging schedule, it will appear that unpaid accounts are aging; 20 percent of March receivables are outstanding instead of 13.3 percent and quarterly receivables outstanding are 23.75 percent instead of 18.33 percent.

Aging Schedule: Increase in March Revenues

	January	February	March	First Quarter
Charges (AR)	$ 100,000	$ 100,000	$ 200,000	$400,000
Outstanding at end of quarter	0	$ 15,000	$ 80,000	$ 95,000
Age of receivables outstanding	0%	3.75%	20%	23.75%

If the payment pattern is known, however, this distortion is avoided. Assume all payers pay 60 percent of their balances in thirty days, 25 percent in sixty days, and 15 percent within ninety days. According to this payment pattern, the percentage of receivables outstanding by month is expected to be as follows:

	January	February	March	First Quarter
Charges (AR)	$ 100,000	$ 100,000	$ 100,000	$300,000
Payment pattern:				
January	$60,000	0	0	
February	25,000	$60,000	0	
March	15,000	25,000	$60,000	
% revenues outstanding	0%	15%	40%	

Now increase March charges as before. Notice that if payment patterns do not vary when revenues are increased, the percentage unpaid by month incurred remains the same:

	January	February	March	First Quarter
Charges (AR)	$ 100,000	$ 100,000	$ 200,000	$400,000
Payment pattern				
January	60,000	0	0	
February	25,000	60,000	0	
March	15,000	25,000	120,000	
% revenues outstanding	0%	15%	40%	

If the actual schedule of revenues outstanding is found to differ from that predicted from past payment patterns and the deviation is significant and/or persists, then it would indicate a change in payments that deserves attention.

Purchase Cash Management Services

Even if the patient receives the completed bill at the time of treatment and pays the provider in cash or by check, the collections stage would not be eliminated. First, cash and checks must be credited to the provider's bank account. There is a small cost to deliver the day's receipts to the local bank. In order to restore available cash balances, checks received from payers or patients must be cleared through the banking system before they can be credited to the provider's bank account. As bank check clearing processes have become more efficient, the time in which a check is in transit from the payer's bank to the provider's bank, or "float," has become shorter, reducing the collections stage. These improved check processing systems are part of the cash management services offered by banks (Moynihan, 1996).

In order to access bank cash management services, the health care organization must have a checking account with the bank and maintain a minimum cash balance in the account to avoid bank fees. Once in place, checking accounts support the bank's other cash management services, such as **sweep accounts** (Sagner, 1994). A sweep account "sweeps" cash deposits received in the provider's account during the day that are above the minimum balance required into an interest-earning account, typically a **money market mutual fund** which is a portfolio of short-term securities.

Another service banks offer for improved cash management is the provision of **lockbox services.** With a lockbox system, patients and third-party payers mail their payments to post office boxes, where they are collected daily by a local bank. The local bank deposits the checks in the provider's account, where they can be transferred to an interest-bearing account or be used to pay bills. With lockboxes, providers may maintain several checking accounts in different banks, or deposits may be consolidated in a single bank. Lockboxes are especially important for health care providers whose facilities are geographically dispersed.

The process of consolidating payments in a single bank is called **concentration banking.** It can be done with or without lockbox services. Checks from several banks are consolidated using a **depository transfer check,** a check drawn on local banks payable to a lead bank that holds the provider's account. Electronic depository transfers enable transfers from local banks to a lead bank in the same day. Wire transfers through the Federal Reserve system also facilitate large payments from a third-party payer's bank to the provider's bank.

In addition to transactions and short-term investment services, banks provide working capital financing. Banks charge fees for cash management services. If fees are less than the opportunity cost on funds that would remain in circulation and earn no interest without these services, then their purchase is cost-effective.

Sell Accounts Receivable

Selling (or **factoring**) accounts receivable is another strategy for shortening the cash conversion cycle (Flaum and Pecoulas, 1995; Mamo, 1994). When accounts receivable are sold, the bank or collection agency pays cash to the provider for the right to collect payment on outstanding accounts. The collection agency commands a discount for the cost of collecting and the risk that some of the accounts will be uncollectable. Suppose accounts receivable are valued at $500,000. Assume the probability of collecting these accounts in full is 90 percent and it costs 10 percent to collect. The collections agency will pay no more than $400,000 (80 percent) for the receivables. This 20 percent discount is the cost of more rapid conversion of the organization's receivables to cash. The age of accounts sold will affect the size of the discount because the odds of collecting are much lower as accounts age.

Banks that buy receivables often **securitize** them (Folk and Roest, 1995). When receivables are securitized, banks working through brokers resell portfolios of accounts receivable to investors. The security issued is typically a discount bond whose par value is returned to investors at maturity as the receivables upon which the security is based are collected. One problem for health care organizations that sell receivables to collection agencies is the compromise in public relations if the agency is overly aggressive and inflexible in its attempt to obtain payment on outstanding accounts.

Offer Discounts *Large Payers*

Another strategy to shorten the collections stage is to offer a discount to payers who pay quickly. Services that are not reimbursed at the time of delivery are provided to patients on a credit basis. Credit costs, which include collections costs and the opportunity costs of funds that are tied up in accounts receivable, are built into the overall costs of providing services and reflected in billed charges. A discount from charges will lower the charge needed to cover costs, because the costs of collection are reduced. In addition, cash reimbursed sooner can be invested in interest-earning assets. Thus the provider should offer a discount only so long as the savings from reduced costs of credit plus the interest earned on speedier collections are greater than the amount of the discount.

A Case in Point. Assume that the provider offers a 1 percent discount if claims that are due in forty-five days are paid within fifteen days. This discount is described as **1/15 net 45**; it says that a **1** percent discount is offered on bills paid within **fifteen** days, with the **net** outstanding balance after 15 days payable in full within **forty-five** days of the original billing date. Given a billed charge of $500,000, payment within fifteen days will reduce the amount due by $5,000. The health care provider will receive $495,000 in cash thirty days sooner if the payer takes the discount.

Suppose $495,000 can be invested at 4 percent for thirty days, or 8.2 percent of the year. The provider can earn $1,627 on this cash balance:

$$\text{Interest earned} = \$495,000 \ (.04)(.082) = \$1,627.$$

Total receipts to the provider over the forty-five-day period are now:

$$\text{Total revenues} = \$495,000 + \$1,627 = \$496,627.$$

(continued)

At first glance it might seem that the provider has lost money by offering the discount since only $496,627 is received rather than the $500,000 in billed charges. This does not take into account, however, the reduced credit costs to the organization with early payment. When the payer pays within fifteen days, billing and collections costs are eliminated for thirty out of the forty-five-day period. Thus the original billed charge overstates underlying costs.

Assume the cost of offering credit is 10 percent of the billed charge. A portion of these costs will be avoided if the payer pays early. For thirty days, or 8.2 percent of the year, if the payer accepts the discount, the avoided cost is $4,100:

$$\text{Cost of credit for 30 days} = \$500,000(.10)(.082) = \$4,100.$$

Billed charges would be $495,900, not $500,000, after collection costs for thirty days are removed. Compare $495,900 to $496,627, the amount the provider receives if the payer takes the discount and the funds are invested for thirty days. Obviously this discount, which earns $727, is cost-effective for the organization.

Estimating the Length of the Cash Conversion Cycle

These four stages thus make up the cash conversion cycle. Recall that in Chapter 7, the average collection period was reported for health plans and providers. This financial ratio measures the number of days a dollar remains on the books in accounts receivable before being converted to cash. This interval of time begins when charges are recorded by the internal billing system and ends when payment is received and deposited in the provider's bank.

A Case in Point. What is the cash conversion cycle for Suburban Medical Center? First, assume that there are no start-up costs; Suburban is fully operational. Next assume service delivery at Suburban takes six days based on the average length of stay of its patients. An additional four days are required to prepare and mail patient bills. Finally, bills take fifty-two days on average to collect and be deposited in Suburban's bank. Thus, the cash conversion cycle in this hospital is sixty-two days.

$$\begin{aligned}
\text{Cash cycle} &= \text{Service delivery} + \text{billing} + \text{collections} \\
&= 6 \text{ days} + 4 \text{ days} + 52 \text{ days} \\
&= 62 \text{ days}.
\end{aligned}$$

The average collection period measures the billing and collections stage of the cycle. Thus in Suburban Medical Center the ACP would be 56 days.

Although a single cycle has been described, each day begins a new cycle. So long as volumes, reimbursement, costs, and payer mix remain the same, the cycle will remain relatively stable over the year. The situation is changed if conditions affecting the cash conversion cycle change. Higher volumes and reimbursement will increase the amount of outstanding cash in the cycle and increase cash requirements. A change in the payment patterns of individual payers or a change in the payer mix to slower-paying groups also will increase the need for cash.

A Case in Point. Assume Suburban Medical Center has net patient revenues of $110,000 per day and costs per day are $100,000. Assuming the cash conversion cycle is stable, then each day in the cycle, the hospital will collect $110,000 from patients whose treatment was completed fifty-six days earlier. Each day the hospital incurs costs of $100,000 on new patients coming into the system. The hospital will show $10,000 profit deposited in the bank each day.

Now assume inflation rises so that costs per day are $115,000. At the same time, net patient revenues are increased to $125,000 to cover these costs. The problem is that daily revenues of $110,000 received from previous patients who were treated fifty-six days earlier are insufficient to cover current costs of new patients of $115,000. Cash balances will be depleted. Temporary financing must be sought to bridge the gap until the higher revenues begin to arrive fifty-six or more days later. Note that with permanent changes in volume, inflation, or the cash conversion cycle, the organization will have a permanent, increased need for cash and working capital.

In hospitals, the average collection period averaged 56.7 days in 1996. In HMOs the average collection period was considerably shorter, at 9.5 days. Why do managed care plans have shorter collections cycles than hospitals? To answer this question, we turn to the stages of the cash conversion cycle in a managed care plan.

The Payer Perspective

So far, the cash conversion cycle has been examined for the provider of health care services. Cash is depleted as health care is given and restored as payers reimburse caregivers for services. Insurers and managed care organizations have a different pattern of cash flows. The cash conversion cycle in a prepaid health plan begins with a stockpiling of cash from premium collections, followed by cash depletion as funds are used to administer and pay claims. Cash from premium revenues is invested in high-yielding short-term assets, earning interest income, until funds are used to reimburse providers. Capitated health care providers, like managed care plans, have a similar need to manage capitation revenues to ensure that operating cash is available to support covered services.

Information management essential (handwritten)

Except for start-up, the cash conversion cycle in a prepaid health plan is almost the mirror image of the cycle for providers:

1. Start-up stage (cash outflow)
2. Premium collection stage (cash inflows)
3. The service delivery/expense accrual stage (cash outflows)
4. Provider reimbursement stage (cash outflows)

In a well-run prepaid health plan, profits remain after all providers have been reimbursed.

The Start-up Stage

During start-up, health plans must price and market their services to employers and their employees. Cash is used to support plan development and growth. Typical costs include (1) the costs of space and equipment, (2) marketing costs related to advertising as well as the salaries, benefits, and travel expenses of the plan's sales force, and (3) the staff and supply costs associated with plan administration. Plan administrative costs include support staff and supplies for information systems, underwriting, finance and claims administration, human resources management, and customer services.

During start-up, the health plan prices its package of health benefits using group rates set by plan actuaries. Premium rates are developed from capitation rates (see Chapter 2) and depend on the type of rating system applied to the group being rated: community rating, community rating by class, adjusted community rating, or experience rating. These rates are then adjusted for the administrative costs associated with plan size and types of households covered, for contingency reserves, and for taxes and required returns to owners in proprietary firms. Premium rates are set well in advance of enrollment to enable current and prospective employer groups to decide whether to contract for the following year with the plan.

Start-up costs may be large in a new health plan because of extensive development and marketing costs. Minimizing cash requirements of the start-up stage, as in the case of providers, involves avoidance of excess built-in administrative expense and fixed costs that will overly burden the plan's ability to compete for enrollees. Premium rates must be set low enough to ensure sufficient enrollment but high enough to cover costs. Plan growth and stability depends on the adequacy and competitiveness of the quoted rates and the attractiveness of the panel of plan providers. If rates are too low, the plan will be at risk of failure because it will be unable to cover basic medical care expenses of plan enrollees, much less the extraordinary medical costs of enrollees who become extremely ill. Likewise, if rates are too high, the plan may not enroll enough members to spread risk adequately. Many start-up HMOs fail because they do not become large enough to reduce objective risk, administrative costs remain high relative to enrollment, and utilization management is inadequate.

The Premium Collection/Accounts Receivable Stage

As enrollment begins, the cash outflows of start-up are offset by inflows from the collection of premiums. Health plans bill employers monthly for premiums and expect to be paid by the beginning of the month when coverage is in force. These payments are typically made in line with the employer's payroll cycle. A health plan's accounts receivable stage is thus relatively short when compared with that of health care providers. As premiums are collected and deposited, positive cash flows accumulate to significant cash balances. The only exception to the initial buildup of cash in a managed care plan is when plan providers are capitated. Premium revenues are transferred directly from the managed care plan to providers who have accepted risk. Capitated contracts thus provide working capital to providers and deprive health plans from the short-run use of these funds (Jacobs, 1995).

The average collection period in a managed care plan is considerably shortened because premiums are expected on or before the first of the month when coverage is in force. Suppose premium bills go out on the fifteenth of the month before premiums are due and are to be received by the thirtieth. With bank clearing times of five to six days and assuming on average that employers pay within the fifteen days, the average collection period would be about twenty-one to twenty-two days.

The amount of premium revenues received by the health plan depends on current enrollment. Bills must be adjusted monthly for changes in enrollment status of plan subscribers. Poor coordination between the health plan and employers makes management of premium receivables problematic. Incorrect enrollment data results in the delivery of services to persons who are no longer covered or in the delay or denial of reimbursement for a legitimate claim. Such confusion over enrollments will be transferred to capitated providers whose payments may be delayed by the health plan. Thus, disagreement over eligible enrollees may lengthen the cash conversion cycle. Electronic billing shortens the premium collection stage, as do better enrollment verification systems.

The employer, or payer, typically enrolls new subscribers. This information must be provided promptly to the health plan for accurate and timely billing to occur. Various billing systems have been developed to reduce the cost and delay of enrollment verification. In a self-billing system, the employer verifies its enrollment using the monthly premium invoices received from the health plan and adjusts the next premium bill to incorporate any changes that have occurred. Alternatively, the health plan may take the responsibility of making adjustments prior to billing employers based on enrollment information that has been supplied to the plan.

Since premium revenues will be used primarily to pay provider claims over the following months, they are converted into short-term, interest-bearing assets. Management of short-term investments is therefore very important for efficient health plan operations.

Short-term investments are defined as financial assets that mature in one year or less. Because interest can be earned overnight and premium revenues to be invested are large, the health plan gains by moving cash into interest-earning assets even for short periods of time. Short-term investments include money market mutual funds, government Treasury bills, negotiable bank certificates of deposit, and commercial paper. Bank **certificates of deposit (CDs)** are short-term notes issued to the public by banks. Negotiable CDs can be bought and sold before they mature. **Commercial paper** consists of short notes—typically issued for thirty-, sixty-, or ninety-day periods—that are sold to the public by corporations.

Important considerations in short-term investments are liquidity, safety, and yield. *Liquidity* is the speed and cost of converting an asset to cash. *Safety* can be found in instruments that are traded in large secondary markets and are issued by the federal government, banks, or very large, well-established corporations. Investments traded in markets with few buyers and sellers and which lack backup of a government guarantee or corporate cash contain more risk. Like banks and insurance companies, health plans are also obligated by state regulators to hold reserves, or to invest in guarantee funds, to ensure their ability to pay bills when they become due. These reserves must be available to the health plan for unusual expenses and therefore cannot be invested in high-risk assets.

Cash requirements vary by type of health plan. Cash needs are much greater for staff model HMOs as compared with other plans because cash balances in these plans support service delivery as well as the administration of the insurance service.

The Service Delivery/Medical Expense Accrual Stage

During service delivery and medical expense accrual stage of the health plan's cash conversion cycle, cash outflows relate primarily to administrative costs of managing utilization and estimating and reserving for the cost of medical services. Unless the plan has underestimated its ongoing medical expenses and is experiencing financial distress, these costs should be well below available cash resources from premium revenues.

To the extent that providers delay billing for services, the financial manager must estimate medical expenses incurred during the month to match premium revenues received. To do this, systems to track ongoing utilization and costs must be in place. Precertification and utilization review are methods managed care plans use to stay in control of medical expenses and to anticipate the size of their accrued medical expense liabilities. (Utilization management is described in Chapter 12.)

In addition to estimating ongoing medical claims expense, utilization review combined with utilization management will reduce medical expense liabilities. If the health plan shortens the length of stay and treatment costs through utilization management, the service delivery stage is shortened and the opportunity for the plan to use premium revenues to earn interest and support plan administration expense is reduced. If the shortened length of stay results in lower medical expenses, however, this benefits the health plan as well even though it must pay providers more quickly.

Some utilization expense may not be subject to careful monitoring and control. This includes out-of-plan utilization, emergency care, care that was not precertified by the plan, and provider billing errors. These incurred but not reported (**IBNR**) liabilities must be estimated from past experience and adjusted for changes in enrollee patterns of utilization and in the current environment so that cash can be available when claims are received (Ryan and Clay, 1994).

Those activities that shorten the billing stage for the provider shorten the medical expense accrual stage for the health plan. Improved health information systems and electronic billing shorten this stage of the cash conversion cycle in both entities.

The Provider Reimbursement Stage

Provider invoices become claims in process of collection and accounts payable on the health plan's books. During this stage the managed care plan must (1) assess whether claims are legitimate, (2) coordinate benefits of dually covered enrollees, and (3) obtain reinsurance recoveries. Coordination of benefits and reinsurance recoveries lengthen the cash conversion cycle in an managed care plan.

During *claims verification,* enrollments are verified, billed services are compared to entitled benefits, and billing errors are detected before payment is initiated. This activity depends on how aggressively and efficiently the claims processing department functions and the relative costs of doing so. Payment delays on the part of the health plan lengthen the provider reimbursement stage and conserve cash but may result in provider dissatisfaction with the health plan and tougher contract negotiations later. Some payment delays may be due to enrollment disagreements between the plan and provider, as well as whether services that have been provided are covered by the plan. Provider withholds also extend claims processing time and conserve health plan cash.

In *coordinating benefits,* the health plan may choose to pay the claim and obtain reimbursement from the primary or secondary insurance carrier later. Alternatively, the plan may direct payment to the other carrier for reimbursement and delay payment to providers until payment is received from the other payer. Thus coordination of benefits provides an additional source of revenues to the managed care plan to cover medical expenses of its enrollees.

Reinsurance recoveries are also initiated during this stage. Once medical expenses on a single enrollee have mounted to a level sufficiently high to meet the deductible so reinsurance can be activated, the plan can submit its claim for recovery of expenses above the deductible to the reinsurer.

Health plans begin to experience significant cash outflows as verified provider claims are paid. Short-term investments must be liquidated and payments mailed to providers and deposited in their accounts. Mailing and bank clearing times extend the time when cash remains invested in interest-bearing accounts and earns income for the health plan. In this case, the health plan gains from the float—the time elapsing after checks to providers have been sent and the check has cleared through the banking system and been deposited in the provider's account.

Cash Conversion Cycle in the Health Maintenance Organization

A staff model HMO integrates the cash conversion cycle of the provider with that of the prepaid health plan into one organization. In theory at least, the staff model HMO is in a better position to reduce net working capital requirements. Since payer billing and provider retroactive reimbursement are eliminated, the staff model HMO cash flow cycle is simplified to:

1. Premium collections phase (cash inflow)
2. Service delivery phase (cash outflow)

One of the efficiencies gained by the staff model HMO, in theory at least, is a reduction in the administrative costs associated with claims processing, billing, and collections. Premium collections go directly from payers to provider-insurers. No bills must be generated by providers since they are now employees of the health plan. Claims processing is eliminated and utilization management becomes an integral part of the health care delivery system. With accurate internal reporting, utilization can be monitored and controlled to achieve efficiencies for the plan. Provider sponsored organizations, recently approved by Congress, which eliminate the middleman—the insurer—have the potential to reduce health care administrative costs if they are effectively managed.

Financing Working Capital

Working capital needed for start-up, service delivery, billing, and collections stages must be financed. Sources of short-term funding include spontaneous liabilities, accounts payable, and short-term debt. Net working capital, by definition, is financed with long-term debt or equity.

Spontaneous Liabilities of Health Care Providers

In provider organizations, **spontaneous liabilities** are obligations to make future payments created as a direct result of providing services. They include accrued supply and payroll expenses, and taxes. For example, suppose hospital staff are paid at the end of the month. Staff services are used for one month, and employee wages and benefits during that period are accrued on the books. These accrued payroll expenses are obligations to employees that involve no cash outflows until the end of the month. As a result, cash to meet payroll does not have to be borrowed from a bank or obtained by asset liquidation when reimbursement for health services delivered during the month is delayed. In essence, the health care provider "borrows" these funds from employees during the thirty-day period. Cash balances are thereby conserved. When employees are paid more frequently, spontaneous liabilities available for financing current assets are reduced, increasing the organization's need for cash.

Spontaneous liabilities are also created by medical supply companies that provide supplies on credit rather than cash on delivery. Suppliers encourage prompt payment after supplies are delivered by offering a discount when the account is paid in full within a certain number of days after receipt. Providers incur no cost from trade credit when they pay before the discount period has ended. For example, suppose a drug supplier provides pharmaceuticals on 2/15 net 30. This means that if the provider pays within fifteen days of delivery, a 2 percent discount is offered off the invoice price. After day 15, the provider must pay full price . A spontaneous liability is created from day 1 through day 15, during which time drugs can be used to deliver services without an expenditure of cash.

A Case in Point. Recall that the health care provider in Table 10-1 obtained $500,000 from investors. The managers had purchased $180 in medical supplies, reducing cash on hand by the same amount. Total assets of the firm remained at $500,000. Now suppose that supplies are purchased on credit. The result of this transaction is shown on the balance sheet:

Balance Sheet (thousands of dollars)

Assets		Liabilities and Equity	
Cash	$225	Accrued payroll	$120
Inventory/supplies	180	Accounts payable	180
Prepaid expenses	275	Current liabilities	200
Current assets	680		
		Equity	480
Total assets	680	Liabilities and equity	680

By using a spontaneous liability to medical suppliers, the health care organization increases total assets to $680 and conserves its cash.

Sometimes arrangements are made with third-party payers to provide interim cash payments when patients have extended periods of treatment in a hospital or nursing facility. Such arrangements will offset the depletion of cash during this period, providing a source of funds to support working capital investments. Such prepayments are shown as a liability on the balance sheet and are a source of financing for short-term assets.

At one time, Medicare prepaid hospitals for services, based on historical utilization and costs, and then settled accounts after services were actually delivered. These created spontaneous liabilities for hospitals in the form of accrued medical expenses of Medicare beneficiaries using hospital services. When hospitals and other providers received these **periodic interim payments (PIP)**, they did not have to finance working capital out of their own cash balances. With prepayments, the federal government and other federal programs bore the opportunity cost on the use of these funds. When PIPs were eliminated, this cost was transferred to hospitals, increasing their need to borrow temporarily from banks and to convert short-term, income-earning assets into cash.

In summary, a health care organization can maximize the use of spontaneous liabilities by delaying paying for medical supplies until the end of the discount period and by paying workers biweekly or monthly instead of weekly. Prepayment also increases the spontaneous liabilities of the organization and reduces the amount of the provider's cash tied up in the cash conversion cycle.

Spontaneous Liabilities in Managed Care Plans

Monthly premiums from employers and monthly capitation from health plans are payments for services to be delivered to enrollees during the month. These monthly payments provide regular cash inflows to the plan or the provider to support ongoing operations.

In a prepaid health plan, premium revenues create a spontaneous liability—the accrued medical expense of plan enrollees. Over the month, as health services are provided to plan enrollees, the health plan is accruing an obligation that must be met when bills from providers are received. Delays in provider billing enable the health plan to use premium revenues temporarily for other purposes. In other words, the health plan "borrows" premiums from payers and invests them temporarily in interest-earning assets or spends them on plan administration (Scott, 1997). The longer it takes for the settlement of claims, the greater is the plan's ability to conserve cash. Because the health plan bears the financial risk of unanticipated medical expenses—or objective risk—it is critical that this uncertain liability be estimated and managed.

Providers must monitor their accounts receivable to identify and manage slow payments and delinquent accounts. Health plans and capitated providers must monitor their accrued medical expense for problems in utilization management and for miscalculations of the actuarial rating assigned to an enrolled group. If utilization is deviating from what is expected but is found to be necessary for the enrollees seeking service, then premiums may be insufficient to cover accrued medical expenses. Future ratings and related premiums must be adjusted to reflect the higher-than-expected medical expenses of the plan's enrolled groups. Also reserves must be increased temporarily to support expected future claims.

Claims are of three types: claims received and paid, claims received but not yet paid, and claims incurred but not yet reported. Claims received can be used to create a **lag report** to help the health plan understand the billing patterns of its providers and estimate its accrued medical expenses. Lag reports are cross-tabulations of the behavior of two variables over time. Lag reports for health plans can be constructed for the month that a claim was received by the month that service was delivered, the month that a claim was received by the month a claim was paid, and the month that a claim was paid by the month that service was delivered.

Table 10-2 shows a lag report for the month of receipt of claim by the health plan by the month that service was provided, which shows how long it takes for providers to submit claims for services delivered in a given month. The table indicates that a majority of providers bill the health plan in the second and third month after services are rendered. This is shown by diagonal entries for the second and third months.

Lag reports allow the construction of **completion factors,** which show what percentage of the claims for a given month are received in each month following service delivery. The completion factor for the month of January for total claims received through June for January services is .1174. This means that 11.74 percent of bills for January services were received in the month of service. The completion factor is obtained by dividing the $25 claim received in January for services delivered in Jan-

Table 10-2   Lag Report for Hospital Service Claims

Month of Service	January	February	March	April	May	June	Total
		Month Claim Received (thousands of dollars)					
January	25	**100**	**60**	20	3	5	213
February		18	**115**	**70**	15	6	224
March			20	**112**	**85**	14	231
April				16	**120**	**65**	201
May					22	**130**	152
June						19	19
Total	25	118	195	218	245	239	1,040

uary by total January bills for the six-month period ending in June, or $213. The completion factors for services delivered in January derived from the lag report are shown below:

	January	February	March	April	May	June	Total
January	.12	.47	.28	.09	.01	.03	1.00

These completion factors can be used to estimate future claims. If on average 12 percent of January bills are received in January, then accrued expenses for January are equal to the claim for January services times 1/completion factor. Suppose the bill for January is $32,000. The accrued hospital expense for January using the January completion factor is therefore:

$$\$32{,}000 \times 1/.1174 = \$272{,}572.$$

Like aging schedules, lag reports are distorted by plan growth, monthly and seasonal variability in health services utilization, and variability in the severity of patient illness.

Another method to monitor accrued medical expense is the **specific inventory method** (Ward, 1995). When applied to hospital services, this method estimates the average expense per patient-day based on utilization reports and claims data. To arrive at accrued expense for the month, average expense per day derived from current and past claims data is multiplied by the number of days reported by utilization management. This method depends critically on good information from the utilization management staff.

Utilization management will not be able to capture total medical expense in the current month, however. Some claims for the month are IBNR. IBNR claims result from out-of-plan utilization, emergency care, care that was not precertified by the plan, and provider billing errors. The medical expense per day estimated by the specific

A Case in Point. Suppose average hospital cost per day for Physicians Medical Plan is estimated to be $1,000. Utilization management reports 200 inpatient-days for the month of January. The total reported expense for January is therefore $200,000.

Assume the IBNR factor is .28. This means that actual claims have tended to be 28 percent higher on average than predicted by utilization management statistics. The estimated hospital expense for the month of January using this information is therefore:

$$\$1,000\ (200) \times 1.28 = \$256,000.$$

inventory method must therefore be adjusted upward for IBNR expense to arrive at total expense for the month. An IBNR expense factor is derived from past unreported claims experience and applied to the cost-per-day estimates.

Anticipating cash required for claims reimbursement by the health plan depends on these estimates of medical expenses that are being incurred in the current month. These expenses will then be shown on the income statement, and because these claims have yet to be paid, they will be shown as an outstanding liability on the balance sheet (Mensah, Considine, and Oakes, 1994). Sufficient cash and near-cash equivalents must be maintained on reserve to reimburse providers when these claims are received by the health plan (Pallarito, 1995).

Trade Credit, Lines of Credit, and Other Short-Term Loans

Spontaneous liabilities finance only a portion of current assets, so health care providers and insurers must seek other sources of financing of their current assets. Short-term sources of financing of working capital include trade credit, lines of credit, and other short-term loans.

Trade credit is used when a provider elects not to take advantage of the supplier's discount. Trade credit is a very expensive source of short-term financing. Suppose a medical supplier offers terms of 1/15 net 45. By paying within fifteen days, the provider obtains a 1 percent discount from billed charges. Otherwise she must pay the bill in full within forty-five days. By failing to pay within fifteen days, the provider is taking out a temporary loan from the supplier for the balance due for the remaining thirty-day period. The interest cost on this loan is quite high The provider pays 1 percent for the use of each dollar of billed charges that remains unpaid from day 15 to day 45. For this thirty-day period, the effective annual interest rate is not 1 percent, however. The interest rate for thirty days must be multiplied by the number of thirty-day periods in the year. The effective annual rate is 12.17 percent since there are 12.17 thirty-day periods in the year.

A Case in Point. Suppose Doctor's Clinic receives a shipment from a medical supply company with an invoice of $100,000 and the terms are 2/10 net 30. Payment within ten days reduces the bill to $98,000. Instead Doctor's Clinic finds it needs cash, so the discount is not taken and the supplier is paid the full amount on day 30. By forgoing the discount, Doctor's Clinic is able to use the $98,000 it owes the supplier for twenty more days, at a cost of $2,000. The interest rate paid for the use of $98,000 for twenty days is:

$$\text{Interest rate} = \frac{\$2,000}{\$98,000} = .0204 = 2.04\%.$$

This is not the annual rate of interest, however. To find the effective annual rate (**EAR**) on this loan, the twenty-day rate must be multiplied by the number of twenty-day periods in the year:

$$\text{Number of 20-day periods in the year} = \frac{365}{20} = 18.25$$

$$\text{EAR} = 18.25 \times .204 = 37.23\%.$$

The effective annual rate would be 37.23 percent. Typically, trade credit is far more expensive than a bank loan or line of credit. Good financial management involves taking advantage of discounts and finding other ways to finance short-term cash needs. To maximize the benefits of the spontaneous liability created by trade credit, the account should not be paid until day 10.

Bank loans to finance working capital are usually in the form of a **line of credit.** Banks make available on demand a given amount of money—a line of credit—that can be borrowed at any time to meet daily expenses. To obtain a credit line, a checking account is usually opened with the bank. In the recent past, organizations desiring credit lines also had to maintain a minimum amount of cash—called **compensating balances**—in their checking accounts on a daily basis. With increased competition among banks and low interest rates, most commercial banks no longer require the maintenance of compensating balances to access a line of credit. Cash budgeting enables the financial manager to predict temporary excess cash needs and maintain the appropriate size of a credit line to cover temporary future expenses.

Another source of short-term financing for health care organizations is to obtain loans against accounts receivables. Receivables are used as collateral for the loan and are committed to repaying the loan as they are collected. Also, very large health care organizations may be able to issue commercial paper to the public.

Finally, long-term debt and equity may be used to finance temporary working capital needs. These financing sources are usually more costly than short-term financing. Moreover, use of long-term debt for short-term assets increases risk because it violates the principle of maturity matching.

Matching the Maturity of Assets and Liabilities

An effective strategy to reduce financial risk is **maturity matching** (Anderson, 1993). Maturity matching involves financing current assets with liabilities of the same maturity. For example, trade credit due in ten days would be funded by an asset that could be converted to cash in ten days. The rationale is that assets converted to cash at a certain time should be financed by liabilities with the same maturity so that both are extinguished simultaneously. If a long-term asset, for example, is financed by a short-term liability, then the organization is subject to interest rate risk when the short-term loan is up for renewal. If market rates are higher than the income earned on assets, the organization will experience losses. If a short-term asset is financed by a long-term liability, then when the asset is reinvested, the marginal cost of financing may turn out to be greater than the marginal return on the asset, again reducing profits.

Rather than match each asset with a corresponding liability, maturity matching can be achieved by matching the average maturity of current assets with the average maturity of current liabilities. A better matching strategy is duration matching (West and Glickman, 1997). **Duration** measures the *effective* maturity of an asset or a liability. A five-year discount bond, for example, has the same maturity as a five-year coupon bond but a longer duration. The coupon bond generates interim cash flows that must be reinvested before the bond matures. The discount bond's cash flows are received only at maturity. Thus, duration of a discount bond is the same as its maturity. The duration of the coupon bond would be shorter because of the earlier return of some of the cash flows of the investment.

The principle of maturity matching can be used when making a decision about how to finance working capital. First, it is necessary to consider whether short-term assets to be financed are permanent or temporary. Minimum cash balances, accounts receivable, and inventory levels maintained continually over the life of a project are permanent assets. As such, according to the matching principle, they should be financed with long-term debt or equity. Replenishing temporary shortages of cash or inventories, on the other hand, should be financed by short-term debt that is eliminated when the shortage disappears.

The managed care plan must match its short-term investments to the arrival of expected medical claims. Holding cash in excess of that needed to reimburse providers is very costly since these funds could be invested long term. Holding too little cash or cash equivalents will force liquidation of long-term investments to meet payment commitments. Furthermore, claims from earlier periods must not be financed by cash derived from current premium revenue. Not only is there an opportunity cost to doing so—what could have been earned on those revenues had they been invested— but also borrowing from future enrollee premiums to meet current expenses is a very risky financing strategy. In this case, the managed care organization is operating with insufficient cash reserves to meet payment commitments (Murata, 1994).

Conclusion

If the health care organization and the external operating environment are stable, the cash inflows and outflows are highly predictable and cash budgeting is a relatively straightforward process. Under these circumstances, the organization can easily recognize unfavorable variances in cash flows when they arise and respond appropriately. When the organization is growing or contracting, reimbursement and health care delivery are changing, or the environment is uncertain, the cash conversion cycle becomes much less predictable.

The challenge for the health care provider is acquiring sufficient cash to support operations until it is paid, minimizing the time it takes to be paid and investing wisely in other current assets. The challenge for the managed care organization is proper investment of premiums until they are needed for payment and predicting, tracking, and managing utilization and claims by enrollees. The health care provider borrows cash to finance services that are likely to be provided in the future for which payment will be delayed. The management care plan invests cash it receives in advance for services that are likely to be used in the future. For both types of organization, accurate prediction of utilization and costs is crucial to managing working capital.

Case 10-1: Developing a Cash Budget for a Physician Group Practice

Page-Smith Medical Group (PSMG), is a twenty-eight-member multi-specialty physician group practice that plans to increase patient volume by accepting a contract with GoodHealth, a nationally known health maintenance organization. The group will be paid a fixed amount per member per month of $38.50 for all enrolled members. Also PSMG agrees to be responsible for all physician services including referrals to physicians outside of PSMG. Therefore, the cost of referrals must be absorbed by the group. Hospital admissions, other than emergency admissions, will require precertification from GoodHealth. The costs of nonemergent hospital admissions that have not been precertified will be charged to PSMG.

The business manager of PSMG, M. J. Varga, needs to develop a monthly cash budget for the plan. He has the following information.

Expected monthly capitation rate (pmpm) in 1998:	$38.50
Start up expense for space renovation, marketing and administration incurred in July through December 1997	$175,000
Maximum available clinic capacity enrollment	12,000
First year average enrollment in the plan	9,975

Enrollment by month enrolled:

Jan	8,000	Jul	10,900
Feb	8,200	Aug	11,200
Mar	8,400	Sep	11,400
Apr	8,600	Oct	11,600
May	8,800	Nov	11,800
Jun	8,900	Dec	12,000

Expected utilization rate (per year per enrollee)	3.75 visits
Copayments:	$10 per visit
Treatment costs per visit	$77.89
Estimated cost of referrals:	$2.45 pmpm

Additional monthly administrative expense related to the GoodHealth contract.

Personnel	$102,000
Rent	4,500
Equipment rental	6,785
Utilities	1,350
Insurance	2,800
Depreciation	3,000
Miscellaneous	2,779
Total	$120,304

Create a cash budget for the year. In doing so, answer the following questions.

1. What are average treatment costs per member per month?
2. What is the maximum amount of cash that will be needed in the first year to support operations until the plan becomes profitable? In which month will this occur?
3. What is the cost per member per month of monthly practice expense? What happens to this fixed expense as enrollment rises?
4. What is the effect on the cash budget if copayments are not collected at the time of service but are received in the next month?
5. What is the impact on the cash budget if GoodHealth delays the monthly capitation payment to PSMG for the current month's enrollees until the next month?
6. What is the impact on the cash budget if PSMG pays its bills for physician referrals two months following the month in which the expense is incurred.
7. Discuss the risks and management issues related to this contract.

References

Anderson, A. M. (1993, July). Enhancing hospital cash reserves management. *Healthcare Financial Management, 47*(7), 91–95.

Flaum, D. B., & Pecoulas, G. A. (1995, Spring). Securitizing health care receivables: Legal and structural issues. *Commercial Lending Review, 10*(2), 45–53.

Folk, M. D., & Roest, P. R. (1995, September). Converting accounts receivable into cash. *Healthcare Financial Management, 49*(9), 74–78.

Hauser, R.C., Edwards, D. E., & Edwards, J. T. (1991, Fall). Cash budgeting: An underutilized resource management tool in not-for-profit health care entities. *Hospital and Health Services Administration, 36*(3), 439–446.

Jacobs, S. E. (1995, April 24). Why we love capitation. *Medical Economics, 72*(8), 51–56.

Mamo, D. (1994, October). Receivables financing as a source of working capital. *Nursing Homes, 43*(8), 28–31.

Mensah, Y. M., Considine, J. M., & Oakes, L. (1994, January). Statutory insolvency regulations and earnings management in the prepaid health-care industry. *Accounting Review, 69*(1), 70–95.

Moynihan, J. J. (1996, October). New disbursement services need new RFPs. *Healthcare Financial Management, 50*(10), 95.

Murata, S. K. (1994, December 12). IBNR—The second most dangerous acronym in medicine today. *Medical Economics, 71*(23), 8.

Pallarito, K. (1995, March 20). Reserves needed to cushion capitation. *Modern Healthcare, 25*(12), 66–67.

Ryan, J. B., & Clay, S. B. (1994, November). An overview of IBNR. *Healthcare Financial Management, 48*(11), 18–20.

Sagner, J. S. (1994, October). "Sweeping" an organization's bank balances. *Healthcare Financial Management, 48*(10), 74.

Scott, J. S. (1997, June). Floating on a sea of money? *Healthcare Financial Management, 51*(6), 28–30.

Ward, D. (1995). Operational finance and budgeting. In P.R. Kongstvedt (Ed.), *Essentials in managed health care*. Gaithersburg, MD: Aspen.

West, J., & Glickman, S. (1997, February). Improving investing outcomes through interest rate management. *Healthcare Financial Management, 51*(2), 80–81.

Chapter 11

Utilization Management Under Capitation

Capitation is one of the approaches used to reduce costs by changing the way providers are reimbursed. However, changing the reimbursement method will not, by itself, resolve the problem of increasing health care costs. Within this reimbursement framework, utilization management has become a tool that managed care companies use to reduce utilization while trying to maintain quality.

Learning Objectives

Upon successful completion of this chapter, the learner will:

- Understand the methods used in utilization management.
- Understand the methods used to control provider behavior.
- Understand the role of financial incentives in controlling utilization.
- Understand the need to control patient behavior.
- Understand the process of utilization management.

Key Terms

case management	preventive services
clinical pathway	prospective review
concurrent review	retrospective review
discharge planning	second surgical opinion
financial credentialing	utilization management

Introduction

Economists and health care providers are using innovative measures to address the problem of exploding health care costs. In many instances, they have attempted to address the issue through different methods of provider reimbursement—typically passing the risk to the provider with the intent that this change will curtail the use of services. Capitation is one of the approaches used to reduce costs by changing the way providers are reimbursed. Nevertheless, changing the reimbursement method will not by itself resolve the problem of increasing health care costs.

Utilization management has entered the scene as one method by which managed care companies have sought to reduce costs while maintaining quality. The MCO can be an IDS or a third party risk taker. They want to make sure that appropriate services are readily available to eligible beneficiaries when they require them, but at the same time to limit the inappropriate use of services. This balance is a delicate one that requires applying the insights of quality measurement and management that focuses on improving overall processes. Quality of care is one of the major objectives of utilization management. When it is successful, it is accomplished by a multidimensional assessment of the physician provider, the institutional provider, and the managed care organization.

Within the framework of the capitated system, utilization management and quality assessments are conducted primarily from the perspective of the managed care company and the provider. These two elements of the health delivery system are important, but they are not the only stakeholders in the process. A core element has often been absent from the process: the patient.

Apart from those instances where patients are surveyed to determine the level of satisfaction attained by their managed care company and provider, patients, who establish the expectations for the delivery of health care, generally have not been recognized as part of the process of establishing quality of care measurements. Their vital insight is missing from the overall formula. In the ideal circumstances, there will be a close and understanding relationship among the health care manager, the physician, and the patient.

Objectives of a Utilization Management System

The health care system has had to develop systems that govern the use of resources in the delivery of health care. Managed care has had as one of its primary objectives that it would lower health care costs in the United States. But health care professionals and patients have worried that if this is the sole objective, quality might decline. Thus, methodologies have been developed to safeguard quality while still effectively dealing with resource utilization. Utilization management programs seek to address this issue.

The typical health plan contains financial incentives to reduce utilization as well as utilization controls that mandate how resources will be used. The utilization management component is integrated into the administration of the health plan and is made part of the day-to-day activities of both the physician and the patient as it relates to the delivery of health care. These programs communicate that the health plan is designed to be used in a responsible way and that all of the stakeholders in its use have a mutual responsibility to keep quality and affordable medical treatment at their proper levels.

Utilization management takes many forms, but the most common activities usually are preadmission review, concurrent review, retrospective review, discharge planning, and second surgical opinion.

These mechanisms will be discussed in the last part of this chapter. First, a discussion of the behavioral dimensions of utilization management is in order.

Control of Provider Behavior

One of the major issues in controlling resource utilization in health care is the resource-ordering preferences of physicians. This problem is compounded in systems where the coordination of patient management is not tightly controlled—for example, if a patient has the option to see any physician he or she wishes. As the patient goes from one physician to another, each new physician has no way of knowing what previous diagnoses have been made or what treatments were prescribed unless the patient reveals that information. Thus, the structure of most managed care plans addresses this issue in terms of attempting to limit free use of the system. In a strict sense, these mechanisms are not part of a utilization management system, but they do bear heavily on how such a system is administered.

Gatekeeper Model

This is a practice used by managed care organizations and other risk takers that controls the use of multiple physicians by a beneficiary. In its purest form, a patient may initiate an appointment for medical care only with his or her primary care physician. All other physician visits are made only with the specific referral of the PCP, who is thus the gatekeeper to the use of other physicians and services.

The avowed reason for this approach is to ensure that the medical care that the patient receives is appropriate both from a cost and a quality point of view. Most managed care companies emphasize that this mechanism is not specifically designed to cut down on the patient's choices for health care, but rather focuses on appropriateness. They argue that the patient is not always in a position to know what specialist is needed and therefore should not be making these choices, which could result in expensive and inappropriate treatment. A further reason concerns maintaining continuity of care when specialty physicians see patients out of the context of their total treatment plan. Of course, specialty physicians can obtain medical records, but only if the patient is fully knowledgeable of the treatments that he or she has received and knows or can remember where the medical records reside.

The gatekeeper model met with some resistance relative to the patient's ability to choose a physician, but in general this approach has been accepted in terms of patient experience, and it is generally agreed that it has been quite successful in reducing inappropriate utilization while maintaining an acceptable level of quality.

Practice Standards and Protocols

One of the reasons for inappropriate use of health care resources is that care of the patient is based on clinical judgment. When a physician is treating an illness that occurs infrequently and has not had personal experience with it, he or she might make inappropriate clinical choices. This does not necessarily mean that the physician is a poor clinician; rather, it suggests that clinical management of illnesses, particularly those that are obscure or rare, is a complex undertaking.

In cases like this, practice standards or **clinical pathways** are a useful tool in guiding the physician through the clinical management process. A clinical pathway (*clinical protocols* and *practice standards* are synonyms) is a protocol for the treatment of a particular disease entity that specifies the clinical activities that should take place and in what time frame. Clinical pathways generally exist in the inpatient acute care setting; some do exist in the ambulatory area, but they are not as prevalent.

These mechanisms are useful for the reasons outlined, but they are not a panacea by any means. Indeed, they offer only limited usefulness in determining the appropriate use of medical resources in the treatment of disease.

First, the development of clinical pathways is a time-consuming process that involves getting consensus on the part of practicing physicians for the proper treatment of a particular disease entity. This includes not only the clinical judgment of the treating physicians of the particular health care entity but also, under ideal circumstances, a complete review of the medical literature on the treatment of the disease. As medical knowledge and insights change, it is necessary periodically to update the clinical pathways in order to reflect the best current thinking in the treatment of the disease. For all of these reasons, most health care organizations have only a few of the diseases that they treat covered by clinical pathways.

The second issue is identifying when a physician departs from the pathway and determining what reasons have caused this departure. For a variety of valid reasons, the treatment might depart from the pathway—for example, medical complications that occur through no fault of anyone or when there are multiple diagnoses. Of course, there are also instances where the actual treatment departs from the pathway for no apparent reason, and this is the condition that clinical pathways are designed to identify. A fairly extensive infrastructure is required to track down the outcomes of the clinical pathways and to distinguish whether there are good and valid reasons for departing from the pathway or whether there is no apparent reason for the deviation.

This leads to the third issue in using clinical pathways: determining what to do when physicians vary their practices from the clinical pathway. Of course, if there are good and valid clinical reasons for deviating from the pathway, no one should argue with that variation. Nevertheless, someone must make the determination of whether the reasons are clinically valid, and the ability to do that takes resources and infrastructure. If it is determined that there are no valid clinical reasons that the physician deviated from the pathway, someone must do something about the deviation. The organization must decide what approaches are appropriate. In general, punitive measures have not been effective except with physicians who show no inclination to change their patterns of practice over a period of time. In general, using the opportu-

nity to increase the knowledge of the physician with some kind of educational vehicle is the preferred course of action.

Selection and Monitoring of Network Providers

Managed care companies sometimes try to reduce resource utilization by selecting
only those physicians, hospitals, and other health care organizations that have demonstrated cost-effective patterns of practice over time. This is sometimes referred to as
financial credentialing.

The rationale is fairly straightforward. If physicians are selected who have historically managed the utilization of health resources for their patients in a cost-effective
and responsible manner, it is quite likely that they will continue that pattern as part of
the network. More specifically, if one physician has an average cost of $3,000 for man-
aging pneumonia in patients in a specific age category while another physician has an
average cost of $5,000 for managing a similar group of patients, the medical costs to the
managed care company would be substantially less for the first physician than the second. Of course, the comparison must be statistically valid and the sample of patients
must be similar so a fair comparison can be made. Those doing the comparison must
be sure to consider that the age and other demographics about the patient population
being compared are the same, the secondary diagnoses are essentially the same, and
the institutions in which the patients are treated are essentially the same.

This brings a second factor into focus. Just as the physician's cost-effective behavior is important in managing the utilization and costs of a patient's treatment, so is the
health care organization in which the patient is treated. Health care institutions can
increase or decrease the costs of rendering care to the patient in a variety of ways.

The overall cost structure of the institution and the cost-effectiveness of its operation is one factor that can change the level of costs. If a health care organization has
a higher personnel complement or tends to have relatively more costly equipment,
these factors will contribute to the overall cost structure of the organization. Therefore,
services offered at that organization will necessarily be more costly than in an institution with lower costs of doing business.

Another factor is the systems in place to promote timely completion of treatment
and diagnostic studies. If the systems promote timely delivery of treatments and services, the overall costs are lowered by reducing the patient's length of stay. Some have
argued that the overall costs are actually not lowered in this scenario because the same
services are being rendered to the patient; the only difference is that they are being provided in a more compressed time frame, possibly resulting in higher unit costs. There
is some validity to this argument, but it is probably not as convincing as it sounds at
face value. In the individual departments, this is possibly true, assuming that there is
no slack capacity. If there is slack capacity, compacting the actual treatment and procedures process by improving the infrastructure and systems could produce some
long-term efficiencies by eliminating the need for the costly slack capacity. In the
nursing care on the floors, the same rationale holds. If there is inefficiency caused by
patients waiting for treatments or services, waste is occurring, and to the extent that
it can be eliminated, costs would be reduced.

A third factor is the systems and procedures in place to promote cost-effective treatment and diagnostic studies. Apart from scheduling issues, there are other efficiencies that might contribute to more cost-effective management—for example, effective inventory management, standardization of supplies, and cost-effective purchasing practices that will get the best price on the needed supplies.

Thus, a physician can be made to appear ineffective in managing the utilization of resources used to treat a patient by ineffective hospital management of the processes. The overall cost structure of the hospital, the timeliness with which treatments and diagnostic studies are completed, and the cost-effectiveness of the way they are conducted all affect the cost of treating the patient and the utilization patterns surrounding the treatment of that patient.

Managed care organizations are just as interested in using cost-effective health care organizations as they are in including cost-effective physicians in their network. The more cost-effective the components of the network, the less costly will be the medical care rendered by the network. Careful monitoring of the quality is necessary to ensure that lower costs do not accrue at the expense of acceptable quality.

Financial Incentives to Providers

Financial incentives to providers should be mentioned in the context of utilization management. Keep in mind that the aim of utilization management is to promote the cost-effective use of health care resources in treating patients while maintaining a level of quality that is acceptable to the community. A number of vehicles have been developed that provide financial incentives to produce this type of behavior. Following are some of the most commonly used vehicles.

Sharing in the Bottom Line of the Plan

In order to promote financial incentives for a physician or institutional provider to manage resources wisely, managed care organizations sometimes structure a health care plan to allow providers to share in their profitability after all of the costs are covered. This kind of plan usually takes the form of paying the health care providers at a nominal rate, such as 75 percent of resource-based relative value units. Furthermore a specified amount—perhaps 15 percent of the premium—is set aside for the company's administrative activities. After these and any other costs are paid, the resulting profit of the plan is shared by the health care providers and the managed care plan. Thus, the lower the utilization that would result in a higher net profit of the plan, the more there is for the providers to share.

Various other parameters are sometimes also made part of such a plan, including the condition that the providers meet specific utilization targets before they are allowed to participate in sharing in the profitability. Obviously, whenever there are financial incentives for providers to reduce utilization, there is also the potential danger that inappropriate levels of services will be withheld. Thus, there is a requirement that concurrent with such a plan, quality measurement vehicles be present to ensure appropriate levels of utilization. There are many variations on the way these financial incentives are structured. Only the general form is presented here so readers can gain an insight into the mechanism used to reduce utilization of clinical resources by offering financial incentives to the providers.

Risk Pools

Typically risk pools are set up to discourage overutilization of specialty services. Those sharing in the risk pool are usually the specialty provider, the primary physician, and the network, which could be either a managed care company or an integrated delivery network, depending on who is taking the risk. It is usually structured with a target budget for specialty services. Some part of each payment, perhaps 10 percent, is withheld and put into the risk pool. At the end of the year, if the target budget for the specialty services is not exceeded, each of the participants shares in the risk pool. The incentive for the primary care physician is to refer a patient for specialty services only when required. The incentive for the specialty physician is to provide only required services. The incentive for the network is to manage the risk related to providing the services.

Usually the primary and specialty physicians share only in the upside risk, not in the downside risk. (See Chapter 8 for a discussion of this subject.) That is, if the target budget is met, they share in the withhold that was actually part of the originally negotiated fee, but they do not share in the savings that accrue as a result of having a positive variance for the target budget. Normally providers would share in the savings only if they are also financially responsible for participating in any negative budget variances as well.

Capitation

Under capitation, the managed care company has shifted the risk for both price and volume to the provider. Under this form of reimbursement, the volume part of the equation deals directly with the subject of utilization management. Thus under capitation, the financial incentive to reduce utilization is complete. This financial incentive to reduce utilization, like the others, must be balanced by a comprehensive quality program that will identify any cases of underutilization that occur.

Control of Patient Behavior

As in the case of physician behavior to overutilize services, there is a similar temptation on the part of patients. When the health care delivery system permits this behavior, human beings will respond to the incentives embedded in the system. This is referred to as **market failure;** it describes a system where adequate incentives, financial and otherwise, are not in place to encourage appropriate behaviors. In the case of the market failure of the health delivery system as it relates to overutilization of resources, the following issues can cause the failure (see also Chapter 1):

- Problems created by the way the insurance system is structured
- Informational disparities between physicians (the seller) and patients (the buyer)
- Inability of consumers to search for lower prices and higher quality in an emergency

This situation is compounded in a system where the coordination of patient management is not tightly controlled, which is actually part of the structure of the insurance system. The insurance system has made some attempts at addressing these structural issues, and they are listed below. Each has strengths and weakness, but all are impaired because there is no single approach being taken across the entire industry. One of the questions thus raised is the core issue of whether it is better to have a single payer system, which would likely be regulated by the federal government, or continue with the current market-driven approach that has many strengths but standardization of structure is not one of them.

Some of the things that the insurance industry has done to try to deal with these market failure issues are listed below.

Co-payments and Deductibles

This is a methodology insurers and managed care organizations use to discourage excess utilization by patients. Whether the reimbursement methodology by the risk taker is indemnity insurance, a discount from billed charges, per diem, case rate, or capitation, the patient is often subject to co-payments and deductibles. A *deductible* amount is the amount a patient must pay before the risk taker pays for any services. For example, if a patient has a $250 annual deductible, he or she must pay for $250 worth of medical bills before the risk taker participates in reimbursing the provider. It might take several office visits or diagnostic tests before this deductible is satisfied. The deductible amount is usually reset annually and can apply to either an individual or an entire family. A *co-insurance* is an amount that is paid each time the patient receives health care and is usually a percentage of the bill for services, although it can also be an absolute amount, such as a $5 co-pay for a pharmacy prescription.

Assume that the deductible is satisfied and a patient goes to a physician's office. The bill is $50. If the patient has a 20 percent co-insurance, the patient will pay $10 and the risk taker will pay $40. Co-insurance and deductibles have been used for some time by risk takers to discourage inappropriate patient-induced demand for services, but because of the relatively low level at which the thresholds have been set, they have not been overly effective.

Explicit Limits on Utilization

Some risk takers place explicit limits on the amount of services that they will permit in certain categories. For example, a risk taker may limit the number of mental health visits on either an annual or lifetime basis. Although this cap certainly does limit utilization, perhaps more than in most other categories of reducing utilization of health care services, the question arises about whether this is in the best interest of the patient from a health status point of view. The issue of quality monitoring certainly comes into focus in this type of situation.

Another example of explicitly limiting utilization of services is in the case of a lifetime reserve, when such a provision is part of the benefit plan. In some cases, a risk taker will impose a lifetime reserve on services obtained. This is usually a relatively large number, ranging from $500,000 to $1 million, but it nonetheless can have a significant effect on people who have a catastrophic illness.

Promotion of Preventive Services and Healthy Lifestyle

This strategy for reducing utilization of health care services is of relatively recent origin. Increasingly, there is a realization that if the population can be made healthier, the utilization of resources in the treatment of illnesses will decrease. For example, if fewer people in the population were smokers, there would be less heart disease and certain forms of cancer, which would lead to consumption of less costly resources in the treatment of these diseases. Although the opinions are not unanimous that prevention programs will reduce the utilization of health resources and thus reduce the escalating costs of health care, there is general agreement that these programs are worthwhile. A second example of **preventive services** is the immunization programs for youth, which result in low rates of serious childhood diseases.

One of the problems with the strategy of promoting prevention services is that in the market-driven health care system in the United States, there is no mandate that health promotion is a consistently worthwhile use of resources, so some health plans include health promotion as a benefit and others do not. The entity taking the risk for the health of the population is the one that will benefit if the population is healthy. In most cases, this is the insurer or the managed care organization, except when providers are capitated, in which case they are responsible for the health of the population. (See Chapter 3 for a fuller discussion of the relationship between risk in the population and the financial costs and risks of providing health care for a defined population.)

The nature of this problem emerges in the following scenario. Suppose that managed care company A believes that preventive services will reduce the long-term costs of providing health care for its covered lives, but company B does not believe this is the case. Company A includes preventive services in the benefits to its beneficiaries, believing that in two to three years, they will benefit from lower utilization of health care services. Company B does not believe this is the case and does not include preventive services as a covered benefit. Three years later, one of the employers offering company A its health care coverage switches to company B. After having paid for the preventive services for three years, company A loses the covered lives at the very time it expected to benefit from the investment, and company B benefits without making any investment whatsoever. This is one of the difficulties with a market-driven health care delivery system that has no systematic way to standardize services that might benefit the population by reducing utilization and the attendant costs associated with it.

The Utilization Process

The actual utilization management process is usually applied to the inpatient acute care setting, although some approaches in the ambulatory setting are emerging. The primary process of the utilization management process is in these areas:

- Reducing the number of hospital admissions
- Controlling the length of stay
- Ensuring appropriate medical treatment
- Promoting the most cost-effective use of provider services.

In order to achieve these objectives, a specific process must be in place that is managed by either the risk taker or the provider, or both. Sometimes the risk taker (the managed care organization) delegates the responsibility for utilization management to the provider; sometimes the risk taker retains that responsibility. In either case, the process and the objectives are essentially the same.

The methodologies that are used in a utilization management program are:

- Prospective review
- Second surgical opinions
- Concurrent review
- Retrospective review
- Case management
- Discharge planning

Prospective Review

Prospective review is a synonym for preadmission review. This is the first step in the overall utilization management process. This type of review is conducted for any elective or nonemergency admission when it relates to an inpatient acute care admission. Prospective review can also be conducted for certain procedures in the ambulatory setting. When done in the ambulatory setting, it usually relates only to procedures with a relatively high cost, such as advanced radiology procedures or ambulatory surgery.

Prospective review is conducted to evaluate the physician's proposed treatment plan and determine its medical necessity. This review also determines the level of care required for the proposed treatment and sometimes suggests that it be done on an ambulatory basis rather than an inpatient acute care basis.

The health professionals conducting this review use medical criteria established by either the managed care company or the provider. The information received from the attending physician proposing the treatment plan is then evaluated against the medical criteria, and a determination is made. Other processes are sometimes involved with prospective review—for example:

- *Emergency admissions.* When a health treatment plan involves an emergency action, the evaluation for appropriateness of treatment usually takes place within twenty-four to forty-eight hours of the event. Findings are generally not retrospective determinations, but they sometimes terminate benefits on a concurrent basis. It is usually the joint responsibility of the family and the provider to make the information available to the reviewing agency within the specified time frame.

- *Appeals.* If there is an adverse determination, there is the opportunity to appeal the finding. A second physician often takes part in the appeal process. Most managed care companies are quite specific on the point that the prospective review process relates only to the question of whether the organization will reimburse for the medical services rendered. They usually indicate that having the service remains the patient's option and that the final decision is the patient's. Although the patient can elect to have the service and pay for it himself or herself, the cost of most major medical procedures often renders this a moot issue.

- *Preadmission testing.* This is a procedure where clinical laboratory and radiology examinations are administered on an ambulatory basis prior to the inpatient acute care episode. This is an example of accomplishing the same testing in a lower-cost environment and is often part of the overall prospective review process.

- *Delayed reviews.* As in the case of emergency admissions, there are sometimes extenuating circumstances that prevent the patient from going through the prospective review process. When this is the case, there is usually a requirement that the patient, the family, and/or the physician provide the needed information within twenty-four to forty-eight hours of the procedure.

- *Duration of approval.* Approval for an admission or ambulatory procedure is usually not good for an indefinite period of time. Rather, the approval is given for a specified period of time, usually not exceeding thirty days.

- *Identification of case management candidates.* For some prospective review processes, the identification of potential candidates for **case management** is accomplished at the time of this preadmission review. Case management is a communication activity in which health care professionals use specific communication protocols to make sure that complex cases are appropriately managed. Case management is applied to cases likely to be particularly difficult or complex.

- *Timeliness of the review.* Some managed care plans specify that the prospective review will be carried out on a timely basis and that the determination will be given within a specified period of time.

Second Surgical Opinion

This methodology requires that whenever an elective surgical procedure is prescribed, the opinion of a second physician who is qualified to do the procedure must be sought and he or she must agree that the procedure is necessary. The second physician could be a community physician or someone selected by the managed care company. If the two physicians disagree, a third opinion is sought to break the tie.

The use of **second surgical opinion**s was a popular tool in utilization management a few years ago, but more recently it has not enjoyed as much popularity. Many managed care companies have concluded that this approach is not warranted when comparing the cost associated with getting the second opinion with the number of times that the course of treatment was actually changed.

Concurrent Review

Concurrent review involves an evaluation of the care while it is being given. As in the case of prospective review, established medical criteria are used by qualified medical personnel to compare length-of-stay norms with the care that is actually being rendered. These utilization management evaluations are conducted to determine whether the continued stay is medically necessary and that the resources being used are appropriate. In most cases, the anticipated length of stay is assigned at the time of admission, based on the diagnosis and treatment plan. The utilization management process then reviews the care throughout the patient's stay to validate that the anticipated treatment plan is being carried out.

If the case is complex or if there are complications associated with the treatment of the patient, the utilization management personnel usually consult with the attending physician and specialists to determine whether any additional days of stay should be authorized.

During the concurrent review process, the reviewer monitors such things as the appropriateness of the level of care and delays that might be compromising the efficiency of the care, and determines whether the treatment plan is being carried out. This includes monitoring whether testing beyond the original treatment plan is being carried out. In addition, the reviewer monitors the handling of the case to determine whether unrelated patient conditions that do not require intervention in the acute care setting are also being eliminated.

Retrospective Review

As the name implies, **retrospective review** is conducted after the patient is released from care, whether it is an inpatient acute care episode or an ambulatory procedure. This evaluation is conducted by reviewing the medical record to determine whether there are patterns of practice by physicians for either underutilization or overutilization. Records are usually pulled on a random basis to identify treatment trends and help focus potential areas for future prospective and concurrent reviews.

In addition, retrospective reviews are sometimes conducted on a focused basis to study the results of treatment for a particular diagnosis or an individual physician. If there is reason to believe that patient care is not being carried out in accordance with expected norms of treatment, additional studies are undertaken, and appropriate educational efforts are implemented to try to correct the problem.

Case Management

Case management can be carried out on an inpatient acute care basis or an ambulatory care basis. The most common application of case management is in complex inpatient acute care scenarios that require significant coordination of resource utilization across a broad spectrum of health professionals. The focus of the activity is on meeting the complex health care requirements of the patient by improving the communication among the professionals managing the care of the patient. The aim of the process is to coordinate the use of the resources and promote a cost-effective outcome while maintaining an acceptable level of quality.

Critical pathways are often used in case management because the pathways have already charted the most cost-effective course to a desired outcome within a specified time frame. These plans make use of the literature in the field to identify the best practices of the medical profession in treating the particular disease entity.

Discharge Planning

Discharge planning is a process that coordinates the resources of the organization to achieve a timely discharge for patients who no longer require inpatient acute care services. It plans to expedite the discharge process so the patient can be placed in the most appropriate level-of-care setting. It addresses and coordinates many services that might not be medical in nature, such as home health care, rehabilitation services, use of durable medical equipment, and transportation.

This utilization management function attempts to get rid of the barriers that prevent patients from being discharged on a timely basis and that often frustrate the patient's overall recovery process. This process often begins at the time of the patient's admission and is carried on throughout the patient's stay in the hospital. It monitors and updates the needs of the patient on the basis of the progress being made in the treatment plan and ultimately comes up with a plan that facilitates an effective transition into the post-discharge environment into which the patient passes.

Conclusion

Utilization management is critically important to the effective functioning of the managed care process. Given the objective of managed care to render quality care in a cost-effective manner, it is mandatory that processes be in place in all health care organizations that promote cost-effective actions on the part of health care professionals.

Utilization management focuses on changing provider and patient behavior. In order to be successful in this activity, it is necessary that the incentives of the risk taker, the providers, and the patient be aligned. To the extent that any of these stakeholders perceives the activity to be an adversarial relationship, as unfortunately some do, the outcome is likely to be less than successful. Chapter 13, on quality and outcomes management, underscores the importance of the stakeholders' working together to achieve the objective of quality health care at a cost-effective price.

Utilization management makes a significant contribution to the cost-effectiveness of the cost/quality equation because its focus is primarily on preventing overutilization of services and ensuring that services are provided at the appropriate level of care. However, the quality dimension is less obvious in the utilization management process and requires that quality be systematically addressed outside the framework of utilization management to make sure that enough is actually done for the patient.

Review Questions

1. What issues must be considered to ensure that financial credentialing is fair?

2. Discuss the ways in which health care organizations can influence changes in the costs associated with rendering health care.

3. Discuss the financial incentives that managed care companies sometimes use with health care providers to promote more efficient utilization patterns.

4. Discuss the concept of market failure, and describe the methods managed care companies use to try to prevent it.

5. What is the purpose of utilization management programs? Discuss the vehicles that are used to encourage proper utilization.

6. Discuss the processes that are used to apply and implement a prospective review activity in a health care facility.

Chapter 12

Cost Accounting and Control Under Capitation

This chapter discusses cost accounting and control in a capitated reimbursement environment. Many of the financial issues are quite different under capitation than is the case under traditional reimbursement models. Indeed, for the most part, the financial incentives under capitation are directly opposite those of traditional reimbursement systems.

Learning Objectives

Upon successful completion of this chapter, the learner will:

- Understand the effects of various revenue-generating strategies on the profitability of the organization under various reimbursement models.
- Understand the behavior of inpatient acute care costs under capitation.
- Understand ambulatory care costs under capitation.
- Understand how costs are defined in various disciplines.
- Understand fixed and variable costs.
- Understand marginal costs.
- Understand variance analysis.

Key Terms

accounting costs

activity-based costing (ABC)

cost centers

economic costs

product line costing

profit centers

variance analysis

Introduction

The role of managing an organization under capitation is a relatively new experience for many health care professionals. Capitation represents a significant departure from most reimbursement models and in many ways reverses some of the economic incentives that drove the health care system for decades. Of course, this change from unrestricted use of resources to one of systematically considering the necessity for use of diagnostic and treatment services for each patient encounter is not entirely inappropriate because health care costs have been escalating over the years and one of the reasons for these increases is that the existing financial incentives did not include curtailing use of unneeded tests and procedures.

These changes in the way the reimbursement system works require additional knowledge and experience on the part of health care managers in order to optimize the use of the organization's resources. This chapter addresses the need for a better understanding of how financial incentives work within the framework of capitation and the role that costs play.

Understanding Costs

In its most fundamental form, the capitated reimbursement system has changed the focus of organizational management of health care providers from a revenue orientation to a cost orientation. When looking at the algorithm for determining the profit of an organization, the two main variables are the revenue flow into the organization, which incrementally increases the level of profitability for the organization as revenue increases, and the expenses of doing business, which reduce the level of profitability of the organization as costs increase. Conversely, if costs are reduced and the revenue remains the same, profitability will increase.

Within reasonable parameters, there is little that an organization can do to improve the revenue portion of the profit algorithm under capitation, at least on a per capita basis. That is, given the enrolled lives that a provider covers and the negotiated per member per month (PMPM) reimbursement that is received, the revenue is fixed on the basis of the number of covered lives and the negotiated rate PMPM that pays for the health care of the covered lives. On the other hand, management has significant latitude for actions related to managing the organization's costs. From the perspective of maintaining or improving the profitability of the organization in a capitated environment, the primary management action must be focused on controlling or reducing costs.

Thus, in an environment that has significant levels of capitation (or in other ways places the economic risk of serving the covered lives on the provider), a premium is placed on skills related to managing costs because reducing costs is the primary method by which profitability can be improved.

Table 12-1 shows the financial results of various management actions that might be taken within a fee-for-service reimbursement environment and a capitated environment. Of course, most health care markets are not limited to these two reimbursement mechanisms; the two extremes are provided here for purposes of illustration.

Table 12-1 Financial Effect of Management Actions Under Two Reimbursement Scenarios

	Fee for Service		Capitation	
	Maximize Resource Use	**Reduce Costs**	**Maximize Resource Use**	**Reduce Costs**
Revenue	Desirable	No effect	No effect	No effect
Expenses	Undesirable	Desirable	Undesirable	Desirable
Net profit	Desirable	Desirable	Undesirable	Desirable

When using the strategy to maximize resource utilization under a fee-for-service reimbursement mechanism, there is a desirable effect on revenue (increase in revenue) and an undesirable effect on expenses (increase in expenses). On balance, however, there is a desirable effect on the net profit of the organization because the increase in expenses will almost always be less than the increase in revenue. The incremental increase in revenue has to cover only the variable cost of the services rendered. This means that in the case of doing an additional radiograph, the incremental variable costs are the radiographic film and other similar direct costs for doing the procedure. The equipment is already there, as are the personnel and other fixed costs; the organization has to pay for them regardless of whether the additional radiograph was performed. Therefore, the incremental expenses for doing the procedure are those where additional costs are incurred as a direct result of doing the procedure. Under these conditions, it is axiomatic that the incremental revenue associated with doing the additional procedure will exceed the incremental expenses of providing the services. Of course, this assumes that the incremental medical procedure is performed on an individual on whom reimbursement will be obtained.

Similarly, when using the strategy to reduce costs under a fee-for-service reimbursement system, there is a desirable effect on the net profit of the organization because of the interaction of the strategy on the revenue and expenses of the organization. Reducing costs has no effect on the revenue of the organization but has a desirable effect on the expenses of the organization (decreases expenses), with a net effect of increasing profitability.

Thus, both strategies—maximizing the use of resources (increasing revenue) and reducing costs (reducing expenses)—have a desirable effect on the net profit of the organization in a fee-for-service environment. This obviously provides more options for managing the profitability of an organization.

However, when using the strategy to maximize resource utilization under a capitation reimbursement setting, the result for the net profit of the organization is quite different from the fee-for-service environment. Indeed, the effect is opposite what was previously experienced. Specifically, we see no effect on the revenue of the organization because, by definition, capitation pays the health provider a fixed rate PMPM regardless of how many or how few resources are consumed in providing the health care needed. At the same time, as the maximization of resource use strategy is applied, there is an undesirable effect on the expenses of the organization because any incremental use of health services will create an incremental increase in direct costs.

When using the strategy to reduce costs under capitated reimbursement system, there is a desirable effect on the net profit of the organization if all other things are held equal. Since reduction of costs has no effect on the revenue of the organization, the defining property of the profitability of the organization is its expenses in providing the health care to the lives it covers. Reducing costs under a capitated environment has a desirable effect on the expenses of the organization and thus a desirable effect on its profitability.

In conclusion, under a fee-for-service reimbursement environment, both a cost reduction and a resource maximization strategy will improve the profitability of a health care organization. This means that one can have a desirable effect on both the revenue and the expenses of the organization. By contrast, under a capitation reimbursement environment, maximizing the use of resources has an undesirable effect on the profitability of the organization because it increases the expenses of the organization but does not create any additional revenue. In completing the scenario for the capitated environment, a cost reduction strategy allows the organization to improve its profitability by reducing its costs (expenses).

Ultimately three factors directly affect the financial success of an organization as it manages operations in a capitated environment:

1. Managing the utilization of health services
2. Managing the costs of the organization
3. Managing the enrollment

Managing Utilization

One of the reasons that managing utilization of health care services is difficult is that most health care providers do not have the luxury of being reimbursed under a single payment system. The health care system of the United States is a pluralistic payment system that uses many different methodologies to reimburse health care providers, ranging from fee for service to capitation. Each methodology carries different economic incentives with it, and at the polar extremes of fee for service and global capitation, the financial incentives are directly opposite.

In a fee-for-service environment, profitability can be optimized by maximizing revenue as well as by reducing costs. However, in this context, reducing costs means that the organization reduces the operating costs of the organization, such as personnel costs, supplies costs, or overhead costs. It usually does not mean reducing costs from the perspective of doing fewer procedures, which would be a reduction of costs to the risk taker for the covered lives. The financial incentives of the fee-for-service reimbursement system are twofold: (1) to maximize revenue by increasing the volume of services and (2) to reduce the operational costs of the health care provider.

In a capitated environment, profitability is optimized primarily by reducing costs. Revenue is fixed, given the number of lives the health care provider covers and the negotiated rate. The only way revenue can realistically be increased is if there is an increase in the number of covered lives.

By contrast, reducing costs will increase the profitability of the organization. Costs can be reduced in two ways. The first is a reduction of the organization's direct costs. The second way is not available in the fee-for-service environment, and that is because in the capitated environment, the provider assumes risk for the health status of the lives it covers. Stated differently, the organization that assumes the economic risk for the health status of the covered lives, whether it is a managed care organization (under a fee-for-service environment) or the provider (under a capitated environment), experiences an additional cost of doing business: the cost of the medical services that are consumed, which is another way of saying that the organization assumes the risk for the health status of the population. Controlling these costs is referred to as *utilization management*, a particularly important issue in the context of having to pay for services outside the organizational structure covering the beneficiaries. This could happen for at least two reasons. First, people are likely to go to the nearest emergency room when they suffer a sudden illness or are involved in an accident. This being the case, the organization responsible for providing the care to the patient is responsible for paying the health care organization providing the emergency services. (This would be the case only if the health care organization was globally capitated to provide all services. In some instances, managed care organizations are willing to retain the risk for emergency services provided outside the network and for out-of-area services, but they will reduce the PMPM capitation by the appropriate amount.) The second way that a health care organization having responsibility for a particular beneficiary might have to pay an outside health care provider for health services is an out-of-area health care requirement. People are mobile, and they may have health care needs during the course of their travels. When this is the case, the health care organization with responsibility for the health care needs of a particular beneficiary has to pay the provider giving the urgent health care services.

Thus, in the capitated environment, the health care provider assumes these additional risks and costs as part of its budget. As such, the organization can improve its profitability by reducing the costs of providing medical services just as it can improve its profitability by reducing the other operational costs of the organization.

As a result, when a health care provider is reimbursed on a capitated basis, managing the utilization of health care services is crucially important to a sound economic outcome. In this environment, managing utilization is equivalent to reducing costs.

Managing Costs

Managing costs is central to effectively managing the profitability of a health care organization covering lives in a capitated environment. In order to manage costs, it is necessary to understand their nature and the elements that drive them. Under a capitated reimbursement system, costs arise from providing inpatient acute care services and from providing ambulatory services. As this subject is discussed, a number of mathematical algorithms will be given. The variables contained in those algorithms are as follows:

A = number of admissions
$AACMI$ = average ambulatory case mix index
AAM = average admissions per member
AC = ambulatory costs
ACA = average cost per admission
$ACMI$ = average case mix index
ACV = average cost per visit
AVM = average visits per member
CL = covered lives
CPA = cost per admission
CPV = cost per visit
IC = inpatient costs
V = number of visits

Inpatient Acute Care Costs Under Capitation

In its most fundamental form, inpatient acute care costs are a function of the following algorithm:

Inpatient costs (IC) = Number of admissions (A) × cost per admission (CPA).

When a manager tries prospectively to determine the costs that will be experienced, whether for budgeting purposes or as information useful for managing the organization, it must be recognized that both the number of admissions and the cost per admission can be determined from experience. Both have algorithms that define them. In a managed care environment where a provider is responsible for a specific population of beneficiaries, this formula is:

Admissions (A) = Number of covered lives (CL)
× average admissions per member (AAM)

and

Cost per admission (CPA) = Average cost per admission (ACA)
× average case mix index ($ACMI$).

Given these algorithms and the assumptions provided, it is possible to determine the inpatient costs associated with a group of covered lives:

Number of covered lives (CL) = 5,000
Average admissions per member (AAM) = .070
Average cost per admission (ACA)(case mix = 1.0) = \$4,000
Average case mix index for the facility ($ACMI$) = 1.1

(Depending on the level of sophistication desired, whether the information is being used for budgeting purposes or for information on which to base management decisions, the manager can adopt the methodology that uses average cost per admission and average case mix index, as was the case with the algorithm given here, or the costs of each individual type of admission and the specific case mix indexes can be used. The latter, while providing a more refined view of the costs being experienced, is also much more intensive in its computational requirements.)

In order to calculate the inpatient costs (IC), we must know the number of admissions (A) and the cost per admission (CPA). The number of admissions is given by:

$$
\begin{aligned}
A &= CL \times AAM \\
&= 5{,}000 \times .070 \\
&= 350.
\end{aligned}
$$

The cost per admission is given by:

$$
\begin{aligned}
CPA &= ACA \times ACMI \\
&= \$4{,}000 \times 1.1 \\
&= \$4{,}400.
\end{aligned}
$$

Given the number of admissions (A) and the cost per admission (CPA), the inpatient costs are given by:

$$
\begin{aligned}
IC &= A \times CPA \\
&= 350 \times \$4{,}400 \\
&= \$1{,}540{,}000.
\end{aligned}
$$

Thus, a health care organization that had agreed to provide inpatient acute care services for 5,000 covered lives could expect the costs associated with providing those services to be approximately $1,540,000. Note that the data on which these calculations were based are merely estimates. Changes in the average admissions per member, the average cost per admission, or the average case mix index could affect the costs in a positive or negative way. In addition, a change in the number of covered lives will also have an impact on the costs of providing health care for those lives. This variable differs from the three noted above; the additional covered lives will incur additional costs but also produce additional revenue, and if the organization is managing the lives in a way that produces profit at the lower level of covered lives, it will experience incremental profit on the additional covered lives.

Ambulatory Costs Under Capitation

Ambulatory care costs are also a function of an algorithm:

Ambulatory costs (AC) = Number of visits (V) × cost per visit (CPV).

Two additional algorithms define the number of visits and the cost per visit:

$$\text{Number of visits }(V) = \text{Number of covered lives }(CL)$$
$$\times \text{ average visits per member }(AVM)$$

and

$$\text{Cost per visit }(CPV) = \text{Average cost per visit }(ACV)$$
$$\times \text{ average ambulatory case mix }(AACMI).$$

Given these algorithms and the assumptions provided below, it is possible to determine the costs associated with providing ambulatory health care for a defined group of covered lives:

Number of covered lives (CL) = 5,000
Average visits per member per year (AVM) = 4
Average cost per visit (CPV)(case mix = 1.0) = \$75
Average ambulatory case mix $(AACMI)$ = 1.1

(As in the case of calculating costs for covering inpatient acute care services under capitation, it is possible to have varying degrees of sophistication in computing the costs associated with ambulatory care. Wherever averages are used in the calculation, a more sophisticated result can be obtained by using the specific data used in calculating the averages.)

To calculate the ambulatory costs (AC), we must first calculate the number of visits (V) and the cost per visit (CPV). The number of visits is determined by:

$$\begin{aligned} V &= CL \times AVM \\ &= 5,000 \times 4 \\ &= 20,000. \end{aligned}$$

The cost per visit is determined by:

$$\begin{aligned} CPV &= ACV \times AACMI \\ &= \$75 \times 1.1 \\ &= \$82.50. \end{aligned}$$

Having calculated the number of visits (V) and the cost per visit (CPV), it is a simple matter to determine the annual ambulatory costs:

$$\begin{aligned} AC &= V \times CPV \\ &= 20,000 \times \$82.50 \\ &= \$1,650,000. \end{aligned}$$

Finally, the total cost of providing ambulatory health care for the 5,000 covered lives in this example can be determined by the following formula:

$$\begin{aligned} \text{Total cost } (TC) &= \text{Inpatient costs } (IC) + \text{ambulatory costs } (AC) \\ &= \$1,540,000 + \$1,650,000 \\ &= \$3,190,000. \end{aligned}$$

Thus, given the assumptions about the actuarial behavior of the covered lives, a manager would know that the costs associated with providing health care for the 5,000 beneficiaries in this example would approximate $3,190,000.

Later in this chapter when the management of costs is addressed, the use of this information will be discussed including the technique of **variance analysis.**

Managing the Enrollment

A health care organization—both health care providers and managed care companies—is interested in managing the enrollment of beneficiaries from several perspectives. This activity includes such issues as maintaining the membership of beneficiaries and strategies to improve quality and reduce costs while maintaining the satisfaction of the members receiving health services.

Maintaining Membership

One of the central issues of providing health care in a risk environment is maintaining sufficiently large numbers of covered lives so that the risks are actuarially sound. This concern is real not only for the health care provider but for the managed care company taking the risk. As a result, health care organizations undertake various programs aimed at maintaining the current membership as well as acquiring new members, among them, quality measurement activities, customer satisfaction activities, and marketing activities. In general, quality is important because there is a danger that the plan members might perceive that other activities designed to reduce costs are endangering their health or causing them to receive suboptimum health care. To whatever extent this belief exists in the plan membership, it is critically important that the perception be corrected with meaningful data.

This leads to the second activity of monitoring and understanding the level of satisfaction of the beneficiary. To manage the enrollment effectively, a manager must know whether the beneficiaries are satisfied with the health care they are receiving. Typically both the managed care companies and the health care providers use various vehicles to measure patient satisfaction.

Reducing Costs

A second part of managing the enrollment is that of reducing costs while maintaining quality and member satisfaction. This is no mean achievement and requires extraordinary attention to the task.

One of the activities that has great potential for reducing costs in the long run, while improving member satisfaction in the short run, is that of preventive services. Providing appropriate preventive services often has the desirable health effect of improving the overall health status of the group being served. Preventive services also have the desirable effect of improving the satisfaction of the group members because they perceive that they are receiving something extra with their health care services.

From the risk taker's perspective, however, there is also a limitation associated with providing preventive services to its group. If the costs are immediate and the benefits are long term, the strategy will work only if the group members are retained over the long term. If they instead shift coverage to a different health plan, the risk taker suffers the undesirable effect of having paid for the preventive services and watching a competitor, who did not pay for the services, benefit from them.

Other strategies can also be employed to reduce costs, but the risk taker must always be aware that cost-cutting measures can have a potentially adverse effect on members' satisfaction, thus raising the possibility of losing membership. For example, there is a danger that plan members will view utilization management strategies and reduction of operational costs either as compromising quality or as a reduction in their health care benefits or both. Therefore, each cost-cutting activity must be carefully evaluated by the risk taker and provider relative to its effect on the quality of the service and, ultimately, the effect on the satisfaction of the member.

Cost Definitions

When a health care organization undertakes a contract embodying financial risk for providing health care to a defined group, it is mandatory that it know its costs of doing business and understand the dynamics of the costs it is experiencing. Typically health care professionals have applied costing models to inpatient acute care episodes of illness and in particular have based the costing on clusters of individual diagnosis related groups (**DRGs**) or some other form of **product line costing.** While it is necessary and important that the costs of inpatient acute care episodes be known, the health care provider should not lose sight of the fact that significant services provided to their covered lives will be outside the context of the inpatient acute care environment. This is particularly true in the case of physician providers.

As with all other information resource management, there are costs associated with obtaining information, and the activity of acquiring information about the expenses of doing business for the health care organization is no different. Managers must always assess the costs of obtaining information compared to the value of that information. That is, they must determine how much the organization will pay for information in order to reduce the uncertainty about some future state or event. In general, as more information is assembled about a particular issue, the uncertainty about the outcome will be reduced. At some point, the cost of obtaining more information exceeds the value of the information in the decision-making process because almost everything is already known and additional information adds little to the knowledge base for making the decision, but it does increase costs. This view about the expenses associated with acquiring information applies to the activity of determining the cost of providing health services, whether it relates to departmental costing or product line costing.

It might seem a simple matter that an organization would be able to determine the costs of doing business. Unfortunately, this is not the case, because a variety of assumptions can be made about how the costs are allocated as well as the fact that there are several concepts of how costs should be defined. Two of the most prominent of these definitions are **economic costs** and **accounting costs.**

Economic Costs

The economic cost of an item is defined as the resources required to acquire the use of some item or service. This concept is derived from the classical economic concept of opportunity cost. This is the concept that comes into play when an organization decides to acquire some resource but not others because of limited resources. The opportunity cost of acquiring this resource is the value of the alternatives that were not selected.

When resources are scarce and there is competition for them, organizations must choose among alternatives because it is not possible to acquire everything that is desired. An example of opportunity cost in the health care field might be if an organization was considering whether to acquire a magnetic resonance imaging unit (**MRI**) or build an ambulatory surgical center but could not afford to do both. Given that the organization selected the MRI, the opportunity cost of the MRI would be the value of the ambulatory surgical center. If there were multiple alternatives in the selection process, there would be multiple economic costs for the MRI, each a function of its comparison with an individual alternative. In an economic sense, value ultimately is determined by a utility function of the people making the decision. Given that it is impractical to measure precisely all decision makers' utility functions relative to each decision alternative, in a broad sense, that is what happens when satisfaction measures are taken relative to the performance of a health care organization.

Accounting Costs

The accounting cost of an item is a simplification of the market's value for the asset over a specific period of time. This manifests itself in the depreciation expenses associated with an asset. Given the example of the MRI, the depreciation expense is the accountant's estimate of the costs of using the asset during a given period of time, usually a year. Since there are multiple depreciation methodologies, it immediately becomes apparent that depreciation expense is nothing more than an estimate. Some of the methodologies that are commonly used include straight line, sum of the year's digits, and double declining balance.

For purposes of illustration, assume the simplest possible case with the following values:

Method of depreciation:	Straight line
Value of the asset:	$1,400,000
Useful life:	Seven years
Residual value:	$0

Since there is no residual value for the asset at the end of its useful life, the annual depreciation expense for the asset would be $200,000 in each year of its useful life. This means that the accounting cost of the asset is $200,000 each year the organization uses it. Furthermore, this is the annual estimated cost of acquiring, installing, using, and disposing of the asset over its seven-year life. If a different depreciation method had been used, the assumed annual cost of the asset would be different.

Some accountants and economists discuss a "true accounting cost," which is possible only when very sophisticated microcosting techniques are used. This method attempts to document and accumulate every cost associated with carrying out an activity. There has been some success with this technique in the manufacturing sector of the economy, largely because its automated manufacturing processes lend themselves to using electronic data gathering techniques. However, because of the uniqueness of most health care work processes, this costing technique has been largely unsuccessful in this sector.

Managers must consider the cost of obtaining the information compared to the value of the information. Only if the additional information adds materially to the reduction of uncertainty in the decision-making process, and thus to the accuracy and value of the ultimate decision, can it be justified.

Accounting for Costs

Determining and measuring costs is an imprecise activity; nevertheless, we must deal with the issue that the costs of doing business must be determined with a sufficient level of confidence that the information can be used to make rational business decisions.

There are several types of costs. For example, the combined category of fixed costs and variable costs constitutes the full cost of an item or service. Variable costs are those that in aggregate vary directly with the number of patients served. By contrast, fixed costs are those that in total do not vary with the number of patients served. Of course, these definitions of variable and fixed costs take into consideration that the total amount of patient care activity does not vary significantly over time. For example, some fixed costs, like personnel, will become semivariable if the number of patients seen is significantly increased. Clearly additional staff members are required at some point in order to be able to serve the patients. In general, however, if there is not significant variability in the volume of services, the definitions of variable and fixed costs are satisfactory.

We will use the example of the MRI equipment to illustrate variable and fixed costs. Recall that the annual depreciation for the MRI unit is $200,000. (There are fixed costs other than depreciation, but for purposes of simplifying this example, only depreciation is considered.) These costs are fixed and will be incurred whether one patient is served or many. We make the following assumptions:

Fixed costs   = $200,000

Variable cost = $150 per procedure

Volume   = Varies from 1,000 units to 1,500 units

Table 12-2   The Behavior of Variable and Fixed Costs

Volume (V)	Fixed Cost (FC)	Variable Cost per Unit (VC)	Total Variable Cost (V × VC)	Full Cost (V × VC) + FC
1,000	$200,000	$150	$150,000	$350,000
1,500	$200,000	$150	$225,000	$425,000

Table 12-2 provides these insights into the behavior of fixed and variable costs:

- The fixed cost remains the same regardless of the variability of the volume of services.
- The unit variable cost remains the same on a per patient basis.
- The total variable cost increases with the increase or decrease of the volume of services.
- The full cost increases with the variability of the volume of services, but this increase is driven by the increase in variable costs and is not influenced by the fixed costs. Thus, in an environment of increasing volumes of service, total costs increase at a less rapid rate than do variable costs.

An additional dimension of this relation is shown in Table 12-3, where the average cost is calculated. Here we observe an additional dimension of the relationship of fixed costs, variable costs, volume, and average cost:

- The full cost increases with the variability of the volume of services, but this increase is driven by the increase in variable costs and is not influenced by fixed costs.
- The average cost decreases as the volume increases. This is due to the ability to spread the fixed costs over a larger number of units of service.
- The cost of providing an MRI exam is not a single value that is universally true. Rather, the imputed cost of doing the examination varies with the number of examinations performed. This means that the fixed costs are shared as the volume increases or decreases, but the variable costs remain the same on a unit basis regardless of the volume of services.

The concept of marginal costs is an additional dimension that must be considered in certain decision-making settings. Suppose that a managed care company indicates

Table 12-3   The Behavior of Average Cost

Volume	Fixed Cost	Total Variable Cost	Full Cost	Average Cost
1,000	$200,000	$150,000	$350,000	$350.00
1,500	$200,000	$225,000	$425,000	$283.33

to the health care provider that it is willing to contract 1,000 MRI exams per year to the health care provider, but instead of paying the market rate of $400 per examination, it is willing to pay only $250 per examination. In Table 12-3 we note that the actual cost of doing the exam varies from $283 to $350, depending on the volume of services provided. The managed care company is willing to pay only an amount that is less than cost for a defined incremental number of examinations. Assume that the provider is currently doing 1,000 examinations and has the capacity to do 2,500. Should this business be accepted? The answer is yes, as long as the organization has excess capacity (in this case 1,500 units), and there are no other purchasers willing to pay more than $250. This illustrates the concept of marginal cost.

The reason this is a prudent decision is that under the conditions outlined, any incremental business that pays a price that is greater than the variable cost will increase the profit of the organization. This is because the fixed costs can be spread over more units of service. Stated differently, all of the fixed costs are embodied in the first 1,000 units, so the average cost of the additional 1,000 units for the managed care company is simply the variable cost, which is $150 per unit.

Table 12-4 provides several insights into the behavior of marginal costs and the effect on the profitability of the organization:

- Taking the incremental business, even though it is below the average cost for the procedure, increases the profitability of the organization if the organization has excess capacity that can accommodate the volume.
- The total average cost of the procedure is lowered from $350 per unit to $250 per unit. This is because the fixed cost of $200,000 is spread over 2,000 instead of 1,000 units.
- The profitability of the organization increases from $50,000 at 1,000 units to $150,000 at 2,000 units, even though the incremental price is $150 less than the $400 the organization was being paid for its original 1,000 units.

There are some significant limitations with this costing model, not the least of which is the fact that the unit costs vary with the volume of services provided. The difficulty is the matter of how the fixed costs can be appropriately allocated to each unit of service. One approach to this has been the emergence of activity-based costing (ABC) in

Table 12-4   The Behavior of Marginal Costs

Volume	Average Cost	Reimbursement	Total Cost	Total Revenue	Profit
1,000	$350	$400	$350,000	$400,000	$50,000
Additional managed care volume					
1,000	$150	$250	$150,000	$250,000	$100,000
2,000	$250		$500,000	$650,000	$150,000

the manufacturing sector. This approach attempts to determine the cost of products by improving the accuracy of allocating fixed costs and overhead on the basis of how they are actually consumed. This approach can be useful where the activities of production are standardized and predictable, but due to the unique nature of health care and the way that it is delivered, ABC has not been widely accepted or used in the health care field.

As the financial management of health care organizations is refined, more accurate and effective costing models will be developed. If the health care delivery model moves in the direction of product lines, the ability to allocate the costs more accurately will be improved because the cause-and-effect relationships can be developed between the health care product and the overhead that is allocated, a condition that will more closely approximate ABC.

Managing Costs

In most organizations, the basic vehicle used to manage costs is the operating budget. It measures both the revenues and expenses as they flow through the organization and provides the targets for both that are expected to occur. These operating budgets are usually broken down into departmental summaries and sometimes even divisions within a department. All of them roll up into the single organizational budget.

All of the cost analyses discussed in this chapter have intensive information requirements. Thus, it is mandatory that organizations plan for effective information systems when they develop cost analysis systems. Information is a resource of the organization and contributes in a direct way to the effectiveness of the organizational decision-making process. Without timely, accurate, and cost-effective information to support decision making, the effectiveness of the organization will be reduced.

Operating Units

In most organizations, there are two different types of operating units, each using the operating budget in a different way: **profit centers** and **cost centers.**

Profit Centers

Profit centers, sometimes referred to as revenue centers, are departments within an organization experiencing both revenue and expenses—for example, a Radiology department. Hence they are centers having "revenue," or they are centers having a "profit" resulting from their operations.

Managers use their operating budgets to manage the appropriate financial outcomes for their departments, including maintaining an appropriate relationship between revenue and expense. Because there can be deviations in either direction from budget for the revenue or the expenses, or both, all financial decisions must include both sides of the equation.

The core of the operating budget is a forecast of the anticipated volume of services. This information allows the manager to develop certain expected relationships that should hold throughout the budget year—including such key indicators as revenue per procedure, variable expenses per procedure, supplies per procedure, and paid hours per procedure. Key indicators like these and others allow the organization and the manager to determine whether they are outside the financial operating parameters that the organization has set. For example, if variable costs are assumed to be $150 per procedure but there is no way to determine whether that target is being met on a current basis, management control of the venture is lost.

Having a current understanding of the revenue per procedure is equally important to effective management of operating budgets. If the revenue per procedure changes from projections, the deviation could signal changing reimbursement patterns, changing payer mix, or collection problems. It is important for the manager to understand that changes from the target require explanations and sometimes actions to correct them.

Finally, these key indicators allow managers to do a meaningful evaluation of the appropriate increases in variable expenses when volumes are increasing. It is not enough simply to say that the expenses are up because the volume is up. The question is whether the expenses are up in an appropriate ratio to the increases in volume. The key indicator of variable expense per procedure is one method by which these changes can be evaluated.

Without these insights into costs and their behavior, it is difficult to evaluate the performance of an organization at the departmental or divisional level. It is particularly important that these dynamics be well understood in the capitated environment because of the significant additional risk shifted to the health care provider.

Cost Centers

Cost centers are the departments or divisions of an organization having a budget for expenses but no revenue. As such, their budgets contribute only costs to the overall budget of the organization. An example might be a human resources department.

All of the points made about expenses that were discussed for profit centers are equally applicable for cost centers, plus the department must project the number of services it performs. In a human resources setting, these operating parameters could include the number of employees served or the number of job applications taken. This projection allows the department to develop its own key indicators with regard to the expenses it generates for the organization—for example, hours paid per employee, total expenses per employee, or hours paid per job application.

As in the case of the profit center, the cost center needs a set of key indicators for monitoring its performance. Since cost centers usually become part of the organization's overhead and ultimately a part of the fixed costs, it is crucially important that they be controlled and not be allowed to increase without valid reasons.

Assessing Performance

In addition to the matters discussed relative to profit centers and cost centers, it is important that an organization assess other kinds of financial performance. One of the most effective tools to assess financial performance is the use of variance analysis.

Whether consciously or unconsciously, most organizations have a plan to identify exceptions to their operating plan and then to act on the causes in order to correct them. Whether this is called management by exception or some other terminology is used, the end result is the same. Budget variance analysis is one of these management-by-exception tools. An organization usually establishes certain rules that act as triggers for investigation—for example:

- All variances from a standard (variable cost per procedure)
- All variances from an absolute amount (budgeted fixed costs)
- All variances from a budget line item greater a certain percentage (say, 10 percent)
- All variances from a budget line item greater than a fixed amount (say, $1,000)

These or other rules allow the organization to identify deviations from their expected financial plans for operation and then to analyze the reasons for the deviations and take action where warranted. Variance analysis is an inquiry into the reasons for a departure from actual performance relative to an expected target. More sophisticated analyses of this type could include use of confidence intervals from the statistical theory field. This would allow the decision maker to establish certain ranges within which there is a certain probability of occurrence.

Variances usually occur because of deviations in volume or deviations in cost, or both. When discussing variations under capitation, the volume deviations can occur either because of changes in the number of covered lives or because the utilization rate has changed (average admissions per member or average visits per member). By contrast, under capitation, the cost variances accrue due to changes in the case mix intensity of the patients seen or the factors of production or productivity measures (employees per patient, supplies per patient, or some other similar measure of productivity). Using the data developed already in this chapter, we can demonstrate how variance analysis can take place. Table 12-5 provides the original data (budget) as well as some additional data reflecting the actual operation during the budget period. The formula for computing the variance is:

$$\text{Variance} = \text{actual} - \text{budget}.$$

Thus, given the actual operating statistics, the budget for inpatient costs was exceeded by $516,320 (column 3), while the budget for outpatient costs was overspent by $329,208 and the budget for total costs was exceeded by $845,528. These budget variances are caused by volume-related variables, cost-related variables, or both.

Inpatient Variances

Volume-Related Variances

Volume-related variances can be caused by changes in enrollment or the rate of utilization, or both. Using the variables set out earlier in this chapter plus the superscript *b* to denote budget values and the superscript *a* to denote actual values, the notation

Table 12-5   Budget to Actual Comparison

	Budget	Actual	Variance	Percent
Number of admissions (*A*)	350	408	58	16.6%
Cost per admission (*COA*)	$4,000	$4,200	$200	5.0
Covered lives (*CL*)	5,000	5,100	100	2.0
Average admissions per member (*AAM*)	.070	.08	.01	14.3
Average case mix index (IP) (*ACMI*)	1.1	1.2	.1	9.1
Number of visits (*V*)	20,000	21,420	1,420	7.1
Cost per visit (*CPV*)	$75	$77	$2	2.7
Average visits per member (*AVM*)	4	4.2	.2	5.0
Case mix (OP) (*AACMI*)	1.1	1.2	.1	9.1
Inpatient costs (*IC*)	$1,540,000	$2,056,320	$516,320	33.5%
Ambulatory costs (*AC*)	$1,650,000	$1,979,208	$329,208	20.0
Total costs (*TC*)	$3,190,000	$4,035,528	$845,528	26.5

for budgeted admissions would be A^b. Using this notation and the numbers in Table 12-5, the formula to determine the enrollment variance is:

$$\text{Inpatient enrollment variance } (IEV) = (CL^a - CL^b) \times AAM^b \times COA^b \times ACMI^b$$
$$= (5,100 - 5,000) \times .07 \times \$4,000 \times 1.1$$
$$= \$30,800.$$

This formula determines the amount of variance due to changes in enrollment by using the difference between the budgeted covered lives and the actual number of covered lives as the factor that is applied to budgeted admissions per member, budgeted cost per admission, and budgeted case mix. Thus, the amount of the total inpatient variance of $516,320 that is due to the increased enrollment is $30,800.

The second part of the volume-related variance is the part due to variations in utilization. The inpatient utilization variance is given by the following formula:

$$\text{Inpatient utilization variance } (IUV) = (AAM^a - AAM^b) \times CL^a \times COA^b \times ACMI^b$$
$$= (.08 - .07) \times 5,100 \times 4,000 \times 1.1$$
$$= \$224,400.$$

This formula determines the amount of variance due to changes in utilization by determining the difference between the budgeted utilization rate and the actual utilization rate as the factor that is applied to actual covered lives, budgeted admissions, and budgeted case mix index. According to this formula, the amount of the total inpatient variance of $516,320 that is due to the increased utilization is $224,400.

Cost-Related Variances

The second part of the variance analysis is an examination of the changes in the costs of doing business. As in the case of the volume variance, the variances due to cost are composed of two parts: the productivity variance and the case mix variance.

In order to determine the amount of cost variance due to changes in productivity within the organization, the following formula is applied:

$$
\begin{aligned}
\text{Inpatient productivity variance } (IPV) &= (COA^a - COA^b) \times ACMI^a \times CL^a \times AAM^a \\
&= (4{,}200 - 4{,}000) \times 1.2 \times 5{,}100 \times .08 \\
&= \$97{,}920.
\end{aligned}
$$

This formula determines the amount of variance due to changes in productivity by using the difference between the budgeted cost per admission and the actual cost per admission as the factor that is applied to the actual case mix index, actual number of covered lives, and actual admissions per member. Thus, the amount of the total inpatient variance of $516,320 that is due to the decreased productivity of the organization is $97,920.

The final calculation, and the second of this subgroup, determines the amount of the cost variance due to the change in case mix. The result is provided by the following formula:

$$
\begin{aligned}
\text{Inpatient case mix variance } (ICMV) &= (ACMI^a - ACMI^b) \times COA^b \times CL^a \times AAM^a \\
&= (1.2 - 1.1) \times 4{,}000 \times 5{,}100 \times .08 \\
&= \$163{,}200.
\end{aligned}
$$

This formula determines the amount of variance due to changes in case mix by using the difference between the budgeted case mix and the actual case mix as the factor that is applied to budgeted cost per admission, actual covered lives, and actual admissions per member. Thus, the amount of the total inpatient variance of $516,320 that is due to the increased level of the case mix is $163,200.

Aggregating this information, Table 12-6 shows the cumulative results of this analysis of the inpatient side of the cost variance. It accounts for all of the inpatient cost variances identified in Table 12-5.

Table 12-6   Cumulative Results of Inpatient Cost Variances

Variance	
Inpatient enrollment variance	$ 30,800
Inpatient utilization variance	224,400
Inpatient productivity variance	97,920
Inpatient case mix variance	163,200
Total inpatient variance	516,320

Ambulatory Variances

Outpatient cost variances can be determined in the same way as inpatient variances.

Volume-Related Variances

Given the data presented in Table 12-5, the ambulatory volume-related variances can be caused by changes in enrollment or the rate of utilization, or both. The formula to determine the ambulatory enrollment variance is:

$$
\begin{aligned}
\text{Ambulatory enrollment variance } (AEV) &= (CL^a - CL^b) \times AVM^b \times CPV^b \times AACMI^b \\
&= (5,100 - 5,000) \times 4 \times \$75 \times 1.1 \\
&= \$33,000.
\end{aligned}
$$

This formula determines the amount of variance due to changes in enrollment by using the difference between the budgeted covered lives and the actual number of covered lives as the factor that is applied to budgeted visits per member, budgeted cost per visit, and budgeted case mix. Thus, the amount of the total ambulatory variance of $329,208 that is due to the increased enrollment is $33,000.

The second part of the volume-related variance is the part due to variations in utilization. The ambulatory utilization variance is given by the following formula:

$$
\begin{aligned}
\text{Ambulatory utilization variance } (AUV) &= (AVM^a - AVM^b) \times CL^a \times CPV^b \times AACMI^b \\
&= (4.2 - 4.0) \times 5,100 \times \$75 \times 1.1 \\
&= \$84,150.
\end{aligned}
$$

This formula determines the amount of variance due to changes in utilization by determining the difference between the budgeted utilization rate and the actual utilization rate as the factor that is applied to actual covered lives, budgeted visits, and budgeted case mix index. According to this formula, the amount of the total ambulatory variance of $329,208 that is due to the increased utilization is $84,150.

Cost-Related Variances

The second part of the variance analysis is an examination of changes in the costs of doing business. As in the case of the volume variance, the variances due to cost are composed of two parts: the productivity variance and the case mix variance.

In order to determine the amount of cost variance due to changes in productivity within the organization, the following formula is applied:

$$
\begin{aligned}
\text{Ambulatory productivity variance } (APV) &= (CPV^a - CPV^b) \times AACMI^a \times CL^a \times AVM^a \\
&= (77 - 75) \times 1.2 \times 5,100 \times 4.2 \\
&= \$51,408.
\end{aligned}
$$

This formula determines the amount of variance due to changes in productivity by using the difference between the budgeted cost per visit and the actual cost per visit as the factor that is applied to the actual case mix index, actual number of covered lives, and actual visits per member. Thus, the amount of the total ambulatory variance of $329,208 due to the decreased productivity of the organization is $51,408.

Table 12-7   Cumulative Results of Ambulatory Cost Variances

Variance	
Ambulatory enrollment variance	$ 33,000
Ambulatory utilization variance	84,150
Ambulatory productivity variance	51,408
Ambulatory case mix variance	160,650
Total ambulatory variance	329,208

The final calculation, and the second of this subgroup, determines the amount of the cost variance due to the change in case mix. The result is provided by the following formula:

$$\text{Ambulatory case mix variance } (ACMV) = (AACMI^a - AACMI^b) \times CPV^b \times CL^a \times AVM^a$$
$$= (1.2 - 1.1) \times \$75 \times 5100 \times 4.2$$
$$= \$160,650.$$

This formula determines the amount of variance due to changes in case mix by using the difference between the budgeted case mix and the actual case mix as the factor applied to budgeted cost per visit, actual covered lives, and actual visits per member. Thus, the amount of the total ambulatory variance of $329,208 that is due to the increased level of the case mix is $160,650.

Aggregating this information, Table 12-7 shows the cumulative results of this analysis of the ambulatory side of the cost variance. It also shows that all of the ambulatory cost variances identified in Table 12-5 have been accounted for.

Thus, the total variance, consisting of the inpatient variance and the ambulatory variance, is $516,320 plus $329,208, or $845,528 as shown in Table 12-5.

Flexible Versus Fixed Budgets

Flexible budgets are budgets that are adjusted for the volume of services rendered. When an operating budget is prepared, certain assumptions are made, including volume of services. Since the actual volume of services is rarely exactly what was predicted in the budget, there will be budget volume variances. In those cases, the organization has several options:

- Conduct the traditional variance analyses, which will identify the volume variances, and add them as explanations in the financial reports.
- Create a revised budget.
- Use the concept of a flexible budget.

The fundamental premise of a flexible budget is that fixed costs do not vary with changes in volume of service, but variable costs fluctuate in direct proportion to the volume of service. Of course, this assumes that an organization is able to identify all of its fixed costs and all of its variable costs. It then adjusts the budget for the variable costs associated with any volume changes.

One of the problems with a variable budget is that the variable costs differ according to the services being rendered. The variable costs associated with doing an MRI exam, for example, are significantly different from the variable costs associated with a liver profile in the laboratory. Since health care organizations offer thousands of services, the choice is either to identify the variable costs associated with each service or to average the variable costs across divisions, departments, or the entire organization. As one moves along this continuum of cost aggregation, from the individual procedure to the division, to the department, or ultimately the entire organization, the level of precision declines. The larger the range of services over which the variable costs are averaged, the more prone the organization is to introducing bias due to changes in service mix.

In conclusion, although the idea of a flexible budget has intellectual appeal, the actual application of the idea is much more difficult to achieve. In the current environment, few health care organizations have adopted flexible budgeting as a method to account for operations.

Correcting Variances

All variances have causes, and not all variances are undesirable. An organization must first identify the variances, then determine whether they are desirable or undesirable, and if undesirable, correct them. In some cases, the causes are outside the direct control of the organization. This is the case with overutilization of resources by physicians who are not employed by the health care organization. In the case of managed care organizations, unless it is operating in a staff model, it is also the case that many of the undesirable variances are created by physicians over which the managed care organization has little direct control. This makes it necessary to use other vehicles to influence utilization.

Incentives

One method to influence the adverse utilization patterns that result in undesirable variances for the organization is to build in incentives for appropriate utilization and behavior. One of the most common is the use of financial incentives. Of these, one of the most noteworthy is the use of a capitation reimbursement model.

Capitation provides powerful financial incentives to restrict the utilization of resources that are not needed. The direct effect is to curtail undesirable utilization variances. Although other reimbursement models that share or transfer risk to the health care provider have similar effects, they usually do not provide as strong a financial incentive to restrict utilization as does capitation.

Profiling

Another method of creating incentives for appropriate utilization is the concept of physician profiling, which usually addresses patterns of treatment and outcomes of those treatments. The concept of financial profiling beginning to emerge here addresses the issue of how many resources a physician consumes in the process of treating a patient. Whatever the subject of the profile, it has a twofold purpose. First, in theory at least, it is used to identify excess utilization so that appropriate education can take place. Second is to identify physicians who will be made a part of a network when it is formed and eliminate those who do not demonstrate appropriate patterns of utilization, either when the network is formed or on the basis of continuing patterns of resource use.

Critical Paths

This methodology establishes a series of protocols for treating individuals with specifically identified diagnoses. A critical pathway for each diagnosis is identified as one having the potential to reduce inappropriate utilization. The treatment protocols are usually created by the practicing physicians of an organization and specify what services and procedures should be performed and the sequence in which they should be offered. Assuming that the course of treatment is uncomplicated, each patient is treated in the same way, and extraneous testing and treatment are minimized.

Conclusion

The role of managing an organization under capitation is a new experience to many health care professionals. As such, it is something for which they have often not been trained. In addition, the reimbursement methodology demands behaviors that are quite different from under the other forms of reimbursement to which they have become accustomed.

This chapter discussed the financial issues that must be identified, analyzed, and resolved if the organization is to be successful financially. The paradigm of rendering health care services is changing, and the reimbursement system is a significant part of this change. If the people who are managing the organization under the new paradigm are not aware of its dynamics and do not address issues resulting from it, the future viability of the organization is in danger.

Case 12-1: City Hospital Managed Care—Part I

You have just become the president of City Hospital. Managed care is just beginning to develop in the metropolitan area that City Hospital serves and your chief financial officer has told you that several managed care companies are anxious to establish a contract with City Hospital. The CFO wishes to know how to proceed. You indicate that it will be necessary to gather information on how you want to proceed in order to provide a baseline for negotiations with the managed care company. The managed care company stated it expected that 6,500 covered lives would select the City Hospital network.

You want to pursue this initiative and wish to ascertain what additional hospital specific information is required in order to determine what costs will be encountered in serving this group of patients. In response, the chief financial officer of the organization provides the following information. You need to determine which pieces of the information are useful and whether additional information is required.

Case mix index for inpatient services	= 1.24
Case mix index for outpatient services	= 1.15
Average cost per admission (if case mix = 1.0)	= $4,625
Average annual admissions per member	= .064
Average cost per ambulatory procedure (if case mix = 1.0)	= $67.50
Inpatient admissions per year	= 9,845
Outpatient encounters per year	= 22,567

1. Is any additional information required to determine baseline costs related to this initiative?
2. Is any of the information provided superfluous?
3. How many total admissions should be projected for the year?
4. What is the cost per admission?
5. How much annual cost should the health care facility expect in serving these patients?

Case 12-2: City Hospital Managed Care—Part II

Assume the conditions cited in Case 12-1. As the president of City Hospital you wish to have a feeling for how much risk you have in terms of the potential variability of the risk factors. You ask the CFO to do a sensitivity analysis of the various risk factors and provide a report to you about the amount of increased or decreased costs that City Hospital will encounter if the various risk factors are greater than the average patient served at City Hospital, or less than the average patient. In the report, you want the CFO to answer the following questions.

1. If the average annual admissions per member is .068, will this increase or decrease the profitability of the organization? Why? If this is the only variable that changes, how much will it increase or decrease the profitability of City Hospital?
2. If the case mix index for the facility is 1.21, will this increase or decrease the profitability of the organization? Why? If this is the only variable that changes, how much will it increase or decrease the profitability of City Hospital?
3. If the number of covered lives is greater than 6,500, will this increase or decrease the profitability of the organization? Why?

Case 12-3: City Hospital Cardiac Catheterization Department—Part I

You are the manager of a catheterization laboratory at City Hospital. As part of your efforts to improve the profitability of your department, you have been having discussions with several managed care companies in an effort to arrange an exclusive provider relationship. The accounting system has not always been able to provide all of the management information you desire in order to make informed economic decisions. Now that you are in conversations with several managed care companies to potentially become an exclusive provider of cardiac catheterizations for them, you must know the current financial status of your organization. You have asked the CFO to provide you with current financial information about the department's operations and financial status. The following information about the financial performance of your department was provided to you.

Allocated fixed costs	= $285,000
Variable cost per procedure	= $375
Annual volume	= 550 procedures
Reimbursement per procedure	= $850

In anticipation of working out a contract with one or more of the managed care companies to be the exclusive provider of cardiac catheterizations, the newly appointed president of City hospital asks you to provide the following information.

1. What is the annual variable cost of your department?
2. What is the annual total cost in your department?
3. What is the total cost per procedure for cardiac catheterizations?
4. What is the fixed cost per procedure for cardiac catheterizations?
5. What is the excess of revenue over expense for your department?
6. What are the strengths and limitations of the data provided?

Case 12-4: City Hospital Catheterization Department—Part II

You are the department head of the cardiac catheterization department and have been trying to get one of the managed care companies in the city to use City Hospital as the exclusive provider of cardiac catheterizations. One of the managed care companies has now indicated that it wishes to negotiate with City Hospital to become the exclusive provider for cardiac catheterizations and estimates that approximately 200 catheterizations are anticipated annually. The managed care company indicates that they have an opportunity to contract with a competitive hospital for $525 per catheterization and if City Hospital is willing to provide the service at $500 per catheterization, they can have the contract.

The CEO of City Hospital is uncomfortable about accepting the contract because the contract price of $500 per procedure is substantially less than the current cost per procedure of $893.18. The CEO has asked you to provide him with a written recommendation about what course of action City Hospital should take in negotiating the contract. Your report should include at least the following information:

1. Provide a rationale for whether or not City Hospital should accept the contract to do cardiac catheterizations for $500 on an exclusive provider basis.
2. What will be the new average cost per procedure if the contract is accepted?
3. What will the new fixed cost per procedure be if the contract is accepted?
4. What will the profitability of the cardiac catheterization department be if the contract is accepted?

Case 12-5: City Hospital Budget Variances for a Managed Care Group

City Hospital has had a contract with a managed care company to provide health care services for a specified group of patients. This contract has been in effect for the last year. The CEO of City Hospital wishes to know how well the hospital did in managing the contract and asks you to provide a report containing specific information about how well the organization did compared to its budget to provide services for this group of covered lives. The following information shows the budget information for this group of patients as well as the actual performance for the past year.

Budget to Actual Comparison

	Budget	**Actual**
Cost per Admission (COA)	$3,750	$4,125
Covered Lives (CL)	4,875	5,125
Average Admissions per Member (AAM)	.065	.061
IP Average Case Mix Index (ACMI)	1.1	1.05
Cost per Visit (CPV)	$68	$66
Average Visits per Member (AVM)	4	3.8
OP Case Mix (AACMI)	1.1	1.2

The CEO has seen this information and as part of the report he has asked you to prepare, he wants you to address the following questions.

1. What is the total inpatient cost variance from budget?
2. What amount of the inpatient cost variance is due to actual enrollment differences when compared to budget?
3. What amount of the inpatient cost variance is due to utilization changes?

4. What amount of the inpatient cost variance is due to productivity changes?
5. What is the number of budgeted and actual ambulatory visits?
6. What is the total ambulatory cost variance?
7. What amount of the ambulatory cost variance is due to changes in the enrollment?
8. What amount of the ambulatory cost variance is due to changes in ambulatory utilization?
9. What amount of the ambulatory cost variance is due to changes in productivity?
10. What amount of the ambulatory cost variance is due to changes in case mix?

Review Questions

1. Explain why doing an incremental medical procedure will produce additional profit for an organization under a fee for service environment.
2. Explain why doing an incremental medical procedure will reduce the profitability of an organization under a capitated environment.
3. Discuss the relationship between economic costs, utility functions, and customer satisfaction.
4. Discuss how managing utilization will have a desirable effect on utilization in a capitated environment. What issues compound this management problem?
5. In calculating profitability under capitation, how is a change in the number of covered lives different than a change in average number of admissions, average cost of admissions or average case mix index?
6. Discuss the financial benefits and limitations for a risk taker offering preventive services to beneficiaries.
7. Define and discuss the relationship between fixed costs, variable costs, total costs, and average costs.

Chapter 13

Quality and Outcomes Management

This chapter looks at the relationship between the clinical practice of medicine and the importance of measuring the quality of that practice. There are multiple groups within the health care system that have a vital and sometimes conflicting interest in the way clinical care is delivered. The ability to assess and monitor quality is therefore essential to the process.

Learning Objectives

Upon successful completion of this chapter, the learner will:

- Describe the participants in the quality monitoring process.
- Explain the interests of the participants in the process.
- Discuss the continuous quality improvement process and explain its relationship to quality monitoring in the delivery of health care.
- Describe the infrastructure required to monitor quality.
- Identify and explain the role of various health care organizations in the quality monitoring process.
- Explain the relationship between technology assessment and the quality monitoring process.

Key Terms

carrier

credentials verification organizations

Foundation for Accountability

Health Care Financing Administration (HCFA)

Health Plan Employer Data and Information Set (HEDIS)

National Committee for Quality Assurance (NCQA)

quality assurance

Quality Assurance Reform Initiative (QARI)

report cards

shadow systems

technology assessment

Introduction

For several reasons quality is interwoven with managed care. On the one hand, there is the danger, and sometimes the belief on the part of the general public, that since one of the primary paradigms of managed care is to reduce costs, the managed care company might become more motivated by the economic outcomes than the clinical outcome. From another perspective, the managed care companies recognize the power of this potential belief on the part of the public, and many adopt specific steps designed to build quality into their product. This chapter examines the dynamics of this topic and the tension between the financial incentives for efficiency and the requirement for clinical quality. The issues surrounding this problem are numerous, complex, and interrelated.

As the penetration of managed care increases throughout the country, monitoring quality is one of the most important activities that a managed care company or health care provider can undertake. Distinguishing the fine line of demarcation between reducing unnecessary treatment and withholding services when they should be rendered is difficult. Such activities as reducing unnecessary treatment, providing preventive care, and coordinating the continuity of care can be viewed as being on either side of this line, depending on the interests of the individual viewing it.

In this chapter some of the concepts that are used to monitor quality will be examined.

Participants and Quality Concepts

A number of organizations have joined in the process of monitoring the quality of health care that is delivered; they examine various parts of the total health care delivery system. Some address issues related to payers, while others focus on issues related to providers. In some instances, they are quasi-public organizations, providing information to anyone wishing to investigate the quality status of the health care delivery system.

As the number of government-funded enrollees in managed care programs has increased, state and federal governments have become increasingly interested in the quality of the health care product as well. They have worked with insurers, providers, and consumers to attempt to improve quality. The Medicaid **Health Plan Employer Data and Information Set (HEDIS)** was implemented with the assistance of the **National Committee for Quality Assurance (NCQA)** and was designed to provide data required to evaluate the health status of the population being served. This vehicle evaluates enrollee satisfaction by assessing the performance of the **carrier**. This methodology was released to the states for use in early 1996. Medicare HEDIS has been developed on a parallel track by the **Health Care Financing Administration (HCFA)** and the Kaiser Family Foundation. Its implementation is in process.

Another organization formed to monitor quality is the **Foundation for Accountability,** a joint effort between private and public health care purchasers (Hadley and Wolf, 1996). The objective of this group is to increase the ability of health care purchasers to compare quality between care delivered in a managed care setting and a fee-for-service setting.

Yet another initiative occurred in 1994 when the NCQA, in collaboration with the Picker/Commonwealth Program, implemented a research program directed at learning more about consumers' attitudes toward report cards on providers. This was a joint research effort between NCQA and two private sector organizations that focuses on gaining greater insight into the consumer's understanding of the managed care delivery system and their comfort level in using it. The research produced several findings, including the following:

- Consumers would be willing to use information on how a health plan works, what it costs, what the covered benefits are, an assessment of the quality of care, and an evaluation of the overall satisfaction with care if such information was available.

- Consumers indicated their highest level of interest is in information on costs of coverage, technical competence, information and communication provided by physicians, coordination of care, and access—in short, the actual delivery of clinical care.

- Consumers wanted an unbiased, expert source of information about health care quality.

The findings concluded by saying that depending on the health status of the consumer, the information needs would vary.

In addition to the work that has been done on report cards for health care providers, a considerable amount of work has addressed the matter of measuring quality. Patient surveys have played a large role in this activity. However, one of the significant limitations of these measures is that not all patients perceive quality in the same way. As a result, individual patient priorities are not always addressed. For example, one patient might assess quality in terms of the amenities of the institution, while another might evaluate it on the basis of the quality of communication between the health care providers and the patient. If the instrument measuring quality fails to address one of these measures, the results will be biased because they will not adequately reflect all patients' assessment of quality.

The needs perceived by patients vary with whether the subject is an inpatient or an ambulatory patient. One study (Cleary and Edgna-Levitan, 1996) found that hospital inpatients placed a high priority on the following:

- Respect for the patient's values, preferences, and explicit needs
- Coordination of patient care
- Having information available to them
- Having meaningful communication with the caregivers
- Experiencing patient education
- Physical comfort and pain management
- Having the involvement of family and friends in their care
- Experiencing systematic transition and continuity of care to their home

Patients experiencing ambulatory care are interested in a different set of needs—for example:

- Having access to care
- Having the care coordinated when multiple modalities are involved
- Having satisfactory experiences in specific patient care processes, such as waiting times in the office and the ability to get timely appointments
- Receiving assistance from the office staff relative to receiving and/or scheduling tests and procedures
- Receiving follow-up care and information

Using Continuous Quality Improvement

The conventional wisdom is that there is an inverse relationship between maintaining or improving quality and decreasing costs. However, study on ambulatory patients demonstrated a positive correlation between quality and cost (Harris, 1994). A simple example might be the case of prescribing antibiotic pharmaceuticals. In some quarters, there has been a temptation to prescribe a broad-spectrum antibiotic for any infection, reasoning that it will "get whatever is there." As more and more has been learned about microorganisms' developing resistance to antibiotics when they are used frequently, thereby rendering them less effective when they are really needed, the realization has emerged that a more specific prescribing methodology is required. Taking cultures to determine the particular organism and then prescribing the specific antibiotic to treat that organism (often a second-generation antibiotic, which is much less expensive) has become the standard of care. In this case, it is clear that the less expensive treatment protocol is also the one providing the highest-quality clinical outcome. As costs were reduced, quality increased.

Continuous quality improvement (CQI) is a core issue in improving the health status of the population. Many health care organizations are adopting this approach to improve both their efficiency and effectiveness. Indeed, the NCQA Standards for Accreditation of Managed Care Organizations requires the health care organizations it accredits to demonstrate improvements in the quality of clinical care and service it provides.

As CQI is becoming more a part of the health care delivery system, there is a much greater realization that reduced costs do not necessarily equate to a lower level of clinical quality. Rather, the CQI model postulates that higher quality and lower costs are parallel outcomes of a good management process.

The CQI model operates on the assumption that no process is perfect and that there is always opportunity to improve a process by eliminating parts of it that cause rework and waste. In the case of the antibiotic example, the process is inefficient in that use of broad-spectrum antibiotics when they are not needed can result in their not working when they are needed; so a person who could be helped by a straightforward broad-spectrum antibiotic therapy instead requires much more rigorous therapy that costs a great deal more, if the patient can be helped at all. This example demonstrates not only that lower costs can result in higher quality, but also that higher costs can lead to lower quality. Thus, processes that cause rework or inefficiency are waste and must be eliminated.

Data Requirements for Quality Improvement

One of the central tenets of CQI is making decisions on the basis of data. A person must know how the system is performing before it is possible to make judgments about whether it is performing properly and whether its processes require redesign. Many techniques have been developed to help in this analysis.

In a health care organization, CQI has the same requirements. Suppose that the organization is interested in improving the process of having the ambulatory medical record available at the time of the patient encounter. Some of the information required before it would even be possible to determine whether there is a problem, much less whether the process requires improvement, are as follows:

- Is the record a manual record?
- Is there more than one copy of the manual record?
- If more than one copy of the record exists, do you know all of the locations where medical records are kept?
- If more than one copy of the record exists, who has responsibility for each copy of the record?
- Which record is considered the master record?
- Are there multiple geographical locations where the record is needed?
- Is the record required at multiple locations on the same day?
- Is there an effective and reliable record tracking system to locate the record?
- What is the current process for making the record available?

Some of these questions might seem quite basic, but they all have importance to an organization attempting to find the most efficient and effective way possible to make the record available to the clinician at the time of seeing the patient. In fact, the list contains hints about areas where the process can be improved and greater efficiency can be achieved while simultaneously providing a higher quality of service to the physician and the patient.

- *Having the record available at the time the patient is seen.* Many organizations operating with a manual record and having multiple sites of service are unable to have an integrated record available wherever the patient is seen. Rather, they resort to local records that report what happened to the patient at that site but do not reflect things that might have happened to the patient at other sites, including inpatient acute care hospitalizations. Thus, having a complete record available to the clinician at the time the patient is seen provides a paradigm shift in quality because the clinician is able to evaluate all phases of the patient's health status.

- *Having multiple records.* When an organization is unable to have the complete record available, it often resorts to keeping records on the patient at each location where he or she is seen. In many cases, the record contains only that information related to the visits at the particular site. In other instances, attempts are made to include other important parts of the patient's health record. In either case, keeping multiple records is a costly activity. When attempts are made to include key parts of records from other sites, it becomes even more expensive to maintain the processes that keep the record updated. This is an obvious candidate for process improvement.

- *Distributing the record to multiple locations.* If the organization attempts to transport the master record from one location to another as the patient is seen at various sites, a process must be in place that (1) can immediately determine the current location of the record, (2) determine in advance the time and place where the record will be needed, and (3) has a transportation system in place that can accomplish the distribution.

Sophisticated systems are required to ensure that any of these three conditions is known or can be accomplished. The potential for **shadow systems,** which are systems whose purpose is to make sure other systems are performing properly, and rework is high in this type of process. Again, because of the potential for duplication of effort and rework, this kind of process is a candidate for process improvement in the CQI context.

While it would be premature to venture any speculation on the solution to the process improvement scenario cited above, one could define part of the potential solution as having an information infrastructure that makes the complete record available to any practitioner at any location within the organization where the patient might be seen. The technology needed to achieve this goal is available today and is being used by many organizations having the foresight to plan for this condition. Part of the solution is having a well-thought-out information strategic plan that anticipates and addresses the issues that will be faced in the future. To the extent that "the future is now" and an organization might not have planned for the required infrastructure, it underscores the importance of working that much harder on information infrastructure problems in order to make up for the lost time.

In this relatively well-defined area of record availability for a clinician in the ambulatory setting, there are multiple opportunities for process improvement that can lead to decreased cost and increased quality. If the record-keeping solution is an electronic information system that can make key parts of the ambulatory and acute care record available to the clinician wherever the patient is being seen, then many of the potential problems envisioned by the questions being posed would melt away. The question that must be addressed by the health care organization is whether the cost of having the information available is less than or equal to the value of having it available. In each instance cited, an improvement in the process would almost certainly result in decreased costs and increased quality to both the practitioner and the patient.

Infrastructure Requirements for a Quality Program

As health care organizations move toward installing quality improvement programs, there is sometimes a blurring of the distinction between CQI programs and **quality assurance (QA)** programs, which are often used to satisfy accreditation and managed care program requirements. Both are important and necessary, but they are also quite different.

CQI assumes that every process can be improved and that the result of the improvement will simultaneously produce better efficiency and higher quality. QA is designed to identify key indicators of quality that can be monitored as measures used to determine whether the quality within the organization is improving or declining.

QA programs are in place in all health care organizations because they are required for accreditation as well as participation in many managed care programs. (This will be discussed in greater detail later in this chapter.) By contrast, CQI is a process that is adopted within an organization because management is interested in improving performance while not losing sight of quality. In other words, QA responds to the requirements of the external environment, while CQI responds to the internal needs of the organization. Both are necessary, and there can be overlap between the activities of each. For example, a QA monitoring indicator might suggest a problem with the length of time that patients remain on a respirator in a critical care unit of the organization. The CQI methodology might look at processes related to the use of respirators in the critical care units and formulate ways in which the processes could be improved. In an oversimplified way, it can be said that strong point of QA is identifying problems, while CQI undertakes ways to improve the processes related to the problems identified within the organization.

In order for a CQI process to be successful, there is a primary prerequisite that the entire organization be committed to it, from the executive level on down. In organizations where CQI works well, it is because it is viewed as a management philosophy or a way in which organizational decisions are made. If the executive level of the organization is not in tune with this approach, it is not likely that it will be successful. For example, if operational decisions in an organization are micromanaged by the executive level, it is not likely that a CQI process would be successful because one of its basic tenets is that problems are solved at the lowest level of the organization—that is, decisions relative to the solutions to those problems are also made at that level. Thus, one important element of the infrastructure of an organization that wants to use the CQI process is organizational commitment.

This commitment is important from several points of view. In addition to executive endorsement, certain resources are required to make it work—for example,

- Education to introduce and implement the CQI process
- Human resources required to make it work, such as meeting time for the personnel engaged in the process improvements
- Information resources to provide the data required to make the decisions relative to process improvement

Unless these organizational resources are made available to provide the infrastructure for a CQI process, it is unlikely that the venture will be successful. (Among the excellent surveys that provide a more complete understanding and broader insights on the subject of quality improvement in the health care sector are McLaughlin and Kaluzny, 1994, and Hospitals and Health Services Administration, 1995).

Quality Indicators

Quality indicators in the world of health care organizations provide guidelines of organizations accrediting health care providers as well as payers and serve the public in making decisions relative to selecting a managed care company or a health care provider.

National Committee for Quality Assurance (NCQA)

The NCQA "is an independent, not-for-profit organization dedicated to assessing and reporting on the quality of managed care plans, including health maintenance organizations" (www.ncqa.org). Its governance includes individuals on its board of directors representing employers, consumer representatives, labor representatives, health plans, quality experts, regulators, and representatives from organized medicine. Its mission is to promote "improvements in the quality of patient care provided through managed health plans. NCQA's primary function is to develop and apply oversight processes and measures of performance for health plans. NCQA is committed to providing information on managed care quality to the public, consumers, purchasers, health plans and other interested parties" (www.ncqa.org).

The activities of the NCAQ have a twofold focus: accreditation and performance measurement.

In its accreditation activities, the NCQA has positioned itself as the dominant player. As of June 1997, more than half of the 630 HMOs in the country had been reviewed by the organization, were scheduled for review, or had a decision on accreditation pending with NCQA. It began accrediting managed care organizations in 1991. In addition to its activities with the mainline managed care organizations, NCQA has recently released standards that will be applied to behavioral managed care organizations. Finally, NCQA is also engaged in reviewing **credentials verification organizations** and will provide certification to organizations doing this work.

The NCQA has been in the forefront in developing report cards of performance and uses HEDIS for reporting.

The NCQA uses over fifty standards, falling into six categories, to evaluate health care organizations seeking its accreditation. The categories are as follows and address the questions given (www.ncqa.org/accred.htm, p.2):

1. *Quality improvement.* Does the plan examine the quality of care given to the members? Does the plan coordinate all parts of the delivery system? How does the plan make sure members have access to care in a timely manner? Does the plan demonstrate it makes improvements in care?

2. *Physician credentials.* Does the plan follow NCQA guidelines in credentialing its physicians? Does the plan investigate the training and experience of all physicians in accordance with NCQA guidelines? Does the plan make investigations into malpractice and fraud for all of its physicians? Does the plan keep a record of physician performance and use that information for evaluation of physicians?

3. *Members' rights and responsibilities.* Does the plan communicate to its members how to access health services? Does the plan communicate how to choose a physician or how to change physicians? Does the plan communicate how to make a complaint? Does the plan do anything about satisfaction ratings and complaints?

4. *Preventive health services.* Does the plan encourage preventive health? Does the plan encourage physicians to deliver preventive services?

5. *Utilization management.* Is the process to decide what health services are appropriate for individuals well defined and used consistently? If payment for services is denied, does the plan respond to appeals by individuals and physicians?

6. *Medical records.* Do the plan's medical records meet the standards of the NCQA for quality of care? Do the medical records demonstrate physician follow up on abnormal test findings?

These questions provide a general insight into the focus of NCQA as it examines a candidate for accreditation. NCQA is rigorous in its approach to quality in managed care organizations and seeks to help the public assess and evaluate the qualifications of a managed care organization. As is the case with any other accreditation process, it does not guarantee the quality of the product. However, in this case, the NCQA indicates that "plans that are accredited have demonstrated that they provide the consumer protections required by NCQA standards and that they closely monitor, and are continuously improving the quality of care they deliver" (www.ncqa.org/accred.htm, p. 3).

A detailed set of standards is available from NCQA.

In addition to accrediting managed care organizations, the NCQA has begun accrediting organizations that verify physician credentials—credentials verification organizations. The focus of this program is to ensure that the NCQA standards related to physician credentials are carried out appropriately. Areas of investigation are (www.ncqa.org/accred/cvotext.htm, p. 2):

- Licensure
- Hospital privileges
- Drug Enforcement Agency registration
- Medical education and/or board certification
- Malpractice insurance
- Liability claims history
- National Practitioner Data Bank queries
- Medical board sanctions
- Medicare/Medicaid sanctions
- Provider application

Reviewing credentials for physicians is just one area where managed care organizations sometimes delegate the authority to carry out the task. This is done in those cases where the organization does not have the resources to carry out the task and does not wish to invest in the infrastructure that would be required. The NCQA has an interest in how these delegations are carried out because its accreditation assumes that all activities are carried out according to standards, regardless of whether the tasks are delegated. In that respect, the relationship between the managed care company and the organization to which the responsibilities are delegated must be clearly defined. From the perspective of the NCQA, the managed care organization may delegate the authority to carry out specified activities to another organization, but the responsibility or accountability for those activities remains with the managed care organization. The NCQA allows many activities to be delegated, but there are particular ones that cannot be delegated. These are listed in NCQA written documentation and on the Internet (www.ncqa.org/accred/delgqa.htm, p. 2).

The NCQA maintains a vital interest in the quality of health services delivered by the health care organizations it certifies. As the environment changes and the level of sophistication evolves, the standards by which the managed care organizations are judged change.

Health Plan Employer Data and Information Set

During the past several decades, health care costs have risen steadily and at a rate higher than the general inflation of the economy. As a result, purchasers of health care have sought relief and have done so in the context of finding managed care organizations that could provide a quality product at the lowest price. In the context of history, it seems much more difficult to keep managed care organizations accountable for quality than for costs. Stated differently, both the users of health care and the purchasers are more uncertain about the quality of the product than about the price.

Experience has shown that it is difficult both to define quality and to measure it. In 1989 a consortium of HMOs, large corporations, and benefits consulting organizations developed the first version of the Health Plan Employer Data and Information Set (HEDIS). As the process evolved, it became the goal of the consortium to convert the model into a set of standards that would be accepted by NCQA. By 1991, this goal became a reality, and HEDIS began working with NCQA.

As HEDIS has evolved, it has had both proponents and opponents. Some have suggested that a problem in the past versions is that HEDIS did not adequately address outcomes (Kimball-Baker, 1994). These criticisms, which focus on the issue that HEDIS is too process oriented, cite a number of examples, such as measuring the percentage of children who are immunized but failing to determine whether the health status of the population is actually improved, quantifying how many females receive mammography but failing to answer the question of how long women who have breast cancer live past detection, and failing to deal with the issue of adjusting for demographic factors. In the case of a plan having a high percentage of women who do not seek prenatal care, an undesirable score on the proportion of low-birthweight babies would be expected. HEDIS critics maintain that it should adjust for such demographic variables. Though it is far from perfect, there is evidence that its popularity has grown and that it is becoming much more accepted as a set of measures for ascertaining whether quality is being improved in health care organizations.

HEDIS has now become a set of measures used by managed care plans to demonstrate improvement in various quality standards specified by the data set. Version 2.0 of HEDIS, originally released in 1993, has been used by many health plans to provide a focus for their quality improvement plans required under NCQA.

In 1992 NCQA took on the responsibility for directing the development of HEDIS in an effort to devise a set of performance measures that could compare the results of health plans across multiple constituencies and thereby produce a model focusing on quality improvement in the health care market. It has been widely embraced by a variety of constituencies, ranging from employers to state and federal regulators, to consumer groups. Estimates are that up to 90 percent of all health plans collect some HEDIS data.

In March 1997 HEDIS 3.0 Volume 4, *A Road Map for Information Systems*, was released by NCQA. Over the course of the preceding year, approximately 100 experts from many fields had engaged in an extensive study to determine how health plan information systems must operate in order to support future quality improvement performance measurement efforts. Representatives from the fields of information practitioners, information system vendors, employers, policymakers, and health plan representatives participated in the study, which identified a number of barriers to efficient operation of current information systems to measure quality performance—for example, incomplete databases, lack of quality control in gathering and managing the data, and the lack of ability and inclination to share data across systems.

If systems can be developed that would have the ability to overcome these barriers, there would be a number of beneficiaries (www.ncqa.org/news/isrel.htm, p.1):

- For patients, it will mean that important clinical information will follow them from provider to provider and even from health plan to health plan, making care more continuous.

- For providers, the framework will help alert them to: new therapies; possible pharmaceutical contraindications; relevant facts from patients' medical histories; scheduled preventive interventions; and other important information.

- For Health plans, the framework will facilitate more comprehensive performance measurement activities, as well as more effective care management and quality improvement initiatives.

The work of the NCQA is important to advancing the state of the art of quality measurement. The work of the committee is broken down into seven elements (www.ncqa.org/news/isrel.htm , p. 2):

- A comprehensive set of data elements that are routinely collected by health plans and used to support performance measurement.
- Linkages between systems which ensure that data can be easily and reliably transferred.
- Standardization across all patient care settings specifying consistent structure, content, definition and coding of medical information.
- Data quality screening to constantly monitor and improve the validity and reliability of information.
- Confidentiality and security of patient records achieved through tight controls over data use and access.
- Automation of clinical information, via the adoption of computerized patient record keeping.
- Data sharing between health plans, providers and public agencies in support of performance measurement and improvement efforts.

The ability to overcome the barriers that will make these benefits possible probably has less to do with the technological issues related to hardware and software than it does with the cultural issues related to the willingness of long-time competitors to share information. However, it is important to recognize the importance of the work done by NCQA because it again underscores the critical importance of having appropriate health information available to decision makers. The implementation of the road map is targeted to take place over the next ten years. An executive summary of the *Road Map for Information Systems* can be found on the NCQA World Wide Web page (www.ncqa.org/hedis/isexsum.htm), as well as in printed form from NCQA.

HEDIS 3.0 has evolved to a sophisticated reporting state that in many cases exceeds the information capabilities of the health care organizations reporting on the data set. There are seventy-one separate elements in the reporting set measures, falling into the following eight categories:

1. Effectiveness of care
2. Access/availability of care
3. Satisfaction with the experience of care
4. Health plan stability
5. Use of services

6. Cost of care
7. Informed health care choices
8. Health plan descriptive information

HEDIS has made an important contribution to the field of quality measurement and has been successful in promoting a standard method for systematically reporting a set of quality measures that are widely used across the health care industry. Now that a fair degree of consensus has been achieved in terms of the need for such a reporting mechanism, attention can be turned to refining the measures to reflect and measure more accurately the entire population of people receiving health care in the United States. This refinement should include, but not necessarily be limited to, a more meaningful look at whether the needs of the elderly and the indigent are being addressed by the health care organizations in the market.

Report Cards

Since the aim of NCQA and HEDIS is to provide information to the public that will promote more rational decision making relative to selection of managed care organizations and health care providers, it is necessary that a mechanism be available to communicate this information. One such mechanism is a **report card,** which is a communication mechanism, often in written form, that reports a general broad scope of performance for health care providers and managed care companies. It reports on preselected variables in order to provide information that allows consumers to compare providers. Although the intended use of report cards is to promote provider accountability to potential consumers, they can also evolve into effective marketing and advertising vehicles when the information they communicate is above community norms.

One of the problems with report cards when they are used to change provider behavior is that they sometimes lack the details that would help an individual provider improve in the manner that CQI would advocate. The criticism has been made that instead, report cards give a general or insufficiently specific account of performance. Indeed, in some instances this information is used as a vehicle for determining whether a provider is included in a managed care network, thereby making it much more of a punitive vehicle than a quality improvement tool.

Not everyone thinks that quality reports based on HEDIS are appropriately suited for provider's programs for quality improvement. It is sometimes assumed that individual plans that meet report card criteria are improving quality at the individual provider level when in fact this might not be the case at all. It is the problem of averages where there are some very good performances and some that are not so good. Furthermore, there is a problem with the assumption that all providers deal with the same level of acuity. As these measures evolve, they should show outcomes adjusted for severity of illness and base their results on representative samples of provider populations.

Medicare

Managed care within Medicare has experienced an extraordinary growth. A fact sheet distributed by the HCFA notes that as of January 1, 1997, more than 4.9 million Medicare beneficiaries were enrolled in 336 managed care plans, or approximately 13 percent of the entire Medicare population. There are three types of plans by which a person can become a Medicare beneficiary:

1. *Risk plans.* The managed care plan is paid a capitated amount, which approximates 95 percent of the average expenses for a fee-for-service beneficiary in a given county. The plan must provide all normal Medicare covered services. The plan assumes all of the risk related to Medicare coverage for the beneficiary. As of January 1, 1997, risk plans accounted for 248 of the 336 managed care plans.

2. *Cost plans.* The plan is paid a predetermined amount for each beneficiary each month, based on a projected budget. At the end of the year, retrospective adjustments are made for any variances in the budget. The plan must provide all Medicare covered services. The beneficiary may go outside the plan to receive services, and this becomes a part of the retrospective annual settlement.

3. *Health care prepayment plan (HCPP).* These plans are similar to cost plans except that they do not cover Medicare Part A services. However they do provide for these services and might file Part A claims on behalf of the beneficiary.

Approximately 75 percent of all Medicare beneficiaries have access to at least one plan. Membership in the Medicare managed care plans is concentrated in the states of California, Florida, Oregon, New York, Arizona, and Hawaii.

The elderly population generally want information relevant to their age and health status. They are not interested in services they would not use, such as childhood immunization status, treating children's ear infections, or low-birthweight babies. They tend to have a different set of information needs from other segments of the population. They frequently do not understand what managed care is and sometimes express concern that it represents "second-class" care. Cost is a major concern to them, as is the overall level of quality of care that reflects their age and health status.

This elderly population have significant concerns about the availability of appropriate health care. Given the choices available to them in the form of managed care options, they will change plans when they feel their needs are not being met (www. hcfa.gov/facts/f960900.htm). A study showed that the following questions were most predictive of a Medicare beneficiary's future disenrollment (Lewin and Jones, 1996):

- Were complaints taken seriously by the doctor?
- Did their primary HMO doctor provide Medicare services, admit them to the hospital, or refer them to specialists when needed?
- Did they perceive that their HMOs were giving too high a priority to holding down the cost of medical care instead of giving the best medical care?

- Did they perceive their health worsening as a result of the medical care that they received in their HMO?
- Did they experience long waits in their primary care doctor's office?

These are quality issues in the eyes of a Medicare beneficiary, and there must be a communication mechanism in place to address these concerns. A significant emerging quality issue in the eyes of health care consumers is that they need comparative information about all health delivery options, not just managed care, in order to make informed decisions. Furthermore, they need information that will allow them to evaluate the trade-offs between access, cost, and quality. With regard to the Medicare population, managers of health care organizations would do well to keep in mind that unlike many employed persons who receive assistance from the benefits department of their employers in screening and evaluating their health plan options, most Medicare beneficiaries can rely on only their own judgment and information.

Medicaid

As in the case of Medicare, Medicaid managed care has become a rapidly growing way for Medicaid recipients to receive their medical care. In the 1990s, Medicaid has become one of the fastest-growing publicly funded health care programs, due in large part to the managed care options that are being widely offered around the country. (Cotter, Smith, and Rossiter, 1996). Since January 1, 1993, Medicaid managed care has increased by 170 percent. The HCFA reports that as of June 30, 1996, approximately 13 million Medicaid recipients, or 35 percent of all Medicaid recipients, were members of a managed care plan.

As of January 1, 1997, forty-eight states offer a managed care option for Medicaid recipients. Because of the mandated services, states have had to seek Medicaid waivers in order to be able to set up the alternative programs under a managed care format. In general, these changes in format anticipate achieving savings, which can be used to increase the number of people who can be covered under the Medicaid program. There are two waivers that can be used (www.hcfa.gov/facts/1960900.htm, p. 2):

Section 1915(b) waivers permit states to require beneficiaries to enroll in managed care plans. To receive such a waiver, states must prove that these plans have the capacity to serve Medicaid beneficiaries who will be enrolled in the plan. States often use Section 1915(b) waivers to establish primary care case management programs and other forms of managed care. Through January 1997, HCFA had approved 96 Section 1915(b) waivers.

Section 1115 demonstrations allow states to test new approaches to benefits, services, eligibility, program payments, and service delivery, often on a statewide basis. These approaches are frequently aimed at saving money to allow states to extend Medicaid coverage to additional low-income and uninsured people. Since January 1, 1993, comprehensive health care demonstration waivers have been approved for 15 states, and nine already have been implemented. When all 15 are implemented, 2.2 million previously uninsured individuals are expected to receive health coverage.

Quality Measures on Federally Funded Programs

As managed care Medicaid programs have grown, there is an increasing awareness of the need for quality oversight of the plans. As in the case of commercial managed care plans, there is the potential for the incentives for cost reduction to overcome the incentives for good quality. As a result it became apparent that quality measures must be applied, and several initiatives have emerged.

Medicare HEDIS has been an effort, joined by the Kaiser Family Foundation, that aims at developing a system designed to measure the performance of Medicare managed care plans. As with other HEDIS reporting mechanisms, the central focus is to improve the quality of care to the beneficiaries receiving services from a managed care company while minimizing new reporting requirements for the companies. Health plans providing services to Medicare beneficiaries began submitting Medicare HEDIS data in January 1997.

Medicaid HEDIS evolved as a venture with NCQA and is designed to address Medicaid managed care issues, which can vary state by state. The data are designed to allow all of the stakeholders in the Medicaid programs to have information that provides the ability to judge the effectiveness and performance of the Medicaid managed care plans. Medicaid HEDIS was released in February 1996.

The **Quality Assurance Reform Initiative (QARI)** is a collaborative effort of the HCFA, states, and other interested parties aimed at creating a monitoring mechanism designed to improve the quality of care for Medicaid managed care programs. In 1993 the organization published a range of guidelines that states might use in setting up a quality improvement program. In collaboration with the Kaiser Family Foundation, these guidelines were tested between 1993 and 1995, with the results reported in *Health Care Quality Improvement Studies in Managed Care* (1995). Historically the collection of quality measurement data has relied heavily on claims data. Under QARI, some of this is changing in that it is creating a patient-level database that profiles practice parameters. It uses claims data when they are available and eligibility information when they are not. The QARI program places heavy emphasis on the importance of information for patients as well as for providers. It also envisions creating a state database on key health outcomes at the population level and will include such data elements as health outcomes, processes of care utilization, and customer satisfaction.

Foundation for Accountability (FAcct) is an organization encompassing HCFA, consumer groups, and health care purchasers whose focus is developing outcome measures that compare the clinical work done in the fee-for-service arena with work done in the managed care field. This work is just beginning. In the spring of 1997, the group released outcome measures in diabetes, depression, and breast cancer.

Technology Assessment

The complex issues related to **technology assessment (TA)** have also contributed to the need for quality measurement. With the evolution of technology in health care, quality issues have become important. TA is the activity of determining the cost-effectiveness, safety, availability, and clinical effectiveness of procedures and medical devices as they move from the experimental stage of their development into the mainstream of medical clinical use. It is important that these quality issues be kept in focus in order to minimize inappropriate actions on the part of any of the parties interested in their clinical use.

The federal government has certainly always been viewed as being deeply involved with TA and the implications that it has for the delivery of clinical care. In addition, there are national subscription services that provide TA information to their subscribing members. A consortium of insurers and managed care companies engages in TA. Finally, some individual managed care organizations have TA capabilities within the confines of their own organizations.

As important is this quality oversight is, there has not been a focused and successful effort to coordinate the activity of technology assessment. Richard Rettig of the RAND Corporation, in a study for the Office of the Assistant Secretary of Planning and Evaluation and the Agency for Health Care Policy and Research, said:

> The efforts, largely unsuccessful, to establish a national technology assessment capability in the federal government or in the non-profit sector reveal this deeply-rooted societal ambivalence toward medical technology—we wish to control health care costs but not at the expense of innovation, quality and clinical progress. Society, however is not a decision maker and societal ambivalence toward TA is seldom found at the level of the interested parties. Indeed political opposition to TA by those developing new health and medical care products and bringing them to the market has been expressed strongly and with great effectiveness over two decades. (aspe.os.dhhs.gov/health/xstechas.htm, p. 1)

The federal government has not assumed a central role in TA, primarily because there has not been enabling legislation to do so. With the failure of health care reform legislation in 1994, the large corporate purchasers of health care recognized that if there was to be a successful effort to control costs and maintain quality, it would be necessary to do it from the private sector. Managed care organizations became central to this process because they are among the core stakeholders in the delivery of health care and because of their important role in the financing of health care activities. However, their role was somewhat different from the way TA had been practiced in the past. Formerly, TA was an activity that had a population focus and dealt primarily with the issue of whether the technology was viewed as good and acceptable on a global basis. With managed care, the focus changed to analysis of particular sectors of the health care delivery system and attempts to determine whether physicians and health care organizations are using the technology in appropriate ways. Appropriateness is often judged on the basis of such variables as cost-effectiveness, safety, availability, and clinical effectiveness of procedures.

As TA is being used more and more by managed care organizations, its focus is on managing the care of the patients. That is, the technology assessments are being used to decide whether to provide coverage to patients. The variables of cost-effectiveness, safety, availability, and clinical effectiveness of procedures are sometimes viewed differently by the various stakeholders in health care delivery. For example, some insurance companies refused to pay for bone marrow transplantation for breast cancer patients until they were forced to do so by litigation. At the same time, patients and health care practitioners saw the treatment as beneficial.

These are difficult decisions. The line between being right and being wrong is often blurred. Thus, TA becomes a critically important element in quality measurement, and this quality measurement activity must be well rounded and include the views of all of the stakeholders in the health care delivery process.

TA is a complex analytical process with a direct effect on the level of quality provided to health care recipients. It has many dimensions and is certainly more than simply cost-effectiveness, although cost-effectiveness is part of its focus. However, when TA is conducted on a comprehensive basis, it must also include safety, availability, and clinical effectiveness of procedures as part of its measurement criteria.

Conclusion

Quality is intimately intertwined with the delivery of health care. Each significant player in the health delivery system has reasons to see health care delivered in a way that is not consistent with health practice standards—for example:

- Patients sometimes want more services than are warranted.
- Practitioners sometimes want to provide more services than are consistent with practice standards.
- Payers sometimes want to provide fewer services than are needed.
- High-tech researchers sometimes want to provide their services in lieu of the practice standards.

With these and other conflicting interests vying, it is important that there be a mechanism that assesses quality on the basis of empirical fact. This is difficult and underscores the importance of that body being independent of the areas of self interest.

The measurement of quality in the United States health care system is evolving and has not yet reached a steady state. It might never reach a steady state. However, it is important that the process continue. Without it, the health care system stands to lose much, and that could include its integrity and the confidence of the people who use it.

Review Questions

1. Discuss the similarities and differences between inpatient and ambulatory quality issues. To what do you attribute this phenomenon?
2. Discuss the relationship between costs and quality. Does the relationship demonstrate a positive or a negative relationship?
3. Discuss the similarities and differences between continuous quality improvement and quality assessment.
4. Describe the role and activities of the National Committee for Quality Assurance.
5. How effective do you feel HEDIS has been in measuring quality? Give reasons for your position.
6. To what extent are the NCQA elements designed to improve quality measurement also applicable to health information managers in managing medical records in a provider organization?

References

Cleary, P., & Edgna-Levitan, S. (1996). What information do consumers want and need? *Health Affairs, 15*(4), 42–56.

Cotter, J., Smith, W., & Rossiter, L. (1996). System change: Quality assessment and improvement for Medicaid managed care. *Heath Care Financing Review, 17*(4), 97–115.

Hadley, J., & Wolf, L. (1996). Monitoring and evaluating the delivery of services under managed care. *Health Care Financing Review, 17*(4), 1–4.

Harris, M. M. (1994). Managing the quality of managed care delivery systems. *Journal of Ambulatory Care Management, 17*(4), 59–66.

Hospitals and Health Services Administration. (1995). Special Issue on Continuous Quality Improvement, *40*(1).

Internet URL, http://www.hcfa.gov/facts/f960900.htm. Medicare beneficiaries may enroll or disenroll in a Medicare managed care plan at any time and for any reason, with the only requirement being that a 30 day notification be given.

Internet URL, http://aspe.os.dhhs.gov/health/xstechas.htm.

Internet URL, http://www.ncqa.org/.

Internet URL, http://www.ncqa.org/accred.htm.

Internet URL, http://www.ncqa.org/accred/cvotext.htm.

Internet URL, http://www.ncqa.org/accred/delgqa.htm.

Internet URL, http://www.ncqa.org/hedis/isexsum.htm.

Internet URL, http://www.ncqa.org/news/isrel2.htm.

Kimball-Baker, K. (1994). HEDIS: Searching for the gold standard. *Medical Marketing and Media, 31*(9), 60–64

Lewin, M., & Jones, S. (1996). The market comes to Medicare: Adding choices and protections. *Health Affairs, 15*(4), 57–61.

McLaughlin, C. P., & Kaluzny, A. P., (1994). *Continuous quality improvement in health care: Theory, implementation and application.* Gaithersburg, MD: Aspen.

Chapter 14

Future Impact on Managers of Health Care Organizations

This chapter looks at the issues that are likely to be major factors in the future of health care organizations. Since health care managers will encounter these complex and often formidable complicating factors in their working environment, it is important that they be familiar with these issues. Certainly no one can predict exactly what the future health care environment will look like, but its history, the current environment, and some responsible speculation about the future are presented in this chapter.

Learning Objectives

Upon successful completion of this chapter, the learn will:

- Understand the impact of the international marketplace on future health care delivery systems.
- Understand the impact of technology on how medicine will likely be practiced in the future.
- Understand the dynamics of health care and prevention services, how they interrelate, and why prevention services are important to the future.
- Understand the role of federal, state, and local governments in the evolution of the health care system.
- Understand the impact of the increasing role the patient is likely to play in the evolution of health care.

Key Terms

availability rating | globalization
centers of excellence | graduate medical education
demographic profiles | health profiles
economic rationing | public health issues
educational rationing | telepresence
environmental factors | telerobotics
exogenous variables | virtual network
geographic rationing | World Health Organization

Introduction

Health care managers of the future will be dealing with a much more formidable array of issues than is currently the case. This is because the environment in which health care is delivered will be significantly different. Some of the forces of change will be the same, such as the impacts of technology, government regulatory agencies, and accreditation agencies. Only the outcomes will be different with regard to these environmental forces. In addition, there will be new elements affecting the environment, such as the **globalization** of health care and the customer perspective. All of these forces acting together will produce a new environment in which health care managers must operate.

There are many perspectives from which we might view the impact of future changes in the health care system on health care managers. Many internal and **exogenous variables** will be material in determining the outcome. A few of the perspectives from which the future of health care delivery in the United States can be viewed include the following:

- The lessons of history
- The impact of the globalization of health care
- The impact of technology
- The impact of changing methods of clinical treatment
- The impact of federal, state, and local government policy
- The impact of regulatory agencies
- The impact of the financing mechanism
- The customer perspective

There is a great deal of difference between a description of the ideal health care system for the future and the system that the future might bring. Furthermore, commenting on what the future might be is little more than speculation that has some basis in history and a modest understanding of that history. There are many exogenous variables that must be considered when discussing various scenarios that might evolve in the future delivery of health care. Some of the elements that must be considered include predicting what role the federal government will play and predicting how states and local government will interact and react in the politics of health care. In addition, the role of all of the stakeholders in the private sector will shape the future. Currently there is a struggle for control among institutional providers, individual providers, payers, and employers. In addition, the patients, who currently have little to say about what is happening in health care, are becoming increasingly militant. When we consider all of these elements, which have an effect on shaping the future of health care in the United States, and then put them into the perspective of how health care management might perform within that framework, the complexity of the issue becomes apparent.

This chapter provides a frame of reference that describes what some of the global issues are likely to be if current trends continue. You can use this general frame of reference to speculate on how that environment might affect the future health care delivery system and the people working in it.

The Perspective of History

When we think of the future of health care in the United States, we often think of managed care as the most likely model, and it is quite possible that managed care will the primary form of health delivery over the next ten to twenty years. We also usually think of managed care as being the newest model in a long list of health care delivery models in the twentieth century, as well as being on the leading edge of this activity as we move into the twenty-first century. But someone once said, "There is nothing new under the sun," and that is certainly the case with regard to managed care as a delivery vehicle for health care.

The perspective of history tells us that as early as the twenty-first century B.C., the Babylonians had a managed care system during the forty-three-year reign of Hammurabi, which ended about 2150 B.C. (Edwards, 1904, p. 150). The Code of Hammurabi included such elements as the following (Spiegel, 1997):

- A specifically defined rate schedule for general surgery, eye surgery, fractures, and other defined health care services
- Fees set according to a sliding scale based on the ability to pay
- Universal health care coverage for the population
- Owners (employers) who were responsible for the health care of their slaves (employees)
- Objective outcome measures to assess quality of care
- Data collection and outcomes management as a vehicle to evaluate patient care
- Patients' rights that were publicly announced and communicated to the entire population

The Code of Hammurabi outlined the behavior that was expected in conducting business, holding property, moral and ethical behaviors, and health care. Everyone living in Babylon received health care under the conditions outlined by the edicts of the code, but it was a three-tiered system, and not everyone received the same treatment. Distinctions were made on the basis of social standing in the society.

The Code of Hammurabi makes clear that physicians in the Babylonian culture were respected citizens and should be rewarded with adequate fees, but it also clearly stipulates that they were to be held accountable for the quality of work they performed. The sliding fee schedule based on ability to pay is set out in sections 215 through 217 of the code:

> If a doctor has treated a man with a metal knife for a severe wound, and has cured the man, or has opened a man's tumor with a metal knife, and cured a man's eye; then he shall receive ten shekels of silver. If the son of a plebeian, he shall receive five shekels of silver. If a man's slave, the owner of the slave shall give two shekels of silver to the doctor. (Edwards, 1904, p. 63)

The code provides insights too into the quality of the outcomes that were expected and the penalties that are levied if the appropriate outcomes were not achieved:

> If a doctor has treated a man with a metal knife for a severe wound, and has caused the man to die, or has opened a man's tumor with a metal knife, and destroyed the man's eye; his hands shall be cut off. (Edwards, 1904, p. 64)

These and other expected outcomes and standards by which quality was maintained might be considered extreme in our own time, but they had the same intent as we experience today. Specifically, the interest then, as it is now, was to make sure that the patient received the best possible care and had the best possible chance for having a desirable outcome.

Babylonians kept meticulous records on clay tablets of virtually every facet of its activities. Medical treatments and their outcome were no exception, and thousands of such tablets have been recovered. As a result, the first medical records emerged and were used as the basis for outcomes management.

Of course, we are exaggerating the parallel between the Babylonian health system and managed care of today in order to make a point: that there are certain basic precepts that govern how health care is provided to a population. These precepts include the fact that all people should have access to health care and that people receiving care should be able to expect to receive high-quality services that produce the desired outcome.

The Global Health Care System

Unlike other sectors of the United States economy, the health care system has been substantially insulated from what is happening in the rest of the world. (There are some exceptions to this broad statement—for example, medical technology and pharmaceuticals that are developed and manufactured overseas and sold in the United States and the impact of foreign medical school graduates' receiving graduate medical education and setting up practices in the United States.)

Increasingly, though, links are being demonstrated that tie the health status of a nation to other parts of the world. The following headlines from *The Newsletter of the Pittsburgh International Health Network* give an insight into the range of health care issues that are taking on an international flavor (pw1.netcom.com/~jborton/pih-nmn21.htm):

"U.S. Hospital Competition for International Business Heats Up"

"University of Pittsburgh Medical Center Partners with Italian Hospitals Group"

"Aetna Moves into Brazilian Insurance Market"

"Columbia/HCA Goes Global"

"Cuba to Train South African Doctors"

"Brazilian Heart Procedure Acclaimed in U.S."

"Cigna Moves into Indian Market"

As trade and commerce have become international in scope, it has been necessary to recognize the importance of individual human beings to making the system work, and each of these human beings manifests some level of health status and health needs. Wherever they might be in the world, they need to have health care available to them. A further complicating factor is that the quality of health care varies throughout the world, and individuals might therefore find themselves in a situation where their health status is compromised because of the role they play in international commerce. Increasingly international business leaders are recognizing that health care is a significant factor in their overall operations, as well as their overall costs of doing business.

Just as there are significant problems with the mobility of health care coverage within the framework of the United States health care system, so also there are problems in trying to transport health care coverage across national borders. There are enormous differences for a person trying to obtain health care in a different national environment, true whether one is from the United States trying to receive health care elsewhere in the world or whether one is a foreign national trying to receive health care in the United States:

- The delivery systems are different.
- The financing mechanisms are different.
- The reimbursement mechanisms are different.
- The quality of care is different.
- The general levels of expectations relative to outcomes are different.
- The methods for gaining access to health care are different.

As the economic framework of the world is forcing internationalization of business activities, so also it will become necessary to put a health care framework together that can effectively operate in this international environment and provide a level of care that has some commonality and meets the expectations of the global community.

The guiding principle of health care policymakers in the developed nations has historically been that the health of the population can be improved by increased economic resources. But, in fact, the health status of the population has tended to remain about the same, and policymakers must come to grips with the fact that factors other than health care affect health status. These **environmental factors** include the following:

- Educational level of the population
- Economic status of the population
- Status of the environment
- Social structure of the population
- Housing status of the population
- Nutritional status of the population

It is difficult to deal effectively with health status if these factors are ignored because of their significant impact on the level of the population's health, regardless of the capabilities of the existing health care delivery system.

There is now a shifting perspective in the health care delivery system that takes **public health issues** much more into account than in the past. This has enormous implications for health care managers. For health information managers it is no longer possible to view health records as individual encounters in an acute care setting or even as individual encounters within the framework of an integrated delivery system (**IDS**). Health status must be measured on a population basis, and as such the information must be available on a community-wide basis or, even more broadly, on a national or global basis. Furthermore, if this trend continues, health records in the future will probably contain data that address public health and environmental factors.

This new paradigm will cause health policymakers and practitioners to shift their view from providing health care to a population (after they have become ill) to improving the health status of the population (before they become ill). In order to shift to this new paradigm of health, it will be necessary for the delivery system to change its approach in these ways:

- Create a process that allows for a systematic reallocation of economic resources from health care to other social issues having the potential to change the health status of the population. Areas of future focus must include such social and environmental issues as housing, nutrition, education, wage earning potential, and social well-being.
- Create an awareness within the health provider sector that these changes are desirable and required.
- Create an infrastructure that can accurately and meaningfully measure the cost and quality of health care currently being delivered.

- Create an infrastructure that can accurately and meaningfully measure the health status of the population.

- Create an infrastructure that can accurately and meaningfully measure the changes in **demographic profiles** and **health profiles** of the population and draw valid conclusions from the data, resulting in health policy that improves the overall health status of the population.

- Bring state and federal public policy into alignment relative to social and health issues. For example, a system that provides an incentive not to work because the income threshold to qualify for Medicaid is set too low manifests conflicting public policy agendas.

Ultimately politicians and health policymakers must understand the importance to health of global economic development. This is at the heart of the globalization of health and is central to an understanding of how the health care delivery system will change. Factors that will be critically important to the success of global economic trade in the future include the health of the workforce, the economic strength of the health care sector and its ability to employ people, as well as a full recognition of the costs of failing to prevent disease in the population.

These changes will have an enormous influence on how health care is practiced and managed and in particular how health information management functions as part of the health delivery system's management team. It will be necessary not only to change the paradigm of what health care is but also to understand the changing nature of how it is delivered and documented. Virtually every facet of health care management will have to be reexamined with a view toward changing and improving the processes so they are consistent with the changing paradigm.

The Impact of Technology

Technology—not only hardware that is brought to bear on diagnosing and treating illness but also pharmaceutical research and innovative ways of using currently available diagnostic and treatment tools—is rapidly changing the way health care is being delivered. Capabilities that could only be dreamed about a few years ago are being researched and developed. For example, "Test-tube replacement organs are moving closer to reality, according to Harvard researchers who say they have grown some animal parts. The two surgeons . . . say the technique shows promise for transplants and correction of birth defects" ("Test tube replacement organs," 1997). And, "The technology to reliably transmit high-resolution visual imagery over short to medium distances in real time has led to the serious consideration of the use of telemedicine, **telepresence**, and **telerobotics** in the delivery of health care. These concepts may involve, and evolve toward: consultation from remote expert teaching centers; diagnosis; triage; real-time remote advice to the surgeon; and real-time remote surgical instrument manipulation (telerobotics with virtual reality)" (www.fedworld.gov/ntis). These are just two of many examples that could be cited as remarkable technological developments.

These and other developments like them have enormous implications for how health care managers will perform their jobs in the future. For example, where will the medical record reside in the case of health services performed by telepresence or telerobotics? Who will own the record? Who will be responsible for it? How will physician signatures be handled? How will acquisition of cloned organs be documented? These and other similar questions will come into focus as these technological advancements take place.

In addition to issues related strictly to health information management, other health disciplines will be subject to change as technology imposes its mark on health care delivery. Operational issues related to the delivery of the services will be subjected to significant changes in process. Legal issues related to the changes will have to be examined and tested. Ethical issues will arise and be examined as technology advances. And, of course, the ever-present financing issues will come more under scrutiny as technology evolves.

Prevention Services

Prevention services are often viewed as a vehicle that can add significantly to the health of the population. Immunizations for infants and youth as well as promotion of healthy lifestyles are often cited as examples to illustrate the cost-effectiveness of prevention services in improving the health status of the population. If we view this as a global issue, and not simply a domestic issue in the United States, the work of the **World Health Organization (WHO)** serves as an excellent example of what can be done to promote health in both underdeveloped countries and highly industrialized countries.

The Expanded Programme on Immunization (EPI), for example, is an entity of WHO with responsibility for making safe and effective vaccines available in all countries at an affordable price. Some of its achievements are quite remarkable in improving the health status of the world's population (www.who.ch/programmes/gpv /genglish/brochure.htm):

- It is estimated that 3 million child deaths a year are prevented.

- Approximately 80 percent of the world's children are immunized before their first birthday against diseases the EPI seeks to eradicate.

- Polio cases worldwide are down by over 80 percent since 1988. The disease has been eradicated in the Americas and is targeted to be eradicated globally by the year 2000.

- In 1996 the global EPI network immunized approximately 75 percent of the world's children under age five against polio (450 million children).

- On a worldwide basis, the work of the global EPI network has reduced measles deaths by at least 95 percent over the past two decades in over half of the countries of the world.

- Four new candidate vaccines (including a DNA vaccine) have been developed to protect against tuberculosis, which kills 3 million people a year worldwide.

In the face of results like this in the single area of immunization, it is difficult to argue against the notion that prevention activities improve the health status of the population. When we include the many other prevention initiatives that are ongoing in health care systems around the world, the impact that this initiative can have becomes clear.

Traditionally, prevention initiatives have been in the domain of public health organizations and applied mostly to the underprivileged and medically indigent. The emerging trend suggests that these initiatives are becoming more widely accepted in the population and being made more a part of the traditional health care delivery system. It should be noted that in the United States, immunizations have long been accepted as a prevention modality, but other modes of preventive services, such as lifestyle changes, have not enjoyed a similar level of acceptance.

Once again, this obviously has significant implications for how health care is delivered, documented, and practiced. Delivery of preventive services is accomplished on a mass (screening) basis and is designed to reach the largest number of people with the expenditure of the least amount of resources. The documentation of these activities evolves to community logs of activities rather than individual medical records.

Many of these types of health services are delivered by less highly trained health care professionals than is the case with the care of people who are ill. This does not mean that preventive services are less important or of lesser significance. Rather, the fact that the services can be delivered less expensively on a per capita basis, with lesser trained people, while still having major positive impacts on the health status of the population, is a manifestation of the importance of what the people involved with these services are doing.

Changing Methods of Treatment and Delivery

In Chapter 5 we postulated that the methods of delivering health care in the future might be quite different than they are today. They could include what is being called a **virtual network**. One dimension of the virtual network is that it is far less expensive to construct because it does not require that the assets of the participating organizations be merged by purchase or some other form of acquisition. By contrast with an asset merger, the virtual network requires only that the participating entities agree on a framework for working together. This framework would have to include consideration of governance structure, decision-making protocols, and the conditions under which an operating unit may exit the entity.

A virtual network sometimes includes a number of new concepts about the needs of patients and how patients will respond to certain treatment protocols. These protocols are built on ideas that are coming out of research in the public health field—for example:

- Patients who are physically and mentally able to do so should be permitted to manage their own health care. They would make more of the decisions related to treatment modalities than is currently the case—more of the decisions would be taken out of the physician's purview.

- A variety of reliable ways must be found to give people information about their own health interests.
- Since a large part of the population has accepted radio, television, computer networks, and electronic databases as reliable sources of information, use of these media should be explored in disseminating health information.
- Technology and communication must be brought together to focus on people's day-to-day health needs.
- Effective communication in all forms is the key to better health among people who are physically and mentally able to understand the implications of the information.

These unconventional approaches to health care will require a different approach to the delivery of health care and preventive programs.

As some of these ideas come into practice, health managers will start to think differently about the health delivery process. For example, if the delivery model agrees that physically and mentally capable patients should be permitted to manage their own health care, it must also take into consideration that physicians and institutions will not be the primary entity controlling resource utilization. This is a markedly different paradigm than is now the case and much different from many health care organizations' plans for the future. If the health delivery model that emerges permits physically and mentally able people to manage their own health care, the delivery system must consider its future charter from a number of perspectives:

- Who actually controls resource utilization?
- How is resource utilization controlled?
- How is reimbursement administered?
- How is the system financed?
- How is the care of the patient documented?
- How is the health record of the individual maintained?
- How is the health record of the individual used and made available to those who need to see it?
- How do we ensure that the best and most cost-effective methods of prevention and treatment are used?

A shift from the current institutional-based delivery system to a system based on individual initiative has enormous implications for how health care and preventive services are delivered. The shift from one model to the other need not be disruptive to the health delivery system, nor does it need to disenfranchise any of the current stakeholders. For example, it is difficult to argue that having physically and mentally capable people directly involved with determining the type of health care and preventive services they receive is a bad thing. To the contrary, many health care professionals feel this area needs improvement. If this actually is the case, and more involvement of patients in their own care would improve the process of delivering health care and preventive services, then the model can be changed by the institutional-based delivery systems that now control the process. It requires only modifying the current system and appreciating the point of view of the patient, who in some instances is currently being left out of the decision-making process.

Although there is no level of certainty that treatment and delivery will change in the future, there are signs that the current system is not working as well as might be expected. Some patients are dissatisfied with the treatment they receive. This can be a function of the allocation process of either the managed care company or the institution providing the care. The dissatisfaction can stem from long waits, lack of provider choice, lack of involvement in choices about treatment modalities, and other items of convenience or perceived service. Regardless of the origin of these dissatisfactions, the patient's interests are not always considered in the process of delivering health care or preventive services. To the extent that these current shortfalls of the system are recognized and addressed, they are certain to have significant implications for the future form of the delivery system and the way that it is managed.

The Policy Perspective on Health Care Availability

Rationing is a fact of life in the delivery of health care throughout the world. In general it takes one of two forms.

The first is the system that exists in the United States, where rationing takes place on the basis of whether the individual is able to gain entry into the health care system. The 35 million people in the United States who are either uninsured or underinsured are ample evidence that many are excluded from the system. However, once someone gains entry to the system, he or she usually has access to virtually all of the services that are provided, regardless of complexity or cost.

The second rationing model is one that is used in most of the other developed nations of the world. This approach stipulates that everyone has access to the health care system, but not necessarily everything within the system is available. Furthermore this rationing system often involves capital rationing as well, which controls the amount of technology available, sometimes resulting in long waits for elective procedures.

Neither of these two approaches is desirable, but given the available resources to provide health and prevention services, it is rarely possible for a nation to afford to make every service available to every person.

Although rationing on the basis of economics is the most prevalent and certainly the one most discussed, there are other more subtle forms of rationing that take place. In general, rationing of health care takes place in four forms: economic, geographic, educational, and availability.

Economic Rationing

Economic rationing means that health and preventive services are unavailable to some parts of the population because funds are not available to pay for them. Examples of this process have been discussed.

Geographic Rationing

In the United States, rationing on the basis of geographic location occurs when facilities are not available in the location where they are needed. Most commonly, this occurs in the rural areas of the country or in urban poor areas. An additional dimension of this issue is transportation. In urban areas, people sometimes live within a few miles of available health care resources but have no transportation to get there. Sometimes affluent citizens have difficulty understanding that there are many people who do not own automobiles and whose only way to travel is by public transportation. This problem is compounded by the fact that health care resources in the affluent suburbs tend not to be located on public transportation routes, and few of the medically indigent population have the means to travel by taxi. Thus, many people are denied health and prevention services because of where they live.

We often speak about the surplus of physicians and hospital beds. Simultaneously we speak of medically underserved areas of the country and have even set up federal programs under Medicaid to address this problem. The problem would be better defined not as areas being underserved or having surpluses but rather as having an acute problem with the appropriate distribution of the medical resources. The reason for this maldistribution of resources is mostly a social and cultural issue. Physicians and health care organizations tend to want to operate in large, affluent areas because that is where they are most comfortable being. These resources tend not to be as available in smaller and/or less affluent areas because the health care providers tend not to be as comfortable in those areas. Most of the health provider stakeholders falling into this latter category will protest that they do their share of charity work for society, but even here, there are often wide variances in the amount of charity work that an inner-city urban hospital does compared to those located in affluent suburbs of large urban areas.

Of course, it must also be recognized that there are economic dimensions of this discussion as well. For example, it is not realistic to suggest that there should be a hospital in every rural community. However, it is equally unrealistic not to acknowledge that redistributing some of the excess capacity of the health care system, both physicians and technology, would significantly improve the current situation.

Thus **geographic rationing** is actually a policy issue that must be resolved in terms of better distribution of the excess resources that are already part of the health care system and are currently being financed under the existing system. In this context, there is some validity to the argument that the problem of access to the health care system in the United States is not one of resource availability but rather one of distribution of those resources.

Educational Rationing

Educational rationing occurs when people lack the knowledge to obtain the health and preventive care they require. Several reasons can cause this to happen. One example occurs when people are not aware that they ought to be doing certain things relative to receiving health and preventive services. For example, routine mammography is a widely accepted medical care norm in the health care community. However, in areas where this type of education is not prevalent, it would not be unusual to find a lack of knowledge about the importance of receiving this service. (Of course, the issues of economic and geographic rationing also come into play.)

A second kind of educational rationing occurs when people do not have the knowledge about how to gain access to the system. For example, the process of becoming a Medicaid recipient is relatively complex, and some people who are eligible to become a beneficiary might lack the knowledge of knowing that they qualify. They might also lack the knowledge of how to make the application.

Availability Rationing

Availability rationing occurs when the medical resources required to provide the service are not available. This is rare in the United States, but it does occur. This is a type of rationing that does not have a co-dependency on the ability to pay. In the case of availability rationing, the problem does not resolve itself with the ability to pay for the service. Rather the availability of the service is dependent on an external supply over which the system exercises little control.

You might think that availability would not be a problem in the United States, and in fact in general this has been a problem only when the commodity is quite rare or limited for some noneconomic reason—for example, donor organs, which are in short supply for organ transplant candidates.

The Role of Government

Federal, states and local government will certainly play a role in the evolution of the health care system of the future, although the federal government's initiative to reform the health care system in the early 1990s was unsuccessful. This initiative attempted to address some of the central issues of the health care delivery systems, but due to the powerful lobbies of a number of interest groups, as well as the fact that it might have been too comprehensive and expensive in its approach, it failed. Thus, the United States health care system must still resolve the following issues in the future:

- Approximately 35 million individuals in the United States have no health care coverage or inadequate coverage.
- There is gross excess capacity of the health care system in some parts of the country and significant shortages in other areas.
- Health care coverage often limits other dimensions of a person's life, such as an inability to transfer some health benefits when changing jobs because of preexisting medical conditions.
- There is a maldistribution of physician and technological resources.
- The market-based system is jeopardizing graduate medical education.
- There is a need to maintain quality in the face of continuing pressures to reduce costs.

Although the initiatives of the federal government to take responsibility for the health care delivery system have been rebuffed by other interest groups and the population at large, increasingly it has been focusing on the important dual responsibilities of reducing costs while maintaining appropriate quality. Bruce C. Vladeck, the administrator of the Health Care Financing Administration (HCFA), said in 1997:

> Meeting the beneficiary's health care needs is our reason for being. The way we do that is through purchasing services on the beneficiary's behalf. In the last couple of years, as we have gone through the process of reexamination and restructuring to keep up with the changing world around us, we have identified the agency's core work with the term, "Beneficiary-Centered Purchasing" . . . In the simplest terms, beneficiary-centered purchasing means that we want to ensure that the services we pay for are of the best possible quality at the best possible price. Value means you get what you pay for and you pay for what you need. In other words, services must be appropriate to the needs of the beneficiary and they must be cost-effective. (www.hcfa.gov/speech/utd.htm, April 16, 1997)

It seems likely that the intent of HCFA is to create broader and more meaningful relationships with private sector entities and to collaborate with both public and private sector purchasers of health care. In the past, Medicare has been limited by law from exploring alternative ways of paying for care. The beneficiary-centered purchasing initiative would provide Medicare with additional flexibility in terms of exploring different methods of payment for Medicare. It would move experimental-payment methodologies from the category of demonstrations to common usage. It would include the following approaches (www.hcfa.gov/speech/utd.htm):

- **Centers of excellence** contracting, in which Medicare pays selected high-quality facilities a flat fee for all services associated with a particular surgical procedure.
- Competitive bidding, in which Medicare would set market-based payment rates for nonphysician Part B services, such as medical equipment and laboratory services.
- Global payment purchasing, in which Medicare would selectively purchase services directed at specific conditions or individual needs.
- Flexible purchasing authority, in which Medicare would be able to negotiate alternative administrative arrangements with providers, suppliers, and physicians who agree to provide price discounts to Medicare.

Because the federal government is the largest purchaser of health services by virtue of being the financing vehicle of Medicaid and Medicare, it is able to use its leverage on the market that private sector risk takers are usually unable to exert. Because of the overall pressure on the federal budget, coupled with the private sector pressure for lower prices, the level of aggressiveness on the part of the federal government in seeking value in the purchase of health services is likely to increase.

At the same time that the federal government is collaborating with the private sector in financing health care, it is also working with the private sector in measuring and assuring quality (see Chapter 11). It is comforting to see that there is a recognition that reducing costs alone is not enough. It is also necessary to measure the outcomes and make sure that quality is not declining.

This systematic and continual pressure for lower costs, while maintaining acceptable levels of quality, will introduce new challenges for health care managers. The ability of providers to shift costs to other paying entities is diminishing; the result is that real efficiencies in providing better value in health care will have to be real gains in efficiency *and* effectiveness.

A related issue to financing health care by the federal government is the financing of **graduate medical education** defined as the activity of training physicians in specialties after they have graduated from a medical school. The costs of this training are rarely covered entirely by the resources of the sponsoring institution. As a result, this training must be subsidized. In the past, it was possible to shift some of the costs to the private sector, just as the costs of providing charity care were shifted. However, with the reduction of managed care reimbursement, the ability to subsidize medical education has been severely reduced. Medicare has explicitly participated in paying for the education of physicians but insists it should not be the sole supporter of this education. From time to time, there has been the threat that this participation would be reduced or eliminated. Therefore the position of the federal government on this issue is of vital interest to medical schools and hospitals engaged in the training of physicians.

In general, the federal government is the only purchaser of health services that explicitly pays for graduate medical education. The view of the HCFA is that medical education has similarities to a public good, just as police departments and fire departments are public goods; they benefit society as a whole, and in the absence of a subsidy, there would be an undersupply. The HCFA view goes on to suggest that "just because the government has an obligation to help meet society's need for medical education does not mean that Medicare has the obligation to pay for the entire subsidy. The role of other large purchasers of care must also be evaluated so that they can assume a parallel role in supporting this service" (www.hcfa.gov/speech/alphactr.htm).

A final issue related to federal policy is that of the government's role in dealing with the uninsured, actually much more of a political issue than a moral or ethical one. The Democratic Clinton administration takes the position that it tried to obtain health care reform in the early 1990s and included universal coverage as part of that proposal. This proposal was defeated by a coalition of interest groups that believed the current environment was better than the one being proposed.

It appears that any strategies for resolving this problem at the federal level will involve incremental rather than global changes. This incremental approach resulted in passage of the Health Insurance Portability and Accountability Act in 1996. Given the estimate that approximately 25 million of the people changing jobs are self-employed or have preexisting conditions that might bar them from another group plan, this represents a substantial step forward in reducing the number of people who are uninsured or underinsured. The Clinton administration is interested in further advances and is likely to propose a premium subsidy for the temporarily unemployed and their families. This proposal, if passed, would assist unemployed people with their COBRA payments until they find new employment. COBRA, or the Consolidated Omnibus Budget Reconciliation Act, requires employers to continue to offer health care benefits to most employees and their beneficiaries when group coverage is eliminated. This provision is part of a larger act (COBRA) that covers many other issues.

Both initiatives focus on the segment of the population that is either employed or temporarily unemployed. They do not address the broader problem of universal access to health care. On the other hand, it is a beginning and certainly reduces the overall problem that currently exists.

All of the potential and actual changes in federal policy will challenge health professionals of the future. If nothing else, they will change the way health care is delivered and will change the balance of power in the health delivery system. Health professionals of the future will have to be innovative in their approach to managing this complex environment.

The Patient's Perspective

Throughout this book, we have noted that patients are disenfranchised, with no real voice in the way the health care system operates. However, there now are signs that this is being considered, and in several ways:

- Measuring patient satisfaction from the provider's viewpoint
- Measuring patient satisfaction from the payer's viewpoint
- Increasing political and legislative pressure arising from patient dissatisfaction

Some health care providers understand that patients' satisfaction is an important dimension of the organization's business and financial success. Sometimes this understanding arises from a continuous quality improvement perspective within the day-to-day operations of the organization, and sometimes it results from a focused marketing perspective. Regardless of the origin of the attention to patient satisfaction, the results have sometimes added the patient perspective to decisions relating to the delivery of health care.

As a result of the increasing scrutiny the managed care companies have become more attentive to the level of patients' satisfaction. Certification by the NCQA requires that there be a mechanism in place to regularly monitor the level of patient satisfaction with regard to the services that the managed care company provides. As in the case of the provider's interest in the level of patient satisfaction, this awareness of patients' views has increased the level of input by the patient, with the result that patients are at least minimally influencing important decisions about their own care.

Where the provider and managed care organization patient satisfaction measures do not identify issues that patients believe are important, political and legislative pressures sometimes play a role. For example, when managed care organizations in some states restricted the inpatient length of stay for a normal vaginal delivery to twenty-four hours, there was sufficient patient dissatisfaction that a successful legislative action was initiated that mandated at least a forty-eight-hour stay. When problems must be resolved by these means, it is obvious that the satisfaction measurement techniques used by the managed care companies and providers do not adequately identify or deal with the true problem areas.

Put in the context of health and preventive care of the future, it seems likely that increasingly patients will have more to say about the services that they consume. This change will impose additional dimensions to the health care manager's role. Managers will no longer simply worry about the adequacy of reimbursement and the management of the organization's resources in the context of budget integrity. In addition, they must be aware of and responsive to patients' level of satisfaction with the services rendered.

The Financial Perspective

The final topic is the question of how we pay for health care. Considerable material in other chapters has addressed how the financing system works and how various entities within it manage the finances and operate their organizations. This section will not duplicate that material but rather will discuss the overall financial structure within which the financing mechanism works and out of which financing policy evolves.

When we speak about the financial dimensions of reforming the health care system, the question is the same as when speaking about the use of other resources in the delivery of health care. In a country that is spending 14 percent of its gross domestic product on health care (almost twice as much as most other industrialized countries), it is not realistic to think that additional allocations of the country's resources will be made to health care. Therefore, if the future changes in the health care system that have already been described in this chapter are to materialize, it will probably occur because the system is able to reallocate the use of resources.

Many people, including in the General Accounting Office in the federal government, believe that there is little question of whether the country can afford to make health care available to all of its citizens (Canadian Health Insurance, 1991). The current pluralistic payment system in the United States creates significant waste and inefficiency, in part because of the requirement that every health care provider be aware of and comply with the multiplicity of rules and regulations in each individual health care plan and the obvious corollary that it takes people and systems to comply with those diverse regulations. In addition to the expenses created on the provider side of the equation to comply with the payer rules, costs are introduced because of the duplication of efforts and administrative services within the many payment systems. A Government Accounting Office report stated, "If the universal coverage and single-payer features of the Canadian system were applied in the United States, the savings in administrative costs alone would be more than enough to finance insurance coverage for the millions of Americans who are currently uninsured. There would be enough left over to permit a reduction, or possibly even the elimination of the co-payments and deductibles, if that were deemed appropriate" (Canadian Health Insurance, 1991). If this is true, it is a compelling reason for health care policymakers to consider how it can be improved from a delivery and a financing point of view. Because the question of how the health care delivery system is financed in the United States is clearly an issue of enormous economic importance, it must be a central consideration in any contemplated reforms.

The way health care is financed is not simply a matter of how much money is available to fund the system; in addition, it addresses the far more important consideration of how resources are allocated. Previously in this chapter, the subject of using more preventive services to improve the overall health of the population was explored. This kind of reallocation of priorities and resources is certainly not the only approach to redesigning the health delivery system, but it is a focal point that illustrates the importance of appropriate allocation and use of resources.

A basic question is which, if any, of the stakeholders in the health care system will initiate the changes that are sorely needed. There is actually no shortage of participants who want to control the financing of the health care system. Indeed, the payers, the physician providers, and the institutional providers have all taken aggressive steps to replace the other and thus control the system. However, a successful solution will have to do more than benefit some special interests; rather, it must resolve the problems of all of the stakeholders in the health delivery system: payers, providers, regulators, and patients.

Conclusion

It is no longer possible to think of health care as an institutionally based phenomenon that centers around a hospital, group of hospitals, or other health care organizations. Health care is no longer an episodic series of transactions having a beginning (admission) and an end (discharge). Rather, it is a continuum of health status not only of individuals but of the population as a whole. As the health system evolves, perhaps along the lines of the points outlined in this chapter, people increasingly will receive their health and prevention care in differing modes.

Thus, there are significant implications of health care availability and delivery for the managers of health care organizations. Even if managers elect not to become directly involved in the solution to these problems, they will nevertheless be involved by the solutions that others bring. As the health care system moves into the next century, universal health care should become a central policy priority.

The health delivery system of the future is not going to be of a single type—not entirely preventive care or entirely care of the sick and injured. Nor will it be entirely a low-tech hands-on process or entirely a high-tech approach. It will be a mix of the best elements of the health delivery system and should evolve according to the desires of the population.

Whatever the form that it takes, many of the elements related to its management will become more complex. Health care managers of the future will have to work within the framework of a system that is not pure. The patients will not "belong to a physician," nor is it likely that they will receive all of their care within a single institution, although it is possible that it would be received within a single organization. Medical information will not reside in a single location. Health care—care of the sick and injured and preventive care—will be provided by multiple entities within a community. Given the history of the health care system in the United States, it is likely that the payment system will continue to be a pluralistic one, even though, on the basis of history, it appears to be less efficient than a single payer system.

Thus, as the health delivery system evolves, it will become more and more complex. Those managing its operations must become more skilled in making it efficient and effective.

As we move from the twenty-first century B.C., where the Babylonians had a form of managed care under the Code of Hammurabi, to the current status of health care in the United States and the rest of the world, and then look into the future to try to anticipate what the future might hold in the twenty-first century A.D., we can say that nothing has changed while at the same time everything has changed. Certain basic expectations have not changed:

- That all people deserve certain levels of health care. The nature of the basic level of health care is decided by society as a whole.

- That health care practitioners will be professionally responsible in their delivery of clinical care.

- That there is a financial cost associated with receiving health care. That cost evolves either to society or the individual or both.

- That those providing the health care have a right to make a reasonable living in plying their skills.

Other things have changed significantly and will continue to change as health care evolves:

- Technology
- The legal and regulatory environment
- Delivery vehicles
- Financing mechanisms
- Our scientific understanding of disease processes and their care

When viewing health care from the perspective of over four thousand years of history, it is gratifying to see that certain basic principles have survived, and these represent some important values of society. While taking some comfort in this insight, it is also important to note that in the theory of systems, organizations that do not interact with their environment or fail to change as a result of that interaction usually pass out of existence.

It is the responsibility of health care managers to distinguish between the things that are good and lasting, and therefore ought to be retained, and the things that are not functioning properly or are not providing optimum outcome, and therefore require change. Managers who can distinguish between these two conditions will succeed in the complex and increasingly uncertain field of health care.

Review Questions

1. List and discuss the stakeholders and factors that are likely to determine the form of the future health care market in the United States.
2. List and discuss the factors leading to the globalization of the delivery of health care.
3. List and discuss the environmental factors that affect the health status of the population.
4. What changes are necessary if the health care system is to shift its primary focus from care for illness to the health status of the population?
5. Discuss some of the likely problems that health information managers will face in the future when dealing with health care documentation.
6. How do you think preventive service will evolve in the United States health care system?
7. List and discuss the issues that must be resolved to create an improved health care system for the future.

References

Army Institute of Dental Research. *Quantitative 3-d imaging topogrammetry for telemedicine applications*. [On-line]. Available: http://www.fedworld.gov/ntis.

Canadian Health Insurance: Lessons for the United States. (1991). *United States General Accounting Office*. Washington, D.C.: U.S. Government Printing Office.

Edwards, C. (1904). *The Hammurabi Code and the Sinaitic legislation*. London: Kennikat Press.

Internet URL http://pw1.netcom. com/~jborton/pihnmn21.htm. *Newsletter of the Pittsburgh International Health Network*, December 1996 , February 1997, March 1997.

http://www.who.ch/programmes/gvp. *Global Programme for Vaccines and Immunizations (GVP)*. [No Author].

Spiegel, A. D. (1997, May). Hammurabi's managed health care—circa 1700 B.C. *Managed Care*.

Test tube replacement organs are moving closer to reality. (1997, April 23). *Wall Street Journal*, pp. 1, B2.

Vladeck, B. C. (1997, January 10). Federal responsibility for the uninsured and for graduate medical education. Remarks to Alpha Center, Health Affairs and the Robert Wood Johnson Foundation National Policy Conference on Financing for the Nation's Safety Net. [On-line]. Available: http:\\www.hcfa.gov/ speech/alphactr.htm

Vladeck, B. C. (1997, April 16). HCFA of tomorrow. Remarks to Health Care Financing Administration/University of Texas at Dallas Health Symposium, Dallas, TX. [On-line]. Available: http:\\www.hcfa.gov/speech/utd.htm.

Appendix

Appendix   DRG Table

DRG	DRG Name	Relative weight	Geometric mean LOS
1	Craniotomy Age >17 Except for Trauma	3.0907	7.2
2	Craniotomy for Trauma Age >17	3.0511	7.9
3	Craniotomy Age 0–17	1.9484	12.7
4	Spinal Procedures	2.3858	5.5
5	Extracranial Vascular Procedures	1.5041	2.9
6	Carpal Tunnel Release	0.7582	2.2
7	Periph & Cranial Nerve & Other Nerv Syst Proc with CC	2.4717	7.3
8	Periph & Cranial Nerve & Other Nerv Syst Proc w/o CC	1.2142	2.2
9	Spinal Disorders & Injuries	1.2646	5.1
10	Nervous System Neoplasms with CC	1.2184	5.3
11	Nervous System Neoplasms w/o CC	0.7879	3.2
12	Degenerative Nervous System Disorders	0.9370	5.0
13	Multiple Sclerosis & Cerebellar Ataxia	0.7832	4.7
14	Specific Cerebrovascular Disorders Except TIA	1.1889	5.1
15	Transient Ischemic Attach & Precerebral Occlusions	0.7241	3.2
16	Nonspecific Cerebrovascular Disorders with CC	1.0452	4.6
17	Nonspecific Cerebrovascular Disorders w/o CC	0.6161	2.8
18	Cranial & Peripheral Nerve Disorders with CC	0.9399	4.5
19	Cranial & Peripheral Nerve Disorders w/o CC	0.6293	3.2
20	Nervous System Infection Except Viral Meningitis	2.5786	8.0
21	Viral Meningitis	1.4866	5.4
22	Hypertensive Encephalopathy	0.8594	3.7
23	Nontraumatic Stupor & Coma	0.7777	3.3
24	Seizure & Headache Age >17 with CC	0.9578	3.9
25	Seizure & Headache Age >17 w/o CC	0.5821	2.8
26	Seizure & Headache Age 0–17	0.9601	3.6
27	Traumatic Stupor & Coma, Coma >1 hr	1.2670	3.4
28	Traumatic Stupor & Coma, Coma <1 hr Age >17 with CC	1.1707	4.4
29	Traumatic Stupor & Coma, Coma <1 hr Age >17 w/o CC	0.6383	2.8

Appendix   DRG Table (*cont.*)

DRG	DRG Name	Relative weight	Geometric mean LOS
30	Traumatic Stupor & Coma, Coma <1 hr Age 0–17	0.3295	2.0
31	Concussion Age >17 with CC	0.8369	3.4
32	Concussion Age >17 w/o CC	0.5109	2.2
33	Concussion Age 0–17	0.2071	1.6
34	Other Disorders of Nervous System with CC	1.0385	4.2
35	Other Disorders of Nervous System w/o CC	0.5941	3.0
36	Retinal Procedures	0.6265	1.3
37	Orbital Procedures	0.9725	2.6
38	Primary Iris Procedures	0.4826	1.9
39	Lens Procedures with or without Vitrectomy	0.5406	1.5
40	Extraocular Procedures Except Orbit Age >17	0.7341	2.2
41	Extraocular Procedures Except Orbit Age 0–17	0.3354	1.6
42	Intraocular Procedures Except Retina, Iris & lens	0.5676	1.5
43	Hyphema	0.4119	2.9
44	Acute Major Eye Infections	0.6072	4.3
45	Neurological Eye Disorders	0.6730	2.9
46	Other Disorders of the Eye Age >17 with CC	0.7234	3.7
47	Other Disorders of the Eye Age >17 w/o CC	0.4623	2.7
48	Other Disorders of the Eye Age 0–17	0.2955	2.9
49	Major Head & Neck Procedures	1.8074	3.9
50	Sialoadenectomy	0.8143	1.7
51	Salivary Gland Procedures Except Sialoadenectomy	0.8367	1.9
52	Cleft Lip & Palate Repair	1.2768	2.2
53	Sinus & Mastoid Procedures Age >17	1.0682	2.3
54	Sinus & Mastoid Procedures Age 0–17	0.4790	3.2
55	Miscellaneous Ear, Nose, Mouth & Throat Procedures	0.8366	2.0
56	Rhinoplasty	0.8830	2.1
57	T&A Proc, Except Tonsillectomy &/or Adenoid. Only, Age >17	1.0182	2.7
58	T&A Proc, Except Tonsillectomy &/or Adenoid. Only, Age 0–17	0.2720	1.5
59	Tonsillectomy &/or Adenoidectomy Only, Age >17	0.8238	2.3
60	Tonsillectomy &/or Adenoidectomy Only, Age 0–17	0.2072	1.5
61	Myringotomy w Tube Insertion Age >17	1.1181	2.8
62	Myringotomy w Tube Insertion Age 0–17	0.2933	1.3
63	Other Ear, Nose, Mouth & Throat O.R. Procedures	1.2444	3.1
64	Ear, Nose, Mouth & Throat Malignancy	1.1568	4.4
65	Dysequilibrium	0.5177	2.5
66	Epistaxis	0.5605	2.8
67	Epiglottitis	0.7866	3.1
68	Otitis Media & Uri Age >17 with CC	0.6831	3.5
69	Otitis Media & Uri Age >17 w/o CC	0.5160	2.9

DRG	DRG Name	Relative weight	Geometric mean LOS
70	Otitis Media & Uri Age 0–17	0.3892	2.7
71	Laryngotracheitis	0.6688	3.0
72	Nasal Trauma & Deformity	0.6364	2.7
73	Other Ear, Nose, Mouth & Throat Diagnoses Age >17	0.7660	3.4
74	Other Ear, Nose, Mouth & Throat Diagnoses Age 0–17	0.3332	2.1
75	Major Chest Procedures	3.1958	8.3
76	Other Resp System O.R. Procedures with CC	2.6427	8.7
77	Other Resp System O.R. Procedures w/o CC	1.1150	3.5
78	Pulmonary Embolism	1.4264	6.6
79	Respiratory Infections & Inflammations Age >17 with CC	1.6258	6.8
80	Respiratory Infections & Inflammations Age >17 w/o CC	0.9121	4.9
81	Respiratory Infections & Inflammations Age 0–17	1.5091	6.1
82	Respiratory Neoplasms	1.3329	5.4
83	Major Chest Trauma with CC	0.9716	4.6
84	Major Chest Trauma w/o CC	0.5260	2.8
85	Pleural Effusion with CC	1.2212	5.3
86	Pleural Effusion w/o CC	0.6715	3.1
87	Pulmonary Edema & Respiratory Failure	1.3639	4.9
88	Chronic Obstructive Pulmonary Disease	0.9705	4.6
89	Simple Pneumonia & Pleurisy Age >17 with CC	1.1006	5.4
90	Simple Pneumonia & Pleurisy Age >17 w/o CC	0.6773	4.0
91	Simple Pneumonia & Pleurisy Age 0–17	0.7940	3.7
92	Interstitial Lung Disease with CC	1.1947	5.3
93	Interstitial Lung Disease w/o CC	0.7423	3.7
94	Pneumothorax with CC	1.1857	5.1
95	Pneumothorax w/o CC	0.5974	3.2
96	Bronchitis & Asthma Age >17 with CC	0.8005	4.2
97	Bronchitis & Asthma Age >17 w/o CC	0.5887	3.3
98	Bronchitis & Asthma Age 0–17	0.6298	2.3
99	Respiratory Signs & Symptoms with CC	0.6710	2.4
100	Respiratory Signs & Symptoms w/o CC	0.5109	1.8
101	Other Respiratory System Diagnoses with CC	0.8518	3.5
102	Other Respiratory System Diagnoses w/o CC	0.5295	2.3
103	Heart Transplant	16.5746	32.1
104	Cardiac Valve Procedures with Cardiac Cath	7.3563	10.8
105	Cardiac Valve Procedures w/o Cardiac Cath	5.7109	8.3
106	Coronary Bypass with Cardiac Cath	5.5843	9.8
107	Coronary Bypass w/o Cardiac Cath	4.0812	7.3
108	Other Cardiothoracic Procedures	6.1282	9.4
109	No Longer Valid	0.0000	0.0
110	Major Cardiovascular Procedures with CC	4.1964	7.7

Appendix   DRG Table (*cont.*)

DRG	DRG Name	Relative weight	Geometric mean LOS
111	Major Cardiovascular Procedures w/o CC	2.2409	5.4
112	Percutaneous Cardiovascular Procedures	2.0025	3.1
113	Amputation for Circ System Disorders Except Upper Limb & Toe	2.6579	9.7
114	Upper Limb & Toe Amputation for Circ Systems Disorders	1.5363	6.4
115	Perm Pace Implnt with AMI, Hrt Fail or Shock or AICD lead or Gen Proc	3.5476	6.7
116	Oth Perm Cardiac Pacemaker Implant or PTCA with Coronary Art Stent	2.5321	3.5
117	Cardiac Pacemaker Revision Except Device Replacement	1.1950	2.7
118	Cardiac Pacemaker Device Replacement	1.5889	2.0
119	Vein Ligation & Stripping	1.1997	3.1
120	Other Circulatory System O.R. Procedures	1.9158	5.0
121	Circulatory Disorders with AMI & Major Comp Disch Alive	1.6537	6.0
122	Circulatory Disorders with AMI w/o Major Comp Disch Alive	1.1446	3.9
123	Circulatory Disorders with AMI, Expired	1.4695	2.7
124	Circulatory Disorders Except AMI, with Card Cath & Complex Diag	1.3565	3.6
125	Circulatory Disorders Except AMI, w/o Card Cath & Complex Diag	0.9738	2.3
126	Acute & Subacute Endocarditis	2.4879	10.0
127	Heart Failure & Shock	1.0199	4.5
128	Deep Vein Thrombophlebitis	0.7807	5.6
129	Cardiac Arrest, Unexplained	1.1414	1.9
130	Peripheral Vascular Disorders with CC	0.9410	5.1
131	Peripheral Vascular Disorders w/o CC	0.6040	4.1
132	Atherosclerosis with CC	0.6749	2.7
133	Atherosclerosis w/o CC	0.5360	2.1
134	Hypertension	0.5760	2.8
135	Cardiac Congenital & Valvular Disorders Age >17 with CC	0.8336	3.4
136	Cardiac Congenital & Valvular Disorders Age >17 w/o CC	0.5709	2.4
137	Cardiac Congenital & Valvular Disorders Age 0–17	0.8131	3.3
138	Cardiac Arrhythmia & Conduction Disorder with CC	0.7962	3.2
139	Cardiac Arrhythmia & Conduction Disorder w/o CC	0.4982	2.2
140	Angina Pectoris	0.5993	2.6
141	Syncope & Collapse with CC	0.7005	3.1
142	Syncope & Collapse w/o CC	0.5231	2.3
143	Chest Pain	0.5200	1.9
144	Other Circulatory System Diagnoses with CC	1.0904	3.9
145	Other Circulatory System Diagnoses w/o CC	0.6401	2.3
146	Rectal Resection with CC	2.7356	9.3
147	Rectal Resection w/o CC	1.5885	6.3
148	Major Small & Large Bowel Procedures with CC	3.3883	10.6
149	Major Small & Large Bowel Procedures w/o CC	1.5495	6.5
150	Peritoneal Adhesiolysis with CC	2.7109	9.1

DRG	DRG Name	Relative weight	Geometric mean LOS
151	Peritoneal Adhesiolysis w/o CC	1.2645	4.9
152	Minor Small & Large Bowel Procedures with CC	1.9139	7.2
153	Minor Small & Large Bowel Procedures w/o CC	1.1634	5.2
154	Stomach, Esophageal & Duodenal Procedure Age >17 with CC	4.1851	10.8
155	Stomach, Esophageal & Duodenal Procedure Age >17 w/o CC	1.3350	3.9
156	Stomach, Esophageal & Duodenal Procedure Age 0–17	0.8374	6.0
157	Anal & Stomal Procedures with CC	1.1824	4.0
158	Anal & Stomal Procedures w/o CC	0.6272	2.2
159	Hernia Procedures Except Inguinal & Femoral Age >17 with CC	1.2548	3.8
160	Hernia Procedures Except Inguinal & Femoral Age >17 w/o CC	0.7177	2.3
161	Inguinal & Femoral Hernia Procedures Age >17 with CC	1.0573	3.0
162	Inguinal & Femoral Hernia Procedures Age >17 w/o CC	0.5856	1.7
163	Hernia Procedures Age 0–17	0.8660	3.1
164	Appendectomy with Complicated Principal Diag with CC	2.3412	7.5
165	Appendectomy with Complicated Principal Diag w/o CC	1.2270	4.7
166	Appendectomy w/o Complicated Principal Diag with CC	1.4582	4.3
167	Appendectomy w/o Complicated Principal Diag w/o CC	0.8373	2.5
168	Mouth Procedures with CC	1.1187	3.2
169	Mouth Procedures w/o CC	0.6903	2.0
170	Other Digestive System O.R. Procedures with CC	2.7587	8.1
171	Other Digestive System O.R. Procedures w/o CC	1.1146	3.7
172	Digestive Malignancy with CC	1.2867	5.3
173	Digestive Malignancy w/o CC	0.6744	2.9
174	G.I. Hemorrhage with CC	0.9925	4.1
175	G.I. Hemorrhage w/o CC	0.5366	2.7
176	Complicated Peptic Ulcer	1.1011	4.5
177	Uncomplicated Peptic Ulcer with CC	0.8556	3.8
178	Uncomplicated Peptic Ulcer w/o CC	0.6241	2.8
179	Inflammatory Bowel Disease	1.1100	5.2
180	G.I. Obstruction with CC	0.9153	4.4
181	G.I. Obstruction w/o CC	0.5204	3.1
182	Esophagitis, Gastroent & Misc Digest Disordrs Age >17 with CC	0.7664	3.5
183	Esophagitis, Gastroent & Misc Digest Disordrs Age >17 w/o CC	0.5496	2.6
184	Esophagitis, Gastroent & Misc Digest Disorders Age 0–17	0.5930	2.7
185	Dental & Oral Dis Except Extractions & Restorations, Age >17	0.8424	3.5
186	Dental & Oral Dis Except Extractions & Restorations, Age 0–17	0.3192	2.9
187	Dental Extractions & Restorations	0.7049	3.0
188	Other Digestive System Diagnoses Age >17 with CC	1.0727	4.3
189	Other Digestive System Diagnoses Age >17 w/o CC	0.5488	2.5

Appendix   DRG Table (*cont.*)

DRG	DRG Name	Relative weight	Geometric mean LOS
190	Other Digestive System Diagnoses Age 0–17	0.8786	3.3
191	Pancreas, Liver & Shunt Procedures with CC	4.3490	11.1
192	Pancreas, Liver & Shunt Procedures w/o CC	1.7057	5.6
193	Bilary Tract Proc Except only Cholecyst with or w/o C.D.E. with CC	3.2666	10.6
194	Bilary Tract Proc Except only Cholecyst with or w/o C.D.E. w/o CC	1.6688	5.9
195	Cholecystectomy with C.D.E. with CC	2.7112	8.2
196	Cholecystectomy with C.D.E. w/o CC	1.6075	5.5
197	Cholecystectomy Except by Laparoscope w/o CDE with CC	2.3085	7.2
198	Cholecystectomy Except by Laparoscope w/o CDE w/o CC	1.1693	4.1
199	Hepatobiliary Diagnostic Procedure for Malignancy	2.3523	7.9
200	Hepatobiliary Diagnostic Procedure for Non-malignancy	3.0210	7.5
201	Other Hepatobiliary or Pancreas O.R. Proc	3.4752	11.1
202	Cirrhosis & Alcoholic Hepatitis	1.3255	5.3
203	Malignancy of Hepatobiliary System or Pancreas	1.2605	5.2
204	Disorders of Pancreas Except Malignancy	1.2117	4.9
205	Disorders of Liver Except Malig, Cirr, Alc Hepa with CC	1.2144	5.0
206	Disorders of Liver Except Malig, Cirr, Alc Hepa w/o CC	0.6543	3.2
207	Disorders of the Biliary Tract with CC	1.0507	4.1
208	Disorders of the Biliary Tract w/o CC	0.6039	2.4
209	Major Joint & Limb Reattachment Procedures of Lower Extremity	2.2337	5.3
210	Hip & Femur Procedures Except Major Joint Age >17 with CC	1.8267	6.5
211	Hip & Femur Procedures Except Major Joint Age >17 w/o CC	1.2541	5.0
212	Hip & Femur Procedures Except Major Joint Age 0–17	1.1311	3.9
213	Amputation for Musculoskeletal System & Conn Tissue Disorders	1.6513	6.4
214	No Longer Valid	0.0000	0.0
215	No Longer Valid	0.0000	0.0
216	Biopsies of Musculoskeletal System & Connective Tissue	2.1082	7.4
217	WND Debrid & Skn Grft Except Hand, for Muscskelet & Conn Tiss Dis	2.8033	9.2
218	Lower Extrem & Humer Proc Except Hip, Ft, Femur Age >17 with CC	1.4576	4.4
219	Lower Extrem & Humer Proc Except Hip, Ft, Femur Age >17 w/o CC	0.9631	2.9
220	Lower Extrem & Humer Proc Except Hip, Ft, Femur Age 0–17	0.5800	5.3

accelerated depreciation   Gives the investing organization a higher tax deduction by increasing the percentage of an asset's purchase cost that can be expensed early in its life. Allowed by the tax code.

accounting costs   The market value of the items or service being acquired.

accounts payable   As part of current liabilities, bills from suppliers that are currently due and payable.

accrual accounting   Documents the activity of the organization, measured in dollars, at the time that services are performed.

accrued expenses   Expenses incurred by the organization during a reporting period but not yet been paid (e.g., payroll expenses).

accumulated depreciation   Total depreciation of the purchase price of an asset obtained by adding annual depreciation expenses incurred to date.

active repository   A system whose sole purpose is to gather selected information into a common database and provide the ability to produce, quickly and easily, ad hoc reports for decision makers, regardless of the diverse origin of the data. It can switch data from one system to another and in some cases becomes the primary system for some information users.

activity ratios   Efficiency ratios that measure how many dollars of revenue on the income statement are turned over on a given dollar of assets. Also called *turnover ratios*.

activity-based costing (ABC)   A method that attempts to determine the cost of products by improving the accuracy of allocating fixed costs and overhead on the basis of how they are actually consumed.

actuarial approach to capitation   A method that calculates a capitation rate for each health service covered by the plan.

adjusted annual per capita cost (AAPCC)   The estimated cost of treating a Medicare patient in a given risk class in the fee-for-service system in a local area. Consists of 122 rating cells and is used by health maintenance organizations to determine average payment rates expected from Medicare from a given group of Medicare enrollees.

adjusted community rate   Derived from a community rate charged by a health plan to commercial payers after adjusting for average utilization differences of a group of enrollees.

adjusted community rating   A prospective experience rating approach to premium rate setting used by health maintenance organizations. It adjusts the capitation rate of some groups in the plan to reflect the expected medical expense of the group based on past cost experience.

adverse selection   Arises when those most at risk for a particular adverse health event join the risk pool and those with the least risk withdraw from the pool. As a result, actual medical expenses are higher than expected, creating a loss for the plan. Community-rated plans are more sensitive to adverse selection.

aging schedules   Reports used by accounts receivables managers to show how many months that current unpaid bills have been on the books at a given point in time.

allowable costs   Reasonable accounting costs that the payer permits the hospital to include on its bill to the payer.

ambulatory diagnostic groups (ADGs)   *See* ambulatory patient groups.

ambulatory patient groups (APGs)   Like diagnosis related groups, an attempt to group these patients based on relative cost weights for purposes of reimbursement.

amortization   A measurement of the consumption of a financial asset. To amortize an asset is to reduce its value on the balance sheet over time.

annual update factor   An adjustment to the prospective payment system rate made annually to account for inflation and improvements in efficiency in all hospitals.

annuities   Financial instruments that pay or require payment of a fixed lump-sum payment each period.

arrearages   Overdue obligations to preferred stockholders when the organization is unable to meet a dividend payment.

at risk   A situation in which reimbursement is determined on a prepaid basis and defines coverage within certain parameters. An organization accepting global capitation for a defined population accepts a specific number of dollars per member per month and accepts the risk of providing all of the health care needs that population encounters.

availability rationing   Rationing that occurs when the resources required to provide the services are unavailable—for example, donor organs for organ transplant candidates.

average age of plant   Measures the relative age of long-term assets that distort organizational efficiency comparisons among peers. Found by dividing accumulated depreciation by depreciation expense.

average collection period (ACP)   Average number of days it takes the organization to collect payment from all payers.

average payment period (APP)   Average number of days the organization takes to pay its suppliers.

average payment rate (APR)   The average per member per month payment that a local health maintenance organization can expect from Medicare based on the adjusted annual per capita cost of its enrollees. *See* adjusted annual per capita cost.

balance billing   The practice of charging the patient for the unpaid difference between billed charges and Medicare customary, prevailing, and reasonable charges.

balance sheet   Shows the dollar value of what the health care organization owns at a point in time and the corresponding obligations to creditors and shareholders who put up cash to finance their purchase. Also called the *statement of financial condition*.

best practices   Fixed protocols by which patients are treated within disease categories that are generally agreed on by most experts as providing the best results. Also referred to as *critical path*.

binomial distribution   A distribution of outcomes of an event that can have only two possible results: heads or tails, win or lose, male or female.

blended rate   A payment derived from a weighted average of the provider's own operating costs and a federal rate.

bond covenants   Creditor restrictions on the total amount of debt an organization can incur at any one time.

bond insurance   Insurance purchased by the organization that issues bonds to protect bondholders from the possibility that the issuing organization cannot meet its payments.

book value   The adjusted value of an asset after subtracting accumulated depreciation from the original purchase price.

break-even analysis   An analysis of the volume of goods or services that must be sold by the organization in order to recover its fixed and variable costs given the price it expects to receive. This analysis can also be used to set the price charged in order to cover fixed and variables costs if volume is known.

business risk   The variability of net income of an organization with no debt. Net income variability can arise from uncertainty of revenues, amplified by the degree to which the expenses of the organization are fixed.

call option   Gives the issuing health care organization the right to buy back its outstanding bonds before maturity, usually for a stated fee, known as a call premium.

call premium   The fee paid by the organization that issues a bond for the right to buy back bonds before they mature.

capital asset pricing model (CAPM)   A model to assess the return required by market investors on individual stocks. It is derived from a theory of how investors value market securities in the presence of economy-wide risk that cannot be diversified away.

capital budgeting   The process of deciding which long-term assets to acquire to fulfill the mission and goals of the organization.

capital structure   The relative amounts of debt and equity used to purchase assets.

capitalization   Financial ratios that measure the organization's use of financial leverage in acquiring its assets. Also referred to as *capital structure ratios*.

capitation   A method of reimbursement whereby a health care provider is reimbursed a fixed amount each month for each covered life, regardless of the amount of health care services consumed by the insured.

carrier   The organization responsible for providing administrative services in conjunction with taking the risk for health care coverage. Usually an insurance company or a health maintenance organization.

carve-outs   Parts of routine health care delivery that are contracted separately ("carved out") from the rest of the medical services received (e.g., behavioral medicine services, laboratory services).

case management   Management that focuses on meeting the complex health care requirements of a patient by improving the communication among all professionals taking care of him or her.

case mix index   In hospitals, measures patient acuity derived from a weighted average of diagnosis related groups' cost weights assigned to patients.

case rate pricing   A reimbursement method where the health care provider is paid a single amount for care of the patient during a specific illness. Diagnosis related groups are an example of this type of reimbursement.

cash accounting   A method of accounting that reports activity only when cash is received and paid, regardless of when the related services were actually performed.

cash conversion schedule   Traces out the pattern of cash outflows and inflows of an organization over time.

cash equivalents   Short-term securities that are readily converted to cash without a loss in return.

cash flow to total debt   A leverage ratio that reveals the amount of cash relative to total debt outstanding.

centers of excellence   In the context of this book, specially recognized and designated health centers that provide particular health services to a defined population for a contractually agreed-on price; usually selected on the basis of national reputation in a specific area of expertise, such as cardiac transplantation.

certificates of deposit (CDs)   Short-term notes that banks use to borrow money from the public to raise cash. Negotiable CDs can be bought and sold in secondary markets before they mature.

clinical integration   Focuses on organizing the provision of clinical care by systematizing the services to the patient in a way that produces the best possible outcomes at the lowest possible cost.

clinical pathway   A protocol for the treatment of a particular disease entity that specifies the clinical activities that should take place and in what time frame. They generally exist in the inpatient acute care setting and are not as prevalent in the ambulatory area.

co-insurance   *See* co-payment.

co-payment   The amount of the bill that the beneficiary is required to pay for each health care encounter; can be specified as an absolute dollar amount or as a percentage of the bill for the encounter. Also referred to as *co-insurance*.

commercial paper   Short-term notes sold to the public by large corporations as a means of raising temporary cash.

common procedural terminology (CPT) codes   Codes developed by the American Medical Association to classify and bill for physician services.

common size ratios   Standardized ratios constructed from the financial statements by dividing each entry by some common denominator.

common stock   Certificates of ownership in an organization that guarantees no regular dividends.

community rating   An insurance risk rating system whereby the premium charged to enrollees in each group in the plan is based on the expected cost of providing health services to all enrollee groups covered by the plan.

comparative analysis   *See* horizontal analysis.

compensating balances   Minimum cash balances that must be maintained in a bank checking account to access bank lines of credit or other services.

completion factors   Factors that show what percentage of total claims for services provided in a given month are received in each month during and following service.

composition ratio analysis   An approach to financial statement analysis that relies on constructing standardized ratios from the financial statements of different-sized but otherwise similar health care organizations.

compounding   Interest that is paid on interest earned in a previous period. Compounding increases the effective annual rate of return to the investor or the amount of interest paid by the borrower.

concentration banking   The process of consolidating payments in a single bank.

concurrent review   An evaluation of the care of a patient while it is being given by using medical criteria established by qualified medical personnel to compare length-of-stay norms with the care that is actually being rendered. The evaluation is conducted to determine whether the continued stay is medically necessary and that the resources being used are appropriate.

consolidated balance sheet   Reflects the aggregation of the balance sheets of all entities in an organization.

consumer price index (CPI)   An index created by the United States Bureau of Labor Statistics that is a weighted average of prices faced by a typical urban consumer for goods and services normally consumed; used to measure changes in the cost of living, or consumer inflation, and to remove price effects from dollars spent by consumers at different points in time.

contingency reserve   Balance sheet accounts, often required by state insurance regulators, dedicated to providing for the payment of unexpected future subscriber or enrollee health care claims.

continuous quality improvement (CQI)   A process that assumes that every process can be improved and that the result of the improvement will be both better efficiency and higher quality.

continuum of care   The entire range of clinical services that a patient might use, ranging from wellness initiatives and patient education to tertiary and quaternary care in the acute care setting.

contractual allowances   Dollar amounts that must be subtracted from gross revenues to account for special discounts and other reimbursement arrangements with third-party payers.

contribution margin   The difference between the price and variable cost incurred in delivering a unit of service. Measures the amount earned per unit that can be used to cover fixed costs.

conversion factor   A national average payment rate set prospectively and used to convert relative value units for a physician service into the amount the physician can expect to receive from Medicare.

coordination of benefits   Revenues obtained from other insurers that also cover enrolled members of a managed care or commercial insurance plan.

corporate finance   A management discipline concerned with financing and investing decisions.

corporate risk   The degree to which the project's rate of return is correlated with the rates of return on the cash flows of the entire organization.

cost centers   Departments within an organization having expenses but no revenue—for example, the human resources department. Management is therefore focused on managing costs.

cost finding   A strategy to minimize accounting costs that could be allocated to a cost-based payer in order to maximize reimbursement.

cost of goods sold   An income statement entry that reports the supply expenses in a manufacturing organization.

cost shifting   A pricing strategy that charges higher rates to payers paying billed charges to cover costs uncompensated by other payers.

cost-based reimbursement   A third-party payment system that pays the provider on the basis of reasonable costs incurred in treating the payer's enrollees or beneficiaries.

cost-benefit analysis   Applies capital budgeting techniques to nonmarket and governmental activities.

coupon   Regular cash payments over the life of a bond. The coupon is derived from the coupon rate, which is multiplied by the face value of the bond.

coupon rate   On a bond, the interest rate that establishes the amount of the coupon paid regularly to investors.

covered services   Health care services reimbursed under a health care plan.

cream skimming   A practice whereby managed care organizations target and market insurance to companies with healthier subscribers.

credentials verification organizations   Entities whose business is assisting managed care and other health care organizations to evaluate and verify the credentials of health care practitioners.

critical path   *See* best practices.

current assets   Short-term assets that are expected to be converted to cash in a year or less. Also referred to as *working capital*.

current asset turnover   An efficiency ratio that measures how many dollars of revenue are produced from a dollar of current assets.

current liabilities   All short-term obligations of the organization that must be met within a year.

current portion of long-term debt   A current liability of the organization indicating the amount of principal owed during the year on outstanding long-term bonds.

current ratio   The amount of current assets available to cover current liabilities.

customary, prevailing, and reasonable (CPR) charges   A reimbursement system according to which physicians receive the lowest of three alternative fees: billed charges, the seventy-fifth percentile of customary charges of all physicians, or the physician's median charge over a prior twelve-month period.

data warehouse   A system architecture where data are taken from diverse production systems and make ad hoc reporting available to organizational decision makers regardless of the origin of the data. Also referred to as *data repository*.

days' cash on hand   A liquidity ratio that calculates the ability of the organization to pay its ongoing expenses with cash and short-term marketable securities.

debt service coverage ratio   A leverage ratio indicating the regular ability of the organization to cover debt service out of operating cash flows plus interest. Debt service is principal payments plus interest due to creditors.

deductible   The amount the beneficiary must pay before the payer makes any payment to the health care provider; usually stated in terms of an absolute dollar amount and can be applied to each individual or to the entire family when family coverage is involved.

deferred tax liability   A liability entered on the balance sheet to avoid reporting lower profits when using accelerated depreciation. Straight-line depreciation is used in reports to shareholders.

demographic profiles The ability to measure the demographic characteristics of a population—for example, on age, income, education, and similar other measures.

depository transfer checks Checks are used to concentrate payments received by several banks at one bank.

depreciation expense A noncash expense to the organization to account for the wearing out of a long-lived real asset.

diagnosis-related groups (DRGs) Derived from over 495 diagnosis-related categories derived from the International Classification of Diseases, 9th Revision, Clinical Modification codes to determine hospital reimbursement. Each DRG is assigned a cost weight to reflect the average resource costs of treating patients in that group.

direct service delivery plan A health plan in which the insurer not only reimburses providers directly for services and establishes prices and reimbursement in advance but also restricts eligible service providers and sometimes oversees and manages the delivery of health services to members.

discharge planning An activity that coordinates all of the resources of the organization, including medical and nonmedical activities, to achieve a timely discharge for patients who no longer require inpatient acute care services and their placement in the appropriate level-of-care setting.

discount bonds Bonds that do not pay coupons and return only the face value at maturity.

discounted cash flow analysis Converts future cash flow to present values to assess the financial implications of alternative investment opportunities.

discounted fee-for-service system Reimburses caregivers on the basis of a percentage discount from prices or billed charges.

discounted payback period (DPP) Uses discounted future cash flows of the project to calculate the payback period.

diversification strategy A strategy by which organizations enter into a range of related businesses rather than concentrating on a core activity. Integrated delivery systems are examples of this strategy, whereby the organization attempts to provide all of the activities related to health care.

dividends Portion of net income returned to investors.

downgrade Used by bond rating agencies when an organization's excessive debt or other factors increase the risk of default on its bonds. Downgrades increase the cost of debt to the borrowing organization.

downside risk The risk associated with losses that a managed care organization and/or provider experiences as a result of providing health care services.

DuPont analysis Analysis that decomposes return on equity into its three underlying components: profitability, efficiency, and financial leverage.

duration Measures the effective maturity of an asset or liability by taking into account the cash flows of a security that occur prior to maturity.

economic costs The amount of resources that it would take to acquire the use of some item or service.

economic profit Occurs when a project is found to make more than its opportunity costs.

economic rationing Rationing that occurs when health and preventive services are unavailable to the population because of a lack of funds to pay for them.

economies of scale   An economic concept that suggests that as the volume of work increases, the unit cost of that work will decrease because fixed cost is covered and the only incremental costs of additional business are the variable costs.

educational rationing   Rationing that occurs when people lack the knowledge to obtain the health and preventive care they require.

effective annual rate (EAR)   The amount of return earned (or interest paid) when interest is compounded during the year.

efficiency   A measure of financial performance that looks at how well the organization's assets and liabilities are being managed and used to provide services.

employee assistance programs (EAP)   Services usually provided by employers to employees aimed at dealing with employees' personal problems (e.g., substance abuse, marital problems, financial problems) that inhibit productive work.

environmental factors   Factors that traditionally have not been regarded as health care issues but nevertheless affect the health status of the population—for example, education and housing.

equity financing ratio   A leverage ratio that measures the percentage of the organization's assets funded by equity.

equity multiplier   The inverse of the equity financing ratio.

excess revenues over expenses   *See* net income.

exogenous variables   Variables outside the control of the people managing a particular enterprise—for example, laws and regulations.

expense/budget approach to capitation   An approach in which total revenues and total expenses for the managed care plan's operations are projected for the coming year.

experience rating   An insurance risk rating system that uses the prior experience of an individual or group of enrollees in a single health plan to determine and set future premiums for that individual or group.

face value   The amount paid on a security at the end of its life, or at maturity. Also referred to as *par value*.

factoring of receivables   Selling receivables for cash to a bank, collection agency, commercial factor, or other purchaser.

fee-for-service (FFS) system   A payment system in which a health care provider charges a specific price for each identifiable and distinct unit of service or good sold in the course of treating a specific patient.

financial accounting   A business discipline concerned with developing and keeping accurate, timely, and comparable data that reflect real activity and performance of the organization.

financial credentialing   The process of building and maintaining a health delivery network that includes only those physicians and health care organizations that have historically demonstrated a pattern of cost-effective health care.

financial leverage   The relative amount of debt financing used to acquire its assets. Ratios to measure it are also called *capitalization* or *capital structure ratios*.

financial management   The efficient and effective use of financial resources to achieve the mission and goals of the health care organization.

financial risk   Any exposure to a possible gain or loss resulting from a monetary investment. In health insurance, the insurer loses invested capital when medical expenses are higher than expected and makes a financial return when medical expenses are lower than expected.

fixed asset turnover   An efficiency ratio that measures how many dollars of revenue are produced from a dollar of fixed assets.

fixed costs   Costs that do not change with the number of units of service provided (e.g., interest, rental expense, managerial overhead).

flotation costs   Costs associated with issuing bonds. They tend to be considerably lower than the cost of issuing stocks.

for-profit   A status under the Internal Revenue Code whereby the organization is subject to all taxes levied against ordinary business institutions.

Foundation for Accountability (FAcct)   An organization involving the Health Care Financing Administration, consumer groups, and health care practitioners whose focus is to develop outcome measures that compare the clinical work done in the fee-for-service arena with work done in the managed care field.

functional integration   Focuses on integration by service line or function. This view attempts to make the individual functions of the total organization as efficient as is possible while attempting to capitalize on gaining efficiency by specialization within the functions.

fund accounting   An accounting system used by not-for-profits to account for the use of donated funds and grants that are restricted as to their use.

gatekeeper   Usually primary care physicians who attend to the general health needs of the population and are solely responsible for referring patients to specialty and subspecialty physicians.

general fund   In fund accounting, records activities of the organization that are not restricted by the external funding agency.

geographic rationing   Rationing that occurs when facilities are unavailable where they are needed, with the result that people are unable to obtain health and preventive services.

globalization   In the health care delivery system, the expanding environmental effects that the global community will have on health care delivery in the United States and the rest of the world.

goodwill   The appreciation in the value of assets of an acquired organization over what is currently shown on the balance sheet. An equal amount of new equity is posted on the right side of the balance sheet.

graduate medical education   That part of a physician's education after he or she has earned the M.D. or D.O. Residencies in clinical specialties are the primary example.

gross domestic product (GDP)   The total dollar spending for consumption, investment, and government goods and services over a given period of time—usually quarterly or annually.

gross revenues   The total revenues of a health care organization before any adjustments are made for contractual discounts.

HCPCS codes   Treatment codes based on the common procedural terminology codes developed by the American Medical Association to classify physician services as well as additional codes for nonphysician services.

Health Care Financing Administration (HCFA)   The federal body that makes and administers policy related to all federally funded health care initiatives.

health maintenance organizations (HMO)   The prototype managed care organization in which delivery and financing of health services are combined into a single organization.

Health Plan Employer Data and Information Set (HEDIS)   A set of measures the managed care plans to demonstrate improvement in various quality standards specified by the data set.

health profiles   The ability to assemble health status indicators for a population—for example, on immunizations and preventive initiatives.

health status risk   Uncertainty surrounding the chance that a person will experience an adverse health event and require treatment. Health status risk, and its avoidance or reduction, is the concern of public health professionals.

health system   A method of organization that focuses primarily on integration of similar entities, which in many instances are acute care hospitals.

horizontal analysis   Financial statement analysis that compares the financial performance and condition of an organization to a group of peer organizations.

horizontal integration   The integration of similar entities.

income statement   Shows the activity (what was produced and the related costs) of an organization over an interval of time. Also known as the *statement of revenues and expenses*.

incremental costs   Costs that arise as a direct result of an investment. Only incremental costs should be included in cash outflows.

incurred but not reported expense to current liabilities (IBNR)   A leverage ratio for managed care plans that shows the estimated amount of claims that have not yet been billed as a proportion of current liabilities.

indemnity insurance plans   Plan that reimburses enrollees directly for their medical expenses. These types of plans have not typically interfered with provider decisions except when they involve fraud. Consumer decisions are influenced by co-payments and deductibles, as well as maximum benefits clauses.

independent practice association (IPA)   A method of organizing independent physician practitioners in a way that allows them to operate collectively with regard to business practices (e.g., managed care contracting , billing, practice management).

individual providers   Individual physicians, allied health professionals, and other licensed caregivers who provide health care to the community.

inflation   The persistent rise in the average level of prices.

inflation rate   The rate of increase in prices over a period of time.

initial public offering   Sales of shares in a company that previously had not issued shares to the public.

institutional providers   Usually facilities such as hospitals, ambulatory surgery centers, and ambulatory treatment centers that provide health care services.

intangible assets   Assets that add value to the organization that typically cannot be seen, held, or separated from other assets used (e.g., reputation, patents, an experienced workforce).

integrated delivery networks (IDN)   Groups of institutional providers and individual providers organized into a single health care delivery network. This integration often comes from entities with diverse backgrounds and are carried out with the purpose of making the total organization more efficient and providing more leverage for negotiation within the marketplace. Also referred to as *integrated delivery system.*

integrated delivery system (IDS)   *See* integrated delivery network.

interest rate risk   Risk that borrowers (lenders) bear when the possibility exists that they will be locked into high (low) coupon rates on long-term debt when market prices fall (rise).

internal rate of return (IRR)   The discount rate that makes a series of future cash flows exactly equal to an initial dollar amount invested.

investment bankers   Bankers that help organizations find buyers and place (sell) their bonds. Commercial bankers provide business loans to organizations.

issuance costs   Costs of marketing and selling stock, fulfilling legal requirements, and meeting Securities and Exchange Commission regulations.

just in time (JIT)   Inventory management systems that minimize the cost of inventory to the organization by delivering supplies as close as possible to the time they will be used.

lag report   Cross-tabulations of the behavior two variables over time. They assist the health plan in understanding the billing patterns of its providers in order to estimate monthly medical expenses.

law of large numbers   A law from mathematical statistics that states that in a given sample of identical individuals, the standard error of the expected loss will decline as the sample size increases. The standard error of the estimated loss is the objective risk of a group in the same risk class. The insurers can reduce their objective risk by increasing the number of members in a given risk pool.

line of credit   An arrangement through a bank to provide loans up to a certain amount at any time that can be used to meet daily expenses.

liquidity   A property of assets that indicates how easily and quickly they can be turned into cash.

liquidity ratios   Ratios that measure the organization's ability to meet short-term payment commitments to workers, suppliers, and creditors.

loading   The amount added to the expected medical expenses, or pure premium, of a health insurance plan to cover the cost of plan administration, taxes and profits. The price of financial security when insurance is purchased.

lockbox services   A system whereby patients and party payers mail payments to a post office box, where they are collected daily by a local bank and immediately credited to the provider's account.

long-term assets   Assets that are expected to take more than a year to be "used up" and returned as cash to owners.

long-term debt-to-equity ratio   A leverage ratio that reveals the relative use of long-term debt to finance assets. Also called the *debt-to-equity ratio.*

managed care   The outside involvement or intervention in the health treatment decisions made by physicians or patients.

managed care integration   An integration method that organizes to provide the entire continuum of care, including physician and hospital services.

managerial (cost) accounting   A financial management discipline that develops cost and productivity statistics to be used internally by management to plan, budget, and determine pricing.

marginal cost of capital   The opportunity cost of the next dollar raised to finance a project.

market failure   A system in which adequate incentives, financial and otherwise, are not in place to encourage appropriate behaviors. In the health care sector, it usually results in overuse of services.

market portfolio   Shares in a portfolio containing, in theory, all securities available in the economy.

market risk   Risk measured by the variability in the returns on the market portfolio that cannot be eliminated by diversification.

maturity   The length of time that cash is left invested. Typically used when referring to bonds.

maturity matching   Financing assets with liabilities of the same maturity.

mean   Mean expected or average value of an outcome or an event.

Medicaid   A state-administered program, funded jointly with the federal government, to provide access to acute and long-term health services to the poor.

medical care risk   Arises from uncertainty about actual services that will be used to treat an adverse health event and the costs per unit of treatment. Physician practice patterns have a major effect on variability in services provided. Volatility in health care inflation can contribute to uncertainty in cost per unit. Together, health status risk and medical care risk determine objective risk of the insurer.

medical loss ratio   The ratio of realized medical expenses to the total premium received by the health insurance plan.

medical price index (MPI)   A weighted average of the prices of a fixed market basket of health goods and services consumed by the typical urban consumer, which is used to construct the health care component of the Consumer Price Index.

medical underwriting   Occurs when the capitation and premium rate are based on an individual's own medical expense risk rather than group risk. It often results in the denial of coverage in the presence of preexisting conditions.

Medicare   A federally financed entitlement program that provides access to acute health services and health insurance coverage to the aged and disabled.

Medicare cost reports   Reports required to be filed by hospitals and other providers that receive Medicare reimbursement with the Health Care Financing Administration documenting direct and overhead expenses on which payment is based.

Medicare risk contracts   Capitated contracts between the Health Care Financing Administration and federally qualified health maintenance organizations or comprehensive health plans.

modified cash basis of accounting   A system that uses a cash basis for most items but also shows noncash expenses like depreciation and prepaid expenses.

modified internal rate of return (MIRR)   An alternative to the internal rate of return (IRR) decision rule for capital budgeting that removes the overstatement of expected returns present in the IRR.

money market mutual fund   An investment fund made up of a portfolio of short-term assets whose cash flows are used to pay returns to investors.

moral hazard   An incentive-created insurance for insured individuals to use more services or expose themselves to greater health risk than would be expected in the absence of insurance. Also referred to as *insurance-induced demand*.

mutual fund A portfolio of stocks and bonds.

National Committee for Quality Assurance (NCQA) An independent, not-for-profit organization that evaluates how a health plan manages all parts of its delivery system.

National Health Expenditures (NHE) The total dollars spent by consumers and government for health-related goods and services.

net assets The net worth, or community equity, of the not-for-profit organization. Before 1996, referred to as *fund balances.*

net income margin The total profitability of the organization after adding nonoperating gains.

net operating income The item on the income statement that remains from revenues earned from providing health services after all related expenses have been taken into account.

net patient revenues Gross revenues adjusted for contractual allowances. This measure of total revenues shows what the organization expects to be paid for the delivery of services.

net present value (NPV) The discounted present value of a project's future cash flows after subtracting the initial cash outflows of the project.

net working capital The difference between the value of current assets and current liabilities. Must be funded by long-term debt or equity.

net worth The difference between available assets and outstanding liabilities; represents the owner's equity in the organization—what remains after all creditors have been paid.

nonoperating gains and losses Revenues net of expenses resulting from activities or investments not directly related to the principal activity of the organization.

nonparticipating physicians Physicians who choose not to accept Medicare fees as payment in full.

normal distribution A distribution of outcomes that take the form of the bell-shaped curve.

not-for-profit A status under the Internal Revenue Code whereby the organization is not subject to income taxes but is required to adhere to the expectations under the code that the entity will not allow any of the profits to inure to the benefit of individuals and that it will be a service organization to the community. Most not-for-profit health care institutions are covered under section 501(c)3 of the Internal Revenue Code.

objective risk The average difference between expected and actual claims experience of an insured group. In health insurance, objective risk results from both health status risk and medical care risk.

operating margin A profitability ratio that measures the income from providing health-related services as a percentage of operating revenues.

opportunity cost The amount that could be earned or the benefit obtained from a resource's next best use.

organized delivery system *See* integrated delivery network.

paid-in capital Cash invested to start up an organization.

par value *See* face value.

passive repository A warehouse for data that gathers and stores the information in preparation for ad hoc reporting requests. Its sole function is to provide an integrated reporting capability from diverse systems within an organization.

pass-through payments Separate payments to hospitals under the prospective payment system that are independent of health care services delivered to patients.

patient encounters   Office visits, specific treatments, lab work, and other services provided to patients.

payback period (PP)   Measures the number of years until the project's cash outflows just equal the project's cash inflows.

payer fiat   A pricing methodology whereby the payer unilaterally sets the reimbursement rate without negotiation or consultation with the health care providers.

payer mix   The proportion of revenues expected from different payers.

per diem pricing   A reimbursement method where the health care provider is paid an amount for each day of care the patient receives. Usually associated with inpatient acute hospital care.

per member per month (PMPM)   The reimbursement methodology most common to capitation. It is a negotiated amount that a health care provider agrees to receive for each covered beneficiary each month in return for providing specified services for a defined population.

periodic interim payments (PIP)   Medicare-made cash payments to hospitals and other providers in a regular basis, supplying working capital for hospital operations. Adjustments to PIPs received were made retroactively based on realized utilization.

perpetuity   An annuity that never ends. It provides a fixed cash payment to the owner forever.

physician integration   An integration strategy organized around physician practices. While organizing to provide the entire continuum of care, the focus of this approach to integration is the physician practice.

pluralistic payment system   A multiplicity of reimbursement systems in the same health care delivery system.

point of service   A method of providing medical services to enrollees where they have a choice of physicians to see. Rather than having to go to a particular clinic for services, the enrollee may choose the office of any physician who is part of the network.

precautionary demand for money   Occurs when organizations and households keep cash on hand as a buffer against uncertain timing and size of future bills.

precertification   In the inpatient acute care setting, requires the physician to seek approval from the managed care company for elective admissions and elective procedures and, sometimes, outpatient elective procedures.

preferred stocks   Securities that pay regular, fixed dividends to stockholders.

premium rate setting supply   The process of constructing a premium to charge an individual or group subscribers for insurance coverage.

prepaid expense   Cash payments made in advance for future services; shown as an asset on the balance sheet. As the asset is used up over time, it becomes an expense on the income statement.

present value   The value today of funds received or paid out at some future time. Obtained by discounting future cash flows by their opportunity costs.

preventive services   Services that focus on keeping the population healthy or improving the health status of the population (e.g., immunizations, smoking cessation programs, and nutritional programs).

primary care   Physician services that address the broad health needs of the population. These physicians often serve as the gatekeepers of managed care organizations.

primary care physician (PCP)   The physician who address the broad health needs of the population. These physicians usually serve as the gatekeepers of managed care organizations.

probability distribution   A pattern of different possible outcomes along with the relative frequency, or probability that each outcome will occur.

product line costing   A way to determine costs based on services offered rather than along departmental lines. Heart transplantation, for example, is a product line that crosses many departments.

profit centers   Departments within an organization having both expenses and revenue—for example, the radiology department. Management therefore is focused on managing the appropriate relationship between revenues and costs.

profitability index (PI)   Used when the organization has limited access to funds and therefore must ration available cash among several profitable alternatives.

pro forma income statement, cash flow statement and balance sheet   Projected financial statements that show a project's expected performance.

prospective experience rating   A rating system in which the premium set in the following year is based on the experience of a group in the previous year.

prospective payment system   A Medicare reimbursement system developed in the early 1980s that pays a fixed fee, set in advance, for a defined episode of hospital treatment based on a patient's diagnosis-related group.

prospective payment system (PPS) rate   A national average price per discharge developed by the Health Care Financing Administration using the average operating costs reported by all hospitals in their 1981 Medicare cost reports.

prospective review   A review conducted for any elective or nonemergency admission when it relates to an inpatient acute care admission and certain ambulatory procedures, with the goal of preventing inappropriate utilization of health resources before it occurs.

provider panel   Caregivers who are contracted and authorized to provide health services to the members of a managed care company.

provision for bad debts   A noncash expense that reflects the estimated loss of revenue on uncollectable accounts. Also used to adjust patient accounts receivable on the balance sheet.

public health issues   Issues related to the health status of a population that generally have not been considered part of the traditional health care system (e.g., prevention initiatives such as smoking and screening programs).

pure premium   The insurance premium before adding administrative profits and expenses. It is equal to the expected medical loss per member of the covered group.

pure risk   Uncertainty about the outcome of a chance event that results only in a loss. (e.g., acute illness, loss of a job, untimely death, property damage, natural disaster).

put option   An option to investors that gives them the right to sell bonds they have purchased back to the organization before maturity.

quality assessment   The process in a health care organization designed to identify key indicators of quality that can be monitored as measured and used to determine whether the quality within the organization is improving or declining.

Quality Assurance Reform Initiative (QARI)   A collaborative effort by the Health Care Financing Administration, states, and other interested parties aimed at creating a monitoring mechanism for improving the quality of care for Medicaid managed care programs.

quick ratio   Relates to the organization's ability to meet short-term liabilities with more liquid components of current assets.

reinsurance recoveries   Payments to a health plan from another insurance company that has guaranteed the health plan against the losses of very high-cost enrollees.

reinvestment risk   The possibility of a higher return when proceeds from one investment must be reinvested in the market at a lower rate of return.

relative value unit (RVU)   The amount of services determined to be appropriate to perform a specific health care procedure. Resources include human resources, capital resources, and operational supplies.

report cards   A communication mechanism, often in written form, that reports a general broad scope of performance for health care providers and managed care companies.

repository   When applied to information systems, a system architecture where data are taken from diverse production systems and make ad hoc reporting available to organizational decision makers regardless of the origin of the data.

resource-based relative value system (RBRVS)   A system established by Medicare to reimburse participating physicians based on relative resource utilization measured by relative value units and cost adjustment factors.

resource-based relative value unit (RBRVU)   A measure of relative resource consumption associated with providing a service and intended to correlate with the price paid for the item.

restricted funds   Presented in fund accounting as individual balance sheets for each major donor.

retained earnings   The portion of net income kept by the organization for future use. It is added to the balance sheet as both an asset and an increase in owner's equity.

retrospective experience rating   A rating system in which adjustments are made in the premium at the end of the contract year to account for under- or overutilization of services. Objective risk can be fully transferred to the payer in such a system.

retrospective review   A review conducted after the patient is released from care (an inpatient acute care episode or an ambulatory procedure) and looks at the medical record to determine whether there are patterns of practice by physicians for either under- or overutilization of services.

return on equity (ROE)   Measures the net income of the organization as a percentage of equity invested. Shows the financial return to investors after all creditors have been paid.

risk   Uncertainty about the outcome of a future event. If a risky event can be characterized by a known probability distribution, then risk can be quantified using some measure of variance of the distribution.

risk aversion   Characterizes people who are willing to pay more than the expected cost of a loss in order to transfer that risk to a third party. People who would pay no more than the expected value of the loss are called *risk neutral*. People who would buy insurance only at a price below the expected loss are *risk lovers*.

risk-based Medicare programs   A movement to shift the responsibility for providing Medicare services from the federal government to the private sector. It capitates the private sector payer in return for providing all services to the Medicare beneficiary.

risk lovers   *See* risk aversion.

risk management Involves the management and control of the organization's uncertain liabilities.

risk neutral *See* risk aversion.

risk pool A mechanism used by risk takers to have the health care providers participate in the economic risk of insuring the population of patients covered by the plan. Usually funded by withholding some percentage of the reimbursement to health care providers. *See* withhold.

schedule of revenues outstanding A way to measure payment patterns. Shows billed charges outstanding as a percentage of the amount originally billed.

second surgical opinion A utilization management technique that requires a second surgeon to verify the need for an elective surgical procedure before it is permitted to be performed.

secondary markets Markets in which securities that were previously issued by firms to raise capital are traded among market investors.

securitization Banks' reselling, through securities brokers, accounts receivables they have purchased to market investors in the form of a short-term security. The cash flows from receivables are used to pay investors.

service benefit plans Insurers that pay providers directly for services rendered to members, designate participating providers, and negotiate reimbursement contracts with providers.

shadow systems Systems kept in local locations that are used to ensure that the organizational systems can be serviced. They often duplicate information and work that are done elsewhere in the organization but are maintained in the local workplace in order to provide control and reliability in handling the important information.

short-term assets Assets that are converted to cash in a year or less.

specialty care physicians (SCP) A physician who takes care of specific types of diseases. Under most managed care protocols, referral must be from a primary care physician.

specific inventory method When applied to hospital services, estimates the average expense per patient-day based on utilization reports and claims data.

speculative demand for money Holding cash for future investment opportunities.

speculative risk Uncertainty about the outcome of a chance event that can produce either a gain or a loss (e.g., investing in the stock market, starting a business, investing in a college education, lending money with interest, betting on the lottery).

spillover effects The indirect consequences of a proposed project on the revenues and costs of other ongoing activities in the organization.

spontaneous liabilities Obligations to make future payments created as a direct result of providing services.

staff model A model in which the physicians of an organization, often a health maintenance organization, work for that organization on a full-time basis.

stakeholders Any individuals or organizations with a vital interest in the outcome of a particular event.

standard deviation The average dispersion of outcomes around the mean outcome.

statement of cash flows A financial statement that shows the sources and uses of cash in an organization over a specified period of time and the cash balance remaining at the end of the period.

stop loss insurance   Insurance that a health care provider or risk taker purchases, usually from a commercial insurance loss, to cover catastrophic cases.

sunk costs   Cash expenses that have already been incurred by the organization.

supplier-induced demand   Additional services initiated or prescribed by the physician that are not cost-effective and would not be chosen by a patient with complete information about the expected efficacy of additional treatment.

sweep account   An account that "sweeps" cash deposits received during the day that are in excess of the minimum balance desired into interest-earning investments.

tangible assets   Assets that are physical in nature. They may be real (e.g., land, buildings, equipment, vehicles, supplies) or financial (e.g., cash, stocks, bonds).

technology assessment   The activity of determining the cost-effectiveness, safety, availability, and clinical effectiveness of procedures used and medical devices as they move into the mainstream of medical clinical use.

telepresence   The ability to observe (e.g., medical treatments) and provide advice by electronic means over long distance.

telerobotics   The ability to manipulate automated instruments electronically over distance.

time line   A visual representation of cash paid or received during the year.

time value of money   The difference in the value of money received or spent at different points in time because of opportunity costs and inflation; each year of an investment project to aid in the analysis of the financial implications of the project.

total asset turnover   An efficiency ratio that measures how many dollars of revenue are produced from a dollar of total assets.

total loss distribution   The combination of the two distributions consisting of the likelihood of illness and the size of the illness once a person has become ill.

transactions demand for money   Based on the need to have cash available to pay bills. The primary reason for keeping and carrying cash.

trend analysis   *See* vertical analysis.

turnover ratios   *See* activity ratios.

unbundling   A charging strategy in which each individual item involved with providing a procedure is charged to the payer. For example, in a radiology examination, the films used would be charged in addition to the technical and professional components of the procedure.

underwriting risk   The objective risk accepted by an insurer. Underwriting risk, measured by the standard error of estimated losses for a group to be covered, declines as the size of the group increases.

upcoding   The assignment of the highest legitimate diagnosis-related group code to a patient discharge to maximize reimbursement for patient treatment.

upside risk   Risk associated with profits that a managed care organization and/or provider experiences as a result of providing health care services.

usual and customary   Devised by payers keeping track of charges made for each health care service in the community and then calculating the mean price and quartile breaks for each procedure. The seventy-fifth or ninetieth percentile is usually considered the usual and customary price for the community.

utilization management   A methodology that addresses the issue of controlling use of resources in the delivery of health care while also measuring the quality associated with the delivery of that care.

variable costs   Costs incurred each time a service is provided (e.g., labor hours, supplies).

variance analysis   An inquiry into the reasons for a departure of actual performance from an expected target.

vertical analysis   Financial statement analysis that examines trends in financial performance and condition over time.

vertical integration   The integration of related entities in order to provide the entire range of services required by a purchaser.

virtual network   A network constructed by relationships rather than ownership and control vehicles.

volume performance standards   Adjustments by the Health Care Financing Administration to conversion factors for physician reimbursement to offset the overall cost effect of a possible increase in physician volumes in response to prices set by the resource-based relative value system.

weighted average cost of capital (WACC)   A single measure of the opportunity cost of funds to an organization or an individual project that incorporates the relative weights and the opportunity costs of each source of financing for the organization.

withhold   An agreed-on amount withheld from a health care provider's reimbursement to be used to cover excessive resource utilization. When the provider operates within specified utilization parameters, the amount is returned at the end of the year.

working capital   Refers to the short term assets, and liabilities, used to support the operations of the health care organization.

World Health Organization (WHO)   The health care arm of the United Nations designed to improve the health status of the nations of the world; pays particular interest to Third World nations.

yield to maturity   The discount rate that equates the current market price of a bond with the present value of its future cash flows. What an investor who holds a bond over its entire remaining life will earn.

Index

Accelerated depreciation, 174
Accounting costs, 324–325
Accounts payable, 167
Accreditation, 91–92
Accrual accounting, 160
Accrued expenses, 167
Accumulated depreciation, 173
Active repository, 113
Activity ratios, 185
Actuarial approach, 50–53
Adjusted annual per capita cost (AAPCC), 146
Adjusted community rate (ACR), 147
Adjusted community rating (ACR), 53
Adverse selection, 39, 219
Aging of population, 18
Aid to Families with Dependent Children (AFDC), 5, 145
Allowable costs, 125
Ambulatory care, 81–101
  growth of, 82–86
    incentives by managed care companies to shift
      delivery site, 84
    incentives under Medicare to shift delivery site,
      82–83
    logistical issues, 84–86
  models of, 86–91
    physician services, 86–88
    other models, 89–91
  quality and managed care, 91–100
    accreditation, 91–92
    applying the quality concept, 98–100
    quality measures in ambulatory care, 92–98
Ambulatory costs under capitation, 320–322
Ambulatory diagnostic groups (ADGs), 94
Ambulatory patient group (APG), 140
Ambulatory sites, shifts to, 218–219
Ambulatory variances, 333–334
Amortization, 171
Annual update factor, 133
Annuities, 233
Arrearages, 239
Assets, 164–166
  characteristics of, 164–165
  liquidity, 165–166
Availability of health care, 370–372
Availability rationing, 372
Average age of plant, 186
Average collection period (ACP), 186
Average payment period (APP), 186
Average payment rate (APR), 147

Balance billing, 142
Balance sheet, 159, 162–168, 247
  assets, 164–166
  effects of income statement on, 172–176

  liabilities and owner's equity, 167–168
Best practices, 87
Billed charges, 75
  discount from, 75–76
Binomial distribution, 30
Blended rate, 135
Blue Cross/Blue Shield, 40–42, 124, 125
Bond covenants, 177
Bonds, 234–237
  call and put options, 237
  valuation, 235–236
Book value, 173
Break-even analysis (BE), 126–130, 261
Budget management under capitation, 198–221
  budgeting under capitation, 202–215
    building the budget, 214
    economic scenario for health care provider,
      204–205
    economic scenario for managed care company,
      203–204
    operating budgets under capitation, 214–215
    setting the price, 205–214
  environmental factors, 217–219
  financial factors, 215–217
  pluralistic reimbursement environment, 199–202
Budget variances, 330–334
Business risk, 44

California Care, 96
Call option, 237
Call premium, 237
Capital asset pricing model (CAPM), 242–243
  versus discounted cash flow analysis, 243–244
Capital budgeting, 164, 222–270
  cash flows and time value of money, 225–230
  evaluating annuities and perpetuities, 233–234
  evaluating a series of lump-sum payments, 230–233
  finding opportunity cost of debt, 237–239
  in health care organization, 247–261
  opportunity costs and capital budgeting, 224–225
  required return on stocks and bonds, 234–237
  stock valuation and opportunity cost of equity,
    239–244
  using decision tools to assess capital projects, 261–265
  weighted average cost of capital, 244–246
Capital costs, 136–137
Capitalization ratio, 187
Capital structure, 167
  decisions, 176–177
  ratio, 187
Capitation, 43, 72
  cost accounting and control under, 314–340
  managing budget under, 198–221
  reimbursement, 77

Capitation (*cont.*)
 use of, by government payers, 146–148
 using community rating, 49–53
  actuarial approach, 50–53
  expense-budget approach, 50, 51
 utilization management under, 300–313
Case management, 310–312
Case mix index, 134
Case rate pricing, 201
Cash accounting, 160
Cash budgeting and working capital management,
  271–299
 cash budgeting, 274
 cash conversion cycle, 274–290
 cash, working capital, and net working capital, 273–274
 financing working capital, 290
Cash conversion cycle, 274–290
 in health maintenance organization, 289–290
 payer perspective, 285–289
  premium collection/accounts receivable stage,
   287–288
  provider reimbursement stage, 289
  service delivery/medical expense accrual stage,
   288–289
  start-up stage, 286
 provider perspective, 274–278
  billing stage, 277–278
  collections/accounts receivable stage, 278–284
  estimating the length of cash conversion cycle,
   284–285
  service delivery stage, 277
  start-up stage, 276–277
Cash equivalents, 273
Cash flows and time value of money, 225–230
 periodic compounding and discounting, 228–229
 periodic compounding and effective annual rates,
  229–230
 simple compounding and discounting, 225–227
Cash flow statement, 159, 177–179, 247
Cash-flow-to-total-debt ratio, 189
Center for Healthcare Industry Performance Studies
  (CHIPS), 179
Center of excellence, 373
Centralized control, 114–115
CHAMPUS (Civilian Health and Medical Program of
  the Uniformed Services), 68, 70
Child Health Assistance Program, 145
Clinical integration, 105, 106
Clinical pathways, 303
Code of Hammurabi, 362–363
Co-insurance, 73, 216, 307
Common procedural terminology (CPT) codes, 143
Common-size ratios, 181
Common stock, 168
Community rating, 3
 system, 39
  and capitation, 49–53
Comparative analysis, 179
Compensating balances, 295
Competitive health plans (CHPs), 146
Completion factors, 292

Compounding of interest, 226
Concurrent review, 311
Consolidated balance sheet, 165
Consolidated Omnibus Budget Reconciliation Act
  (COBRA), 375
Consumer Price Index (CPI), 9–11
Continuous quality improvement (CQI), 91, 95,
  344–348
 data requirements for quality improvement, 345–347
 Infrastructure requirements for a quality program,
  347–348
Continuum of care, 103, 108
Contractual allowances, 169
Coordination of benefits, 170
Co-payments, 68, 307
Corporate finance, 19, 20
Corporate risk, 259
Cost accounting and control under capitation, 314–340
 accounting for costs, 325–328
 cost definitions, 323–325
  accounting costs, 324–325
  economic costs, 324
 managing costs, 328–336
  assessing performance, 329–334
  correcting variances, 335–336
  flexible versus fixed budgets, 334–335
  operating units, 328–329
 understanding costs, 315323
  managing costs, 318–322
  managing the enrollment, 322–323
  managing utilization, 317–318
Cost adjustment using relative value units, 142–144
Cost-based reimbursements, 124, 125–133
 incentives under, 126–130
 problem of cost shifting, 130–132
 services covered by, 132–133
Cost centers, 329
Cost finding, 126
Cost of debt, 237–239
Cost of goods sold, 175
Cost outlier payments, 136
Cost shifting, 130–132
Coupon, 235
Covered services, defining, 216–217
CPI. *See* Consumer Price Index
Cream skimming, 39
Credentials verification organizations, 349
Critical path, 87, 336
Current assets, 166
Current asset turnover, 185
Current liabilities, 167
Current portion of long-term debt, 167
Current ratio, 184
Customary, prevailing and reasonable charges (CPR),
  142

Data requirements for quality improvement, 345–347
Data warehouse, 113
Day's cash on hand, 184
Debt-service-coverage ratio, 189
Decentralized control, 114

Decision tools to assess capital projects, 261–265
  break-even analysis, 261
  discounted payback period, 263
  internal rate or return, 263
  modified internal rate of return, 264
  net present value, 263
  payback period, 261
  profitability index, 265
Deductibles, 68, 216, 307
Deferred tax liability, 174
Delivery methods, future, 368–370
Demographic profiles, 366
Depreciation expense, 171
Diagnosis-related group (DRG), 6, 76, 134–135, 201, 323
Direct service delivery plan, 42
Discharge planning, 312
Discount bonds, 235
Discounted cash flow analysis, 225, 239–241
  versus capital asset pricing model, 243–244
Discounted fee-for-service system, 124
Discounted payback period (DPP), 263
Disease prevention, 90–91
Disproportionate share payments, 138–139
Distribution effects of health care inflation, 12
Diversification strategy, 104
Dividends, 172
Downgrade bond rating, 177
Downside risk, 210
DRG. *See* Diagnosis-related group
DuPont analysis, 190
Duration matching, 296

Economic costs, 324
Economic profit, 234
Economic rationing, 370
Economies of scale, 105
Educational rationing, 371–372
Effective annual rate (EAR), 229–230
Efficiency ratios, 185–187
Ellwood, Paul, 41
Employee assistance programs (EAP), 90
Enrollment, managing, 322
  maintaining memberships, 322
  reducing costs, 322–323
Environmental factors, and health status, 365
Equity financing ratio, 188
Equity multiplier, 190
Excess revenues over expenses, 171
Exclusive provider organization (EPO), 46–47, 73–74
Exogenous variables, 361
Expanded Programme on Immunization (EPI), 367
Expected value, 29
Expense-budget approach, 50, 51
Expenses, 171
  of HMO, 203–204
Experience rating system, 39
Explicit limits on utilization, 307–308

Face value, 235
Federally qualified health maintenance organizations
  (FQHMOs), 146

Fee-for-service (FFS) system, 122
Financial accounting, 19–20
Financial credentialing, 304
Financial incentives to providers, 305–306
  capitation, 306
  risk pools, 306
  sharing in the bottom line of plan, 305–306
Financial information, integrated with clinical and
    outcomes data, 112
Financial leverage ratios, 187–189
  cash-flow-to-total debt, 189
  debt-service-coverage, 189
  equity financing, 188
  IBNR-expense-to-current-liabilities, 189
  long-term debt-to-equity, 188
Financial management, 19
  and managed care, 19–21
Financial performance, 156–197
  balance sheet, 162–168
  capital structure decisions, 176–177
  effects of income statement on balance sheet, 172–176
  financial statement analysis, 179–190
  financial statements, 158–162
  income statement, 169–172
  operating ratios and, 190–195
  statement of cash flows, 177–179
Financial perspective, future considerations, 376–377
Financial ratio analysis, 181–190
  efficiency ratios, 185–187
  financial leverage ratios, 187–189
  limitations in use of, 194–195
  liquidity ratios, 184–185
  profitability ratios, 190
Financial risk, 35
Financial statements, 158–162
  accrual versus cash accounting, 160–162
  analysis, 179–190
    composition ratios, 181
    financial ratio analysis, 181–190
  and not-for-profit organizations, 159–160
  types of, 159
Fixed asset turnover, 185
Fixed costs, 126
Flexible versus fixed budgets, 334–335
Flotation costs, 239
For-profit entities, 60
Foundation for Accountability (FAcct), 343, 356
Functional integration, 105, 107–108
Fund accounting, 168
Future of health care organizations, 360–380
  changing methods of treatment and delivery,
      368–370
  financial perspective, 376–377
  global health care system, 363–366
  impact of technology, 366–367
  patient's perspective, 375–376
  perspective of history, 362–363
  policy perspective on health care availability, 370–372
  prevention services, 367–368
  rationing, 370–372
  role of government, 372–375

Gatekeeper, 210
    model, 302
GDP. *See* Gross domestic product
General fund, 168
Geographic rationing, 371
Global health care system, 363–366
Globalization, 361
Goodwill, 165
Government, role of, 372–375
Gross domestic product (GDP), 9
Gross revenues, 169
Group Health Cooperative, 98–100
    Web site, 98
Group model HMO, 45–46, 72

HCFA. *See* Health Care Financing Administration
HCFA's common procedure coding system (HCPCS),
    143
HCPCS codes, 143
Health care costs, controlling, 19
Health Care Financing Administration (HCFA), 8, 69, 343
Health Care Investment Analysts (HCIA), 179
Health care organization
    capital budgeting in, 247–261
        adjusting discount rate for project risk, 258–261
        determining opportunity cost of capital, 258
        initial cash flows, 250–252
        operating cash flows, 252–257
        process overview, 247–250
        salvage value, 257–258
Health care provider, economic scenario of, 204–205
Health insurance
    profitability and costs of, 36–40
        health status risk, medical care risk, and total risk,
            37–38
        managing health plan risks, 38–40
Health Insurance Portability and Accountability Act of
    1996, 374
Health insurers, 41–42
Health maintenance organization (HMO), 5, 7–8, 28,
    41, 44–47, 60, 72
    criticisms of, 47–48
        compromising quality for cost, 47
        favorable and adverse selection, 47
        poor market information, 47–48
    exclusive provider organizations, 46–47
    expenses, 203–204
    group model, 45–46, 72
    independent practice association, 46, 72–73
    methods of reimbursing for services, 71–73
    network model, 46, 72
    point-of-service plans, 46, 60
    revenue stream, 203
    staff model, 45, 60, 72
Health Maintenance Organization Amendments of
    1988, 7
Health Maintenance Organizations Act of 1973, 5, 7, 40
Health Plan and Employer Data Indicator Statistics
    (HEDIS), 193, 343, 350–353
Health profiles, 366
Health promotion services, 90–91

Health Security Act of 1994, 2–4
Health status risk, 32, 37–38
Health system, 104
    reform, 2–9
Hill-Burton Act, 4
HMO. *See* Health maintenance organization
Home Health, 90
Horizontal analysis, 179
Horizontal integration, 104
Hospital reimbursement, 125–141
    cost-based reimbursement, 125–133
    diagnosis-related groups, 134–135
    effects of PPS, 139–141
    implementation, 135–139
        capital costs, 136–137
        cost outlier payments, 136
        disproportionate share, 138–139
        medical education, 137–138
        patient transfers, 136
    prospective payment system, 133
Hospitals
    expansion of, 4
    occupancy, 14
Hospital services, pricing under capitation, 211–214

IBNR claims, 167
IBNR-expense-to-current-liabilities ratio, 189
IDN. *See* Integrated delivery network
Imaging, 89
Incentives for appropriate utilization, 335
Income statement, 159, 169–172
    effects on balance sheet, 172–176
        depreciation and the value of assets, 173–175
        distribution of net income, 172–173
        estimation of uncertain liabilities and risk
            management, 175–176
        expenses, 171
        net operating income and net income, 171–172
        total revenues, 169–170
Incremental costs, 260
Indemnity insurance plans, 42
Indemnity insurance reimbursement systems, 71
Independent practice association (IPA), 46, 72–73, 107
Individual providers, 59, 63
    competition with institutional providers, 64–65
Inflation
    and effect on Medicare, 6
    rate, 9
Infrastructure requirements for a quality program,
    347–348
Initial public offering (IPO), 168
Inpatient acute care costs under capitation, 319–320
Inpatient care delivery, 58–80
    evolution of risk, 74–78
        billed charges, 75
        capitation reimbursement, 77
        discount from billed charges, 75–76
        per day reimbursement, 76
        per stay reimbursement, 76
    evolving managed care market, 59–68
        competition among institutional providers, 62–63

competition of institutional providers with individual providers, 64–65
competition of providers with employers, 66–67
competition of providers with payers, 65–66
disenfranchised patient, 67–68
pluralistic payment systems, 68–74
government reimbursement systems, 68–71
private sector, 71–74
Inpatient variances, 330–332
Institutional providers, 59, 61
competition among institutional providers, 62–63
competition with individual providers, 64–65
Insurance
and income in price of health care, 15–17
See also Health insurance; Risk and insurance
Insurance providers, 34–36
Intangible asset, 164
Integrated delivery network (DN), 63, 89, 103
Integrated delivery systems, 102–119, 165
basics of, 103–105
and capitation, 217
future considerations, 116–118
information needs of, 108–114
architectural constructs of information integration, 113–114
coordination of clinical services, 109–113
standardization of data elements, 108–109
role of governance, 114–116
centralized control, 114–115
decentralized control, 114
role of physicians, 115–116
types of integration, 106–108
clinical, 106
continuum of care, 108
functional, 107–108
managed care, 108
physician system, 106–107
Interest rate risk, 237
Internal rate of return (IRR), 232, 263
Inventories, 175
Investment bankers, 239
Issuance costs, 239

Just-in-time (JIT) system, 175

Kaiser Family Foundation, 356
Kennedy-Kassebaum Health Insurance Portability and Accountability Act of 1996, 39

Laboratory services, 89
Lag report, 292
Law of large numbers, 34
Leakage, 202, 219
Liabilities, 167
Line of credit, 295
Liquidity, 165–166
Liquidity ratios, 184–185
current ratio, 184
day's cash on hand, 184
quick ratio, 184
Loading, 36

Long-term assets, 166
Long-term debt-to-equity ratio, 188
Lump-sum payments, evaluating, 230–233

Managed care, 2
ambulatory care, 81–101
delivery of inpatient care, 58–80
dominance of , 8–9
early forms of, 40–41
emergence of, 1–26
financial management and, 19–21
health insurers, 41–42
initiatives to curb spending, 6–8
as model of integration, 108
organizations, 40–42
plan characteristics, 42–47
health maintenance organizations, 44–47
preferred provider organizations, 43
premium rate development, 48–49
reimbursement systems, 71–74
exclusive provider organizations, 73–74
health maintenance organizations, 71–73
preferred provider organizations, 73
self-payment systems, 74
Managed care organizations, (MCOs), 43
Management decision support, 111–112
Managerial (cost) accounting, 19, 20
Marginal cost of capital, 258
Market failure, 306
and escalating health care costs, 18
Market portfolio, 242
Market risk, 242
Matching maturity, 296
Maturity of an investment, 230
MCO. *See* Managed care organization
Mean, 30
Medicaid, 4–5, 68, 70, 373
managed care initiatives, 148–149
quality issues, 355–356
reimbursement, 145–146
Medical care risk, 32, 37–38
Medical education costs reimbursement, 137–138, 374
Medical Group Management Association (MGMA), 193
Medical loss ratio (MLR), 36–37
Medical Price Index (MPI), 10–12
Medical record information, availability of, 112–113
Medical savings account (MSA), 19
Medical underwriting, 49
Medicare, 4–5, 6, 42, 68, 69, 373, 374
and ambulatory care, 82–83
cost plans, 354
health care prepayment plan (HCPP), 354
Part A, 132
Part B, 141
quality issues, 354–355
resource-based relative value system, 142
risk plans, 354
Medicare cost reports, 126
Medicare risk contracts, 146–147
problems in, 147–148
Medicare Trust Fund, 6, 39

Military medical services, 70–71
MLR. *See* Medical loss ratio
Modified accelerated cost recovery system (MACRS), 174
Modified cash basis of accounting, 162
Modified internal rate of return (MIRR), 264
Moral hazard, 16–17, 39
MSA. *See* Medical savings account
Mutual fund, 242

National Committee for Quality Assurance (NCQA), 91–92, 343, 348–350
National health care spending
  distribution effects of inflation, 12
  effect of quality on prices, 12
  price changes in spending, 9–11
  problems with the Medical Price Index, 11–12
  reasons for increased spending, 17–18
    aging of the population, 18
    growth of technology, 18
    market failure, 18
  utilization per capita, 12–13
National health expenditures, 2, 8–9
  growth of, 8–9
Net assets, 168
Net income, 171
  distribution of, 172–173
    dividends, 172
    retained earnings, 173
Net income margin, 190
Net operating income, 171
Net patient revenues, 169
Net present value (NPV), 263
Net working capital (NWC), 167, 251–252
Network model HMO, 46, 72
Network providers, selection and monitoring, 304–305
Nonoperating gains (losses), 170
Nonparticipating physicians, 142
Normal distribution, 30
Not-for-profit organizations, 60
  financial statements, 159–160

Objective risk, 32
  reducing, through group insurance, 33
Occupational health, 90
Operating margin, 190
Operating ratios and financial performance, 190–195
  HMOs and other managed care plans, 191–193
  hospitals, 191
  physician practices, 193–194
Operating revenues, 169
Opportunity costs, 130, 224–225, 237–244
Organized delivery system (ODS), 103
Outcomes. *See* Quality and outcomes management
Outpatient surgery, 89
Owner's equity, 167–168

Paid-in capital, 168
Par value, 235
Passive repository, 113
Pass-through payments, 135

Patient
  and health care delivery, 67–68
  satisfaction with health care, 375–376
  scheduling, 109
  transfers, 136
Payback period (PP), 261
Payer fiat, 68
Payment systems, 200
Peer review organization (PRO), 139
Per day reimbursement, 76
Per diem pricing, 201
Periodic compounding and discounting, 228–229
  and effective annual rates, 229–230
Periodic interim payments (PIP), 291
Per member per month (PMPM), 201
Perpetuity, 233
Personal health care spending, 121–122
Personal Responsibility and Work Opportunity Act of 1996, 5
Per stay reimbursement, 76
Physician integration, 105, 106–107
Physician reimbursement, 141–149
  cost adjustment using relative value units, 142–144
  impact of RBRVS, 144
  Medicaid managed care initiatives, 148149
  Medicaid reimbursement, 145–146
  Medicare's resource-based relative value system, 142
  non-Medicare use of PPS and RBRVS, 145
  use of capitation by government payers, 146–148
Physicians
  nonparticipating, 142
  role of, 38, 64–65
    in governance of organization, 115–116
  supply of, 14
Physician services
  and ambulatory care, 86–88
    clinical practice impact, 88
    economic impact, 87–88
  pricing under capitation, 205–206
Physicians practice plan (PPP), 40
Pluralistic payment system, 68
Pluralistic reimbursement environment, 199–202
  health care environment, 199–200
  payment methodologies, 200–202
    risk for health status of the population, 201–202
    risk for price, 201
    risk for volume of services given, 201
Point-of-service entities, 60
Point-of-service (POS) plans, 46
PPS. *See* Prospective payment system
PPS rate, 133
Practice standards and protocols, 303–304
Precautionary demand for money, 272
Precertification, 65
Preferred provider organization (PPO), 40, 43, 71, 73
Preferred stock, 168
Premium rate setting, 48–49
Present value, 226
Preventive services, 308, 367–368
Prices of health care
  causes of increases, 13–17

expansion of insurance, 15–17
  increases in intensity of services, 17
  national income growth, 15
Pricing issues under capitation, 205–214
  hospital services, 211–214
  physician services, 205–206
  primary care physicians, 206–209
  specialty care physicians, 209–211
Primary care, 105
Primary care physician (PCP), 202
  pricing services under capitation, 206–209
Probability distribution, 30
Productivity of organizations, 218
Product line costing, 323
Profiling, 335–336
Profitability index (PI), 265
Profitability ratios, 190
  operating and net income margins, 190
  return on equity, 190
Profit centers, 328–329
Proforma income statement, 247
Prospective experience rating, 40
Prospective payment system (PPS), 6, 124, 133
Prospective review, 309–310
Provider panel, 65
Provision for bad debt, 171
Psychiatric services, 89
Public health issues, 365
Pure premium, 36
Pure risk, 29
Put option, 237

Quality
  of health care goods and services, 12
  and managed care, 91–100
    accreditation, 91–92
    applying the quality concept, 98–100
    quality measures in ambulatory care, 92–98
Quality and outcomes management, 341–359
  participants and quality concepts, 342–344
  quality indicators, 348–358
    Health Plan Employer Data and Information Set, 350–353
    Medicaid, 355–356
    Medicare, 354–355
    National Committee for Quality Assurance (NCQA), 348–350
    quality measures for federally funded programs, 356
    report cards, 353
    technology assessment, 357–358
  using continuous quality improvement, 344–348
Quality assurance (QA), 347
Quality Assurance Reform Initiative (QARI), 356
Quick ratio, 184

Rationing of health care delivery, 370–372
  availability, 372
  economic, 370
  educational, 371–372
  geographic, 371

Reform in the U.S. health system, 2–9
Registration of information, 109–110
Reimbursement
  hospital, 125–141
  Medicaid, 145–146
  physician, 141–149
  systems, 71–74
Reinsurance recoveries, 170
Reinvestment risk, 237
Relative value unit (RVN), 69
Report cards, 353
Repository, 113
Resource allocation 110–111
Resource-based relative value system, 124, 140
Resource-based relative value unit (RBRVU), 83
Restricted funds, 168
Retained earnings, 173
Retrospective experience rating, 40
Retrospective review, 311
Rettig, Richard, 357
Return on equity (ROE), 190
Return on stocks and bonds, 234–237
  bond valuation, 235–236
  call and put options, 237
Revenues, 169–170
Revenue stream of HMO, 203
Risk
  business, 44
  corporate, 259
  downside, 210
  financial, 35
  health status, 32, 37–38, 201–202
  in inpatient care delivery, 74–78
  interest rate, 237
  market, 242
  medical care, 32, 37–38
  objective, 32
  for price, 201
  pure, 29
  reinvestment, 237
  speculative, 29
  underwriting, 35
  upside, 210
  for volume of services given, 201
Risk and insurance, 28–36
  pooling of risks, 34–35
  reducing objective risk through group insurance, 33
  risk described, 29
  risk reduction and the law of large numbers, 34
  role of insurance providers, 34–36
  statistical properties of risk, 30–33
Risk aversion, 36
Risk-based Medicare programs, 69
Risk lover, 36
Risk management, 38–40, 175–176
Risk neutral, 36
Risk plans, 354
Risk pool, 34, 210, 215–216, 306

Salvage value, 257–258
Secondary markets, 237

Second surgical opinion, 310
Self-payment systems, 74
Service benefit plan, 42
Shadow systems, 346
Simple compounding and discounting, 225–227
Single-payer system, 19, 377
Skilled nursing facilities (SNFs), 140
Specialty care physicians (SCP), 205
    capitating the specialist, 218
    pricing services under capitation, 209–211
Specific inventory method, 293
Speculative demand for money, 272
Speculative risk, 29
Spillover effects, 257
Spontaneous liabilities
    of health care providers, 290–291
    of managed care plans, 292–294
Staff model of HMO, 45, 60, 72
Stakeholders, in health care delivery system, 59
    relationship among, 61, 62
Standard deviation, 30
Standard error (SE), 34
Statement of cash flows, 159, 177–179, 247
Stocks, 234–235
    valuation and opportunity cost of equity, 239–244
        applying discounted cash flow analysis, 239–241
        capital asset pricing model, 242–243
        discounted cash flow analysis versus capital asset
            pricing model, 243–244
        incorporating cash flows of a growing company,
            241–242
Stop loss insurance, 217
Sunk costs, 250
Supplier-induced demand, 15, 17

Tangible asset, 164
Tax Equity and Fiscal Responsibility Act of 1982, 8
Technology
    future impact of, 366–367
    and rising prices in health care, 18
Technology assessment (TA), 357–358
Telepresence, 366, 404
Telerobotics, 366, 404
Temporary Assistance for Needy Families (TANF), 5
Third-party payment systems, 120–155
    alternatives to fee-for-service, 124–125
    hospital reimbursement, 125–141
    physician reimbursement, 141–149
    traditional payment systems, 122–123
Time value of money, 225
Total asset turnover, 185
Total loss distribution, 31
Trade credit, 294
Transactions demand for money, 272
Treatment methods, future, 368–370
Trend analysis, 179
Turnover ratios, 185

Unbundling charges, 69, 123
Underwriting risk, 35

Up-coding, 139
Upside risk, 210
U.S. health system reform, 2–9
    dominance of managed care, 8–9
    health reform efforts, 4–6
    managed care initiatives, 6–8
Usual and customary (U&C) basis, 70
Utilization of health care, 12–13
Utilization management under capitation, 300–313,
    317–318
    objectives of utilization management system,
        301–308
        control of patient behavior, 306–308
        control of provider behavior, 302–306
    utilization process, 308–312
        case management, 311–312
        concurrent review, 311
        discharge planning, 312
        prospective review, 309–310
        retrospective review, 311
        second surgical opinion, 310

Variable costs, 126
Variance analysis, 322
Variances, 30, 330–334
    ambulatory, 333–334
        cost-related, 333–334
        volume-related, 333
    correcting, 335–336
        critical paths, 336
        incentives, 335
        profiling, 335–336
    inpatient, 330–332
        cost-related, 332
        volume-related, 330–331
Vertical analysis, 179
Vertical integration, 104
Veterans Administration, 70
Virtual integration, 117
Virtual network, 368
Vision services, 90
Vladeck, Bruce C., 373
Volume performance standards, 143

Weighted average cost of capital (WACC), 244–246
Withhold, 46, 215
Working capital, 273–274
    financing, 290–297
        matching maturity of assets and liabilities, 296–297
        spontaneous liabilities in managed care plans,
            292–294
        spontaneous liabilities of health care providers,
            290–291
        trade credit, lines of credit, and other short-term
            loans, 294–296
World Health Organization (WHO), 367

Yield to maturity, 237

How to Use the Computer Disk

The computer disk contains exercise spreadsheets that correspond to the case studies presented in Chapters 1, 2, 6, 7, 8, 9, 10, and 12 of the book. The cases, the problems and questions they pose, and the accompanying spreadsheets will enhance learning by reinforcing concepts through application.

In the spreadsheets you will find partially completed data that directly correlates with the specific case. Your job is to complete the missing information, based on concepts you are learning in the book. In many cases, this means that you need to derive and input formulas at designated places in the spreadsheet to perform the necessary calculation. The worksheet cells you should focus on are highlighted in the spreadsheet.

Computer System Specifications

The disk was prepared on a PC using **Windows**® operating systems (versions 3.1 and 95). The files should be easy to port to a **Macintosh**® because we used common file structures.

To work through the computer-based exercises you will need to have a commercially available spreadsheet program previously installed on the computer. You may also want to use a word processing program to view the cases and answer the questions on-line (all of the cases are also printed in the book). We used Microsoft® Excel for the spreadsheets (.xls file extension) and Microsoft Word for the cases (.doc file extension). The .xls files can be loaded directly or imported into other common spreadsheet programs such as Lotus® 1-2-3®. The .doc files can be either loaded directly or imported into other common word processors such as Corel® WordPerfect®. We used Microsoft® Excel version 5, which can be read by the two most recent versions of nearly any spreadsheet software program on a PC or a Macintosh.

For Technical Support: 1-800-245-6720

General Information

We recommend that you not overwrite the spreadsheet files we've provided. Instead, as you complete the exercises you should save your work to a new file—preferably onto a different disk. If something happens to your original disk files, you will find all of the original files posted on Delmar Publishers' Allied website for you to download. www.delmaralliedhealth.com (Look for and select the listing for this book.)

On the disk you will find a folder for each of the eight chapters of the book that present cases. The folders are named as follows: **chap1**, **chap2**, **chap6**, and so on. Each chapter folder contains all the case studies presented within the chapter (.doc files) and a corresponding spreadsheet file (.xls file) that you can use to calculate, track, and report the information described in the case. The case studies are named by chapter and case number, as sequenced in the book; for example **Cs6-3.doc** is the third case presented in Chapter 6. The spreadsheet that goes with that same case is named **Ch6-3.xls**.

Instructors may sometimes prefer that students turn in their work electronically (either on disk or by e-mail) rather than turning in just a print-out of the completed spreadsheet for a particular case. This will allow for better assessment of how well the student understands the underlying mathematical formulas that need to be developed inside the spreadsheets.

How to Get Started

1. To start, make sure the computer power is turned on and the system is booted up, ready for action.
2. Next, insert the disk into the $3\frac{1}{2}$-inch disk drive on the computer.
3. Browse the disk for the chapter and case number in which you are working. Here's how to browse in Windows 95, choose *Start* (lowest left corner of your screen); in the Start menu choose *Run...* and then click the *Browse* button. In the *Look in:* window, locate the $3\frac{1}{2}$-inch disk drive (usually labeled as *A:*), and then select the folder that corresponds to the appropriate chapter in the book.

If you are fairly new at using a spreadsheet program, you will benefit from first viewing the tutorial spreadsheet file provided on the internet web page established for this book. You can get to that page from www.delmaralliedhealth.com. If you are using Excel, review the file named **TEACHME.xls**. If you are using Lotus 1-2-3® you should review the file **TEACHME.wk4**. These files illustrate the basic spreadsheet operations you will use in solving the problems presented in the cases.

How to Use on a Windows-based PC

If you are using Microsoft® Excel: To begin working in one of the spreadsheets you may simply double click on the filename/icon for that .xls file. Excel will launch and the spreadsheet will load. If Excel is already running, you may load the spreadsheet by choosing *File > Open...* and then browse for the file on the $3\frac{1}{2}$-inch disk drive.

If you are using Lotus 1-2-3®: To begin working in one of the spreadsheets, launch Lotus 1-2-3. Choose *File > Open...* and then select the .xls file from the $3\frac{1}{2}$-inch disk drive. When you save your work, it will be saved as a 1-2-3 file, which has a file extension of .wk5 or .wk4, depending on the version of 1-2-3 you are using.

How to Use on a Macintosh Computer

If you are using a Macintosh computer running operating system 7 or newer, you should be able to read the disk as it is, as long as the extension "PC Exchange" is enabled in the Apple Control Panel. If you are using an older version of the operating system you will need to transfer the files using a file transfer utility such as Apple File Exchange.

When you insert the disk into the disk drive, if an icon for the disk appears on the desktop, labeled as a PC disk, then you're all set. To proceed, launch your spreadsheet program, choose *File > Open...* and then browse the disk for the appropriate file. To view the Case document, follow the same procedure—launch your word processing program, and then choose *File > Open...* and select the case document.

If, when you insert the disk into the disk drive, you see a dialog box telling you the disk has not been initialized, be sure to *Cancel* and *Eject* the disk. Do not initialize it. Here's what to do next. If you are running operating system 7 or newer, choose the *Apple menu* (top leftmost corner of your screen), and choose *Control Panel*. Now choose *Extensions Manager*. A checklist of available extension utilities will appear. Select the one called *PC Exchange*, and then close the window. Your Mac should now be able to read the PC disk.

If you are running an earlier version of the operating system, you will need to use the *Apple File Exchange* utility (if not already on your system, this utility was included on a disk called Apple Utilities that came with most systems). If it's already installed on your computer, you may find it in a folder called Apple Utilities; or it may be in your System folder in a Utilities folder. Double click the *Apple File Exchange* icon to launch the program. The Exchange window will split into two windows: you will want it to display your hard disk contents on one side, and the $3\frac{1}{2}$-inch floppy disk drive on the other side. Insert the disk into the disk drive, and select that disk drive as the one to look at. Before transferring the entire contents of the disk to your Mac, you should do a few trial transfers to make sure the transfer settings work for you. You can adjust some of the transfer settings from a pull-down menu. After you have the details worked out, you may want to copy the entire contents of the disk over to your system. If you need to put the files on another floppy disk, you can copy them to the hard disk temporarily, and then move them to a different floppy disk when you are done with the PC disk. If you need to transfer files back to a PC disk, simply reverse the transfer steps.

How to Learn More About Using Spreadsheets

International Thomson Publishing (ITP) has many excellent books and tutorials that will guide you through the fundamental concepts and skills you'll need to become proficient at building spreadsheets. Course Technology, an ITP publishing group, offers their "Illustrated" series designed to show you the ropes in a graphical, easy-to-follow manner. For product descriptions and ordering information, we invite you to visit the Course Technology website: http://www.course.com/templates/catalog/default.cfm
Here are a few titles we suggest:

- *Microsoft® Excel 7 for Windows 95—Illustrated Standard Ed.* by Shaffer and Reding; ISBN 0-7600-3523-7
- *Lotus® 1-2-3® 97 Double Diamond Ed.* by Shelly & Cashman; ISBN 0-7895-1200-9
- *Corel® Quattro Pro® 7 for Windows® 95—Illustrated Standard Ed.* by Salkind; ISBN 0-7600-3753-1

Also, be sure to download and review the tutorial file we created for you (TEACHME.xls, TEACHME.wk4). You will find the file in the Delmar Publishers Allied Health web section for this book. www.delmaralliedhealth.com

License Agreement for Delmar Publishers
an International Thomson Publishing company

Educational Software/Data

You the customer, and Delmar incur certain benefits, rights, and obligations to each other when you open this package and use the software/data it contains. BE SURE YOU READ THE LICENSE AGREEMENT CAREFULLY, SINCE BY USING THE SOFTWARE/DATA YOU INDICATE YOU HAVE READ, UNDERSTOOD, AND ACCEPTED THE TERMS OF THIS AGREEMENT.

Your rights:

1. You enjoy a non-exclusive license to use the enclosed software/data on a single microcomputer that is not part of a network or multi-machine system in consideration for payment of the required license fee, (which may be included in the purchase price of an accompanying print component), or receipt of this software/data, and your acceptance of the terms and conditions of this agreement.

2. You own the media on which the software/data is recorded, but you acknowledge that you do not own the software/data recorded on them. You also acknowledge that the software/data is furnished "as is," and contains copyrighted and/or proprietary and confidential information of Delmar Publishers or its licensors.

3. If you do not accept the terms of this license agreement you may return the media within 30 days. However, you may not use the software during this period.

There are limitations on your rights:

1. You may not copy or print the software/data for any reason whatsoever, except to install it on a hard drive on a single microcomputer and to make one archival copy, unless copying or printing is expressly permitted in writing or statements recorded on the diskette(s).

2. You may not revise, translate, convert, disassemble or otherwise reverse engineer the software/data except that you may add to or rearrange any data recorded on the media as part of the normal use of the software/data.

3. You may not sell, license, lease, rent, loan, or otherwise distribute or network the software/data except that you may give the software/data to a student or and instructor for use at school or, temporarily at home.

Should you fail to abide by the Copyright Law of the United States as it applies to this software/data your license to use it will become invalid. You agree to erase or otherwise destroy the software/data immediately after receiving note of Delmar Publishers' termination of this agreement for violation of its provisions.

Delmar Publishers gives you a LIMITED WARRANTY covering the enclosed software/data. The LIMITED WARRANTY can be found in this product and/or the instructor's manual that accompanies it.

This license is the entire agreement between you and Delmar Publishers interpreted and enforced under New York law.

Limited Warranty

Delmar Publishers warrants to the original licensee/purchaser of this copy of microcomputer software/data and the media on which it is recorded that the media will be free from defects in material and workmanship for ninety (90) days from the date of original purchase. All implied warranties are limited in duration to this ninety (90) day period. THEREAFTER, ANY IMPLIED WARRANTIES, INCLUDING IMPLIED WARRANTIES OF MERCHANTABILITY AND FITNESS FOR A PARTICULAR PURPOSE ARE EXCLUDED. THIS WARRANTY IS IN LIEU OF ALL OTHER WARRANTIES, WHETHER ORAL OR WRITTEN, EXPRESSED OR IMPLIED.

If you believe the media is defective, please return it during the ninety day period to the address shown below. A defective diskette will be replaced without charge provided that it has not been subjected to misuse or damage.

This warranty does not extend to the software or information recorded on the media. The software and information are provided "AS IS." Any statements made about the utility of the software or information are not to be considered as express or implied warranties. Delmar will not be liable for incidental or consequential damages of any kind incurred by you, the consumer, or any other user.

Some states do not allow the exclusion or limitation of incidental or consequential damages, or limitations on the duration of implied warranties, so the above limitation or exclusion may not apply to you. This warranty gives you specific legal rights, and you may also have other rights which vary from state to state. Address all correspondence to:

Delmar Publishers
3 Columbia Circle
P. O. Box 15015
Albany, NY 12212-5015